INTERNATIONAL TERRORISM IN THE CONTEMPORARY WORLD

Contributions in Political Science
Series Editor: Bernard K. Johnpoll

American Democratic Theory: Pluralism and Its Critics
William Alton Kelso

Doves and Diplomats: Foreign Offices and Peace Movements in Europe and America in the Twentieth Century
Solomon Wank, EDITOR

The Capitol Press Corps: Newsmen and the Governing of New York State
David Morgan

31
56

INTERNATIONAL TERRORISM IN THE CONTEMPORARY WORLD

edited by Marius H. Livingston
with Lee Bruce Kress and Marie G. Wanek

WITHDRAWN

Contributions in Political Science, Number 3

Tennessee Tech. Library
Cookeville, Tenn.

GREENWOOD PRESS
WESTPORT, CONNECTICUT • LONDON, ENGLAND

290316

Library of Congress Cataloging in Publication Data
Main entry under title:

International terrorism in the contemporary world.

(Contributions in political science; no. 3 ISSN 0147-1066)
Papers presented at a symposium held at Glassboro State College in 1976.
Bibliography: p. 471.
Includes index.
1. Terrorism—Congresses. I. Livingston, Marius H.
II. Kress, Lee Bruce. III. Wanek, Marie G. IV. Series.

HV6431.I56   301.6′33   77-84773
ISBN 0-8371-9884-4

Copyright © 1978 by Marius H. Livingston

All rights reserved. No portion of this book may be reproduced, by any process or technique, without the express written consent of the publisher.

Library of Congress Catalog Card Number: 77-84773
ISBN: 0-8371-9884-4
ISSN: 0147-1066

First published in 1978

Greenwood Press, Inc.
51 Riverside Avenue, Westport, Connecticut 06880

Printed in the United States of America

10 9 8 7 6 5 4 3 2 1

Many nations have recognized the great potential of terrorism; the terrorist is now the spearhead of a developing theory and practice of surrogate warfare.

Disorders and Terrorism
Report of the Task Force on
Disorders and Terrorism, p. 9.

We dedicate this book to all those organizations and individuals, particularly the New Jersey Committee for the Humanities, whose generous contributions and devoted efforts made possible the 1976 Glassboro State College International Symposium: *Terrorism in the Contemporary World.*

THE EDITORS

In Memoriam

Marius H. Livingston, principal editor of this volume, Chairperson of the History Department at Glassboro State College, and Director of the International Symposium, died on December 14, 1977. His death is a great loss to the Department, to the College, and to the history profession.

Lee Bruce Kress
Marie G. Wanek

CONTENTS

PART III—SOME PSYCHOLOGICAL ASPECTS OF INTERNATIONAL TERRORISM

PART IV—SOME POLITICAL CONSEQUENCES OF INTERNATIONAL TERRORISM

PART V—SOME LEGAL PROBLEMS AND INTERNATIONAL TERRORISM

FOREWORD

There is a spectrum of attitudes toward terrorism ranging from paranoia to complacent optimism. Those who are moderate take guidance from the past and reluctantly confess expectation of some continuing terroristic activity.

I reject any pessimistic notion that terroristic forces may shape their own destiny without opposition from the civilized world.

I believe the future for terrorism is, to a meaningful extent, the future ordained for it by the civilized world.

The concept of terrorism seems to escape consensus in definition. Implicit in this difficulty is the realization of its complexity. It does appear, however, that some characteristics of the term have broad recognition.

Many scholars agree that a terroristic act is performed for political objectives, using dramatic techniques of fear and coercion. Others, such as Robert Friedlander, define terrorism as "abominable means used by political fanatics for contemptible ends."

Our choice of words may differ. Our substantive thought may be at odds. But we can still discuss the concept meaningfully.

In the context of terroristic conduct, our planning for the future must include a range of considerations. Among them, certainly, will be:

1. The creation of environments which minimize the spawning of terroristic behavior.

2. The creation of environments which discourage the occurrence of terrorism.

3. The creation of law-enforcement tactical skills which can effectively manage a terroristic occurrence.

4. The creation of proper criminal codes which not only will intimidate the terroristic impulse, but will also provide the juridical framework within which transgressions can be measured.

5. The creation of a penal system—comprised of both programs and policy—which will administer postjuridical disposition.

This list is far from complete. It suggests subconsideration of philosophy, economics, and political science. Given the difficult nature of terrorism, it is an achievement to form even a tentative analysis. From the outset, the analyst, the international lawyer, the world planner, and the scholar are frustrated by the shattering relativism which earmarks a great part of terroristic activity.

For every characterization of terrorism there is a countercharacterization of noble patriotism. For every present moment of confidence in the characterization of a transnational act there is the potential of a future time which, in retrospect, will prove embarrassing.

Terroristic activity is often not psychotic. It carries purpose, aspiration, and a messianic conviction that the future will ultimately venerate conduct otherwise considered treacherous.

Governor Brendan T. Byrne

PART I

General Introduction

MARIE G. WANEK

Symposium Summary

This chapter reorganizes and synthesizes, under a number of key headings, the many ideas on terrorism in general and international terrorism in particular which were developed during a three-day symposium at Glassboro State College in 1976. A wide variety of approaches to the theme of international terrorism was presented—in academic disciplines as well as in opinions regarding the nature of the problem and the degree of its complexity. The content of this chapter reflects primarily the papers included in this book, but some material has been taken from other papers presented at the symposium.*

The Problem of Definition

The fundamental and existential difficulty of coping with the contemporary phenomenon which we so easily in our daily language call "terrorism" was immediately brought into focus: it was impossible to find a universally satisfactory definition of terrorism, and the reasons for this are political rather than semantic.

Violence, and with it terror, goes back beyond the dawn of history: contemporary violence stands on the shoulders of earlier fanatics. Terrorism, however, belongs to our modern, sophisticated technological age. The French Revolution's Reign of Terror and the *Revolutionary Catechism* of the Russian anarchists Bakunin and Nechaev, *Dowling* suggested, mark important steps in the development of modern international terrorism: terror as policy and terrorism as philosophy. *Wilkinson* found the first use of urban guerrilla warfare in the 1848 revolutions. *Gros,* who analyzed terrorism in literature, found the beginning of intellectual rationalization of violence at least as early as Rousseau and spoke of Sartre's discussion of purifying and creative crime.

Within our own generation modern technology has qualitatively changed the nature of terrorism, for states as well as for dissident groups. Official government terrorism is as old as history—from the Egyptians and the Assyrians and the Incas to the Nazis and the Russians, both Tsarist and Soviet—but modern technology has made genocide possible on a truly vast scale. It has also enabled tiny groups to wield enormous powers of destruction—in contrast to a Guy Fawkes who, *O'Ballance* noted, in the early seventeenth century had to laboriously transfer his thirty-six barrels of

---

*Quotations are taken from the papers as delivered at the symposium.

gunpowder to the Parliament building, using "state-of-the-art technology for terroristic motives," *Mengel* added. State-of-the-art technology now poses a much greater threat. Today submachine guns, grenades, plastic explosives, and the like, are easily transported; the mails can be used for remote control by sending letter-bombs; airplanes with hundreds of passengers can be hijacked by a single individual, and nuclear devices could readily be employed. The technological effectiveness is not only in the weapons themselves and in their transportation, but also in communications and especially in the mass media: tool, weapon, and objective.

During the last several decades the world has seen a new development in the history of modern terrorism, namely, transnational terrorism. Perhaps this era opened, suggested *Fearey*, with the hijackings by freedom-seeking refugees from East European Communist countries in the middle and late forties. But during the last decade international terrorism, for both liberation and oppression, has reached epidemic proportions: civil disobedience, tyrannicide, political coups, guerrilla warfare, and wanton terroristic murder.

Even the briefest of historical résumés brings one face to face with the problem of definition. No universally acceptable one was developed by the symposium, but many of the speakers provided their own definitions or outlined the "functions" of terrorism for the purposes of their own papers. The focal concern with international terrorism, and therefore with the complexities of the contemporary international order, made definition that much more difficult: "One man's terrorist is another man's freedom fighter" was a phrase often heard. The majority considered today's overriding problem to be the threat posed to liberal democratic pluralistic societies by reason of the capability of small groups, or even one or two individuals, to disrupt their orderly functioning. Some expressed the view that state terrorism, whatever the political orientation of the particular state, was the more serious, perhaps the only real problem.

The opinion of those who considered international terrorism, regardless of perpetrator, to be the fundamental concern was well expressed by *Mickolus*. He defined it as:

The use, or threat of use, of anxiety-inducing extranormal violence for political purposes by any individual or group, whether acting for or in opposition to established governmental authority, when such action is intended to influence the attitudes and behavior of a target group wider than the immediate victims and when, through the nationality or foreign ties of its perpetrators, its location, the nature of its institutional or human victims, or the mechanics of its resolution, its ramifications transcend national boundaries.

The various approaches to the problem of definition reflected the complex dimensions of the contemporary problems and the varied concerns of the speakers. "Not surprisingly," said *Friedlander*, reflecting others' opinions as well, "given the sovereignty explosion and prevailing international alignments there has been almost a total lack of agreement within the world community on either the causes or the cure of the terrorist phenomenon." He called it "randomized violence," saying that to condone it would mean "to replace the rule of law with the ancient credo of might makes right." Quite a few participants noted that the actual killings, injuries, and property damage resulting from individual and small-group terrorism were minimal compared with the crime statistics of one medium-sized American city, the effectiveness of state violence and terrorism, or the destructiveness of a single bombing raid as an act of war. "Governments which hold many foreign cities under the threat of their nuclear ICBMs," *Vacca* observed, "deserve more severe condemnation than the terrorist who threatens a few dozen people [because] violence is less civilized and more dangerous, the larger the threatening means" over which it disposes. Nevertheless, although the toll in lives and property damage may not be large, the threat to society is great in terms of disruption. *Wolf* suggested that the idea of the nineteenth-century Russian terrorist Stepniak is significant: terrorism would compel a government to neglect everything else. *Mickolus* urged that the symposium consider the indirect costs of terrorism in terms of the flight of capital from countries which experience terrorist campaigns, security costs, such intangibles as the random rerouting of aircraft, and not least, "the costs of all academic and governmental research on terrorism as well as the costs of policy staffs assigned to develop national responses to terrorism, such as the Cabinet Committee to Combat Terrorism."

Facets, Forms, and Functions of Terrorism

If a satisfactory definition of terrorism eluded the symposium, clear identification of some of its functions did not: to many it was clearly warfare. A more precise understanding of what the term terrorism encompasses, *Mallin* argued, would contribute greatly to its satisfactory definition. Many gray areas of violence and intimidation cannot be clearly identified as terroristic. He formulated his definition of political terrorism as the "threat of violence or an act or series of acts of violence effected through surreptitious means by an individual, an organization or a people to further his or their political goals," a "form of military activity." The Black September massacre of the Israeli athletes was "fundamentally a military move. Having failed in four conventional wars to defeat the Israelis," he continued, "the Arabs and Palestinians resorted to unconventional tactics, specifically, terrorism." Soldiers take over when diplomats fail, and terrorists are soldiers, doing battle in city streets and making the vulnerable areas of modern society their targets. Pointing out the changing nature of warfare in a changing world,

Mallin cited a military analyst: given the "rapidly shifting alliances and animosities of the modern world, no nation could be quite sure in any case just which foreign power had (or even *if* some foreign power had) sponsored its disasters, for such violence would lend itself, like underworld money, to political laundering." It is also psychological warfare because it publicizes the terrorists' political cause, demonstrates their capabilities, heartens sympathizers, disconcerts and paralyzes the enemy, and discourages allies. It does material and economic damage. These are military functions; this is warfare.

Several articles, especially *Wilkinson*'s and *Wolf*'s, discuss the value of terrorism to revolution and to urban guerrilla warfare in achieving revolution. To Engels, it would not win revolutions. Lenin and Che Guevara saw terrorism as a hindrance because it provokes police repression and interrupts communications among the revolutionaries themselves. Guevara was concerned about the indiscriminate killings involving both innocent persons and lives valuable to the revolution. Others, by contrast, are not only unconcerned with the innocent victims but see positive gain because the police can be blamed. There are also the fanatical revolutionaries to whom terror and violence have mystical significance; a drug, *Wilkinson* suggested, an addiction to murder in the name of "liberation" and "justice" to sublimate the urge to rebel.

To Carlos Marighella, terrorism was an indispensable weapon of revolution precisely because of the cold-blooded, calm decisiveness it requires: "adequate dedication and well-trained volunteers." Terrorism, Marighella insisted, must be distinguished from urban guerrilla warfare itself, but he noted that the latter has a "higher terrorism potential." It is a powerful means to achieve revolution: "It is necessary to turn political crisis into armed conflict by performing violent actions that will force those in power to transform the political situation of the country into a military situation. That will alienate the masses, who, from then on, will revolt against the army and the police and blame them for this state of things." Debray and others think similarly that terrorism is an indispensable weapon. In *Wilkinson*'s analysis, "[T]errorism may give useful tactical support to guerrilla operations by creating diversions and tying down large numbers of security forces in costly counter-terrorist activity . . . a sustained campaign of terrorist attrition can assist the wider revolutionary struggle by sapping the will of the government and security forces to uphold the law, by undermining public confidence in the government and its capacity to protect the lives and property of citizens, and by helping to create a general climate of fear and collapse."

Wilkinson analyzed the differences between urban and rural guerrilla warfare, their relative advantages and disadvantages, and noted two apparently contradictory developments: there has been a shift from rural to urban guerrilla warfare in even the still largely rural areas of the world along with an ultimate, fundamental commitment to the rural base, "the mystique of the rural guerrilla," in *Mallin*'s words. What this reflects, of course, *Wilkinson* explained, is the rapid spread of urbanization in the developing world without its overwhelmingly rural character being superseded. So Mao and Ho and Castro remain the heroes of Third World revolutionaries. He quoted Marighella: "From the urban front we shall go direct to armed struggle against the *latifundio* through rural guerrilla war." There will be the "alliance of the proletariat, peasantry, and students in a decentralized and mobile guerrilla war."

Recognizing that terrorism is a mode of warfare, *Mallin* asked at what point "does terrorism become the concern of the 'regular' military?" The complexity of contemporary technological society has made of the modern city a kind of vast integrated circuit, and of the nation and perhaps even of the world, a complex of integrated circuits—a "global nervous system" in Brzezinski's phrase. Thus, the potential for disruption, *Mallin* explained, is enormous, even catastrophic. Urban guerrilla warfare (which can involve the use of terror) may have to become a recognized part of regular military training. On the other hand, the prevalence of terror, and especially the potential threat of catastrophic consequences from terrorist use of nuclear technology, *Mengel* said, might necessitate military intervention into the domestic realm in spite of strong democratic traditions to the contrary. Central to his paper were two propositions: that "nuclear technology is reasonably available to terrorists and that the employment of this technology represents such a danger to society that the ultimate force of the state, the military, must be used to counter the threat." We do not know, he mused, why terrorists have not yet used nuclear technology.

Mallin detailed categories of nuclear threat and noted the lack of a popular sense of danger. He pointed out that the nuclear programs of all countries are under government control and that the United States has by far "the largest number of civilian agencies with some nuclear-related function and responsibility." As for weapons, here military responsibility begins only with delivery. He stated that the United States views terrorism as "essentially a criminal activity with political overtones," discussed the duties of various investigative and law-enforcement agencies which have the responsibility in this area, and specifically noted existing laws, such as the 1974 Disaster Relief Act and others which authorize the use of the military "in times of civil disorders and disasters, including a Presidential declaration of a state of national emergency. Although used with discretion in the past," *Mengel* warned, "a reign of nuclear terrorism could result in the broader application of these laws." Adequate mechanisms presently exist in the civilian sector, and society must guard against unwarranted increase in military involvement.

A clearly implicit and often explicit theme of the symposium was the technological nature of contemporary society which makes it vulnerable to terrorism and puts technology in the service of terrorism. The special role of the mass media in the terrorists' scheme of things was often referred to and one paper was devoted to the mass media in relation to terrorism. *Mosse* discussed the impact of television and other mass media on children in conditioning them to violence. She expressed the conviction that television is "potentially the single most important antiviolence device" because, according to the conclusions of Wertham's research, "the opposite of violence is communication." Television "makes communication between all people on earth possible as never before," *Mosse* stated, but she deplored the fact that its benefits are being destroyed by the violence and horror it presents. Racial stereotypes create race hatred which fosters violence. That other very potent mass medium, the press, was the subject of repeated reference. The commitment to a free press in a free society was weighed against concern for the aid press coverage can give terrorists and the danger it can spell for hostages: there were strong opinions on both sides of the argument.

What kind of personality and culture and circumstances produce terrorism? *Storr* distinguished between aggression, some degree of which, he said, is "essential for survival," and cruelty, which he described as "a blot on the human escutcheon [which] is the opposite of adaptive [and] serves no obvious biological purpose." Certain social conditions and attitudes tend to produce cruel behavior: childhood experiences; physical distance producing psychological distance; a "tendency toward obedience" in the expectation that it produces stability and order (thus "clearly adaptive" behavior); and fear. Turning to human cruelty in history, *Storr* cited several examples, including the collapse of the Weimar Republic and its aftermath, which, he explained, "not only throw up pathological leaders, but mobilize paranoid projection on a large scale." Similar themes were echoed in *Dowling*'s psychohistorical analysis. It appeared to him that anarchism and terrorism were expressions of the "Freudian paradigm of 'the return-of-the-repressed' (that is, man's wish to be free and integrated) [and] the Eriksonian paradox of the influence of 'great men' (for example, Bakunin, Sorel, Fanon) with emphasis on personality integration and the 'shared themes' paradigm which might take the form of group, generational, or cohort analysis." He saw contemporary totalitarian movements and late medieval chiliasm as similar phenomena. He considered that anarchism-terrorism is increasing "in direct ratio to control and rationalization in modern technotronic society" as "part of a larger, endemic impulse to resolve the existential isolation of man," often as response to a "breakdown in traditional patterns." There is a belief that violence was purifying, that one used the gun to get rid of the gun, that "morality came from the muzzle of a gun."

In his study of assassination within the context of "various aspects of subjective political culture" in twenty-three countries, *Frank* demonstrated that certain societies are "violence-prone." Assassinations and attempted assassinations will increase, he concluded, in political cultures in which strangers are seen as weak and enemies as passive, respect is highly valued, and being a leader is important and a follower undesirable. He referred to Arendt's notion that negative reaction to bureaucracy, the "rule by Nobody," can be a significant attitude leading to violent political behavior. Social and political discontent as a breeder of violence was heard as a recurrent theme at the symposium. In a paper devoted to Jamaican Black Power ideology, an expression of the Latin American Dependency Theory, *Sandstrom* argued that underdevelopment was not an original condition but was deliberately created by international capitalist investment and domination. These are revolutionary ideologies and they argue for the necessity of violent action against oppressive and repressive political systems. The Jamaican Black Power ideology is representative of Black Power movements throughout the West Indies, among which there is considerable communication. They have two themes: black consciousness and solidarity, and opposition to foreign domination.

In discussing the rising rate of violence, organized crime, and terrorism in a period of history when "remarkable improvement in human conditions has been achieved," *Zinam* observed, quoting McNeill, that "without an increased understanding of the forces that shape the individual, we will forever fail to comprehend the direction that international violence may take." He also noted the importance of carefully distinguishing the meanings of the terms *violence* and *force*. *Zinam* deplored the use of the term violence for all instances of force, "legitimate or illegitimate," because it creates the impression that any use of force is to be condemned and avoided. Yet, he pointed out, "no human society can survive without an adequate use of legitimate coercion and proper use of force," a point also made by others. He proceeded to make the distinction between the concepts of "legality" and "legitimacy." An illegal act violates a formal law; an illegitimate act violates "ethical norms and standards shared by a given community." He explained that the two concepts would coincide in the ideal state but that "in reality positive and natural laws differ and this creates some ambiguity." Proceeding to his discussion of the conditions which give rise to discontent, violence, and terrorism (the "apex of violence"), *Zinam* said: "Frequent occurrence of legitimate, but extralegal acts, indicates that laws do not provide adequate protection of human rights or that they place too many restrictions on law-enforcement agencies so that, to fulfill their duty to society they have to break existing laws." The central question *Zinam* explored, having set up a theoretical framework, concerned what the forces of modernization do to the human propensity for violence, considering subjective and objective factors. Beyond his theoretical discussion he deplored "the gradual spread of the notion that human actions are determined by social circumstances [because it] undermined the basic belief in personal responsibility." One result of this trend is that there has been a "gradual transformation of the revolution of rising expectations into a revolution of rising entitlements and a concomitant lowering of the average societal threshold of frustration."

Occurrences of Terrorism

Several panels were devoted to specific occurrences of terrorism in various parts of the world during this century while two other papers, analyzing trends in transnational terrorism and terrorist manipulation of the democratic process, also cited significant occurrences. *Mickolus* noted that almost half of the reported instances of transnational terrorism have occurred in "Westernized, highly affluent nations." *Wolf* used the examples of Ireland, the Middle East, Latin America, and others to show that essentially a political process is involved. There were detailed discussions of terrorism as used both by incumbent governments against rebels and by freedom fighters against incumbent governments.

In a paper on the former British colony of India, *Khan* explained that both the British and the Indians practiced equally ruthless terror in the Sepoy Mutiny of 1857-58. At that time as later in the twentieth century, terrorism was limited to northern India, usually originating in Bengal. *Smith* pointed out that Mahatma Gandhi's nonviolent movement became a tremendous force because it became a mass movement, which both constitutional reform and terrorism had failed to do. Nevertheless, violence continued, and particularly that between the majority Hindu and the minority Muslim religious communities of India remained an important element. The migration of millions and the slaughter of hundreds of thousands marked the partition between Pakistan and India in 1947. Communal violence, with a dimension of colonialism, also characterizes the terrorist insurgency which began in Northern Ireland in 1969. *Moodie* discussed the extension of frequent and severe terrorism to England by the IRA, the failure of the Constitutional Convention of 1975, and the resumption of violence thereafter. *Fisk* analyzed a special aspect of the British government's response to the unrest in Ulster, namely, the quasi-legal functions given to the military in Northern Ireland for the purpose of temporarily propping up the Royal Ulster Constabulary. The military engaged in police and law-enforcement activities of doubtful legality, as well as far-reaching intelligence activities, for which they specifically received professional training.

West provided a broad analysis of political violence in the Latin American countries, noted certain characteristics, and gave a prognosis for the future. He contrasted Latin American terrorist activities with those of the IRA and certain Palestinian terrorist organizations, noting that the former discriminated carefully in their choice of targets. They concentrated on people rather than property, seizing individuals for ransom selected for their symbolic as well as financial value: foreign diplomats, "local agents of North American imperialism," or prominent members of indigenous elite groups. Latin American terrorists (again in contrast to the IRA and certain Palestinian groups) have not received significant financial assistance from abroad. Therefore they must undertake activities which gain them money and publicity at low risk; they have usually been able to accomplish their goals with traditional weapons. Since the mid-1970s there has been a slight decline in terrorist activity in many of the Latin American countries, probably related to the succession of stronger authoritarian governments in place of the more democratic and weaker authoritarian governments of the 1950s and 1960s. This trend could be reversed if Cuba should decide to take a more active role in other Latin American countries. There might also be an increase in incidents as Latin American terrorists gain access to more sophisticated technology, possibly providing them with a new set of targets such as jumbo jets, supertankers, offshore drilling rigs, nuclear power reactors, and computer and communications centers.

Two papers presented aspects of the effectiveness of terrorism in the recent history of Africa: *Mojekwu* described its role in the independence movements, while *Sundiata* discussed its function in integrating the economically and politically disparate parts of one country. *Mojekwu* demonstrated that when protest "as a legitimate political process produces violence rather than political redress [then] terrorism becomes a technique in the overall strategy to remove the foreign authority." He stated that, over the past two decades, self-determination or liberation groups employing terror-violence were uniformly successful, whereas those who, for whatever reason, did not employ terror-violence, failed to obtain their objectives. He then proceeded to question whether "the carryover of the experiences of colonial terrorism practiced on them" was not in fact so profound that African leaders would be unable in the future to solve domestic problems without resort to terror-violence. An example of its use in the internal affairs of one country, in the context of immediately inherited problems at the time of independence, was the subject of *Sundiata*'s paper. Equatorial Guinea, he contended, presented in extreme form problems faced by many African states, namely, "anomalous boundaries bequeathed by European imperialism." Its president has succeeded by various means, including the use of terror, in keeping his country together in spite of possibly nonviable boundaries and a lopsided economy.

The Baader-Meinhof gang, or Red Army Faction, wrote *Wagenlehner*, emerged in 1968 at the height of the student revolts in Germany. Between 1970 and 1972 the terrorists went to East Berlin several times to fly via East German *Interflug* to Jordan and Lebanon, where they were trained in Palestinian camps in marksmanship and the use of explosives. Nevertheless, they had neither political objectives nor constructive programs, wanting merely to destroy. These terrorists were essentially concerned with the solving of personal problems; although they considered themselves Marxists they were "disappointed middle-class children without revolutionary discipline [or] fundamental political knowledge."

The rather complex evolution of modern Arab terrorism was analyzed in two papers. *O'Ballance* placed the beginning of terrorism in the Middle East with the Assassins of the late eleventh century and the beginning of modern Arab terrorism in 1965 in the context of Arab-Israeli tensions and the Arab refugee problem. It soon became international, carrying out its terrorist activities in various countries and becoming involved in a terrorist network through the training and employment of groups the world over. It also became indiscriminate in its choice of targets. "The Arab whirlwind of indiscriminate terrorism," he wrote, "induced, and then became intermixed with, an Israeli backlash that developed into an underground war that spread to Europe, in which Arab terrorists and Israeli agents eliminated each other." *O'Ballance* pointed to Israel's concern with its survival as a state (in contrast to the primary regard in Western societies for individual lives), which accounts for Israel's policy of "no negotiation."

A more detailed presentation of the rather complicated and intricate development of Arab movements and terrorist organizations was given by *Ellenberg*. He indicated that Arab Palestinian national consciousness and Arab revolts began in the 1920s with the growth of Jewish immigration into Palestine, under terms of the League of Nations Mandate and as the result of the persecution of the Jews in Germany in the 1930s. The PLO became an umbrella organization for many disparate groups, each having its own ideology, each waging its own war against Israel, each acting upon orders of different Arab heads of state. After the 1967 defeat by Israel "the guerrilla organizations found themselves confronted with the need to change their policies and to turn—all of them—to purely terrorist activities, with only formal claim to real anti-Israeli guerrilla activities." They turned increasingly into "professional" terrorist groups and became big business, "among the best paying industries in the world" (quoting Laffin), no longer pursuing political or social objectives. They assisted, and were assisted by, other terrorist groups around the world. In spite of the absence of political goals, *Ellenberg* contended, Yasser Arafat was given political recognition in the United Nations by being invited to speak to its General Assembly.

Most of the concern of the symposium was with terrorism which challenged an incumbent government. However, two major examples of terrorism in the service of the encumbent regime were also discussed: the Soviet Union and Nazi Germany. *Hendel* outlined the reasons for the reign of terror and analyzed the cost to the Soviet Union in terms of its specific objectives.

The terror was an instrument for altering the structure of society "at a rapid rate and from above," for creating a utopia "by the use of political authority" which had but minimal support from below. Stalin believed that a rapid tempo of transformation (and by implication the use of terror) was necessary because Russia was so far behind the advanced nations and was threatened with being crushed. Furthermore, Allied intervention in Russia immediately after World War I had created a sense of fear and suspicion and the conviction of the need for ruthlessness. The cost to the Soviet Union was the destruction of thousands of professional and military personnel and the disaffection of masses of the peasantry; these losses, *Hendel* concluded, slowed rather than hastened the desired transformation.

The Germans of the Third Reich also employed terror as an instrument of national policy: to change their society through the elimination of a race which they considered both inferior and a threat to their national security, namely, the Jews. *Glicksman*'s paper explored the mentality which produced the Final Solution, the barbarism of its methods, as well as the Nazi objective of changing the human species for the ultimate purpose of wiping out other nations and ruling the world—since only the Nordic race was fit to rule the world. In a concluding discussion of anti-Semitism as a historical phenomenon *Glicksman* pointed out that it has been most prevalent among urban rather than rural populations among the various components of the middle class, and as a response to social and economic problems. Another paper discussed how it was possible for the Nazis to get the necessary nationwide cooperation to carry out such a heinous program. Various references were made to the fact that what is ultimately involved, beyond anti-Semitism, the crime against one race, is the issue of a crime against humanity. *Hewsen* pointed out that as many non-Jews as Jews were destroyed in the gas chambers, and that Hitler had felt no concern with world opinion of his Final Solution because previous instances of mass slaughter, for example, of the Armenians under the Ottoman Empire, had been in fact ignored. Lest others become victims at another time, "the victims of the Nazi holocaust—Jew and Gentile alike" should be remembered.

The Free Society's Response to Terrorism

The implicit, and sometimes explicit, concern of the majority of the symposium's participants was that terrorism threatens the liberal, democratic, pluralistic society. *Vacca* suggested "it would be difficult to refute the point of view that no open societies exist anywhere in the world at present and that none has ever existed"; but the general assumption was that, while not perfect, it is the best system yet devised for the fullest development of human potential. One reason such societies are threatened is because terrorists can move about so freely and procure the necessary materials so easily.

Some analyses were made in response to this threat.

Whatever the problems of defining terrorism because of incompatible ideologies, there is no difficulty in describing the experience: "acts or threats of violence intended to affect the social and political life of the community." *Cooper* gave this as his working definition for the purpose of discussing terrorism and the intelligence function. He added certain other key characteristics: it is "clandestine, unlawful activity of a violent and undiscriminating kind [and] fundamentally political." The relationship between society and terrorism is one of warfare, in which victory is gained by studying the enemy's weaknesses. This has been done by terrorist theoreticians, and this is the function of society's intelligence organization. Its task is to gather facts in order that "sensible policies can be developed and sensible decisions made" as well as forecasts for the future. The difficulties in intelligence work in a free society arise from questions of the degree of intrusion into privacy that will be tolerated and the amount of counter-terrorist measures, infiltration activities of the "dirty tricks" variety, society will permit. Both, *Cooper* insisted, are necessary. But the secrecy which is indispensable for effective intelligence work must be subject to control and accountability; there must be safeguards in terms of philosophy, policy guidelines, laws, legislative oversight, and judicial review. He concluded by quoting Senator Strom Thurmond: "We have to strike a balance between protecting our constitutional liberties and protecting our society against those who would destroy it."

Several other speakers also concerned themselves with the issue of intelligence. *Sundberg* described the shift in Swedish government policy from neutrality in the 1950s to hospitality for socialist-oriented refugees in the 1970s. In presenting many examples of terrorist manipulation of the democratic process, their tactics and areas of occurrence, *Wolf* argued that the very ambivalence of free societies concerning the use and methods of intelligence is what lays the democratic process open to manipulation by terrorists. The ambivalence was reflected at the symposium: there were those, such as *Alesevich*, who were concerned that law-enforcement and intelligence agencies were not being sufficiently investigated and controlled; there were others, such as *Yarborough*, who were concerned that they were being hamstrung by too much concern for the rights of criminals.

One paper was devoted to preparedness on the part of one group of potential targets of terrorism, namely, kidnap victims. There are categories of persons of symbolic or ransom value to terrorists who can be prepared for possible exposure to that ordeal. *McClure* enumerated various psychological factors to be taken into consideration concerning both hostage and captor. The course of preparation was based upon a study of more than two dozen victims who had survived the experience. Nevertheless, the writer stressed that since each case is basically unique, it is not possible to prepare for precisely what will be encountered and instruction should not become oversystematized. But *McClure* demonstrated that much can be done. One can become aware of signs that one might be a prospective victim, have one's affairs in order, and understand the basic psychological situation—how one is viewed by a political kidnapper.

Terrorism and the International Order

For centuries the search for order has extended beyond the boundaries of individual nations because the potential disruption of order cannot be controlled by nations individually. International criminal law, explained *Kittrie*, arose out of concern with international piracy, "long considered an offense against all civilized nations." International traffic is being affected today to a degree not experienced since "the heyday of classical piracy." He considered this a matter for serious concern, for "the security of international commerce and travel, diplomatic protection, and the safeguarding of non-combatant civilian populations" are "classical pillars of the international community." *Kittrie* explored approaches to the control of this escalated threat to international order derived from international law and custom. He noted the passing, in the Age of Enlightenment, of the notion of *lese majesté*, and the beginning, in the aftermath of the French Revolution, of the concept of the non-extraditable political offense. But the latter was seldom defined in treaties or domestic legislation. There has been increased concern with the defense of conscience in the last century, he pointed out, and with self-determination and human rights in this century. But the increase in terroristic activities worldwide has caused a renewed concern with international safety and "the old conflict between individual conscience and public order has once more returned to haunt the international arena." The terrorist is distinguished from the traditional political offender by his commitment to violence as a process and as an end in itself, a violence which can affect also the noninvolved even in remote, neutral countries. Proposals for international conventions have not been successful because of the fundamentally different presuppositions between most of the Western world and most of the rest of the world. To the former, terrorism generally connotes indiscriminate commitment to violence, whereas the latter see terrorism in the service of revolutionary and liberation movements. It is the problem of definition, of ideology, of the diverse camps into which the "world community" is divided.

The use of the term "world *community*" [emphasis added] in the same breath with mention of "diverse camps and ideologies" serves indeed to place the heart of the problem in sharp focus. This dilemma was reflected explicitly in certain papers and implicitly in the tone of the symposium. *Sundberg* suggested that the difficulty in developing international law lies in a lack of understanding as to what the word law really means. He explained that it is derived from the Old Norse *lagu*, which is plural and basically means peace. Law to the Norsemen was "not only a collection of prescriptions but the very peaceful society of which the individuals are members." He quotes the *Njal Saga*: "The law only binds the members of the law [not] the foreigner." *Sundberg* went on to explain that international law "by definition is dominated by foreigners." Nevertheless, it is not in fact primarily concerned with foreigners although it appears to be. The main function of international criminal law "is to make your own people," he declared, "accept sacrifices (such as to abide by the law) knowing that the [foreigners] have it worse." Thus the law "influences no actor, but it does create a feeling of solidarity in the local population in general and among victims, past and future, in particular."

These papers and others, including *Evans*'s discussion of the Draft Convention on International Terrorism, introduced by the United States to the United Nations General Assembly in 1972, and an entire panel devoted to the subject of an international criminal court, variously reviewed the history of international conventions. Suggestions were made for other possible approaches to the contemporary problem of terrorism and the international order. They ultimately foundered on the Scylla and Charybdis of divergent ideologies in a world which in fact is *not* a community because there is no sharing of a sufficient core of common values: "What is terrorism to some is heroism to others." *Evans* suggested that the "major lesson" to be drawn from the debates on the United States resolution and subsequent substitute resolutions was that "while terrorism may be perceived in the West in general and in the United States in particular as a humanitarian problem, this is *not* the way it is perceived by most of the rest of the world. Most countries," he pointed out, "regard international terrorism as basically a political manifestation of the struggles against regimes such as South Africa, Rhodesia, and Israel which, it must be admitted, are very unpopular among the community of nations." Nevertheless, the effort must continue to be made. *Kittrie* suggested "a pragmatic step-by-step approach," continued exploration on national and international levels, and "exploring potentials for greater consensus regarding the extradition of political offenders, including terrorists." A balance must be maintained "between human rights and world order." To this end "the principle of proportionality" should be fundamental to any resolutions made: terroristic acts cannot be justified merely on the basis of considerations of conscience; on the other hand, all opposition to established governments cannot flatly be considered unjustified by international standards.

It might be well, *Kittrie* further suggested, to proceed through agencies other than the United Nations because of this organization's politicization. An International Commission on Human Rights ought to be set up, through whose work a "finer line of demarcation would be drawn between non-extraditable political offenses and crimes against humanity." This work might lead to the establishment of an international criminal court. *Bekes, Dautricourt,* and *Murphy* contributed papers addressed to these matters. *Murphy* discussed a research project submitted to the Department of State on the legal aspects of international terrorism limited specifically to the "threat or use of violence by private persons for political ends" international in scope. In his discussion of the legal problems of hijacking and hostages *Bekes* again recognized the problem of freedom fighter versus terrorist. Referring to early efforts, in the context of privateer versus pirate, to distinguish the lawful from the lawless, he discussed the 1970 Hague and 1972 Montreal conventions, ending with a recognition of the near-impossibility of getting these agreements more generally accepted. *Dautricourt,* quoting Donnedieu de Vatres, addressed himself to the undesirable situation of "trial of the vanquished by the victors, sitting on *ad hoc* tribunals" and stressed the importance of the court existing before the crime to be tried is committed. An international criminal court with but "a restricted acceptance" would be better than no preexisting tribunal at all.

The *Mallisons* presented a paper discussing the application of the International Humanitarian Law of Armed Conflict (Law of War) in controlling state terrorism perpetrated on civilians living in occupied territories, in unoccupied territories, and in areas of internal conflict, who "may be terrorized by attacks upon either human or property values." They pointed out that the modern international law of war "traces its origin to the United States Civil War," and emphasized that it "contains doctrines which are applicable to internal or civil conflicts" as well. After brief remarks on the Hague Convention IV of 1907, the writers discussed the work of the Geneva Diplomatic Conference of 1949, which met in the shadow of the grim violations of the earlier convention by both the Nazi and the Japanese militarists during World War II. The Geneva Conference "aimed at preventing the repetition of state terror which characterized that war." The concluding paragraphs of their paper again echoed the recurrent symposium themes of the increasingly evident "realities of international interdependencies" and "increasingly sophisticated weapons technology" which require that "law and legal institutions must at least keep pace." Perhaps the time has come to move beyond the "sixteenth-century conception of sovereignty" which today may be causing us "to deny the existence of common values which we in fact share with those who express conflicting ideologies."

The symposium speakers recognized repeatedly in various ways that there are at present insurmountable obstacles to ending the disruption caused by transnational and international terrorism and that these lie in the absence of a sufficient core of common values worldwide. Nevertheless, they also expressed the conviction that, while individual countries can and must take their own measures of self-defense, in the last analysis it is an international problem, a global problem, and therefore appropriate cooperation is unavoidable. It is, said *Fearey*, "past time for the international community genuinely to address the affliction of international terrorism and take effective action against it." He referred to the technological interdependence of the modern world and concluded: "The international community must catch up with this modernization of barbarism before it is victimized by acts of terrorism as yet only slightly imagined." *Mickolus* called "feeble" the "international response to transnational attacks." The United Nations General Assembly members, he stated, "have quibbled over who is and is not a terrorist, and have not managed to agree on a common definition, much less a solution, to the problem," again reflecting the absence of a sufficient core of common values. *Mickolus* summarized his assessment of the present situation, noting that the actual casualties due to transnational terrorism are comparatively not large. But he warned that they have "lessened societal freedoms and the sense of security, diverted resources to protection against attack, and led to strains in state relations. Concerted and cooperative international action," he concluded, echoing the opinion of others, "will be needed to stem the tide."

Carl van Doren, in the years immediately after World War II when the United Nations was being created, wrote a history of the making and ratifying of the Constitution of the United States which he called *The Great Rehearsal* because he saw certain parallels between 1787 and 1948 and many of the arguments against a strong central government for the United States in 1787 repeated again in 1948 against a strong United Nations. *Sundberg*, noting that the "international arena is dominated by rivalry among nations and not solidarity," suggested that the prevalence of this rivalry "is possibly not imperative." In so saying he also referred to 1787, to the "full faith and credit clause" of the United States Constitution and cited some examples of the application of this attitude in international relations. "But," he concluded realistically, "the international world of today is certainly no Full Faith and Credit World and it presumably will not be much better in the foreseeable future." *Sundberg* concluded that it is "lost labor to work at solutions that presuppose such a world," and one should pursue what can be done in the existing world. Within the context of his paper, for instance, this meant to "start working at refining the doctrines of justification which control the requirement of 'unlawfulness' so that they will perform a useful and foreseeable service rather than be referred to as not the best developed areas of the penal law." Several speakers expressed the opinion that contracting agreements between two or a few nations was for the present a considerably more realistic goal than full-scale international agreements, and should be pursued in the absence of a United Nations treaty or an international court.

Thus there could be discerned at the symposium the dual theme of working realistically within the limits of the present international order and recognizing another reality as well, namely, that the limitations of the present international order are at the heart of the problem. *Dautricourt* pointed out that the "national state and its power policy remain, today, the main values in the world policy and the privileges of its rulers the basic pillars of the international public law." The United Nations, he continued, is "not at all representative of the social conscience of mankind, but only of the interests of national states and of the policies of their rulers." *Vacca* expressed the opinion, in the words of Tinbergen, that the nation state is "unable to solve some of the most important world problems." He went on to recommend that governments should "renounce some of their traditional prerogatives (like deciding on national defense)" and suggested that a "logical step further" would be the "abolition of the nation state." Somewhat less drastically, the *Mallisons* concluded their paper with a quotation from Lasswell stating, they noted, "the central point succinctly": "From your perspective or mine the creative opportunity is to achieve a self-system larger than . . . family, friends, profession, or nation; and inclusive of mankind."

What Is to Be Done

Naturally enough, the symposium was concerned with the future of terrorism, the future of society as affected by terrorism, and what we should do now, in the short run and in the long, to "avoid the future." In his paper on this subject, *Taylor* listed five characteristics of the "future we want to avoid" which "are likely to become more marked and thus to promote an increase of terrorism and violence over the next twenty or thirty years: education, freedom of movement, techniques of destruction and disruption, decay of social controls, decay of conscience." He warned that "the terrorists of the year 2000 have already been born. They are *now* undergoing the experiences which will turn them toward terrorism." The remedies, he suggested, lie in a more realistic and imaginative social policy. Present social policy, *Taylor* considered, "lags far behind sociological know-how here." He concluded by recommending that we "tackle the genuine political injustices and resolve the supposed injustices" and that we "learn to work on an international scale." Various speakers urged continued and expanded study of the trouble spots of the world, and an intensified awareness of all areas of the world so that potential conflict situations can be recognized and defused before they approach the point of violence and terrorism. *Croker* discussed the Gandhian nonviolent protest movement which, if more widely known and understood, might also become more widely adopted as an alternative to violent and terroristic protest. Several speakers warned of the explosive potential inherent in the global maldistribution of wealth and consequent

inequality of opportunity, of the responsibility of the affluent West for
the underprivileged, of the profound discontent and justified grievances of
many peoples across the globe.

The analyses of the present situation and future prospects were as many
and varied as the suggestions about what can be done. They ranged from
immediate pragmatic measures like airport security, through restricting
freedom in the free society in order to preserve it, seriously attacking maldistribution of wealth and opportunity around the world, and making bi- and
trilateral antiterrorist agreements, to stressing the absolute necessity for
fundamental changes in the international order. Scholars were encouraged
to continue their researches with increased cross-disciplinary approaches.
On balance, the general tenor of the symposium was more pessimistic than
optimistic concerning the future, what with terrorism being a "growth industry"; but there were also many expressions of optimism and emphases
upon progress made. Our attention was called to examples of the resilience
of people and societies in the face of overwhelming catastrophe, such as the
destruction of World War II, especially the courage of urban populations in
the face of interminable bombings and the rapidity with which they rebuilt
their cities.

MARIUS H. LIVINGSTON

Preface

A new specter is haunting the world, the specter of international terrorism. It is a new barbarism, a new form of warfare waged by small groups against neutrals or innocent bystanders as often as against actual foes. It is fought primarily not to win territory or even to cause destruction, but to command attention, to instill fear, and to terrorize in the hope of forcing the world to listen and to right an alleged wrong. There is little agreement on what really constitutes international terrorism or on the meaning of terrorism itself. Robert A. Fearey, in the Introduction, defines "this modernization of barbarism" as a form of violence which is essentially criminal and politically motivated and which transcends national boundaries.[1] Of course, international terrorism has been difficult to define partly for obvious political reasons and partly because it is such a relatively new phenomenon. Scholars, politicians, journalists, and others have hardly had time to cope with it. Its rather sudden appearance ten or fifteen years ago roughly coincided with the emergence of new systems of transportation and communication and with the invention of weapons especially useful in terrorist hands. Today these developments continue at a constantly accelerating pace, making it all but certain that, sooner or later, terrorists the world over will acquire atomic, bacteriological, or chemical weapons of mass destruction. Once that disastrous development comes to pass, the world will appreciate the full implications and significance of international terrorism.

Now is the time to consider the future of such a disaster. What may we expect when the first credible nuclear blackmail demand is received by the mayors of cities like New York or London?[2] What options will the authorities have? They won't be able to risk ignoring the terrorists' demands, however outrageous those might be. But will they not probably be equally unable to agree to those demands? It is not easy to imagine the panic and terror such a situation will suddenly create. A city might conceivably be evacuated, but to what purpose? A temporary evacuation, assuming it were logistically possible, would do little more than postpone the crisis. But if the demands were complied with, the authorities would be in the same untenable position as other blackmail victims who have paid and who know they may soon be confronted with new demands. Will there be other options? Of course, attempts might be made to negotiate for better terms to gain time, but those attempts would probably fail and any compromise would surely be regarded as a victory for the terrorists and lead to new demands in the future.

Fearey notes that it is the goal of terrorists to influence public opinion; it is rarely to cause mass murder. It is therefore unlikely that they would use weapons of mass destruction. They would avoid such weapons as potentially counterproductive. Fearey recalls that terrorists have had access for some time to such potential weapons as toxic aerosols, but have not used them. This argument is not reassuring because first, we cannot be sure that such weapons have never been employed since terrorists do not always "take credit" for their deeds, and second, because we must never forget for a moment that terrorists can never be depended upon to act rationally. For example, a bomb was exploded at LaGuardia Airport in New York in 1975, killing many people. As far as is publicly known the incident still remains a mystery.

Fearey's argument also does not pay enough attention to the fanatical and truly *irrational* element among terrorists. He does not seem to consider that relatively *rational* terrorists might resort to threats they do not expect to have to carry out, but later find themselves in situations they can no longer control. Fearey does, however, agree that such future threats are real enough and cannot be ignored.

At a Nobel Peace Prize ceremony held not long ago in Stockholm, solemn warnings were issued regarding nations experimenting with bombs of inconceivably greater power than anything now in existence. It would border on the miraculous if sooner or later such devices did not reach terrorist hands. Bombs might be built that could devastate whole countries or even entire continents.

Fearey adds to these unimaginable prospects the idea that governments themselves might hire terrorists and unleash them against their enemies. We have recently had an opportunity to see what certain African "statesmen" would be capable of doing, if only they had the power. Governments might not even be certain in future scenarios whether they were dealing with individual terrorists, with criminal organizations, with foreign governments, or, indeed, whether anyone at all will step forward to negotiate. The perpetrators of a particular action, intending to create panic only, might prefer to maintain complete anonymity. When terrorists or would-be terrorists acquire weapons of mass destruction, we will be at the threshold of an era of violence without precedent in scope and universality. This may well usher in a new period in history.

Some scholars, notably Walter Lacqueur, insist that international terrorism is not worth all the attention that has been focused on it. They point to the relatively small number of people who have been killed and the modest amount of destruction that has been caused thus far. This interpretation misses the point entirely. The significance of international terrorism does not lie in the number of lives taken or in the amount of destruction inflicted; it lies in the number of lives threatened and in the amount of fear and terror generated. At any rate, terrorism is today only in its infancy. It is too early to make an accurate forecast of its true potential as a new type of warfare.

How has the world gotten itself into such a dilemma? At least part of the answer may be found in the history of Western civilization since the democratic revolutions of the eighteenth and nineteenth centuries and especially since the advent of the industrial revolution, occurring at about the same time. These revolutions profoundly altered the political, economic, and social foundations of society. They liberated and prepared the masses for participation in public life to a degree unprecedented in history. At about the same time, a revolution in education occurred which had for its goal nothing less than the total elimination of illiteracy. A consequence of these developments was an enormous increase in the number of men and women who began to have an impact on political life. This popularization and indeed secularization of public life ushered in a new era in history. More and more people felt entitled to involve themselves in one way or another in the great issues of the day.

At the same time, the industrial revolution increased the opportunities for violence and destruction quite beyond anything known in the past. The process is still very much under way. In fact, the pace is constantly accelerating. Terrorists and would-be terrorists are only beginning to appreciate their opportunities. Already they have used heat-seeking missiles to attack airplanes and other targets. Relatively inexpensive, accurate, and operated by a single individual, such weapons are greatly enlarging the potential scope of terrorist operations. Supersonic, surface-to-air missiles targeted by a laser beam guidance system may be expected in terrorist hands at almost any time. Finally, in the near future, we must be prepared for the specter of terrorists armed with atomic, bacteriological, or chemical weapons. But all of this may be no more than a beginning. In the remaining years of this century and beyond that into the indefinite future, we can expect a cascade of ever more powerful and, at the same time, more portable weapons. Future opportunities to inflict death and destruction on a massive scale will become easier and cheaper all the time.

There are of course numerous other reasons which account for the worldwide increase in violence in the twentieth century. Among these are surely such factors as nationalism, competing economic and political ideologies, and, very importantly, overpopulation. But one of the more fundamental reasons for the rise of violence in the modern world may well be the fanaticism and irrationality that the majority of men bring to public affairs.

Who are these new barbarians, the new international terrorists? A "typical" terrorist probably does not exist, but terrorists as a group seem to have at least some characteristics in common. Perhaps the first of these is a denial that they are in fact terrorists. They see themselves as freedom fighters, patriots, unselfish and dedicated people enlisted in a sacred cause. Fanatics more often than not, they are always prepared to take deadly risks on behalf of their cause. Terrorists tend to regard themselves as legitimate representatives of a nation, or a people, and as the true executors of the public will. They envision themselves as chosen by God or destiny to carry out their deeds, no matter how bloody or destructive. They possess no lack of self-esteem and fully expect to be vindicated by history. Terrorists as fanatics are incapable of accommodation. They see compromise as a form of capitulation, as destruction of their goals. J. Bowyer Bell in his profile of terrorists is more inclined to compare them with the conventional soldiers in certain elite units, such as British commandos or American paratroops.

The men of the IRA or Black September turn out to be rather ordinary. They are violent by profession, imbued with simple idealism and devotion to duty. They possess the *esprit de corps* of the ordinary soldier and do not have much understanding of complex political issues.

Bell's profile, it will be noted, includes the traits of idealism and discipline, but not such traits as exceptional cruelty or lust for power. Terrorists, seemingly, are often ordinary men caught up in extraordinary situations. One is reminded of Hannah Arendt's view of the banality of evil. Terrorists may be fanatics, but they are not necessarily exceptional men; they are often rather ordinary men who do wicked deeds. They are simply newcomers to public issues: naive, emotional, impulsive, often irrational, and fundamentally uninformed.

What is the probable future of this new brand of warfare? Will it become a permanent factor in international relations, or will it be controlled as piracy was in the early nineteenth century? It is doubtless too soon for confident predictions, but some brief comments may be in order. Efforts designed to destroy the menace are sure to grow rapidly. Whether or not these will in time avoid major disaster is another matter. Certainly the terrorist threat will continue to grow, will become better organized, and above all, will become more formidable. It is reasonable to assume that with the proliferation of terrorist successes there will come a corresponding increase in international cooperation to oppose it. This process is already under way as can be seen by the declining number of countries providing sanctuary for international terrorists.

To checkmate terrorists armed with nuclear weapons, however, will be another matter. If literally all countries could be made to cooperate, the job might become manageable. But even assuming such cooperation, and assuming also the use of weapons of mass destruction, the fight against terrorism will be difficult and the price society will have to pay could be exorbitant. Democratic societies, for example, may disappear. Even now they constitute a minority among states. They will become dictatorships in order to mobilize enough power to do the job. Freedom of press and assembly, for example, will become luxuries in a world threatened by fanatics armed with the new weapons. Education, to cite another example, may have to become a state enterprise to a far greater degree than is true already. Democratic systems could not survive such drastic alterations. This process has already taken place in Uruguay, where the struggle against the Tupamaros has led to the destruction of a democratic society.

It is not too much to assume that as soon as terrorism becomes intolerable, democracy is likely to collapse by public demand, so to speak. People will always prefer security over ideology, survival over freedom. But actually there will be no choice in the matter. As soon as terrorists begin to use weapons of mass destruction, society will have no choice but to retaliate. The prospect of a city or a province or an entire country held for ransom will not be tolerated. The demand for effective action, no matter how drastic, will be all but universal.

International terrorism will therefore acquire two implacable enemies, an outraged public demanding action at any price and equally outraged and determined governments fighting for survival. The result will no doubt be the imposition of governmental counter-terror. Most governments have had some experience in this area and should have no trouble in mounting effective systems of counter-terror in very short order. Not the least of the dangers implicit in terrorism is therefore the danger to democratic government as well as the danger to international peace.

In the fight against international terrorism a number of practical measures have already been taken. In addition to some bilateral agreements between nations for joint action, there has also been some progress in the United Nations. In the area of hijacking and sabotage of civil aircraft, three agreements put together by the International Civil Aviation Organization might be mentioned: the Tokyo Convention of 1963 dealing with crimes committed in aircraft; the Hague Convention of 1970 calling for severe punishment of hijackers; and the Montreal Convention of 1971 which broadened the terms of the Hague Convention. No doubt a great deal more must be done by such international treaties and agreements. More action may also be expected from various national governments. In the United States, for example, in July of 1976, an antiterrorist resolution was introduced which called upon the President "to initiate and to engage in negotiation of agreements with other nations to help prevent acts of terrorism by, among other means, denying assistance or asylum to persons who perpetuate acts of terrorism, and by invoking sanctions against any nation which gives assistance or grants asylum to such persons."

It is reasonable to assume that more and more nations, including those from the Third World, will come to see the need for concerted action to protect their vital interests. Steven J. Rosen and Robert Frank, in their work "Measures Against International Terrorism," list a number of other steps nations can take in their own defense. These include:

Coordinated intelligence contingency planning; improved technology of electronic surveillance to detect metals and explosives; more stringent customs procedures;

stepped-up security at embassies and airports; development of screening profiles to identify terrorists; improved aircraft construction to partition passengers from pilots; bilateral and multilateral extradition agreements; direct pressure on states which harbor terrorists; development of clandestine counter-terrorist organizations to combat guerrilla groups or to create incentives for other states to support action against terrorism.[3]

The potential effectiveness of such measures may be gauged by the large degree of success that has been attained in many countries in safeguarding planes and passengers against hijackers. Hijacking has now almost disappeared from this country. It has not, of course, disappeared from the world as a whole, as the affair at Entebbe showed so dramatically. Many other measures will have to be adopted. We must appreciate that to put an end to this menace will be costly beyond anything we can imagine. Indeed, terrorism may even become a permanent threat no matter what we do.

The contributors to this volume have examined international terrorism from many points of view and have arrived at a variety of different conclusions and interpretations. Naturally they have not and could not exhaust the subject. No single volume is likely to do that. But if they have succeeded in stimulating further thinking and research, they will have made a contribution toward the understanding of a complicated and urgent subject.

Nearly all the papers which make up this book were originally presented at the Glassboro State College *Symposium on Terrorism in the Contemporary World,* held on the college campus, April 26-28, 1976. The symposium brought together about one hundred scholars and specialists from the United States and eight other countries. It attracted an audience of several hundred. This may be an appropriate place to express my sincere thanks to all those who contributed to the symposium, which did so much to develop a new interest and a desire to understand this problem among students as well as the general public.

I wish, in particular, to acknowledge a special debt of gratitude to my wife, Ina Livingston, for her extensive help in the preparation of this volume. Carole Pizzillo is deserving of special commendation for additional editorial assistance and typing. Special thanks go to Dr. Eva Aronfreed for her help in preparing for the symposium as well as the present volume.

Notes

1. Robert A. Fearey, "Introduction to International Terrorism," p. 25.

2. Attention is called to a recent novel by Richard Harris titled *The Mesada Affair.*

3. Steven J. Rosen and Robert Frank, "Measures Against International Terrorism," *International Terrorism and World Security,* David Carlton and Carlo Schaerf, eds. (London: Croom Helm Ltd., 1975), p. 68.

ROBERT A. FEAREY

Introduction to International Terrorism

International terrorism* is distinguished by three characteristics. First, as with other forms of terrorism, it embodies an act which is essentially criminal. It takes the form of assassination or murder, kidnapping, extortion, arson, maiming, or an assortment of other acts which are commonly regarded by all nations as criminal. Second, international terrorism is politically motivated. An extremist political group, convinced of the rightness of its cause, resorts to violent means to advance that cause—means incorporating one or more of the acts cited above. Often the violence is directed against innocents, persons having no personal connection with the grievance motivating the terrorist act. Finally, international terrorism transcends national boundaries, through the choice of a foreign victim or target, the commission of the terrorist act in a foreign country, or an effort to influence the policies of a foreign government. The international terrorist strikes abroad or at a diplomat or other foreigner at home, because he believes he can thereby exert the greatest possible pressure on his own or another government or on world opinion.

The international terrorist may or may not wish to kill his victim or victims. In abduction or hostage-barricade cases he usually does not wish to kill—although he often will find occasion to do so at the outset to enhance the credibility of his threats. In other types of attacks innocent deaths are his specific, calculated, pressure-shock objective. Through brutality and fear he seeks to impress his existence and his cause on the minds of those who can, through action or terror-induced inaction, help him to achieve that cause.

On September 6, 1970, for example, the Popular Front for the Liberation of Palestine hijacked three airliners flying from Europe to New York, diverted them to airports in the Middle East, and moments after their passengers had been evacuated, blew them up. The terrorists' purposes were: to attract world attention to the Palestinian cause; to convince the world that the Palestinians could not be ignored in a Middle East settlement or there would be no lasting settlement; and to demonstrate that they had destructive powers which they were prepared to use, not just against Israel but far afield against other governments and peoples, until their aims were achieved.

*While this paper is limited to a discussion of international terrorism, much of what is said is applicable also to indigenous, or national, terrorism such as that within Northern Ireland, Argentina, and many other countries.

Another recent and vivid example occurred on December 21, 1975. Five professional international terrorists—a Venezuelan, two Palestinians, and two Germans—took control of the OPEC (Organization of Petroleum Exporting Countries) ministers and their staffs in Vienna, killing three persons in the process, demanded and received publicity for the "Arab rejectionist" cause over the Austrian national radio, and finally released the last of their understandably shaken hostages in Algeria. Their purpose appears to have been to pressure the more moderate Middle East governments into tougher oil and anti-Israel policies.

Historical Origin

Terrorism as a form of violence for political ends is as old as history, probably older. It is said to have acquired its modern name from the French Reign of Terror of the mid-1790s. The first use of international terrorism is hard to pinpoint. However, historians will recall the Moroccan rebel Raisuli's kidnapping of an American and an Englishman in 1904 in a successful attempt to force the United States and British governments to pressure France into compelling the Sultan of Morocco to comply with Raisuli's ransom, prisoner-release, and other demands.

Perhaps the opening phase of the international terrorist threat we face today, though itself a reaction to oppression and terror, was the hijackings by freedom-seeking escapees from the East European Communist countries in the middle and late forties. In the early sixties the stream of hijackings from the United States to Cuba commenced. Terrorist groups around the world saw the potential for publicity in hijackings and began to use them for attention-getting political objectives. Beginning about 1968, Palestinian and other violence-oriented political groups in several parts of the world began to extend their terrorist activities to countries—or to the diplomats of countries—not directly involved in the dispute giving rise to the violence.

Modern Terrorism

What have we learned from our study of terrorism and from our practical experience with it? How does one combat terrorism? It is done basically in three ways:

Intelligence. If you can learn his plans ahead of time, you can sometimes forestall the terrorist. It was through intelligence that the terrorists armed with SA-7s were apprehended at the edge of the airport in Rome before they could destroy their intended Israeli Airlines target. The CIA, the FBI, and other intelligence agencies coordinate their antiterrorist efforts through the Cabinet Committee Working Group.

Physical security of target installations and people. Here again, we have improved our position significantly since 1972. U.S. civil airport security has been strengthened to the point where, in combination with bilateral and multilateral antihijacking conventions, we have not had a successful commercial hijacking in the United States in three years—although there was, of course, the recent terrible bombing at LaGuardia airport. The security of our diplomatic posts abroad has been upgraded with such safeguards as armored limousines, more marine guards, closed-circuit TV systems, and careful briefing of personnel.

Apprehension and punishment of terrorists. To achieve this key objective we seek international cooperation. The threat is international and can be met only by international means. A major focus of the United States effort and initiative with other nations has been in the antihijacking area. We took the lead in negotiating in the International Civil Aviation Organization three conventions on hijacking and aircraft sabotage. The general idea of all these conventions, now ratified or adhered to by about seventy countries, is to deter terrorists by internationalizing their criminal acts and thus providing legal means of apprehension and punishment.

But we have not been altogether successful. Hijacking has declined sharply, but more because of improved airport security than the antihijacking conventions—except for our highly effective bilateral agreement with Cuba. Too few countries are willing to arrest, try, and severely punish international hijackers and saboteurs, or indeed international terrorists of any kind. United States efforts for the adoption of enforcement mechanisms to give teeth to the international aircraft-hijacking and sabotage conventions' sanctions, by denying air services to noncomplying countries, have been completely unavailing. Our proposed convention in the 1972 U.N. General Assembly which would have obliged participating states to prosecute or extradite international terrorists coming under their control, at safe-haven destinations or in other ways, won the support of only about half a dozen nations. It did, however, serve as the genesis of the United Nations convention to protect diplomats and foreign officials, adopted in 1973 but still awaiting the necessary ratifications to come into effect.

The Rand Corporation recently calculated, on the basis of experience since 1968, that there is an 80 percent chance that an international terrorist involved in a kidnapping will escape death or capture. The terrorist kidnapper has a close to even chance that all or some of his ransom demands will be granted. Worldwide publicity, normally an important terrorist objective, is achieved in almost every case. For all crimes of terrorism (as opposed to just kidnapping), the average sentence for the small proportion of terrorists caught and tried is less than eighteen months.

In a word, outside the hijacking area, the efforts of the United States, as well as of a small but, hopefully, growing number of other governments, to make terrorism unprofitable for the terrorists have made little headway.

An additional and very important way to combat terrorism is to encourage and assist other nations to alleviate the inequities and frustrations from which international terrorism mainly—though by no means entirely—arises. Unfortunately, effective action to alleviate these inequities and frustrations is in many instances a very long-term proposition. The trend in most countries and regions is the other way. The awakening political consciousness of oppressed, poverty-stricken, or otherwise frustrated peoples on every continent threatens an increasing resort to terrorism in areas now relatively free of it.

U.S. Policies in Terrorist Incidents

From time to time Americans abroad are assassinated or abducted by international terrorist groups. United States policy, with respect to assassinations, seeks to deter or thwart such attacks through intelligence warning and physical security in cooperation with the host government. If an American is nevertheless assassinated, our government does its utmost to insure that the murderer is brought to justice and that intelligence and security measures in that country affecting American citizens are intensified.

With respect to abductions, our policy was made clear by Secretary Kissinger at Vail, Colorado, in August 1975:

The problem that arises in the case of terrorist attacks on Americans has to be seen not only in relation to the individual case but in relation to the thousands of Americans who are in jeopardy all over the world. In every individual case, the overwhelming temptation is to go along with what is being asked.

On the other hand, if terrorist groups get the impression that they can force a negotiation with the United States and an acquiescence in their demands, then we may save lives in one place at the risk of hundreds of lives everywhere else.

Therefore it is our policy . . . that American Ambassadors and American officials not participate in negotiations on the release of victims of terrorists and that terrorists know that the United States will not participate in the payment of ransom and in the negotiation for it.

The following month, at Orlando, Florida, the Secretary said:

When Americans are captured, we are always in great difficulty because we do not want to get into a position where we encourage terrorists to capture Americans in order to get negotiations started for their aim. So our general position has been—and it is heartbreaking in individual cases, always heartbreaking—that we will not, as a Government, negotiate for the release of Americans that have been captured.

. . . we will not negotiate . . . because there are so many Americans in so many parts of the world—tourists, newsmen, not only officials—that it would be impossible to protect them all unless the kidnappers can gain no benefit from it.

For these reasons, the United States government has not and will not pay ransom, release prisoners, or otherwise yield to terrorist blackmail. Nor will it negotiate with respect to any of these matters. We urge the same policy on other governments, private companies, and individuals. We rely for the safe return of American hostages on the responsibility under traditional international law of a host government to protect all persons within its territories, including the safe release of hostages. We consider it the host government's sovereign right to decide during an incident how it will fulfill this responsibility.

This may sound somewhat cold and unfeeling. But be assured that those of us charged with managing cases of Americans abducted abroad feel keenly both the plight of the hostage and our government's legal and moral responsibility to exert every appropriate effort for his safe return. The local United States embassy abroad, and the task force at home, go to work with all the experience, energy, and imagination they can muster. They stay in close and continuous contact with the host government, supporting it with all practicable intelligence, equipment, technical services, and other assistance and advice it may request, *except* advice on how it should respond to demands from the abductors. This decision is considered to be the exclusive responsibility of the host government, taken in awareness, however, of our own government's policy not to accede to terrorist demands.

Sometimes a host government proves unwilling or unable to discharge effectively its responsibility to secure the hostage's release, perhaps because he has been seized by a rebel or outlaw group within the country. In such cases we may nominate an intermediary to the host government, enlist the assistance of a third government, or conduct discussions with the abductors ourselves. But if we hold such discussions they are strictly confined to such matters as the well-being of the hostage and to humanitarian and other factors arguing for his unconditional release. There are no negotiations. The host government is kept closely informed.

So we do not allow ourselves to be rendered helpless as a result of our no-concessions policies or the failure of a host government to fulfill its obligations under international law. Sometimes the terrorist has decided in advance to execute the hostage or stubbornly holds to his demands to the point of fulfilling his threat to execute. But in the more typical case the terrorist is not anxious to kill the hostage and when he sees, usually over time, that he is not going to succeed in his blackmail effort, he will begin to have second thoughts and events will move toward release. We recently witnessed this process in the Netherlands, British, and Irish governments' patient but firm handling of the Moluccan, Balcombe Street, and Herrema incidents. The year 1975 saw an encouraging trend of greater firmness by a number of NATO governments in their handling of terrorist incidents. It also saw a welcome trend of a higher level of terrorist arrests and trials and of sterner laws against terrorism, notably in Germany.

Some argue that we are misreading the situation—that acceding to terrorist demands to save an American hostage's life would have no, or insignificant, effect on the safety of other Americans abroad or on our effort to combat international terrorism. Such reasoning is tempting, but I for one would be reluctant to assume the responsibility of following it. On the other hand, we have repeated, convincing evidence that our government's no-negotiation, no-concession policy is widely known by terrorist groups abroad, that it is believed, and is having important deterrent effect.

The United States has not yet had to face seizures or attacks within its own territories by international terrorist groups. Would our government, as a host government responsibile for dealing with such incidents at home, practice the same firm no-concession policy it has urged on other governments, including occasions when our own citizens have been abducted abroad? The answer is yes. We are convinced of its soundness. And we have seen other governments, faced with a series of terrorist incidents of a type we have thus far been spared, conclude from hard experience that firmness is the only course. We have dealt as firmly as the law allows with domestic terrorist organizations, such as the Black Panthers, Symbionese Liberation Army, Weather Underground, and Puerto Rican Liberation Armed Force. I do not think the United States government will be found wanting if, unhappily, the international terrorist menace reaches our shores.

International Cooperation Against Terrorists

Several principal issues and requirements regarding the international terrorist threat can be identified as we look to the future. First, how are we to achieve more effective international cooperation for the apprehension, trial, and punishment of international terrorists?

This objective is as intractable as it is central. Most countries apparently remain unwilling to apply strict legal sanctions to international terrorists. In the Third World, where most of the difficulty lies, many countries sympathize with the political aspirations of groups which practice terrorism. There is the sympathy of Arab governments for the Palestinian cause, including approval of terrorist attacks on Israel and, in the case of the radical Arab governments, approval and support of Palestinian terrorist attacks in Europe and elsewhere as well. There is the sympathy of newly independent countries, many of which used terrorism to help achieve their freedom, for anticolonial terrorist groups. And there is the sympathy of practically all Third World governments for terrorists striking against repressive authoritarian regimes, particularly in the developed world. Third World governments generally accept the terrorists' argument that the weak and oppressed, with their pleas for justice unheeded, and lacking the means for conventional war, have no alternative to terrorism—that terrorism in a perceived "just" cause is not criminal but patriotic and heroic.

We, with our Judeo-Christian tradition, can understand this reasoning up to a point, but can never accept it. We believe there can be no justification, in any circumstances, for the deliberate killing of innocent individuals. We recognize that the alternatives to terrorism, centering on peaceful protest, constructive proposals, and negotiation, often involve frustration and delay. But we believe that, in an interdependent world attempting to move away from violence before it is too late, they offer the only acceptable means of change.

For reasons different from those put forward by Third World countries, most advanced countries are also disinclined to commit themselves to clear and unequivocal sanctions against terrorists. Sometimes they are inhibited by political or commercial interests from offending governments that support or condone terrorism. Or they are concerned that if they convict and imprison terrorists this will attract more terrorists to their territories seeking, through further violence, to free their comrades. Or they are reluctant to see rights of political asylum weakened. The Communist giants, the Soviet Union and China, appear to share our conviction that hijacking, aircraft sabotage, and other forms of international terrorism are a criminal threat to civilized society and should be stopped. But they also share the Third World's belief that terrorism as an instrument of "wars of national liberation" is acceptable, and they support such terrorism.

A succession of major international terrorist incidents during 1975, culminating in the seizures in Vienna and the Netherlands, appears to have somewhat enhanced awareness of the common danger presented by international terrorism. Venezuela and Colombia have jointly proposed a new consideration of the problem by the General Assembly in the fall. The United States earnestly hopes that this increased awareness and concern is widespread and that antiterrorism proposals in the 1976 General Assembly will find a different atmosphere and reception from that accorded the convention we proposed in 1972. In an address in Montreal in August 1975, Secretary Kissinger urged the United Nations once again to take up and adopt our 1972 proposals, or some similar convention, as a matter of the highest priority. In December our representative on the U.N. Sixth Committee reiterated this position.

All stand to suffer if the present apparently heightened interest in the control of international terrorism is allowed to die without result and has to be reawakened by further terrorist acts of even more serious proportions than those suffered in 1975.

Effectiveness of Terrorism

Second, how effective has international terrorism been for the terrorists' purposes?

Clearly, international terrorists have had tactical successes, as recently evidenced at Kuala Lumpur and Vienna, and have achieved their objectives of publication or broadcasting of manifestos, release of imprisoned comrades, or extortion of ransom. And these successes have been achieved at small cost to the terrorists—most have escaped to safe havens, or, if caught, have later been rescued by comrades or served very short terms. On the other hand, international terrorist groups have fruitlessly suffered suicidal losses in attacks within Israel. And such groups operating in Europe and elsewhere have in a number of cases suffered heavy casualties while achieving none of their purposes, except dubious publicity, as in the Baader-Meinhof seizure of the German Embassy in Stockholm in April 1975 or the earlier mentioned South Moluccan, Balcombe Street, and Herrema incidents.

How about terrorist groups' attainment of their fundamental political goals—the causes their abductions and attacks are intended to serve? Here, too, the overall record is hardly a source of encouragement for terrorists. Certainly the Baader-Meinhof Gang and the Japanese Red Army have not succeeded in advancing their nihilist, world revolution cause significantly. The kidnappings and murders of United States and other diplomats in Brazil, Guatemala, Argentina, and elsewhere have won the terrorists no discernible political gains. The terrorism perpetrated by South Moluccan extremists in the Netherlands achieved world publicity, as sensational crimes are wont to do. But the terrorism was essentially negative in its consequences for the South Moluccan cause, embarrassing the group's responsible members and outraging the Netherlands government and people.

As for Palestinian terrorism, the Palestinian cause is unquestionably more widely known as a result of the terrorism than would otherwise be the case. But against this must be set the revulsion of all civilized peoples over the crimes committed by Palestinian terrorist groups at Lod, Munich, Khartoum, within Israel, and elsewhere. And terrorist attacks have contributed importantly to the hatred and bitterness which impede a Middle East settlement from which the Palestinians might hope to achieve their goal of a Palestinian state. The decline in Palestinian terrorism within the past two years suggests that the more moderate Palestinian leaders have come in part, at least, to share the view that terrorism is counterproductive to the attainment of Palestinian objectives.

International terrorism, in short, is no success story, for the Palestinians, the South Moluccans, or any other group.

Terrorism As a World Problem

Third, how deeply need we be concerned about international terrorism as a world problem?

Up to now international terrorism's toll in dead and wounded and property damage has been relatively small. This is true of all forms of terrorism, compared with the casualties and property losses of even the most minor conventional wars. But it is particularly true of international terrorism. It has been estimated that some 800 people have been killed, including terrorists, and some 1,700 injured, in all international terrorist incidents from 1968 through the present. Year by year this is no more than the crime rate of one moderate-sized American city, intolerably high as that rate is. Property damage, principally in destroyed aircraft, has been equally limited.

But international terrorism's limited toll in lives and property thus far is only part of the story. There are a number of things we should note and ponder:

1. Most of the world's airports are now manned by guards and inspectors, aided where possible by expensive X-ray machines. Even so, no air traveler is secure from terrorist attack.

2. United States and other nations' embassies in Beirut, Buenos Aires, Nicosia, and many other capitals are heavily guarded, in sharp contrast with, and derogation of, their diplomatic function. Diplomats can no longer go about their business in any capital without varying degrees of fear of being kidnapped or killed.

3. The world's leading statesmen work and travel under costly and inhibiting restrictions.

4. Mail received at potential target addresses, such as the Department of State, must be X-rayed for explosives before delivery.

5. State authority is weakened as governments accede to terrorist demands for release of prisoners, ransom, and publicity.

6. The principles and standards of justice are impaired as the perpetrators of horrible acts of violence are given short sentences or let free.

None of these conditions has reached critical proportions. But in combination they signal a potential for mounting, serious erosion of world order if we do not succeed in bringing the international terrorist threat under control.

Future of Terrorism

What of the future? Although terrorism, particularly international terrorism, has resulted in a relatively small toll in killed and wounded and property damage, this could soon begin to change. New weapons are constantly enlarging terrorists' destructive capabilities.

Particularly rapid advances are being made in individual weapons development as we and other advanced nations seek to equip our foot soldiers with increased, highly accurate firepower. There is obvious risk of growing quantities of these weapons coming into the hands of terrorists, weapons which are as capable of being employed against civil aircraft, supertankers, motorcades, and speakers' podiums as against military targets. The Soviet SA-7 heat-seeking, man-portable missile has already, as I mentioned, been found in the hands of terrorists.

And there are more serious hazards. As nuclear power facilities multiply, the quantity and geographical dispersion of plutonium and other fissionable materials in the world will increase greatly. The possibility of credible nuclear terrorist threats based on illicitly constructed atomic bombs, stolen nuclear weapons, or sabotage of nuclear power installations can be expected to grow. Even more plausible would be threats based on more readily and economically produced chemical and biological agents, such as nerve gas and pathogenic bacteria.

Would terrorists actually use such weapons? Probably not. They could already have attacked cities with toxic aerosols, for example, but have not done so. Terrorists, at least the rational ones, fundamentally seek to influence people, not kill them. The death of thousands, or tens of thousands, of persons could produce a tremendous backlash against those responsible and their cause. But the possibility of credible nuclear, chemical, and biological threats, particularly by anarchists, is real. Although the chances of such threats being carried out may be small, the risk is there and must be met.

There is a further danger—one of international terrorist groups for hire, which we may already be seeing in an incipient stage. A government might employ such groups to attack, alarm, or subvert another government or international organization. Powerful pressures might be brought to bear through a small, deniable expenditure by the aggressor government.

The future, some believe, holds a prospect of reduced resort to open warfare but of a high level of subversive and terroristic violence and insecurity originating with governments or subgovernmental elements using, or threatening to use, against our vulnerable modern societies, the frightening small, or even more frightening mass-effect, weapons I have cited. A world of many Ulsters might be statistically safer for the average man than the world of the past sixty years of repeated major conflicts. But it would be a more nerve-wracking and unsettled world of continuing low-level violence and threatened mass-destruction terrorist attack.

Conclusion

Man's inhumanity to man is not confined to war. Terrorism, too, inflicts brutal suffering on the innocent. We see its toll daily in atrocious acts of indigenous or international terrorism.

To combat the latter the United States presented to the 1972 General Assembly the carefully formulated draft Convention for the Prevention and Punishment of Certain Acts of International Terrorism (mentioned earlier). The idea of the convention was simple. States should be left to deal themselves, under their domestic law, with acts of terrorism against persons within their own territories, except diplomats and other internationally protected persons. However, when terrorists sought to export terrorism by blackmailing states through acts committed on the territory of other states or in international air or waters, international law should impose obligations on the states party to the convention to prosecute or extradite such terrorists coming under their control. Had this convention come into force with a full range of parties, international terrorism would have been dealt a heavy, perhaps fatal, blow. There would today be no safe havens.

Instead our proposal foundered in a discussion of definitions and of the causes of international terrorism. It was argued that we had ignored the problem of terrorism practiced by repressive governments—state terrorism—to which group terrorism is often a response. It was further argued that international terrorism practiced in a just cause, such as the self-determination of peoples and human rights, could not be considered criminal.

Our reply to the first of these arguments was, and is, that there is a wealth of existing law and ongoing effort in the field of state action, including state terrorism. Although these laws and effort have not given us a perfect world, mixing the problem of international terrorism with the problem of state terrorism would not assist the reduction of either.

With respect to the causes of terrorism, we pointed out that none of the many states which have won their independence the hard way, including our own nation, engaged in the type of international violence which our draft convention sought to control. Our proposal was carefully restricted to the problem of the spread of violence to persons and places far removed from the scene of struggles for self-determination. We further noted that even when the use of force may be legally justified, there are some means which must not be used, especially when directed against innocents. This principle has long been recognized in the rules of war. Certainly if a state, acting in a situation where its very survival may be at stake, is legally precluded from resorting to atrocities, individuals or groups purportedly seeking to advance some self-determined cause should be similarly limited.

Terrorism is an affront to civilization. Like piracy, it must be seen as outside the law. In Secretary Kissinger's words, in August 1975 in Montreal, "It discredits any political objective that it purports to serve and any nations which encourage it." The United States is not wedded to its 1972 proposal, but it is firmly wedded to that most precious of human rights, the right of the innocent person to life. It is time—past time—for the international community genuinely to address the affliction of international terrorism and to take effective action against it. The technological interdependence of the modern world enables the terrorist to carry out and publicize acts of terrorism in ways that were beyond reach a few decades ago. The international community must catch up with this modernization of barbarism before it is victimized by acts of terrorism as yet only imagined.

J. BOWYER BELL

Terror: An Overview

In recent years terror has become trendy, not only in the number of spectacular and often gruesome incidents but also as a subject for academic analysis and a concern to policy makers. Munich, Vienna, Rome, and Athens have been transmuted into a litany of massacres: a macabre grand tour. Diplomats have been kidnapped and murdered, ending their careers in as diverse sites as the basement of the Saudi Arabian Embassy in Khartoum and an official limousine in the streets of Guatemala City. Transnational executives have been shot in Argentina, American military advisers in Iran, and unlucky tourists standing in the wrong line in various air terminals. And it has not been only the weak seeking to bomb their way into prominence if not power. The threatened have resorted to governing by torture or responding to provocation with authorized assassinations. Fanatics in the grip of some compelling fantasy mimicking revolutionary violence have hijacked aircraft while babbling half-digested political slogans, or shot at the President of the United States in the cause of the environment. Nor have those who employ the tactics of extortion or coercion for financial gain been absent—kidnapping in Italy has become a veritable cottage industry, exploited not only by criminals but by sound businessmen eager to sell potential victims insurance. To many we appear to live in an era of violence, a time of terror.

Yet, even the most casual discussion of terrorism soon reveals what might be called the definitional problem. Some see almost any violent, asocial act as terrorism. Others stress the reasonableness of revolutionaries or the violence of governments. Some see "terror" as a technique employed by an international conspiracy directed from Moscow or Havana, others as the result of disturbed minds. There is no consensus, nor even in many cases a recognition, that the discussion is carried out at cross-purposes about subjects few have ever seen even at the point of a gun. A paucity of data has, however, never deterred the academic mind; rather, one suspects, the contrary. Thus, attracted to the recent spurt of spectacular acts of violence, scholars have rushed into print almost as fast as the journalists, fashioning typologies, defining, explaining, and usually prescribing. And yet the definitional problem remains: who is a terrorist, what is terrorism? The term, of course, now is pejorative, the label of the threatened ("There are no guerrillas in Rhodesia, only terrorists"), where once in the nineteenth century it was conventional, convenient revolutionary usage for those who used a special kind of violence against the state. Today in revolutionary circles there are no terrorists, only guerrillas or freedom fighters or fedayeen. No matter, the term will not go away; and thus it might be wise to sketch out some bounds.

First, we appear to be concerned with a cluster of violent deeds: murder—especially of the innocent—mutilation and torture, kidnapping and hijacking, extortion, bombing, theft, arson. A more classical form of terrorism is clearly present when these deeds are choreographed for special effect, make up a series rather than a discrete display, and are rationalized with political purpose. From a violent act alone without a context of explanation the disinterested eye cannot determine if the deed could be popped into a terrorist pigeonhole. Is a man killing a woman "terrorism"? Does it decrease the possibility if we know they are man and wife? But what if one is king and the other queen? Then is it an act of passion or of state? Thus for analytic purposes one approach is certainly to define the motives of the actors. Certainly some violent deeds are performed solely for profit, for instance, Murder, Inc.; others, even if given a patina of politics, such as robbing banks for the cause, seem largely criminal. And for various reasons violent crime, such as the kidnapping and mutilation of Getty, has seemed less fruitful for analysis than has political crime, such as the kidnapping and conversion of Patty Hearst.

Secondly, many acts, such as the long series of American assassinations, have come at the hands of seriously disturbed individuals whose subsequent explanations have been a mix of fantasy and the current political trend. Arthur Bremer, who shot Governor George Wallace, did not even bother to have a "cause"; all he wanted was recognition—better to be wanted for murder than not wanted at all. Most of those who hijack airplanes, for example, can be explained in psychological rather than political science terms. Then there are psychotic "terrorists." Some scholars find such types gravitate to various organizations such as revolutionary parties or the police force. Others insist that this is rarely so and that the criminals and the psychopaths lie outside an examination of terrorism.

There are, of course, societies where violence appears endemic, neither mad nor criminal, but habitual, the custom of the tribe. Again, such ritual barbarism has been of major concern to anthropologists and rarely to other social scientists except when some cannibal king disturbs the transnational order. What has been of concern is violence used for political purpose. There have regularly been those swift to point out regime-terror, either rule by reliance on torture and judicial assassination or by resort to the tactics of their opponents, seeking out and shooting down their enemies wherever they may be found. Every state involved in an irregular war has been so tempted and most have succumbed. And where the state has held back, often others, vigilantes of order, have not. Policemen kill rather than arrest suspects in Brazil; assassins wander the lanes of Belfast and the roads of South Armagh. And, no matter how awful the deeds, somehow the cloak of the state gives them some small legitimacy, for, to many, a suspect shot down by an agent of the state fails to conjure up the same distress and outraged indignation reserved for murder without proper banners—revolutionary violence without legitimate sanction. Mostly and perhaps rightly so terror is seen as a revolutionary tactic, sometimes a revolutionary strategy, and, to those even marginally threatened, a clear and present danger.

For the revolutionary, quite aware that power comes from the barrel of a gun, recourse to violence, often the last option, is a legitimate means to shape the future. The present is intolerable and violence the only way. As one Palestinian fedayi said, "We would throw roses if it would work." Since it does not, they throw bombs. But within revolutionary violence, there are as well various categories of intention. Within the organization discipline may be maintained by force, informers murdered, for example, while outside the core support may be acquired from the reluctant, dues collected, strikes imposed, by coercion. A revolutionary, unlike the state, has no conventional means to tax the people, imprison the culprit, or draft a new brigade.

Mostly, however, it is the use of violence as an offensive weapon that has attracted attention: a campaign of functional violence, for example, killing policemen, that may provoke, and often is intended to provoke, counter-violence. In fact, some revolutionary operations are fashiòned to be manipulative, to include a role for the authorities. There are as well deeds that will not swiftly advance the revolutionary toward power but only prominence. Frustrated without the means to act on events, the revolutionary chooses terror. A spectacular assassination or the televised negotiations over the fate of hostages can maintain the organization as well as propagate a message. The victims are not the targets, only the means. It has been this facet of revolutionary violence—the murders in Munich, the kidnapping of the OPEC ministers, the slaughter in the Lod airport—that has kindled a concern with what most see as a novel form of transnational terrorism. For most in democratic countries, the quibbles about appropriate revolutionary violence collapse when a bomb goes off in a crowded pub or women and children are machine-gunned in an airport lounge. Terror like love may be difficult to define but readily recognizable to the involved.

There are several considerations fundamental to a discussion of terrorism. Clearly, the definitional problem is crucial. When there is not a generally agreed subject matter, then any discussion goes on at cross-purposes. One man's terrorist need not be another's patriot, but limits and bounds need to be recognized. Is every asocial violent act for whatever purpose to be included? Are generalizations to be made about terrorists that include or exclude those involved in authorized regime-terrorism? Do psychopaths count whether they are in or out of a revolutionary organization? Was the Symbionese Liberation Army a handful of psychopaths acting out self-destructive fantasies, a group of asocial criminals hiding in radical rhetoric, or a serious manifestation of America's political maladies? Were their crimes simply crimes? Or do some organizations and deeds lie outside easy categories? What of the strange world of the surviving Japanese Red Army terrorist who predicted that victims and murderers would be reunited in the stars? Was he a madman, a kamikaze hired with slogans, or was he representative of a Japanese warrior tradition, a revolutionary samurai? Does Squeaky Frome count? What of the fedayi who drank the blood of the murdered Prime Minister Tal of Jordan, gunned down in the lobby of the Sheraton Hotel in Cairo? Are conventional rural guerrilla campaigns in or out as terror campaigns—murder from the ditch, ambushes at night? Does assassinating a tyrant make you a terrorist? Or is assassination not murder? Does placing a symbolic bomb in an empty laboratory make you a terrorist? What if you shoot a man on orders of the state or in pursuit of gain? Can you be a terrorist? No matter what the answers, recent experience has indicated that the word slips and slides with hopeless imprecision. Terrorism has too often become a tag in the service of various predilections and postures, a stump for explanations filled with outraged indignation. And yet what is to be done?

A second consideration is that once there is agreement, more or less, on the limits and bounds of terrorism some caution must be displayed on the nature of those being examined. Active revolutionaries are for analytical purposes often elusive, the captured or interned no longer in the live state, and the retired apt to adjust memory for present cause. Historians have long had to make do with evidence at one remove; some would truly prefer to read Napoleon's mail than talk to the man, and historians have often produced most germane analyses of revolutionary movements and the revolutionary mind. Contemporary social scientists, however, use other tools that are, in the case of the terrorist, often difficult to apply. Certainly much can be learned from existing records, from interviews, from some of the customary means of investigation; but it would be wise to be wary about generalizations concerning men on the run, men without names, living covert lives whose real nature largely lies beyond academic capacity to investigate with customary rigor.

A third obstacle to an examination of terrorism has been an inclination of much of the academic community and most of the policy makers to see the subject as novel. Violence often of the most unsavory kinds has long been with us, beginning with Cain and Abel. The slaughter of innocents, torture for sport, the destruction of whole peoples, the sordid litany of every civilization has been the stuff of history. For present purposes, however, the existing mix of today's revolutionary violence is founded on the aspirations of the enlightenment, the rise of nationalism, the arrival of industrialism, all of which inspired some to seek radical change by violent means, to create new nations, new societies, a new world. In various forms this revolutionary aspiration has been a significant aspect of Western history for more than two centuries. Thus the public and the press may have only recently discovered the Provo IRA bombers in Belfast, but Irish rebels spring from a long and often bloody history. The IRA, for example, is a direct descendant of the Irish Republican rising of 1798, has organizational ancestors from 1848, and a structure little changed since 1916.

In point of fact, the mad bomber and the assassin have long been with us. Contemporary society has not suddenly and for the first time been held to ransom by gunmen. We are not uniquely vulnerable to bombers. The revolutionary tactics of anarchists made life at the turn of this century far from easy. Thus the inclination to see the tactics of Black September or the Japanese Red Army as quite new is an historical fallacy.

Obviously nothing today is as it was even in the recent past; nevertheless, contemporary violence stands on the shoulders of earlier fanaticism. The primary difference may be not so much in the revolutionaries but in the growing interdependence and sophistication of the new international society. In any case, even if there is no consensus on the bounds of terrorism, no ready means to investigate the practitioners, and little realization of the historical roots of the phenomenon, there is ample indication that the past violence will be prologue.

The prospect of more massacres, more assassinations, seems to many strange just as the world begins to enter an era of detente and interdependence. Over the last generation and especially the last decade, the old differences between nations at least have been eased. Great transnational conglomerates stretch over much of the world. Populations move more freely, communicate more easily, enjoy similar pursuits, and use identical machines. Germans watch American television serials, drive Japanese cars, wear Italian shoes, and vacation in Ireland. It is in fact this trend toward universality that has engendered a violent reaction in the name of specialism—a Basque republic before the language is lost and the country filled with Dutch summer houses. Other frustrated rebels see the ubiquitous consumer culture as an intolerable new imperialism with color television the opiate of the masses. They seek, like the Baader-Meinhoff group in Germany, somehow to strike the first blow against tyranny. There are, too, those who take up arms to defend the old ways, to prevent a novel future. Except in those efficient authoritarian states sufficiently brutal to crush any potential revolt—one Budapest or Prague a decade—and those efficient democratic states sufficiently flexible to accommodate legitimate dissent, the prospect for revolutionary violence and often counter-terror seem quite real. Terrorism appears a growth field and society easily vulnerable. There will be new and more lethal weapons for the desperate, perhaps some feel even a nuclear option, and congruently there will be new targets—supertankers, nuclear power facilities, giant computers, communication networks.

It should be stressed that imminent disaster is not at hand. The IRA cannot bomb down London or Black September end air travel. The strategic bombing campaigns of World War II revealed just how resilient society and cities could be under stress. Terrorists have neither the capacity nor the desire to kill great masses; only rulers have had both. It was Caligula who wanted the world to have one neck to cut, not Spartacus. What revolutionaries can do is to demand a price for peace, a strategy of attrition. FRELIMO could not win in the Mozambique bush but could in Lisbon. Those who have no real hope of pursuing such an extended campaign, those who lack not the will but the resources, those most frustrated have instead of attrition and patience chosen to stage spectacular and violent displays— kidnappings stretched out over three continents, massacres set for prime-time coverage, assassinations of the important, and random murder of the innocent. They make propaganda by the deed, and their violence can be seen in living color via satellite by hundreds of millions. The result is that the perception of much of the public by means of the manipulated media has been warped. There have really been very few victims, but the target— massed viewers—has been again and again shocked and outraged. They and their leaders have in indignation called for a response to such provocation. And the nature of that response has seldom been the subject of reasoned arguments. The threat is seen as new and lethal to open society, to democratic norms—and *something* must be done. In reality, as noted, the threat is not new but may, indeed, be lethal to an open society if the public and policy perception continues, as the revolutionaries desire, to be exaggerated.

There are thus two factors present in almost all examinations of terrorism, the analytical focus and the prescriptive: what is happening and what should be done about it. The existing and more recent analysis of terrorism, however defined, has been understandably discipline-bound. Historians go for root causes in narrative prose, lawyers to covenants and codes, psychologists to the mind of the assassin, political scientists to discrete data accumulation. In nearly every case the ultimate form is remarkably similar; the problem is serious or otherwise why bother? The cherished means is deployed—charts and graphs appear or philosophical essays or case studies of deviant behavior—and then there is a prescriptive summation. Since there is no agreed definition of terrorism, since few investigators have access to the subject, and since most exaggerate its novelty and seriousness, the results have often left something to be desired.

One or two admonitions on the means of analysis might be in order. First, revolutionary activity is very difficult to quantify, and counting is a most popular academic sport. Those who rely on aggregate data, for example, face two problems: (1) the data from conventional sources is at best partial—I have been to wars that didn't make the *New York Times Index*; (2) many events of considerable significance never take place—aborted assassination attempts, failed coups, shots that miss and go unrecorded.

Those who want to create a composite statistical account of the revolutionary, for instance, an IRA volunteer, can marshal the record of the captured, the failed or foiled, but not of the covert activists. And those who want not to count but to talk must recognize that the specimens they see in the zoo are not those of the wild. Finally, there has been a tendency to shape generalizations about selected terrorists across cultural boundaries, assuming that Arabs and Germans and Irish if they perform certain acts then share certain characteristics. In some cases this may be true—youth and dedication and daring—but not very revealing; however, to find meaningful links, for example, between a middle-aged Belfast bookie, a medical graduate of the American University in Beirut, a retired Greek colonel, and a Latin American priest, is a task not lightly to be undertaken and not likely to be productive given the available data.

Another difficulty with the analysis of terrorism is that for many it has proven difficult to be disinterested. In fact, a number have begun at the end, with prescription, rather than at the beginning. At present those concerned, whatever their politics and tools of analysis, mostly clump about two general postures. At one extreme are those who feel that most terrorists are warped, their politics pathological and consequently unamenable to accommodation. Since their demands are essentially nonnegotiable—what did Oswald want that could be given?—the appropriate response is placed on coercion, protection, and punishment. Order is to be defended by stringent law, cunning safeguards, and expanded security forces. Some sketch out as well a great conspiracy, seated in Havana or Moscow, to manipulate these rebels without a cause for a very real Communist cause. This threat, too, must be met by appropriate force, a swift and measured defense of Western society. Those who would sympathize with the mythical Guevara are dupes or innocents. Others less interested in international conspiracies or the pathology of the rebel mind insist, too, that swift, effective coercive force is essential to protect democratic society. Ineffectual or uncertain governments in Italy after World War I, in Germany during the depression, in Uruguay more recently, failed to keep their houses in order and democracy died. Tough-minded professors insist on the death penalty, on no deals with hostage-holders, on no talks with terrorists.

At the other pole are those who concentrate on the reasoned demands of the revolutionaries, who believe that in many cases accommodations or at least a dialogue is possible. They stress the reasons behind the massacres, the roots of violence, and the remedies to ease real frustration. They put less stress on maintaining order by coercive law and more on the necessity for justice. Where law is stressed the focus is on international agreements and compacts, on United Nations resolutions, on consensus building, on the end of sanctuary rather than on punishment. While there thus tends to be a left-right, liberal-conservative dimension to the two poles, this is not always the case. What does remain true is that the posture of the investigator quite often determines the result of his or her analysis.

Consequently, there has at times been more interest in accumulating sympathetic "evidence" or defining the nature of terrorism, so as to buttress long-held positions, than in value-free investigation. Those who oppose nuclear power are criticized for wishful thinking when they fashion doom-laden terrorist scenarios and defend themselves by stressing the inadequacy of present safeguards. The hypothetical "terrorist" is dragged back and forth in this argument, first bogie and then strawman. All the special pleading makes it remarkably difficult for the responsible to sift out some useful reality. Even the predictions of future prospects vary immensely.

With all of this, there have been certain comforting developments. Much more useful information is available concerning the pathological end of the terrorist spectrum. A variety of techniques and tactics is evolving in preventive profiles, in hostage-bargaining, in various safeguards. More important, an increasingly informed debate is under way on various aspects of such violence: the appropriate response of the press and media, the scope and effectiveness of legal remedies, the actuality of the revolutionary threat to open societies. Yet there clearly continues to be a need for sophisticated interest in various quarters in discovering more rigorous answers, more effective approaches, a greater consensus.

In summary, then, there appears to be a continuing phenomenon with inadequate analytical tools. There is no consensus and no common language; in fact, it may be that the very word *terror* is a hindrance in the investigation of violence. That investigation has been hampered by the emotive quality of those violent deeds, and a focus solely on violent deeds removed from context—the analysis of a technique—is a limited venture. One murder is much like another. Giving them numbers often is of little help; those who inform us that out of thirty-two recent cases of kidnapping eleven ended fatally can tell us nothing of the thirty-third. Using these violent deeds as a fulcrum, however, there is much that can be done and often much that is of more than academic interest. Still, there are far more questions than answers. Who are these people? What are their motives? Are there valid generalizations to be made about the mind of the assassin, the profile of a sane bomber? If the subjects remain elusive, should investigation be postponed? How great is the threat to society? Does the past, even the immediate past, reveal patterns of violence? How does a democratic society respond? How have representative governments reacted recently and to what effect? And for those in positions of responsibility, how best to cope? No one has yet fashioned compelling or definitive conclusions.

EDWARD MICKOLUS

Trends in Transnational Terrorism

In the last decade the world has seen the rise of a new type of actor on the global stage: the transnational terrorist. Groups of them have engaged in numerous types of acts to gain headlines and increase public awareness of their causes, being willing to engage in the assassination of government leaders, sabotage of critical facilities, bombing of embassies and foreign corporations, assaults on military installations, skyjackings, kidnappings of diplomats and businessmen, and the take-over of embassies and holding of their staffs for ransom. How great is this problem? Is it worsening? Are there any trends we can discover? Can any nation consider itself safe from such attacks? Are certain nations being singled out? What groups are engaged in such activity? What is it they want? Why do they resort to these methods? And, finally, what does the future hold in store for the world?

Defining Terrorism

Definitions of terrorism vary tremendously, both among governments and among individual researchers. Incidents considered terrorist by South Africa are merely the legitimate acts of freedom strugglers in the eyes of many Third World nations. Indeed, it has become so difficult to satisfy all the governments of the world, that in the United Nations one does not officially discuss "international terrorism" but rather Item 92: "Measures to Prevent International Terrorism which Endangers or Takes Innocent Human Lives or Jeopardizes Fundamental Freedoms, and Study of the Underlying Causes of those Forms of Terrorism and Acts of Violence which Lie in Misery, Frustration, Grievance and Despair, and which Cause Some People to Sacrifice Human Lives, Including Their Own, in an Attempt to Effect Radical Changes." Such a view borders on accepting the motivations of the terrorists, and is also difficult to translate into action. For purposes of the present discussion, we can consider our research to be concerned with:

The use, or threat of use, of anxiety-inducing extranormal violence for political purposes by an individual or group, whether acting for or in opposition to established governmental authority, when such action is intended to influence the attitudes and behavior of a target group wider than the immediate victims and when, through the nationality or foreign ties of its perpetrators, its location, the nature of its institutional or human victims, or the mechanics of its resolution its ramifications transcend national boundaries.

We can further isolate transnational terrorism from other forms of violence by making the following distinctions: *International terrorism* is such action (as described above) when carried out by individuals or groups controlled by a sovereign state. Examples include attacks in Europe against Palestinian liberation groups by Israeli intelligence agents and the anti-Basque campaign recently launched in the south of France by the Spanish police. *Transnational terrorism* is such action when carried out by basically autonomous non-state actors, whether or not they enjoy some degree of support from sympathetic states. Examples include the kidnappings of United States businessmen overseas, the hijacking of international flights, and the machine gun attacks on international airports by members of the Popular Front for the Liberation of Palestine. *Domestic terrorism* is that behavior which has the aforementioned characteristics of extranormal violence, but does not involve nationals of more than one state. It is the domestic parallel to transnational terrorism in that it is carried on by basically autonomous non-state actors, but only affects citizens of one state. The bombings in New York City by the Weather Underground, attacks by the Irish Republican Army and Ulster Defense Association upon the civilian population in Northern Ireland, and attempted assassinations of governmental leaders by nationals of that state are examples. *State terrorism* includes terrorist actions conducted by a national government within the borders of that state, and is the domestic parallel of international terrorism. Examples include genocide in Nazi Germany, the pogroms in the Ukraine, and tortures in police states. Schematically, we can locate transnational terrorism as being one cell of political terrorism, as shown in Figure 1.

Figure 1: Types of Political Terrorism

		Direct involvement of nationals of more than one state?	
		YES	NO
GOVERNMENT CONTROLLED	Yes	International	State
OR DIRECTED?	No	Transnational	Domestic

Other types of nonpolitical terrorism, such as criminal terrorism in which the sole object is personal gain, are beyond the scope of the present inquiry.

Transnational terrorism has often been described as violence for effect. It differs from military concepts of war as a strategy in that it does not attempt to hold a specific piece of territory by dint of military engagement. Rather, it attempts to give the impression that the terrorist group is able to strike with impunity, that its small, numerically weak band should be considered a credible threat, and that governmental authorities cannot guarantee security to members of the society under its protection. Hence, while wars, be they civil wars, colonial wars, international wars, or irredentist battles for a territory, may lead to great fear in noncombatant populations, their primary objective is the securing of populations and territory tactically as well as strategically.

Annual Trends

Not all activities of groups which have engaged in acts of terrorism can be classed as terrorist. While the Montoneros in Argentina may kidnap businessmen and conduct armed attacks upon military and police facilities, they also engage in more widely accepted political pursuits, such as funding political parties, conducting meetings to discuss politics, and the like. While such activities are the work of the same organization, we somehow do not normally consider the latter actions to be terrorist in nature when engaged in by others. It is the use or threat of use of extranormal violence which disturbs us. There are basically two general types of such violence: (1) incidents in which the terrorists attempt to injure or kill individuals and/or damage or destroy property, and (2) incidents in which individuals are taken hostage, and destruction of property and injury to the hostages are conditional upon the response of a target group to the demands of the perpetrators. In Table 1, we note seven kinds of destructive incidents and four types of hostage situations.[1]

The latter are described as follows: *Kidnapping* is an incident in which a diplomat or businessman is taken to an underground hideout and held for monetary ranson, release of prisoners, publication of the group's manifesto, or against some other demand. *Barricade and hostage* situations include incidents in which the terrorists seize one or more hostages but make no attempt to leave the original scene of the crime. Negotiations are carried on with the perpetrators themselves effectively being held hostage, unable to leave the scene freely. Such scenarios frequently occur at the end of an incident in which the seizure of hostages was not the terrorists' primary aim—for example, a bank holdup in which the robbers, discovered by the authorities before they are able to escape, seize any hostages who happen to be handy; or an attack on an airport lounge or residence in which hostages are seized as pawns to be used to secure free passage from the site of the murders. *Skyjackings* involve the alteration of the direction of an airline flight due to actions by the terrorist. We can distinguish between those situations in which the hijacker is merely seeking a means of transportation to a nation giving him asylum (the old "Take this plane to Cuba" demand), situations in which the hijackers force the pilot to land the plane, release the crew and passengers, and blow up the plane without making any ransom demands (engaged in for the shock value of the action), and incidents in which the skyjackers make specific demands upon governments or corporations, threatening the safety of the passengers and crew.[2] *Takeovers of non-air means of transportation* involve hijackings of such transport media as trains, ships, and automotive vehicles.[3]

Destructive incidents are described as follows: *Bombing* involves the attempt, notwithstanding degree of success, to explode a device which will cause some amount of damage. Timing mechanisms are usually employed, and the incident is not considered part of a general armed assault. *Letterbombs* are devices sent through the mails and intended to explode when attempts are made to open the envelope. They range in size from a large parcel to a first-class letter. *Armed attacks* involve assaults upon facilities using missiles, hand-held weapons, grenades, thrown bombs, and/or incendiary devices. They range from machine gun and grenade assaults upon airport lounges to rifle shots aimed at an embassy from a fast-moving car. *Murder and assassination* involve the attempt to kill a specific individual for political purposes.[4] *Arson and molotov cocktails* are devices to set afire a selected installation. Bombs of an incendiary nature are included in this category, rather than with the explosive types. *Theft and break ins* involve the forcible entry of facilities and an attempt to acquire money or documents from the installation illegally. Robbery of individuals by political terrorists is also included here. *Sabotage* entails the attempted damage of facilities by means not involving explosives or incendiary devices.

We can see trends in such incidents over the past eight years. Kidnappings are by far the most popular hostage incident, showing a wavering but rising trend line over time. In 1975 we witnessed more kidnappings than in any other year in recent memory. Moreover, the probability that the kidnappers will successfully seize a hostage in the attempt has grown dramatically since the beginning of the 1970s. We have also seen a steady rise in barricade and hostage incidents, with no known failures to take hostages in the eight years studied. Again, 1975 saw the establishment of an annual record in this category as well. The situation changes with respect to aerial hijackings. Improvements in security procedures made in 1973, as well as the unwillingness of countries to grant asylum to hijackers have made this type of incident a comparative rarity. Non-air transportation takeovers are infrequent annoyances rather than common threats. Overall, if we consider kidnappings, barricade situations, non-air takeovers, and only those skyjackings which involve hostage negotiations, we find an erratic rise in the total number of incidents, with a rise in the probability of successfully seizing hostages.

In the category of destructive acts, bombings have become the most popular type of activity, and are a continuing threat to embassies, consulates, and corporation facilities. The IRA and PFLP have also been targeting bombs against more generalized civilian populations. Letter-bombs appear

Table 1. International Terrorist Incidents, 1968-1975

INCIDENT TYPE	1968	1969	1970	1971	1972	1973	1974	1975	TOTAL
Kidnapping	1	4	28	15	11	30	21	32	142
Barricade and Hostage	0	0	2	1	4	8	11	17	43
Skyjacking	33	79	70	37	38	19	7	6	289
Takeover of Non-Air Transportation	0	0	3	0	1	0	1	1	6
Bombing	29	55	42	45	61	90	33	78	433
Letter-bomb	2	1	1	1	147	49	1	3	205
Armed Attack	2	6	6	9	4	10	7	10	54
Murder or Assassination	6	4	10	6	5	11	3	18	63
Arson or Molotov Cocktail	0	1	10	8	1	15	1	6	42
Theft or Break In	0	4	6	0	0	1	2	3	16
Sabotage	0	0	0	1	3	0	1	0	5
TOTAL	73	154	178	123	275	233	88	174	1298

to follow no pattern, with the 1972 and 1973 peak years showing a wave of bombings by two groups, rather than worldwide bombings by many organizations. It appears that most letter-bombs are sent from the same post office on the same day, but that the targets are worldwide. Because of their general unreliability in successfully harming the chosen target as well as the technical sophistication required to make them, there does not seem to have been an imitation of letter-bombing techniques by observing terrorist groups. (Many letter-bombs are intercepted by police or explode in post offices, injuring innocent workers and leading to negative publicity for the terrorists.) Armed attacks and murders appear to be following a cyclical trend, which may be slowly rising, with 1975 setting annual records in both categories. Arsons peaked in 1973, a year in which, subtracting intercepted letter-bombs, the greatest number of incidents occurred. Thefts and sabotage are comparatively rare. While the total number of incidents appears to have peaked in 1972 and 1973, we can by no means say that terrorism no longer presents a threat. Methods which have proven too difficult to engage in or relatively ineffective, such as skyjackings and letter-bombs, respectively, have been replaced by other methods which appear to the terrorists to satisfy their goals. This gloomy conclusion is further supported by Table 2 and Figure 2, which present statistics on all casualties from transnational terrorist operations. Here we find a very disturbing rise in deaths, injuries, and total casualties.[5]

Table 2. Annual Casualties from Terrorist Actions (includes terrorists, police, foreign and domestic noncombatants)

YEAR	KILLED	WOUNDED	TOTAL
1968	11	31	42
1969	12	46	58
1970	73	60	133
1971	18	73	91
1972	142	273	415
1973	90+	455	545+
1974	330	461	791
1975	155	468	623
Total	831	1967	2798

Geographic Trends

What have transnational terrorists chosen as the sites of their operations? Tables 3 and 4 give us some idea of the location of the more frequent types of attacks.[6]

Conventional wisdom argues that most terrorism occurs in emerging Third World nations. While this may be true for cases of domestic terror-

Figure 2. Annual Casualties from Terrorist Actions

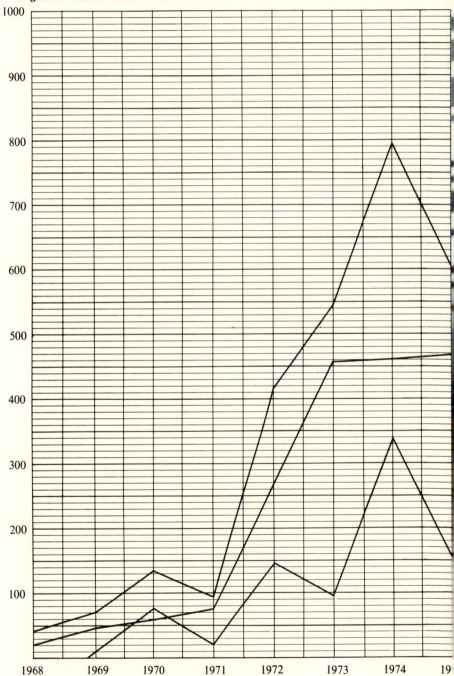

Table 3. Location of Incident, by Country, Region, and Type

LOCATION	B&H	SKY-JACK	KID-NAP	MURDER	ARMED ATTACK	BOMB	LETTER-BOMB	ARSON	TOTAL
ATLANTIC COMMUNITY									
Austria	2	1	—	1	—	1	—	1	6
Belgium	—	—	—	1	—	1	1	2	5
Canada	—	2	2	1	—	2	—	—	7
Cyprus	—	—	—	2	2	1	—	—	5
Denmark	—	—	1	1	—	2	—	—	4
France	4	5	3	6	4	18	1	1	42
Gibraltar	—	—	—	—	—	—	1	—	1
Greece	2	4	—	1	2	25	—	—	34
Ireland	—	—	2	—	—	3	1	1	7
Italy	—	5	1	3	—	16	—	6	31
Netherlands	4	1	—	—	—	5	—	1	11
No. Ireland	—	—	2	1	5	8	—	—	16
Norway	—	—	—	1	—	—	—	—	1
Portugal	—	1	—	—	—	1	1	—	3
Spain	1	2	2	4	—	3	—	2	14
Sweden	2	1	—	1	—	4	—	—	8
Switzerland	—	3	—	—	1	3	6	—	13
W. Germany	1	6	1	3	3	16	1	3	34
UK	3	2	1	3	1	57	31+	—	98
US	—	98	—	6	5	106	7	10	232
MIDDLE EAST									
Algeria	1	1	—	—	—	—	—	—	2
Bahrain	—	1	—	—	—	—	—	—	1
Dubai	—	2	—	—	—	—	—	—	2
Egypt	—	5	—	1	1	—	—	—	7
Iran	—	2	1	3	—	3	—	—	9
Iraq	—	1	—	—	—	—	—	—	1
Israel	6	1	1	—	4	8	1	—	21
Jordan	1	1	3	4	1	6	—	1	17
Kuwait	1	—	—	1	—	—	—	—	2
Lebanon	1	10	9	3	10	13	4	2	52
Libya	—	1	—	—	—	—	—	—	1
Morocco	—	—	—	—	—	2	—	—	2
Saudi Arabia	—	—	—	—	—	1	—	—	1
Sudan	1	—	—	—	—	—	—	—	1
Syria	—	—	—	1	—	—	—	—	1
Tunisia	1	—	—	—	—	—	—	—	1
Turkey	—	3	4	—	1	23	1	4	36
Yemen	—	2	—	—	—	—	—	—	2
LATIN AMERICA									
Argentina	1	8	39	3	4	59	—	1	115
Bahamas	—	1	—	—	—	—	—	—	1
Bolivia	—	1	4	—	—	—	—	—	5

Table 3. Location of Incident, by Country, Region, and Type (continued)

LOCATION	B&H	SKY-JACK	KID-NAP	MURDER	ARMED ATTACK	BOMB	LETTER-BOMB	ARSON	TOTAL
Brazil	—	8	7	2	—	1	1	4	23
British Honduras	—	1	—	—	—	—	—	—	1
Chile	—	2	—	—	—	5	1	—	8
Colombia	—	23	5	1	1	1	—	—	31
Costa Rica	—	2	—	—	—	—	—	—	2
Cuba	—	1	—	—	—	—	1	—	2
Dominican Republic	1	2	2	—	—	—	—	—	5
Ecuador	—	6	—	—	—	1	—	—	7
El Salvador	—	—	—	—	—	3	—	—	3
Guatemala	—	—	4	2	—	—	—	—	6
Haiti	1	—	—	—	—	1	—	—	2
Honduras	—	1	—	—	—	1	—	—	2
Jamaica	—	1	—	—	—	—	—	—	1
Mexico	—	11	4	—	—	12	—	—	27
Netherlands Antilles	—	1	—	—	—	—	—	—	1
Nicaragua	1	1	—	—	—	—	—	—	2
Panama	—	1	—	—	—	—	—	1	2
Paraguay	—	—	1	1	—	—	—	—	2
Peru	—	1	—	—	—	3	—	—	4
Puerto Rico	—	3	—	—	—	3	—	—	6
Uruguay	—	1	9	—	2	1	—	—	13
Venezuela	—	6	2	—	1	1	—	1	11
AFRICA									
Angola	—	2	3	—	—	—	—	—	5
Chad	—	—	1	—	—	—	—	—	1
Ethiopia	—	4	11	2	1	1	—	—	19
Kenya	—	1	—	—	—	—	—	—	1
Somalia	—	—	1	—	—	—	—	—	1
South Africa	1	1	1	—	—	—	—	—	3
Spanish Sahara	—	—	1	—	—	—	—	—	1
Tanzania	—	—	1	1	—	—	1	—	3
Uganda	—	—	1	—	—	—	—	—	1
Zaire	—	—	—	—	—	—	1	—	1
Zambia	—	—	—	—	—	—	1	—	1
ASIA									
Afghanistan	—	—	—	1	—	—	—	—	1
Australia	—	2	—	—	—	5	—	—	7
Bangladesh	1	—	—	1	—	1	—	—	3
Burma	—	—	1	—	—	—	—	—	1
Cambodia	—	—	—	—	—	3	—	—	3
India	—	3	—	—	—	—	54	—	57

Table 3. Location of Incident, by Country, Region, and Type (continued)

LOCATION	B&H	SKY-JACK	KID-NAP	MURDER	ARMED ATTACK	BOMB	LETTER-BOMB	ARSON	TOTAL
Japan	—	2	—	1	1	1	—	2	7
Malaysia	1	—	—	—	—	—	—	—	1
Nepal	—	1	—	—	—	—	—	—	1
New Zealand	—	—	—	—	—	1	—	—	1
Pakistan	1	—	—	1	1	—	—	—	3
Philippines	1	4	2	2	—	—	—	—	9
South Korea	—	2	—	—	—	—	—	—	2
S. Vietnam	—	3	—	—	—	—	—	—	3
Thailand	1	1	1	—	—	—	—	—	3

EAST EUROPE

Czechoslovakia	—	6	—	—	—	—	—	—	6
Finland	—	1	—	—	—	—	—	—	1
Poland	—	4	—	—	—	—	—	—	4
Romania	—	2	—	—	—	—	—	—	2
USSR	—	5	—	—	—	—	—	—	5

OTHER ACTIONS

Takeover of non-air means of transportation: Poland—2;
    Cuba, Lebanon, Thailand, US—1

Theft or break in of facilities: US, Uruguay—3; Lebanon—2;
    Argentina, Ireland, Japan, Jordan, Portugal, Sweden, UK—1

Sabotage not involving bombs: Jordan, Kuwait, Netherlands, UK, W. Germany—1

Table 4. Location of Incident, by Region, and Incident Type

LOCATION	B&H	SKY-JACK	KID-NAP	MURDER	ARMED ATTACK	BOMB	LETTER-BOMB	ARSON	TOTAL
Atlantic Community	19	131	15	35	23	272	50	27	572
Middle East	12	30	18	13	17	56	6	7	159
Asia	5	18	4	6	2	11	54	2	102
East Europe	—	18	—	—	—	—	—	—	18
Latin America	4	82	77	9	8	92	3	7	282
Africa	1	8	20	3	1	1	3	—	37
Total	41	287	134	66	51	432	116	43	1170

ism, it does not seem to be correct when analyzing transnational forms of political terrorism. Nearly half of the incidents reported in the past eight years have occurred in what are considered to be Westernized, highly affluent nations.[7] The United States reports more bombings and skyjackings with international implications than all of Latin America combined. Again, discounting the inflationary impact of the letter-bomb figures, transnational terrorism is very infrequent in the developing countries of Asia and Africa. Eastern European nations have been virtually immune to attacks, suffering only sporadic skyjackings by people seeking political asylum in Western nations. Latin America outdistances the Middle East for second place in total number of incidents. Argentina leads the world in kidnappings of foreigners, and is second to the United States in the bombings of foreign facilities. Middle Eastern nations do not have terrorist groups with developed undergrounds which would be useful in attacking the types of targets they seek (for example, few Israeli diplomatic or military installations) and so do not engage in certain types of incidents on Middle Eastern soil to the extent that one would otherwise expect. Rather, they have resorted to the barricade and hostage scenario. Latin groups, on the other hand, do have the developed undergrounds, and have not needed to resort to barricades. Hence, we see that at times logistic constraints may rule out the imitation of tactics by other groups.

Are certain nations being singled out as victims of attacks? In Tables 5 and 6 we find that while many nations' cities suffered in one or two incidents, Westernized, industrialized nations are the most popular targets of attacks. The United States alone has witnessed its citizens fall victim in over 30 percent of all events,[8] with the British also facing a serious security

Table 5. Victims of Terrorist Actions, by Nationality and Region

NATION	NUMBER OF INCIDENTS	NATION	NUMBER OF INCIDENTS
NORTH ATLANTIC		LATIN AMERICA	
Austria	7	Argentina	18
Belgium	2	Bahamas	3
Canada	11	Bolivia	2
Cyprus	1	Brazil	14
Denmark	3	British Honduras	1
France	24	British West Indies	1
Greece	18	Chile	11
Holy See	2	Colombia	27
Ireland	6	Costa Rica	3
Italy	29	Cuba	14
Netherlands	15	Dominican Republic	7
Portugal	7	Ecuador	8
Spain	34	Haiti	2
Sweden	4	Honduras	2
Switzerland	14	Jamaica	1
West Germany	36	Mexico	22
United Kingdom	121	Netherlands Antilles	2
United States	435	Nicaragua	3

Table 5. Victims of Terrorist Actions, by Nationality and Region (continued)

NATION	NUMBER OF INCIDENTS	NATION	NUMBER OF INCIDENTS
ASIA			
Australia	5	Panama	4
Bangladesh	1	Paraguay	3
Hong Kong	1	Peru	3
India	9	Puerto Rico	7
Indonesia	4	Uruguay	5
Japan	12	Venezuela	13
Malaysia	1		
Nepal	1	**EAST EUROPE**	
New Zealand	1	Czechoslovakia	8
North Korea	1	East Germany	1
Pakistan	1	Finland	1
P.R. China	1	Poland	9
Philippines	6	Romania	2
Singapore	2	USSR	30
South Korea	3	Yugoslavia	12
South Vietnam	4		
Taiwan	1		
Thailand	1	**AFRICA**	
		Angola	1
MIDDLE EAST		Ethiopia	14
Algeria	7	Gabon	1
Dubai	1	Ivory Coast	1
Egypt	12	Kenya	1
Iran	7	Liberia	1
Iraq	5	Malawi	1
Israel	71	Mozambique	1
Jordan	19	Nigeria	1
Kuwait	3	Rhodesia	1
Lebanon	22	Senegal	1
Libya	2	South Africa	5
Morocco	1	Tanzania	1
Palestinians	20		
Qatar	1	**OTHER**	
Saudi Arabia	10		
South Yemen	1	CENTO	3
Syria	1	OAS	2
Turkey	11	foreigners (i.e.,	
United Arab		source inspecific	
Emirates	1	about nationality	
Yemen	2	of victim)	26

Table 6. Victims of Terrorist Actions by Region

REGION	TOTAL NUMBER OF INCIDENTS	REGIONAL VICTIMIZATION INDEX
North Atlantic	769	42.7
Middle East	197	10.4
Latin America	176	7.3
Eastern Europe	63	9.0
Asia	55	3.1
Africa	31	2.2
Other	31	n.a.

problem. The Regional Victimization Index[9] illustrates the preference of terrorists in choosing North Atlantic targets. Again we find that transnational terrorism has not yet affected Asia and Africa to the extent it has other regions. Eastern European communist nations have been relatively safe when one discounts skyjackings by domestic dissidents. Only the USSR and Yugoslavia find themselves subjected to other attacks, by the Jewish Defense League and Croatians, respectively. The immunity of these nations may be due to their verbal and material support of many of the contemporary terrorist groups. In the Middle East, it is not surprising to find Israeli citizens most harassed. The more moderate nations in the Arab-Israeli conflict also find themselves singled out for attack, with Palestinian terrorists frequently ambushed by unknown attackers.[10] Latin Americans frequently involve non-Latins as victims, with those perceived to be rich capitalists being singled out. Overall, nationals of the poorer nations who are victimized are most often their nation's ambassador to another country, or a manager or president of a multinational corporation's local subsidiary. Hence, although no one country can feel perfectly safe from terrorist attack, the problem appears to be primarily one for Westernized, capitalist nations.

Links of Terrorist Groups

Contacts between terrorist groups and with sympathetic governments appear to be growing. Various groups have been funded, armed, and trained by nations such as the Soviet Union, the Chinese People's Republic, Cuba, North Korea, and radical Arab nations. It has been reported that Colonel Qaddafi recently gave Carlos Marighella $2 million for his attack on the OPEC ministers' meeting in December, 1975. Soviet-made Kalashnikov machine guns and SA-7 Strela portable missiles have been discovered in the hands of arrested terrorists. It has been argued that governments have found conventional forms of warfare too expensive, and may resort to hiring mercenary terrorist groups to disrupt enemy societies,[11] a tactic which is far cheaper and can be plausibly denied.

But what is far more disturbing to many are the growing contacts between terrorist groups. Palestinians have apparently trained Latin Americans, members of the Baader-Meinhof Group of West Germany and of the Irish Republican Army, and Japanese anarchists. Latin groups which have acquired fantastic ransoms[12] have been reportedly funding less affluent, but possibly more violent, smaller groups. Such groups have held many world-wide meetings, including the recent one in Trieste of a score of European separatist groups, the confederation of four major Latin American guerrilla groups, and the frequent meetings of the members of the Palestine Liberation Organization, which at times has served as the forum for ten separate groups which have engaged in terrorist tactics. Such groups have also conducted joint operations, such as the skyjackings and barricade-and-hostage episodes of the Japanese Red Army and the Popular Front for the Liberation of Palestine, as well as kidnappings engaged in by coalitions of MR-8, ALN, and VPR in Brazil. Terrorist groups have also engaged in operations designed to secure the release from prison of members of their own and other organizations. If such trends continue, and terrorists are able to rely upon each other for funding, training, arms, and technical skills, they may develop a greater autonomy from their current nation-state mentors, and not be subject to what restraints are now placed upon their activities by these nations. More spectacular, grisly incidents may be the result.

The Economics of Terrorism

In economic terms, how great a problem has transnational terrorism been? In answering this question, we could simply tally the number of individuals killed and wounded due to terrorist attacks (see Table 2) and add the dollar damage caused by bombings, armed assaults, arson, and sabotage, the amount of ransom paid in hostage situations, and dollar losses due to thefts and extortion payments. The casualties total far less than deaths from automobile accidents in one year in the United States. But this considers only the direct costs of terrorism. We should also note the flight of foreign capital from nations experiencing terrorist campaigns, as well as decisions not to invest in those countries in the first place. Added in should be opportunity costs for hostages, and opportunities lost while a given corporation consolidates its losses after an attack. The cost of security measures taken to prevent attacks is also high, and must include the expense of metal detectors, skymarshals, bodyguards, security training for corporation, airline, and embassy staffs, as well as more intangible costs, such as randomly rerouting airline flights, ships, motorcades, and home-to-office travel to evade attacks. Other intangibles include the personal anxiety faced by victims and possible victims of attacks, as well as whatever anxieties are faced by the terrorists themselves.[13] Finally, we could include funds required for academic and governmental research on terrorism and for maintenance of policy staffs assigned to develop national responses to terrorism, such as the Cabinet Committee to Combat Terrorism. When all of the above factors are considered, transnational terrorism is indeed an expensive problem.

But is such activity cost-effective? We need to assess the cost-effectiveness of terrorism for the terrorists themselves. What does it cost to launch a terrorist operation in terms of manpower, arms, time, planning, money, security precautions, and so on, and what types of benefits may the guerrillas expect from such actions?[14] The answer to the first part of the question depends upon the type of operation envisioned—simple arson requires a Coke bottle, gasoline, and a wick, whereas some kidnappings by the Tupamaros in Uruguay involved more than fifty persons.

What is it that terrorists are seeking? Strategically, some groups aspire to control of the apparatus of the state. As far as can be determined, no campaign of terrorism by itself has ever led to the fall of a government, although the independence of Algeria and Israel can be attributed in part to pressure on colonial authorities by sustained attacks by the FLN and Irgun, respectively. At a somewhat lower level, many seek policy changes, ranging from greater autonomy for a province of the country to increased wages for union members.

At a tactical level, terrorists have sought changes in sentences, elimination of torture, or the outright release of specified political prisoners, including members of their own groups. Monetary ransoms are also frequently mentioned, along with extortion payments.[15] Terrorists have met with varying degrees of success in such endeavors.

But where terrorism has proven to be overwhelmingly effective is in the securing of publicity for the groups' actions and views. Dramatic actions are able to attract sensation-seeking television and newspaper coverage, which tends to give an impression of strength which the group does not possess. Among other objectives, terrorists are attempting to demonstrate that they can attack at will, and that government is unable to guarantee the security which is its duty to society. They attempt to embarrass the government and corporations viewed as exploiters by releasing damaging information secured in interrogation of hostages or by theft of documents, as well as by clever maneuvering of hostage negotiation situations. For example, the terrorists may demand that the government donate food to poverty-stricken peasants, casting themselves in the role of Robin Hoods while forcing the government into the position of refusing a charitable demand or giving in to a group of criminals. Corporations refusing monetary ransoms are portrayed as caring more about finance than the lives of the hostages. Terrorists also use such media coverage as a forum for expounding their political views, frequently demanding the publication of the group's manifesto as well as granting interviews to press reporters. In these ways, a small group can acquire the publicity of a major political campaign.

Identity and Motivation of Transnational Terrorists

Despite common conceptions, terrorists differ as to types of tactics chosen, motivations, and their respect for life. Table 7 identifies the groups which engaged in the more prevalent forms of transnational terrorism,[16] which is summarized regionally in Table 8.

Again we note that Latin American groups, along with the ELF, with their extensive undergrounds, are able to engage in standard kidnap situations which require great resources. Middle Eastern groups, lacking this infrastructure, have resorted to actions which leave them more open to police attack, but which also receive greater press coverage and involve a larger number of hostages per incident, that is, barricade and hostage events and skyjackings. They also have a near-monopoly on armed assaults and assassinations, tactics which also do not require large support groups.

Very few groups exhibit an extensive repertoire of tactics. Only the ELF, PFLP, IRA, JDL, ERP, URA, and Black September have consistent ability (or prefer) to vary their operations. Most other groups appear to specialize in only one type of incident; for example, the Puerto Rican FAIN consistently chooses to bomb selected targets. Many other groups, which may engage in a great deal of domestic terrorism, have surfaced into the transnational level only once or twice, such as the FAL, ELN, and FLQ. Finally, many groups mentioned in Table 7 are names given to cover the organization behind the incident. For example, many have reported that Black September was an appendage of El Fatah, and would engage in particularly gruesome operations which would shock the world and bring great publicity to the Palestinian conflict, but would not bring public outcry against El Fatah itself. Such ploys may have also been used by anti-Castro Cuban groups.

Unfortunately, we have no well-developed theory which suggests why some groups choose to engage in terrorism and others do not. One can point to feelings of relative deprivation, and note inequality of distribution of land and income, lack of political participation of the masses, the shock of changing societies, and so forth. One could also note a given society's history of other forms of violent behavior and attempt to create a theory based upon a culture of violence view. Still others could point to racial, religious, ethnic, or linguistic antagonisms within the society. These macro-level explanations must then be linked to a discussion of the weakness of the groups which are attempting to articulate their grievances. Terrorism appears to be engaged in by small bands, rather than large organizations with extensive popular support, and has been called the weapon of the weak. Finally, these societal and organizational factors must

Table 7. Group Claiming Responsibility for Incident by Country of Members' Nationality, Region, and Incident Type

COUNTRY	GROUP	KID-NAP	B&H	SKY-JACK	BOMB	ARMED ATTACK	MURDER
AFRICA							
Angola	Popular Movement for the Liberation of Angola (MPLA)	3	—	—	—	—	—
Chad	Toubou rebels	1	—	—	—	—	—
Ethiopia	Eritrean Liberation Front (ELF)	11	—	7	1	1	2
French Somaliland	Liberation Front for the Somali Coast	1	—	—	—	—	—
Spanish Sahara	Saharan nationalists	1	—	—	—	—	—
Zaire	People's Revolutionary Army	1	—	—	—	—	—
ASIA							
Bangladesh	Bengali guerrillas	—	1	—	—	—	—
Burma	Shan insurgents	1	—	1	—	—	—
India	Kashmiri nationalists	—	—	1	—	—	—
Japan	United Red Army	—	4	1	—	1	—
Nepal	Nepalese Communist Party	—	1	1	—	—	—
Pakistan	Black December	—	1	1	—	—	1
Philippines	Kabataang Makabayan	—	1	—	—	—	—
	Moro National Liberation Front	—	1	—	—	—	—
	Philippine nationalists	2	—	—	—	—	—
South Molucca	South Moluccans	—	3	—	—	—	1
Thailand	Pattani Liberation Front	1	—	—	—	—	—

NORTH AMERICA						
Canada						
Canadian-Hungarian Freedom Fighters Federation	—	—	—	—	—	1
Quebec Liberation Front	2	—	—	—	—	—
Puerto Rico						
Armed Commandos of Liberation	—	—	—	—	—	—
FALN	—	—	—	17	—	—
Puerto Rican Resistance Movement	—	—	—	1	—	—
United States						
Black Panthers	—	—	5	—	—	—
Black Revolutionary Assault Team	—	—	—	3	—	—
Jewish Armed Resistance	1	—	—	—	—	1
Jewish Defense League	—	—	—	7	2	—
Republic of New Africa	—	1	1	—	—	—
Revolutionary Action Party	—	—	—	2	—	—
Revolutionary Affinity Group 6	—	—	—	1	—	—
EUROPE						
?						
National Youth Resistance Org.	—	—	—	2	—	1
Cyprus						
EOKA-B	—	1	—	—	—	—
France						
Action for the Rebirth of Corsica	—	—	—	2	—	—
Committee of Coordination	—	—	—	1	—	—
Greece						
EAN—Greek Anti-Dictatorial Youth	—	—	—	1	—	—
Greek Militant Resistance	—	—	—	1	—	—
Greek People	—	—	—	1	—	—
Popular Revolutionary Resistance Group	—	—	—	—	—	—
Resistance, Liberation, Independence (AAA)	—	—	—	4	—	—

Table 7. Group Claiming Responsibility for Incident by Country of Members' Nationality, Region, and Incident Type (continued)

COUNTRY	GROUP	KID-NAP	B&H	SKY-JACK	BOMB	ARMED ATTACK	MURDER
EUROPE (continued)							
Italy	Ordine Nero (Black Order)	—	—	—	1	—	—
Portugal	ARA	—	—	—	1	—	—
Spain	ETA—Basque Nation and Homeland	3	—	—	—	—	1
	GARI	1	—	—	1	—	—
	Hammer and Sickle Cooperative	—	1	—	—	—	—
Switzerland	Les Beliers-Jura	—	1	—	—	—	—
United Kingdom	Black Liberation Front	—	—	—	—	—	—
	IRA-Provisional Wing	1	2	2	45	5	1
West Germany	Baader-Meinhof Group	—	1	—	3	—	—
	Holger Meins Commando	—	—	—	—	—	—
	Meinhof-Antich Group	—	—	—	1	—	—
	Second of June Movement	1	1	—	—	—	—
Yugoslavia	Ustasha and other Croatians	—	1	1	5	—	2
MIDDLE EAST AND NORTHERN AFRICA							
Algeria	Soldiers of the Algerian Opposition	—	—	—	2	—	—
Iran	Iranian Peoples' Strugglers	—	—	—	1	—	2
	Iranian terrorists	—	—	1	1	—	1
Israel	Masada-Action and Defence Movement	—	—	—	1	—	—
Jordan	Jordanian National Liberation Movement	—	—	1	—	—	—

Country	Organization						
Lebanon	Lebanese Revolutionary Guard	1	—	—	1	—	—
Palestine	Revolutionary Socialist Action Organization	—	—	—	—	—	—
	Action Organization for the Liberation of Palestine	—	—	—	—	1	—
	Al Saiqa	—	1	—	—	—	—
	Arab Liberation Arm	—	1	—	—	—	—
	Arab Liberation Front	—	1	—	—	—	—
	Arab Nationalist Youth for the Liberation of Palestine	—	—	2	—	—	—
	Arab Nationalist Youth Organization for the Liberation of Palestine	—	—	1	—	—	—
	Black September	—	3	2	11	3	7
	Eagles of National Unity	—	—	1	—	—	—
	Eagles of the Palestine Revolution	—	1	—	—	—	—
	El Fatah	1	1	3	4	—	1
	Moslem International Guerrillas	—	1	—	—	—	—
	Nationalist Organization of Arab Youth	—	—	—	—	2	—
	Nationalist Youth Group for the Liberation of Palestine	—	—	—	1	—	—
	Organization for the Victims of Zionist Occupation	—	—	1	—	—	—
	Organization of Sons of Occupied Territories	—	—	1	—	—	—
	Organization of Victims of Occupied Territories	—	1	—	—	—	—
	Palestine Liberation Army	1	—	—	—	—	—

Table 7. Group Claiming Responsibility for Incident by Country of Members' Nationality, Region, and Incident Type (continued)

COUNTRY	GROUP	KID-NAP	B&H	SKY-JACK	BOMB	ARMED ATTACK	MURDER
MIDDLE EAST AND NORTHERN AFRICA (continued)							
	Palestine Liberation Organization (PLO)	—	—	—	1	—	—
	Palestine Popular Struggle Front	—	—	1	2	1	—
	Palestinian guerrillas	—	1	3	9	11	7
	Popular Democratic Front for the Liberation of Palestine (PDFLP)	—	1	—	—	—	—
	Popular Front for the Liberation of Palestine (PFLP)	2	4	14	17	4	2
	PFLP-General Command	—	1	—	—	—	—
	Punishment Squad	—	1	—	—	—	—
	Seventh Suicide Squad	—	1	—	—	1	—
	Squad of the Martyr Patrick Arguello	—	—	—	—	—	—
Turkey	Turkish People's Liberation Army (TPLA)	4	—	1	1	—	—
LATIN AMERICA							
Argentina	Argentine rightists	—	—	—	—	—	1
	Comite Argentino de Lucha Anti-Imperialisto	—	—	—	5	—	—
	ERP—People's Revolutionary Army	11	—	3	11	2	—

Country	Group						
	FAL—Argentine Liberation Front	1	—	—	—	—	—
	FAP—Peronist Armed Forces	—	—	—	15	—	1
	MANO—Argentine National Organization Movement	1	—	—	—	—	—
	Montoneros	4	—	—	1	—	—
	Peronist guerrillas	—	—	—	1	—	—
Bolivia	Bolivian peasants	1	—	—	—	—	—
Brazil	ELN—National Liberation Army	1	—	—	—	—	—
	ALN—Action for National Liberation	3	—	—	—	—	—
	MR-8—Revolutionary Movement of the 8th	1	—	1	—	—	—
	VAR-Palmares—Armed Revolutionary Vanguard-Palmares	—	—	1	—	—	—
Chile	Chilean refugees	—	1	1	—	—	—
	Leftist Revolutionary Movement	1	—	2	—	—	—
Colombia	ELN—National Liberation Army	1	—	—	—	—	—
	Invisible Ones	1	—	—	—	—	—
	United Front for Guerrilla Action	—	—	—	—	—	—
Cuba	anti-Castro Cubans	—	—	—	14	—	—
	Cuba Movement 4	—	—	—	1	—	—
	Cuba Power 76	—	—	—	1	—	—
	Cuban Scorpion	—	—	—	1	—	—
	Cuban Youth Group	—	—	—	7	—	—
	El Poder Cubano	—	—	—	20	1	1
	Secret Organization Zero	—	—	—	1	—	1
	Youths of the Star	—	—	—	1	—	—

Table 7. Group Claiming Responsibility for Incident by Country of Members' Nationality, Region, and Incident Type (continued)

COUNTRY	GROUP	KID-NAP	B&H	SKY-JACK	BOMB	ARMED ATTACK	MURDER
Dominican Republic	Dominican guerrillas	—	—	—	1	—	—
	United Anti-Reelection Command	1	—	—	—	—	—
Guatemala	FAR—Revolutionary Armed Forces	2	—	—	—	—	1
Haiti	Coalition of National Brigades	—	1	—	—	—	—
Mexico	Armed Communist League	—	—	1	—	—	—
	Mexican guerrillas	1	—	—	—	—	—
	Peoples Revolutionary Armed Forces	1	—	—	—	—	—
	23rd of September Communist League	1	—	—	—	—	—
Nicaragua	FSLN—Sandinist Front of National Liberation	—	1	1	—	—	—
	MoPoCo	1	—	—	—	—	—
Uruguay	OPR-33—Organization of the Popular Revolution-33	1	—	—	—	—	—
	Tupamaros	6	—	—	1	2	—
Venezuela	People's Revolutionary Army-Zero Point	—	—	1	—	—	—
	Red Flag	1	—	—	—	—	—
OTHER							
Unknown		3	—	2	193	19	24
Individuals or groups who engaged in incident as a one-time event, and were not involved in a campaign of terrorism		4	3	230	5	4	6

Table 8. Region of Nationality of Group Claiming Responsibility for Incident by Incident Type

REGION	KID-NAP	B&H	SKY-JACK	BOMBING	ARMED ATTACK	MURDER
Africa	18	—	7	1	1	2
Asia	4	10	4	—	1	2
North America	3	—	6	33	2	2
Europe	6	7	3	69	5	5
Middle East	7	19	32	51	23	20
Latin America	44	3	11	82	5	6

be further linked to a study of the type of personality who would be attracted to this kind of political expression. Other groups have arisen to become vigilante terrorists, established to fight "primary" terrorist groups. Examples of such pairings include the Ulster Defense Association versus the IRA, the anti-ETA versus Basque nationalist, the JDL versus the PLO, and the Argentine Anti-Communist Alliance versus the ERP and numerous other Argentine leftist groups.[17] Much work remains to be done in explaining terrorists' motivations and the causes of their behavior. A preliminary typology of transnational groups is offered in Table 9.

But given that political terrorism by autonomous actors may be caused by the aforementioned societal, organizational, and personality factors, why

Table 9. Types of Terrorists

GROUP TYPE	EXAMPLES
separatists or irredentists	ETA, ELF, IRA, Corsicans
Fedayeen	PFLP, PDFLP, El Fatah, Al Saiqa
ultra left anarchists	Japanese URA, Baader-Meinhof Group and its splinters
Latin guerrilleros	ERP, Montoneros, ALN, ELN
criminal gangs	Mafia, groups who publicly cloak their actions in political rhetoric, but whose intent is personal gain
psychotic individuals	security guard who seized Israeli Embassy in South Africa in 1975
hoaxes	Brian Lea's kidnapping in Uganda
cover names	Black September, Cuban groups

do some groups choose to internationalize their struggle and involve citizens of foreign countries? A number of reasons can be offered. Their grievance may well be a country perceived by them to be exploiting, rather than their home government. Thus, they choose American and Western businessmen as victims of attacks. The terrorists may also believe that attacking foreigners will lead the victim's government to exert pressure upon the host government to capitulate to the terrorists' demands. We have also noted the lack of an underground of some groups. Being unable to engage in prolonged military confrontations with the army, they resort to spectacular incidents to give a false impression of strength. Publicity is increased if the target is a foreign diplomat, rather than a backwater village. This publicity may have a contagious effect upon other groups, who observe the success of these operations. Finally, groups such as the Japanese Red Army preach world revolution, and are insensitive to territorial borders.

Responding to the Terrorist Threat

Unfortunately, the international response to transnational attacks has been feeble. The United Nations General Assembly members have quibbled over who is and is not a terrorist, and have not managed to agree on a common definition, much less a solution, to the problem. They have managed to approve a convention on the protection of diplomats, but only nine nations have ratified this 1973 agreement, and it is not yet in force. Other relevant conventions include the 1963 Tokyo Convention on Offenses and Certain Other Acts Committed on Board Aircraft, the 1970 Hague Convention for the Suppression of the Unlawful Seizure of Aircraft, the 1973 Montreal Convention for the Suppression of Unlawful Acts Against the Safety of Civil Aviation, and the 1971 OAS Convention to Prevent and Punish Acts of Terrorism Taking the Form of Crimes Against Persons and Related Extortion that Are of International Significance. Unfortunately, many states which support terrorist groups have refused to ratify these conventions. Effective sanctions against states which disregard the prosecution-or-extradition clauses have not been created. And finally, these conventions cover only a small part of what can be viewed as terrorist acts.

Bilateral treaties have also been resorted to, among the most important being an agreement between the United States and Cuba on skyjacking, which has effectively shut off the flow of hijackers to that island nation. But the right of asylum in Latin American countries is a time-honored tradition in Latin international law. Government leaders recognize that they may one day be requesting asylum when and if they are ousted from power in the next revolution. It is not in their personal interest to restrict this practice in any way, and any proposals to place a global, regional, or bilateral ban on the granting of asylum to political offenders (either the terrorists instigating the incident or the prisoners whose release is demanded) will be met with great resistance in these countries.

On the national level, many governments have resorted to draconian measures to root out terrorist groups, torturing prisoners, establishing strict curfews, and creating a quasi-permanent police state. But this may be precisely what the terrorists are attempting to provoke. Such measures must be applied nationwide if the government is to have a reasonable expectation of hitting all of the group's cells. Unfortunately, many individuals uninvolved in the hostilities will be adversely affected by such measures, and can be expected to resent such incursions on their liberties deeply. It is the terrorists' hope that this animosity will surface, and the government will be faced with a nationwide revolutionary movement with broad popular support.

Suggestions are also made to establish a no-ransom policy, which would hopefully deter terrorists from engaging in future incidents. But the acquisition of money or the release of prisoners may merely be bonus effects of the incident, with the real purposes of the terrorists being served by the extensive media coverage which their operations receive.

All governments have had or may have to face this growing problem. No one solution, such as toning down present media coverage, will stop terrorism. But a combined program of greater security measures, worldwide cooperation by governments and other concerned parties, better intelligence efforts, a well-thought-out incident negotiation policy, attempts to meet the justified grievances of those whom the terrorists claim to represent, and self-restrained media may well bring about a lessening of the problem.

The Future of Transnational Terrorism

We can only speculate on what the trends we have seen may portend for the future. Among the possibilities are:

1. Terrorists may shift from one type of political terrorism in our fourfold table to other types. For example, governments may co-opt stateless revolutionary transnational groups, and send them to disrupt the societies of their perceived enemies. Domestic terrorists may discover that going transnational gives them greater publicity and more leverage in bargaining with governments. Domestic terrorists may come to power and discover that they must resort to state terrorism to keep revanchist populations in line.

2. Transnational terrorists may choose new victims for their operations. Installations using sophisticated but delicate equipment are particularly vulnerable, and much damage to valuable facilities can be caused by the simple bomb. Possible targets may include offshore drilling rigs, the Alaska

pipeline, airport control towers, the BART computer, and nuclear reactor sites.

3. We shall probably observe increased cooperation among transnational and domestic groups, with more joint operations, intergroup training, funding, arming, and so on. This may result in greater autonomy from sympathetic governmental sponsors, with the subsequent lack of restraints this implies.

4. With highly destructive weapons becoming cheaper and more easily carried, we may see the use of more sophisticated weapons by terrorists, and more spectacular incidents. With the large number of incidents occurring in any given year, terrorists must resort to increasingly theatrical attention-getters to attract any publicity to their cause. A bombing of an embassy goes virtually unreported, buried on the back pages next to the classified ads. But an attack on a nuclear facility by groups using hand-held launchers of heat-seeking missiles would capture the front pages for days (if not the facility).

5. With the increasing sophistication of terrorist technology, *some* of their operations may in fact become less destructive. For example, clandestine bugging of some embassies is a relatively simple task once entry has been gained. Rather than setting time-bombs during an enemy take-over, could a guerrilla technician more profitably spend his time in such activities as planting listening devices in strategic locations, giving the group information about future precautions which will be taken by the embassy to prevent more incidents of that type, or about embassy-police liaison regarding the conduct of the nationwide search for the perpetrators?

6. High-speed jet airliners and international telephonic communications will continue to make the planning and execution of transnational events on any continent easier than they were even a decade ago.

7. Finally, there is the possibility of what many view as the greatest horror story of the near future: a nuclear bomb in the hands of terrorists. There are a number of unanswered questions: Why has no one yet stolen nuclear material? Why would a group want to steal it? What are the characteristics of a group wishing to kill thousands of people? Or of a group who would use the bomb to ransom a city? What types of demands could be made, and agreed to, which could not be made in incidents threatening a lower level of destruction? What effect would such an attack have upon the group's public support? What would be the reaction of the public to such a situation of high stress? Do any existing groups possess the requisite skill to manufacture a bomb? Would it be more cost-effective for them to resort to other methods, such as chemical or biological warfare, aerosol attacks, sabotage of major life-support systems, or plutonium dispersal devices? Is the theft of nuclear material to make a bomb the only type of terrorist threat to society involving nuclear facilities?

If present trends continue, the future for the world looks bleak indeed. Casualties due to transnational terrorism amount to less than 3,000, not a large figure compared to other statistics, such as conventional warfare, accident, and illness. Yet such actions have lessened society's freedoms and sense of security, diverted resources to protection against attack, and led to strains in state relations. Concerted and cooperative international action will be needed to stem the tide.

Notes

1. In the tables and figures, only incidents of transnational terrorism, as defined, are included. Events related to the Vietnam conflict are not included, nor are the numerous cross-border raids between Arabs and Israelis against military targets. Plots to engage in actions classified as terrorist, but which were discovered before the carrying out of the operation, are not included, nor are threats to engage in such actions.

Data were obtained from chronologies provided the author by the U.S. Department of State, the Federal Aviation Administration, the Rand Corporation, the United States Information Agency, the United States Senate and House of Representatives, staff reports for Congressional committees, Facts on File, plus reports from the Associated Press, New York Times, Washington Post, Chicago Tribune, Detroit Free Press, The Economist, and many of the books on terrorism mentioned in the bibliography. Because of omissions in reporting for some incidents, grand totals for the tables presented herein may disagree.

2. Skyjackings must have the attributes of our definition of transnational terrorism to qualify for inclusion. Incidents which did not involve a crossing of a border (such as events involving the payment of ransom and parachuting of the hijacker from the plane within the territorial confines of the nation of embarkation), domestic attempts to hijack a plane to another country which involved no injuries in the resolution of the incident, and incidents which involved only one nationality of passengers, crew, hijacker, and destination and embarkation point of the flight are thus not included.

3. While skyjackings and non-air take-overs can become barricade and hostage situations, these incidents are not treated as such if they occurred in transit. Hence, the multiple skyjackings of the PFLP in September 1970 are treated as skyjackings, although negotiations were conducted on the ground.

For a discussion of trends in hostage situations, what the terrorists seek, and the policy debate over the proper response to such demands, see Edward Mickolus, "Negotiating for Hostages: A Policy Dilemma," *Orbis* 19, 4 (Winter 1970).

4. A score of definitions has been offered for assassination. Rather than attempt to distinguish between the political murder of a low-level official and a high-level official (if such an arbitrary cut-off point could be established), the motivations of the killer, and so forth, a general category of political murder and assassination is used. To qualify for inclusion, such acts must satisfy the conditions of the transnational terrorism definition.

5. The casualty totals for 1974 are all the more distressing when it is noted that the data currently on file in the ITERATE Project (*I*nternational *T*errorism: *At*tributes of *T*errorist *E*vents), which is based upon the sources mentioned in note 1, are incomplete. The author has had access to classified and proprietary data on the eight years studied, and is able to state that the present sources are not reporting all incidents. Hence, the rather comforting decline in the number of terrorist events shown in Table 1 for 1974 is misleading, and is due to error in the data, rather than restraint by the terrorists.

6. The location of an incident is considered to be the place in which the incident began, while its year is that date on which it became known to individuals other than the terrorists that a terrorist incident was taking place. In the case of skyjacking, the location is the nation in which the plane had last touched ground before the hijackers made their presence as hijackers known. If the embarkation point is not known, the location is considered to be that nation in which the plane landed and the negotiations took place, where appropriate. If both of the above do not apply, the nation of registry is used.

7. The location of an incident need not be a nation-state. Protectorates, colonies, and mandated territories may also experience terrorism, and are considered by the government to be different types of security and administrative environments, not comparable to the metropole. Hence, areas such as Puerto Rico and Gibraltar are included as locations, despite the legal citizenship of their residents.

8. The grand total for Tables 5 and 6 is greater than that for Table 1 because of the multiplicity of nationalities of victims in some incidents.

9. The Regional Victimization Index is computed for each region by dividing the number of incidents in which any citizen of that region was the victim of an attack by the number of nations in the region whose citizens were reported as victims in at least one attack.

10. However, reports frequently allege these attacks to be the work of members of Israeli intelligence.

11. An interesting discussion of this possibility is included in Brian M. Jenkins, *International Terrorism: A New Mode of Conflict,* Research Paper No. 48, California Seminar on Arms Control and Foreign Policy (Los Angeles: Crescent Publications, 1975).

12. Ransoms in Latin America have ranged from as low as a tractor demanded and received by Bolivian peasants to $60 million in cash, $1.2 million in food for peasants, and the publication of a manifesto in selected foreign newspapers, received by the Montoneros from Bunge y Born in 1975.

13. Such neuroses have been described in the work of Frantz Fanon.

14. The author and Henry McFarland of the Economics Department of Northwestern University are presently conducting research on the economics of kidnapping, noting the utility to the terrorists of their demands being met, publicity garnered, etc., against the costs of the operation, such as the expectation of arrest, conviction, and jailing, the probability of release in subsequent incidents, the monetary costs of the operation, etc.

15. Despite the popularity of the United States as a provider of hostages, this government is rarely the target of terrorist demands. Terrorists have tended to single out corporations or make demands which do not mention a particular target

(for example, "We want $4 million for his safe return") when holding American hostages.

16. The name of the group claiming responsibility for the incident is what is reported, rather than the identity of the group which police or the press speculate as having been involved. Often groups give cover names to be able to deny the responsibility of the umbrella organization for particularly hideous crimes or for operations which failed to achieve the objectives of their perpetrators. Actions which are less frequent than those mentioned in Table 7, and the groups responsible for such incidents, include:

Theft: 4 Jewish Defence League (US)
       3 Palestinians, Tupamaros (Uruguay)
       2 Irish Republican Army (UK)
       1 Japanese students, Ethiopian students, ERP (Argentina), unknown
Arson: 27 unknown
       5 Revolutionary Force 7 (US)
       2 Palestinians
       1 Black September, Irish Republican Army, Jewish Defence League, Movement of Youthward Brothers in War of the Palestinian People, Proletarian Revolutionary Action Group (Chile or Italy), Puerto Rican Liberation Front, Bandera Roja (Venezuela), National Liberation Armed Forces (Venezuela), one-timers
Sabotage: 2 Black September, unknown
       1 PFUP
Letter-bomb: 80 Palestinians
       59 Black September
       40 Irish Republican Army
       24 unknown
       3 El Poder Cubano
       1 Yanikian Commandos (Turkey)
Non-air take-over: 5 one-timers
       1 Palestinians

When the nationality of the perpetrators is known, but no organizational name is available, it is so noted, for example, "Palestinians" or "Iranian guerrillas."

17. Vigilantes do not appear to conduct transnational operations.

PART II

International Terrorism in Selected Parts of the World

DENNIS CLARK

Terrorism in Ireland: Renewal of a Tradition

Since 1969 Northern Ireland has been in the grip of violent events that have resulted in military rule for that unhappy province in all but a formal legal sense. Americans are confronted by various obstacles in comprehending what has transpired in Northern Ireland over the last six years. The mass media have acted as a distorting filter through which news of varying adequacy has been channeled to the United States. Americans in general also have a tendency to see Ireland as a strange amalgam of historical mythology and Irish Tourist Board caprice. Finally, Americans, as a people with a tradition strongly conditioned by Anglo-Saxon modes of thought, share that same lamentable miscalculation about Ireland that has been almost endemic among the English and those who share their cultural presumptions. For these reasons, in addition to the importance of the subject itself, it is appropriate to review the implications of recent Northern Ireland events.

Those familiar with Irish history cannot help but be aware of its violence. The clan system itself produced generations of internecine warfare in a warrior-oriented clan society. Accounts of revenge and ferocious deeds loom with immense significance throughout the recently edited ten-volume *History of Ireland* issued by Gill and Macmillan.[1] The modern political and agrarian history of Ireland contained certain features that made for the repeated appearance of guerrilla activity and terror tactics. The indigenous and largely disaffected Irish people ruled by England until 1921 never really had a standing military establishment of their own through which to enforce their political views. The lack of a professional military element among the Irish Catholics who composed the overwhelming majority of the population constantly left the way open for the innovation of irregular military groups and insurrectionary elements. Further, the odds against the Irish as minority dissenters within the orbit of English imperial institutions were always so very great that direct military challenge to British overlordship was usually clearly impractical. This fact made guerrilla activity and terror tactics a strategic necessity in the long conflict with England.

The very tradition of implacable opposition to English rule bred a nationalist atmosphere in which terrorist schemes were more likely to occur. Each episode of such activity was glorified *ex post facto* in a nationalist tradition that was immensely popular and represented powerful cultural forces of oral and musical folk tradition. The nineteenth century produced the Fenian Brotherhood in the 1860s, and this group was responsible for the bombing of Clerkenwell prison in England that resulted in twelve dead, one hundred

twenty wounded, forty premature births in a nearby lying-in hospital resulting in twenty infant deaths, and widespread fear of the Fenians in England.
While the purpose of the bombing was not political but to free prisoners, the
terror it produced had political effects. In the 1880s revolutionary agents
from Irish societies in the United States, especially the secret Clan-na-Gael
brotherhood, undertook plots to bomb London subways, shipyards, London Bridge, the House of Commons, and other facilities.[2]

In the twentieth century Irish nationalists carried out one of the first anticolonial wars of liberation, and their struggle was replete with numerous
acts of arson, bombing, mining, kidnapping, assassination, and revenge
slayings. One slaying at least was arranged as a trans-Atlantic mission
when Pa Murray came from County Cork to New York City in the wake of
the Anglo-Irish War to kill an informer on the streets of New York. Irish-
American supporters of the Irish nationalist movement were led by men
who believed in the power of the "desperate deed," the terrible act that would
strike terror into beholders.[3]

Lest it be forgotten that this propensity for terror tactics was somehow a
peculiarly Irish quality, it will bear recall that England's record in Ireland
itself was a potent factor in perpetuating the Irish in the tactics of terror.
Terror-producing actions were part of the strategy of subjugation carried
out by English adventurers and colonists who were always in a harassed
minority numerically. The names of Oliver Cromwell, Sir Walter Raleigh,
and even the poetically sweet-singing Edmund Spenser are remembered in
Ireland for their practice or advocacy of terror. The overlord complex of English presence in Ireland was also reinforced by a strident racism characteristic of English imperial undertakings, for the Irish in ages past and until
early in this century were deemed by the English to be a separate "race." The
imputation of inferiority to the "other" race was, of course, freely acknowledged and acted upon. Finally, the numerical inferiority of the English themselves acted as a stimulus to a sort of paranoia that often marks colonizers,
and this psychological condition frequently led to instability of judgment
and administration resulting in excesses of all kinds.

Thus, just as the British in India in 1919 had to face the responsibility for
the atrocity and massacre at Jallianwalla in the Punjab, so devious Lloyd
George had to contend in the House of Commons with questions involving
execution of hostages, random arson and military murder, and the uncontrolled excesses of spies and provocateurs serving as adjuncts to the English military forces in Ireland.[4] If the Irish lacked a professional military
organization to place a conservative hand on terror tactics, the English, who
had a professional military organization in the country, never seemed to be
able to maintain it in a professional posture because of the assumptions of
racism, social alienation, and demographic imbalance.[5] Hence, Hayes-
McCoy, the leading military historian of Ireland, asserts that guerrilla war-

fare is the most characteristic form of conflict in the island's history, and to his list of geographical factors and perennially incomplete conquests can be added the causes noted above.[6]

To this history must be added the fact that the hard-line Irish Republican nationalist tradition has been a minority belief within Ireland itself in the twentieth century, with the possible exception of the period of euphoric struggle in the 1920s.[7] The predominantly rural Irish population is and has been essentially conservative, though a tough antagonist when aroused. This social and political conservatism has not shared the ideological and doctrinaire Republican tradition for the most part. Nor has the new Irish bourgeoisie shared the hard-line IRA outlook. The long-postponed enjoyment of even a modicum of consumer repose is not lightly gambled away for political goals by this class. The Republican response to this indifference and tepidity has always been to insist upon the Biblical doctrine of the "saving remnant," the principle that change comes about through minorities and the dedicated minority is unbeatable. Terence MacSwiney, who died on a hunger strike while imprisoned by the English in 1920, announced the cardinal precept: "It is not those who can inflict the most suffering who will win, but those who can endure the most." MacSwiney also said: "We ask no mercy and we will accept no compromise." The Irish Republican Army members of today have been indoctrinated with such propositions.[8]

Those who see something new in the international links of contemporary terrorism must recall that the major modern disruptions in Ireland known as the Rising of 1798, the Young Ireland disorders of 1848, the Fenian rising of 1867, the agrarian violence of the 1880s, and the Anglo-Irish War of the 1920s all proceeded with substantial overseas inspiration and aid either from Europe or America. The international ties of the Provisional IRA are very much a reminder of the international dimension of revolutionary activities that grew up in the nineteenth century. If the Fenian Brotherhood of the 1860s reached to Australia, South Africa, and the mining camps of the American frontier, it should be in no way surprising that the Provisional IRA should be seeking aid in Libya or in Amsterdam.

If what has been stated above can be accepted as the basis of a rough historical description of modern Irish revolutionary tradition, what is there that is new in the campaign of the Provisional IRA in the last six years? What differences, elaborations, and new emphases have developed in Ireland since 1969? First, there does seem to have developed a higher tolerance for civilian casualties among the revolutionaries. Old Tom Barry, legendary guerrilla leader of the flying columns of the 1920s, parted with the IRA leadership in 1939 over the planning of a bombing campaign in England that portended extensive civilian casualties. Tom Barry's code was one of personal combat, so much so that he was renowned for saying, "There are no bad shots at ten yards range." Between January 1, 1969, and March 1, 1976, combined British army, Ulster Defense Reserve, and Royal Ulster Constabulary casualties have totaled 376, while civilian deaths totaled 1,096 including IRA deaths.[9] In addition, of course, there have been dreadful maimings of civilians. It is evident that these civilian casualties have been a "bearable cost" to those engaged in the warfare in Northern Ireland. They include the thirteen people killed by English gunfire in Derry in January 1972 and others killed by military actions of English forces, as well as the victims of terror-bombs in shopping areas.

Although the Anglo-Irish war of the 1920s produced many civilian casualties, the attitude toward purposeful assaults on civilians by the Irish Republican Army of the time was quite clear. Such assaults were seen to be a secondary result of military action, not a primary target to produce political results. The English forces, however, did pursue purposeful assaults on civilians in attempts to cow the Irish population.[10] The change in priorities between the 1920s and the 1960s on the part of the IRA might be explained by several factors. In Ireland, as elsewhere, modern social influences have changed the context of life. Urbanization has proceeded, although at a slower rate than in most other European countries. Yet, it was from the towns and cities that the leadership for the modern Irish revolutionary movement arose.[11] This same urbanization has contributed in Ireland as elsewhere to an increasing impersonality in local life. Northern Ireland is the most modernized portion of Ireland, and it is here, I believe, that the forces of impersonality have proceeded furthest. This has had two effects. It has made it easier for those engaged in the fighting to depersonalize their efforts and to inflict civilian casualties. And this same depersonalization has made the tribalization or retribalization of Ulster society into religious and local groups of antagonists easier. Finally, the violence itself has acted as a polarizing influence, for its horror, shame, and brutality have helped to dissolve the bonds of sociability in Northern Ireland. If the Ulster struggle can be characterized as a "civil" struggle, then the savagery of the conflict is commensurate to that kind of fighting.

Second, the media coverage of the Ulster violence has dramatized it according to the vastly increased capacity of modern communications. This is especially true of television and film coverage of the violent events. The magnifying effect of this coverage has been enormous, and the respective propaganda uses of the media have been duly pursued by all parties. While the dissidents in the Tyrol and the Basques in Spain have been largely barred from media exposure, those in Northern Ireland have been able to achieve broad exposure. Although Irish agitation often achieved worldwide notice in the days when Irish members were part of the English Parliament in Westminster, and although the news media have often dramatized the IRA, the power of television has enhanced even further the profile of Irish agitation in our time. This development has made the Irish issue more acute than it might have been without televised scenes of bombings and arson. It has added to the political potency of the situation.[12]

Third, within the framework of modern Irish history, the counties of Ulster have played a particularly vibrant role. Many of the leaders of the independence movement in the 1920s were of Ulster origin.[13] Ulster was traditionally the home of the battle sagas of Irish literature and of the great clan leaders, the O'Neills and the O'Donnells. As such it held a special place in the nationalist hagiography and sentiment. The exclusion of six of the traditional Ulster counties from an independent Ireland had a particular irony and provocative effect for a nationalist tradition that had looked to Ulster for so many models. The events since 1969 have served to reaffirm the Ulster nationalist leadership and to reactivate one of the traditional slogans of Irish rebellion: "The North began . . . ." Within Ireland, then, the nationalists of the North, who have always felt they were oppressed in a special way, have asserted again their intense localism and their claim to nationalist primacy, a primacy that would be a threat to Dublin and a rejection of the bureaucratization of the nationalist tradition under the government of the present Irish Republic. This is an elaboration of the indigenous insurrectionary tradition.

Fourth, the intellectual isolation of the Northern Ireland nationalist insurgents represents a change from the revolutionary pattern of the past. While it would be unrealistic to expect a renewal of that extraordinary literary and artistic upsurge that accompanied the burst of Irish nationalism in the early part of this century, the isolation of the Provisional IRA from the intellectual leaders of Ireland today is notable in a nation where nationalism and intellectual leadership have long been strongly intertwined. It is true that some of the artistic brilliance extolling the 1916 Easter Rising and the struggle for independence was an exercise in retroactive creativity, yet much of it was also contemporaneous with the actual events of the struggle. Today there are few writers, indeed, who are partisans of the Provisional IRA, and it does seem that the hard-pressed men of the North are estranged from the most powerful current of modern Irish cultural life. Perhaps this is due to a lack of *intellectual leadership* among the Provos themselves. Perhaps it is due to the narrowness of the Ulster conflict and its reference to religious loyalties that contradict humane sentiments.[14]

Fifth, the new international dimension of the insurgency of the nationalists in Ulster is in strange contrast to the localism of that conflict. Since 1969 the Provisional IRA has built a network overseas in England and the United States that is composed largely of Irish-born people. It is the most successful overseas effort by Irish dissidents since the 1920s. This construction has been easier than previous ones because of better communications, but it still represents a most diligent effort in the face of English pressure and the watchfulness of American authorities. It is indicative of what can be achieved by small numbers of dedicated men in the midst of hostilities. It has much to say about the capacity of dissidents to garner support from afar in the future.[15]

These brief observations about terror in Ireland have attempted to highlight the ways in which contemporary insurgency is related to the historic traditions of nationalism of that country. The revitalization of illegal insurrectionary activity in Ireland since 1969 could have profound effects upon the Irish Republic. It has already reopened that historic rift between England and Ireland that had been made quiescent by the creation of an independent Irish state. Deepening economic troubles or the rise of some charismatic leader could spread the turmoil of the North to all Ireland. The insurgents in Ulster did much to bring down one antidemocratic regime that England sustained in Northern Ireland, ending still one more chapter of folly in the incredible story of Ireland's English problem.[16] If social unity and reconstruction are to come to Ireland as a whole, they will come only in some movement that transcends the powerful nationalist militancy that has been such a formative influence in Irish life for 200 years. Any such movement, however, must produce cultural changes that discredit terrorism. In various places and times terrorism has been the result of mental illness, social hysteria, or political immaturity. In Northern Ireland it has been the result of the stubborn refusal of men to share power among themselves, and of morbid, flagrant, and incorrigible English policies of repression and abuse. In Ulster the cult of violence has been carefully cultivated by an enormity of historic malice and desecration of human rights.

Notes

1. James Lydon and Margaret MacCurtain, eds., *The Gill History of Ireland,* 10 vols. (Dublin: Gill and Macmillan, 1972-76).

2. Thomas N. Brown, *Irish-American Nationalism* (Philadelphia: Lippincott, 1966). Throughout I use the term "terrorist groups" in the sense defined by J. R. Reber: "Terrorist groups are groups which conspire and act without regard for legal constraints, committing acts of violence with or without previous threats against any target deemed appropriate for the achievement of a political or economic goal. Terrorism is a tactic that includes kidnappings, executions, sabotage and any other action that will support the goals of the terrorist group." *London Times Literary Supplement,* August 22, 1975.

3. The most notable of these men was John Devoy who lived in New York. The most successful was probably Joseph McGarrity of Philadelphia. Sean Cronin, *The McGarrity Papers* (Tralee: The Anvil Press, 1972).

4. L. P. Curtis, *Apes and Angels: A Study in Anti-Irish Victorian Prejudice* (Bridgeport, Conn.: Conference on British Studies, 1968). For a critique of the English imperial mentality see Barnett Corelli, *The Collapse of British Power* (London: Eyre and Methuen, 1972). England's violent record overseas contrasts with the

touted nonviolence in England extolled by Richard Clutterbuck, *Protest and the Urban Guerrilla* (New York: Abelard-Schuman, 1973). This book exculpates British troops for the deaths in Derry on Bloody Sunday (1972).

5. For instances of terrorism see Calton Younger, *Ireland's Civil War* (New York: Tapplinger Co., 1969), chaps. 6 and 7; Sean O'Callaghan, *Execution* (London: Frederick Muller, 1974); Brigadier General F. P. Crozier, *Ireland Forever* (London: Jonathan Cape, 1932), p. 184.

6. G. A. Hayes-McCoy, *Irish Battles* (London: Longmans, 1969).

7. Sean O'Callaghan, *The Easter Lily* (New York: Roy Publishers, n.d.).

8. Alice Macardle, *The Irish Republic* (London: Corgi Books, 1968).

9. *Fortnight* (London), March 5, 1976.

10. Crozier, *Ireland Forever,* passim.

11. Oliver MacDonough, *Ireland* (New York: Prentice-Hall, 1968), pp. 68-94.

12. Paddy Heron, "Television's Role in Reporting Ulster Violence," *Harrangue, A Political and Social Review* (Belfast), no. 2 (Summer, 1974).

13. F. X. Martin, "McCullough, Hobson and Republican Ulster," in F. X. Martin, ed., *Leaders and Men of the Easter Rising* (London: Methuen and Co., 1967), pp. 95-108.

14. Contrast the writings on Ulster since 1969 with the material in William Irwin Thompson, *The Imagination of an Insurrection* (New York: Harper and Row, 1967). The role of the artist in Irish politics is examined by Conor Cruise O'Brien, "Passion and Cunning: The Politics of W. B. Yeats," in G. A. White and Charles Newman, *Literature in Revolution* (New York: Holt, Rinehart and Winston, 1972), pp. 124-42.

15. The author currently has under contract a book on the American support groups for the IRA.

16. Various interpretations of the success and failure of the IRA since 1969 are given in: Clutterbuck, *Protest and the Urban Guerrilla;* Robert Moss, *The War for the Cities* (New York: Coward, McCann and Geoghegan, 1972); Robin Higham, ed., *Civil War in the Twentieth Century* (Lexington: University of Kentucky Press, 1974), especially J. Bowyer Bell, "Societal Lessons and Patterns: The Irish Case," pp. 217-28. For views of Irish and English governmental roles see Calton Younger, *A State of Disunion* (London: Muller, 1972), and James Kelly, *The Genesis of Revolution* (Dublin: Kelly Kane Publishers, 1975).

ROBERT FISK

The Effect of Social and Political Crime on the Police and British Army in Northern Ireland

In early 1970, the Ministry of Defence began publication of a four-page card to be issued to every soldier serving in Northern Ireland. It was printed on yellow paper, marked "Restricted"—the lowest security classification— and carried a long and occasionally confusing list of instructions about when a soldier may or may not open fire on a civilian in the province. It began with sensible enough advice. "Never use more force than the minimum necessary to enable you to carry out your duties," was one of the general rules. If a soldier had to open fire, the card said, "fire only aimed shots." But a warning should be given before opening fire, "preferably by loud hailer." If a guard is approached by a stranger who is behaving suspiciously, the card went on, the soldier is at the second challenge to apply the safety catch of his weapon and shout: "Stand still I am ready to fire." But soldiers could fire *without* warning in certain circumstances: when hostile firing was taking place, where delay could lead to serious injury (but then only if the person had a firearm), or at a vehicle if the occupants were opening fire.

The disclosure that such a document existed created a predictable burst of anger from the Ministry of Defence at the time.[1] *The Guardian* reporter responsible for breaking the story was virtually sent to Coventry by the army in Northern Ireland, and complaints were made to his editor about his lack of "responsibility." But then something very strange emerged from the government—an admission that while the card's instructions had been drawn up by civil servants at the Ministry of Defence, a soldier who obeyed them to the letter could still find himself in court charged with manslaughter. In other words, this carefully worded document had no legal standing. Nothing could have more dramatically illustrated the quasi-legal functions (as opposed to the legal role) of the army in Northern Ireland nor the vagueness with which these functions were conceived.

A glance at James Callaghan's memory of the first British military involvement in Belfast during the current war[2] is enough to illustrate the speed with which the military authorities were, quite unprepared, plunged into the latest Irish conflict. When the first troops entered Derry in August of 1969—they belonged to the Prince of Wales's Own—they crossed the Craigavon Bridge with bayonets fixed to their self-loading rifles. Officers at that time thought that their presence would be a very temporary one and for two years afterward their superiors announced (at least to the press) that the Irish Republican Army could be beaten by military means. The army, after all, knew that they themselves were only in the province "in support of the civil power"; they were temporarily propping up the Royal Ulster Constabulary because for a number of reasons the police were unable to cope.

But from the start, there was an ambiguity not only about the army's functions but also about its enemy. The IRA, when they clearly emerged in the shape of the Provisionals in 1970, were described in fashionable if slightly easy terms as "thugs and murderers"; they were—and the RUC still repeat this—common criminals with no genuine political aspirations. Merlyn Rees, the Northern Ireland Secretary of State, has repeated this within the past six months, comparing the sectarian murders along the Irish border with the work of the Mafia in the United States. Yet British ministers and their civil servants found within three years that it was politically expedient to treat with the IRA. The men condemned as "thugs and murderers" were invited to talk to senior British ministers in Cheyne Row. Men like Frank Steele, one of the Foreign Office's most able negotiators, were chatting amiably to the IRA within eight days of the resumption of hostilities in Belfast. Indeed, Sean MacStiofain remembers Steele approaching him on the secret flight back to Ireland with the words: "I hope you're not going to start your bloody stupid campaign again."[3] It was only five days later that a British colonel in the Royal Artillery found himself negotiating directly with Seamus Twomey, then the IRA Brigade Commander in Belfast, in an army post in the Lenadoon housing estate.

It was little wonder, then, that as the years went by in Northern Ireland the army's activities became not less but more complex and confusing. Yet from the start of their campaign against the IRA—a campaign which gained some veracity for the IRA when a British general actually said the army was "at war" with them, thus giving extremists the dignity of a legitimate army—there was an extralegal dimension to the military actions. The Special Powers Act in Northern Ireland—which has since been replaced by the slightly less draconian Emergency Provisional Act—enabled soldiers to search houses almost at will, to arrest men and hold them for longer periods than would be allowed in Britain, to draw up massive intelligence files, to carry out spying operations in plain clothes and, in August of 1971, to assist in the internment of hundreds of people without trial. On the day after internment at least eleven men were subjected to a severe form of interrogation involving sensory deprivation. This was carried out by experts in deprivation techniques who came from the Ministry of Defence in London.[4] To this day, the government has not been prepared to say who gave permission for this treatment of prisoners nor where the interrogations even took place. At least three of the men have since received 30,000 pounds compensation from the British government.

The purpose of such observations is not to attach any credence to the sectarianism or validity to the methods of extremists in Northern Ireland.

Nevertheless, in a period of three years, the actions of these extremists placed the army in a precarious moral position. Was the army to act as an armed police force or as a paramilitary wing of the police force? In the event, it took a middle—and therefore more disturbing—line of action.

Thrust into a vacuum in which the police had no real authority, the army found itself quite unwillingly acting as more than an auxiliary to the RUC. In theory, military units in Northern Ireland awaited a request for help from the police before becoming involved in civil disturbances. In practice, this strategy became less and less applicable and the army increasingly came to take over the functions of the police. This came about not through any subversive conspiracy on the part of the army but because the police were unable to operate on their own in districts where the IRA was particularly strong. The military machine, being by nature bureaucratic, also took upon itself various functions on the periphery of the army's daily duties. Thus soldiers became not only policemen, patrolling the streets as the police might do elsewhere in the United Kingdom, but also community relations experts, housing assistants, intelligence men, and plain clothes officers. The intelligence corps provided an alternative to the Special Branch. The plain clothes army patrols, assisted in early 1974 by men from the 22d Regiment of the SAS from Bradbury Lines camp in Hereford, became a kind of unofficial CID, operating quite outside the control of the RUC, under the immediate and exclusive control of the Commander Land Forces at Lisburn in County Antrim. The army, in effect, became the civil power itself.

This peripheral theatre of activity was to have immediate and sometimes embarrassing results. Genuinely and at times justifiably worried about the trust which could be placed in the RUC, the army began closing off their intelligence files. Battalion and company intelligence records were marked "for UK eyes only"; in reality this meant British eyes only and police detectives who wished to see these records were required to seek permission from the battalion commanding officer. The records themselves, which have since been placed onto a computer filing system at army headquarters at Thiepval Barracks, went into astonishing detail of the lives of thousands of people. Every three months, each company in Belfast (battalions broke into companies for billeting for both tactical and administrative reasons) carried out a survey of their area. Householders were questioned about their friends, relatives, hobbies, holidays, and interests. Widespread "screening"—the indiscriminate if temporary arrest of large numbers of civilians in Catholic areas and their subsequent questioning—helped to build up these files. In the company headquarters at the Henry Taggart Memorial Hall in Ballymurphy, an area of West Belfast, were literally thousands of photographs of Catholics, male and female. If one was arrested, a disc was placed over the lower part of the photograph and a soldier added the word "taken" or, in some cases, "zapped." I was once given an extraordinary example of the depth of such intelligence filing. In an armored vehicle in West Belfast, I was asked by the sergeant escorting me to request any piece of information about any house in the area. I named a house in White-rock Road which I had visited since I had friends who lived there, and I asked the color of the sofa. After speaking briefly over the radio to his head-quarters, the sergeant told me, quite correctly, that the relevant piece of fur-niture was brown.

It was not surprising that soldiers began to take a personal, almost jeal-ous attitude toward their intelligence gathering. In 1973, the army secretly printed another rule card, this time on blue paper, which set out instructions for troops when they wished to arrest members of the public. Much of the document was made up of mundane and rather obvious advice about treat-ment of a prisoner but one of the first rules instructed soldiers to hand ar-rested men over to the Royal Military Police for interrogation and only to the RUC *if releasing the arrested man was the only other alternative.* The army at first denied that such a card existed, later admitted its existence when *The Times* published a photograph of the card. The army then said that the rule had been "misinterpreted" and that the police knew about it all along. On the day of publication, the reporter responsible—myself—was telephoned by a very senior policeman in Belfast with a request to show him the card pri-vately. Neither he nor any of his colleagues, he said, had ever seen the doc-ument. So sensitive was the army that the Chief Information Officer at Lisburn complained to *The Times* that their Belfast correspondent's work was "snide and misleading." The same officer then sent a classified signal to all three military brigades in Northern Ireland instructing them not to give me any information. The Ministry of Defence at first denied that any such order had been sent but immediately admitted it—and rescinded the instruc-tion—when *The Times* acquired a copy of that classified signal as well.

The army's relationships with the police, however, were not the only doubtful area of activity. A black propaganda section was set up at Lisburn under the command of a lieutenant colonel who had been trained in psycho-logical operations at the United States psyops school at Fort Bragg. This department forged Sinn Fein posters and IRA documents. In early Decem-ber 1974, for example, they gave assistance to troops of the Gloucestershire Regiment stationed at Hastings Street barracks to forge a Sinn Fein news-paper called *The Vindicator*.[5] But they also distributed bogus information to the press to the effect that a leading Protestant politician had been involved in the kidnapping of the honorary West German consul Thomas Nieder-mayer—this information was disseminated by a major in 39 Brigade who now works as public relations man to an English county council—and built up long personal files on newspapermen which suggested their contacts. My own file was drawn up for the army's Special Investigation Branch by Major Geoffrey Cox, a former SAS officer who invited himself to my home in Belfast while serving as second in command to the third battalion of the parachute regiment. Since *The Times* had been told to suspect this officer's intentions, the file contains totally false information.[6] More recently, the same military department forged journalists' press cards for soldiers working on plain-clothes surveillance duties in Belfast.[7]

But what has worried the RUC most has been the army's relationship with the law itself. On at least three occasions, innocent men have been killed by soldiers operating on duty in plain clothes in Belfast. One sample will suffice. Patrick McVeigh, a Catholic from Andersontown, was shot dead in an apparently sectarian murder in 1972. The army and police both told the press that the culprits were unknown.[8] But months later his inquest revealed that soldiers in plain clothes firing from a civilian car had been responsible. The soldiers' testimony was unsworn and no one was charged. There were other, less lethal incidents. An army captain and an NCO were charged in the Belfast courts after a bus queue in Andersontown had been sprayed with machine gun fire. Both were accused of possessing a Thompson submachine gun in February of 1973[9] when the incident took place and in evidence the captain said that the ammunition had been handed to him by the special branch. The Thompson submachine gun is normally used by the IRA. The men were not convicted and the army said later in private conversations with journalists that their weapon had also been acquired "legally."

Many people have in fact been shot dead while not engaged in any terrorist activity by *uniformed* soldiers in Northern Ireland. Figures compiled in mid-1974 by *The Times* showed that at least sixty of the 150 people shot dead by soldiers had no known terrorist affiliations. This figure is not a final one; the army claims it does not have a figure for the number of people they have killed and the Dublin magazine *Hibernia* produced a table a week later claiming that of 156 persons killed by British troops, eighty-six had no known terrorist affiliations.[10] On January 12, 1973, for instance, Elizabeth McGregor was shopping when she was killed; Robert Johnston and Robert McKinney, his brother-in-law, were shot driving home in a car on September 7, 1972. Taxi driver Thomas McIlroy was killed while changing a wheel on his car on February 2, 1972. The army has sometimes acknowledged mistakes—an elderly woman killed on the edge of the Ardoyne, for example, and a Protestant plumber in the same area whose piping was mistaken by soldiers for a rifle.

At times, the army's shooting tactics were shown in the courts to have been far outside the framework laid down by the quasi-legal yellow card. Evidence was given in a Belfast court that a soldier in the Ardoyne fired at a man carrying a gun and saw the man fall. Then when the man called for help and tried to crawl away the soldier fired at him again, killing him. This only came to light at the inquest on the dead man; he was indeed carrying a gun for—far from being an IRA member—he was himself a uniformed soldier, shot by mistake by his own colleague. Such incidents were inevitable for, in spite of the yellow card, General Freeland, a former GOC, had said three years before[11] that anyone seen carrying arms would be shot dead. In the Ardoyne on the night of August 9, 1971, a soldier in the Green Howards shot and killed Sarah Worthington because he thought she was a looter. The army said at the time that it had not shot her—a dangerous statement in view of the inflammatory sectarianism in Belfast—but the inquest revealed the truth. No criminal proceedings were instituted. In fact, of the sixty fatal shootings involving soldiers firing at innocent persons, only seven had resulted in charges of unlawful killing being laid against military personnel.[12]

The British government, as well as the police, became worried when they found that the army was handing information on suspected IRA men over to members of Protestant paramilitary groups. The purpose of this was to gain information from Protestants about Catholic neighbors who may have been members of the IRA although the Ulster Defence Association and other groups kept their own files on Republicans to which the army information was added. Information was handed over by military authorities on a regular basis on frequent occasions; for instance, a Life Guards squadron in East Belfast handed over information about Catholics to the UDA in August 1972. Last year, a loyalist handed *The Sunday Times* military documents marked "Restricted" that he said had been given him by British soldiers. The documents were genuine and contained the names of Provisional IRA suspects in the Ardoyne area of Belfast who had been photographed during army screening operations. One was described as an "acid bomber," another as "assistant explosives officer in Provo A Company."[13]

For their part the police, whose morale has been upheld in a remarkable way during the assaults of the last seven years, now find themselves a virtually sectarian force. Each year, at the passing out parade for new police recruits at Enniskillen, the Northern Ireland Chief Constable appeals to Catholics to join the force. There are no official figures of Catholic membership issued by the authorities although unofficially it is believed to be around 9 percent or lower. The police are not, in essence, a sectarian force nor do they have any particular desire to be used as a political tool by Protestant governments. Indeed, the Police Federation in Northern Ireland has said on three occasions in the past two and one-half years that it never wishes to be used as a political weapon. Yet official government reports on the violence in Northern Ireland have shown that the police cannot always be relied upon to perform in the manner which should be expected of them. The Scarman report referred to wild shooting by the police in Divis Street in 1969, where they were responsible for the killing of a youth and an off-duty soldier, and suggested that policemen went on the rampage around Catholic homes in the Bogside area of Derry in the same year. (Evidence given before the inquiry included eyewitnesses who saw policemen swigging beer from bottles before the Bogside operation.)

Yet the effect of the continuing violence upon the police in Northern Ireland has led them to question not so much their function as their role, a diametrically opposite but not entirely unconnected problem to that facing the army. Almost 2,000 under strength (their total at present is just 4,800) they have no chance of taking back the security initiative from the army. Lord Scarman in his report said that "once large-scale communal disturbances occur they are not susceptible to control by police . . . there are limits to the efficiency of the police and the criminal law: confronted with such disturbances the police and the ordinary processes of the criminal law are of no avail."[14] Left to their own devices, the police have "soldiered on" to the promises of politicians who have continued to say that the RUC will ultimately remain the only law-enforcement agency in Northern Ireland. They have lost sixty-one dead to date—a further fifteen reservists have been killed—although there is no concrete sign that they have become more acceptable in Catholic areas.

Catholics and Protestants complain that even the complaints procedure within the RUC is partial. Figures released by the Northern Ireland police authority for 1972 certainly suggest that—compared to the rest of the United Kingdom—the RUC is a pristine force. In England and Wales in that year there were 9,872 complaints against the police of which 1,100 were considered substantiated by the end of the year.[15] That represents 11 percent. In Northern Ireland there were naturally far fewer complaints because the population only numbers one and one-half million. But of the 850 complainants, only forty-four had had their complaints substantiated by the end of the year. That represents only 5 percent.[16]

Whatever interpretation is put upon these figures (and one need hardly add that completely opposite interpretations can be—and are—put upon them) the chief constable's report for 1974, the latest available in Ulster, suggests that the police have improved in both efficiency and crime detection.[17] There were, for example, 669 explosions in 1974 compared to 1,007 the previous year. The report also drew attention to the reports of intimidation which had decreased in twelve months by 20 percent. Yet the reality behind this was obscured by these figures. An appendix to the report that included statistics from the various police divisions in Northern Ireland and D Division in Belfast, where Catholics are surrounded by a large Protestant district, showed a remarkably different picture. The area covered by the division includes some of the most dangerous interface roads in North Belfast and the local report read as follows: "Intimidation is a continuing problem but firm police action has resulted in a significant decrease in the number of cases reported during the year. One hundred and seventy cases were recorded compared with 431 in 1973 but unfortunately no detections were made. . . ."[18] In other words, the *reports* of intimidation fell but the success rate was in fact nil.

The police impotence when faced with intimidation is only a symptom of deeper problems. Intimidation is the greatest social disease between the two communities in Belfast but there seems little trust in the police even in Protestant areas. During the UWC strike, the government believes that the police did nothing to prevent the Protestant strikers from staging a virtual coup d'etat. Certainly there were numerous examples of policemen watching idly as loyalists built barricades. There were examples of the army doing just the same. What happened in May of 1974, however, was that the police showed no *will* to combat crime. Since most of them were Protestants, they had been brought up at the same schools and in the same estates as many of the strike pickets. Politically, some identified with the strikers—one RUC man was a strike leader's bodyguard—and this led to an extraordinary situation. Roadblocks were built around Stromont Castle; indeed Merlyn Rees's permanent secretary, Frank Cooper, had to shout down the telephone to the police to demand that the blocks be removed. During the entire strike, in which four people were killed and no fewer than 862 roadblocks were built and when Northern Ireland was paralyzed by the strike which was backed by the Protestant private armies, only seventy-one people were ever charged with offenses. Of these thirty-one were taken to court over only one incident, an attack on a public house in County Antrim in which two men were killed.[19]

That the police should, ideally, be free and capable of operating anywhere in Northern Ireland is not questioned by the government but the recent disputes involving the appointment of a new chief constable and the government's decision to allow Provisional IRA men to be taken off the army's suspect lists during the cease-fire suggests that the preservation of the police force in its present form is not high on the government's list of priorities. It was not by chance that it was an officer at North Queen Street police station who leaked the documentary evidence about the army's instruction not to arrest Seamus Twomey.

The effect of violence upon the police and army is, in the short term, one of function and role. There are, of course, other complications. The courts had their function changed when internment with quasi-legal trial at Long Kesh was introduced; Long Kesh itself turned out to be run not by the prison authorities nor by the army, which guards the perimeter, but by the prisoners themselves. Northern Ireland's social and political crisis was then played out in miniature *within* the prison. On Boxing Day 1973, a prisoner was beaten to death in a Republican hut at the Kesh, but no one was ever charged with his murder. At Magilligan prison in County Derry warders just prevented Republican prisoners from hanging one of their fellow inmates. For over two years, deep distrust has also been expressed by Catholic politicians in the part-time Ulster Defence Regiment. The UDR is part of the regular army but in its early days members of the Protestant paramilitary UDA were allowed to join.[20] In 1971, 18 percent of the membership were Catholic. Since then, partly because of IRA intimidation but also due to Catholic reluctance to join a force of auxiliaries whose members were already turning up in the courts for Protestant paramilitary offenses, Catholics have been less willing to join the group. Five UDR members have been charged variously with murder and arms offenses within the past seven weeks in Northern Ireland, one of them with the assassination of the Miama showband pop group in County Down.

What the army and police lack in Northern Ireland is a set of specific, legally defined ground rules of operations. This should be on paper and it should be open to inspection. The distrust which has been built up against the security forces in the province has been caused as much by suspicion of their activities as by misbehavior or unacceptable policies adopted by army and police officers. Junior officers in the British army would welcome such ground rules as much as civil-rights organizations. They could, at least in theory, take into account the Bill of Rights for Northern Ireland which is at present being studied by a British government commission.

If this needs defining in a more blunt—if less precise—way, then we might say that all British citizens should have the right to know all the conditions and rules under which they may be interrogated, arrested, imprisoned, or even killed by the representatives of their state.

Notes

1. Though not, curiously, when *The Times* printed a photograph of the entire card on its front page in February 1972.

2. *A House Divided* (Collins, 1973), p. 2. In 1967, Northern Ireland was dealt with by the General Department of the Home Office, a body which also covered such matters as the administration of state-owned pubs in Carlisle and "the protection of animals and birds."

3. See MacStiofain's tortuous and hopelessly partial account of his time in the IRA, *Memoirs of a Revolutionary* (Cremonesi, 1975), p. 285.

4. Simon Winchester, *In Holy Terror: Reporting the Ulster Troubles* (Faber, 1975).

5. *Times* (London), 11 December 1974.

6. *Times* (London), 25 March 1975.

7. *Times* (London), 15 February 1976.

8. Robert Fisk, *The Point of No Return; The Strike That Broke the British in Ulster* (Andre Deutsch, 1975), p. 102, fn. 1.

9. *Irish Times,* 28 February 1973.

10. *Hibernia Review* (Dublin), 30 August 1974, p 10.

11. On 28 June 1970.

12. Although lesser charges of unlawful discharge of arms had been instituted.

13. *Sunday Times* (London), 8 June 1975, p. 1.

14. *The Scarman Report* (April 1972), p. 17.

15. 1,203 cases were still under investigation.

16. 208 cases (24 percent) were still under investigation.

17. Chief Constable's Report 1974.

18. Chief Constable's Report 1974, p. 76.

19. Robert Fisk, *The Point of No Return,* pp. 99-100.

20. Peter Blaker, the Tory Under-Secretary for the Army, said in January 1973 that "there is no obligation on a UDR member to tell us if he belongs to the UDA or not, since this is not an illegal organization." This practice was later changed.

MICHAEL MOODIE

The Patriot Game: The Politics of Violence in Northern Ireland

> Come all you young rebels, and list while I sing,
> The love of one's country is a terrible thing,
> It banishes fear with the speed of a flame,
> It makes us all part of the patriot game.
>
> IRA Song

Like beauty, patriotism in Northern Ireland is in the eye of the beholder. Those who are committed to the creation of a thirty-two county Irish republic claim it as readily and as self-righteously as those who affirm their loyalty to the British crown. It is only one of the differences that has divided the Ulster community for the last four centuries and continues to make it a province of the United Kingdom where governing without consensus remains the rule.

In 1839 Gustave de Beaumont remarked that "Ireland is a small country where the greatest questions of politics, morality and humanity are fought out." The period between the collapse of the Sunningdale power-sharing agreement in May 1974 and the dissolution of Ulster's Constitutional Convention in March 1976 might lead one to conclude that the problems of Northern Ireland remain as far from resolution today as they were in the nineteenth century. Events in Northern Ireland during that period, however, may prove to be a turning point in the history of the province, providing the impetus for action that shatters the existing stalemate.

Political developments in Northern Ireland during these two years follow a pattern of action and reaction between three sets of actors: the Ulster Protestants, the Catholic faction in the province, and the British government.[1] It has been said that the Catholics in Northern Ireland are preoccupied with the British Army, while the Protestants are preoccupied with the Catholics. During the past year, however, both communities in Ulster have been keenly conscious of the British government's policies emanating from Westminster. It is the interaction of these three groups, therefore, that is the focus of this analysis. While the discussion concentrates primarily on the acts of violence relating to the Ulster troubles, it must place those acts in the political context created by the interactions of Protestant, Catholic, and British politicians.

The British government has made a number of attempts to resolve the conflict in Northern Ireland through political channels. As recently as November 1973 a resolution of the Ulster dispute appeared to be in sight. In July 1973, following a poll in which a majority of the Northern Ireland electorate voted to remain part of the United Kingdom, the British government passed the Northern Ireland Constitutional Act. The purpose of the act was to replace direct rule of the province from London with an Assembly and an Executive representing both the Catholic and Protestant communities of Ulster.

Despite strong opposition to the provisions of the act by hardliners in both Protestant and Catholic communities, plans for its implementation went ahead into 1974. To fulfill the act's provision for a Council of Ireland, a tripartite conference at Sunningdale, including both the British and Irish prime ministers, agreed to establish a Council of Ministers and a Consultative Assembly to deal with such noncontroversial issues as tourism and transportation between the Irish Republic and Northern Ireland.

Ratification of this agreement by the Northern Ireland Assembly in May of 1974 prompted militant Protestant leaders in control of Ulster's labor unions to call a general strike. Appealing to Protestant fears that the Council of Ireland would be a first step toward unification of Ulster with the Irish Republic, the Protestant leaders enlisted mass support for their action. Supported and policed by Protestant paramilitary groups, the strike all but shut down the province.[2]

Brian Faulkner, leader of the provincial government's coalition of moderate Protestants and Catholics, favored negotiations with the strikers. This course was resolutely opposed, however, by Secretary of State for Northern Ireland Merlyn Rees, who refused to be coerced into talks by the strikers. Faulkner and his fellow Unionists in the government resigned, and the power-sharing agreement outlined in the Sunningdale Agreement collapsed. London was forced to abandon its new arrangements and revert to direct rule.

In July 1974 the British government announced new plans for Ulster, calling on the people of Northern Ireland to devise a settlement themselves by holding a Constitutional Convention the following year. Both Britain and Northern Ireland were back where they had started in March 1972 when direct British rule was first imposed on the province. No prospects to an end of the stalemate were in sight.

The Aftermath of Sunningdale

The events following the Protestant general strike can be divided into four distinct phases: (1) May through Christmas 1974, a period characterized by an increasing level of sectarian violence by both Catholic and Protestant militants in Northern Ireland, and by a growing willingness on the part of the Provisional wing of the Irish Republican Army to extend its terrorist activities to Britain; (2) Christmas 1974 through March 1975, when the IRA and the British government agreed to a shaky cease-fire that was marked by stops and starts, but was generally upheld by both sides; (3) April through May 1975, when the campaign and elections for the Constitutional Convention were held, and (4) May 1975 to March 1976, which included the failure of the Constitutional Convention to achieve a satisfactory framework for provincial government and the return to a level of violence comparable to that after the general strike. Each of these phases saw new elements introduced into the Ulster equation. Taken together, their consequences could set Northern Ireland on a new course. Whether that course is toward the tragedy of civil war or toward an acceptable resolution of the conflict is not clear.

THE VIOLENCE: MAY-CHRISTMAS 1974

Following the Protestant strike in Northern Ireland the old pattern of violence and counterviolence between warring Catholic and Protestant factions reappeared. As Christmas approached, however, two new factors emerged. First, the Provisional wing of the Irish Republican Army[3] demonstrated its intention to focus its terrorist activities increasingly on targets in England, with the goal of forcing the British to withdraw their troops from the province. Second, the Provos were forced to reconsider their long-term strategy.

Shortly after the downfall of the power-sharing Executive the IRA resumed its Ulster bombing campaign through a series of explosions in Londonderry and Belfast.[4] At the same time it signaled its intention to intensify its terrorist attacks in England by exploding a bomb in Westminster Hall, the most historic section of the Houses of Parliament.[5] Sporadic bombing by the IRA had plagued the British throughout 1974, but the last six months of the year found the tactic increasingly used in England in situations that would draw considerable publicity. In July, for example, an unannounced bomb attributed to the IRA exploded at the Tower of London, killing one and injuring forty-two.[6] The terrorist campaign in England culminated in November when IRA bombs destroyed two crowded pubs in the heart of Birmingham, killing fourteen people and injuring at least one hundred.[7]

The reaction of the English to this last in the series of IRA attacks was one of outrage and immediate action. Roy Jenkins, the Labour government's home secretary, introduced sweeping emergency legislation that would outlaw the Irish Republican Army in Britain, give the police unprecedented powers of arrest and detention, and impose restrictions on travel between England and the Republic of Ireland. The IRA promised to step up its bombing campaign if the antiterrorism bill was passed, but the measure became law on November 29, 1974.

True to its word, the IRA exploded bombs at well-known locations throughout London, including Picadilly Circus, Oxford Street, and even at the home of former Prime Minister Edward Heath.[8] The violence in Britain stopped only after an uneasy cease-fire between the IRA and the British government was announced for the Christmas holidays.

The extension of frequent and severe terrorism to England by the IRA raised three important issues. First, it resulted in the imposition of unprecedented peacetime internal security measures in a country that has long prided itself on its unusual respect for civil liberties. Second, it stimulated a reaction in the British populace that could have major ramifications for future popular attitudes in England toward the Ulster problem and could generate popular pressures for ending the British involvement in Northern Ireland. Third, it served to demonstrate the direction of the IRA's future operations.

The laws passed by Parliament in reaction to increasing IRA terrorism provided wide-ranging powers to the British government for dealing with the problem. The measures, described as "draconian powers" by Roy Jenkins in his speech to the House of Commons, authorized the government to bar or expel from Britain any suspected IRA member or accomplice. Not only was the IRA outlawed in England for the first time, but any public support for the organization and the wearing of its traditional parade uniform were also banned. Moreover, the police were empowered to search and arrest without warrants, and the time of detention prior to the initiation of formal judicial proceedings was extended.

Despite the severity of the measures and the expressed concern that the new powers might entrap innocent bystanders and deprive them of their legal rights, Jenkins reportedly indicated that even stricter options, such as the reinstitution of capital punishment and a system of national identity cards, might have to be implemented.[9] In a country such as Britain, where the preservation of civil liberties has always assumed a high priority, these measures represented drastic deviations from normal practice, and they demonstrated the impact that IRA activities were having.

In addition to prompting the British government to pass such legislation, the IRA's bombing campaign in England shook the apathy of the British populace toward the "Irish Problem" and succeeded in raising the average Briton's awareness of the threat of terrorism. At stores and theaters people were asked to open their bags for inspection; it was common to see motorists checking the trunks and exhausts of their cars for bombs before driving away. Attendance at London's West End theaters slumped, as did tourism in general.[10]

While the Londoners and other Englishmen did not panic, the disruption of their daily routine forced them to experience an unease that had long been a fact of life for the people in Belfast. Some backlash against the Irish was inevitable, although it was largely verbal and few violent incidents were reported. Nevertheless, the large Irish concentrations in the cities of London, Manchester, and Glasgow make them convenient targets for retaliatory attacks should the IRA resume its "English" bombing campaign in the future.

The impact of the bombing campaign was not lost on the IRA. As one IRA source noted: "Last year taught us that in publicity terms one bomb in Oxford Street is worth ten in Belfast. It is not a lesson we are likely to forget in the future."[11] By initiating a major terrorist campaign in England the IRA was hoping to fuel the desire among the English populace to withdraw from Northern Ireland altogether and let the province fend for itself. Although most Englishmen have thus far viewed the British military presence in Ulster as necessary for the prevention of civil war, the continuing economic crisis in Britain, an increasing casualty rate as a result of further bombings, the dislocation of daily life, and the atmosphere of fear engendered by indiscriminate terrorism could all contribute to a change in that perception and increase popular pressure on the British government to pull the troops out.

The Provisional IRA's decision to focus on England as its target demonstrates its recognition of Britain as the actor whose policies will have the most important impact on the ultimate course of events in Northern Ireland. This recognition was also apparent in another major IRA decision in the second half of 1974: a reevaluation of long-term strategy that led to the Christmas cease-fire.

Late in 1974, senior members of the Provisional IRA met with prominent Protestant churchmen from the North at a small hotel in Feakle, County Clare. There they were confronted with a forceful explanation of how the IRA's terrorist campaign was counterproductive, and that the only way to achieve its goals short of civil war was some form of agreement with the Protestants. As one account of the meeting later described it:

[E]ven the most bigoted and blinkered of freedom fighters had to see, in the mental stocktaking forced on them by eight hours of talks at Feakle, that the Provisionals were far from winning the military war, and perilously close to defeat in the battle for minds.[12]

Following the meeting with the Protestant clergy a fundamental division appeared within the ranks of the Provos.[13] Some members advocated further violence at the risk of provoking civil war or of losing what popular support they did have; others argued that it was time for a temporary cessation of the bombings and the start of political negotiations. The "political" faction apparently won the first round, since authorization was given to make contact with the Northern Ireland Office about a cease-fire.

The December split within the Provisionals is important in that it provides evidence of a "moderate" IRA faction that seems to be more in line with the prevailing sentiment of Ulster's Catholic community. That community had given its support to the political leadership of the Catholic

Social Democratic and Labour Party which favored some form of eventual compromise with the Protestants. Aware of Protestant strength in the wake of the general strike, many Catholics in Northern Ireland shifted their emphasis from fighting old battles to avoiding future ones.[14] That there is an element of the IRA with similar sentiments could have positive implications for the future. It at least allowed for the successful implementation of a tenuous cease-fire and the temporary restoration of some form of normality in Northern Ireland.

THE CEASE-FIRE: CHRISTMAS 1974-MARCH 1975

The IRA called a halt to its violence on December 22, 1974. The following months saw a cease-fire that was marked by stops and starts, but the Christmas truce initiated the first prolonged respite from the sectarian warfare and terrorism that had plagued Northern Ireland since 1969. Although there were isolated incidents of sporadic or retaliatory violence, for some time the major actors demonstrated a desire to keep their part of the bargain.

The first phase of the cease-fire broke down after twenty-five days. In a statement announcing the resumption of hostilities in mid-January, IRA Provisionals accused the British government of not living up to its promises of gradually releasing all prisoners held under detention orders and reducing the activities of the British army in the province. Subsequent meetings between British officials and the Provisional Sinn Fein—the political wing of the Provisional IRA—smoothed over these differences sufficiently to allow the IRA to announce a new cease-fire in early February.[15]

To safeguard and monitor the cease-fire the British government established a series of "incident" centers in sensitive Catholic areas across Northern Ireland. The purpose of these centers was to receive information or complaints from both the Provisionals and the British army about the cease-fire's operation in order to head off mistaken judgments should any serious incidents occur. The centers represented the most elaborate and formal structure of contacts with the Provisionals that the British government had ever accepted. It also reflected a change in policy for the British government which, only a month earlier, had refused to consider talks with representatives of the IRA.[16]

In addition to the growing communication between the British government and the IRA, two other important factors emerged during the period of the cease-fire. First, Ulster's would-be rulers were forced to think seriously about the possibility of Northern Ireland "going it alone." Second, the cease-fire led to serious divisions and disputes within the competing Catholic and Protestant factions.

The implications of Northern Ireland's potential independence strongly emerged in the months following the declaration of the Christmas cease-fire. Green Papers were produced to demonstrate the extent to which the province depended economically on the rest of the United Kingdom for its financial prosperity. Local Ulster television broadcasts, described in the media as "unprecedented," found Ulster economists discussing the economic implications of Northern Ireland's independence.[17] One Belfast economist said, for example, that a unilateral declaration of independence (UDI) by Northern Ireland along Rhodesian lines would mean a fall of one-fifth in unemployment, sickness, invalidism, and supplementary benefits as well as considerable reductions in family allowances.[18]

The economic impact was not the only problem of independence receiving serious attention from Northern Ireland's leaders during the first months of 1975. Another was the problem of policing. Six months before the cease-fire, the Royal Ulster Constabulary (Northern Ireland's police force) was totally ineffective in combating Ulster's violence. As one newspaper described it:

> [T]he Unionists were demanding a third force home guard, a better armed police force and calling for what amounted to raids on Roman Catholic housing estates. The main Catholic Social Democratic and Labour Party were refusing to talk about the Royal Ulster Constabulary until it had been reformed. The Provisionals' only reaction was to shoot them.[19]

It was this sorry situation to which *The Economist* testified in its comment that "Even children regarded the police as enemies."[20]

During the cease-fire, however, there occurred some thawing of the attitudes toward the police. Crime-prevention exercises in Catholic neighborhoods elicited a large response. The IRA began to discuss ways in which Catholic areas should be policed, and the Unionists' threat to create their own paramilitary patrols turned out to be a publicity stunt.

The police authorities' autonomy is inevitably restricted until Northern Ireland has a form of government acceptable to both Catholic and Protestant communities. Nevertheless, these developments indicated that continued tact and even-handedness on the part of the RUC could ease the problems confronting the police if they are asked to assume the burden of maintaining order in Ulster without the help of the British Army. If Ulster should become independent, effective performance by the police would be crucial.

A development during the cease-fire that was as important as the emergence of prospects for independence was the internecine feuding that broke out within Catholic and Protestant militant organizations. The split within the Provisional wing of the IRA continued as the militant faction became increasingly angry with what they believed were meager responses by the British government to their moratorium on violence. The militants got their way when the IRA returned to offensive action in February, but the offensive was short-lived in the wake of the initiatives of the Labour government's Northern Ireland office.

A split more serious for the peace of the province was the bloody feud that erupted between the Official Wing of the IRA and the break-away Irish Republican Socialist Party. The IRSP split from the Official IRA in December 1974, claiming that the Officials were "reformists" and not committed to their espoused Marxist-Leninist ideology. There was some suspicion, however, that behind the ideological accusations lay the desire of some Official IRA men, unhappy with the three-year truce maintained by the Officials, to return to violence.[21] Whatever the reasons for the split, the Officials blamed IRSP gunmen for numerous shootings and for the murder of Official IRA officers. Countercharges of murder and violence were hurled back by the IRSP. The situation reached an uneasy resolution only after the IRSP announced that it was disbanding in Belfast in order to isolate the gunmen responsible for the shootings.

A similar feud also flared up between rival Protestant extremist groups. The Protestant dispute, between the leftist-oriented Ulster Volunteer Force (UVF) and the more right-wing Ulster Defence Association (UDA), broke out after the murder of two UDA officials in North Belfast. It appeared to be part of a more long-standing quarrel between the two organizations, stretching back to the time of the 1974 general strike, about which of the two groups should take the profits of local loyalist clubs.[22] The feud, which caused at least two deaths and countless shootings and bombing incidents, was based as much on left-right ideological differences between the groups as on allegations of racketeering.

Although the Protestant violence ended with a settlement between the UDA and the UVF, their dispute (as well as the Catholic quarrels) demonstrates that even if the differences between Northern Ireland's Catholics and Protestants were resolved, violence could erupt in the province over other issues. The question of Ulster's future commitment to socialism as the road to progress could be one such issue. The UVF and the IRA "Officials," both espousing a strong commitment to socialism, were confronted with challenges that had nothing to do with religion. Such challenges could very likely be repeated if either group was in a commanding position in Ulster.

A further implication of the fratricidal warfare that erupted during the cease-fire must be noted. By not being a party to the violence, the Provisional IRA's image as the Protestants' "enemy" was downplayed. As a consequence, it left the Protestants with no immediate external target against which to direct their violence. As a result, the Protestants turned against themselves. For both Catholics and Protestants, membership in a paramilitary organization confers a certain status on an individual. It might be postulated, then, that in the absence of an external threat, the internecine fighting in the Protestant community represented a necessary justification for the continuation of these organizations as new "enemies" were discovered in their own ranks.

By feuding, however, the Protestants discarded the strongest card they had to play in the Northern Ireland situation, the threat of another province-wide general strike. Implementation of such a strike requires close coordination among all elements in the Protestant community. As long as they are divided, the Protestants are not strong enough to implement a strike and hence cannot have great impact on British policy in Ulster.

THE CONSTITUTIONAL CONVENTION CAMPAIGN: APRIL-MAY 1975

The run-up to the elections for Northern Ireland's Constitutional Convention, announced for May 1 by the British Government, saw the continuation of the Provisional IRA's cease-fire, but one that was increasingly pockmarked by incidents that threatened to bring it crashing down.

As the cease-fire wore on, disaffected Provisional IRA elements continued to press for the resumption of violence in the face of what was regarded as a lack of major concessions by the British. Hopes for a relatively peaceful period before the convention were shattered in early April when sectarian violence was responsible for ten deaths over a single weekend, and it appeared that local IRA commanders in Belfast, Londonderry, and Newry were given a free hand in deciding how to react to further violence.[23]

The fact that the cease-fire survived at all during what was called "one of the bloodiest weekends the province has seen since 1972"[24] was evidence of the lengths to which both the IRA and the British government were willing to go to insure that it was maintained. Behind-the-scenes contact between the British government and the Provisional Sinn Fein was continual, and it was stressed by both sides that the Provisional IRA had played no known part in the violence.[25] The Provos did issue two warnings that the cease-fire was only conditional, but the British compromised by intensifying British Army patrols in the most vulnerable areas between Catholic and Protestant strongholds.[26]

Sporadic violence plagued Northern Ireland as the convention approached, dampening whatever hopes existed for dramatic results that would force some movement away from the status quo. Pre-convention reporting was quite pessimistic; that pessimism was warranted as "loyalist" hardliners captured 54 percent of the vote and thirty-six of the seventy-eight convention seats.

While the Constitutional Convention was in session, events in Ulster developed along two separate, but closely interrelated, tracks. On the one hand, Northern Ireland's politicians unsuccessfully attempted to arrive at an acceptable constitutional formula for the province. On the other, the cease-fire between the British and the Irish Republican Army was almost totally discredited as political violence in the province escalated severely. The deterioration of the security situation and the shortening of political tempers as a result of the abortive convention were mutually reinforcing.

On the political front the crux of the problem created by the election results, a problem central to any successful resolution of Northern Ireland's stalemate, was "power-sharing," a formal arrangement ensuring that the political views of both Catholics and Protestants would be represented in a provisional government. To the "loyalists" such an arrangement has come to be seen as a device leading to Northern Ireland's dissolution as a province of the United Kingdom and its incorporation into the Irish Republic. As a consequence, the United Ulster Unionist Council, the successful umbrella organization for Protestant loyalists during the election campaign, stated in the clearest terms possible that it would not share power with those whom they considered Republicans.

However, the Social Democratic and Labour Party, the Catholic representatives during the election, emphasized with equal clarity that they would accept nothing less than guaranteed seats in any future government.[27] The SDLP also indicated its desire to incorporate an Irish dimension into any constitution that emerged, although it was prepared to have a British link included as well.[28]

Thus the convention reached an impasse with neither side willing to compromise on an issue as vital as the distribution of power within the state. The Protestant moderates did so poorly in the election that any potential mediating role they could have played had to be ruled out. The Protestant hardline majority, intent on implementing its constitutional plans, submitted a majority plan deemed unacceptable by the British government. Although Britain's Secretary of State for Northern Ireland reconvened the convention for one month to attempt to make some progress toward a devolved system of government, on March 5, 1976, he was forced to dissolve the convention in the face of no progress. It was obvious that a new British policy would be required.[29]

As it became increasingly apparent that the convention would not achieve a compromise, the security situation seriously deteriorated. This period began with the lowest number of British troops in Ulster since the spring of 1972, but it ended with large numbers of additional troops being sent to the province, including elements of the crack Special Air Service Regiment. The period during which the convention was in session closed with the ominous warning of one Belfast Protestant spokesman that 1975 had been the year of the politicians and that 1976 would be the year of the "paramilitaries."[30]

RETURN TO THE VIOLENCE: MAY 1975-MARCH 1976

The three months following the opening of the convention found the cease-fire between Britain and the IRA uneasily maintained. The IRA Provisionals concentrated their efforts on sociopolitical activities, supporting the political wing of Sinn Fein and policing their own areas. Nevertheless, the IRA used the period to rearm and regroup, and while there were few confrontations between the army and the IRA, the continued sectarian killings were enough to lead many to question whether the cease-fire could be maintained.[31] Given the tender of political frustrations that stemmed from the deadlocked convention, it was inevitable that sparks would set the province on fire again in a blaze of widespread political violence.

The return to violence in Ulster during the second half of 1975 and early 1976 is important in four respects. First, it demonstrated that the limitations imposed on the counter-terrorist activities of the British Army make it impossible for the Army to control certain segments of the province. Second, the IRA provided evidence of its conviction that terrorism in England could be efficacious by a series of bombings in London and elsewhere. Third, the return to violence stimulated increasing disenchantment among militant Protestant paramilitaries. Fourth, and most important, the renewed violence convincingly demonstrated that a solution to the Ulster troubles is not solely in the hands of Northern Ireland's politicians.

A considerable portion of the violence during the latter half of 1975 and early 1976 occurred in the "deadly triangle" of South Armagh, southwest of Belfast. Writing anonymously in *The Guardian* a British Army officer noted, "The Provisionals have declared this area the Independent Republic of South Armagh, and regrettably this assertion is not so very far from the truth."[32] With its wild terrain and uncharted stretches of bog, the area is one of the most suitable for terrorist and guerrilla activities in Europe. The British Army has never successfully ambushed an IRA patrol or inflicted heavy casualties in this region.

The lack of success by the British Army in South Armagh is due to the geographical advantages of the region for the terrorists and the disadvantage of the limitation on army action. In addition to its difficult terrain, South Armagh's border with the Irish Republic provides the IRA men in the area with a safe refuge for retreat. It goes without saying that the IRA in South Armagh—perhaps its major stronghold in Ulster—uses the geography of the area to its best advantage.

Combined with these factors, the relatively small size of the British contingent in South Armagh and the limits placed on its activities ensured continued anarchy in the region. The IRA, not the army, held the initiative, forcing the army to react to incidents rather than create them. The task of trying to defeat the terrorists fell to just one infantry battalion of 600 men. This force was doubled, however, after fifteen people were murdered in the area one weekend in January 1976.[33] Despite the increase, Merlyn Rees has been quoted as acknowledging that ten battalions could not prevent killings in the area.[34]

Irrespective of the size of the British army force in South Armagh the restrictions under which it operated also seriously curtailed its effectiveness there. For example, it was not allowed to use automatic weapons from helicopters, grenades, mortars, or Claymore mines. The level of army intelligence was also quite low, and the arrest and screening of suspects was stopped. In addition, restraints with respect to vehicle checks and personal identification made it more difficult for the army to prevent border crossings by IRA members.

In early January 1976 a contingent of the Special Air Service Regiment (SAS), specially trained to deal with insurgents and guerrilla warfare, was dispatched to South Armagh.[35] While the introduction of SAS elements appeared to have reduced violence in the area, the level of violence there is likely to remain relatively high. The events in South Armagh in the last half of 1975 and early 1976 indicate that the British army will have an extremely difficult time restoring order to the area unless it is allowed to go on the offensive.

The second important factor in the return to violence during the Constitutional Convention was the IRA's reversion to terrorist activities in England, London in particular. For the most part, those activities constituted a bombing campaign similar to that prior to the cease-fire of Christmas 1974.[36] However, one incident that stimulated considerable outcry against the terrorists was the door-front assassination of Ross McWhister, an outspoken British conservative who had offered $100,000 for aid in capturing the Irish bombers. Such assassinations had been frequent in Northern Ireland, but McWhister's murder was the first of its kind by the IRA in England.

These terrorist activities were viewed as instigated by the London branch of the Provisionals or a breakaway group from the IRA. In either case the new wave of bombings in London demonstrated that the Irish terrorists viewed the earlier bombings as a success, and they sought to use the new bombings as a pressure point against British policymakers. While the bombings have had little effect on British policy thus far, they have increased logistical problems for the British government. In London, for example, one thousand additional policemen were assigned to the subways after two explosions in March 1976.[37]

The return to violence in Northern Ireland while the Constitutional Convention was in session stimulated a third important element—a growing militancy in the Protestant paramilitary organizations and their increasing disillusionment with Protestant politicians and the British government. The Labour government's decision to reject the report of the convention and extend direct rule against the wishes of Ulster's Protestant majority generated considerable discussion among these militants about another province-wide general strike as well as the possibility of some form of independence from Britain.

Loyalist hackles were already up about the British government's cease-fire policy with the IRA, the continued release of detainees and the increase in violence, especially the murder of ten Protestants in South Armagh.

While it was hoped that the government's security initiatives of early 1976, including the deployment of the SAS, would be sufficient to postpone the Protestants' threatened action, the response of the Wilson cabinet to the convention plan regenerated those threats.

The disarray in the ranks of the Protestant politicians contributed further to the militancy of the loyalist paramilitaries. The mood of disillusionment with the politicians can be judged by a statement of Sam McCormack, brigade commander of the East Belfast Ulster Defence Association: "Two years ago we had control of this place. We handed it back to our politicians, and what happened? Nothing. They went back to squabbling, jockeying with each other. They had the power and they lost it. . . ."[38]

The militant mood of the Protestant paramilitaries, the division among Protestant politicians, and the need for a new initiative by the new British prime minister, James Callaghan, make it likely that some kind of independence for Ulster will be an increasingly dominant topic of conversation. While it is controversial, the idea already has received support from a few influential politicians including Glenn Barr, a prominent loyalist spokesman and Ivan Cooper and Paddy Devlin of the SDLP. Although independence would create serious problems for both Catholics and Protestants in Ulster, it remains an alternative still open to discussion.

If independence for Ulster is pursued as a viable option the manner in which it is attained would be extremely important. In this regard, the attitude of the Protestant paramilitary groups would be crucial. An independence negotiated by Ulster's politicians with the paramilitaries standing aside would probably eliminate many of the factors used by the IRA to justify its violence. However, if an independent Ulster is established as a result of the type of coup d'état and UDI frequently discussed by the Ulster Defence Association and other loyalist groups, extremely serious problems would result. The economic dependence of Ulster on the rest of the United Kingdom would provide London with a very influential lever over a new Ulster government. Under such circumstances it is also likely that the IRA would intensify its activities rather than curtail them.

The militant mood of the Protestant paramilitary organizations created by the rising sectarian violence during the Constitutional Convention pushed those groups to the brink of action. If further initiatives from the new British government are not quickly forthcoming, it appears that it would take very little to push those groups into taking direct offensive action. That action might be only a province-wide strike, but, given the intensity of the militancy, it could also be an attempt to gain power in the province and declare Ulster independent.

The fourth important lesson provided by the increasing violence during the Constitutional Convention is that the future of Northern Ireland will not be determined solely by the politicians. It was argued by many that the rise in the number and intensity of acts of violence by the IRA was for the purpose of bringing down the convention or, at least, ensuring its failure. The Protestant paramilitary organizations demonstrated their political importance during the same period by the pressure they were able to bring to bear on loyalist politicians and in their criticism of the policies of the Wilson government.

Most reliable estimates indicate that if civil war erupted in Ulster the Catholic and Protestant paramilitary organizations could mobilize at least 20,000 men. In addition to such major groups as the Catholic IRA and the Protestant UDA, both sides include a number of fringe groups, largely composed of disaffected members of the larger organizations, who are responsible for many of the blatant acts of sectarian violence. Both the Protestant and Catholic paramilitary organizations are capable of sectarian savagery, and they all seem to be waiting in the wings for an opportunity to mobilize their resources.

In Ulster private armies are accepted by most of the population as a fact of life. The fact that these organizations, both Catholic and Protestant, have the will and weaponry to inflict injury and destruction on a scale unprecedented in Irish history gives them an influential role in determining the future of Ulster. Their importance is further enhanced by the disarray among the ranks of the politicians in the province. Given the importance of these private armies, the British must deal with them directly as well as with Ulster's politicians if solutions to Northern Ireland's problems are to be found.

Considerable discussion has focused on the need for Prime Minister Callaghan to take a new initiative in Northern Ireland. He will be faced with hard choices from a number of unattractive alternatives. Difficult decisions, however, will not be limited to Downing Street. The events of the period between the collapse of the Sunningdale Agreement in May 1974 and the dissolution of Ulster's Constitutional Convention in March 1976 demonstrate that the conflict in Northern Ireland will be entering a new phase and that every party to that conflict will adapt to suit its own interest.

Conclusion

It must be recognized that the period for which Britain can assume responsibility for Ulster's future is limited. The extent of this limitation is today unknown. Yet a convergence of private and public views on the eventual necessity for some form of British disengagement from Northern Ireland appears to have begun. There will come a day when the indefinite postponement of Britain's withdrawal will not be allowed. It is in the interest of everyone who is party to the Northern Ireland dispute that some agreement be achieved before that day is reached.

Conor Cruise O'Brien, Dublin's minister of posts and telegraphs and one of the Irish government's spokesmen on Ulster affairs, once likened the consideration of solutions for the crisis in Northern Ireland to a search for "alternative routes to the cemetery."[39] Any progress toward solving the fundamental problems of Northern Ireland must take cognizance of three facts. First, the present situation can no longer continue. The destruction—physical, psychological, and emotional—that has been wrought in Ulster by endless years of sectarian strife is something that cannot be tolerated by civilized society. Moreover, the British public is making it increasingly clear that it believes it should not be expected to bear such a burden.

Second, the history of Northern Ireland demonstrates that neither segment of Ulster's community can be coerced into accepting the positions held by the other. Britain must unambiguously communicate to all parties that it will not force Ulster's Protestants into a unified Ireland. At the same time, Britain should welcome any initiatives and changes in the Irish Republic that would make it easier and more palatable for the Protestants to draw closer to the South. Conversely, the assurance of civil and human rights for Northern Ireland's Catholics must assume a high priority at Westminster and be clearly defined to all parties as such.

Third, the Irish dimension of the Northern Ireland problem cannot be ignored; Ulster shares a common border with the Irish Republic. The last effort to take this factor into account, Sunningdale's "Council of Ireland," failed disastrously. Nevertheless, it will have to be addressed if conflict in Ulster is to end.

Much of the responsibility for the future of Northern Ireland rests with the British government; however, it is not theirs alone. The Catholics and Protestants in the province, politicians, and paramilitaries must all be actively involved in any attempt to resolve Ulster's basic problems if violence in Northern Ireland is to end. The alternative is an open-ended conflict more violent and more destructive than the province has yet seen.

Notes

1. There have been several recent contributions to the historical background of the crisis in Northern Ireland. Among them are Robert Kee, *The Green Flag: A History of Irish Nationalism* (New York: Delacorte Press, 1972), Lawrence J. McCaffery, *The Irish Question: 1800-1922* (Lexington: University of Kentucky Press, 1968), and D. G. Bayce, *Englishmen and Irish Troubles, 1918-1922* (Cambridge: Cambridge University Press, 1972). Works focusing on recent Ulster events include Richard Rose, *Governing Without Consensus: An Irish Perspective* (Boston: Beacon Press, 1971), The Sunday Times Insight Team, *Northern Ireland: A Report on the Conflict* (New York: Vintage Books, 1972), and Simon Winchester, *Northern Ireland in Crisis: Reporting the Ulster Troubles* (New York: Homes and Meier, 1975). For an interesting presentation of the argument that, since the time of the Tudor conquest of Ireland in the sixteenth century, British policy has been the

major cause of the "Irish Question," see Patrick O'Farrel, *Ireland's English Question* (New York: Schocken Books, 1971).

2. For a more detailed discussion of the events leading to the Protestants' general strike, see *Ulster: Consensus and Coercion* (London: Institute for the Study of Conflict, *Conflict Studies*, no. 50, October 1974).

3. In December 1969, the IRA divided into two factions. The minority that broke away, known as the Provisional wing, disagreed with the Marxist line of the Officials and returned to the Republicanism and violence that had earlier characterized the IRA. The Officials have been observing a truce since 1972. There was a second split from the Official Wing of the IRA in December 1974, when the Irish Republican Socialist Party (IRSP), also with a Marxist orientation, was formed. See J. Bowyer Bell, *The Secret Army: The IRA,* 1916-1974 (Cambridge: The MIT Press, 1974).

4. *New York Times,* 20 June 1974.

5. *New York Times,* 18 June 1974.

6. *New York Times,* 18 July 1974.

7. *New York Times,* 22 November 1974.

8. *New York Times,* 23 December 1974.

9. *Christian Science Monitor,* 3 December 1974.

10. *New York Times,* 24 December 1974.

11. *New York Times,* 26 February 1975.

12. *Guardian* (Weekly), 1 February 1975.

13. *Ibid.*

14. *New York Times,* 26 February 1975.

15. *New York Times,* 10 February 1975. The interim was not without violence, however. Five bombs exploded in Belfast, for example, only hours before the renewed cease-fire was announced.

16. *New York Times,* 8 January 1975.

17. *Times* (London), 7 March 1975.

18. *Ibid.*

19. *Ibid.*

20. *Economist,* 5 April 1975, p. 17.

21. *Times* (London), 8 March 1975.

22. *Times* (London), 17 March 1975.

23. *Times* (London), 7 April and 9 April 1975.

24. *Times* (London), 9 April 1975.

25. *Ibid.*

26. *Economist,* 12 April 1975, p. 17.

27. The loyalists did indicate that they were willing to consider establishing back-bench committees with minority representation that would have a part in reviewing legislation. They have ruled out, however, any guarantee of positions in the government for the minority.

28. *Economist,* 19 April 1975, p. 17.

29. British Information Services, "Northern Ireland: Constitutional Convention Dissolved," *Policy Statements,* no. 15/76, 5 March 1976.

30. *Times* (London), 5 August 1975.

31. *Times* (London), 13 January 1976.

32. *Guardian* (Weekly), 4 January 1976.

33. *Times* (London), 7 January 1976.

34. *New York Times*, 7 January 1976.

35. *Times* (London), 8 January 1976.

36. At one point, however, there was an apparent shift of tactics in the IRA (or in the breakaway group responsible for the bombings) away from car-bombs to explosives tossed through windows of restaurants. When this tactic led to the capture and arrest of Michael Wilson, "the most wanted terrorist in Britain," the tactics reverted to earlier practices of car-bombs and bombs in subways.

37. *New York Times*, 19 March 1976.

38. Quoted in *New York Times*, 29 March 1976.

39. *Observer*, 6 February 1972.

JACOB SUNDBERG

The Antiterrorist Legislation in Sweden

The Buildup of Leftist Privileges

During the 1960s a policy of involvement gradually succeeded the neutral and more prudent Swedish policy of the 1950s. The Greek coup d'etat of August 21, 1967, particularly incensed leading socialist circles and created a strong reaction. Efforts were made to cultivate the birth of a Greek resistance movement, partially directed by the dethroned Greek politican Professor Andreas Papandreou. He was invited to direct his fight against the Greek regime from Sweden. He cooperated with Anthony Brillakis, head of the Greek Communist party, to establish terrorist activities in Greece.

The new policy of involvement led the Swedish government to abandon its previous demands that refugees who had been given asylum in Sweden refrain from political activity there.[1] Instead, it was decided that foreigners could enjoy the same freedom as Swedes to engage in political activity.[2] Since they were not allowed to participate in the Swedish elections, the formula mainly operated to allow the Papandreou type of political activity. This change in attitude (hereinafter called the Papandreou policy) for the first time had the effect of attracting refugees from outside of the socialist camp. Sweden now turned into a haven for an ever-increasing number of people whose socialist views led to their persecution and repression by some dictatorship or other.

Under the new socialist leadership of the mid-1960s, Sweden entered into an era of virulently anti-American policy which dominated the subsequent period and at times reached such heights that the American ambassador was withdrawn. Part of this policy was due to the intense support for the socialist regime that took over in Chile in 1970 under President Allende. In the increasingly polarized Chilean society that developed after the take-over, the Swedish government sympathized more with those seeking to destroy the managerial and middle classes and to establish a dictatorship of the revolutionary left, than with the opponents of the regime. The Cuban regime took a similar attitude and concentrated on Chile after 1970, moving its headquarters for revolutionary activity from the Paris embassy to the new Cuban embassy in Santiago.[3] The Pinochet coup of September 11, 1973, was felt in Sweden to be an enormous setback.

Pressured by the leftist forces on which the position of the new Swedish leadership depended, the government allowed large numbers of Chilean refugees and other Latin American revolutionaries, stranded by the Pinochet coup, to live in Sweden. The government provided language training, jobs, homes, and money. By early 1974, Sweden with a population of only eight million had received some 400 Chilean refugees, while countries like the almost three times bigger DDR in the socialist camp and revolution-exporting Cuba, had limited the number of refugees to seventy and 100 respectively, fearing that the exiles could become a source of domestic unrest.[4] Permission to engage in foreign politics inherent in the Papandreou policy had the effect of conferring upon Sweden the character of being to some extent a base for staging a counter-coup in Chile. The increasingly hostile Swedish attitude toward Chile was accompanied by an increasingly friendly attitude toward Cuba. In 1971 annual aid to Cuba started with 2.5 million SwCr (Swedish Crowns). By 1975 aid had risen to an annual amount of 60 million SwCr, in spite of the surprising Cuban reexportation of aid to many African and some Asian countries.[5]

Sweden was spared participation in World War II; that war did, however, impose increasing vigilance upon Sweden. In the late 1930s, the Swedish agency of internal security started to register Communists and Nazis. In a move to please the victorious Soviet neighbor, such registration of Communists ceased in 1945, but was reinstated in 1948 in the wake of the Prague coup of 1948. On June 19, 1963, disaster struck the internal security organization of Sweden with the prosecution of Colonel Wennerstrom. This spy scandal, the greatest ever to affect Sweden, exposed numerous and serious shortcomings in the security system. A Parliamentary committee was set up to study the guidelines for processing security questions. One result was the adoption of an act on April 9, 1965, with guidelines for all kinds of police registers, even for those of the internal security people. Another was the publication in 1967 of a broad report on how to strengthen internal security.[6]

However, the Soviet decision after the Six-Day War to give all-out support to the Arabs created confusion in Sweden.[7] Together with the anti-American policy that was the hallmark of the new socialist leadership in Sweden, there followed a polarization of opinion with increasingly leftist forces on one side, and the pro-United States and pro-Israeli forces and their increasingly demoralized sympathizers on the other. The leftists, on which the new leadership depended, made a show of force and the suggestions of the Parliamentary Committee were inexplicably set aside. The Personnel Control Ordinance issued on June 13, 1969, to supplement the Police Register Act contained, contrary to what the committee had proposed, strict guidelines for what could be entered into the police registers. A dramatic innovation was also inserted in Article 2 which read: "No annotation in such a register may be made on the mere basis that somebody has expressed a political opinion by belonging to an organization or in some other way."

This ordinance was followed by guidelines adopted by the National Police Board on December 17, 1970, which read in part:

It is, however, a well-known fact that certain political extremist movements represent views that purport to subvert democratic society by violent means. The risk is evident that a member of or sympathizer with such an organization is prepared to take part in anti-societal activity. Therefore such a person must be controlled by the security service. The grounds for the registration however are not to be found in political opinions as such but must be based on the risk of anti-societal activity. It may happen that a person is a member of or sympathizer with such an organization without being prepared to take part in an anti-societal activity. If this is the case, he shall not be registered.[8]

This meant a considerable setback for the idea of strengthening internal security, particularly where fellow travelers were concerned—a category that Münzenberg had employed so masterfully in the service of Soviet policy during the Spanish Civil War. All existing registrations of membership in the Communist party were destroyed by the police, unless the entry could be supported by supplementary information.[9] Even the military security service destroyed what duplicates it might have had.[10]

In May 1973 a new blow was dealt to Swedish security. On the cabinet level the decision had been taken to set up, outside of the civil and military service, a separate intelligence outfit called IB (Informations Byran). This outfit succeeded in disguising itself so well that even among high military men in intelligence work its existence was not known. However, it had some contacts with Israeli intelligence.

The leftist forces, associated with Palestinian militants through a group called Action Group Palestinian Front and headed by Marina Stagh, set out to destroy it. On May 3, 1973, the extreme left published an issue of a paper called *Folket i Bild/Kulturfront* with a ten-page report on the Swedish intelligence service. This report was written by the husband of Mrs. Stagh, Jan Guillou, a French citizen. After a great deal of confusion in government circles, Guillou and his assistants were finally arrested on October 10, 1973, on the charge of espionage. Ultimately, a ten-month jail sentence was imposed (*certiorari* denied September 1974). The matter came before the ombudsman who said, among other things, referring to the fact that an IB agent had infiltrated the militant leftist organization: "An infiltration—because after all that is what is here in issue—into political and other associations that are not illegal, always constitutes a violation of the freedom of association that is guaranteed to Swedish citizens."[11]

The Introduction of Other Conflicts

Internal security was also threatened by the introduction of other quarrels. The great immigration from Yugoslavia that had taken place during the 1960s had also brought Croatian separatists. The political activity of these separatists in Sweden, long overlooked by the Swedish police, but perfectly permissible under the new Papandreou policy, was sufficiently uncontrolled to make the Communist government in Yugoslavia nervous. Sending in political agents to counteract the activity of the Croatians, they involved themselves in murder and legal proceedings in Sweden. Most attention was attracted by the Asanov trial in 1970. In February 1971 Yugoslav security agents reportedly succeeded in inducing their Croatian adversaries to occupy the Yugoslav consulate in Gothenburg in order to extort the release of one Miljenko Hrkac, sentenced to death in Yugoslavia as a Croatian terrorist but in reality apparently a Yugoslav security agent.[12] Eventually the Croats assassinated the Yugoslav ambassador to Sweden, a former general believed to have had a bloodstained past in the Yugoslav security service.

This problem, too, was taken up by the Swedish security service. Said the ombudsman in a review of the task of supervising extremist organizations among certain immigrant groups:

The operations of these organizations are often not directly aimed against our country and its institutions, but against other members of immigrant groups or against the institutions of other countries. What has happened, and it is not necessary to review that, has shown that it is necessary to supervise such organizations. This should be a task for the general police. Several circumstances, among others the secret nature of these extremist organizations and their conspiratorial ways of operating, however, make it difficult for the police to find out about the activity of these organizations. Nor should it be overlooked that some of these foreign extremist organizations have connections with certain domestic extremistic movements. The security service with its special work methods is in this respect a better instrument although it, too, seems to have considerable difficulties. A special problem is whether members of foreign extremist movements should be listed in the register of the security department.[13]

The Hijacking Incident and the Adoption of the Antiterrorist Act of 1973

On September 15, 1972, an SAS airliner was hijacked by a Croatian band and the Swedish government gave in to their demands that they release from prison seven Croatian prisoners serving sentences for a number of political crimes, the most famous being the murder of Ambassador Rolovic, mentioned previously.

That event made the Swedish government set up, on September 22, 1972, a commission under the chairmanship of Minister Lidbom to draft legislation aimed at preventing acts of political violence in Sweden having international implications.

The immediate result of the hijacking incident was the revision of the 1969 Personnel Control Ordinance. On September 22, 1972, the famous innovation of 1969 concerning the nonregistration of "political opinion" was supplemented by the addition: "More precise regulations relative to the application of this rule will be issued by the King in Council." The addition conferred upon the government the authority to issue further directives in the practical application of the rules for registration.

The government used the occasion to state in a Royal Letter to the National Police Board that there were organizations and groups that pursue political activities calling for violence and threats to achieve political goals. It then added:

Furthermore there are organizations that operate, in this realm or in other states, politically subversive activities that include resort to violent means or threats. Information about a member of or a sympathizer with such an organization or group shall be entered into the police register of the security department.[14]

In an interview the same day, the minister of justice, Lennart J. Geijer, confirmed that "already membership or sympathies" should be registered.

The leftist organizations, which at that time already controlled all newspapers of national distribution except one,[15] immediately reacted by noting the dangers of press censure as a result of aggressions overseas by various "liberation" movements.

THE LIDBOM REPORT

The Lidbom Commission delivered its report on December 8, 1972.[16] In the main, the report proposed the enactment of a law that tried to develop, in harmony with the 1971 Montreal Convention (although this was not mentioned and the convention at that time had not been ratified by Sweden and was not in force),[17] cooperation between the different national police forces so that the Swedish police could act upon information received from foreign police forces. The overriding principle throughout the proposed law was that it should not deal with penal law issues, but only with the administration of aliens, thereby, as a windfall, avoiding any collision with the European Convention on Human Rights.[18] A foreigner who was suspect because of foreign police tips could be expelled from Sweden, or his entry into Sweden could be refused. Essentially, the proposed legislation attempted to make clear the conditions under which measures would be taken against a foreigner who belonged to or was active in an organization or a group that might resort to violence in Sweden for political purposes. Such a foreigner would be refused admission into Sweden or would be expelled from the country. It was proposed that the National Police Board should be empowered to make a list of foreigners to be expelled pursuant to this rule (hereinafter called the *terrorist list)* but directives for how to draw up the list were to be issued by the king in council.

The Lidbom Report caused an uproar in leftist quarters who saw their privileges obtained during the Palme government in danger of being eroded. They mounted a counteroffensive.

The proposed drafting of a terrorist list, and the bases for making entries therein, were the major bones of contention. Evidently, it was another form of a police register that seemed to follow principles other than those developed in the recent past for police registers. More specifically, the 1969 addition on "opinion-registration" was missing. The language of the bill was that antiterrorist measures could be taken against a foreigner and he could be entered into the terrorist list, if there was "a well-founded reason to believe that he belongs to or is active for a political organization or group that might resort to violent means, threats or constraints."

When the bill was presented, Mr. Lidbom defended the terrorist list idea further. First, the legislation was aimed only at "such groups as have already in action demonstrated that they systematically resort to violence in any country whatsoever to achieve their ends." Second, "it will be almost exclusively a list of persons who have never been in Sweden. We will receive the information from, among others, Interpol, and the police of foreign countries. We will check the information as far as it is possible." However, he admitted, "it cannot be excluded that foreigners will be refused entry at our borders although they neither are active for, nor belong to any terrorist organization. But the alternative is that we do nothing at all."[19] Incidentally, Yugoslavia is a member of Interpol.

Eventually the authors of the bill tried to fend off the opposition by stating that the legislation only required neutrality since it was directed against foreigners who used violence on Swedish soil.[20] Mr. Lidbom promised that the legislation would not be used without prior cabinet permission, except against two specified movements: the *Ustasja* and *Black September.* A terrorist movement acting on foreign soil to change political conditions anywhere other than in Sweden remained privileged.

The act was passed on April 13, 1973. It was re-moved on April 26, 1974 (SFS 1974, no. 178), and June 5, 1975 (SFS 1975, no. 355). It expired December 30, 1975, and was finally replaced by a slightly different act partly integrated into the Aliens Act, and partly reenacted as a separate act (see SFS 1975, nos. 1358 and 1360, respectively).

THE APPLICATION OF THE ACT

The terrorist list was drawn up by the National Police Board pursuant to directives issued by the king in council on April 13, 1973. It named two *organizations* and used the following language: "those organizations or groups that may be referred to as the so-called Ustasja movement." This all-inclusive description seemed to cover everything from the purely cultural organization HOP to more militant groups such as HNO-Drina and down to HRB, the Croatian Revolutionary Fraternity, an outright fighting corps with military manuals and the like. Furthermore: "that or those groups within the Palestinian liberation movement that may be assumed to be attached to 'Black September.'" This was also a very broad description that certainly threatened parts of the pro-Palestinian movement cleverly built up in leftist circles after the Six-Day War. On September 28, 1973, new directives added to the list: "the organization, or groups that may be referred to as the Japanese Red Army." This was also an all-inclusive formula that may have meant, although this was by no means clear, the Red Army Faction or Rengo Sekigunha, in contradistinction to the Chukakuha, a middle-core faction, and the Kahumaruha, a revolutionary Marxist faction.

After the attack on the Stockholm embassy of the Federal Republic of Germany in late April 1975 in which Lt. Col. Baron von Mirbach was shot, the Baader-Meinhof group was added to the list. The following formula was used: "the organization or group that can be referred to as the Red Army faction, also called the Baader-Meinhof Group." By this, presumably, was meant the organization known as the Red Army Faction in Germany.

Thus the list was limited to four organizations. The principles for selecting organizations have been discussed. Goran Melander suggests:

. . . it appears that it is a condition for being considered as a dangerous organization in the sense of the Anti-Terrorist Act, that the organization—on the basis of its prior activity—has performed an act of political violence outside the country against which it is active. It then does not matter whether the terrorist act took place in Sweden or abroad.

However, it seems that it is the presence of some member of or collaborator with the organization in Sweden that makes it eligible for entry into the list. Tomislav Rebrina, who commanded the group which hijacked SAS flight 130, belonged to HNO Drina, which thus was associated with a violent operation in Sweden. No such operation could be ascribed to Black September or the Japanese Red Army, but at the time of their addition to the list, group members were believed to be in Sweden.

However that may be, one will find the list of organizations highly selective and not a very significant contribution to the international fight against terrorism. All liberation movements can be accused of resort to politically inspired violence outside the country they have picked for an adversary, simply because it is part of their tactics to operate from a neighboring country, and their discipline is maintained, contributions collected, and supporters recruited under pressure that certainly involves threats of violence or outright constraint. Even if Sweden has not taken note of such disciplinary murders as those in which the Algerian FLN engaged and which surfaced in the famous Ktir Case,[21] recruitment for the Palestinian cause and the extortion of contributions under threats of violence occasionally do come to light in Swedish universities and sometimes are even brought to the attention of the police.

It may be suggested that this list of organizations has in reality only a limiting function. Nobody can be put on the list as a presumed terrorist without his membership in one of the listed organizations first being positively established. By the end of 1975 the list included slightly fewer than eighty *persons*, all of them residing abroad. This list was, in all its versions, approved by the National Police Board *in pleno* and copies thereof were, successively, submitted to the king in council.[22]

It has been asserted that the question of membership in terrorist organizations alone seldom acquires decisive importance. This was ascribed to the fact that "it is a characteristic feature of the organizations and groups in question that they are of an extremely secret nature. Experience has shown that it is primarily other circumstances relating to the relationship of the person concerned to the organization and its activity that becomes decisive."[23] By this is meant, presumably, that information coming from foreign police departments is always directed at a certain individual and includes material on his past activity in connection with acts for which a certain listed organization has taken credit, so that membership by itself cannot be said to have independent importance.

Expulsion of presumed terrorists has been an issue in twelve cases. Board requests for expulsion have been submitted to the king in council and have been granted in about half the cases. In 1974, decisions to expel were taken against three Yugoslavs and one Japanese (Akira Kitagawa). In 1975, the decision was taken to expel another Yugoslav as well as the five-member band of Germans that took the West German embassy in order to extort the release of the Baader-Meinhof defendants. In six of these cases, the requests were either turned down or withdrawn, the latter presumably because the alleged terrorists had left the country anyway.

The decision to expel could not be executed in any of the Yugoslav cases because the persons concerned enjoyed political refugee status. Instead, the presumed terrorists were subjected to directives which imposed certain limitations and conditions for their continued presence in Sweden. These directives established limitations relating to residence and employment which were not to be changed without prior permission. The presumed terrorists were also to register regularly with the police.[24]

The basic weakness in the Swedish approach to terrorism has turned out to be the existence of the status of political refugee because it has often prevented the execution of a decision to expel. This comment by the chief prosecutor in Stockholm seems pertinent:

Since it justifiably can be said that in most cases under the new Act those foreigners to whom it applies are such as may invoke political refugee status, the conclusion seems warranted that the Committee has attempted to make political activity at one and the same time a ground for returning and expulsion, on the one hand, and a bar for such measures on the other.[25]

Political refugee status was to be granted to the presumed terrorist if he, in the country to which he was sent, risked "political persecution." What was meant by this extremely imprecise formula was very unclear; still, it was pivotal. The heavily leftist Swedish mass media were almost able to limit the application of the act to the Baader-Meinhof group by singling out the Federal Republic of Germany. They focused on the societal monopoly on violence and on attorney privileges in communicating with clients and accused Germany of being a country that had abandoned the rule of law.[26] If that was synonymous with "political persecution," the murder squad could look forward to some time in a Swedish jail (probably no longer than the master-spy Col. Wennerstrom, who eventually was pardoned by the Palme government) and thereafter remain in Sweden on social welfare, if not otherwise. So what was meant by "political persecution"?

To take the Swiss example relating to the former prohibition barring women from taking part in general elections, this certainly was a violation of the declaration of human rights, but it could not be considered persecution, since the prohibition was not based on race, nationality, and so forth, but on sex, which is not mentioned by the Refugee Convention as a basis for persecution.

"It is difficult to understand," says Dr. Melander, "why a violation of human rights should not be considered to be persecution—of course on condition that this violation is founded on . . . political opinion."

It was considered advisable to look more closely into the matter of "political persecution" in Japan. Eventually, after some on-the-spot research, it was concluded that people could be expelled to Japan without risking political persecution.

With such definitions of "political persecution" it is hard to send a presumed terrorist anywhere. Daniel Patrick Moynihan, the United States delegate to the United Nations, has reminded us that there are no more than two dozen genuine democracies remaining in the world. The rest are nations that have adopted or accepted autocratic forms of government, socialist or not. He was prepared to produce a list of forty-five military governments and thirty-five governments installed by military coups. Certainly all of these would fail to meet the Human Rights test. On the other hand, the rule of law might conceivably be a lot better in some of these countries (for example, Switzerland) than in the genuine democracies because the rule of the majority is no guarantee that the majority will stick to the laws it has enacted.

Kyoichi Shimada was a Japanese student residing in Sweden with his wife. Occasionally he was interrogated by the police. The Japanese embassy in Stockholm asserted that he was guilty of passport irregularities and asked the Swedish police to deprive him of the fake passport. In early February 1975, Haruyuki Mabuchi, counselor at the Japanese embassy in Stockholm, sent a circular letter to airlines, shipping lines, and others, warning them about Shimada's presence in Sweden and identifying him as a member of the Red Army Faction.[27] Late in March the Swedish Embassy in Athens received a letter signed by the Red Army threatening an attempt to release two Japanese, Nishikawa and Tohira, recently sent home from Sweden (without resort to the Anti-Terrorist Act). On June 27, 1975, the Carlos affair started with the murder of two French DST agents in Paris and revealed, as it developed, the worldwide terrorist connections among the Japanese, the Latin American, the Palestinian and the Baader-Meinhof people.[28] It followed the Japanese Red Army's attack on the Swedish embassy in Kuala Lumpur and the taking of the Swedish chargé d'affaires Bergenstråhle hostage.[29] These developments put the Shimada situation into the forefront. The National Police Board now requested his expulsion and the decision to do so was made on September 2, 1975. The decision was executed. Back in Japan, however, it turned out that the case of the Japanese police against Shimada was weak, and he was detained in prison merely on charges of having obtained a false passport.

On the same occasion, Kitagawa was expelled and flown to Japan. There being no case against him, he reportedly was released.

Notes

1. Melander, *infra* note 3, p. 70.

2. Kungl Proposition (1971), no. 109, p. 4.

3. *Annual of Power and Conflict 1973-74* (Institute for the Study of Conflict, London), p. 8.

4. Shaw, *International Herald Tribune,* 8 January 1974, p. 3.

5. For years, reportedly some 2,000 Cubans have been working on aid in primarily African countries but also in Southern Yemen and Vietnam. See *International Herald Tribune* 24-25 January 1976, p. 2, and 2 January 1976, p. 1. The size of the Cuban military expeditionary force to Angola had by the end of 1975 risen to some 7,500 men: official confirmation of the intervention was given by Premier Fidel Castro on December 18, 1975. See *International Herald Tribune,* 20-21 December 1975, p. 1.

6. "Handläggningen av säkerhetsfrågor," *Statens Offentliga Utredningar,* 1968, p. 4.

7. For a scholarly report, see Moshe Ma'oz, "Soviet and Chinese Relations with the Palestinian Guerrilla Organizations," *Jerusalem Papers on Peace Problems* 4 (March 1974).

8. Quote as per the Offical Ombudsman report (hereinafter quoted as JO only) 1973, p. 52 f. Translation mine.

9. JO 1973, p. 87.

10. JO 1973, p. 72; JO 1975/76, p. 160 f.

11. JO 1975/76, p. 167.

12. In connection with the removal of Yugoslav Minister of the Interior Radovan Stijacic, his resort to provocative tactics came to light. In 1973, the Belgrade periodical *Nin*, attempting muckraking, reportedly disclosed materials suggesting that Hrkac had had status of *agent provocateur*: see report by Wattrang in the Stockholm daily *Expressen*, 14 October 1973, p. 13.

13. JO 1973, p. 48.

14. As per report by Sune Olsson in *Svenska Dagbladet*, 23 September 1972.

15. The last independent daily, *Göteborgs Handels-och Sjöfartstidning*, closed on September 8, 1973. Its editor in chief, Bjorn Ahlander, attracted general attention by an unsuccessful attempt to control his leftist "cultural" editor who expanded into general politics. Dr. Ahlander's demise was speeded by attacks against him that were administered by the future, supposedly "conservative" editor in chief of *Svenska Dagbladet*.

16. Ds Ju 1972: 35, reprinted in *Kungl Proposition* 1973: 37, pp. 20-116.

17. ICAO Doc 8966. It did not enter into force until January 26, 1973; the Swedish instruments of ratification were deposited on July 10, 1973. See *Sveriges Överenskommelser med främmande makter* (hereinafter SÖ) 1973, no. 48.

18. SÖ 1952, no. 26.

19. *Expressen*, 13 February 1973.

20. See further J. Sundberg, "Thinking the Unthinkable or the Case of Dr. Tsironis" (ch. V, sec. 4) in Bassiouni, ed., *International Terrorism and Political Crimes* (Springfield, 1975), p. 448, at 458.

21. *Arréts du Tribunal Féderal Suisse* 87-I-134.

22. *Proposition* 1975/76: 18, p. 151.

23. Anna Greta Leijon in *Proposition* 1975/76: 18, p. 207.

24. *Proposition* 1975/76: 18, p. 151.

25. *Överåklagaren i Stockholm dnr ÖÅ ADI* 493-72, comments of January 9, 1973, signed L. Hiort.

26. Right after the attack on the embassy, *Dagens Nyheter* in three consecutive articles published a major attack on the Federal Republic, written by Frank Hirschfeldt, which subsequently was made the basis of much anti-German comment in other leftist mass media. See *Dagens Nyheter*, 22, 23, and 27 April 1975.

27. The newspaper story was more dramatic. It claimed that in December 1974 the Japanese government asked the Swedish security police to find and arrest Kyoichi Shimada, believed to be the mastermind behind the Lydda Massacre, who had taken refuge in Sweden after the wrecking of a plan to seize the Japanese embassy in Oslo (Norway). When the Swedish service failed to find Shimada, the Japanese government secured Swedish permission to send three Japanese security agents to Sweden for the search. Then Mabuchi sent his circular letter.

28. Cook, *International Herald Tribune*, 8 September 1975, pp. 1, 5.

29. *Time*, 18 August 1975, p. 18.

SAMUEL HENDEL

The Price of Terror in the USSR

Terrorism in modern times has conventionally been thought of as a form of guerrillalike warfare waged by "rebels," *outside the law,* in the attempt to overthrow or modify the policies or conduct of established regimes. But there is a form of terror by rulers of established states, *acting within or under color of the law,* on so massive and pervasive a scale, and often so bereft of any rational justification, as to dwarf comparison with that of "conventional" terrorists, however well- or ill-conceived their causes or blemished their actions by indiscriminate murders or assassinations. Such in recent history was Hitler's Holocaust, and so, too, were Stalin's purges.

Sweep and Scope of Terror

During the first years after the Bolshevik revolution, no Communist party leaders were executed; and it seemed that they had learned the lesson of the French Revolution which led the revolutionists to send the citizenry to death in droves.

But consider the composition of the Politburo in 1924 when Lenin died. Of seven, Zinoviev and Kamenev were executed and Tomsky committed suicide in 1936; Rykov and Bukharin were shot in 1938; Trotsky was killed in Mexico in 1940. Only Stalin survived.

About fifty Bolshevik leaders were tried in the purge trials of 1936 to 1938 but scores of men, some of equal or greater prominence, disappeared without any public trial. No sphere of leading Soviet cadres went unpunished. Among the purged were a majority of the Central Committee and of the Bolshevik "Old Guard," senior officers of the armed forces, heads of the Soviet Police, leading officials of the Union Republics and Komsomol, heads of industrial trusts and enterprises, foreign communist leaders, and prominent scientists, writers, scholars, and artists. As Khrushchev conceded at the 20th Communist Party Congress in February 1956, "Many thousands of honest and innocent Communists have died as a result of [the] monstrous falsification of . . . cases."

With so little regard for its leading cadres, it is small wonder that the wider scope of Soviet terror, beginning in 1928 with the mass deportation of kulaks to forced labor camps in northern Siberia, culminated in the Great Purges of 1936 to 1938 with *millions* of innocent people suddenly transformed into saboteurs, terrorists, traitors, and enemies of the people. During the war, millions more in several Soviet nations were expelled en masse from their homelands for dubious loyalty and, as Khrushchev explained, "The Ukrainians avoided meeting this fate only because there were too many of them. . . ."

After the war, the USSR followed the policy of treating tens of thousands of voluntary and involuntary "returners" as contaminated by their contact with the West and dispatched many of them to forced labor camps. Reportedly, also, large-scale deportations have taken place from incorporated areas of Estonia, Latvia, and Lithuania.

Why the Terror?

It is well to admit that in dealing with this question, we are at least partly in the realm of speculation about motives which were no doubt mixed and at times probably unconscious.

1. *Terror is a consequence of the attempt to organize a resistant and recalcitrant society in accordance with a doctrinaire theory and plan.*

In his provocative analysis, Barrington Moore, Jr. *(Terror and Progress, U.S.S.R.)* suggests that terror as a system of power stems from "the attempt to alter the structure of society at a rapid rate and from above. . . ." He goes on to explain:

The essence of the situation appears to lie in the crusading spirit, the fanatical conviction in the justice and universal applicability of some ideal about the way life should be organized, along with a lack of serious concern about the consequences of the methods used to pursue this ideal. . . . The attempt to change institutions rapidly nearly always results in opposition by established interests. The more rapid and more thorough the change, the more extensive and bitter is the opposition likely to be. Hence organized terror becomes necessary. . . .

George F. Kennan agrees that terror was the inevitable outcome of the attempt "to put a utopian vision into practice by the use of political authority" in a country where active popular support of the Bolsheviks was minimal and where even the class they professed to represent, the proletariat, was only a tiny minority.

The crusading spirit and fanatical conviction of the Bolsheviks of which Barrington Moore wrote was perhaps best exemplified in Leon Trotsky's *The Defense of Terrorism* written in 1920 (when he was a leading Bolshevik): ". . . The revolution does require of the revolutionary class that it should attain its end by all methods at its disposal—if necessary by an armed rising: if required, by terrorism."

It is noteworthy that in the very midst of Khrushchev's denunciation at the 20th Communist Party Congress of the appalling uses of terror by Stalin, he felt it necessary to add that these were not "the deeds of a giddy despot" but that "He [Stalin] considered that this should be done in the interests of the Party, of the working masses, in the name of defense of the revolution's gains."

2. *"Terror functioned as prod as well as brake."*

The quote is from Merle Fainsod who in *How Russia Is Ruled* also comments that:

The arrests of responsible technicians and officials frequently produced serious setbacks in production, but as their replacements acquired experience, order was restored, and production began to climb again. While many functionaries reacted to the purge by shunning all responsibility, others responded to the fear of arrest by working as they had never worked before.

The removal of high-level bureaucrats and officials provided a form of upward mobility and advancement for thousands of mostly younger, ambitious, grateful men and women determined to prove their loyalty and worth.

3. *Terror was used to provide cheap, expendable "slave" labor on a massive scale for work projects under inhospitable conditions in the vast spaces of the North and Far East.*

The main area of Soviet concentration camps was in the Kolyma goldfields, where the annual death rate among miners is estimated to have been about 30 percent. The millions of slave-laborers worked in a variety of other fields as well including lumber camps, agriculture, and construction and, as Robert Conquest in his brilliant study, *The Great Terror: Stalin's Purges of the Thirties,* has noted, "played an important economic role, and indeed became accepted as a normal component of the Soviet economy." [But he adds the judgement that, as often is the case with involuntary labor, much of it was "valueless" and its total cost was "much in excess of the value of its output."]

4. *Terror was used to punish past "mistakes" or "offenses" and prevent future ones.*

As Khrushchev himself pointed out in 1956, Stalin's "mass repressions" occurred at a time when there was no danger to the party or the Soviet state, when the opposition "was completely disarmed," when many of the former oppositionists had "changed their views and worked in the various sectors building socialism." "It is very clear," he added, "that in the situation of socialist victory there was no basis for mass terror in the country."

It was, then, to settle old scores and inhibit existing opposition, of which, however unorganized and disorganized, there no doubt was some, and to prevent incipient opposition, that Stalin deliberately and coldbloodedly began a new reign of terror which once initiated fed and battened on itself and became increasingly arbitrary and indiscriminate. Examples abound.

Obvious targets were former members of such opposition parties or groups as the Socialist Revolutionary Party and the Jewish Bund. So also were those who had individually or as part of a group or faction within the Bolshevik party opposed Stalin's policies on, for example, the speed and techniques of collectivization, the emphasis on socialism in one country, the Nazi-Soviet Pact, growing inequality in wage payments, the treatment of old Bolsheviks, and the application of terror itself. Those who had opposed Stalin on these and other issues, whatever the merits of the positions taken, in time became the victims of his malevolence. And not only they but also a special category became victims, "wives of enemies of the people" who were specifically marked for conviction "in the first degree," meaning extinction, in a memorandum signed by Yezhov, then head of the NKVD, and formally approved by Stalin and Molotov in the 1937-1938 period. As a kind of ultimate absurdity, one noted physicist, a perceptive victim, Alexander Weissberg, in *Conspiracy of Silence* commented that "Hundreds of thousands of people were arrested during the Purge for no other reason than that at some time in the past the Soviet authorities had done them an injustice." Aleksandr Solzhenzitsyn *(The Gulag Archipelago, I)* explains:

By and large, the *Organs* had no profound reasons for their choice of whom to arrest and whom not to arrest. They merely had over-all assignments, quotas for a specific number of arrests. These quotas might be filled on an order basis or wholly arbitrarily. [For example,] person marked for arrest by virtue of chance circumstances, such as a neighbor's denunciation, could be replaced by another neighbor.

5. *Scapegoats were made the instruments of terror to explain failures and deficiencies.*

Again, numerous examples may be cited. Among the earliest was the 1928 trial of fifty Russian and three German technicians and engineers in the coal industry charged with sabotage and espionage. Convictions were based entirely on the "confessions" of some of the accused with no other evidence introduced. Ten years later, as pointed out by Stephen F. Cohen in *Bukharin and the Bolshevik Revolution,* in the 1938 purge trial of Bukharin and others, counts in the indictment "were clearly fabricated to explain away spectacular failures of Stalin's leadership since 1929, for example, the charge that Bukharin and others organized 'kulak uprisings' and poisoned livestock during collectivization, and conspired to deprive the urban population of consumer goods, partly by instructing their agents to mix glass into foodstuffs."

The logic used by the prosecutor, Andrei Vyshinsky, in the Bukharin trial to explain economic failure was as simple as it was fraudulent:

In our country, rich in resources of all kinds, there could not have been and cannot be a situation in which shortage of any product should exist. . . . It is now clear why there are interruptions of supplies here and there, why, with our riches and abundance of products, there is a shortage first of one thing, then of another. It is these traitors who are responsible for it.

Whatever other purposes these and other cases served, they clearly provided scapegoats to explain economic failures and deficiencies and deflect or blunt criticism that might otherwise have been directed at the leadership of the regime.

6. *Terror was used in bitter internecine struggles for personal power.*

Robert Conquest in *The Great Terror* concludes that "We do not need to posit a conscious long-term plan to say that in a general way the drive for power was Stalin's strongest and most obvious motivation" for the use of terror. This is a judgment shared by Roy A. Medvedev, a Soviet dissident, in *Let History Judge,* truly called "a monumental study of the whole Stalin epoch." In a long chapter on "The Problem of Stalin's Responsibility," he writes:

What, then, were the basic motives of Stalin's crimes? The first and most important was undoubtedly Stalin's *measureless ambition.* This incessant though carefully hidden lust for unlimited power appeared in Stalin much earlier than 1937. Even though he had great power, it was not enough—he wanted absolute power and unlimited submission to his will. [Emphasis in original.]

The evidence Conquest and Medvedev supply in support of their power thesis is compelling but in my mind not wholly persuasive. The motives of men in complex historical conditions and circumstances are seldom referable to any single source. That is not to deny that Stalin's lust for power was probably *one* of his strongest—partly conscious, partly unconscious—motivations. But it seems to me erroneous to elevate the struggle for naked power from its role as a vital part of a complex explanation to the status of virtual self-sufficiency. If we were seeking, for example, to explain the impulses that guided Hitler would it be sufficient to reduce a complex amalgam to a manic thrust for power?

7. *Terror was used out of fear of intervention, attack, and subversion by the West.*

As John M. Thomson *(Allied and American Intervention in Russia, 1918-1921)* has commented, ". . . The interventionist attempt [by Western powers during and after World War I] left an ugly legacy of fear and suspicion . . . and it strengthened the hand of those among the Bolshevik leadership who were striving to impose monolithic unity and unquestioning obedience on the Russian people."

The attempt to destroy Bolshevik power at its birth left a residue of great bitterness and created an encirclement psychosis in the USSR intensified by the rise of Hitler.

Even before Hitler came to power, Stalin, in a speech at the First All-Union Conference of Managers of Socialist Industry in February 1931, rejected the idea that the tempo (and inferentially the terror) associated with rapid industrialization should be reduced. "To slacken the tempo," he said, "would mean falling behind. And those who fall behind get beaten." Old Russia, he maintained, was continually beaten because of her backwardness—by the Swedes, Poles, Lithuanians, British, French, and Japanese. Prophetically he added, "We are fifty or a hundred years behind the advanced countries. We must make good this distance in ten years. Either we do it, or we will be crushed." [The Nazi attack came in June 1941.]

8. *Terror was a consequence in part at least of Stalin's personal paranoia that (a) the revolution would be betrayed or destroyed if power were not concentrated in his hands and (b) he was surrounded by personal enemies and enemies of the people.*

The evidence, I believe, is overwhelming that Stalin suffered from paranoia which convinced him that he was surrounded by personal enemies and enemies of the people. In my judgment, this explains at least in significant and major part, not only the indiscriminate nature of the purges but the fact that they were often directed against his own friends, allies, and dedicated supporters. Khrushchev in his de-Stalinization speech in 1956 explained:

Stalin was a very distrustful man, sickly suspicious; we know this from our work with him. He could look at a man and say: "Why are your eyes so shifty today?" or "Why are you turning so much today and avoiding to look me directly in the eyes?" The sickly suspicion created in him a general distrust even toward eminent party workers whom he had known for years. Everywhere and in everything he saw "enemies," "two-facers" and "spies."

It is noteworthy, too, that Roy Medvedev who, as we have seen, maintains that the first and most important and basic motive for Stalin's crimes was undoubtedly his "measureless ambition" and desire for "absolute power and unlimited submission to his will," concedes that "the story about Stalin's mental illness is not entirely unfounded." He adds:

It is not difficult to detect pathological elements in his behavior: Morbid suspiciousness, noticeable throughout his life and especially intense in his last years, intolerance of criticism, grudge-bearing, an overestimation of himself bordering on megalomania, cruelty approaching sadism. . . .

Nonetheless, Medvedev insists that:

Despite all the pathological changes in his personality during the last twenty years of his life, which took on the characteristic features of paranoid psychopathology, despite the fact that his behavior clearly shows not only acute moral degeneration, but also serious psychic derangement—I am profoundly convinced that *Stalin was beyond doubt a responsible* (vmeniaemyi) *man, and in most cases was fully aware of what he was doing.* And no court, including the court of history, can excuse and explain Stalin's actions by reference to incompetence. [Emphasis in original.]

Nor, in my judgment, can one explain Stalin's conduct without reference to his paranoia. That paranoia was compounded by bitter, internecine conflicts over Bolshevik policy during which, again and again, Stalin was persuaded or rationalized that oppositionists' success would betray or destroy the revolution. Thus it is not difficult to believe that Stalin increasingly was convinced that the safety of the revolution depended on the concentration of power in his hands and his alone. From Stalin's point of view, for example, opposition to "socialism in one country" or the Nazi-Soviet Pact could only have led to attacks from the West and the destruction of Soviet power.

But did Stalin care about the revolution or was he a Marxist in any sense? Medvedev categorically asserts that "in fact Stalin was not a Marxist" although he "often wrote and spoke like a Marxist." "He could not," says Medvedev, "ignore the Party's ideology or avoid the use of Marxist terminology." Again, I consider this an oversimplification. While it is unquestionably true that fundamental tenets of Marxist theory were perverted, attenuated, or even abandoned, in a process begun by Lenin himself, including commitment to socialist democracy and the withering away of the state—perversions brought to appalling proportions by Stalin—there is I think little reason to believe that Stalin was not a Marxist in *any* important sense. All his life, beginning with his early years when he joined the Bolshevik movement, Stalin shared its belief in the abolition of private property (which Marx and Engels wrote "summed up" the essence of their theory). While it is possible to argue, as W. W. Rostow has, that Stalin's sole concern in his industrialization and collectivization programs was with "achieving and consolidating his dictatorship," it seems more reasonable to suppose that Stalin supported and imposed the socialist organization of the economy, that is, production for use and not for profit, as a central, unalterable aspect of a creed for which he and many other Bolsheviks had languished in tsarist prisons and in which he continued to believe.

The Hazards and Price of Terror

There is no doubt that while terror served as a goad, its more pervasive and dominant effect was to function as a brake and deterrent on production. As Khrushchev remarked in 1956, "due to the numerous arrests of party, Soviet and economic leaders, many workers began to work uncertainly, showed overcautiousness, feared all which was new, feared their own shadows and began to show less initiative in their work."

The Soviet Union paid a heavy price for its reliance on torture and terror in other respects. As Conquest has observed, "Far from the Great Purge eliminating a Soviet fifth column, it laid the foundation for one throughout the country in 1941-45. This was the first war fought by Russia in which a large force of its citizens joined the other side."

What is more, experience with terror in the Soviet Union demonstrated: a secret police is not easy to control; it tends to become an *imperium in imperio,* exaggerate dangers and even deceive the leadership to enhance its importance; and it is wasteful of manpower both in the talented people it destroys and the masses of spies it employs. It is, in sum, generally counterproductive because, as a trade union leader explained as early as 1920, "You cannot build a planned economy in the way the Pharaohs built their pyramids."

One of the most impressive illustrations of the counterproductive effects of the widespread and indiscriminate use of terror relates, in fact, to the brutal process of collectivization. Alec Nove *(Was Stalin Really Necessary?)* points out that "the attempt to collectivize all private livestock ended in disaster and a retreat." He quotes from the *official* handbook of agricultural statistics:

LIVESTOCK POPULATION
(Million of Head)

	1928	1934
Horses	32.1	15.4
Cattle	60.1	33.5
Pigs	22.0	11.5
Sheep	97.3	32.9

He adds:

Its consequences were profound. Peasant hostility and bitterness were greatly intensified. For many years there were in fact no net investments in agriculture, since the new tractors merely went to replace some of the slaughtered horses. Acute food shortage made itself felt—though the state's control over produce ensured that most of those who died in the resulting famine were peasants and not townsmen. But once all this happened, the case for coercion was greatly strengthened, the need for police measures became more urgent than ever, the power of the censorship was increased, freedom of speech had still further to be curtailed, as part of the necessities of remaining in power and continuing the industrial revolution in an environment grown more hostile as a result of such policies.

The conclusion is, I think, clear. Whatever the uses of terror to accomplish the objectives of rapid industrialization and collectivization, the great transformation would have been effected much more quickly and efficiently if Stalin had not destroyed tens of thousands of scientists, engineers, teachers, doctors, and writers; if millions of innocent people had been permitted to work as free men rather than as slave laborers; if the peasantry had not been provoked into mass resistance; if the finest Soviet officers had not perished before the war; and if moderating the tempo had brought greater loyalty and cohesion.

Note

This study has drawn on a large variety of sources dealing with terror in the USSR but particularly upon the following: Barrington Moore Jr., *Terror and Progress, U.S.S.R.* (Harvard University Press, 1954); Merle Fainsod, *How Russia Is Ruled* (Harvard University Press, 1963); Robert Conquest, *The Great Terror* (The Macmillan Company, 1968); Nikita Khrushchev's address to the 20th Communist Party Congress in 1956 as set forth in Samuel Hendel, ed., *The Soviet Crucible,* 4th ed. (Duxbury Press, 1973); Aleksandr Solzhenitsyn, *The Gulag Archipelago, I* (Harper & Row, 1973); Stephen F. Cohen, *Bukharin and the Bolshevik Revolution* (Vintage, 1975); Alec Nove, *Was Stalin Really Necessary?* (Allen & Unwin, 1964); Roy A. Medvedev, *Let History Judge* (Vintage, 1973); Samuel Hendel, "The U.S.S.R. After Fifty Years: An Overview," in Samuel Hendel and Randolph L. Braham, eds., *The U.S.S.R. After 50 Years* (Alfred A. Knopf, Inc., 1967); and Evgenya Ginzberg, *Precipitous Journey* (Flègon Press, 1967).

MARVIN MAURER

The Ku Klux Klan and the
National Liberation Front:
Terrorism Applied to Achieve Diverse Goals

Introduction

The Ku Klux Klan (KKK) of the 1860s and the National Liberation Front (NLF) of the 1960s are considered polar opposites in terms of their goals and tactics. The latter is described as part of a nationalist movement whose aim was to rid South Vietnam (SVN) of foreign domination and a native "fascist" regime ensconced in Saigon. By contrast the KKK is portrayed as an immoral collection of racist thugs who irresponsibly terrorized blacks and moderates alike.

However, in an era long before "terrorism" became a field of study the Klan enjoyed widespread support by "well-meaning" citizens in this country. Klansmen were regarded as heroes as typified in the 1915 extravaganza film, *The Birth of a Nation*. In this film vanquished Southern whites were terrorized by white and black politicians and their easily controlled sex-crazed black troops dressed in Union blue. These ruthless predators threatened old and cherished family values. The aged, the meek, and above all white women were murdered, abused, and humiliated. In desperate response, bands of hooded men rallied to the call of justice. Under the white hoods and robes were "clean-cut" veterans of the defeated Confederacy.

Similarly the NLF passed around stories about village folk heroes avenging horrible outrages against the people. For instance, a 1963 clandestine newspaper told of Bau Bau, an ordinary young peasant whose bride was kidnapped by the enemy. She resisted. Infuriated, the troops stripped her, raped her, and took out her liver and devoured it. The husband then joined a guerrilla band and learned the art of war. He soon avenged the outrage.[1]

Of course, the propaganda scenes in *The Birth of a Nation* were reverse images of what actually happened. It was the newly liberated blacks and white moderates who were victimized and terrorized by the KKK. Since World War II, the Klan has been stripped of its myths; and the American government and the defunct Government of Vietnam (GVN) are more likely to be linked to atrocities and bombings, while the tactics of the NLF are rarely reviewed, let alone popularized.[2] The NLF waged a terror and propaganda campaign designed to destroy the leadership and morale of SVN. So thorough was this campaign that Douglas Pike called its effect genocidal.[3] If a goal of political terror is to win the public opinion battle among significant populations, then both the KKK and the NLF succeeded.

Understanding the phenomenon of political terror entails more than realizing that unarmed civilians are the main target. Terrorism is a *tool* which enables insurgents to disrupt moderate, decentralized social political systems. It is especially effective against weak, pluralist, democratic regimes.[4] Political terrorism is associated with those historical periods when sharply divergent value systems are clashing for power. In the nineteenth century a democratic America was unable to thwart a racist insurgency; while in the 1960s the same nation was unable to stem "a war of liberation." In both cases the United States government was not defeated militarily. Its withdrawal symbolized its considered opinion that the governments it supported could not halt their respective insurgencies.

Two ideologically different insurgencies were selected for this study to determine whether their tactics and ethics were similar. Both overcame weak, pluralist, or fragmented, and even partially democratic governments. Both deliberately utilized terror as part of an effort to reach their goals and both sought and received the support of powerful groups and leaders outside their territories. Their opponents were no match for nor were they able to grasp the significance of these insurgencies. This study seeks to review the events of two different areas and eras and link them together on a comparative basis in order to determine how political terrorist groups armed with different ideologies were capable of determining the fate of millions of people as well as the course of history.

The key problem can be expressed either in the form of a question or as a hypothesis. Given a weak, rural, decentralized, pluralistic political system, what techniques would an insurgency adopt to topple it? Or, given a similar situation—a rural society, weak leaders, ineffective and insufficient military forces backed by a powerful democratic state—then similar organizational responses can be expected from opposing insurgencies.

The NLF is an easier organization to deal with because its organizers and leaders were theoretically oriented. Their insight into the sociology of power and organization, albeit from a Marxist-Leninist view, can be counted as original contributions to social thought. The Klan's leaders and their supporters did not have a theory of insurgency. At best they came up with apologies and moral declamations. However, thanks in part to the excellent study by Allen W. Trelease,[5] it is possible to describe the Klan's actions and subsequent successes in terms utilized to examine the NLF.

Thomas Perry Thornton's ideas are extremely useful in studying both insurgencies. Insurgency terror is designed to disrupt a social order allegedly having superior conventional military forces. The insurgents seek to secure the support of the population or neutralize it so that the power of the government is undermined. Insurgents not only propagandize the populace but seek to break their connection with the government by whatever means possible. Thornton suggests that terrorism is a form of "investment." An effective, but limited application of terror enables its users "to project an image many times larger than their actual strength."[6] Terrorism is a variant of classical guerrilla warfare. The latter consists of hit-and-run tactics against a superior armed force. Terrorism is a form of warfare aimed at civilians or individuals—whether they be police or military. Its purpose is to secure a sociopsychological victory in that a cowed populace accepts its version of events and disclaims or is hostile to those set forth by the government.

The Setting in SVN: Disorganized Pluralism

Both the defeated Confederacy and SVN were in a state of leaderless confusion after 1865 and 1954 respectively. Both were susceptible to the claims of opposing groups seeking to press their plans for reconstruction. Both areas had a pool of fighting talent from having fought the French and the Union armies respectively.

After 1954 Vietnam was divided in half. The Vietminh, led by the brilliant and redoubtable Ho Chi Minh,[7] defeated the French. As a result the latter ceded control of North Vietnam to the Democratic Republic of Vietnam (DRV). The transfer of power was ratified in July 1954 in Geneva. The peace agreement was signed by the Communists and the French. In the South, Ngo Dinh Diem came from the United States to replace the French and their puppet administration. Diem and his American supporters hoped to develop a nationalist regime independent of Hanoi. According to Philippe Devillers, assumption of leadership by Ho Chi Minh and Diem "decisively marked the end of the colonial period in Vietnam history and the beginning of its modern period of independence."[8]

The Geneva agreement called for a nationwide election in two years. Apparently there was a consensus that the DRV would win the elections and by 1956 Vietnam would be completely under Communist rule. With some reluctance the DRV accepted the partition which roughly divided Vietnam's 127,000 square miles and some 32 million people in half. Hanoi mistakenly hoped that their "democratic" (that is, Communist) friends in France would pressure the French government to live up to the terms of the Geneva agreement. Also, Hanoi figured there was no capable leadership to unify fragmented Vietnam or to lead what Robert Scigliano describes as a collection of "states within states."[9]

Diem and his supporters dashed Hanoi's hopes for an easy and early unification. Neither Diem nor the United States signed the Geneva agreement and the French lost control of the situation in the South. Diem surprised all parties by his ability and skill in thwarting the assorted religious sects and their private armies as well as pro-French factions. On October 23, 1955, France's agent Emperor Bao Dai was voted out of office and Diem became head of a new republic.[10]

On paper, the new constitution made President Diem an imposing executive with vast powers to implement policy, wage war, and suspend the legislature as he required. Also, on paper, Diem abolished village autonomy and asserted control over the major cities to create an administrative system more centralized than that of the French and "surpassed only by the Communist bureaucracy in the North."[11]

Diem was granted considerable leeway to assert his leadership because Hanoi was too occupied with its own efforts to establish party supremacy. A fierce repression took place in the North resulting in mass executions of dissidents and peasants who were especially bitter at losing their lands to a collectivization program. (The Communists promised land ownership for the peasants before they took power.)

This helped Diem, too, as word of these mass executions and repressions reached the South. Some one million refugees fled the North carrying the story of terror. Also, the DRV itself conceded that "excesses" and "mistakes" had occurred. (Estimates of executions reached as high as 500,000.)

Almost one in twelve South Vietnamese were refugees. (Refugee movement was permitted under the terms of the Geneva agreement.) The refugees, predominantly Catholic, as was Diem, provided administrative talent for the GVN. In addition to their being anti-Communist, they were free of the factional and religious politics plaguing SVN. Ultimately they would prove to be a liability to Diem as he would be accused of ignoring indigenous SVN groups.[12] (Ironically, and without anticipating the theme of this paper, Scigliano points out that "the Diem regime . . . assumed the aspect of a Carpetbag government in its disproportion of Northerners. . . .")

After the initial successes in stabilizing his regime and reducing the chaos in SVN it became apparent to all sides that Diem was a disaster. Two views developed. The first, and most prevalent, was that Diem set up a repressive police state. For example, Philippe Devillers writes that "to make good the lack [of village intelligence] they [Diem's police and army] resorted to worse barbarity, hoping to inspire an even greater terror among the villagers than that inspired by the Communists. And in that fateful year of 1958 they overstepped all bounds. The peasants, disgusted to see Diem's men acting in this way, lent their assistance to the Communists, . . . going so far as to take up arms at their side. . . ."[13]

In effect, Devillers and others contend that the guerrilla warfare and revolt against the Saigon government was inspired by the brutality and police terror of the Diem regime. The Lao Dong Party (NVN's Communist party) also claimed that the NLF was formed because "the repressed and terrorized people of the South needed an organizational base for their general uprising." It was not Hanoi that initiated the guerrilla war to unify the country, but rather the NLF was formed because of "the seething discontent in the South."[14] In 1958 and 1959 the battle spread and became more intense. Scattered guerrilla warfare passed into the coordinated efforts of the NLF's leadership.

Another view stressed was that Diem was not a totalitarian or a brutal tyrant. He was instead a failure as a leader and ultimately isolated himself from every sector of support in SVN. Douglas Pike argued that Vietnam was never a nation because the population's loyalties were neither directed to the state nor to the capital city. If there was a basic loyalty it was to the kinship or family system.[15] The families were spread over 2,500 villages which in turn were subdivided into some 16,000 hamlets.[16] SVN was also composed of disparate religious groups with their private armies. The army was a separate body riven with strong family and regional ties. Cambodians, Montagnards, and Chinese were among the nationality groups. There was little to tie them together. Rather than show loyalty to Saigon as a national capital a spirit of *doc lap* (independence) prevailed among the social components in SVN.[17]

In sharp contrast to the Communists who forcibly unified the North, Diem failed as he initiated those policies which lost maximum popular support. He severed his local contacts by abolishing elected village councils and mayors. He sought to be repressive and centralize power, but did not succeed.[18] Pike suggests that a more accurate account was that his "government was disorganized." He was incapable of compromise with the non- and anti-Communists. His rigid conservatism alienated his American supporters because he failed to realize that SVN needed "radical solutions for its economic and political problems."[19]

Diem's supporters lacked organizational skill and their reactions to the NLF were crude and hysterical. Without the capability to compromise and work with other groups, Diem alienated one major group after another. Pike concludes that Diem literally tore the social fabric of SVN apart. He writes that "at one point in 1954, Diem controlled little more than a dozen square blocks of downtown Saigon . . . and that by the time open armed attacks began in 1960 he had only slight political control over most of the country and still no control at all over isolated areas." Diem did not know what was happening in the countryside. He pretended there were no problems at the local level. Local officials were left to shift for themselves.[20]

The Communists inadvertently substantiated the "weakness" theory. They claimed that "in many villages . . . [Diem's] machine was deteriorated. . . ." The NLF reported demonstrations by all social elements against Diem. University students protested against harsh examinations; merchants and tradesmen objected to higher taxes. Buddhists demonstrated, and unions organized and went on strike. Even anti-Diem landholders were active in protest. In effect, the NLF inadvertently reported the prevalence of a full-blown pluralism.[21]

Diem's successors also experienced strikes, street protests, and a constant barrage of criticism. Buddhist students at the University of Saigon protested against the government, prayer groups were assembled in opposition, and a Buddhist newspaper attacked the Ky government with impunity.[22]

Throughout the period the American press periodically reported that Saigon closed down or banned newspapers or arrested student protestors. As late as February 3, 1975, President Thieu closed down five opposition papers. These were antidemocratic actions but on second thought where did these papers and student groups come from to be banned so repeatedly in wartime Saigon? Similarly Diem's critics pointed to his loss of voter confidence. Bernard Fall reports that Diem lost about one million votes between 1955 and 1961. "In Saigon where foreign journalists could watch the polls, Diem got 354,000 votes out of a total of 732,000. . . ." In the same letter he argues with those who contend the South Vietnamese are strangers to the electoral process.[23]

On May 6, 1966, an Associated Press report quotes an unidentified diplomat stationed in Saigon. "There is no Vietnam south of the 17th Parallel. . . . [It] . . . is a group of feuding religious groups, of defiant warlords . . . of entire areas under Communist control" and all sorts of groups including seventy political parties, a divided Buddhist religion, and the like. He concluded that only American aid and arms were holding the place together.

Fall contends that post-1954 SVN was a more prosperous society in contrast to its northern counterpart. Its food situation "is better than that of the agriculturally poorer and overpopulated north. . . ." Rubber and coal production went up and by 1961 SVN surpassed the North in the growth of rice, the number of cattle, and the output of electricity and textiles. Left on its own, Fall contends, SVN would have been economically viable. However, the NLF campaign took its toll. In 1963, SVN exported 300,000 tons of rice, but by 1966 it had to import 475,000 tons.[24]

Neither Diem nor his successors were able to establish a viable state. While the Buddhists and others prevented Saigon from developing any order in 1964 and 1965, no major province, city, or population group voluntarily defected to the Communists. Instead South Vietnamese "voted with their feet" against the Communists and chose refugee status even up to the final collapse in 1975. The refugees turned SVN into an urban country.[25] Even in its weakest period Premier Ky agreed to hold elections. In spite of an NLF effort to urge a boycott of the election, 80 percent of the voting population went to the polls.[26]

The situation in SVN then was one of increasing production until the NLF insurgency took its toll and a government resulted that was neither capable of providing the inspiration to unify the country nor willing or able to use the repressive skills of the Communists in the North.

The Situation in the American South

Prior to World War II, American historians "maintained that the Radical Republicans, who dominated the Congress . . . and the carpetbaggers, scalawags and Negroes who controlled the southern legislatures by their corruption, political opportunism, and vindictiveness made Reconstruction the most disgraceful episode in American history."[27] All of the faults of the moderates were brought to the fore while the Confederates were idealized. William A. Dunning described Reconstruction as a "struggle through which the southern whites, subjugated by adversaries of their own race thwarted the scheme which threatened permanent subjection to another race."[28] "Redemption" finally took place, it was argued, on a state-by-state basis as the South's natural leaders took power and as the North came to its senses when it withdrew its forces from the South in 1877, ending "The Tragic Era."[29] Thus, it was argued that given the hopeless inferiority of the Negro, the only chance for reconciliation between the North and the South was to accept "Southern racial attitudes."[30]

Even progressives began to abandon efforts to create a democratic society. Edwin Godkin, editor of the *Nation,* and a one-time supporter of the Negro, wondered if the latter were worth "the interests of 55 million whites on this continent." The blacks' interests appeared remote. Business was booming and the hopelessly situated Negro would jeopardize this if he received more support.[31] It was this background that provided the rationale, apologetics, and "understanding" of the Klan.[32]

But claims that white insurgency was a response to unprecedented abuse are not supported by the evidence. The great mass of pro-Confederate whites regained their rights as citizens. There were no mass arrests or executions of defeated Confederates. By 1872 former leaders were serving as state governors, members of Congress, and even in the cabinet.[33] At home the Confederate leaders were blamed for the costly, unnecessary war by their fellow southerners. The Confederacy was idealized and hatred and bitterness arising in the aftermath of defeat were transferred to the army, the moderate whites, and free Negroes.

While "the defeated nation" did not experience punitive retaliation in any great degree, its economy was in ruins. Land values dropped to record lows and of course the value of slave property was lost forever. Poverty was everywhere. Women and children who were once in good circumstances were reduced to begging. The army and the Freedmen's Bureau distributed rations by the millions to impoverished whites.[34] Nevertheless Union forces were hated. In an 1865 issue of *Harper's Weekly* a vivid picture shows Richmond ladies snubbing Union soldiers as they were about to receive government rations.[35]

With the Confederate military machine in ruin there were no bonuses for the disbanding Confederates. Southern agencies were not functioning. Indeed the infrastructure of churches, schools, law-enforcement agencies, and economic enterprises was not performing. Not until 1877 did cotton production equal the 1860 level. The point is that poverty and the psychological pains of defeat were not caused by the Republicans but stemmed from the defeat of the Confederacy.

The complete disruption of the slavocracy left the social and political order in a state of flux. While "the principle of national unity had indeed triumphed," Don Fehrenbacher asks "on what terms . . . and by what methods, was the conquered South to be reincorporated in the system it had tried to destroy?"[36] Various factions were preparing to press their version of the social order on the South.

The first government's assignment was to fill the vacuum left by the defeated Confederacy.[37] In addition to providing orderly rule and preventing Confederates from securing positions of power, it was buffeted by the controversies taking place between a proconservative presidency and the Radical Republicans in Congress.

In 1865, the Johnson administration began to outline steps to restore civil government and ultimately to pave the way for the southern states to rejoin the Union. The army's function was to support the civilian authority of the newly appointed provisional governors and other officials. It also assisted the Freedmen's Bureau in the performance of its relief and rehabilitation duties. The army interfered with civilian government when the latter attempted to enforce Confederate values. In some cases it had to set aside local elections "because too many unpardoned rebels had been elected." It also had to exercise political authority in the absence of functioning civilian courts.[38] In effect, its range of duties was immense as it presided over the transition from war to recovery.

The army of occupation veered toward the passive as social groups jockeyed for power. Several factors accounted for this development which functionally aided the more aggressive and able conservatives. The North was increasingly reluctant to support a large army. The 202,000-man force of 1865 dropped to 60,000 by 1866 and to 20,117 by 1867.[39] Also, the quality of these forces changed. Seasoned fighting troops were replaced by less efficient and less-motivated men. For a while poorly trained Negro troops outnumbered whites, but these men were mustered out by 1866. In effect, the army was unable to provide the power to resist the return of conservatives to positions of power.

John Hope Franklin concludes that the rapid reduction of Union forces revealed a lack of determination to resist the conservatives. At every opportunity conservatives demonstrated their unity and capacity to secure power. Franklin points out that from the very beginning Northerners were naive to believe that conservatives would be "regenerated by Northern ideas and free institutions." A regeneration was taking place "but only on the basis of Southern ideas and Southern institutions." Without adequate civilian talent, the army had no choice but to let the ex-Confederates take over as legislators, sheriffs, judges, and so forth. This meant that postwar rehabilitation would be for whites only.[40]

The basic values and goals of the whites throughout the post-Civil War period was exemplified by the Black Codes enacted by the southern states one year after their defeat. According to Franklin, these codes were aimed at controlling and regulating Negro labor. They included a contract system for enforcing work and vagrancy laws which provided a source of cheap prison labor for whites.[41] It was these codes that signaled the totalitarian intent of the conservatives.

While all sides accepted the need for "home rule," the conservatives had their special version based on white supremacy. Congress strongly reacted to these efforts and proceeded to replace "Reconstruction Confederate Style" with their own version of reconstruction.

The Reconstruction Act of 1867 divided the South into five military districts "to provide for the most efficient Government of the Rebel States." Enfranchised males were to elect delegates to write new constitutions. With congressional approval of these constitutions, and the states' approval of the Fourteenth Amendment, the former states would be readmitted to the Union.[42]

Southern conservatives and their northern Democratic supporters bitterly resented "the military despotism of Congressional Reconstruction and called for state regulation of the suffrage question." The Democratic party vote in 1868 reflected considerable northern hostility to Reconstruction. Nevertheless the army enfranchised 703,400 Negroes and 660,000 whites. For the first time "Negroes were voting and holding office."[43]

Reconstruction sought to graft a democratic society onto the old South. However, Negroes were not out to overturn social relations nor challenge the Confederate right to own property.[44] Negroes sought equal rights and opportunities as well as education and landownership. Negro gains provoked the insurgency, but it is important to remember that it began before Reconstruction and before the Negroes voted or held office. As with the NLF, pretext has to be distinguished from intent. The Klan insurgents sought to reestablish white supremacy before they were allegedly provoked.

The Confederates, for the most part,[45] had full access to the polls and were able to control hundreds of county and local government positions as well as a majority of the newspapers in the South.[46]

From the beginning of their forced merger with the Union, conservatives were determined to restore a labor system subordinating the Negroes. They felt especially threatened when Reconstruction governments passed laws assuring Negroes access to public (but still racially separate) education. Their concept of life was challenged as new laws sought to provide rights for all citizens.

Conservatives charged that public monies were being wasted and pleaded the right to protect themselves. This meant that for the first time ex-plantation owners were being taxed to support services never provided for and especially for services for Negroes. To them this was equivalent to inflicting humiliating conditions of barbarism on a superior race.[47]

The moderate leaders of the South were unable to establish their control because in spite of their commitment to the democratic processes they lacked the power to control their foes. They were unable to preserve law and order or make sure that democracy would prevail. Freedom of the press, open and fair courts, and a competitive legislative system did not fulfill the intended function of providing constructive debate so that opposing groups might reconcile or compromise their differences. The conservatives utilized all available outlets to destroy the governments that provided these liberties.

President Grant did not understand the dimensions of the threat to Reconstruction nor was he encouraged to take action by significant interests in the North. For the most part he preferred that southern officials "exhaust their own military resources first" to quell reported violence and terror.[48] Those military resources—the militias—were very weak for the most part. They were manned by poorly trained Negroes and frightened whites.[49] The use of Negro troops spurred the insurgents to maximize their efforts to destroy Republicanism in the South.

The ability of the conservatives successfully to play up exaggerated claims of abuse and objectionable conduct on the part of Unionists was one of the hallmarks of their strength. They accused the Radical Republicans of being in league with northern business to exploit the whites in the South. Recent studies now challenge this long-held contention. Northern concerns were profit-oriented, of course, and they often opposed the Radical Republicans for these reasons. (Their actions are reminiscent of American firms selling such goods as oil and steel to the North Vietnamese in spite of efforts in SVN.) Also, Northern business interests opposed the taxation required to support a military presence in the South.[50]

Critics invariably raised the corruption issue. Franklin agrees that it was a blight, but no one had a monopoly on the practice in 1860 America. Corruption "was bisectional, bipartisan, and biracial." He concludes, though, that the matter of corruption is pertinent to the survival of a weak government confronted by a fanatical insurgency. "The tragedy of public immorality in the Southern states was only part of a national tragedy. The added misfortune of the South was that it could least afford it, not only because of poverty and political instability but because . . . critics . . . were anxious to find excuses to discredit any efforts to reconstruct the South."[51]

Terror As Communication: The NLF

A difference between the NLF and the KKK was that the latter had a visible and enduring hate object—the Negro. The NLF was more likely to create its objects. As a given hate symbol faded, for example, the French or Diem, new ones were found. In spite of this difference both were adept in the art of propaganda. Even though both made serious errors and committed abuses and engaged in corruption, their opponents were ineffective in capitalizing on any openings.

Neither superior economic performance nor improving living standards deterred the insurgents or strengthened the legal governments. Indeed it was these "healthy" developments that aroused the insurgents and resulted in their intensifying their efforts. Both the NLF and the KKK feared that their opponents might develop effective service bureaucracies. Thus, while "the white South was willing to tolerate colored clowns in office, it bitterly resented any Negro who showed political intelligence or ability. . . ."[52] Hanoi created the NLF to interdict SVN's economic progress as well as to disrupt any order achieved between 1954 and 1959. (Critics of the Diem regime suggest that he failed to take advantage of SVN's superior output in shipping surpluses to the North. Whether this would have influenced Ho Chi Minh is arguable, but Diem's critics do acknowledge the economic gains.)

Terrorism was the most effective way to destroy the government and the social system. Both insurgencies wanted to avoid direct confrontation with the ARVN or the Union army. While both armies were passive in dealing with the insurgents they had superior power. The insurgents were careful not to assault or provoke the military. Bernard Fall points out that guerrilla movements learn that disrupting the civilian system is far less costly than directly confronting a country's armed forces.[53]

General Vo Nguyen Giap suggests that "the War of Liberation is a protracted war . . . in which we must rely mainly on ourselves for we are strong politically but weak materially, while the enemy is very weak politically but stronger materially." Put another way, the theory of guerrilla war is resorted to when "one does not have the controls ordinarily available to rulers embarked on creating a nationwide political military establishment." Thus, by a long war of attrition or the achievement of "a thousand victories" the enemy will finally become exhausted and the once superior forces will have become dispersed and disorganized.[54]

The theoretical capacities and originality of the founders of the NLF were far superior to those of the KKK. Giap envisioned that the liberation front would proceed through a three-stage program before the enemy could be overthrown. The stage concept appears applicable also to the insurgency process which finally defeated the Reconstruction government.

Each stage has the effect of securing a physical and psychological momentum. "The military objective is to break the government's hold on the population; the political objective is to break the psychological ties."[55] The first stage is the psychological warfare stage, as well as the time for the formation of small groups or cells. In the second stage small-unit assaults are organized whereby towns or villages are temporarily and symbolically held. The small units carry on assaults on the enemy's forces and seek to slash at his infrastructure. The third stage is set so that the insurgents are able to carve out and hold enclaves or liberated areas.[56] It is possible for all three stages to operate at the same time in that some areas are more amenable to one stage rather than another. Bernard Fall describes how the NLF established "resistance base areas in . . . Mekong Delta provinces. They proceeded to seal off Saigon from the rice-rich and densely populated delta areas."[57]

The NLF's actions and agit-prop activities were subordinated to the achieving of a "central socio-psychological objective."[58] This was to sever the populace's links with the government in any way possible. Every means was employed to eliminate rival power centers. It included the infiltration of the government apparatus and those of other institutions. Ultimately, they hoped the populace would swing over to the NLF and a broad coalition would be formed leaving the government totally eviscerated.[59] When the NLF thought of a broad coalition, there was no requirement that it be reeted with joy; it meant having the power to manipulate organizations and groups, while the government had lost the capacity to do this.

The NLF was very concerned about American efforts to forestall their drive for power. Unlike the French, the Americans were stressing the use of economic and political "tricks" (that is, reforms) to win over the people. The Americans pressed the government to initiate land reforms, encourage self-protection efforts, expand education, and halt corruption. It hoped that SVN would have a written constitution and provide for regular elections. As part of a counter-insurgency concept, the Americans hoped to develop a reform-oriented pluralistic system, including the expansion of the free trade union movement, to counter the NLF.

The insurgents were not simply seeking to take over "the turf," that is, to replace "the old gang" with a "new" one. Pike points out that the most impressive feature of the NLF was the totality of its goals. It sought to create a new system of property relations and new forms of production as well as a new social and legal order. It also sought to create the basis for an entirely different way to recruit and provide leaders.[60]

As the NLF sought to build a new order it conducted a massive campaign of violence to destroy the GVN. Terrorism was an integral part of its "communicational view of social change."[61] Its purpose was to eliminate any leader, official, or group that could possibly sustain an infrastructure independent of the NLF. Political terrorism was aimed at de-energizing the effectiveness of institutions not controlled by the NLF.

With the formation of the NLF on December 20, 1960, terror increased dramatically. Bernard Fall reports that between 1957 and 1958, 452 village chiefs were killed and by June 1960, the rate climbed to about fifteen a week. In a speech before Congress on May 25, 1961, President Kennedy reported that minor officials were being killed at the rate of 4,000 a year.[62] Fall reported that more than 1,000 officials were murdered in 1964 and another 400 were done away with in the first four months of 1965. The terror rate declined as the NLF "chewed up" the GVN's infrastructure.

The key victims of terror were the natural leaders—the village chiefs and their families, government officials including school teachers, social workers, medical personnel, police officials, and the like, as well as religious figures. For example, on February 2, 1961, a priest was slain. In Phuoc Trach village, Go Dau Ha district of Tay Ninh province, a dozen guerrillas killed three villagers including a seventeen-year-old Cao Dai priest "who gained a reputation for his militant hostility in the pulpit, charging that the NLF was basically anti-religious. He was stabbed to death and the guerrillas withdrew."[63]

In another incident, taken from an Associated Press survey of terroristic events, the NLF moved into a Mekong Delta town. The guerrillas called for forty-eight-year-old village Chief Nguyen Van Thanh to answer for crimes committed against "the revolutionary struggle to destroy imperialism." The chief previously ignored the request of local Vietcong (NLF) leaders to cooperate with them. Thanh was not a strong supporter of the government nor a particularly efficient leader. The NLF added a "disliked and corrupt policeman, a popular school teacher, and an innocuous census taker" to face them. The chief, his wife, and three-year-old daughter were forced to squat on the muddy ground when the show trial began. The policeman was not deemed worthy of a trial—he was simply shot. The school teacher was slashed with a knife and she bled to death. The village chief was strangled and his wife and child riddled with bullets. The charges were spying, stealing tax money, and stifling "the just revolutionary aspirations of the people." They pinned the charges to the chief's body and an NLF agit-prop worker explained to the assembled villagers why the executions were needed.[64]

Acts of terror were not kept secret. The NLF utilized them as communicational and educational tools. They were widely publicized to reach as much of the populace as possible.

Corrupt and venal officials were subject to terroristic punishment. It was their deaths that were most likely to be published overseas. Pike stresses, though, that the main victims were the successful leaders, the men and women of integrity who were able to develop and maintain an alternative infrastructure.[65] In a sense, this is also a logical position, for a successful pluralistic system would end the leadership vacuum the NLF hoped to fill. For about a six-year period or more, the NLF wiped out or converted an entire class of Vietnam villagers. As early as 1961, village after village was depopulated of its natural leaders, the men most important to rural society.

Whether terror consisted of an execution, a kidnapping, a sniping, a blowing up of a busload of school girls, or the shooting up of a hamlet, "the psychological objectives" were to create fear and uncertainty and to demonstrate that the GVN and its police and army were unable to provide security. The act of terror was designed to break the people's psychological ties with the GVN.[66]

As noted previously, these acts were genocidal in that the population was losing its capacity to identify with traditional values as the keepers of these values were eliminated. The populace no longer had the resistance to withstand the input of another ideological system, the one provided by the NLF.

To achieve their goals the insurgents rejected any possibility of compromise. Cadres were singled out for being too soft. All achievements of the GVN were ignored and all faults or grievances, whether real or not, were exaggerated. (The Communist propaganda machine played up these defects in the West in order to turn public support away from the Americans.[67] To put it another way, in another vernacular, the NLF was able to transmit all the failures of the GVN through "the copperheads" who sent them out all over the democratic world.)

To succeed at genocide the victims must be seen as totally repulsive. If there was any feeling permeating the NLF it would be "hate." Hate functioned as an "energizer" to commit the most bloody of acts.[68] Among the most dramatic phenomena of the twentieth century has been the (dubious) achievement of totalitarianism to couple hate with modern technology to destroy tens of millions of people. The power of hate as an organizational tool can also be seen in the KKK.

The Ku Klux Klan Terror

After the American Civil War two opposing forces sought to press their values on what Samuel Eliot Morison calls "the Shattered Empire." One of these forces received inspiration and backing from the Radical Republicans. (Perhaps it is not too far-fetched to suggest that the impetus for democratic reforms in SVN were supported by an analagous group of Americans in the 1960s.) The significant feature distinguishing the southern Republican party from the conservatives was that it sought to include all southerners as participants in the political system.

The conservative forces were composed of those whites whose "cardinal test of a Southerner . . . whether expressed with the frenzy of a demagogue or maintained with a patrician quietude" was support for white supremacy.[69] Even though their fighting forces were totally defeated, a highly skilled and racially motivated pool of personnel was available for the insurgency. These defeated Southerners rapidly organized themselves for they feared that "Yankee ideas" of equality would penetrate the South.[70] Even before Reconstruction reforms got under way, Southerners revealed their intentions by passing the Black Codes. Morison notes that not even the half million free Negroes composed of mechanics, truck farmers, barbers, small businessmen, and the like, were given any chance to participate in the South controlled by the ex-Confederates.

The Radical Republicans reversed the conservative laws and forced them out of office. Given their military weakness they had to give way. However, they did not relent and started an intense propaganda barrage and insurgency effort to secure their version of "home rule" for the South. Within a decade, they succeeded in establishing their version of the Solid South.

"The resistance movement," to use Kenneth Stampp's phrase, was especially suited to the rural vastness of the South. Klan units were quickly formed because of the common experience local men had in serving in Confederate units. Guerrilla bands were as much a part of the South as secret organizations were part of the history of SVN. They supplemented the legal forces to control slavery. Posse service was particularly common and important in tracking down runaway slaves.[71]

The key to Klan morale and unity was the common hatred whites had for blacks, and more particularly, for those who sought to press their claims as free citizens.

The most important way to reassert conservative authority was to defeat the Republican party. To this end, local Democrats throughout the South kept dossiers on anyone who supported or voted for Republicans.[72] First, economic sanctions and other forms of social pressures were tried to dissuade Republicans from going to the polls. If these sanctions failed the Klan resorted to physical intimidation and terror. Its effectiveness in keeping voters from the polls proved to be a major factor enabling Democrats to secure local posts throughout the South and, subsequently, would result in the capture of state legislatures. Once in office, the Democrats would throw the government's resources into the war against the Republicans.

In retrospect, it was an immense achievement that hundreds of thousands of blacks voted, for they had just emerged from slavery. The Klan had to persuade sufficient numbers of voters to stay away from the polls to assure Democratic victories.

Klan violence during elections was not isolated to single events. Trelease argued that the KKK conducted large-scale coordinated campaigns. In Louisiana, between the elections of April and November 1868, "1,081 people were killed. This represented a deliberate campaign of terror by the white population against the blacks throughout the state."[73] Klan terrorist activities extended beyond the systematic disruption of the voting processes. Terror was aimed at destroying all organizational activities that would have encouraged the development of a free, pluralist South. It was aimed at destroying moderate leaders or institutions that improved opportunities for Negroes. For example, the Klan was particularly hostile to white teachers of Negroes, especially white females. They were forced to live in Negro homes and then would be accused of sexual misconduct. Terror included intimidation, sniping, assassination, and lynching, which may or may not have been preceded by a mock trial.

Klan tactics varied. Usually an action would take place at night with about a dozen Klansmen fully hooded and sheeted. A typical target was a Negro suspected of violating some "white man's values." The Klansmen had all the advantages with them—"darkness, disguise, superior numbers and armaments." Their victims had an ingrained fear of the Klan and had little or no military skills. In a given night the Klan group might visit several Negro cabins to inflict their "lessons" and "punishments."[74] Before the terror ended, thousands of people of both races experienced beatings, shootings, rape, hangings, or forced exile, loss of money, property, and crops.[75]

In Texas, Republicans "had been publicly slated for assassination and forced to flee their homes." Maj. Gen. James Curtis reported on the situation in Texas counties in 1868. "The right of franchise is a farce. Numbers of Negroes have been killed for daring to be Radicals, and their houses have so often been broken into by their Ku Klux neighbors in search of arms that they are now pretty well defenceless." The officer was careful to note that only Negroes who voted Republican were terrorized. "No more notice is taken here of the death of a Radical Negro than a mad dog. Yet, a Democratic Negro who was shot . . . was followed to his grave . . . by a long procession (including some of the most aristocratic and responsible white men in this city)."[76]

The ritualistic nature of the terror is illustrated by the following: Capt. George W. Smith, a young Union army veteran, was attacked in jail with obvious collusion of local officials. "The door burst open and the crowd surged in upon him as he fell, and then, man after man . . . fired into the dying body. This refinement of barbarity was continued while he writhed, and after the limbs had ceased to quiver, that each one might participate in the triumph."[77]

Klan violence was designed to send a "message." Its purpose was to instill fear and paralyze Republicans, Negroes, and even military officers, sheriffs, and other officials. The Klan was encouraged to spread fear through terror because they were rarely prosecuted. Efforts to use military force against the Klan produced a nationwide chorus of protest. In Congress, Democrats, whose strength kept increasing, were more concerned about "persecution" and "harassment" of Klansmen than tales of terror against their victims. Ironically, the Klan's defenders invoked every legal technicality to defend it, including the hated Fourteenth Amendment.[78] "All of the safeguards for the accused in the Anglo-Saxon system of justice were mobilized to enforce the higher law of supremacy."[79]

The insurgency utilized the freedom allowed for *all* to destroy the Republicans. The latter's regard for civil liberties enabled the Democrats to capture government after government, but they were unable to protect the voting rights of their supporters. Law-enforcement officials abetted the Klan and usually these officials were Klansmen as well as Democrats. It would be appropriate to describe the Democratic party in the South as a legal arm of conservatives, as the Klan was the insurgent arm.

The Klan's ability to use the resources of a democratic system enabled it to have an effective communication system. The ease with which it was able to communicate enabled it to interdict arms shipments and anticipate many of the actions of its foes. In addition to controlling the countryside, it was frequently better armed than the state militias.

William Pierce Randel argues that this "underground government" destroyed the moderate governments of the Reconstruction era. He also argues that a "determined minority, convinced of the rightness of its cause" can defeat an effort backed by a wearying majority. Not only were the moderates checked at every point in the South, but the voters in the North felt events in the South becoming more and more remote.[80] In effect, the more a democratic society permits insurgents to function, the more it is subject to collapse.

The Klan was formed by one John Kennedy and fellow ex-Confederates in Pulaski, Tennessee, in 1866. The name, the rituals, and the secret oaths were patterned from Kennedy's fraternity experience while at college. Gradually, as the organization grew the initial organizers faded away. A loose hierarchy developed, including dens, provinces, dominions, realms, and "the Invisible Empire of the World." These units coincided with the traditional levels of government in the states.

The Klan's stated purposes were to form "an institution of Chivalry, Humanity, Mercy and Patriotism . . . embodying in its genius and its principles all that is noble . . . and patriotic." It intended "to protect the weak, the innocent and the defenseless . . . and . . . the Constitution. . . ." It opposed "negro equality, both social and political," and was "in favor of white man's government."[81] Thus, the Klan claimed to be a defensive body dedicated to defending white supremacy.

However, as with other political terror groups, it required a distorted image of reality to justify murder and torture of innocent victims. Trelease argues that it was the fanatical and fantasized hatred of the Negro that "ener-

gized" the Klan.[82] It institutionalized the feelings and urges as well as the
disparate guerrilla activities in the South. It caught on and spread. In the
first four months of 1868 the Klan expanded from half a dozen counties in
middle Tennessee "to every State between the Potomac and the Rio
Grande."[83]

Conservative leaders quickly realized the value of the insurgency. It enabled them to secure "liberated" areas outside of the major cities. In order to
do this a conservative infrastructure had to be developed and protected. *The
Nashville Press and Times* of July 12, 1866, provides an example of the
process. It reported that the mission of a secret organization "is to prevent
the employment . . . of Unionists in any capacity whatever, as day-laborers,
clerks, book-keepers, teachers, physicians, lawyers or mechanics. In all
cases rebels are to be employed, and the members of the association pledge
to starve out or drive out every Union man from that part of the country."[84]

In 1868, the Klan was able to flaunt its power in many southern towns.
Thus in Pulaski, Tennessee, on July 4, 1868, 300 to 400 Klansmen demonstrated in full regalia. "They performed military maneuvers in the square
and along the streets, in perfect order without any word of command being
uttered."[85] (This, too, suggests these men were once members of well-
trained Confederate units.)

Increasingly the liberated areas expanded as the Republican strength
atrophied. *The Aberdeen Examiner* of Monroe, Mississippi, provides a
vivid example of the insurgency's prowess by 1875. The people of Jackson
were able to secure weapons in large numbers. "At the call of the County Executive it was easy . . . to put seventeen hundred well-mounted horsemen into line, that could be transposed into a brigade of cavalry at a moment's
notice. . . . In addition . . . over 100 square miles of territory were so
thoroughly connected by courier lines . . . that we could communicate with
every voter within its borders within a few hours."[86]

As the insurgents took over state militias and sheriffs' offices, "the police state" quality of life became more entrenched. Moderation gave way to
racial totalitarianism. The Klan proved to be an effective arm in recovering
power from the Republicans.[87]

The media waged a vicious and ceaseless campaign against the moderates. No positive ideas were proffered to deal with any of the problems in the
South. Claims of Klan violence were treated as exaggerations, mistakes, or
lies. When proof of atrocities was available the press usually found a reason that explained the need for the action. Similarly, Democrats in Congress had stock answers. Even with the overwhelming evidence of the thirteen volumes compiled by the Joint Committee to investigate the Klan, the
Democrats refused to accept the findings.[88]

The Klan enjoyed a preponderance of support from the population in the
South because it was either admired or feared. Its capacity to inflict pain and

death with relative impunity helped dissolve the Republican infrastructure. There was little or no military protection against the terror. A state adjutant general wrote that in Arkansas "all we can do now is to show the rebels that we can march through any county in the State whenever it is necessary." (The GVN made similar statements.) By 1868, this was not possible in many states.[89] Maj. Lewis M. Merrill of the United States Army concluded that those in favor of a civilized community were in complete disarray and disorganization.[90] Congress concluded that "terror seemed on the verge of engulfing, tearing apart the very fabric of society. . . ."

The Klan ultimately wore down the North. Trelease describes its final victory. "Every year brought the downfall of additional Republican state governments. This was not the work of scattered Ku Klux bands . . . but of open white paramilitary organizations and wholesale intimidations . . . violence and rioting."

Conclusion

While the difference between the situations in both areas was great, there were enough common elements to make comparisons about them meaningful. Both legal regimes encountered implacable foes determined to force different world views on their respective peoples. Both regimes had ineffective military support and both failed to secure sufficient support from interest groups within their areas or from their overseas or northern supporters.

Neither government was able to mount an effective ideological alternative to counter the insurgents. The insurgents' superior organizational abilities and superior agit-prop teams enabled them to replace their opponents' infrastructure with their own. The insurgents were able to sever their respective countrysides from the governing forces. Both were absolutely determined not to make any accommodations or to accept any reforms that might prop up their respective foes.

These two insurgencies enshrouded their terror with an ideological mystique based, in part, on the total hatred of their opponents. They were sufficiently confident of their beliefs to take whatever actions were needed to illegitimatize their opponents' legal apparatus. Both were successful in that they were able to make their gruesome atrocities acceptable to important opinion groups. Aside from the differences of historical events, both could be described by a common theory of action.

Notes

1. Douglas Pike, *Viet Cong: The Organization and Techniques of the National Liberation Front of South Vietnam* (Cambridge; The M.I.T. Press, 1966), pp. 87-8.

2. For example, the world's media reported the Communists commemorate the 1968 My Lai massacres. See *New York Times,* 21 March 1976.

3. Pike, *Viet Cong,* p. 248.

4. Thomas Perry Thornton, "Terror as a Weapon of Political Agitation," in Harry Eckstein's *Internal War: Problems and Approaches* (New York: The Free Press, 1964), p. 72.

5. Allen W. Trelease, *White Terror: The Ku Klux Klan Conspiracy and Southern Reconstruction* (New York: Harper and Row, 1971).

6. Thornton, in Eckstein's *Internal War,* pp. 78, 83.

7. For a review of Ho Chi Minh's commitment to Stalinism and his capacity to exercise ruthless methods in liquidating his competitors see Robert Shaplen, *The Lost Revolution* (Harper and Row), pp. 31-54.

8. Philippe Devillers, "Ngo Dinh Diem and the Struggle for Reunification in Vietnam," *The China Quarterly* 9 (January-March 1962) pp. 2-23. Reproduced in Marvin Gettleman, ed., *Vietnam* (New York: Fawcett, 1965), p. 217.

9. Robert Scigliano, *South Vietnam Under Stress* (Boston: Houghton Mifflin, 1964), p. 19.

10. *Ibid.,* pp. 22, 23.

11. *Ibid.,* pp. 27-28, 33-34.

12. *Ibid.,* p. 54.

13. Devillers, *Ngo Dinh Diem,* p. 224.

14. Pike, *Viet Cong,* p. 79. (He challenges Devillers's thesis.)

15. Pike, *Viet Cong,* pp. 6, 57-8.

16. Scigliano, *South Vietnam,* p. 33.

17. Pike, *Viet Cong,* p. 6.

18. Bernard Fall, "The Viet Cong—The Unseen Enemy in Vietnam," *New Society* (London), 22 April 1965. Reprinted in Marcus G. Raskin and Bernard B. Fall, eds., *The Viet-Nam Reader* (New York: Vintage, 1965), p. 255.

19. Pike, *Viet Cong,* p. 57.

20. *Ibid.,* pp. 73, 80, 88.

21. *Ibid.,* pp. 88-9 and Scigliano, *South Vietnam,* p. 218.

22. *New York Times,* 17 April 1966.

23. *Ibid.,* 8 May 1966.

24. Bernard B. Fall, *The Two Vietnams: A Political and Military Analysis* (rev. ed.) (New York: Praeger, 1964), pp. 295, 296, 299, 302. Also *New York Times,* 17 June 1963.

25. Samuel P. Huntington, "Vietnam: The Bases of Accommodation," *Foreign Affairs* (July 1968), pp. 642-656.

26. Bernard B. Fall, "Viet-Nam in the Balance," *Foreign Affairs* (Spring, 1966), pp. 1-18 and *Vietnam: Vital Issues in the Great Debate* (New York: Foreign Policy Association, 22 September 1966), p. 10.

27. Kenneth M. Stampp and Leon F. Litwack, *Reconstruction: An Anthology of Revisionist Writings* (Baton Rouge: LSU Press, 1969), "Foreword," p. vii.

28. Don E. Fehrenbacher, "Disunion and Reunion," *The Reconstruction of American History* (New York: Harper Torchbook, 1962), p. 108.

29. Kenneth M. Stampp, "The Tragic Legend of Reconstruction," in Stampp and Litwack, *Reconstruction Anthology,* p. 8.

30. Fehrenbacher, *Disunion and Reunion,* p. 107.

31. Stampp and Litwack, *Reconstruction Anthology,* p. 16.

32. William Pierce Randel, *The Ku Klux Klan: A Century of Infamy* (Philadelphia: Chilton Books, 1965), p. xii.

33. Stampp and Litwack, *Reconstruction Anthology,* pp. 9-11.

34. Richard Hofstater, William Miller, and Daniel Aaron, *The American Republic, II* (Englewood Cliffs: Prentice-Hall, 1959), pp. 4, 6.

35. James E. Stefton, *The United States Army and Reconstruction, 1865-1877* (Baton Rouge: LSU Press, 1967), p. 156.

36. Fehrenbacher, *Disunion and Reunion,* p. 103.

37. Sefton, *U. S. Army and Reconstruction,* p. 8.

38. *Ibid.,* pp. 30, 31.

39. *Ibid.,* pp. 65, 265.

40. John Hope Franklin, *Reconstruction After the Civil War* (Chicago: University of Chicago Press, 1961), pp. 36, 4, 45.

41. *Ibid.,* pp. 46-49.

42. *Ibid.,* pp. 70-71.

43. *Ibid.,* pp. 83, 80, 84.

44. *Ibid.,* p. 91.

45. Rebeccah Brooks Gruver, *An American History* (New York: Appleton, Century and Crofts, 1972), p. 593.

46. Trelease, *White Terror,* pp. xxxviii-xxxix.

47. *Ibid.,* p. xxxiii.

48. Sefton, *U. S. Army and Reconstruction,* p. 217.

49. Franklin, *Reconstruction,* p. 122.

50. Stanley Coben, "Economic Interests Do Not Explain Civil War and Reconstruction," in Charles Crowe, ed., *The Age of Civil War and Reconstruction, 1830-1900* (Homewood, Illinois: The Dorsey Press, 1966), pp. 291, 302.

51. Franklin, *Reconstruction,* p. 151.

52. Samuel Eliot Morison, *The Oxford History of the American People* (New York: Oxford, 1965), p. 719.

53. Fall, *The Two Viet-Nams,* p. 289.

54. "People's War and People's Army," in Pike, *Viet Cong,* pp. 33-35, 57.

55. Pike, *Viet Cong,* p. 39.

56. *Ibid.,* pp. 37-8.

57. Fall, *Viet Cong,* pp. 256-7.

58. Pike, *Viet Cong,* pp. 38, ix.

59. *Ibid.,* pp. 32, 41, 40.

60. *Ibid,* p. 55.

61. *Ibid.,* p. 32.

62. Fall, *Viet Cong,* p. 257.

63. Pike, *Viet Cong,* p. 241.

64. Associated Press, 10 October 1968.

65. Pike, *Viet Cong,* p. 248.

66. *Ibid.,* pp. 246, vi, 38.

67. *Ibid.,* chap. 17, "Externalization: Projecting the NLF Image Abroad."

68. *Ibid.,* pp. 283-5.

69. Morison, *Oxford History,* p. 707.

70. David M. Potter, *The South and Sectional Conflict* (Baton Rouge: LSU Press, 1968); see chaps. I, II, and III on "The Nature of Southernism."

71. Trelease, *White Terror,* pp. xlii, xii.

72. *Ibid.,* pp. 79-80.

73. *Ibid.,* p. 135.

74. *Ibid.,* pp. 58-9

75. *Ibid.*

76. *Ibid.,* pp. 138-139.

77. *New York Tribune,* 31 July 1869; Trelease, *White Terror,* p. 142.

78. Trelease, *White Terror,* pp. 219-222.

79. *Ibid.,* pp. xxxviii-xxxix.

80. Randel, *Ku Klux Klan,* p. x and Trelease, *White Terror,* p. x.

81. Trelease, *White Terror,* pp. 16-17.

82. *Ibid.,* p. xvii.

83. *Ibid.,* p. 27.

84. *Ibid.,* p. 8.

85. *The Pulaski Citizen,* 10 July 1868; Trelease, *White Terror,* p. 38.

86. Vernon Lane Wharton, "The Revolution of 1875," in Stampp and Litwack, *Reconstruction Anthology,* pp. 481-2.

87. Trelease, *White Terror,* p. xlvi.

88. Report of Joint Select Committee to Inquire into the Condition of the Affairs in the Late Insurrectionary States, 13 vols. (Washington, 1872), House Reports, 42nd Congress, 2d Session, no. 22, p. 5286.

89. Trelease, *White Terror,* p. 160.

90. *Ibid.,* p. 369.

THOMAS P. ANDERSON

Political Violence and Cultural Patterns in Central America

In discussing the problem of violence and terrorism in Central America, it is important to avoid the trap of suggesting that there is something in the Central American character that makes Central Americans more violent than other peoples. Indeed, despite the high crime rates in several of these countries, there is no reason to suppose that Central Americans have a greater disposition to personal violence than do New Yorkers. Statistically, they have a good deal less in some categories. Nor, despite the prevalence of terrorism in Guatemala and El Salvador, can anyone claim that terrorism is a Central American characteristic. Such a suggestion would be very amusing to a citizen of Belfast or Beirut.

Rather, it should be noted that there are specific features of violence, both personal and organized, that do have their roots in the cultural formation of the Central American peoples, and that Central America represents a microcosm of Latin America. I will consider, for this purpose, two aspects of the social character of the Spanish Americans of this area: their concepts of manliness and their religion, as these affect both rich and poor, and how these contrast with the attitudes of the Indian community.

I would like to focus my attention on the three neighboring countries of Guatemala, El Salvador, and Honduras and exclude from consideration Nicaragua and Costa Rica, the former because violence there has largely become institutionalized in its governmental processes and the latter because an entirely different set of economic and cultural circumstances have left the Costa Ricans to a certain extent immune to the malady of violence. I should further like to focus on that type of violence associated with political life in the twentieth century: ideological violence.

Ideological violence in Central America begins with the organization of left-wing labor movements in the 1920s. In 1924 the first Guatemalan Communist party was organized, and this was followed by the organization of similar groups in Honduras and El Salvador. Early in 1932 the Communist party of El Salvador led the first organized Communist uprising in the western hemisphere. The revolt began among the peasants in the western part of the country, spread rapidly, and was then drowned in blood by the military. Some 20,000 people were killed. Most of those killed were victims of the military repression that followed the revolt's failure, the *Matanza,* which has been detailed in my book of the same title. So ferocious was this massacre that Communist activity was crushed for four decades.

Instead, violence in El Salvador took the form of coups and counter-coups during the forties and fifties. Then, forestalling more of the same, the military rulers of the country began to encourage what we might call *national violence,* directed, in this case, at the neighboring country of Honduras. Juan Ramón Ardon, in his book *Días de Infamia,* sees this as an attempt of the government to take the people's minds off internal problems which might revive left-wing activities.[1] This culminated in the Soccer War of 1969, which this writer observed going into Honduras during the Salvadorean military occupation of that country's territory.

The Honduran government did not entirely regret the war either, for a great deal of agrarian violence and terrorism, of the type so completely repressed in El Salvador, continued in Honduras on a sporadic basis. Part of this was directed by the banana workers against The United Fruit Company and the other great planters and consisted of burning estates and attacking managers, while part was directed against Salvadorean immigrants and thus had an immediate bearing on the war of 1969. Marco Virgilio Carias, in *La Guerra Inutil,* shows the relation of this Honduran internal violence to government war policy.[2] Since 1970, Communist activity in El Salvador has been very much revived. The *Ejército Revolucionario Popular* and other terrorist groups have killed government ministers and members of the "14 families" and have seized radio stations to broadcast their propaganda.

This Marxist violence may be a revival in El Salvador, but, of course, it is old hat in Guatemala. Guatemala lived under the stern dictatorship of Jorge Ubico until 1944. Then a left-wing movement took over under Juan José Arévalo, and finally, Jacobo Arbenz. This was ousted in 1954. As pointed out by John Gillin and K. H. Silvert,[3] this CIA-backed takeover resulted in a general massacre which I see as little different from the 1932 atrocity in El Salvador. But the snake had been scotched, not killed, and Col. Carlos Castillo Armas was himself the victim of an assassination which signaled the beginning of leftist guerrilla activity lasting through the sixties. Guerrillas of the *Fuerzas Armadas Revolucionarios* seized arms and ambushed patrols of both the warring parties in the Soccer War, along the Guatemalan border. No less than three guerrilla movements of the left have operated in Guatemala in recent years, and there is a right-wing terrorist organization, the "White Hand," which operates in both Guatemala and El Salvador in similar fashion to the Honduran *Mancha Brava.* What is being emphasized in this summary is that violence is indeed endemic in the region. But, the question remains, out of what deeper springs does this violence flow?

First of all, a few words should be said about the cultural roots of this violence in so far as it relates to the *Ladino* (that is, non-Indian) community in these countries. It goes almost without saying that the background of

Central American *Ladinos,* whatever their personal origin, is culturally Spanish and Spanish-American. This gives them a certain definite value system and code by which they live. This code is very much bound up with the much misunderstood term *machismo.* Literally, this means *maleness,* but it means a good deal more, and, in fact, a good deal less as well. Perhaps no one has put its true meaning as well as Julius Rivera in his book *Latin America: A Socio-Cultural Interpretation:* "A Macho gambles with Destiny, ready to win or lose. He gambles with Death, he gambles with God. A burning love affair is a victory over Destiny; a revolution a victory over Death; sin a victory over God. When the three come together, man has accomplished his fulfillment. This is the essential meaning of *machismo.*"[4]

One can see that this is a good deal different from the Anglo stereotype of the *macho.* It is more concerned with defiance than with pleasure. It seeks to temporarily stave off the effects of the immutable laws of life. Like the philosophy of Miguel de Unamuno, it stresses living for what should be rather than what is. In short, the Latin American *macho* is more Don Quixote than Don Juan.

It is possible to discuss the *macho* and his thirst for violence, as Samuel Ramos does,[5] in terms of feelings of inferiority and consequent aggressive behavior, but I would suggest that while this debased style of *machismo* might apply to the Mexican *Pelado,* it has scant application to the revolutionary terrorist who does not simply hurl vulgar insults at his tormentors, but rather faces them, thereby risking their bullets and their torture chambers.

Essential then to this concept of manliness is the willingness to face death, even when it could be avoided. Anyone who has ever ridden behind a Central American bus driver has a new insight into the idea of *machismo.* It would not be too much to say that this is a "death-oriented" society. In part this is due to the circumstances of a life lived, in many cases, close to the margin of survival. A high infant mortality rate (that of El Salvador is estimated by Alastair White at 120 to 140 per 1,000 live births), poverty, and a fierce murder rate (there were 1,313 arrests for homicide in 1969 compared to 243 traffic deaths in that same country of less than 4,000,000) combine to affect the attitude toward death.[6] The church, too, plays its part. Death is given an importance in Latin American Catholicism which is far greater than that assigned in North American Catholicism or Protestantism. The celebrations, with the corpse as the principal guest, that attend the death of a "little angel" (a child below the age of reason) in country towns especially, testify to an orientation quite different from that of the life-prizing gringos. The picnic in the graveyard, mentioned by Huizinga as a phenomenon of the late Middle Ages, still goes on in Central America and Mexico.

With death such an ever-present companion, the emphasis shifts from the length of existence to the quality of its termination. The Mexican poet

Octavio Paz has observed: "Death defines life. . . . Death illuminates our lives. If our deaths lack meaning, our lives also lacked it. . . . Tell me how you die and I will tell you who you are."[7] For a man the best way to die is to go down fighting. John Ruskin once observed that the "roots of honor" for a soldier were his willingness to die—not his willingness to kill. And in Central American society there is a fascination with the soldierly qualities, an acceptance of this role as *the* ideal role for a man. Joining a terrorist organization, under these circumstances, is as natural as joining a baseball team.

While I would like to suggest that these feelings are as intense in Central America as in most of Latin America, I would certainly not want to suggest that they are exclusive to the area. The "little angel" and the kamikaze bus driver are familiar figures from northern Mexico to Patagonia. Certain traits, however, while not exclusive to the area, do take on unusual importance there. The rural machete culture, the role of the educational establishment, and the conflict of Indian and *Ladino* culture are examples.

One aspect of violence which is very Central American is the machete culture of the area. There is a surprisingly complete and technical vocabulary concerning the types and usages of machetes. In lands which raise maize, cane, and fruits, the machete is a very useful tool. But it is more than that. The highly decorated scabbards and the loving care of the blades would tell you that this was primarily a weapon, even if you had never witnessed a Saturday brawl in a rural village. It is the mark of the lower classes that they carry these weapons, just as it is the mark of the upper classes that most men carry pistols. To a Central American peasant the machete is closely tied up with his manhood and his honor. During the Communist uprising of 1932, the participants largely disdained guns in favor of their familiar and beloved weapons. Even today, the *Guardia* in El Salvador carry the machete rather than the billy-club, along with automatic rifles.

In short, this is an armed society. Such societies, whether in the Middle Ages or today, are noted for their excessive politeness in everyday address with acquaintances and strangers. Theodore Roosevelt noted the same thing in the 1880s among his cowboys, and correctly remarked that excessive politeness is always the rule where every man is armed.

A machete society, by its very nature, lends itself to *machetismo* which William S. Stokes characterizes as "a crude, primitive method of mobilizing violence primarily in local, rural politics but occasionally in national, urban areas as well." And, as he points out, "Whoever can command the authority represented by the machete in rural areas possesses political power of an important nature and automatically constitutes a factor to be reckoned with in the affairs of government."[8] Both Maximiliano Hernández Martínez in El Salvador and his rival Jorge Ubico in Guatemala were masters of exploiting the rural, machete-wielding populace.

Too often, however, sociologists and political scientists tend to focus on

violence and terrorism as if they were exclusively lower-class manifestations, linked to the rural village backwaters and to the shanty towns of the
cities. In reality, the present wave of Marxist terrorism in Central America
is actually a product of the universities and the *colegios,* a violence perpetrated in the name of the masses, but not necessarily always implicating
them.

The educational system of any culture is a microcosm of the society itself.
It is hardly surprising that the Central American educational establishments, surrounded by a world which legitimizes the violent response to
social and political situations, takes on itself the aspect of a warfare society. The same sort of politicization that Hugh Thomas has discussed in regard to the University of Habana in the 1930s and 1940s has gone on in the
Central American universities. A university strike, attended with considerable violence, was a key factor in the overthrow of General Martínez in El
Salvador, and similar incidents marked the downfall of Ubico in Guatemala
and that of many later leaders. The degree in which institutions of higher
learning serve as breeding grounds for gunmen suggests that the privileged
student is not as remote from the national life as he might like to think. It is
not even unheard of for university intellectuals such as Abel Cuenca in El
Salvador to end up as leaders of a machete-wielding uprising.

The politics of the university community tend to more extremes than that
of the society as a whole. So the combination arises of a cultural tradition of
violence, in which the attitudes of the elite are only slightly removed from
those of the masses, coupled with a strong revolutionary idealism. When
one adds to this the fact that the intellectual demands of Central American
universities are often not very great, and the prospects of a career arising
out of one's education *per se* rather slim, one sees the potential for violence
becoming more of an academic way of life than the taking of examinations.

So far, this paper has focused on various aspects of *Ladino* society: the
macho character of both the poor, machete-carrying peasant and that of the
pistol-packing university student. At this point it might be well to remember
that one of the distinctive features of society in part of Central America is
the existence of a relatively separate Indian society. In Guatemala, the various Maya peoples make up more than half of the population, and while El
Salvador and Honduras are Mestizo nations, there remain, especially in the
former, isolated Indian communities, such as the Izalco region's *Pipil.*

In communities among the Indians where social institutions like the leadership of the *cacique* and the brotherhood of the *cofradía* remain intact, there
appears to be less violence and tension than in communities which follow
the *Ladino* patterns of culture. Age-old bonds of cooperation and the still
prevailing pre-Hispanic cults maintain a civility not found in the surrounding world. This is not to say that such peoples are not potential participants
of left-wing revolutionary movements. The 1932 Communist uprising in El

Salvador was based squarely upon the Izalco Pipil, while Jacobo Arbenz drew a great deal of his support in Guatemala from Indian "reds."

When such revolutionary violence arises among the *indígenas,* the view of this observer is that it is likely to be much more socially controlled and much more subject to discipline. The Maya of Yucatán, to use an example from that region, formed an entirely separate society and government to pursue their "Caste War" in the late nineteenth and early twentieth centuries. Residents of Felipe Carrillo Puerto (the Chan Santa Cruz of the Maya) testify even today to the orderliness of the Indian government.

One result of the conscious attempts to break down Indian society, particularly in Guatemala, has been to introduce among the indigenous population Latin concepts of rebellion, resistance, and death. In this sense, the central governments have contributed to the radicalization of elements formerly outside the national life and helped to create their own enemies. It is doubtful if the Indian notions of community and conformity will long exist anywhere in the region.

In following the weekly accounts of violence and political terror in Central America, one feels the violence of this region is somewhat parochial even today. Assassinations there are, seizures of property and bombings. And yet, I do not think that it is simply coincidence that this violence has been directed almost exclusively toward fellow Latin Americans and has been largely designed as a direct attack upon those seen as the revolutionary enemy. Random terror has played little part in the region. This might be attributed to the intensely personal views of the Central American. His intense *machismo* may force him to tilt at windmills, but he never mistakes other objects for the windmills he is seeking. As bitterly as the Miss Universe pageant was resented in El Salvador, and as much violence as was brought against it, no effort was made to harm either the spectators or the unfortunate contestants. The interpersonal attitude of Central Americans toward violence has the mitigating quality of sparing the bystander in a way the bystander is not spared in Ulster or in Lebanon.

What I have tried to suggest is that the Central American, while sharing fully in the characteristic attitudes which make resorts to political violence so common in Latin America, tends to bring a style of his own to this violence, a style compounded of the elements of *Ladino* and *Indio* culture within this area.

Notes

1. Juan Ramón Ardon, *Dias de Infamia* (Tegucigalpa: Impresa Calderon, 1970), p. 52.

2. Marco Virgilio Carías, *La Guerra Inutil* (San José: Editorial Universitaria Centro-America, 1971), p. 68-9.

3. John Gillin and K. H. Silvert, "Ambiguities in Guatemala," *Foreign Affairs,* XXXIV (1 April 1956), p. 474.

4. Julius Rivera, *Latin America: A Socio-Cultural Interpretation* (New York: Appleton, Century, Crofts, 1971), p. 5.

5. Samuel Ramos, *Profile of Man and Culture in Mexico* (New York: McGraw-Hill, 1963), pp. 54-60.

6. Alastair White, *El Salvador* (New York and Washington: Praeger, 1973), p. 236, note 20 on p. 250, note 43 on p. 251.

7. Octavio Paz, *The Labyrinth of Solitude* (New York: Grove Press, 1961), p. 54.

8. William S. Stokes, "Violence as a Political Factor in Latin American Politics," in *Conflict and Violence in Latin American Politics,* Francisco José Moreno and Barbara Mitrani, eds. (New York: Thomas Y. Crowell & Co., 1971), p. 156.

EDGAR O'BALLANCE

Terrorism in the Middle East

This paper excludes, except by way of brief reference, what may be thought of as battlefield or urban guerrilla warfare, as expounded by Mao Tse-tung and other authorities, and only terrorism with a political motive will be considered. The hostage system, murder, torture, and terrorism in all forms are not new to the Middle East: they have been carried out for a variety of reasons, and particularly for political ends. In the Middle East terrorist acts probably date at least to the original Old Man of the Mountains, Hassan ben Sabbah, who toward the end of the eleventh century organized and conditioned a fanatical sect, the Assassins, in northern Iran. He later moved to Lebanon, where his followers committed many political murders.

The Cult of the Fedayeen

The Arab fedayeen, or freedom fighters, came into prominence in 1965, when the Fatah organization began to raid Israel, but it was fairly ineffectual and failed, after the Six-Day War of 1967, to instigate Mao Tse-tung-type guerrilla tactics in the occupied territories, where lived some 1.3 million Arabs. Then suddenly in late 1968, something seemed to snap in the Arab mind, and the cult of the fedayeen swept through Arab countries like wildfire and a crop of guerrilla groups sprang up almost overnight, mostly based in Palestinian refugee camps. Early in 1969, Yasser Arafat, the Fatah leader, became chairman of the Palestine Liberation Organization, the PLO, which was supposed to control and coordinate their activities. By mid-1969, mergers and forcible take-overs had reduced the number of guerrilla groups from more than fifty to about a dozen, but they all had different aims, were of varying quality, and were very independently minded; Arafat's control in most cases was less than nominal. Fedayeen activities included terrorist raids across Israeli borders, explosions inside Israel, assassination of Arabs suspected of collaborating with Israelis, attacks on Israeli embassies and El Al offices abroad, and hijacking aircraft.

On December 1, 1968, Arab terrorists attacked an El Al airliner at Athens Airport, causing death and injury. This incident provoked the Israelis, whose policy was one of hard reprisal, to mount a raid in helicopters on the Beirut Airport in which thirteen Arab airliners were destroyed. The first fedayeen hijacking of an aircraft had already occurred on July 23. Other incidents followed in quick succession, and soon the list became long.

Arab adulation, coupled with the fact that they tried to brush aside governments and reach the people directly, caused the fedayeen to become arrogant and to resist national restraints as they strove to become a "power without responsibility" in their host countries. In October 1969, this caused a clash with the small Lebanese army, which showed unexpected determination in preventing fedayeen expansion of its Fatahland base. In September of the following year, fedayeen activities and arrogance in Jordan brought about civil war, during which King Hussein eventually ejected them all from his country by the following July.

One of the more spectacular and dramatic incidents occurred at the World Olympic Games at Munich, on September 5, 1972, when members of the Black September Organization, the BSO, which had arisen from the bitter ashes of fedayeen defeat at the hands of King Hussein, and which had already assassinated the Jordanian premier, were responsible for killing eleven Israeli athletes. This act caused attitudes of moderate Arab governments to harden against the fedayeen, and they took what restricting action they could.

The Israeli Backlash

The Israeli counter was to mount raids on camps in adjacent Arab territory where it was suspected terrorists lived, to blow up buildings, and make air strikes. The Israeli attitude toward bargaining for the lives of hostages was uncompromising. For example, on May 8, 1972, when BSO terrorists hijacked an airliner and flew it into Lod Airport, demanding the release of Arab prisoners held by the Israelis in exchange for the lives of their hostages, Israeli paratroops stormed the plane, to kill or capture the hijackers. In May 1974, the Israelis took similar swift action when Arab terrorists took over a girls' school at Ma'alot, and did so again in March 1975, when terrorists took over the Savoy Hotel in Tel Aviv.

The Arab whirlwind of indiscriminate terrorism inducted, and then became intermixed with, an Israeli backlash that developed into an underground war that spread to Europe, in which Arab terrorists and Israeli agents eliminated each other in a twilight world beyond the imagination of Ian Fleming, but without the glamour of a James Bond, and all too often with a deadly finality.

Postal warfare also developed, which caused many casualties on both sides, as Arabs sent parcel-bombs and letter-bombs to prominent Israelis and Zionists, and Israeli agents sought to eliminate key terrorists. This Israeli backlash did much to frighten Arafat, the PLO, Fatah, and other fedayeen groups into adopting a "responsible" attitude, to openly condemn Arab terrorist activities, to disassociate themselves from them, and to at least make a show of punishing terrorists who were handed over to the PLO.

The International Phase

Restricted by their own organizations and individual Arab states, the fedayeen terrorists found contacts with international terrorist groups, such as the Japanese Red Army. International revolutionaries began to work with them, and one of their first exploits occurred on May 30, 1972, when three Japanese Red Army members arrived at Lod Airport and began firing guns and throwing grenades at passengers, killing twenty-four and injuring seventy-nine, of whom one later died. International terrorists cooperated with Arab ones in a number of aircraft hijackings and other incidents that involved taking hostages: again, the list is long.

A most bizarre incident occurred on December 21, 1975, when a group of six international terrorists, including Arabs, stormed the OPEC headquarters building in Vienna, killing three people, and holding hostages, including eleven oil ministers. The Austrian government provided an aircraft to fly terrorists and hostages to North Africa, where all were eventually released. The leader was identified as Carlos Martinez, a Venezuelan, who had come to be dubbed "The Jackal," a name linked with many notorious terrorist activities. Although he condemned "all moderate Arab statesmen as traitors," it is not yet clear to what extent Arab terrorist groups have been influenced, or even taken over, by international professional revolutionaries, such as Carlos, to become part of a world revolutionary movement, instead of purely an Arab one.

Terrorists Require Favorable Conditions

What makes a terrorist, and what conditions are essential to his success? Arab terrorism, continuing unabated as it still does today, initially began from a sense of frustration, a feeling of helplessness, and the complete inability to achieve anything by using constitutional or peaceful means, a condition that often finds an outlet in violence; its cause can be closely linked with the still unsolved Arab-Israeli dispute. During the Israeli War of Independence practically all the Palestinian leaders abandoned the Arab population remaining in Palestine and the thousands of refugees in scattered camps, and it took a couple of decades for a new generation of leaders and political thinkers to take their place. Determined to achieve something for their cause, embittered and humiliated, these new leaders were not the mindless thugs of the early days of the fedayeen, but were better educated, sharper, and more calculating, and made their mark by careful planning and bold action.

The basic essential for organized terrorism of this nature is that those who participate, subscribe, or give encouragement or aid must have a fixed political ideal, which the Arabs found in their Palestine "problem." Indoctrination convinced them it was not only right, but paramount and compelling. Extreme bravery and selfless dedication were also required and like the assassins of old, the Arab terrorists had to be prepared to die themselves, a supreme sacrifice few, in any race or nation, will deliberately accept. The Arabs have managed to produce a number, small but sufficient, of men and women of this mold.

Terrorist operations are based on creating and exploiting fear, and the Western regard for the sanctity of human life has played into their hands. All too often, when it was a stark choice between death or the survival of hostages, governments chose the latter alternative, while on the other hand Israel, concerned with its survival as a state, rather than with the individual, took a hard, uncompromising line which usually, but not always, paid off. The Israeli principle of no negotiation with terrorists curbed, but did not stop incidents—but at times the cost was high.

Like guerrilla fighters in the field, terrorists must have a sanctuary, and the ideal is to have the cooperation of an adjacent country sympathetic to their cause, as was the case in Vietnam. At first, almost any Arab country, sensing the mood of its people, enthusiastically applauded the exploits of the terrorist fedayeen and welcomed them as heroes. When the terrorists demanded and, where they could, took license from all national restraints in their host countries, national attitudes changed as Arab governments found that hijackings affected their own interests as much as anyone else's, and so took steps to curtail them. Terrorists found themselves progressively unwelcome, unwanted, detained, and finally debarred, which caused the overt fedayeen organizations to attempt to become "responsible," under cover of which, extremists continued their underground activities. Few Arab countries will now readily give sanctuary to terrorists; Algeria and Libya, and also sometimes Syria and Iraq, are the general exceptions, although on occasions all have handed terrorists over to the PLO for trial. So far only President Numeiry, of the Sudan, has been bold enough to bring Arab terrorists to trial himself, but changing Arab attitudes indicate others may follow his example.

Terrorists need supplies, arms, and money, and caught in the coils of their own anti-Israeli propaganda, Arab governments were forced to praise the exploits of the fedayeen and to give them some help, while other aid was initially widely and generously donated by the Arab masses. As governments sought to control the fedayeen within their countries, they also sought to deny this aid to the underground extremists, which they have done with moderate success. President Nasser, of Egypt, had helped and encouraged the fedayeen, giving money, medical aid, intelligence, and radiotime, to operate anywhere except in Egypt, but on his death this almost dried up. Other Arab governments have been far less generous and more selective, generally only supporting those guerrilla organizations they thought they could influence or control; Gaddafi, of Libya, was perhaps an exception, while external non-Arab aid, such as from the Soviet Union or China, has been infinitesimal.

Nasser's place as a provider and encourager of indiscriminate terrorism has been taken by Gaddafi, who on his own admission has staked many a terrorist organization and act—and seems to be still doing so. For example, in January 1976, he called together three extremist leaders, Nayet Hawatmeh, of the DPFLP, Ahmed Jabril, of the General Command of the PFLP, and Carlos Martinez, the latter fresh from his OPEC exploit, to ask for more similar raids, saying he was willing to finance them to impose the will of the "progressive" Arab states, that is, Libya, Algeria, Syria, and Iraq, on the remaining more moderate ones.

The one factor still in favor of the terrorists is that of publicity, which an open society like that of the West allows, and without which their acts would be largely unnoticed, unreported, and unappreciated.

Deduction

While Arab terrorism, unlike perhaps world terrorism, can be said to have reached and passed its zenith, and would probably have been on the fast wane if a solution to the Arab-Israeli problem could have been found, it was given an impetus and twist by the Yom Kippur War of 1973, which opened it up to wider vistas. Arab guerrilla power has been deflated, not by its avowed enemy, Israel, but by Arab governments, none of which supported a Palestinian government-in-exile, nor wanted the Palestinians to speak up independently for themselves.

International terrorists of the caliber of Carlos Martinez, with a global vision, having penetrated Arab terrorist movements, are now probably trying to take them over and bend them to their own international ends. At the OPEC HQ incident in Vienna, the Iraqi chargé d'affaires negotiating with Carlos said to him, "But you are not an Arab?," to which Carlos replied, "We are working for revolution all the world over."

EDWARD S. ELLENBERG

The PLO and Its Place in Violence and Terror

Background

During the last few years, it has become more and more evident that the Palestine Liberation Organization, the PLO, is playing a central role in the steadily developing international terrorist community. Although its so-called raison d'etre is within the Middle Eastern political and historic context, the PLO has lately achieved the role of the main center of international terrorist linkup.

To better understand how this development was possible, it is necessary to take a look at the continuous Jewish-Arab conflict over Palestine. It was this conflict that generated events such as the establishment of the state of Israel, the Arab-Israeli wars, and the birth of the PLO. More tempers are lost in arguing the Arab-Israeli conflict than over any comparable political issue; they usually expire in ignorance and irrelevance as both the pro-Israeli or pro-Zionist and the pro-Arab or pro-Palestinian refuse to understand each other's point of view and to accept that Jewish colonization of Palestine and Arab nationalism emerged almost simultaneously. On the political scene, Zionism and the Arab national movement appeared at about the same time, but Arab Palestinians needed a lot more time to organize themselves than did the Jews.

Before 1917, the date of the Balfour declaration proclaiming that the British government "view with favor the establishment in Palestine of a national home for the Jewish people," there was no specific Arab Palestinian national consciousness. On the contrary, it was even possible for Emir Faisal, the son of Sharif Hussain of Mecca, who in 1921 became King of Iraq, to sign, while "representing and acting on behalf of the Arab Kingdom of Hejaz," an agreement with the leader of the Zionist movement, Dr. Chaim Weizmann, who was to become the first president of the state of Israel thirty years later. This agreement, signed on January 3, 1919, was "mindful of the racial kinship and ancient bonds existing between the Arabs and the Jewish people," and proposed that "immediately following the completion of the deliberations of the Peace Conference, the definite boundaries between the Arab State and Palestine shall be determined" and that "all necessary measures shall be taken to encourage and stimulate immigration of Jews into Palestine on a large scale, and as quickly as possible to settle Jewish immigrants upon the land."

In 1921 and 1929, the first Arab revolts in Palestine took place as a consequence of the growing Jewish immigration in accordance with the terms of the League of Nations mandate. The British administration of Palestine quelled these Arab revolts. The persecution of Jews in Germany caused an increase in the flow of immigrants, both legal and illegal, and at the same time caused new Arab riots in Palestine. The Peel Commission, sent by the British in 1936 to investigate the reasons for these renewed Arab riots, mentioned in its 1937 report that the desire of the Arabs for national independence and their hatred and fear of the establishment of the Jewish National Home were the underlying causes of the disturbances. The report stated that:

about 1,000,000 Arabs are in strife, open or latent, with some 400,000 Jews. There is no common ground between them. . . . Their cultural and social life, their ways of thought and conduct are as incomparable as their national aspirations. These last are the greatest bar to peace. Arabs and Jews might possibly learn to live and work together in Palestine if they would make a genuine effort to reconcile and combine the national ideals and so build up in time a joint or dual nationality . . . .

The Peel Commission, therefore, suggested the partition of Palestine into a Jewish and an Arab state, the latter to be united with Transjordan.

A radical Zionist leader of that time, the late Vladimir Jabotinsky, who not only opposed the idea of partition but even proclaimed the necessity of a Jewish Palestinian state on both sides of the River Jordan, insisted in 1937, during his speech in front of the Peel Commission in the House of Lords, London, that:

the economic position of the Palestinian Arabs, under the Jewish colonization and owing to the Jewish colonization, has become the object of envy in all the surrounding Arab countries. . . . There is no question of ousting the Arabs. On the contrary, the idea is that Palestine on both sides of the Jordan should hold the Arabs, their progeny, *and* many millions of Jews. What I do not deny is that in this process the Arabs of Palestine will necessarily become a minority in the country of Palestine. What I do deny is that *that* is a hardship. It is not a hardship on any race, any nation, possessing so many national states now and so many more national states in the future. One fraction, one branch of that race, and not a big one, will have to live in someone else's state: well, that is the case with all the mightiest nations of the world. . . . That is only normal and there is no "hardship" attached to that.

This was, in 1937, the statement of a Jew, who had grown up as a minority member of an East European country.

Two years later, in 1939, the British government issued a White Paper proposing the establishment within ten years of an independent Palestinian state, "one in which Arabs and Jews share in government in such a way as to ensure that the essential interests of each community are safeguarded." Both Arabs and Jews rejected the White Paper's proposals. Eight years later, on August 31, 1947, the UN Special Committee on Palestine recommended the partition of Palestine into an Arab state, a Jewish state and the City of Jerusalem. On November 29, 1947, the UN General Assembly adopted a resolution on Palestine along the same lines. One day before the termination of the British mandate, on May 14, 1948, the Jews of Palestine proclaimed the state of Israel. On the next day, regular armed forces of Transjordan, Egypt, Syria, Lebanon, and Iraq, supported by contingents from Saudi Arabia and the Yemen, invaded Palestine in clear defiance of the UN Partition Resolution. The results of this Arab invasion and of the ensuing Arab-Israeli war were the following: Israel, having repelled the Arab invaders, occupied various areas allotted to the never-proclaimed Arab state, increasing its share by some 40 percent; Transjordan acquired parts of Palestine west of the river Jordan (now better known as Jordan's Western Bank territories); and Egypt occupied the Gaza Strip, thus leaving virtually no territory to the envisaged Palestine Arab state. A further result of this war was the birth of the Arab refugees' problem, which brings us to the birth of the Palestine Liberation Movement.

There are divergent views not only on the number of the Arab Palestinian refugees but also on how this Arab exodus from Palestine came about (a problem which I tried to analyze as far back as 1964 in a paper, "The Real Extent of the Arab Refugees' Problem") and why this problem is still very much alive. Whereas the official Israeli point of view is that the Arabs left their lands and homes after being incited to do so by Arab governments and organizations, the Arabs insist that their people were evicted at bayonet-point and by panic deliberately incited by the Israelis. One fact should be kept in mind however: long before the establishment of the state of Israel, many Arabs voluntarily sold land to the Jewish colonizers, thus making the creation of Jewish settlements in Palestine possible. Another fact was reported in 1957 by the London-based international Research Group for European Migration Problems: "as early as the first months of 1948 the Arab League issued orders exhorting the [Arab] people to seek a temporary refuge in neighbouring [Arab] countries, later to return to their abodes in the wake of the victorious Arab armies. . . ." Statements to the same effect were made by the Greek Catholic Archbishop of Galilee, Msgr. George Hakim, now Patriarch in Lebanon and Syria, and by the former Secretary of the Arab Higher Committee, Emile Ghoury.

The problem of ending the plight of these Arab refugees is also the object of divergent views. Thus the Israelis and many others insist that the problem could have been solved long ago through their resettlement outside the then state of Israel but still on the lands of historic Palestine, a view shared also by some Arabs like Ghoury, who claimed that "the fact that there are these refugees is the direct consequence of the action of the Arab states in opposing partition and the Jewish state. The Arab states agreed upon this policy unanimously and they must share in the solution of the problem." But the Arab states and leaders opposed such a solution, preferring to leave the refugees in their shabby camps, in order to put pressure on the world community and on the Jewish state. Under the pretext that most of the refugees are unskilled peasants and that the Arab host countries cannot create jobs for them, even the idea of a resettlement of the refugees in the vast Arab regions was flatly rejected. The real reason for this refusal to find a humanitarian solution to the already thirty-year-old refugees' plight was and still is a political one; as long as the problem exists, the Arab states have a case to fight and a cause to defend.

With their numbers continuously increasing and the misery of the conditions in the refugees' camps growing, the Arab refugees became an easy prey to those who, refugees themselves, decided to make a political career. In 1956 a Palestine Arab nationalist organization, the Al Fatah, was created in the Gaza Strip. The word Fatah, which means conquest, was formed by the Arabic initials in reverse order of "Harakat al Tharir al Falastia" or Palestine Liberation Movement. In 1959, Fatah, led by Yasser Arafat, created the military commando organization of al Assifa which, in 1964, developed into an operational force trained chiefly on Syrian territory. In the meantime, in Cairo, under Egyptian auspices and following an agreement at the Arab Summit Conference, the late Ahmed Shukairy, a Palestinian lawyer who represented Saudi Arabia and later Syria in the UN, prepared the charter of the PLO and became the organization's first president. In May 1964, the National Covenant of the PLO was drawn up, suspending the charter launched only a year before. The PLO was proclaimed as "a mobilizing leadership of the forces of the Palestine Arab people to wage the battle of liberation, as a shield for the rights and aspirations of the people of Palestine."

At the time of its proclamation, it was clear that this National Covenant of the PLO was influenced by the political aims of Gamal Abdul Nasser, who as leader of Egypt dreamt of becoming *the* leader of all Arabs. But Article 24 of this covenant specified that "this Organization [PLO] does not exercise any regional sovereignty over the Western Bank in the Hashomite Kingdom of Jordan, or the Gaza Strip or the Himmah Area." In other words, the PLO did not want to or was not allowed or supposed to exercise any sovereignty over those parts of Palestine that were considered parts of an Arab Palestine state but which had been already annexed by other Arab states. The PLO was only allowed to fight against Israel. The conclusion is a clear one: the PLO was meant to be an organization aimed at pushing the Arab refugees to fight against the Jewish State but not at resettling them in the territory of historic Palestine. According to the wishes of Nasser and of Hussein of Jordan, the PLO was not entitled to proclaim an Arab state on the territorities that belonged to the initial Arab parts of Palestine—as mentioned by the UN Partition Resolution—that were not yet occupied by the Israelis, but was only to fight the Jewish state. Again the refusal of the

Arab leaders to find a solution for a large number of the Arab refugees by helping them to create an Arab Palestinian state was evident. They had divided the Arab Palestinian territories among themselves in an effort to maintain the plight of the refugees and to play them against Israel. And the whole world did nothing to stop this shameful action.

After the Israeli victory in the 1967 war and the occupation of the Western Bank, Fatah retreated into Jordanian territory, making Jordan its base of guerrilla operations against Israel. Shukairy was forced to resign as the PLO's president and was succeeded by Fatah's Yasser Arafat, as the head of the already biggest Palestinian organization. The Seven Points adopted in 1969 by the Central Committee of Al Fatah made it clear again that the struggle was against Israel and only in the second place toward "restoration of the independent democratic State of Palestine." In 1967, another guerrilla organization dedicated to the destruction of Israel was founded—the Popular Front for the Liberation of Palestine, led by Dr. George Habash, an avowed Marxist. The second aim of this organization was the creation of a revolutionary socialist Palestine Arab state. Habash decided that his organization must conduct a campaign of terror directed not only at Jews but designed to attract international attention to the plight of the Palestinian Arabs. The Al Fatah, the Popular Front for the Liberation of Palestine, the Syrian-sponsored Al Saiqa, the Popular Democratic Front, and five other smaller groups, despite their ideological differences, are formally united in the PLO. But each is waging its own war against Israel and acting upon orders of different Arab states. In this struggle, the younger Palestinian generations of refugees are used as soldiers, and their camps have become centers of recruitment.

The PLO—A Revolutionary Force

"Arab regimes for decades manipulated the Palestinian question to ensure class collaboration within their own states and at the same time proved incapable of assisting the Palestinian people to assert their self-determination," asserts Fred Halliday, editor of the *New Left Review,* in his book *Arabia without Sultans* (London: Penguin, 1974).

Ronald Segal, general editor of the African Library of Penguin Books and a noted scholar of Middle Eastern affairs, notes in his book *Whose Jerusalem?* (London: Jonathan Cape, 1973) that:

Al Fatah, the largest of the [Palestinian] organizations . . . claims to have had its beginnings in 1956, when Israel occupied the Gaza Strip during the Suez war. The failure of Egyptian power, even under the leadership of Nasser, to protect the Strip persuaded several young Palestinians there of the need for a specifically Palestinian instrument of liberation. The preeminent member of the group, Yasser Arafat, toured the Palestinian diaspora, recruiting support, and in 1959 the ideas of the movement began receiving publicity in "Our Palestine," a Beirut monthly. They were ideas that the victory of Algerian nationalism over France in 1962, after eight years of armed struggle, reinforced. The ideal of Arab unity, so passionately proclaimed by Nasserist Egypt, had held for many Palestinians the promise of their own return. But the collapse in 1961 of the union between Egypt and Syria made a realization of the ideal seem far too remote; and among the young especially, a mood of disillusionment and impatience provided the apostles of an armed Palestinian struggle with a ready response. The Nasser regime sought to control this response, and promoted the establishment in 1964 of the PLO under a leadership safely devoted to the waging of war by words. The Syrian Ba'athists, confronted by a Nasserist propaganda that blamed them for the failure of the union with Egypt, saw a chance to counter-attack and win popular Arab approval by placing themselves in the forefront of Palestinian militancy. Al Fatah set up its headquarters in Damascus and was supplied with military training, weapons and money. In January 1965 came its first strike at Israel. Fearful of Israeli reprisals, suspicious of the Syrian connection, and alarmed by the possibilities of this new Palestinian militancy, the regimes of Egypt, Lebanon and Jordan were quick to indicate their opposition to such activity.

Fatah guerrilla activities were soon stopped by Lebanese or Jordan forces.

After the Six-Day War and the Arab regular armies' defeat, Palestinian faith in this instrument of restoration collapsed, and Al Fatah represented the one course of honor and hope. The call to guerrilla warfare was all the more eloquent, for young educated Palestinians especially, in the intellectual climate promoted by the Vietnam war. Therefore, the Palestinian exponents of guerrilla engagement found it easy to persuade themselves that they could repeat the Vietnam experience in the Middle East. With exaggerated guerrilla claims and with the help of sympathetic press reports, the popular prestige of the Al Fatah increased in the Arab world. In 1968, the Al Fatah came to constitute a formidable military presence within the Jordanian state itself. A clash between the guerrillas and the Jordanian security forces was inevitable and, when it took place, Al Fatah was able to achieve the status of a state within the Jordanian state. Not only did it acquire its own substantial army, but it gained as well its own hospitals, schools, social security system, tax collectors, and virtually sovereign territory. Its financial resources were already considerable. In February 1969, Al Fatah gained control of the PLO with its military and financial network, winning at the same time the long desired and sought after recognition by Arab governments. But—and this is of considerable importance—it was no longer alone in commanding the Palestinian guerrilla commitment.

Other organizations had emerged to reflect old rivalries among Arab regimes or the existence of a new, deep, doctrinal conflict. The Syrians, for instance, considering Al Fatah both too conservative and too independent, sponsored the Al Saiqa group as a Ba'athist alternative, while Iraq backed the Arab Liberation Front. Far more important, however, was the creation of Palestinian organizations professing a Marxist-Leninist revolutionary outlook. Paradoxically, such organizations were born of the Arab Nationalist Movement, the Nasserist answer to the Ba'ath. Following Nasser's failure to make much progress in the Palestinian cause, a search for an alternative ideology had begun among members of the MAN, and two noteworthy Marxist-Leninist groups were formed: the Popular Front for the Liberation of Palestine (PFLP) led by Dr. George Habash, and later, a breakaway from this, the Democratic Popular Front for the Liberation of Palestine (DPFLP), under the leadership of Naif Hawatmeh.

The PFLP—though its leadership consisted, like Al Fatah's, of intellectuals of mainly petty-bourgeois background—held that the guerrilla war had to be made a people's war, by the mass involvement of Palestinians. Such a war, through such involvement, could only occur if it was directed at more than a mere recapture of the homeland. Its dynamic thrust had to be the socialist restructuring of Palestinian society. Yet, as this restructuring could scarcely succeed in isolation, it would be necessary to spread the revolution throughout the Arab world, the proper context of the Palestinian issue.

The noted Arab analyst, Hisham Sharabi, writes in his book *Palestine Guerrillas: Their Credibility and Effectiveness* (Center for Strategic and International Studies, Georgetown University, 1970): "From the beginning, the PFLP upheld the principle of total war: if Israel used napalm to kill civilians, dynamited homes in retaliation for commando activities, and engaged in collective punishment, then the guerillas were justified in refusing to distinguish between civilian and military targets or to limit themselves to a single kind or field of action. The Front, as a result, concentrated on urban sabotage and on 'special' operations, such as plane hijackings and bombings in foreign countries." This statement brings us to the definition of the activities of the PFLP as being mainly terrorist ones.

Knowing that "fiat spectaculum pereat mundus" (the more spectacular, the better) and having received publicity as never before, the PFLP gained rapidly in Arab prestige, influence, and recruitment through these "special" operations. Certainly, the result was also that relations among the various rival Palestinian guerrilla organizations deteriorated rapidly. The confrontation with the Jordanian army in 1970 and 1971 brought a bloody end to the Palestinians' efforts to overthrow Jordan's regime of King Hussein and to take over the power in an existing Arab state where at least half of the population was Palestinian. It also made clear the fact that the PLO as such was but a formally united front, without a real claim of directing the activities of all the Palestinian guerrilla organizations, though these were (and still are) represented on its Central Committee. But the main consequence of the Palestinians' Jordanian defeat in the Hashemite Kingdom's struggle for power was that the guerrilla organizations found themselves confronted with the need to change their policies and to turn, all of them, to purely terrorist activities, with only a formal claim to real anti-Israeli guerrilla activities.

The PLO and Its Terrorist Program

To this terrorist end they were pushed, as well, by Arab leaders who had their own interests at heart and who considered the Palestinians as useful instruments in the pursuance of their own aims. The late King Faisal of Saudi Arabia, for instance, wanted to keep the Palestinians busy with other problems and tasks, in order to avoid their infiltration into his kingdom. So he started allotting to these organizations huge sums and premiums for each killed Jew or Israeli. Libya's head of state, Colonel Gaddafi, himself a fanatic Pan-Arabist, wanted the Palestinians to do a twofold job: to bring unrest and disorder to Egypt, whose new leader, Sadat, is his archfoe, and also to show the whole world that he has a long arm and can with his oil money and his Palestinian mercenaries do whatever he wishes wherever he wishes.

With the huge financial assistance of these and other Arab leaders—each paying for his own reasons and in pursuance of his own aims—the Palestinian guerrilla organizations turned more and more into what we would call professional terrorist groups. Wherever it was possible, they combined terrorist activities with their anti-Israeli aim. But, as John Laffin wrote, in his excellent article "Murder Incorporated," *The Spectator* (London), 30 August 1975):

Terrorism is no longer merely political and no longer national. Whatever the motives for the establishment of groups such as the Palestinian . . . terror groups, their development is largely dictated by economics and the laws of bureaucracy. Terrorism is big business, with low investment costs and immense profits. On a commercial basis, it is among the best paying industries in the world. To speak of it in terms of guerrilla or commando warfare or as a resistance or social struggle is about five years behind the times. The terrorist leaders are entrepreneurs, and terror is merely the commodity in which they principally deal. Other business activities are kidnapping, blackmail, extortion, narcotics smuggling, assassination and gun-running. Privately, some terrorist leaders will admit to the terror label but their well-financed propaganda departments push the notion of resistance and use the terms guerrilla and commando only because they have a certain dignity in the West.

Like the IRA which found it could tap the wealthy Boston Irish community, various other national groups, the Palestinians included, quickly realized that there is money in terrorist activity. The Palestinians started collecting cash from Palestinians living in the United States, Britain, Germany, Kuwait, and other parts of the Arab world. Many "voluntary" contributions have been paid at the point of a knife or gun. Some cases became known to West German authorities, despite the fact that most of those involved were unwilling to report this sort of blackmail and extortion, for fear of consequences. The PLO and its subsidiary companies are now so wealthy that personal contributions are little more than petty cash, but there has been no letup in collections. Principles are invoked as well as profits, and it certainly would be bad business to stop the cash flow.

"The big money to PLO and its subsidiary companies comes from four sources—direct subsidy by the oil-rich countries, hijacking, rewards for terrorist coups, and blackmail," John Laffin writes. He continues by saying,

For obvious reasons, the Palestinians have so far made the most money. The PLO gets its basic funds in grants from Libya, Saudi Arabia, Kuwait and Algeria. President Gaddafi of Libya provides some $100 million annually, plus generous bonuses for outstanding successes—$10 million for the Munich massacre, for example. Altogether, during 1974, the Arab terrorists received over $250 million in subsidies and they got even more in 1975 (around $350 million), largely to cover the greatly increased budget for world publicity in the form of paid advertisements. Their formal recognition by the Rabat Arab Summit as the sole authority representing the Palestinians (which was first of all meant as a slap in the face of Jordan's Hussein) assured them of even greater funds for 1976. Gaddafi of Libya had also helped in many other ways—thus he ordered that 6% be deducted from the salaries and wages of Palestinians working in Libya. This money is sent to Yasser Arafat. Libya also established several terrorist training camps on her territory and permits her diplomats to smuggle arms across international borders. Not a few of the terrorists are given Libyan diplomatic passports for this performance. In 1975, the Libyan Embassy in Athens, Greece, openly advertised its services as a recruiting office for potential terrorists.

Further, Libya has become the haven for all terrorists captured in action and afterward released under duress and pressure, following the capture of hostages, hijacking of planes, and so forth by the respective governments. When the terrorists reach Libyan territory, with a hijacked plane and their hostages, they are certain to get VIP treatment. Hijacking has paid handsomely. The PFLP, for instance, planned the hijacking of a Lufthansa aircraft for three months, then took it to Yemen and ransomed it for a large amount believed to be as much as $10 million.

Rewards and bonuses are an established part of terrorism. Certainly, Gaddafi is the principal rewarder, but in Beirut, before the start of the still continuing civil strife, it was common knowledge that an Arab bank paid head money—a bonus for every Israeli killed in a raid on Israel itself. The bank, however, sponsored by Saudi Arabia and Kuwait, declined to widen the offer to include any Jew killed anywhere. Blackmail linked with extortion and protection is an increasingly profitable part of the industry. Gaddafi of Libya, for example—as John Laffin reports—paid the Black September group to bring back from Italy a Libyan accused of crimes against "the people" during King Idris's regime. The terrorists found the wanted man, but, as he was wealthy, struck a deal with him; he paid them a certain amount and was allowed to go into hiding while they reported to Tripoli that they could not find him. The Black September Palestinian group (so-called to remind the world of the Jordanian massacre against the Palestinians) had started its terrorist activities by killing Jordan's Premier Wasfi Tel in Cairo.

Contracts are commonplace, but only a few get into the news. Black September and another PLO undercover group, Jibaz al-Rasd, have extensive networks in Europe to do work of this nature. They carried out, among others, the contract for the explosion of the Gulf refinery in Rotterdam, in March 1971.

Having so much money at their disposal, the PLO and its different groups and factions also took a lesson from the United States Mafia and made legitimate investment of funds throughout Europe, thus making even more money. Another very important source of revenue is the smuggling of hashish into Europe. It is common knowledge, for instance, that in Frankfurt, West Germany, Palestinian groups of smugglers compete with Israeli smugglers, among others, to cover the big drug market in West Germany.

The PLO, through most of its component organizations, also started to play an important role in assisting other terrorist groups, and this in both directions—both by giving and receiving, thus playing an important role in the terrorist linkup on the international level. It is known that terrorists of various countries have no great interest in one another's activities, but we agree with John Laffin that "expediency has brought them together." The German Baader-Meinhof terrorist gang and its numerous subsidiaries were really happy to receive the PLO's offer to be trained with explosives and firearms in the PLO's camps in Jordan and Lebanon. They got free training and, in exchange, offered the PLO not only their own services whenever needed in Europe or elsewhere but also transported weapons and fabricated passports for them.

Of even greater interest and intensity at one point for the PLO was cooperation with the Japanese Red Army group. The PLO trained Japanese terrorists in their own camps and used them in terrorist attacks like those perpetrated in Holland, France, and Israel, at the bloody 1972 Lod Airport massacre. However, after this kamikaze-type massacre, when the PLO-engaged Japanese terrorists killed twenty-four and wounded seventy-six Christian pilgrims, it became clear to the PLO leadership that they could not use Japanese terrorists in their actions. So the next terrorist allies of the PLO were chosen from among the many South American terrorists. However, although most of the South American terrorist organizations were really interested in getting PLO training, assistance, weapons, and badly needed moneys, they were less enthusiastic about tackling Israelis in Israel or elsewhere. Even the mysterious South American Communist terrorist, better known as Carlos, is said to have refused to do so. They are, however, cooperating with the PLO on other levels, exchanging information and techniques, and getting money and weapons in return.

We shall again quote Laffin, who believes that "Beirut and Damascus might be the terrorist operation centres, but the heart of world terrorism is Tripoli, Libya. Gaddafi underwrites," Laffin insists, "and directs much terrorism and provides the final haven for those terrorists too hot to be taken elsewhere." This fact has been proven many times. Libya has never refused haven to any hijacker and has never brought any terrorist to court. In many instances, there has been no doubt that Libyan money was behind terrorist actions, although there was no apparent reason why Libya would have been interested in providing it. Laffin even charges that Libya gave away arms, ammunition, explosives, and instructions to the IRA. The fact is that most foreign terrorist groups have a permanent representative in Tripoli, Libya—including the Irish IRA. The main backer of the PLO is Libya. Even if the money is not given formally to the PLO as such but to different Palestinian terrorist groups like the PFLP or the PDFLP it serves the same goals.

Another principal backer of the PLO is the Soviet KGB. A recent report of the West German newsmagazine *Quick* stated that, since March 1976, the PLO has had its central European headquarters in Budapest, Hungary, where a group of KGB terrorist specialists is acting as "consultants" and providing "support" to the PLO, which means money and weapons.

For the PLO and its president, Yasser Arafat, the invitation to speak before the U.N. General Assembly (during the presidency of Algerian Foreign Minister Bouteflika), as well as the granting of status of official United Nations observer, meant political recognition by the world organization, but it did not change the facts. Certainly, the PLO leadership started to speak another language and disavowed some terrorist actions of PLO groups, trying to show that it has become conscious of its new political responsibilities. But on more than one occasion, it was clear and beyond any doubt that the PLO is only a facade for terrorist activites carried out by different Arab terrorist organizations, each with its own aims, means, and leaders, and is not at all interested in speaking out with a single voice. The PLO was allowed to be their official speaker, but each organization was dealing in its own way in terrorism.

Again, especially after his United Nations debut, Arafat had to act to maintain his shaken position inside the PLO movement and to counter the maneuvers of those of his competitors who considered him a traitor to the Palestinian cause. To him it became clear that he had to choose a new platform. What he needed was a territory, a state from which he could operate, not a state within a state—he had such a position already in Lebanon—but a state of which to be the leader. The territory he chose was Lebanon, and this is why the PLO started the last Lebanese civil war. That the result was not the expected one is due less to Arafat's mistakes than to the fact that again the PLO was unable to muster and unite all the Palestinian terrorist organizations under its flag. Each Palestinian organization was acting on its own; it was one more proof that no one of the terrorist leaders is likely to give up his activities without force. What else could give them so much authority, prestige, power, and money? All they need, as a matter of fact, is a very small number of simpleminded, deeply indoctrinated young men, eager to kill. And the arsenal for such manpower is there—the refugee camps. For a few dinars, a weapon, and a free-to-kill order, they can get as many young people as they want. The PLO serves their aims only as a front group that is giving them new opportunities and a new status, but nothing more. The rest—that is, money, authority, and power over their own followers—they have with or without the PLO. Having so many different ideological approaches and aims, they do not accept or need a common political platform. Thus, the PLO cannot claim that it is a political forum for all Palestinian organizations. It is what it always was—a linkup of terrorist groups, using a common front name in order to better distract attention from their real activities, which are of a terrorist nature. It is, if we might compare it with a well-known example, a kind of Palestinian Mafia composed of many "families," each acting according to its own ideals and interests and pursuing its own aims, but united when addressing others.

Conclusion

The PLO claims to be a political guerrilla organization aimed at liberating Palestine and creating an Arab state. It is no more. It is a cover organization for a large and diversified number of Palestinian organizations, sponsored by different Arab states and leaders, each with its own ideology and having in common two factors: the desire to exert power over the Palestinian refugees and, if possible, over the Arab people; and the performance of terrorist activities wherever possible to gain more power and pressure over the Arab people. The PLO's recognition as the sole representative of the Arab Palestinians is another Arab farce—because, in fact, the PLO represents a leadership group of Palestinian terrorists, unwilling and unable to find a common language or a common, nationally stated aim.

The PLO plays a dual role: first, by trying to pose to the Western world as a mature political organization, with "diplomats" and "public relations" bureaucrats doing their work in a really brilliant way by good propaganda; and second, by trying to maintain a claim of formal unity of all Palestinian organizations to protect an image of a national organization, while in reality it is nothing more than a cover front.

Therefore, the PLO might claim it is not a terrorist organization. But, in point of fact, its simple claim of being the parent organization for all the Palestinian groups makes it deserving of being considered, globally as a terrorist organization.

CHRISTOPHER C. MOJEKWU

From Protest to Terror-Violence: The African Experience

It is sad to admit that transnational mugging or terror-violence has, to our general dismay, become the most effective weapon in national and international power politics. So far, neither national nor international law has an effective answer against its use.

Hijacking of planes, assassinations, destruction of property, and kidnapping, whether by individuals, groups, or governments, have been on the increase. Paradoxically, the industrialized and affluent democracies are more concerned, because the terrorists have selected them as targets for attack in the hope that these target nations may use their international influence to secure for them some redress of their grievances. These acts of terrorism and violence, these political crimes that produce psychic fear, by and large, should be looked upon as the normal behavior expected of desperate people in our human society. These atrocities, although highly reprehensible, could be acts of protest which our technological and modern society has neglected to look into at the initial stages.

Speaking as an African about Africa, and on the important subject of this symposium, I must observe as Dr. E. V. Walter did, that the terror process involves three actors: the source of violence or the perpetrator, the target of violence, and the victim of violence. I must also assume, as Allen Silver did, that "men who engage in dangerous and desperate behavior . . . have a certain claim to have taken seriously *the meaning which they see in their acts* and wish others to see in them." We must accept that transnational muggers of today are engaged in dangerous and desperate behavior. In this regard, where does freedom fighting end and terrorism begin? Where does mere protest end and violence begin?

Africa has been the target and the victim of international terror and violence, notably from the fifteenth century to the present. The slave raiding and the slave trade in East, North, and West Africa were indeed acts of transnational terrorism. They were acts of terror in which Africa was the target and Africans the victims. The emotional reactions and the social and political consequences continue to live with us on both sides of the Atlantic and in the Arabian peninsula.

The scramble for and the colonization of Africa in the nineteenth century was achieved as a result of terror and violence. The protests and resistance of African kings and leaders to these unwarranted intrusions and impositions by foreign nations were responded to through the policy of "pacification of the natives" which meant more deaths, more terror, more violence, and more banishments for the African kings and rulers: Bai Bureh of Sierra Leone; King Prempreh I, of Ghana; King Kosoko of Lagos, and King Jaja of Opobo are a few examples of these banishments and acts of terror. The victims were a total people, subjugated and exploited! The Hut Tax War of 1890 in Sierra Leone, the Maji Maji rebellion of 1905-6 against the Germans in Tanganyika, the Ashanti War of 1896, the Aba Women's Riot in 1929, and the 1952 Mau Mau uprising in Kenya are examples of protests against not only alien rule and government, but also violence and destruction.

Africa had learned during these processes to submit to some of the atrocities in order not to be totally destroyed. She had learned to stoop in order to conquer. When protest, which is a legitimate political process, produces violence rather than political redress, as in the 1960 slaughter of Africans in the Sharpeville protest rally in South Africa, confrontation and greater violence are bound to follow. When the national power holders have reacted abnormally to these political processes, the so-called rebel groups, that is, the revolutionary heroes, would resort to terror and violence because they were never strong enough to overthrow such foreign domination by any other means. In such a situation terrorism becomes a technique in the overall strategy to remove the foreign authority and maintain Africa's independence. The successful overthrow of foreign regimes through guerrilla warfare, arson, sabotage, and terror-violence in Algeria, Guinea Bissau, Mozambique, and Angola are classical examples of the efficacy of this strategy.

But what about the situation in Zimbabwe (Rhodesia), Namibia, and the Republic of South Africa? The white minority regime in Rhodesia has continued to use terror-violence and fear as a system of governing the majority African population. Mere political protests have led black Africans nowhere. After several years of torture and death for the African majority in Rhodesia, the OAU and the United Nations finally sanctioned that the self-determination of the Zimbabwe people may be achieved by whatever means available to them.

From the Africans' point of view, the introduction of Cuban technicians and Russian assistance in nearby Mozambique, Zambia, and Tanzania at the request of the Zimbabwans in Rhodesia and by the OAU—Africa's regional body—must be viewed by unbiased political analysts as legitimate, desirable and, indeed, as a humanitarian act.

The establishment of zones of terror in the Union of South Africa and Namibia, the creation of the native homelands or Bantustan in Zulu land are clearly aggressive acts by the white minority government of South Africa to enable it to apply the full rigors of fear and intimidation, which is characteristics of apartheid policy. Police brutality against black South Africans is a commonplace event. The target is South Africa, the victims once more are black South Africans. Violence and fear, causing mental and emotional harm, have been and will continue to be applied in these terror zones where black South Africans will be forced to live and congregate. Neither the OAU nor the United Nations has been able, through diplomatic niceties or through international law, to effect any change of heart in South Africa. The ambivalence of some of the democratic superpowers is simply bewildering. It is therefore no wonder that Africans are skeptical about Vorster's concept of dialogue with African leaders. They are doubtful that it will ever produce significant results to assuage the course of violence—a course which South Africa has uncompromisingly set itself.

A survey of the activities connected with self-determination or liberation movements in Africa within the last two decades has shown that groups that have employed terror-violence were always successful in achieving their objectives: Algeria, Guinea Bissau, Mozambique, and Angola are cases in point. Those who either from public policy or for material inadequacy failed to employ the instruments of terror and violence lost in their bid for self-determination and political independence: Southern Sudan and Biafra, and the blacks of Zimbabwe and South Africa. In contrast, the success of Bangladesh but more especially Arafat's Palestinian Liberation Movement, with its supreme appearance at the United Nations, are concrete examples that international practice, if not international law, recognized the international effectiveness of terror-violence as the true "Real Politik." Africa has the capacity to learn fast. Events in Lebanon and in Angola are object lessons. The greater the terror, violence, and firepower, the quicker and more successful the goals will be reached.

But the situation does raise major issues of political sociology and political theory, especially in African domestic affairs. The ability of African leaders to resolve African domestic problems without resort to violence and terror is called in question. These questions must be asked: Is this terror and violence a carryover of the experiences of colonial terrorism practiced against them? Are these the extension of practices, patterns, and measures cultivated during decolonization and during the liberation movements? We must further ask whether all this terror and violence within the state and between states has come to stay. Is it really necessary? Is this state of affairs endemic to Africa, as some historians are apt to spectulate?

Because transnational mugging has paid rich dividends from the days of the slave trade through the colonial period to the present, one must have the capacity to terrorize dramatically. It is my contention that terrorism—violence and terror—will stay with us and that it will be on the increase until human society learns to listen, to talk, and to compromise. So far, "effective" terrorism wins recognition and friends. Power and influence can now be measured by the size and effectiveness of "the barrel of the gun" and all that that implies.

If we turn our attention to African domestic affairs, evidence shows that

Africans have been the causes of terror systems, the targets and the victims—all of their own making. It is a disaster when a system of terrorism exists within a system of national authority. It is a terrible situation when fellow nationals, who are the trustees and custodians of the normal institutions of power, abandon the use of civil authority and the democratic political process, and resort to the use of terror and violence against their compatriots in order to resolve political differences. The savage violence against the Hutu people by the Tutsi powerholders in Burundi, the disappearance of Ugandans from among certain ethnic groups, the wanton destruction of Southern Sudanese people during their civil war, and the slaughter of thousands of Igbos in Northern Nigeria between May 29 and September 29, 1966, are all black chapters in African history. Such terror-violence, sponsored and encouraged by duly constituted political authorities with or without foreign help, can only lead to more protests, more defiance, and more counterviolence. In the four cases above, the targets were in no position to defend themselves or to respond adequately. The victims were old men, women, and children—all Africans.

But the real employment of power and terror in Africa will come when African states reach independence. There will then be no colonialists to fight. Africans will have had time to reflect on their former colonial boundaries. The Spanish Sahara situation, for example, will be a mere trifle. The major boundary issues will come in claims between Ethiopia and Eritrea, between Somalia and Kenya, and over the eventual control of Cape de Verd and the Sao Tome Islands, to mention just a few. There will be the internal continental boundaries to be resolved. There will be claims and counterclaims of rights not only over resources but also between tribal and ethnic groups.

Comparatively speaking, violence in Africa is as yet at a very low ebb. This is because African countries depend on outside support for the procurement of terror equipment, including common items like rifles and ammunition. When Africa is in a position to produce iron and steel, when it has developed a greater technological capacity, when it can produce its own arsenal, then a completely new power situation will emerge, and a new wave of "violence" will sweep across the continent.

Lest we forget, traditional African leaders and kings have always chosen address names which depict courage and bravery, or take names of animals that are credited with brave deeds and courageous behavior: Ingoyama, Agu, Odumodu, Zaki—the lion! Courageous and brave people were never known to be mean persons. They are fair, generous, and reasonable. When traditional Africans went to war, it was to settle a dispute. Dispute settlement in Africa involved negotiation. Justice in Africa was arrived at through negotiated settlements. Dispute settlement in Africa is not conducted as an adversary proceeding. There are no winners and no losers. The parties seek to be reconciled. The conflict is to be settled so that the social and political equilibrium will be restored and the parties concerned can live normal lives. This African concept of conflict resolution—political and social—has gone with the wind of change. Perhaps, African leaders should rediscover the stabilizing concept in African culture—justice.

Ibn Battuta, the Tangerian, who traveled very extensively in Africa and in the Middle East in the fourteenth century, visited the ancient Kingdom of Mali in West Africa in 1352-53. He observed that ". . . they [the Malians] are seldom unjust and have a greater abhorrence of injustice than any other people. Their Sultan shows no mercy to any one who is guilty of the least act of it. There is complete security in their country. Neither travelers nor inhabitants in it have anything to fear from robbers or men of violence. They do not confiscate the property of any white man who dies in their country, even if it be uncounted wealth. On the contrary, they give it to the charge of some trustworthy person among the whites, until the rightful heir takes possession of it."

Such was Africa in the fourteenth century. What would Ibn Battuta write if he returned in the year 2000? This should be food for thought for the African leaders of our time.

I. K. SUNDIATA

Integrative and Disintegrative Terror: The Case of Equatorial Guinea

The Republic of Equatorial Guinea, the only officially hispanicized country in sub-Saharan Africa, has a total area of 10,820 square miles (slightly larger than the state of Maryland) and a population estimated to be 318,000 in 1974.[1] Since gaining its independence from Spain in 1968, Equatorial Guinea has largely slipped from the wider discussion of African affairs. The state, whose two major components are the mainland enclave of Rio Muni (10,039 square miles) and the island of Macias Nguema Biyogo (779 square miles), has only received limited outside discussion because of the supposedly repressive nature of the government of President Francisco Macias Nguema.

In the spring of 1975 exile sources reported the execution of over 300 people, including former members of the government.[2] Communication with the outside world is severely limited. It has been charged that those seeking refuge in the neighboring countries of Gabon and Cameroon are not safe but are kidnapped, returned, and executed. In early 1975, an exile group, the National Alliance for Restoration of Democracy in Equatorial Guinea, appealed in Geneva to international organizations to "denounce the atrocities committed by President Francisco Macias Nguema."[3] In April of 1975, Martin Ennals, the Secretary-General of Amnesty International, urged the Equatorian president to "take all necessary steps to halt these atrocities which have a profound effect on international opinion." He reiterated that more than 300 prominent Equatorians had been executed and that there are "continuing indications that basic human rights [are] consistently violated."

What brought about this state of affairs in Equatorial Guinea (if the reports are to be believed)? Unfortunately, most of the news emanating from the republic is negative. Little attempt has been made to analyze the factors which have given rise to the repression intermittently mentioned in the outside press. Yet, Equatorial Guinea may very well be a prime illustration of the torturous attempt to build a nation within anomalous boundaries bequeathed by European imperialism.

The republic is a state in which terror has had a clearly integrative function. The terror does not represent a form of African "atavism," nor can its leaders be simplistically dismissed as "racist murderers." Civil terror keeps in check the centrifugal forces which would otherwise dissolve the

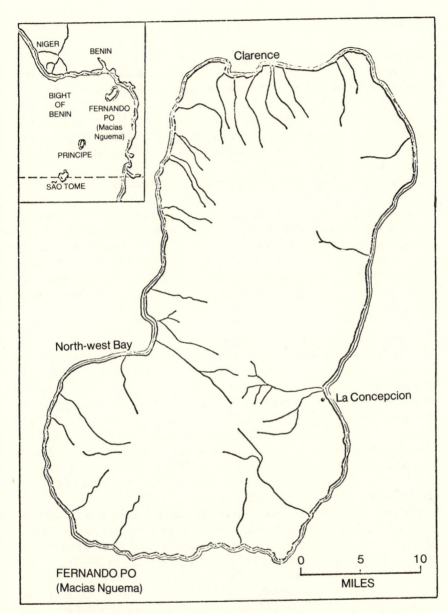

NIGER

BENIN

BIGHT
OF
BENIN

FERNANDO
PO
(Macias
Nguema)

PRINCIPE

SÃO TOME

Clarence

North-west Bay

La Concepcion

FERNANDO PO
(Macias Nguema)

0   5   10

MILES

policy. Equatorial Guinea contains, in extreme form, those problems which bedevil many African states. It possesses neither ethnic nor economic unity. Nor does it possess a political consensus; the country's raison d'etre is rooted in the discredited colonialism of the past. In the presence of a lack of consensus (and until one is created) the rules of Equatorial Guinea must use force as the nation's social cement. Force must also be employed to root out the vestiges of cultural imperialism and to create that national culture which is intended to provide a consensus.

Equatorial Guinea possesses traits which are found in several other states in equatorial Africa, for example, Uganda, Zaire, and the Central African Republic. However, in Equatorial Guinea these are exaggerated by the republic's miniscule size, and peculiar diversity. Within narrow and, perhaps, nonviable confines, an individual and the interest he represents must defend his newly won economic and social position against a plethora of internal and external enemies.

At the time of its independence, there were few surface indications that the relations between President Francisco Macias Nguema's government and Spain would become unalterably embittered or that he would eventually eliminate the members of the ruling coalition which had been put together in the last year of Spanish rule. On October 12, 1968, the Spanish Minister of Information, Fraga Iribane, as representative of Generalissimo Franco, devolved sovereign power to the government of Macias Nguema, saying that it was "the result of a peaceful, friendly, and constructive development" with Franco as its architect.[4]

This seemingly auspicious beginning of Hispanic-Guinean relations was shattered the following year when anti-Spanish demonstrations and speeches by the new president materialized. The great breach between Spain and Equatorial Guinea is traceable to the efforts of Spain and the enemies of Macias Nguema to reverse these "anti-Spanish" tendencies. A former rival of the president, Foreign Minister Atanasio Ndongo, and the Equatorian delegate to the United Nations, Saturnino Ibongo, were asked by Spanish officials to stop supposedly inflammatory broadcasts. After the president refused to heed them, the two attempted a coup. Ndongo briefly took over the presidency, but was soon routed. He and Ibongo were captured. The followers of the ill-fated *putsch* fled to the forest, while the president ordered the arrest of a number of political leaders.[5]

The events of 1969 were something more than a conflict of personalities. They reflected the socioeconomic tensions present in Equatorial Guinea and the problems inherent in the relationship between Fernando Po (Macias Nguema Biyogo) and the mainland enclave of Rio Muni. In 1968 it was estimated that Rio Muni, the poorer of the two major sections of the Republic, had a population of approximately 200,000, while Fernando Po had a population of around 62,612.[6] Rio Muni, with a population composed mainly of fishermen and peasants, had an annual per capita income of $40.

There, as in neighboring Gabon, the predominant ethnic group is the Fang. Fernado Po, together with the island of Annobon, had a more prosperous population, the annual per capita income being $250 to $280 at the time of independence.[7] On the island at least 89 percent of the indigenous population received a primary education. In 1960, exports from then Spanish Guinea totaled more than $33 million, the highest level of exports per capita in Africa ($135). This level was artificially maintained, since Spain bought Rio Muni coffee and Fernando Po cocoa at prices much above the world market price.

The independence of "Spanish" Guinea presented a serious (as was to be seen later) conflict of economic motives and interests. Unified independence would favor the relatively disadvantaged mainland. Separate independence or continued rule by Spain promised to conserve the wealth of the island for its own use (with continuation of advantageous trade terms with Spain). In the year of independence the insular population consisted of roughly 15,000 Bubis (the indigenous Bantu-speaking population), 4,000 Fernandinos (descendants of freedmen landed by the British in the past century), 5,000 Fangs, and a force of 40,000 Nigerian migrant laborers (mostly from Eastern Nigeria).[8]

The metropolitan government had by the 1960s resolved on unified independence for the island and the mainland. A 1963 Basic Law gave the two areas four counselors each in a central Consejo de Gobierno. Opposition to this arrangement was readily evident on Fernando Po where only 5,340 Fernando Po voters voted yes on the new Basic Law, while 7,150 voted no. On the eve of independence one commentator noted, "it seems reasonable to assume that the aggressive Fang (who outnumber the Bubi by a ratio of at least ten to one) will not be satisfied with this distribution of political power, much less economic power, once Spanish rule is lifted."[9] The same writer noted:

In contrast to the economic slowdown and tense relationships on the mainland, Fernando Po is booming with prosperity. The Bubi, who are indirectly benefiting from the flight of Spanish investment from Rio Muni, are disenchanted with continental nationalism. They are now convinced that independence in union with Rio Muni, and the loss of Spanish protection, would open their island to economic and political plunder from a flood of Fang. In the circumstances, this fear is thoroughly justified.[10]

Organized separatist sentiment was not unknown on Fernando Po. In the sixties the Union Bubi was founded under the leadership of Enrique Gori Molubela. The Union Bubi advocated separation from Rio Muni and very strong links with Spain. In 1968, Wilwardo Jones Niger, former mayor of Santa Isabel, founded the Union Democratica Fernandina, a group which was prepared to accept independence for Fernando Po in a federal union with the mainland. An added, but most potent, force urging a separate status for Fernando Po was Spanish economic interests on the island.

Balanced against the centrifugal forces which seemed to promise the separation of Fernando Po from Rio Muni were potent ones which ensured that the two should remain together. International African opinion, as far as it was concerned with Equatorial Guinea, was loath to see Spain remain entrenched in the Bight of Biafra. Metropolitan Spain became convinced that she could trade off the "loss" of Equatorial Guinea for anticolonialist support on the status of Gilbraltar. By the year of independence (1968) there were five contending parties in Spanish Guinea, all but two advocating independence and strong union: MUNGE (Movimento de Union Nacional de Guinea Ecuatorial); MONALIGE (Movimiento Nacional de Liberacion de la Guinea Ecuatorial); IPGE (Idea Popular de la Guinea Ecuatorial); Union Democrática Fernandina; and Union Bubi.

In the late 1960s international opinion, especially within the United Nations, had demanded a quickened pace for Spanish decolonization. A visit by the subcommittee of the U.N. Committee of 24 in August of 1966 strengthened the hand of the unionist parties. Spain had reluctantly consented to extend the invitation in order to counter a proposal by the Algerian Foreign Minister Abdelaziz Bouteflika that the entire committee make a tour of inspection. The subcommittee which did arrive was headed by Gershon Collier of Sierra Leone. It insisted upon talking to MONALIGE and IPGE leaders as well as those of MUNGE. The subcommittee reported to the Committee of 24, which in turn reported to the U.N. General Assembly that the inhabitants of Spanish Guinea wanted and should have independence no later than 1968. Later, in December of 1967, the U.N. General Assembly called on Spain to promise that Equatorial Guinea would accede "to independence as a single political and territorial entity not later than July 1968."[11]

The metropole, moving rapidly toward decolonization before the end of 1968, announced on August 21 of that year that presidential and general elections would be held on September 22 and that independence would be granted on October 12. Thus Fascist Spain, unlike her Fascist neighbor of the time, Portugal, moved to divest herself of her sub-Saharan African holdings before the end of the decade. However, as in many other such situations, a problem revolved around the devolution of power. In a first round of voting, on September 22, no candidate received the required absolute majority: Macias Nguema received 36,716; Ondo Edu, 31,941; Ndong (head of the main wing of MONALIGE), 18,232, and Edmundo Bosio Dioco of the Union Bubi, 4,795.[12] The emergence of Macias Nguema was at hand; MONALIGE had split and the future president was able through a combination of moderation and militancy to secure a power base among several disparate groups. He opposed the draft constitution during the constitutional referendum in August, but campaigned during the election for the maintenance of the union between the two segments of Equatorial Guinea and for close ties with the former colonial power.

One might be able to argue that the abortive Ndongo coup of 1969 was Macias Nguema's Reichstag Fire. His combination of militancy and moderation at the time of independence gave few indications of the direction in which the government would move. After independence the president appointed himself defense minister in a twelve-member cabinet in which MONALIGE held half of the portfolios. The new government also retained the apportionment provided by the constitution: two-thirds of the ministers came from Fernando Po and the rest from Rio Muni. Political offices were parceled out to former rivals, for example, Ndongo and Ibongo. And even the leader of the separatist Union Democratica Fernandina, Wilwardo Jones Niger, was awarded the ambassadorship to Cameroon. The abortive coup brought about a drastic change in this policy of conciliation through accommodation. After the failure of the coup d'état, the president ordered the arrest of a number of opposition leaders, including Pastor Torao (National Assembly president), Ondo Edu, and the Fernandino mayor of Santa Isabel. Later it was reported that all of these men had died in prison, a type of occurrence which later became frequent in Equatorial Guinea. In an effort to crush once and for all the secessionist tendencies of Fernando Po, many Bubi leaders were imprisoned and the president suspended the constitution and assumed authoritarian powers. By the spring of 1975, exile sources estimated that over 300 people had been executed, including eleven members of the transitional government, twenty-two members of the original coalition independence government, nine members of the National Assembly, sixty-seven civil servants and twenty-one police and army officers.[13]

In 1972 Macias Nguema was appointed President-for-Life by the National Unity Party (later renamed the Worker's National Party), the sole political party.[14] At the third congress of the Worker's National United Party (UNP) the party adopted a new constitution which replaced the 1968 independence constitution, suspended since 1971. After approval in a popular referendum it was proposed that the state's structure be unitary, with an exchange of resident officials between Rio Muni and Macias Nguema Island (Fernando Po) and the augmentation of the powers of the presidency.[15] According to a recent source, all citizens are obliged to belong to the governing party and to participate in numerous military exercises.[16]

Supposedly, since 1969 the twin pillars of the Macias regime have been the youth group Juventud en Marcha con Macias and the National Guard. The former has been accused by its enemies of being the Equatorian equivalent of the Ton Ton Macoute of Haiti's Francois Duvalier. Political murder and private extortion have been laid at their doorstep and the same has been said of the National Guard. Whatever the validity of these charges, it is true that the death rate for politicians is unusually high. In March of 1975, the newspaper *West Africa* queried:

Whose body was it which was found in a house in Malabo [the former Santa Isabel], capital of Equatorial Guinea last month? There were reports that M. Miguel Ezegue, the Vice-President, and a close associate of President Macias Nguema, had been assassinated, and that his body showed signs of beating. According to a Presidential spokesman, Mr. Daniel Boyono, however, it was the former Vice-President, Mr. Edmundo Bosio Dioco who died after taking an overdose of drugs. Mr. Boyono said Mr. Bosio's wife had discovered his body, lying on his bed in their house on February 9, with a letter deploring the "attacks and false accusations" against him since he left the government almost a year ago. But the letter pledged Mr. Bosio's respect for "Comrade President-for-Life Francisco Macias." Mr. Bosio had been dismissed by President Macias and some reports say, put under strict house arrest, and allowed to see nobody.[17]

The same periodical later observed that "The suicide of the former vice-president Edmondo Bosio Dioco on the Isla Macias Nguema . . . provides another example of the tendency to commit suicide shown by opponents of the regime."[18]

The Equatorian charge d'affaires in Madrid (his government's only diplomat in Europe) had no explanation of reports on continuing purges in Equatorial Guinea and maintained that there were no more than fifteen political prisoners in the country, ten of these having recently committed suicide. Nevertheless, other sources maintain that between eighty and 100 prisoners committed suicide in their jail cells in Bata in June of 1974 "after their plot to overthrow the government from the safety of their prison cells had been discovered. . . ."[19] The Equatorial Guinean representative to the United Nations labeled accusations of brutality against his country as "products of their [the Western press'] febrile imagination with the sole aim of sullying the name of Equatorial Guinea where their 'masters' [Western interests] have lost the battle."[20] He lashed out at implications of foul play in the case of the former vice-president, "who, for no known reason was found to have committed suicide in a room of his own home where he lived quietly."[21]

The abortive coup of 1969 was the apparent trauma which led Macias Nguema to attempt to forestall any such future subversion through the crushing of opposition. Authoritarian rule was also one means by which to finally extirpate the separatist tendencies which had not been finally laid to rest at the time of the 1968 independence. In 1975 the Equatorian representative at the United Nations cited the events of the post-independence year as those with most significance for Equatorial Guinea:

. . . the thwarted coup of the former Minister for Foreign Affairs Atansio Ndongo Miyone, who was bought by the Spanish colonialists for a price of 50 million pesetas [about U.S. $892,858] and the expulsion of all the Spanish colonial military forces which were still occupying the country together with colonial civilians marked the end of colonialism in Equatorial Guinea and the Guinean people's achievement of awareness in order to direct their own destiny as part of real independence and freedom, as part of unity, peace and justice which symbolize the country and through a peaceful revolution.[22]

Ndongo's attempted seizure of power has fueled the subsequent fear (some would say paranoia) which has characterized national policy. The coup was led by "Men who confused ambition with patriotism, persons who expected something distinct from what they saw on October 12 [Independence Day], groups of people with their consciences reduced through lack of love for their people, carried away with selfishness in order to drive Equatorial Guinea to chaos, selling our people into the hands of a foreign people."[23]

As in certain other central African countries, independent Equatorial Guinea has spawned a "cult of personality" and a program of cultural nationalism. In the Equatorian context these can only be understood against the backdrop of the intensive hispanization which characterized the last years of Spanish rule. In the mid-sixties it was observed that:

More than 90% of all children of school-going age in Guinea actually attend school and nowhere else does one find governmental services and the Catholic Church working in such close liaison. Native cults and aboriginal beliefs are harried with all the vigor of the sixteenth century. African customs are suspect and are harnessed or suppressed altogether in favor of the only true values of triumphant Hispanism: love the Spanish mother country, the Caudillo and the Church. The new urban centers built since the end of the war therefore bear such names as San Fernando, Mongomo de Guadalupe, Sevilla de Niefang and Valladolid de los Bimbiles. Schools, chapels, hospitals are built alongside 'plazas de toros.' In other words, an attempt is being made to bring about a thoroughgoing cultural and political assimilation before it is too late.[24]

It is against this cultural imperialism that the independent government is now reacting. Although seen from the outside this reaction may seem excessive (or even bizarre), it must be remembered that the Franco government's attempts in the other direction were as extreme. It is not surprising that the post-independence relations between the church, the pillar of hispanization, and the African government have grown in abrasiveness. At independence the country was officially more than one-half Roman Catholic. After independence churchmen increasingly ran afoul of governmental policy. Two bishops (Spaniards) were expelled and, in May of 1973, the Spanish nuns of the Immaculate Conception met the same fate. By 1973 most Catholic schools had either been closed or were under the control of the Macias Youth. The forty-one priests, forty nuns, twenty-nine monks, and twenty-seven seminarians who remained in two "Apostolic administrations were reportedly subject to political censorship."[25] By May of 1975 it was being reported that churches on Fernando Po had been converted into warehouses in a drive against "subversive agents of neo-colonialism and imperialism."[26] In July it was reported that all nuns and priests working on the mainland had been jailed, the actual arrests perhaps having taken place in May.[27]

If Roman Catholicism is to be disenthroned, what is to take its place? Although few observers have recognized it, Macias Nguema has attempted to create a national church. As in other such situations, the political leader has been central to the new order. In 1970 the writing of a member of the government adumbrated the later full development of a personality cult:

Slowly like enormous octupi they went about slowly enrolling our Nation in their tentacles of death—'Equatorial Guinea is Suffocated, Equatorial Guinea is not able to breathe' . . . , in this precise instant, in which all appeared lost, there appeared, as if in a dream the Liberator, The father of our constructive revolution. At his side, the National Force, guide of our security. "Juventud en marcha con Macias"—and all the Guinean population rose as one man to the magnetic nationalist cry of "En Marcha con Macias."

Pacific Equatorial Guinea had been provoked and such an attitude wounded our intimate patriotic sentiments. Once on the march we continue and we continue well directed by our Leader [Caudillo] until managing to finally wrench out the colonial nail driven into our Nation.[28]

In 1972 Macias Nguema reportedly announced that he was to become the "only saint" for veneration in Equatorial Guinea,[29] a move which has apparently produced serious difficulties with the church. In July of 1975 it was reported that priests on the island portion of the republic were no longer allowed to celebrate mass. The government said that the religious had shown a "reluctance to read required texts of praise to the President during services."[30] It can be seen that Equatorial Guinea has, like certain of its neighbors, inaugurated a program of *authencité*. Indeed, on his way home from last year's Organization of African Unity meeting in Kampala, Uganda, a member of the Equatorial Guinean government, Sr. Oyono Alogo, declared that the cultural policy of President Mobutu was identical with that of his own country and the president of Zaire was heaped with praise as being in the forefront of African liberation.[31]

The agency of ideological transformation in Equatorial Guinea is to be education (or rather, re-education). Prior to independence there were only a small number of secondary schools (primarily for whites) in Equatorial Guinea. There was a threefold increase in the number and enrollment of primary schools and pupils by 1972. Three higher education institutes had been established; one for primary teacher training, one for administration, and one for secondary education. In that year there were 147 secondary school instructors, ninety-six of them Guineanos. All schools require compulsory political education and secondary schools conduct classes in agronomy. The ruling party has published a text called *Anti-Colonialist Political Education*; emphasis is placed on the centrality of productive labor and the development of a truly national culture.[32]

As early as 1970 the regime was actively seeking to formulate an educational ideology which would obliterate the heavy-handed indoctrination of the late colonial period. The path demarcated at that time (and perhaps modified since then by a shift to the left) was one which rejected the traditional "liberal education" prevalent in the West. At the time it rejected an educational program dominated by Marxist ideology. According to a government publication, there were three ways of approaching education: the individualist-idealist position, the collectivist-materialist position, and "the position that consists of considering the individual, but not individualism, and in considering society but not collectivism."[33] The first position was rejected as being the product of the elitist Greco-Latin tradition of the West. The second position was also rejected, on the grounds that:

The materialist-collectivist position considers education only in the face of society and material goods. It is the position of the Jew Carlos [Karl] Marx, according to which the individual ought to integrate himself completely within a total collectivity. In reality, this theory has never been applied in any country in its extreme conception; and within the purely communist countries the way is opening [for] the idea that the individual counts more and more.[34]

A middle way was urged, one which echoed the "African humanism" so much in vogue in Africa in the last decade:

The third position consists of considering the individual as an entity in [and of himself], but who has to live with a society. Education is for the individual, for his integral development, but this is not unable to unfold itself fully if he does not find his place within the society in which he lives.

The positive affirmation ought to be this: that education ought to have as [its] objective the whole development of the individual, but not only during the years of study, but [also] during all his life. Education ought to prepare the individual for [his] profession and for leisure time. And, as the ultimate end, education ought to expand the development of individual faculties, but not [just] any one of them.[35]

The Limits of Terror

The economic viability of Equatorial Guinea continues to rest on a slender economic base. In 1971 the president lamented that: "It is no secret to anyone that colonial Spain left nothing in our hands except some cocoa and coffee plantations; in fact, a limited agrarian economy. . . ."[36]

On the insular portion of the Republic, the mass exodus of many Spanish *hacendados* threatened the economy with collapse. Plantation work was disrupted and many workers (reportedly 15,000 on Fernando Po) lost their jobs. The majority of the workers were Nigerians of Ibo origin. The satisfaction of the demands of these laborers (a force which, on the island, outnumbered the Bubi, Fang, and Fernandinos) proved to be the prime determinant of the future of its development. In 1970 the Equatorial Guinean government was asked whether or not it would revise the "obnoxious" labor laws maintained under the colonialist regime. Macias Nguema said his government would promulgate a new labor ordinance which would remove all oppressive legislation. In the last month of the year the Equatorian Ambassador to Nigeria, Samuel Ebuka, visited Chief Enahoro, the Nigerian Commissioner for Labour and Information, on the matter of preliminary negotiations for a new labor accord. However, the situation did not seem to improve; on the contrary, it was exacerbated by the departure of from 15,000 to 20,000 Nigerian plantation workers, out of an original total of 40,000.[37]

The end of the Nigerian civil conflict in 1970 gave impetus to the return of workers to their homeland. But more importantly the slowdown in the whole cocoa economy resulted in the nonpayment and disaffection of workers. The Equatorial Guinean Ambassador in Nigeria lamented at the end of 1971 that cocoa production had fallen off because "hundreds" of Nigerians had not recontracted for Fernando Po. He attributed this state of affairs to the dilatory way in which Nigeria contemplated ratifying a new labor agreement concluded earlier in the year. This new agreement increased wages, provided free housing, medical attention, and food, and instituted rigid regulation of working hours.

Equatorial Guinea found itself in the position of a miniscule republic which could only be kept alive by transfusions of labor from a larger and more powerful neighbor. The postindependence series of labor treaties signed between Equatorial Guinea and Nigeria had fallen into desuetude by the middle seventies. The ruling party congress held in Bata (July 9-13, 1973) condemned the continued decline in cocoa production and encouraged the Guineanos to increase production through patriotic effort. In a revised prognostication, published in June, the 1972/73 production of cocoa was estimated to be 15,000 tons. The figure had fallen to half of the 1970/71 level of 30,000 and far short of the 1971/72 estimate of 22,000 tons.[38]

Relations between workers and the government became truly tense in 1972 when approximately fifty Nigerian workers were killed after demonstrating over the arrest of fellow laborers. This action highlighted a signal problem of the Equatorial Guinean rulers. Internally terror might coerce compliance with the dictates of the regime. However, it could not be a truly effective weapon of economic mobilization. A migrant work force can always return home. Force, when employed against praedial labor, was counterproductive. However, the regime seemed unable to successfully shift policy on this issue. Having crushed insubordination among its own nationals, it was loath to grant immunity to the large alien population in its midst. Following the 1972 incident workers again began to desert the island. Only about 12,000 workers were recruited for the cocoa plantations by the end of the year and friction between migrant and local workers was reported. A group of Nigerians returning to Calabar claimed they had narrowly escaped death and that they had been forced to abandon their property.[39]

In the following year arrests and expulsions of Nigerians from Equatorial Guinea caused the Nigerian government to suspend further recruitment. After the expiration of the bilateral labor agreement between the two states in February of 1973, Anthony Enahoro visited Malabo and was satisfied that the terms of previous labor agreements had not been lived up to. In July the Nigerian government refused to send 1,000 workers recruited in Calabar, pending a full investigation and the arrangement of a new agreement.[40] In the spring of 1975, an African newspaper reported:

Douala's [Cameroon] international airport has for some weeks been flooded with hundreds of Nigerian refugees from Equatorial Guinea, writes David Ndifang. The Nigerian Consul on several occasions has been called on by the airport authorities to help to organise the refugees. Many have spent nights at the airport. The twice weekly Nigerian airways flights to Lagos have often been late because of the problem of fitting in the refugees, of whom over 1,000 are said to have been flown out of Douala.

With the exodus of Nigerians who were the backbone of the labour force in the former Fernando Po the plantations, too, came to a standstill. Travellers from Malabo say nationals are no longer permitted to leave the island, and that the entire economy of Equatorial Guinea has virtually broken down. President Macias Nguema, some stories have it, behaves like Macbeth in his last days, as he orders his own bodyguards to be shot for plotting against his life. Mainland Bata, to which political prisoners are dispatched, is called "the land of no return."[41]

Since 1968 Macias Nguema has been able to keep together a state which appears to be both a geographical and economic anomaly. Terror has played an important part in this. However, because of the state's dependence on foreign labor for the production of its major export crop, terror is ultimately dysfunctional. It can keep the state together, but it cannot insure the proper use of labor. In fact, it probably will discourage its deployment. According to his critics, the president of Equatorial Guinea has encouraged the growth of cannabis as a substitute for other export crops. In the long run, force will not be enough to insure the stability of the regime, since it cannot insure the stability of the labor force. As the economic "pie" dwindles, disaffection, even among the Fang associates of the president, is bound to increase. Ultimately, as the amount of wealth that can be squeezed from the existing system decreases, threats to the regime will multiply and those benefiting from the regime will decrease. At that point the instruments of terror devised by the regime are liable to be turned against itself.

Notes

1. United States, Department of State, Background Notes (April 1975), Equatorial Guinea (Washington, D.C., 1975), p. 1.
2. *West Africa,* 21 April 1975, p. 475.

3. *West Africa,* 10 March 1975, p. 282.

4. *African Contemporary Record,* 1968-9, p. 480.

5. *ACR,* 1969-70, B457.

6. Réné Pélissier, "Uncertainty in Spanish Guinea," *Africa Report* (March 1968), p. 18.

7. *ACR,* 1968-9, p. 479.

8. *Ibid.*

9. Pélissier, "Uncertainty," p. 37.

10. *Ibid.*

11. News Brief, *Africa Report* (February 1968), p. 36.

12. News Brief, *Africa Report* (January 1969), p. 22.

13. *West Africa,* 21 April 1975, p. 462.

14. *ACR,* 1972-3, B545.

15. *ACR,* 1973-4, B597.

16. Fode Amadou, "Le Tigre, La Guelle Ouverte," *Afrique-Asie,* 10 March 1975, p. 51.

17. *West Africa,* 10 March 1975, p. 282.

18. *West Africa,* 21 April 1975, p. 462.

19. *Ibid.* This was supposedly the version the government organ *Unidad de la Guinea Ecuatorial* published.

20. Benjamin Ecua Miko, Letter to the Editor, *Africa Report,* July-August 1975, p. 54.

21. *Ibid.*

22. *Ibid.*

23. Buenaventury Ochaga Ngomo, "Nacimiento de la libertad de Guinea Ecuatorial," *Organo informativo del Ministerio de Educación Nacional de Guinea Ecuatorial.*

24. Réné Pélissier, "Spain's Discreet Decolonization," *Foreign Affairs* (April 1965), p. 525.

25. *ACR,* 1973-4, B597.

26. Associated Press, 3 June 1975, Vol. X, Number 22: *Washington Post,* 30 May 1975.

27. *West Africa,* 21 July 1975.

28. Ochaga Ngomo, "Nacimiento de la libertad."

29. Amadon, "Le Tigre," p. 51.

30. *West Africa,* 21 July 1975.

31. Elima *(Kinshasa),* 3 August 1975, p. 1.

32. *ACR,* 1972-3, B546.

33. Ponciano Nvo Mbomio, "Relaciones entre la educación y el desarrollo económico," *Organo informativo del Ministerio de Educación Nacional de Guinea Ecuatorial,* VII (March 1970).

34. *Ibid.*

35. *Ibid.*

36. *ACR,* 1971-2, B504.

37. *ACR,* 1971-2, B504.

38. *ACR,* 1973-4, B598.

39. *ACR,* 1972-3, B545-46.

40. *ACR,* 1973-4, B597.

41. *West Africa,* 5 May 1975, p. 521.

GUNTHER WAGENLEHNER

Motivation for Political Terrorism in Germany

April 2, 1968, at the height of the student revolts, Andreas Baader set fire to a department store in Frankfurt. His explanation was that the fire was necessary to activate the masses. During his defense in court he said that an oppressed minority had a natural right to use any means, however illegal, when legal means are not sufficing. One of his comrades, Fritz Teufel, justified it all the more concisely and clearly when he said: "It is better to set a department store on fire than to manage one."

After a short time in prison, Baader was freed by a group of terrorists which included Ulrike Meinhof. Three people were injured in this action. Meinhof's justification for the use of violence was: "The person wearing a uniform is a pig and not a human being and therefore we have taken a stand against them . . . naturally shots may have to be fired. We want to demonstrate that it is possible to carry on armed opposition and win. Naturally it is important to escape capture. That is essential to success."

Members of the Baader-Meinhof group call themselves revolutionaries and Marxist-Leninists, but prefer the term *Rote Armee Fraktion* (Red Army Faction). They work together with terrorist groups in other parts of the world and learn some of their tactics from them and therefore think of themselves as international. However, they are primarily German and that must be kept in mind in trying to understand their motives. To comprehend the reasons for political terrorism in Germany, one must examine the peculiarities of the German situation.

The Philosophy of the Red Army Faction

Since 1970, thirty-nine persons have become the direct and twelve persons the indirect victims of politically motivated terrorism in the Federal Republic of Germany. Seventy-five persons have been injured in dynamite explosions and an additional one hundred have been threatened with murder. But the various terrorist groups have neither a common philosophy nor any kind of unified structure. Their most important organization is the so-called Red Army Faction (RAF). Its hard core consists of approximately forty members of the Baader-Meinhof group. Since 1972, they have been jailed, although some spectacular kidnappings succeeded in bringing about the release of a few of their members from prison.

The RAF published its program and philosophy in a special brochure titled "Red Army Faction, City Guerrillas and the Class Struggle." According to its philosophy, there is only one difference between the Social Democratic Party of Germany (SPD) and the Christian Democratic Union (CDU), and that is the difference between plague and cholera. The legal Left is clearly helpless. Therefore violence must become the principal method of operation. The revolutionary guerrilla battles in the background where he cannot be touched. He forces others to take responsibility and he demoralizes the police and operates as an opposition force to their power.

The motives of the terrorists are not difficult to understand. At the present moment in history, no one can deny that an armed group, as small as it may be, has a better potential for transforming itself into a large people's army than a group which limits itself to announcing revolutionary slogans.

The revolutionary activities of the RAF are financed mainly through bank robberies. But they do not consider this to be criminal. They justify themselves by saying:

Many people say that a bank robbery is not political. But, financing a political organization is a political question. This is how you solve the revolutionary organization's financial problems. It is right because the financial problem could not be solved in any other way. It is tactically right because it is a proletarian action. It is also strategically right because it serves the purpose of financing the guerrillas.

Violence could certainly not be carried on without the solidarity of like-minded persons. Political work seeks to achieve solidarity. Without solidarity it would be nothing more than repression. All men who support revolutionary solidarity are regarded as comrades. Solidarity is used as a weapon against the courts, police, and other authorities, as well as against spies and traitors when it is effectively employed. Jailed terrorists have tended to become even more radical during their periods of imprisonment, rejecting the philosophy of a free democratic society. The lawyer Mahler, one of the founders of the RAF, stated early in 1972, during a period of imprisonment pending his trial: "Today, to live as a human being and act humanely means to battle against capitalistic expansion and to destroy the bourgeoisie."

In the beginning of 1975, while in prison, the leading figures in the Baader-Meinhof group provided written answers to questions of the news magazine *Der Spiegel*. They drew all criminal prisoners into their revolutionary front. Every prisoner, the leaders maintained, who perceives his situation politically, is a political prisoner, regardless of the reasons for his imprisonment. The question requesting an analysis of the situation in the Federal Republic of Germany was answered in the following way: "An imperialistic center. U.S. colony. U.S. military base. Leading imperialistic power in West Europe, in the EG (European Community). Second strongest military power in NATO. Representative of the U.S. imperialistic interests in Western Europe." To the question of if, according to their reasoning, they are Marxists or anarchists, they spontaneously answered: "Marxists."

However, this point of view is more or less rejected by the Communists in Germany and quite definitely also by those in the German Democratic Republic. Their official organ *Horizont* (horizon) stated in the beginning of 1972: "The Baaders and the Meinhofs are not revolutionaries or Marxists-Leninists. They are disappointed middle class children without revolutionary discipline and without fundamental political knowledge."

In reality the RAF functions as a *Buergerschreck* (frightening of citizens). Its role is certainly exaggerated by the opposition in order to facilitate the launching of an anticommunist witch hunt. The fact is that the German terrorists have been, as a result of their criminal deeds, rejected by the entire population and have even become a burden to the Communists. The Baader-Meinhofs were welcome as long as they merely created disturbances in Germany, but as "Marxist bank robbers" they endanger the Communist reputation.

The Social and Political Background

For approximately two years, from May 1970 to June 1972, the police were unable, despite the most strenuous efforts, to arrest the leaders of the RAF. During those years, twenty and later ten terrorists went underground, robbing banks and attacking city halls for passports, official stamps and seals, and police uniforms. They carried out bomb attacks against police stations, publishing houses, and repeatedly against the United States headquarters in Heidelberg. During these two years, the terrorists frequently crossed the border into East Berlin in order to fly from the East German airport Schoenefeld with the East German airline Interflug to Jordan and Lebanon. There they were trained in Palestinian camps in marksmanship and the use of explosives.

Without a large number of sympathizers, these underground activities would not have been possible. The terrorists received shelter and other help from the intellectual circles from which they originated. The sympathizers were professors, journalists, and other intellectuals—like the fathers of the terrorists themselves. The hatching ground for many terrorists was the German university.

Steeped with the more than 100-year-old Humboldtian educational ideal, the German universities after 1945 did not understand how to adjust themselves to the new situation created by student violence. Traditionally, German students entered a university after passing the *Abitur* examination

(German high school diploma). This was the passport into the academic world. Freedom of instruction and unity between research and teaching had remained the hallmark of the university.

After 1945, reform commissions were set up, but university reforms did not take place. The result was that the distance between the now aging conception of the university and the new demands and conditions continued to grow. The professors barely knew their students. They were remote and inclined to be arbitrary, particularly in the matter of grades and examinations. This lack of communication between professors and students made a mockery of Humboldt's ideal of the university as a community of scholars. The university proved to be an institution which examines everything but itself, and it was incapable of reform.

The only suggestions for reform came from leftist student organizations. From these suggestions arose controversies, and it came to protests against the "Muffle of 1000 Years" and later to violent clashes with the police. All terrorists of the Red Army Faction went through these stages. Ulrike Meinhof's case was quite typical. Two important witnesses of her career were Professor Renate Riemeck, her adoptive mother, and Klaus Rainer Roehl, the man to whom Meinhof was married for many years.

Roehl was the publisher of the leftist periodical *Konkret,* for which Ulrike Meinhof wrote lead articles for some ten years up until about 1969. In the beginning of June 1972, while Meinhof was still living underground, Roehl dedicated a special publication to her, entitled *Documents of a Rebellion.* Renate Riemeck in turn wrote a type of biography, titled *The Truth About Ulrike,* as a refutation that Meinhof had been the chief of a band or that she had been a confused theoretician and a pistol-carrying heroine or even a kind of Rosa Luxembourg.

On the advice of her adoptive mother, Ulrike Meinhof took part in actions of the *Sozialistischen Deutschen Studentenbundes* (SDS—Socialist German Student League) at the University of Muenster toward the end of the fifties. These actions were directed against the atomic arming of the Federal Republic of Germany. Later when the SDS was expelled from the SPD, Ulrike Meinhof became active in the extraparliamentary opposition. But above all, she wrote political articles that were a mixture of leftist politics and sex for the periodical *Konkret.*

In his introduction to a special 1972 issue of *Konkret,* publisher and husband Roehl called on Federal President Heinemann and social democratic sympathizers, radio managers, professors, and ministers, as witnesses for the moral purity of Ulrike. Completely and accurately, Roehl characterized the influence of *Konkret* and in particular that of the columnist Meinhof: "For ten years she greatly influenced an entire generation of all kinds of young people, students, youth officials, ministers, social welfare workers, trade-unionists, writers and journalists. Her thoughts were adopted by students, youth newspapers, by youth groups, organizations, clubs and work groups."

Roehl contends that a cadre of reform politicians could have been recruited. That is questionable, but what is certain is that from those whom Meinhof influenced, the cadres of the radical, leftist student organizations of varying beliefs were recruited. Her starting point was the students' right of codetermination. That meant the administration of the student cafeteria, the student dormitories, and the like, as well as representation in the student parliament.

In a short time, the New Left, which meant anarchist and Maoist student groups, was ruling the student parliaments of ninety German universities. In an election with approximately 30-40 percent of the students participating, the groups of the New Left, the so-called Chaoten, conquered the student parliament and largely dominated the composition of the general student steering committees. The conditions at the universities as well as in the Organization of German Students now became chaotic. The use of force against professors, destruction of furniture, defamatory writings, and disruption of lectures became normal in the universities from 1969 on.

Salvation came less from measures taken by the government than from action by the orthodox Communists of the Moscow school. Their student organization, *Der marxistische Studentenbund Spartakus* (The Marxian Student League Spartacus), first founded in 1968, battled for the leading place in the student parliament, attained it, and then stayed there until 1974 while reorganizing the Organization of German Students. Since then, the more moderate student groups have gained ground. Proportionately, the students' readiness for terrorist activities and violent demonstrations declined. Based on their experience in Germany, the New Left became responsible for the escalation in the use of force until it reached the level of terrorism. But, obviously, one must also question the orthodox Communists' influence on the situation in the Federal Republic of Germany and in particular their influence originating in the German Democratic Republic. It is clear that in the beginning the Communists from the German Democratic Republic actually did influence the student protest movement in the Federal Republic of Germany in every possible way.

Roehl admitted in a later book published in 1974, *Fuenf Finger sind keine Faust (Five Fingers Do Not Make a Fist)*, that until 1964 he had been a member of the illegal *Kommunistische Partei Deutschlands* (Communist party of Germany) and had even received money from it to publish his leftist periodical. Meinhof's leading articles were also financed by the Communists. It was not accidental that the protest movement was concentrated at the Free University in Berlin (FU). The FU had originally been founded as an anticommunist move against the East Berlin compulsory university. However, many students in West Berlin came from the German Democratic

Republic. On top of this, a considerable portion of the students from the Federal Republic of Germany chose West Berlin in order to escape compulsory military service. In any case, Rudi Dutschke, the most important leader of the 1967-68 student revolts, stated in 1975 that it was completely logical that West Berlin played a key role in the student protest movement.

Ultimately, specialists from the German Democratic Republic also aided this development by originating the so-called STAMOKAP theory, which refers to government monopolistic capitalism, which must be overcome. Leftist organizations in the Federal Republic of Germany readily adopted this theory, although no one was certain that it had been imported from the German Democratic Republic. At any rate, its major characteristics do not explain the qualitative jump from the Socialist or Communist camp to the Baader-Meinhof group, otherwise known as the Red Army Faction.

The witnesses for Ulrike Meinhof were also pretty much in the dark. Roehl considers Andreas Baader to have been mainly at fault, not his ex-wife. Frau Professor Riemeck points to the disappointing results of the student revolts of May 1968. Thereafter one could find in Meinhof "the first clues of a readiness to break the law." The last explanation, which really does not explain anything, is that "Ulrike made too many excessive demands in 1968 or that too many excessive demands were made of her."

The Motives

The German terrorists came from the radical leftist students. Consequently we must examine the motives of the German students for the general trend toward the Left. The situation was paradoxical. In elections the German Communist party and the other Communist parties of the New Left combined did not win more than one to two percent of the vote. But, in the student elections from 1969 to 1974, these same Communist organizations were the victors.

This raises the question of why students choose Communist student organizations. The students' answer was: We choose them although they are Communist organizations because they will stand up for the students' interests more than will other organizations. But the real motives lie deeper. They are to be found in a change of conscience of the upper stratum of the educated youth. This change had already been under way for quite a long time.

In the fifties, after the war generation had left the university, a new, young, unbiased type of student took their place. The taboos of the older generation were no longer valid for these younger people. These students wanted extreme freedoms in accordance with the philosophy of a militant democracy. They heaped ironic criticism on the traditional political system. Thus the foundations for the later protest movement were laid down very early.

Opinion polls show that this change in conscience of the upper stratum of the education youth reached a peak between 1965 and 1968. That was made apparent in the regularly repeated question about conscience and ideals. In 1965, 66 percent of the secondary school graduates and university students named freedom, democracy, and human rights as the ideals for which they would consider it worthwhile to fight. In 1968 it was only 18 percent. In 1968 the most named ideal, totaling 20 percent, was "revolutionary change of society," which had not even been mentioned in 1965 or earlier.

Only 35 percent of those questioned were satisfied with the political parties as they existed at the end of 1968. In the entire population, 72 percent were satisfied. However, 19 percent of the students wanted a rightist party and 28 percent of them wanted to choose a party to the left of the SPD or a Communist party. Under these conditions it is not at all surprising that 90 percent of those questioned felt the student demonstrations to be justified. Fifty percent of those said they were justified without any limitations. Twenty-one percent indicated that they would most definitely participate in these demonstrations; 54 percent said probably; only 13 percent said probably not; and 9 percent said they would not under any circumstances.

Three motives for this type of negative sentiment are especially important. The first concerns the conflict between students and the production-oriented industrial society. The necessary abstention from consumption, which is part of the training of present students, is perceived as too rigid and out-of-date. Even if such conditions exist all over the world, German students have given the problem their own interpretations. They are against the "efficiency principle" of an antiquated capitalistic system. Their negative sentiments were demonstrated in the spontaneous founding of a new type of university, a "critical university" without the constraint of being production-oriented.

The second motive for these negative sentiments is the crisis in the understanding of democracy within the upper stratum of the educated youth. After a feeling of superiority in the first years following the war, the general attitude moved to the other extreme. After the collapse of Hitler's totalitarian regime, the German youth were taught that democracy was the only possible form of government and that it was superior to all others. In comparison to democracy, sooner or later Communist countries must prove themselves the weaker.

In the eyes of the students, many events in the East and West shook democracy's position of superiority. In the East it was the scientific and technological inventions such as Sputnik and the space programs, as well as other demonstrations of strength. One example was the building of the Berlin Wall, which the democratic West was incapable of preventing. On top of this also came the realization that the democratic West did not represent *co ipso* an insurance against war and inhumanity. It was not by chance that the protests against the Vietnam war were so strong in Germany.

The third motive for the negative conduct of the students concerns the crisis of authority. They looked in vain for effective authorities in a social order which was determined by the striving for profit. Instead of finding these authorities in their own country, the rebellious youth found them in distant countries with men like Ché Guevara, Mao Tse-tung, and Ho Chi Minh. Gradually the need for authority emerged among the students. These motives for the negative sentiments of the students still do not explain the decision to become terrorists. However, it did make something else clear, which is valid for the entire protest movement in Germany from mere demonstrations to bloody terrorism: The protest movement was exclusively conducted by a negative group. It did not offer any alternative to the democratic order.

This is the point which answers the decisive question about the motives of terrorists. They had no constructive ideas, but merely wanted to destroy. How did they become terrorists? How did they get the Red Army Faction? New investigations in the Federal Republic of Germany were supplying more information about this. Thousands of radical students were questioned. Out of all these, a core of radical leftists were clearly prepared to use force.

The motives, as they themselves identified them, were unpolitical. They actually belong more to the area of psychopathological disturbances. These students became terrorists because they suffered from acute fear and from aggression and the masochistic desire to be pursued. The armed battle appeared to be the right form of confrontation in this situation. It also served as an individual form of liberation. Personal problems and needs provided the inducement. Normally, in the families of radical leftist students the mother was dominant and the father was perceived to be a failure.

The answer to the question of how they became terrorists was amazingly simple: German terrorists were and are basically concerned with the solving of personal problems, be they family, sexual, or professional. The government was felt to be responsible for solving these problems, but since it was not capable of doing so, it was attacked in every possible way. The orthodox Communists are considered *Schreibtisch-Marxisten* (desk-Marxists) and *Schwaetzer* (chatterboxes), who are only concerned with dissertations about Lenin and other academic issues.

The revolutionary battle should liberate one from personal fears. A radical leftist student commented:

Only the seriousness of the revolutionary situation, the possibility of battling on a life or death basis, to attack the enemy and to be pursued by him, can reduce my fears. The schoolbook leftists, the Communist chatterboxes, who would be afraid to place a bomb in their hands can't differentiate anyway between their sexual phantasies and reality. That also means that they will never attain an experience free of fear.

The leaders of the Red Army Faction repeatedly name political and ideological motives for their way of operating. However, their motives and their goals show that German terrorists have no right to that assertion.

Conclusion

The recognition that terrorism in the Federal Republic of Germany is not politically motivated, but is basically psychopathologically motivated, cannot satisfy us, even though the present situation appears to be markedly better than it was a few years ago. The RAF, with a few exceptions, is sitting in prison. Terrorist acts have become less frequent. The more moderate student organizations have been gaining strength in the recent past in student elections. Opinion surveys show that students, including the upper stratum of the educated youth, are now more positively inclined toward government and society than they were a few years ago.

The present situation, however, is far from being safe and secure. The basic problems which led to the negative criticism and eventually to the acts of terrorism have still not been solved. This is true at the university level as well as among the young people. One cannot forget the bitter truth which Montesquieu formulated over 200 years ago: "The coming generation does not deteriorate: it only goes astray as soon as the adults have corrupted it." In the current situation that means that not the youth, but the establishment of the Federal Republic of Germany will have to find the solution for these problems.

ROBERT W. TAYLOR
BYONG-SUH KIM

Violence and Change in Postindustrial Societies: Student Protest in America and Japan in the 1960s

The impact of technology on society has produced a new stage of socio-economic development. In advanced technological societies, the industrial revolution is being replaced by what a group of scholars call "postindustrial society."[1] As preindustrial society was based on the extraction of primary resources from nature, and industrial society was organized around nature fabricated for the efficient production of goods, postindustrial society depends upon the large-scale transmission of knowledge between individuals through cybernetic processes, new telecommunications, and jet transport. The postindustrial society is an analytical construct, not a picture of any specific or concrete society. It is an ideal-type to denote a social framework that identifies a new form of social structure which has a particular set of tendencies: codification of theoretical knowledge as sources of innovation, creation, and productive force; a new character of work which is focused on services among individual persons rather than production of goods and the change of scale in institutions created by the role of technology.

Thus, in the postindustrial society, a new stratification is structured by a service economy, a technologically based industry, and the rise of new technical elites based on codified knowledge. According to sociologist Daniel Bell, the United States, Japan, western Europe, and the Soviet Union will take on such aspects of postindustrial society by the end of the century, and they have to confront the management of these new dimensions.[2] Some scholars stress the advent of the "technetronic age" where society is shaped culturally, socially, and economically by the impact of technology and electronics, and by the bureaucratically structured process of cybernetic gadgetry.[3] As technological change profoundly alters the nature and centrality of industrial activity as a major social institution, capital and heavy industry will no longer generate wealth and productive force. Instead, in the future society, the codification of theoretical knowledge obtained through technetronic, cybernetic processes which are transformed into many systematized forms of physical and social activities becomes the primary productive force and wealth generator.

Critics of the concept argue that postindustrial society is a result of transitional historical forces that can be traced back over a hundred-year span.[4] Postindustrialism, according to their notion, is merely an advanced stage of industrialism and problems imputed to be postindustrial are also endemic to capitalist societies. While we recognize that some conceptual ambiguities exist, as the critics point out, we maintain that the conceptual construct of the postindustrial society is a useful analytical scheme, and as an ideal-type it presents a particular set of tendencies which emerge in advanced technological societies. This paper, therefore, does not deal with the specific historical details of change in advanced industrial societies, but attempts to synthesize the three tendencies of social structure noted above which emerge in postindustrial society in order to analyze violence and functions of conflict in such a societal transformation.

Codification of Theoretical Knowledge

The codification of theoretical knowledge is the growth of the science-based industries of computers, electronics, telecommunications, and optics which were mostly developed after World War II. The utilization of intellectual technology in the form of cybernetics, electronic data retrieval systems, and systems research produce an exponential growth in knowledge. As industrial society was organized around technological efficiency in the production of goods, postindustrial society focuses upon knowledge accumulation and dissemination.

Due to their centrality to theoretical knowledge, the university and the "think tank" such as the Rand Corporation and Brookings Institute in the United States become key institutions. Knowledge is intrinsic to power relations in postindustrial society, and it becomes the controlling factor in decision-making processes, as the technocratic elite administers and manipulates this knowledge.

New Character of Work

Postindustrial society is essentially a service-based society, where work is a socially interactive process between people rather than a relationship between the individual and the machine. In preindustrial society work is extractive and the work force is engaged in such primary industries as mining, fishing, forestry, and agriculture, while industrial societies are goods producing and utilize inanimate energy to engage in the "game against fabricated nature."[5] Postindustrial society is based upon personal-service relationships between highly trained and educated personnel who provide the necessary skills that society demands.

In American society, major structural changes are evident in the shift to postindustrial society. Since 1945, the work force has been transformed from one engaged in manufacturing-related occupations to one where over 50 percent of the work force is involved in service-oriented pursuits, especially in the high skill areas of trade, finance, education, health, and government. While generally blue-collar manufacturing occupations have declined, although blue-collar technical services (auto, transportation) have increased, the development of a new upper-middle-class, urban-based white-collar elite of managerial, professional, and technical personnel has been dramatic. This shift has produced a widening gap between skilled and unskilled, and constitutes a source of violence in postindustrial societies.[6]

Expansion of Institutional Scale

The growth of large bureaucratic hierarchies, the electronic development of the "global village," and the increased physical sprawl of cities are all products of the expansion of institutional scale of postindustrial society. While this tendency is not unique to postindustrial society but is also existent in industrial society, the role of technology and industries based on codified knowledge in increasing the change of scale bears new forms and functions unique to postindustrialism.

The industrial city has given way to the metropolis, where, in American society, over 80 percent of the people live. Large-scale administrative bureaucracies, especially in government, have centralized decision-making, producing a sense of powerlessness among the recipients of their services. In such a process of large-scale institutionalization, the university, the container, the trainer, and the disseminator of technical knowledge evolves into the corporate multiversity. It is this institution which functions as a "knowledge factory to process professional, licensed apprentices for technological corporations, and to do contracted researches."[7]

The three tendencies of postindustrialism explained above interact with each other as the basic elements of the social structure. As shown in Figure 1, the interaction between each of the tendencies forms a web which produces a particular set of social situations along the dimensions of elitism, megalopolis, and the military-industrial complex.

Elitism

Key to the functioning of postindustrial society is the growth of a technocratic elite of managers, professionals, and technicians. It is this group that manipulates the codification of theoretical knowledge and controls the levers of decision-making in the large institutional structures that they administer. James Burnham has developed the concept of management divorced from ownership in modern technological society—as society

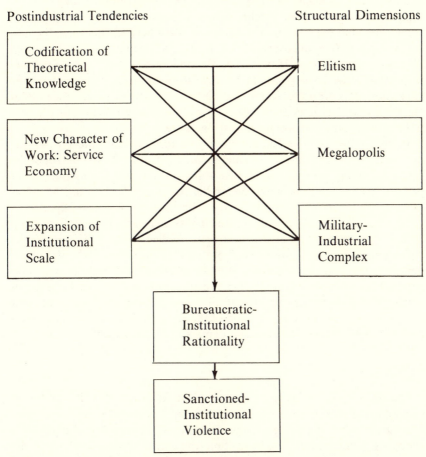

Figure 1. A Web of Postindustrial Society

Postindustrial Tendencies   Structural Dimensions

Codification of Theoretical Knowledge

New Character of Work: Service Economy

Expansion of Institutional Scale

Elitism

Megalopolis

Military-Industrial Complex

Bureaucratic-Institutional Rationality

Sanctioned-Institutional Violence

becomes more complex decisions are made by the technicians rather than the owners.[8] Indeed, in 1968 American stock ownership was dispersed among 24 million people, and high-level management could perpetuate its decision-making control through soliciting the proxies of stockholders to elect their chosen corporate directorship. Yet it can be pointed out that elite management does, in fact, constitute corporate ownership, and that separation of ownership from management is not always clear. As Michael Harrington has noted, "the non-owning managers at the top of society accumulate wealth in the form of special stock deals on profits, investment assets, etc., and must be counted among the golden elite."[9] In fact, a 1967 *Fortune* magazine survey stated that the chairman of the board of General Motors owned only .017 percent of the stock of the enterprise over which he presided, yet this amount totaled $3.917 million.[10]

The technocratic elite is not uniform, but differentiated into high, middle, and low levels. Scholars like John Kenneth Galbraith optimistically perceive that the managers of the "technostructure" defined as the community of technicians and experts moving back and forth between industry, the university, and the federal government, constitute a creative vanguard of a more liberalized democracy.[11] However, as Harrington sees it, the role of the elite in postindustrial society should be understood in negative terms, and the expansion of corporate technology into the university will mean that "fundamental decisions about learning will become a function of the corporate struggle for shares of the knowledge market."[12]

In postindustrial society, therefore, the technocratic elite creates the potential for violence in two distinct areas. First, through its control of the decision-making process and its removal from the direct consequences of decision-making in impersonal hierarchic structures, it alienates the populace.[13] Second, as membership in the elite through technical expertise is basic to attain social, economic, and political power in society, the gap between the technically skilled and the unskilled grows.[14] Therefore, the development of a new "proletariat" of disenfranchised poor who have been denied access to technological codified knowledge through social structural defects becomes a source of violence. Furthermore, the white-collar elites of managerial, professional, and technical personnel who have access to codified knowledge are in full command of the service-oriented productive relations through bureaucratic processes of mass-institutional scale.

Megalopolis

The megalopolis is the locus of postindustrial society. It is its symbol of technological power and social inequality, and by its very nature becomes its central source of glaring violence. The megalopolis is characterized by a sprawling, often mindless, urbanization, the decayed "inner city" slum, the social problems of racism, drug addiction, unemployment, and crime, and the massive ecological problems of air and water pollution.[15] It is managed through office automation in which computers store and process information involved in record-keeping, billing, and mathematical computations, and through production lines consolidated by automatic-transfer and material-handling machinery, and punched tape codes inserted into electronic control devices. In post-World War II American society, rapid suburbanization has decentralized people and services.[16] Since it is no longer necessary to locate near raw materials or energy sources, the industries of postindustrial society—electronics, defense, aerospace, research, and development—have located on the periphery of megalopolitan agglomerations, and this is where urban growth has accelerated. The new white-collar middle class and blue-collar technicians have followed the industries to suburbia and have reinforced the rapid process of decentralization. Consequently, the unskilled, the marginally poor, and the new ethnic minorities, many of whom have migrated from rural societies, have been physically separated from the technocratic elite in a deteriorating urban environment and thus produce the condition of alienation.[17]

Military-Industrial Complex

The public and private economic sectors have merged together in post-industrial society to form the military-industrial complex.[18] Galbraith has noted this development as the essence of "the new industrial state."[19] Partly bureaucratic, and partly industrial, it is almost impossible to detect where government ends and the corporation begins. It is "a new form of corporation: a government-created, government-subsidized, hybrid earning private profits from the tax coffer. . . ."[20] Although in the past, the influence of the American military establishment, hawkish congressmen, and defense industries have exerted pressure on American foreign policy, not until the rise of the Cold War did this develop into an interlocking directorate, joining public and private sectors together. In 1970 it consisted of over five million persons in the armed forces, four million in defense industries, and millions more economically dependent upon them. Universities, through their research and "think tank" capacities, have been intricately connected to this system.[21]

The military-industrial complex is built upon a technocratic elite which utilizes the codification of theoretical knowledge for destructive purposes instead of for life-prolonging needs. The scientists, engineers, and managers who are engaged in developing military weaponry and gadgetry do not use their expertise to solve problems in the areas of housing, education, health care, and transportation, but primarily to promote national technological superiority.

Daniel Bell has pointed out that a major social change occurring in the emergent postindustrial society is resisted by a cohesive force of a "new class" derived from a counterculture reacting against the growth of technocratic society.[22] Such a response to postindustrialism can be understood in terms of the challenge to the sanctioned, institutionalized violence of which sources may be located in elitism, the megalopolis, and the military-industrial complex.

Institutionalized violence is the result of elite control of the hierarchic structures of postindustrial society. It is produced as a response to the interaction of the dimensions of elitism, the megalopolis, and the military-industrial complex to the three established tendencies of postindustrial society. It originates in the application of force by the established authority, the technocratic elite, who preside over the apparatus of collective power (that is, military, police) against the underclasses and the counterculture dissidents for the purpose of protecting existing social and institutional relationships. It produces violence in the form of international warfare through the military-industrial complex, and corporate violence in the form of air and water pollution, and natural resource waste. Latently, there appears a sociopsychological form of violence caused by the theories of the "culture of poverty," racism, and genetic inferiority.[23]

One of the reactions against sanctioned, institutionalized violence is the student activism which arose in the 1960s in the United States and Japan. These student revolts can best be understood as a violent expression of frustration at their powerlessness in decision-making in the university and their lack of control over a destiny engineered more and more by a political-military-industrial technocracy.[24] One of the causal factors of such a deep sense of frustration is perhaps best explained by the concept of alienation.[25] On a sociological level, one can attempt to explain this state by an analysis of the process which affects an individual's relationship to his work and his social relationship with objects and other human beings. Alienation in post-industrial society then, is the feeling of estrangement caused by increased mechanization, bureaucratization, and impersonalization of society. Such estrangement is derived from reification, a social process through which individuals are forced by social conditions to view themselves and others as impersonal objects or things, and thus, lose their personal self-identity. As Karl Marx noted, the transformation of all activities and products into exchange values reduces the individual human being into a mere commodity, and such a transformation is the process of reification.[26]

In postindustrial society, man is dominated by a bureaucratic system of technocratic elites, controlled by the sanctioned-institutional violence of the military-industrial complex. Moreover, he is overwhelmed by various social problems of megalopolis. The domination of society over the individual through such bureaucratic processes tends to adopt totalitarian form. The totalitarian form of the societal dominance occurs through the use of technetronic and cybernetic manipulative control over man, thereby creating a state of alienation.

Reified individuals confront a fundamental question: Is man's fate irrevocably determined by technocratic bureaucracy? Is man doomed to become the slave or a cog or a "cheerful robot" of machines and mythified community? As shown in Figure 2, cohesion of the counterforce represents a possibility in the face of the totalitarian control of the reifying bureaucracy. The counterforce is based upon self-consciousness with clear awareness of reified social reality and mythified community. In recent history, such a force was illustrated by student activism, particularly in the United States and Japan.

An analysis of the American student movement indicates that three themes of protest are prevalent: nonviolent, issue-oriented protest; anti-

Figure 2. Reified Process of Postindustrial Society

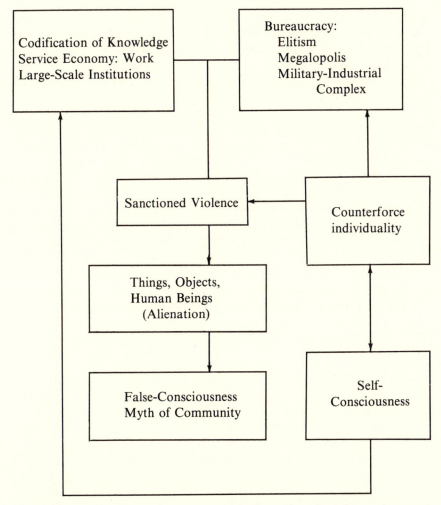

hierarchic, antibureaucratic protest; and disanctioned-confrontation pro-test. Each theme can be viewed along a continuum of escalating counterforce violence in the sixties and is equivalent chronologically to the beginning, middle, and end of the decade.

Nonviolent, issue-oriented protest represents one significant theme of the student movement and was most characteristic of the period of the early sixties. Its idealism was manifested in the presidency of John F. Kennedy, in the social policies of the Peace Corps and the "war on poverty," and its protest was labeled on the nonviolent techniques of social action contained in the civil rights movement. While the student response to alienation was individualized in the 1950s, the student activists of the early sixties sought a collectivized response to the alienation-producing bureaucracies of post-industrial society through specific, concrete examples of social action. They inveighed against racial injustice and segregation through the civil rights movement, they sought peace through nuclear arms control, and they campaigned for the elimination of poverty and social inequality through a more just distribution of wealth. Generally optimistic concerning the responsiveness of authorities to protest, and believing that social criticism could promote constructive social change, student activists engaged in the process of institutionalized politics, often supporting liberal Democratic party candidates to elected office.[27]

The second major theme of the student movement was a direct response to the bureaucratization and increased institutional scale of postindustrial society. The formation of the Students for Democratic Society in 1962 was organized on the vision of a "participatory democracy," where technology and mass education would create new forms of decentralization where people who were alienated from power would develop mechanisms of decision-making and community involvement. In the Port Huron statement, the SDS noted:

We regard men as infinitely precious and possessed of unfulfilled capacities for reason, freedom, and love. In affirming these principles we are aware of countering perhaps the dominant conceptions of man in the 20th century: that he is a thing to be manipulated, and that he is inherently incapable of directing his own affairs. . . ."[28]

It is this populist, egalitarian ideology asserted through the SDS that was to emerge as a central theme of counterculture protest. It emphasized the notion that the true value of society rested with the people and not with the elites, or as Jerome Skolnick aptly states: ". . . it seeks to undermine deferential attitudes towards authority by asserting anti-hierarchial and democratic principles; it defends the rejection of conventional values by celebrating the idea of free expression and individualism."[29]

As the technology of postindustrialism manifested itself in the centralization of political life, the increasing social and economic domination by giant corporate bureaucracies, and the militarization of American life, the ideological counterforce to sanctioned-institutional violence emerged in the student protest movement. Charles Reich referred to this "counterculture protest" as seeking "to transcend science and technology to restore them to their proper place as tools of man rather than as the determinants of man's existence."[30] From an historical perspective, it developed most significantly in the Free Speech Movement at the University of California, Berkeley, in 1964 and at Columbia University in 1968.[31]

By probing the question of the role of the multiversity in postindustrial society, the student movement by the mid-sixties reflected the key influence that this bureaucracy played in society as educator of the technocratic elite. It was the dichotomy between the nature of the university as a "knowledge factory" for the sanctioned violence of postindustrial society which brought the student movement into close scrutiny of the multiversity.

At Berkeley, the FSM developed as a result of the ban that a rigid, archaic administration placed on students who used the campus to advocate off-campus social or political activity. Protesting this restriction, students seized and occupied an administration building and were forcibly removed by the police who were called in by the administration to arrest the students. At Columbia, a similar protest and bureaucratic response occurred. The student protest at Columbia centered around three causes: an unresponsive and highly structured administration drawn from the world of business and finance, who were influenced by corporate interests and the military; a lack of concern for undergraduate teaching and a perceived irrelevant curriculum; and the physical extension of Columbia into the surrounding impoverished black community without consultation of that community.

In both the Berkeley and Columbia actions, student radicals noted the politization of the scientific and technological functions of the university. A Columbia student leader stated: "We see the university as a factory whose goal is to produce trained personnel for the corporations, government, and more universities, and knowledge of the uses of business and government to perpetuate the present system."[32] The multiversity and the bureaucracies of the public and private sector merged, as the large universities functioned due to the research grants provided by governmental agencies and industrial corporations, and the latter functioned as a result of the expert personnel and laboratories provided by the multiversity. Hence, it was the recognition of the non-neutral nature of the university and its implication in furthering the status-quo sanctioned violence of racial injustice and international war in Vietnam that provoked the student occupation of university buildings in the middle and late sixties. The university became the conflict arena over the questions of what kinds of services it should provide, and to whom these services should be provided—to the underclasses to improve their quality of life, or to the technocratic elite to maintain their ruling power.

The third theme of the student protest movement was the desanctioning of institutional violence through a process of delegitimation of elite authority, and the increased resort to counterviolence and confrontation by student radicals. This process occurred as alienation increased and as the realization dawned that channels of nonviolent change were blocked. The failure of domestic social programs to eliminate poverty, racism, and social inequality and to aid the deteriorating cities, and the escalation of the Vietnam war tended to radicalize the student protest movement. When university administrators responded to protest with force and bureaucratic intransigence, the results were a counterforce and violence on the part of the student activists. At Columbia in 1968, when the university bureaucracy resorted to police intervention, it established a counterbelief on the part of student radicals that sactioned violence was illegitimate and should be resisted. Political violence at Columbia radicalized the student body, as Daniel Bell describes:

> In all, about a hundred students were hurt. But it was not the violence itself that was so horrible. Despite the many pictures of bleeding students, not one required hospitalization. It was the capriciousness of that final action. The police simply ran wild.[33]

When student activists went to the Democratic Party Convention in Chicago in 1968 to protest American involvement in Vietnam, the same response and resistance to protest were registered by the city bureaucracy, and resulted in what a citizens' investigatory committee called an extreme example of police violence. Other examples of this same process can be noted in Kent State and Jackson State. Hence, the American student movement in the 1960s developed as a result of a rising resistance to the sanctioned violence produced by the bureaucracies of elitism, megalopolis, and the military-industrial complex in postindustrial society.[34]

Another historical illustration of a new force which reacted against the sanctioned violence of postindustrialism can be observed in Japanese student activism of the late 1960s. It is true that Japanese postindustrial tendencies are not as clear as those we have observed in the United States. However, Japan can be considered as a society which has experienced elements of postindustrialism with her rapidly expanding large-scale institutions, new character of work which is oriented more and more toward a service economy, increased reliance on codification of knowledge based on electronic gadgetry, uncontrollable urban sprawl, and the continued influence of the United States military-industrial complex.

Faced with such an emergence of postindustrial society, Japanese students in the late 1960s reacted violently against the established forces of bureaucracy. In the 1967-68 academic year, campus disputes arose in nearly 200 universities which would be just about half of the total number of four-year colleges and universities in Japan at that time.[35] Nearly 34,000 freshmen could not start classes in the spring of 1968, and there were no graduations in most universities. Sixty-nine universities were still partially barricaded and closed by the students in the summer of 1969. These troubled institutions included almost all of Japan's most prestigious universities—Tokyo, Kyoto, Kyushu, Waseda, Keio, Nihon, and Sophia. One of the most serious campus revolts arose in Tokyo University when medical students protested the outdated methods of intern training. Many students joined with radical students in occupying the main university buildings and stayed behind their barricades for seven months until an 8,500-man riot police force drove them out after two days of battle.[36] After the Tokyo University revolt, almost all of the major universities had disputes and disturbances, and these revolts lasted for about three years.

The immediate stated reasons and purposes of the revolt and protest were different from campus to campus. Some were caused by a tuition hike, inadequate facilities, or the inhumane traditional way of intern training. In other cases, some communist radicals might have wanted to destroy the entire university system; still others might have simply wanted to see an inefficient curriculum changed. However, the Japanese student revolt may be characterized in terms of two closely related efforts of students: a search for self-identity through violent means and a search for a new concept of university.

First, their violent action might be understood in light of the fact that they were in the midst of an identity crisis, and they wanted to find a self-identity through whatever available means. The urgency and seriousness of this crisis was clearly shown in a diary written by a Kyoto University student who was killed during one of the earlier street demonstrations. He wrote the following a few days before his death:

I came into existence 18 years and 10 months ago. What have I done to live during this period? I can feel no sense of responsibility, either for the present or for the future. I constantly find myself doubtful, if not indifferent, and I borrow others' words to defend myself. What on earth am I?[37]

This student was the first casualty in the Japanese student revolt.

What then was the source of such an identity crisis? Japanese youth in the midst of economic prosperity sensed that they were betrayed and cheated by the older generation in the political, educational, and business establishments. They felt that they were being processed in the educational factory by rules and methods which were designed and tailored by the government and the school administrators. They thought that the establishment provided tailored guidelines and requirements in order to produce the most efficient tools or compartmentalized specialists for the creation and maintenance of national economic and political power. Students asked: "What is the meaning of these goods and luxuries for us? More leisure and more consumption for what?" After such a struggle to gain admittance to the university, all they learned seemed to be the irrelevant lecture notes of professors who loyally followed the traditional methods and guidelines printed by the bureaucratic government. Thus, students were lost in the midst of material abundance which was accomplished through the emergent postindustrial techniques, and cried out searchingly for self-identity.

Second, their violent reaction was caused by the rapidly expanded scale of the educational institution. In the history of the modern university in Japan since the Meiji Restoration, the major goals of higher learning were directly incorporated into the national policy for economic and military establishment. However, Japan's military revolution was a total failure when she was defeated in World War II. Yet, Japan has amazingly succeeded in its economic revolution. In only twenty-four years since the end of the war, Japan has become one of the strongest economic powers in the world. In 1970, it was the second-largest producer in the free world, and with an active expansion of foreign markets, especially in the United States and in East and Southeast Asia and including the People's Republic of China, its GNP continues to rise by more than 10 percent yearly. The United States trade deficit with Japan in 1972 was $3.2 billion.[38]

Behind this brilliant economic success, there was a rigid educational system focused on business establishment and market expansion for the service economy. As a Japanese professor put it, the goal of Japanese education was mainly "catching up with the great economic giants of the West."[39] Now, while students enjoyed their economic prosperity, they no longer wanted to be educated to become high-quality technicians, that is, compartmentalized specialists for the maintenance of the bureaucratic establishment.

In the midst of such a conceptual confusion of university education, students strongly proposed a new concept of university. They declared: "We are free to choose what we want to study, free to make decisions on university policy, free to occupy the building or even to destroy it, if it is necessary, as the building itself is not the university."[40] With such a conviction, they wanted to destroy the established authority of the government and of the university administration and some part of the faculty. In this sense, the student revolt was a deauthorization movement.

On another level, the ambiguity of institutional processes created an alienated condition in which the students were situated. Before World War II, there existed an accepted philosophy of higher education in Japan, the Humboldt doctrine, which was based on German idealism supported by an elaborate theory of transcendental ethics. The Humboldt doctrine strongly held that the university is the center of learning which exists for the purpose of educating the social elite. After the war, the American system of mass university education replaced this approach. Although there was a massive increase in student enrollment, the old doctrine of elite education still dominated the postwar university in Japan. In other words, there was no clear educational value system which could cope with the newly expanded mass educational institutionalized patterns. In consequence, such a situation created a serious cultural lag and anomie, in which students were alienated and confused and were searching out new concepts of university. Thus, it may be stated that the student revolt was unavoidable in the absence of an alternative value system which was functionally applicable to the mass, large-scale educational institution controlled by bureaucratic-instrumental rationality. Thus, it was a struggle against emergent post-industrialism.

The Japanese university students were engaged in the protest movement against technocratic irrelevance of their life situation. Their revolt can be seen as a beginning of the violent expression of postindustrial despair. It is a counterrevolution, that is, a reaction against the gasp of the dying order in the emergence of postindustrial society.

In conclusion, the three tendencies of postindustrial society—the theoretical codification of knowledge, the new character of work, and the expansion of institutional scale—have created three sources of bureaucracy in elitism, the megalopolis, and the military-industrial complex. These bureaucracies create both alienation and sanctioned-institutional violence. Postindustrial alienation creates two forms of behavior: one establishes a false-consciousness through social-psychological myths which rationalize existing social structural relationships and social conditions, and the other creates a consciousness built upon individuality and constitutes the foundation for counterforce conflict against the sanctioned violence of postindustrial bureaucracies. The result is a complete social system, where conflict generated through the interaction of counterforce protest and bureaucracy creates innovation and social change which loops back to reflect a change in the basic nature of postindustrial society.

Notes

1. Much research and popular writing has been devoted to the concept of the postindustrial society. The most comprehensive work has been Daniel Bell's *The Coming of Post-Industrial Society* (New York: Basic Books, 1973). Others include: Zbegniew Brzezinski, *Between Two Ages: America's Role in the Technetronic Era* (New York: Viking, 1970); Herman Kahn and Anthony Wiener, *The Year Two Thousand* (New York: Macmillan, 1967) and Robert L. Heilbroner, "Economic Problems of a 'Postindustrial' Society," *Dissent* (Spring 1973), pp. 163-176.

2. Bell, *The Coming of Post-Industrial Society,* p. 483.

3. Besides Bell, Brzezinski, Kahn and Wiener, and Heilbroner, see: Alvin Toffler, *Future Shock* (New York: Random House, 1970), and *The Futurists* (New York: Random House, 1972); John Rasmussen, *The New American Revolution: the Dawning of the Technetronic Era* (New York: John Wiley, 1972); N. Wiener, *God and Golem, Inc.* (New York: Macmillan, 1964) and Marshall McLuhan, *Understanding Media: the Extensions of Man* (New York: McGraw Hill, 1964).

4. See social historian Peter Stern's criticism of the concept in "Is there a Post-Industrial Society?" *Society,* XI, IV (May/June 1974), pp. 10-22.

5. Bell, *The Coming of the Post-Industrial Society,* p. 116.

6. See Victor Fuchs, *The Service Economy* (New York: Columbia University, 1968).

7. Standard works on the rise of the American metropolis are: Blake McKelvey, *The Emergence of Metropolitan America* (New Brunswick: Rutgers, 1968); John

Bollens and Henry Schmandt, *The Metropolis* (New York: Harper, 1970, 2d ed.), and Sam Warner, *The Urban Wilderness* (New York: Harper, 1972). Paul Goodman's "Thoughts on Berkeley" in S. M. Lipset and S. S. Wolin, eds., *The Berkeley Student Revolt* (Garden City: Doubleday, 1965) analyzes the role of the multiversity in post-industrial society.

8. See James Burnham, *Managerial Revolution* (Bloomfield: Indiana University, 1960).

9. Michael Harrington, "Old Working Class, New Working Class," *Dissent* (Winter 1972), p. 332.

10. *Ibid*, p. 331.

11. See John Kenneth Galbraith, *The New Industrial State* (Boston: Houghton Mifflin, 1967). For a review of the Galbraith-Bazelon version of the "new class" theory and the creative function of elites see Christopher Lasch, *The Agony of the American Elite* (New York: Vintage, 1969), pp. 188-204.

12. Michael Harrington, *Toward a Democratic Left* (New York: Macmillan, 1968), p. 90.

13. Bell, *The Coming of Post-Industrial Society,* p. 129.

14. Lasch, *The Agony of the American Left,* p. 174.

15. See Jean Gottman, *Megalopolis* (Cambridge: M.I.T., 1961).

16. See Louis Masoti and Jeffrey Hodden, eds., *The Urbanization of the Suburbs* (Beverly Hills: Sage, 1973).

17. Lasch, *The Agony of the American Left,* p. 174.

18. General works on the military-industrial complex are: Sidney Lens, *The Military-Industrial Complex* (Philadelphia: United Church, 1970); Richard Barnet, *The Economy of Death* (New York: Atheneum, 1969); William Proxmire, *Report From Wasteland: America's Military-Industrial Complex* (New York: Praeger, 1970), and Carroll W. Purcell, *The Military-Industrial Complex* (New York: Harper, 1972).

19. See Galbraith, *The New Industrial State,* and Walter Adams, "The Military-Industrial Complex and the New Industrial State," *American Economic Review,* LVII (May 1968), pp. 652-665.

20. Sanford Gottlieb, "A State Within a State," *Dissent* (October 1971), p. 493.

21. *Ibid.,* p. 492.

22. Bell, *The Coming of Post-Industrial Society,* p. 118.

23. For a detailed analysis of the "culture of poverty" concept see C. A. Valentine, *Culture and Poverty: Critique and Counter-Proposals* (Chicago: University of Chicago, 1968). A conservative interpretation of the "culture of poverty" is contained in Edward Banfield's *The Unheavenly City* (Boston: Little, Brown and Co., 1970), and the theories of genetic inferiority are posited in Arthur Jensen's "How Much Can We Boost I.Q. and Scholastic Achievement"? *Harvard Educational Review,* XXXIX, I (Winter 1969), pp. 1-123, and Richard Herrnstein's "I.Q." *Atlantic,* CCXXVIII (December 1971), pp. 43-58.

24. See Paul Jacobs and Saul Landau, *The New Radicals* (New York: Random House, 1966).

25. M. Seeman, "On the Meaning of Alienation," *American Sociological Review,* XXVI (1961), pp. 753-758.

26. Karl Marx, *Grundrisse der Kritik Politischen Okonomie* (Berlin: Dietz Verlag, 1953).

27. See Jerome Skolnick, *The Politics of Power* (New York: Ballantine, 1969), pp. 79-124.

28. M. Cohen and D. Hale, *The New Student Left* (Boston: Beacon Press, 1967), p. 12.

29. Skolnick, *The Politics of Power,* p. 84.

30. Charles Reich, *The Greening of America* (New York: Bantam, 1971), p. 383.

31. Nelson Blake, *A History of American Life and Thought* (New York: McGraw Hill, 1972), pp. 638-644.

32. Skolnick, *The Politics of Power,* p. 100.

33. Daniel Bell, "Columbia and the New Left," *Public Interest* (Fall 1968), p. 81.

34. See Daniel Walker, *Rights in Conflict* (New York: New American Library, 1969), and James Michener, *Kent State* (New York: Random House, 1971).

35. Mychio Nagi, "University Problems in Japan," *Bulletin,* XXIII (Tokyo: International House of Japan, Inc., 1969), p. 1.

36. *Asahi Shimbun,* 19 August 1969.

37. *Jo Kyo,* Special Edition: "Revolt is Spreading," (Tokyo, Jo Kyo Sa, 1968).

38. For a detailed discussion on this point see B. S. Kim, "Student Activism in Korea and Japan: A Comparative Analysis," *Asian Journal of Columbia University,* I, I (1973), pp. 3-13.

39. Professor Yama Oaka of Waseda University, Tokyo, made this remark at his lecture to American students of the Summer Seminar on Student Activism in Tokyo, August 1969.

40. Interviews with students revolting at Waseda, International Christian, and Tokyo Universities conducted by B. S. Kim in August 1969.

PART III

Some Psychological Aspects of International Terrorism

PART II.

Some Experimental Reports on
Rats, Cats, and Porpoises

JOSEPH A. DOWLING

Prolegomena to a Psychohistorical Study of Terrorism

A serious handicap for those interested in psychohistory is the seemingly compulsive need to justify or rationalize their efforts in acceptable philosophical and methodological terms. This syndrome is of course endemic in all academic fields, but the disease is most acute in so-called interdisciplinary areas. It is doubtful, for example, that American studies can survive another paper on "What Is American Studies?"

Similarly, sessions on psychohistory often lapse into covert or overt debates on the nature of historical knowledge, a thorny enough problem, and are then further exacerbated by the warfare of competing psychological and psychoanalytical schools. John Demos, at an OAH panel, raised the question of relying on psychological theories subsequently abandoned by the originators. My feeling then and now is that one stays with the explanatory system most satisfactorily suited to the historically observed phenomena. To put it more bluntly, theoretical formulations gain credence from the evidence uncovered in historical digging. As H. Stuart Hughes asserts, "An interpretation ranks as satisfactory not by passing some formal scientific test but by conveying an inner conviction . . . a thread of inner logic that will tie together an apparent chaos of random words and action."[1] Thus the historian who finds particular psychological or psychoanalytical insight satisfactory in supplying this "inner conviction" should not be deterred by internecine clinical dispute. Lifton has noted that most of the development in psychohistory has come from the psychological direction, but he also notes that "psychohistory could be an avenue toward the revitalization of psychoanalysis itself. . . ."[2] Although Lifton means this in a somewhat different way than will be argued here, it does suggest that the road between history and psychoanalysis is a two-way street and that too heavy reliance on clinical theory produces an ahistorical Promethean syndrome.

Before one can discuss terrorism in the contemporary world, it is necessary to define "terrorism," for it is a term which covers a wide array of violent or lawless acts from skyjacking through indiscriminate bombing to ritualistic murder and politically inspired kidnappings, assassinations, and destruction of property. To develop some overarching theory to cover such a host of phenomena is demonstrably impossible unless one subscribes to the presently popular belief that all of these events are simple manifestations of man's basic aggressive and destructive nature. The belief that man is by nature "evil" is, as everyone knows, an ancient idea with firm roots in American history. Civilization from this point of view is only a thin skin holding in man's propensity to kill and destroy. Recent works by Konrad Lorenz have given "scientific" standing to the theological belief in original sin. There is neither the time nor the space to engage in a long dispute over man's nature; suffice it to say that I find the arguments of Lorenz and company unconvincing and the postulating of a "destructive human nature" as an explanatory hypothesis inadequate theoretically and self-serving politically and psychologically.[3]

To return, therefore, to a definition of terrorism it seems highly desirable that some agreement be established as to what is meant by the term. It appears to include practically any type of violence involving some interference with the general functioning of society. It does not seem to include gang fights, muggings, and other such violent personal acts. For my purposes I intend to dismiss individual seizures of airplanes and other such non-political actions, even including ritualistic murder, although an analysis of these very well might be revealing in terms of psychobiographies and as revelations of societal disintegration. My concern will be with terror as both a political philosophy and a mode of political action. Or as Roland Gaucher put it, "Terrorism is—or seeks to be—a strategy."[4] Thus, before developing a psychohistorical framework some historical comment is necessary.

Terrorism developed within the anarchist element of the nineteenth century revolutionary movement. The first great disciple of "propaganda by the deed" was the Russian Michael Bakunin, although it is entirely possible that the core of the terrorist argument was supplied by his strange and sinister young friend Nechaev.[5] Together these men produced a most fascinating revolutionary document, *The Revolutionary Catechism,* from the publication of which, in 1869, historians date the emergence of philosophically based terrorism. Bakunin's famous comment, "Let us put our trust in the eternally creative source of life. The urge to destroy is also a creative urge,"[6] could in fact serve as the leitmotif of this discussion. Through Bakunin's personality and involvement in the revolutionary struggles of his time, the idea of terror as a political weapon passed into the revolutionary mentality of Europe and has been gradually developed and refined in other parts of the world. It is not my intention to try to encompass all of these movements but to start with Bakunin in order to establish a typology. Obviously a good deal of Bakunin's thought is tied to the romanticism of his era. The glorification of brigands as the only true revolutionaries, the posing as the man who has "no emotions . . . one science that of destruction," freed from all bourgeois sentimentality, all mark the romantic's belief in his power to re-create the world. In *Faust,* Goethe revealed both the romantic desire to re-create order and his emphasis on the *deed.*[7]

One could argue that the turmoil in traditional patterns of European society which reached catastrophic levels with the French Revolution and the Napoleonic Wars forced men to seek personal and social shelter from their existential dilemma in movements ranging from deMaistre's reactionary Catholicism, through liberal nationalist revolts, to calls for the complete destruction, in Bakunin's words, of "this effete social world which has become impotent and sterile. . . . We must first purify our atmosphere and transform completely the milieu in which we live; for it corrupts our instincts and our wills and contracts our heart and intelligence. The social question takes the form primarily of the overthrow of society."[8] Bakunin resisted Marx and communism as "the negation of liberty and I can conceive of nothing human without liberty."[9] This libertarian rejection of Marxism and the continued glorification of the heroic deed of terror lingered on in Italy and particularly Spain where the Spanish Civil War gave sad testament to this fatal split on the Left.

Anarchism and terrorism tended to fade away in northwest Europe after the failure of the Paris Commune, but in Italy and Spain endemic agrarian distress, reinforced by the impact of the new industrial processes on an old artisan class, carried on the belief in insurrection and acts of terrorism. That this connection with "romanticism" continued is testified to by E. J. Hobsbawm who recounts his attempt to get in touch with the anarchists in the 1950s: "When I tried to make contact . . . I was given a rendezvous at a cafe in Montmartre, by the Place Blanche, and somehow this reminder of a long-lost era of bohemians, rebels and avant-garde seemed only too characteristic."[10]

To the anarchist as terrorist the act itself was to bring society down by actions which destroyed symbols of the oppressive state. This belief in propaganda by the deed not only provided for the removal of an oppressive individual or institution, but would, it was hoped, begin the unraveling of society. Here, and later in George Sorel, there is a contempt for the intellectual, for the organized, and for the elite. Bakunin and Sorel both believed that the proletariat would be educated in violence not in lectures and speeches and that violence itself was purifying. That this strikes many as irrational is of course exactly the point.

Terrorism is not simply the act of a demented few, but represents a deeper endemic impulse against repression in its most fundamental sense. Terrorism increases among political activists, as well as among psychopaths in direct ratio to control and rationalization in modern technetronic society and the seeming failure of other paths of revolutionary activity (that is, the failure of "socialism" in the Soviet Union). To the New Left of recent memory the hero was the urban guerrilla with such violence-glorifying slogans as "in order to get rid of the gun it is necessary to take up the gun." To which Andrew Kopkind added that morality came from the muzzle of a gun. Students informed their professors that "you've got to bring it all down" and Frantz Fanon provided the theoretical framework for many of the committed. "Violence alone," writes Fanon in *The Wretched of the Earth,* ". . . violence committed by the people, violence organized and educated by its leaders, makes it possible for the masses to understand social truths and gives the key to them." Fanon, writes Sartre in presenting him, "shows clearly that this irrepressible violence is neither sound and fury, nor the resurrection of savage instincts nor the effect of resentment. . . . No gentleness can efface the marks of violence, only violence itself can destroy them."[11]

It should be noted that there is no intention to imply that the objective conditions and political forces were the same for all the individuals and movements mentioned. Nor is there meant to be any question of influence, although one might be traced. What is being suggested is that terrorism as advocated in anarchist, anarcho-syndicalist, and romantic Marxism has an emotionally similar quality. "The main appeal of anarchism was emotional and not intellectual."[12] James Joll sees in anarchism "a recurrent psychological need . . . which has by no means disappeared with the apparent failure of anarchism as a serious political and social force."[13] A comment which takes on a more pertinent tone is stated in Hobsbawm's essay, "Reflections on Anarchism," where this old-left Marxist ponders the reasons for a resurgence of anarchism which should have stayed by all rights dead and buried. In fact, as Hobsbawm declares, "it [anarchism] seemed to belong to the pre-industrial period and in any case to the era before the first World War and the October Revolution, except in Spain, where it can hardly be said to have survived the Civil War of 1936-9."[14] Hobsbawm goes on to provide an interesting analysis for this phenomenon; however, I will move on to possible psychohistorical themes before returning to a consideration of anarchism cum terrorism.

The similarities in psychological tone among the movements mentioned, as even Hobsbawm's somewhat incredulous account of modern anarchism agrees, suggest an endemic pattern. However, what is not as clearly perceived, perhaps, is that the slogans and assertions of the anarchists and their psychological descendants represent a form of millennialism. Hobsbawm sees this most clearly in his essay, "The Spanish Background," where he states that "Spanish anarchism is a profoundly moving spectacle for the student of popular religion—it was really a form of secular millennialism—but not, alas, for the student of politics."[15] Further testimony to this aspect of the movement is contained in Joll's analysis of the anarchists' claim that their intellectual predecessors were Zeno and the Stoics, Gnostic heretics, and the Anabaptists.[16] Through all of these philosophic schools runs a belief that the world of corruption and damnation can be overcome or overthrown and that harmony can replace oppression and dissonance. Anarchists believed, as did the later version of the New Left, in the "possibility of a violent and sudden transformation of society." That this belief was combined with a confidence in man's reasonableness and in the possibility of human improvement and perfection is not contradictory. Irrationality and corruption lay in the false social order, not in man. To the antinomians, Christ's grace would free them from "the law" and allow for spontaneous goodness. The millennialist sects of the late medieval period constantly expected the Kingdom of God to arrive after some cataclysmic event, usually found described in the Book of Revelations. Frank and Fritzie Manuel have suggested that "a revealing way to examine the psychic life of Judeo-Christian civilization would be to study it as a paradise cult, isolating fantasies about another world as they found expression in sacred texts, in commentaries upon them, and in their secular adaptation."[17] As already noted, this "paradisiacal" impulse does not disappear with the undermining of the religious traditions which gave it structure. Millennialism is a world-wide phenomenon as well as a modern one.[18] Norman Cohn in his study of medieval millennialism speculates that contemporary totalitarian movements and later medieval chiliasm are more related than superificial analysis would indicate: "The old symbols and the old slogans have indeed disappeared, to be replaced by new ones, but the structure of the basic phantasies seems to have changed scarcely at all."[19]

This is obviously not the place to pursue the problems and manifestations of millennialism, but other examples could be used to further support my assertion that the anarchist-terrorist phenomenon is part of a larger, endemic impulse to resolve the existential isolation of man.[20] If this argument for a "psychic" reality is accepted, at least tentatively, what insights can psychohistorical paradigms afford us?

First let us look at a Freudian explanation which has been used at least in part by Marcuse and Brown. Admittedly, the use of what some call Freud's metapsychology is not too popular with psychohistorians, but I believe it is a valuable initial take-off point. At the risk of oversimplifying or belaboring the obvious, it is necessary to briefly outline Freud's idea of civilization. Civilization develops only through repression of man's basic drives (that is, pleasure principle). Repression is therefore the key to Freud's analysis of man and society. Man must repress himself and culture affords a subli-mated expression of man's drives. The repressive elements of the superego are of course institutionalized in society and although in one sense man makes civilization, civilization in turn acts to repress us. Nevertheless, these basic drives of the pleasure principle are not eliminated, but live on in our unconscious and reveal themselves in fantasies and dreams. Thus, the unconscious contains the memory of the integral gratification of infancy. The adult world, especially the "rationalized" world of modern technology, is seen as a betrayal of the hope and promise of childhood. Freud therefore saw memory, that is, the "true" memory of the unconscious, as constantly erupting into the civilized world of the reality principle. As Marcuse has commented, "The return of the repressed makes up the tabooed and subterranean history of civilization.[21] This endemic eruption gives rise to millennialistic movements, both religious and secular, which strive to recover the lost Eden of the past by projecting it, paradoxically it seems, into a future paradise of harmonious communities, classless societies, or whatever form will overcome man's sense of separation from himself, his fellow beings, and his world.

Now, even if one grants this argument concerning an Edenic myth, certain difficulties arise both for psychoanalysts and historians. Freud's argument rests on the somewhat ahistorical assumption of the traumatic oedipal event which thereafter determines history as a form of a repetition-compulsion syndrome, or, in the words of Norman O. Brown, "it appears to swallow all cultural diversity, all historical change, into a darkness where all cats are grey."[22] Erik Erikson has of course attempted to avoid the reductionism of Freud by tying his analyses into the society of which the subject is a part. He pays attention to the conditions and situations Luther found himself in during social change in sixteenth-century Germany. Since the subjects dealt with in Erikson's book are well-known, I will not belabor them here except to say that Erikson is trying to relate one great man's intrapsychic struggle with himself and his environment and the so-called universalization of that identity struggle. Furthermore, Erikson argues that each culture be examined in terms of its unique version of personality integration.[23] Whatever the events of the "great man" argument, Erikson's attempt places the case history in history and does provide a model for some further explorations in the field.

Before doing so, however, there is a third psychoanalytic paradigm which may help in constructing a psychohistorical model, namely, what Lifton calls "shared psychohistorical themes." This approach, used in similar ways by Kenneth Keniston and Robert Coles, avoids the historical assumptions of Freud as well as some of the difficulties inherent in Erikson's "great man" approach. Without falling too far into the methodological abyss, I will use the following quotation from Lifton as an attempt to summarize his ideas and to then relate it to my argument and then to terrorism.

Within this perspective, all shared behavior is seen as simultaneously involved in a trinity of universality (that which is related to the psychobiological question of all men in all historical epochs), specific cultural emphasis and style (as evolved by a particular people over centuries), and recent and contemporary historical influences. . . . My point is that any shared event is all of these. The weighting of the components may vary, but nothing is *purely* universal, or cultural-historical, or contemporary-historical, everything is all three.[24]

This formulation allows for the Freudian (or, if preferred, the arguments of Becker or Fromm) conception of the return of the repressed as a universal phenomenon. The form it takes depends, of course, on the way in which each society integrates the personality (in Lifton's terms the cultural-historical). The demand of anarchists, as millennialists, turns to terrorism in given historical milieus, usually those in which state power and oppression allow few other perceived solutions. Cohn observed that millennarian movements "have varied in tone from the most violent aggressiveness to the mildest pacifism and from the most ethereal spirituality to the most earth-bound materialism."[25]

The answer lies in examining the traditions handed down by "the great man" (that is, the influence of Bakunin in Spain) and the peculiar space-time of that culture. If, for example, anarchism and terrorism seemed preindustrial, how would one approach the strongly anarchistic and frequently terroristic student involvement of the 1960s? One obvious contemporary-historical factor was the disillusionment of students with the obvious bureaucratization of both the capitalist and the communist worlds. Planned, organized, or "working-within-the-system" politics appeared to go nowhere. The Vietnam War lumbered along and the French C.P. seemed as establishmentarian as the Gaullists. Everywhere it seemed the only way to revolutionize a society which was perceived as life-denying was by spontaneous acts of revolt and terror. Even Hobsbawm recognizes that it was only the "anarchists, the anarchizers, and the situationnistes"[26] who created the massive French movement of 1968. The contemporary-historical situation has, in brief, made the anarchists the most sensitive "to spontaneous elements in mass movements." Only thus could the student movement in the United States succeed as well as it did. Of course, terrorism will wax and wane in developed countries lacking any nationalistic bases for guerrilla warfare led by minority groups.

Although all destruction or terror has its obvious moral and/or psychological price, it should be recognized that terror *per se* may be promoted by life-furthering forces. Terrorism can express a desire for freedom, rooted in man's nature, that is produced by specific times and places, usually in response to a breakdown in traditional patterns, or periods of official or foreign oppression, or struggles for national identity and often reflects the distance between man's potential and limiting social conditions. The rise of violence and terrorism of all types may of course be due to what Lifton calls "a form of radical psychohistorical dislocation associated with the breakdown of viable modes of symbolic immortality."[27] If this is the case, then "the return of the repressed" will take the form of malignant destruction which is, as Erich Fromm argues, a means of establishing one's being alive.

In summation, the Freudian paradigm of "the-return-of-the-repressed" (that is, man's wish to be free and integrated), the Eriksonian paradox of the influence of "great men" (for example, Bakunin, Sorel, Fanon) with emphasis on personality integration, and the "shared themes" paradigm, which might take the form of group, generational, or cohort analysis, seem to be vital aspects of dealing with the historical phenomenon of terrorism.

Notes

1. H. Stuart Hughes, *History as Art and as Science* (New York: Harper and Row, 1965), p. 47.

2. Robert J. Lifton, ed., *Explorations in Psychohistory: The Wellfleet Papers* (New York: Simon and Shuster, 1974), p. 41.

3. Konrad Lorenz, *On Aggression* (New York: Harcourt, Brace Jovanovich, 1966). See Erich Fromm, *The Anatomy of Human Destructiveness* (New York: Holt, Rinehart and Winston, 1973) for an extended refutation of Lorenz and a penetrating analysis of aggression.

4. Roland Gaucher, *The Terrorists: From Tsarist to the O.A.S.* (London: Secker and Secker, 1968), p. x.

5. James Joll, *The Anarchists* (New York: Grosset and Dunlap, 1964), pp. 84-148. George Woodcock, *Anarchism: A History of Libertarian Ideas and Movements* (Cleveland: New American Library, 1962), pp. 145-183.

6. Quoted in Woodcock, *Anarchism*, p. 151.

7. Goethe, *Faust*.

8. Quoted in Joll, *Anarchists*, p. 86.

9. *Ibid.*, p. 107.

10. E. J. Hobsbawm, *Revolutionaries: Contemporary Essays* (New York: Pantheon, 1973), p. 82.

11. Richard Hofstadter and Michael Wallace, eds., *American Violence* (New York: Knopf, 1970), pp. 3-43.

12. Hobsbawm, *Revolutionaries*, p. 83.

13. Joll, *Anarchists*, p. 12.

14. Hobsbawm, *Revolutionaries*, p. 82.

15. *Ibid.*, p. 76.

16. Joll, *Anarchists*, p. 16.

17. Frank E. and Fritzie P. Manuel, "Sketch for a Natural History of Paradise, "*Daedalus*, 101 (Winter 1972), p. 83.

18. Sylvia Thrupp, ed., *Millennial Dreams in Action* (The Hague: Mouton, 1962).

19. Norman Cohn, *The Pursuit of Millennium* (New York: Oxford University Press, 1961), p. XIV.

20. David Smith, "Millennarian Scholarship in American," *American Quarterly* 17 (Fall 1965), pp. 535-549.

21. Herbert Marcuse, *Eros and Civilization* (New York: Random House, 1962), p. 15. One could also apply Jungian and Kleinian formulations at this juncture.

22. Norman O. Brown, *Life Against Death: The Psychoanalytic Meaning of History* (New York: Random House, 1959), p. 11.

23. Erik Erikson, *Young Man Luther* (New York: Norton, 1962) and *Childhood and Society* (New York, 1963).

24. Lifton, *Explorations*, p. 32.

25. Cohn, *Pursuit*, p. xiv.

26. Hobsbawm, *Revolutionaries*, p. 87.

27. Lifton, *Explorations*, p. 38.

ANTHONY STORR

Sadism and Paranoia

While aggression is an identifiable part of the behavioral repertoire of many species, including man, cruelty seems peculiar to the human species. It could, perhaps, be argued that a cat playing with a mouse is enjoying the exercise of power; but it is unlikely that the cat either hates the mouse or is capable of entering into the mouse's presumed feelings of terror and helplessness. Indeed, some authorities would not only deny that predation was cruel in the sense in which we apply the word to human behavior, but would remove it from the category of aggression altogether, confining the use of the word aggression to conflict between conspecifics. Whatever view one takes, there can be no doubt that aggression serves a number of different functions and is essential for survival, while cruelty is not only a blot upon the human escutcheon, but serves no obvious biological purpose. Indeed, one might argue that cruelty is the opposite of adaptive. Edward Wilson has recently contended that reciprocal altruism in human, and to some extent in animal, societies is an adaptive device likely to promote the survival of each participant.[1] In other words, kindness to other human beings is likely to pay in terms of survival and reproductive potential; or as a friend of mine used to put it, "Civility is cheap, but it pays rich dividends." Human cruelty, therefore, is a phenomenon which is not only repulsive, but requires explanation.

Regrettably, the cruel behavior of human beings is far too common to be explicable solely in terms of psychiatric abnormality, or of special social conditions, important though these are. Violent and cruel behavior is a potential in normal people. But let us look at some of the factors which appear to make cruelty more likely, and begin by considering one kind of abnormal person. In any Western society, there are inevitably a few individuals who lack the normal degree of control over immediate impulse. These are the so-called aggressive psychopaths who commit violent offenses of various kinds, and who may show an almost complete disregard for the feelings of their victims. These are the abnormals whom idealists would like to blame for the whole sum of human cruelty, but who are actually too few in number to make more than a small contribution toward it. We do not understand all the reasons for the psychopath's lack of control of violence. As with other psychiatric conditions, the causes are multiple.

As we know, some suffer from genetic abnormalities; others show what appears to be a delayed maturation of the central nervous system, as evidenced by the persistence, in the electroencephalogram, of electrical rhythms characteristic of childhood. Many psychopaths show a failure of socialization, in that they have never formed ties of mutual regard with others, and thus live in a world which they assume to be indifferent or hostile. The development of conscience, that is, of an internal regulator of behavior, appears to depend much more on the wish to preserve love than on the fear of punishment. Since many psychopaths come from homes in which there has been little love and a good deal of physical punishment, it is hardly surprising that they have not developed a normal conscience. A child cannot respond to the withdrawal of something which he has never had; it is understandable that those who have never felt themselves loved or approved of are not affected by disapproval. Although many psychopaths show both a lack of control of hostility and also an abnormal amount of hostility toward their fellows, much of the cruelty which they exhibit appears to be casual rather than deliberate. Thus, they may injure someone whom they are robbing or sexually assaulting because they do not identify with their victim or care what he or she feels, which is obviously a different matter from the deliberate exercise of cruelty. In Holland, criminologists have experimented with confronting violent criminals with their victims. In some instances, this has brought home to the criminal for the first time that his victim is a person like himself, with the consequence that he has wished to make reparation.[2]

It is possible that we may be able to understand the psychopath's lack of control over immediate impulse in physiological terms. Psychopaths are emotionally isolated even if not physically so; and, in other species, isolation appears to produce heightened reactivity to dangerous stimuli, shown by a faster mobilization and a release of systemic norepinephrine.[3] Human beings who, for one reason or another, have not learned to mix with their fellows in early childhood, often show inappropriate aggressive responses, sometimes overreacting because they perceive threat where none exists, sometimes underreacting because they have never learned to "stand up for themselves." In rodents, it has been shown that isolation produces a lower level of tonic aggressive arousal combined with the heightened reactivity to dangerous stimuli already mentioned; it would be worth investigating whether a similar physiological state of affairs occurs in human beings who have been isolated.

Since psychopaths constitute a small proportion of human beings, we cannot explain the human tendency toward cruelty by blaming it upon them alone, though the study of psychopaths may go some way toward helping our understanding. The second factor predisposing toward cruelty is the human tendency toward obedience. The experiments of Stanley Milgram are so well-known that I need hardly refer to them. They are summarized in his recently published book, *Obedience to Authority*.[4] To his surprise, around two-thirds of normal people would deliver what they believed to be extremely painful, possibly near-lethal, electric shocks to a subject whom they thought was engaged in an experiment on the nature of learning because they were urged to do so by the experimenter. The excuse that they were only obeying authority is the one most frequently offered by those arraigned for torture or other forms of institutionalized cruelty, from Eichmann down. Obedience is clearly adaptive in human society as in many animal societies. A stable dominance hierarchy promotes peace within a society, makes possible organized resistance or organized escape if danger threatens, and allows for instant decision making by dominant individuals. It is impossible to imagine a human society functioning at all adequately without a built-in tendency to obey.

However, obedience involving acts of violence and cruelty does not explain the cruelty of those who give the orders. At present, throughout the world, the use of torture appears to be increasing. There are two main uses. First is the obvious one of extracting information. Second is its use for the control of political dissent by creating an atmosphere of terror. It is an interesting and unexplained paradox that, while there is today a general consensus that torture is totally inadmissable, it is more widely employed than ever before. I do not believe that the tendency toward obedience entirely explains the compliance in cruelty of those who carry out cruel orders. It is certainly a powerful factor in military situations such as the Vietnam massacres or the recent execution of mercenaries. But orders to shoot women and children or one's comrades-in-arms are often backed up, in wartime, by the explicit or implicit threat that refusal might bring about one's own execution. Moreover, it is possible to imagine orders which would be resisted more strongly than orders to kill or torture. If an officer ordered his men to eat feces for breakfast, it may be supposed that few would obey, even if threatened with dire penalties.

The third factor conducive to cruelty is distance, whether this be measured in physical or psychological terms. If human fights were confined to fisticuffs, there would not only be fewer deaths, but fewer instances of cruelty. A man who is a few hundred feet above his victims in an airplane will drop napalm upon them without a qualm. He would be less likely to produce a similar effect by pouring petrol over a child and igniting it if he was close enough to do so. Most terrorist acts, like the planting of bombs, result in harm not witnessed by the terrorist; it is significant that the best way of saving lives of hostages held by terrorists is to allow time for a relationship to develop—that is, for psychological "distance" to diminish. Lorenz has argued that human beings possess inhibitory mechanisms against injuring their own kind which are not well-developed and which are easily overcome because they are not armed by nature with dangerous weapons like tusks or claws. Natural selection has not allowed for the invention of weapons which kill at a distance.

By psychological distance I mean the human tendency to treat other human beings as less than human; the phenomenon of *pseudo-speciation*. Many societies maintain out-groups who are treated with contempt and often with cruelty. In Japan, for example, the descendants of a pariah caste, known as Burakumin, are still discriminated against, both socially and economically, although they are no longer labeled as *eta* (filth-abundant), *yotsu* (four-legged), or *hinin* (nonhuman).[5] In a very interesting paper, George de Vos has distinguished between psychological attitudes toward pariah groups, and attitudes toward those at the bottom of the hierarchy in any society.[6] Most of us acquiesce to some extent in the exploitation of the poor and the unintelligent, and are glad to have them do the dirty jobs of society; this is instrumental exploitation, just as torture for the sake of extracting information is instrumental.

However, exploitation of pariah castes goes further than this, and is labeled "expressive" exploitation by de Vos. By this he means the phenomenon of creating an out-group which acts as a scapegoat for the tension within a society, just as individuals may act as scapegoats for the tensions within a family. Pariah castes not only provide a group of people to whom even the humblest member of the legitimate society can feel superior, but are also regarded as disgusting and potentially polluting. A member of such a caste, unlike a member of the lowest class in a society, cannot rise in the hierarchy because he is not allowed to intermarry. Harshly authoritarian and insecure societies have a particular need for scapegoats, just as do harshly authoritarian and insecure individuals. Pseudo-speciation plays on the universal human tendency toward xenophobia, a characteristic found also in other social animals from geese to monkeys. The more easily human beings are relegated to a subhuman category, or perceived as alien, the easier it is to treat them with cruelty. The SS deliberately degraded concentration camp prisoners, forcing them to live in filth, often covered with their own excrement. When the commandant of Treblinka was asked why such humiliation and cruelty was practiced, since the prisoners were going to be killed in any case, Franz Stangel replied: "To condition those who actually had to carry out the policies, to make it possible for them to do what they did."[7]

The fourth factor which influences people in the direction of cruelty is the treatment which they themselves experienced when children. Throughout most of the history of Western civilization, children have been treated abominably. So much is this the case that a recent investigation by ten American historians begins: "The history of childhood is a nightmare from which we have only recently begun to awaken. The further back in history one goes, the lower the level of child care, and the more likely children are to be killed, abandoned, beaten, terrorized, and sexually abused."[8] Studies of parents who batter their children show that, as children themselves, these parents had been deprived of basic mothering and had, at the same time, excessive demands made upon them. According to Steele and Pollock, these parents had been made to feel that all they did was "erroneous, inadequate and ineffectual."[9] Feeling ineffectual leads to demands for absolute, instantaneous obedience, demands which small children seldom, and babies never, are able to meet. A small child who will not instantly obey is perceived as a threat because it has the power to increase the parent's sense of inadequacy, and therefore invites retaliation. Moreover, deprived parents, paradoxical as this may seem, make demands on their children for the affection which, as children, they did not themselves receive, and react with resentment and violence when the children do not appear to give it to them. Baby-battering is an interesting example of how basic biological behavior patterns of protecting and cherishing the immature can be overridden by personal maladaptation. Helplessness is generally inhibitory of violence in humans as well as other primates; but once violence has begun to be used against the helpless, helplessness loses its capacity to inhibit and may actually increase the use of violence. One of the most distasteful features of human cruelty is that it persists even when the victim is utterly at the mercy of his persecutor.

The fact that human beings who have been neglected or ill-treated in childhood seem more prone to treat others with cruelty argues that much human cruelty is really revenge. This is relevant to the dispute which still goes on about the effects of witnessing violence. Does witnessing violence cause ordinary people to feel violent themselves, or does it simply disinhibit those who, consciously or unconsciously, are keeping in check violent impulses with difficulty? This may be the wrong question to ask. I shall argue that all human beings are suffering from some degree of inner resentment derived from infantile experience. On the whole, I agree with Richard Herrnstein and Roger Brown who, in their recent summary of the literature in their textbook, *Psychology,* come down in favor of the view that witnessing violence is disinhibitory of violence rather than provocative of it.[10] I share the dislike which many psychologists show for a so-called hydraulic model of the mind; but clinical experience makes it difficult for me to conceive of any model which does not allow for resentment being in some way stored-up. If one agrees that an accumulation of irritations during a working day may be vented or abreacted by kicking the dog, which is surely a commonplace observation, I see no reason why resentment should not be stored for much longer, even for a lifetime.

The widespread misuse of the word sadism has given rise to the supposition that human cruelty is partially sexual in origin, and the ubiquitous response to sado-masochistic literature is sometimes advanced as evidence that cruelty contains a sexual element. Elsewhere[11] I have argued at length that sado-masochism is not what it seems; that is, to use the terminology employed both by Claire and William Russell and by Abraham Maslow, sado-masochism is *pseudo-sex* rather than sex itself, using sexual behavior patterns to establish dominance relationships, as happens in other primates. So many human beings in Western culture show an interest in sado-masochistic literature or films that it is not possible to argue that such interests are abnormal. Yet there are some people who are particularly plagued by sado-masochistic fantasies and who need such fantasies or rituals in order to become sexually aroused. In my experience, these people have generally felt themselves to be particularly uncertain and ineffective both in sexual situations and in most other aspects of interpersonal relationships; and their fascination with sado-masochism springs from their need to establish dominance (or to have the other person establish dominance) before they can venture upon a sexual relationship.

It seems highly unlikely that torturers are obtaining direct sexual satisfaction when inflicting pain upon their victims, nor do I believe that riot police have erections when wielding their clubs. But the dominance which such people achieve through their cruelty may certainly facilitate their own belief in their sexual potency. Rattlesnakes wrestle with each other in struggles for male dominance. The winner of such a contest, it is credibly reported, immediately goes off and mates, while the loser is unable to do so for some time. The human male needs to feel confidence to achieve sexual arousal, and this confidence may be obtained in all sorts of ways, some of them highly distasteful. But this is not to say that the exercise of cruelty is itself sexually exciting. Part of the confusion about sex and dominance must be laid at the door of Freud. Psychoanalysis has been so concerned with the pleasure principle, and so obsessed with the notion that pleasure must be sensual that it has omitted to consider the pleasure afforded by the exercise of power. In his early writings, Freud does make some reference to an "instinct for mastery." I have suggested that, had he pursued the subject, we might have had a book titled "Beyond the Power Principle."

It seems probably that those who have been harshly treated as children are particularly prone to treat other human beings with cruelty both because they have a particular need to establish dominance and because they wish to be revenged. It is also probable that the casualness and neglect with which infants in the West have been treated has resulted in there being a large number of persons who have a rather marked propensity toward cruelty. Anthropologists are apt to idealize the peoples they study, but it does seem probable that there are still some people in the world who are relatively peaceful and kind, and that this may be related to the way in which they rear their children. I am thinking particularly of the practice of what has been called *extero-gestation* in which the infant is kept in close physical contact with the mother, both by day and by night, until it is independently mobile. Cultures in which this happens consider it pathological for infants to cry.

However this may be, there are certainly a large number of people in our culture who produce evidence of having felt, as infants or young children, that they were helplessly at the mercy of adults who were perceived as threatening. We have only to look at myths and fairy tales to discover many instances of violence emanating from dragons, giants, and other mythological figures who are immensely powerful compared to human beings and who may be supposed to reflect something of the infant's experience of the world. This brings me to the fifth factor which I consider important in the genesis of cruelty—fear. Fear is closely related to pseudo-speciation, and pseudo-speciation is related to myth, since out-groups have projected upon them qualities which can only be called mythological. I mentioned earlier that pariah castes are believed to be polluting. This of course makes them creatures to be feared as well as despised. It is remarkably easy for human beings to be persuaded that other human beings are malignant, evil, and immensely powerful. I am by no means persuaded of the validity of all that is postulated by Melanie Klein and her followers, but I am convinced that there is a paranoid potential in most human beings which is easily mobilized under certain conditions of stress.

The other day I saw a middle-aged man who was being treated for various phobic anxieties. The ostensible origin of his symptoms was an experience at the dentist. He was lying prone, and during part of the dental treatment, found it somewhat difficult to breathe. He therefore attempted to sit up, but the dentist pushed him down, saying "You're bloody well not getting up." He had previously thought that the dentist was somewhat "trendy" and unprofessional, but at this point the dentist's face appeared quite different. He changed, as it were, into a malign persecutor, and the patient lost any sense of being able to resist him. He actually fainted at this point. The situation had been transformed to one in which the patient was in danger of death from an evil and powerful enemy. This same patient was an unusually courageous man who, during the last war, had survived three air crashes without developing phobic symptoms.

We shall never understand human cruelty until we know more about paranoid projection, a mechanism of mind which is far from being confined to the psychotic. Conditions of social stress such as those which followed the Black Death in Europe or which led to the collapse of the Weimar Republic not only throw up pathological leaders, but mobilize paranoid projection on a large scale. The historian, Norman Cohn, has made a particular study of this phenomenon, which is contained in three books, *The Pursuit of the Millennium, Warrant for Genocide,* and *Europe's Inner Demons.* The history of anti-Semitism is a case study in paranoia in which Jews are seen not only as potential dominators of the world, but also as poisoners, torturers, castrators, and ritual murderers. Cohn has demonstrated that the persecution of the Jews has regularly rested upon such beliefs, together with the totally false hypothesis that there was an international Jewish conspiracy dedicated to world domination. "Exterminatory anti-Semitism appears where Jews are imagined as a collective embodiment of evil, a conspiratorial body dedicated to the task of ruining and then dominating the rest of mankind."[12] Within the last thirty years, so Cohn reports, travelers in the remoter parts of Spain have been informed that they could not be Jewish since they had no horns. Examination of the statements of Nazi leaders reveals that they had a megalomaniac sense of mission in which they were playing the noble role of exterminating evil embodied by the Jews. When Irma Grese was taxed with cruelty she said defiantly: "It was our duty to exterminate anti-social elements, so that Germany's future should be assured." As Cohn says: "To hear them on the subject of themselves, one would think that killing unarmed and helpless people, including small children, was a very brave and risky undertaking."[13]

The same paranoid process was at work in the great witch-hunt which took place in Europe during the fifteenth, sixteenth, and seventeenth centuries. Witches were supposed to destroy babies, to engage in cannibalism, to practice incest, to worship the devil, and to come together in a conspiracy of evil at the so-called sabbats. It was when this latter belief took hold that the persecution started in earnest, for the conspiracy was supposed to threaten both church and state. It is interesting that fantasies of evil refer to activities which infringe rather basic biological prohibitions; the destruction of babies, incest, and cannibalism.

In my belief, man's paranoid potential takes origin from the very helpless state in which he persists for a long time after birth, together with the extended period of his total life-span in which he is under the control of others. Thomas Szasz begins his book of aphorisms by stating: "Childhood is a prison sentence of twenty-one years."[14] Whether or not one agrees with him, I think that the relation between childhood experience and the propensity to paranoid fantasy deserves further investigation.

There is, therefore, an intimate connection between feelings of helplessness and the propensity to behave violently. Violence is both a response to threat and a way of reestablishing confidence in one's own power. Terrorism appears to be connected with feelings of helplessness in that it tends to be initiated by people who believe that they have no power to alter events in any other way. Once embarked upon, terrorism has many attractions for those who, for any reason, have taken with them into adult life resentments from infancy and childhood. Just as particular political circumstances throw up particular types of leaders such as, de Gaulle and Churchill, so the circumstances which make sections of the population feel politically powerless throw up those whose psychopathology predisposes them to commit terrorist acts. There will always be sufficient of these in any large population to ensure a supply of terrorists so long as the adverse political circumstances continue. The greatest cruelty which men inflict upon one another seems to occur when persons who have been perceived as threatening and dangerous are finally in the power of those whom they made to feel helpless and frightened.

Notes

1. Edward O. Wilson, *Sociobiology* (Cambridge: Harvard University Press, 1975), p. 120.

2. A. M. Roosenburg, *The Interaction between Prisoners, Victims and Their Social Network,* Ciba Foundation Symposium (Amsterdam: Elsevier, 1973).

3. David M. Vowles, *The Psychobiology of Aggression* (Edinburgh: Edinburgh University Press, 1970).

4. Stanley Milgram, *Obedience to Authority* (New York: Harper and Row, 1974).

5. Hiroshi Wagatsuma, "The Pariah Caste in Japan," *In Caste and Race,* Ciba Foundation Symposium (London: Churchill, 1967).

6. George De Vos, "Human Systems of Segregation," *In Conflict in Society,* Ciba Foundation Symposium (London: Churchill, 1966).

7. Terrence Des Pres, *The Survivors* (New York: Oxford University Press, 1976), p. 61.

8. Lloyd De Mause, *The History of Childhood* (New York[?]: Souvenir Press, 1976).

9. Quoted in Jean Renvoize, *Children in Danger* (London: Routledge, 1974), p. 43.

10. Roger Brown, and Richard Herrnstein, *Psychology* (Boston: Little, Brown, 1975).

11. Anthony Storr, *Human Destructiveness* (London: Sussex University Press, 1972).

12. Norman Cohn, *Warrant for Genocide* (London: Eyre and Spottiswoode, 1967), p. 252.

13. *Ibid.,* p. 265.

14. Thomas Szasz, *The Second Sin* (London: Routledge, 1974), p. 1.

OLEG ZINAM

Terrorism and Violence in the Light of a Theory of Discontent and Frustration

Violence and terror have existed since time immemorial. Yet those who believe in the perfectibility of human nature are puzzled by the observation that violence, organized crime, and terrorism are on the rise despite a remarkable improvement in human conditions. This experience seems to contradict the conventionally accepted notion that crime and violence are caused primarily by poverty and other kinds of human deprivations. Moreover, the increase in violence is proportionately greater in the most prosperous and technologically advanced countries.

The causes of this phenomenon are multifarious and extremely complex. But there is no doubt that it represents a serious and dangerous symptom of social disruption and malfunctioning. As Coser aptly stated, "human beings . . . will resort to violent action only under extremely frustrating, ego-damaging, and anxiety-producing conditions. It follows that if the incidence of violence increases rapidly, . . . this can be taken as a signal of severe maladjustment."[1]

Since the violence syndrome becomes more encompassing and menacing, it is necessary to analyze the historical conditions which have contributed to this problem. There are two major methods of studying social phenomena. One is to obtain the overall data on their incidence and relate them to values of other variables by using statistical methods in order to find some meaningful and useful generalizations. The other concentrates on a legitimate traditional question, "Why does individual A engage in deviating behavior, when individual B does not?"[2] The causes of this type of behavior have their deep roots in the overall social and cultural circumstances. Speaking of the relationship between the individual and international violence, McNeil comments that "Without an increased understanding of the forces that shape the individual, we will forever fail to comprehend the direction that international violence may take."[3]

In the late sixties a commission appointed to investigate the causes of violence found that one of the major obstacles in the way of understanding this social phenomenon was "the lack of a general theoretical framework with which to order our perceptions of the motives and attitudes that impel groups toward violence and the social conditions conducive to it."[4]

The central purpose of this discussion is to analyze the impact of certain selected forces of modernization on the propensity for violence in contemporary society of the postindustrial type. The factors behind preference and opportunity for violence are subjected to an investigation which primarily focuses on the question of what causes a person to decide to act violently rather than within the limits of legitimacy and legality. An attempt is made to explain the rise in violence and terrorism in our modern age in terms of a theory of discontent and a theory of social change of the necessary and sufficient conditions type. The last part deals with an analysis of factors relevant to determining the legitimate use of force with some proposed long-range cultural changes which will eventually lead to a reduction in preference for violence.

Definitions: Power, Force, Violence and Terror

One of the difficulties in conducting research in social sciences is the multiplicity of conflicting, overlapping, and tautological definitions of terms. Though it has been stated that it is useless to argue about conflicting classifications, the use of terms and their definitions is not neutral. This is especially true if the term conveys a pejorative connotation, like violence. Therefore, this section is devoted to defining basic terms for the purpose of this study.

Power is defined here as "anything, the possession of which confers on the possessor the ability to proceed toward the desired goal despite resistance."[5] This definition is akin to Max Weber's concept of power which he sees as "the probability that one actor within a social relationship will be in a position to carry out his own will despite resistance, regardless of the basis on which this probability rests."[6] Nieburg, following Mumford and Walter, views power in terms of the social environment as "the ability to direct human energy (that is, attitudes and behavior) to express or realize certain values by the organization and use, modification and control of both physical and human (that is, behavior itself) materials."[7]

While power conveys on its possessor the capability to use force, force can be defined as an actual application or exercise of power. It is power in action. Force is morally neutral like power, its source. It can be used for both good and bad ends. Violence is defined here as an illegitimate use of force. This distinction between force and violence is stressed by Holmes who decries "the tacit assumption that force and violence are the same. While violence typically involves the use of force," he said, "and we often use 'force' and 'violence' interchangeably, the two cannot be equated. We can use force . . . without in any way involving violence."[8] Gray emphatically supports the distinction between force and violence. "It is important," he wrote, "to keep the meaning of the word violence distinct from terms like power, force, strength and authority," and adds, "it is a sad commentary on our muddled minds that they today are frequently used as synonymous." He insists that "unless we do clarify the difference between force and violence and try to apply it in our lives, thinking and action are surely lamed and even frustrated."[9] Pareto clearly distinguishes force from violence and states that force is a prerequisite for governing and "the foundation of all social organization." For him, use of violence is impractical, foolish, and weakens social order.[10]

However, numerous authorities in the field do not distinguish between the terms force and violence. They define it as "behavior designed to inflict physical injury on people or damage to property,"[11] or "unmeasured or exaggerated harm to individuals, either not socially prescribed at all or else beyond established limits,"[12] or "the display of behavior which inflicts physical injury,"[13] or "the most direct and severe form of physical power."[14] Most of these and other writers as well, while agreeing with this definition, proceed to distinguish between the legitimate and illegitimate use of violence. A good example of a most complete definition of violence as indistinguishable from force is given by Van den Haag. For him, violence is "physical force used by a person, directly or through a weapon, to hurt, destroy, or control another, or to damage, destroy, or control an object." He prefers "to use 'violence' as a synonym for physical 'force' and when necessary to qualify it as legitimate or illegitimate."[15]

The use of the term *violence* to cover all application or threat of force, legitimate or illegitimate, does create the impression that any use of force is somehow condemnable and should be avoided. Yet, no human society can survive without an adequate use of legitimate coercion and proper use of force. Therefore, in this study, the use of the terms force and violence are clearly differentiated. Of course, this procedure requires drawing a line between force and violence. This is very difficult to do because of the distinction between the concepts of legality and legitimacy. An act is illegal if it violates ethical norms and standards shared by a given community. In an ideal state the two concepts coincide—legitimacy and legality are coextensive. But in reality positive nand natural laws differ and this creates some ambiguity. Acts can be legitimate but illegal and legal but illegitimate. Graham and Curr believe that "the legality of acts is determined by formal procedures of community decision making" and "acts are legitimate . . . , if members of a community regard them as desirable or justifiable."[16] These writers, however, apply these terms to distinguish different types of violence and do not use them to separate the concept of force from the concept of violence, as it is done here.

If force is placed in the area circumscribed by the boundaries of legality and legitimacy and violence is placed outside these boundaries, three basic cases should be considered. *Case 1:* The boundaries of legality and legitimacy coincide (an ideal state). In such a case violence is committed by indi-

Figure 1. Definitions: Power, Force, and Violence

POWER

	VIOLENCE	FORCE	VIOLENCE
	PRIVATE CITIZENS		STATE AUTHORITIES

Area of legitimate self-defense and protection of individual and group rights

Area of normal process of law-enforcement by state authorities

Case 1 L = 1	Violence by citizens neither legal nor legitimate		Violence by state authority neither legal nor legitimate
Case 2 1 > L	Legalized violence by individuals and social groups		Legalized violence by the state
Case 3 L > 1	Violence by citizens neither legal nor legitimate		Violence by state authority neither legal nor legitimate

Legitimate but extralegal actions by individuals and groups

Legitimate use of self-defense and protection of individual and group rights

Normal process of law-enforcement by state authorities

Legitimate but extralegal actions by state authorities

L = Legitimacy
l = Legality

viduals and groups if they violate formal law or the ethical standards of the community. State authorities can also commit violence if they overstep the legitimate and legal use of force to attain compliance with the law. *Case 2:* The area of legally permissible use of force extends beyond the limits of legitimacy. In this case one can speak of legalized violence by individuals and social groups as well as of legalized violence by the state. *Case 3:* The area of legitimacy extends beyond the area of legality. This leads to both, legitimate but extralegal actions by individuals and groups and legitimate yet extralegal actions by state authorities. (See Figure 1.)

The division between force and violence is clear-cut in *Case 1*. It is more difficult to define the situations of legalized violence or of legitimate but extralegal use of legalized violence or of legitimate but extralegal use of force, dealt with in *Cases 2 and 3*. The case of legalized violence calls for legislative action to eradicate this gray area by restricting the legal use of force if it violates the moral standards of the community. Frequent occurrence of legitimate but extralegal acts indicates that laws do not provide adequate protection of human rights or that they place too many restrictions on law-enforcement agencies so that to fulfill their duty to society they have to break existing laws.

An important distinction must be made between two basic types of violence: rational and irrational. Blumenthal and Kahn distinguish "between violence that is instrumental and violence that is expressive." "Expressive violence," they write, "arises primarily in response to feelings of hate or rage, while in the case of instrumental violence such feelings are secondary, although they may arise during the course of committing violent acts. Instrumental violence is violence used to some end."[17] The distinction is very important because crimes of passion are difficult to deter or prevent, while most instrumental violence and crime is a matter of calculated risk and therefore potentially controllable. This is especially true for organized crime which tends to flourish when risks are negligible but the potential gains are very substantial. Changes in the law, in the attitudes of law-enforcement agencies, in judges, and the rest of the community can have a strong impact on the spread or diminution of organized crime.

Terrorism is the apex of violence. Once violence is defined, the definition of terrorism is a comparatively easy task. It is important to note that "violence may occur without terror, but not terror without violence."[18] Terrorism is defined by some as "the most flagrant form of defiance of the rule of law,"[19] as "process of terror . . . a compound with three elements: the act or threat of violence, the emotional reaction, and the social effects,"[20] as "a strategy of terror-violence which relies on psychological impact to attain political objectives,"[21] or as "illegal acts of violence committed for political purposes of clandestine groups."[22] In this study, terrorism is broadly defined as the use or threat of violence by individuals or by organized groups to evoke fear and submission to attain some economic political, sociopsychological, ideological, or other objective. Wilkinson distinguishes isolated, spontaneous outbursts of terror from organized terrorism. "Terror may occur in isolated acts and also in the form of extreme, indiscriminate and arbitrary mass violence," he writes. "Such terror is not systematic, it is unorganized and is often impossible to control," in contrast to terrorism which is "a sustained policy involving the waging of organized terror either on the part of the state, a movement or faction or by a small group of individuals."[23]

According to the motivation of terrorist groups, terrorism can be classified as psychopathic, ideological, and pragmatic.[24] In this discussion, the motivations of terrorists are divided into pathological, political, and economic. It is assumed that the political type of terrorism contains ideological, sociopsychological, and military-strategic components. From the point of view of its incidence and territorial spread, terrorism can be either intranational (domestic) or international. On the domestic scene, it can either involve individuals or groups against each other and the state, or the state against its people. Internationally, terrorism may involve individuals and groups in one state against individuals and groups in other states, or states against states. Figure 2 presents this double classification in tabular form.

Since terrorism always contains violence or the threat of violence, the study of factors contributing to the spread of violent behavior contributes also to the understanding of the most important sociopsychological components of terrorism. The causes of violence, moreover, are numerous, complex, and closely interdependent. No one can see the whole picture. Nevertheless, it is the duty of social scientists to contribute as much as they can to shedding some light on this extremely important phenomenon. What follows is an attempt to look at the factors which influence the decision of a person to act violently rather than within the limits prescribed by legality and/or legitimacy. The central question is what do forces of modernization do to human propensity for violence? The proposed theoretical framework which deals with this issue consists of a theory of decision-making based on discontent and a theory of social change based on the power-will hypothesis.

Discontent, Elasticity of Discontent, and Threshold of Frustration

Theories of social change based on the power-will hypothesis, and of decision-making centered on a theory of discontent, were developed by the writer elsewhere.[25] Here, only the most salient and relevant points and relationships are presented and applied to the problem of violence in society.

Though the factors contributing to social change are numerous, complex,

Figure 2. Definitions: Terrorism
TERRORISM

MOTIVATION	INTRANATIONAL-DOMESTIC		INTERNATIONAL	
	Individuals & Groups vs. Others & the State	*State vs. Citizens*	*Individuals & Groups vs. Other Indiv. & Groups*	*States vs. States*
1. PATHOLOGICAL	Revenge against society Destruction of the "Establishment"	Pathological behavior of a tyrannical government caused by excessive fear	Fanatical hatred Movements based on racial hatred	States attempting to destroy other states for the primary reason of hatred
2. POLITICAL contains components of a) Ideological b) Socio-psychological c) Military-Strategic	Terror used by individuals & groups against the state a) To seize control b) To clear the way for takeover by the new regime c) To punish and destroy those in authority	Terror used by state authorities to: a) Control the cities b) Punish and/or destroy potential and actual "enemies"	Assassination of foreign dignitaries for political reasons by individuals or organized groups	Wars of national liberation supported from outside states' frontiers. Assassination of foreign dignitaries. Control over communist "satellites" by fear and intimidation, and so forth
3. ECONOMIC	Domestic organized crime	To enforce and make possible economic exploitation of the population by state authorities through submission	International organized crime	Terror used by states against each other to inflict economic losses

and inextricably intertwined, one can roughly divide them into two categories: ecological and eiconic.[26] This division is necessary because a human being inhabits two realms of existence: ecological (noumenal, objective) and eiconic (phenomenal, subjective). In general, most historical changes can be traced to some combination of factors belonging to these two realms. In Whitehead's terms, "The great transitions are due to a coincidence of forces derived from both sides of the world, its physical and its spiritual natures."[27]

Coincidence of *will*, derived from the eiconic realm, and *power* flowing from the ecological one, represents a sufficient condition for change involving human decision-making. Each of them, taken separately, represents a necessary condition for this type of social change. Equilibrium (a state in which there are no net forces for change) exists when "no one who has power to change it has the will, and no one who has the will has the power."[28]

In an interdependent modern society, power flows mainly from organization. Social roles act as transmission belts which convey power on individuals. The amount of power controlled by the decision-making unit sets the limits to its opportunity function which represents either *what is,* or what *can be.* Power is a necessary component of decision-making and action.

The other necessary condition for decision-making is *will* which is defined as the "determination to use the available power, or to expand presently available power, in order to attain a given goal, despite resistances."[29] The will or determination to act in a particular way depends on the actor's image of the world or *Weltanschauung,* his internalized value systems, and on his overall subjective view of the totality of his situation. In any particular situation of choice a person forms his preference function which expresses what is *desirable* as contrasted with opportunity function which delimits the area of the possible.

Will or the determination to act depends on the following necessary conditions: (1) recognition of the gap between the ideal (I) and actual (A) value of the variable measuring the level of aspirations and the level of attainments respectively, (2) cathection of this gap leading to strong discontent with the gap, and (3) volition leading to the decision to use power to close the gap. To become effective, preference must be coupled with the use of power contained in the opportunity function. Thus, the coincidence of power and will represents sufficient condition for actions leading to social change.

Discontent is at the heart of the process of social change. Without the discontent of those having power, no change will be initiated. Following are basic terms and relationships of the proposed discontent theory:

(1) $g = (I - A)$ .... Aspiration-attainment gap where A is level of attainment and I is level of aspiration.

(2) $d = f(g) = f(I - A)$ .... Personal discontent gap, a measure of absolute deprivation.
(f = "function of").

(3) $G = (I/A)$ .... Aspiration-attainment ratio.

(4) $D = F(G) = F(I/A)$ .... Coefficient of personal discontent, a measure of relative deprivation.
(F stands for "function of").

(5) $E_d = dI/I \div dA/A =$
$dI/dA \cdot A/I$ .... Elasticity of discontent—a ratio of change in the level of aspiration to change in the level of attainment.

Relationship (4) leads to the basic theorem of the theory of discontent: Discontent varies directly with the level of aspiration and inversely with the level of attainment.[30] A case of high elasticity of discontent leads to the apparent modern paradox of rising discontent in the most rapidly advancing economies, revolutions when the revolting group is evidently on its way toward improving its relative power in society, rise in violence, crime, and terrorism in the wealthiest nations of the world, and an increasing occurrence of riots when conditions seem to improve rather than deteriorate.[31]

In a closely interdependent modern social order the preferences of individual decision-makers or decision-making units might conflict. The resolution of conflicting preferences on several organizational levels represents one of the most difficult theoretical problems of sociology and social psychology. Whose preferences will prevail and to what extent depends primarily on availability of power and determination to use it. Figure 3 summarizes the salient features of the proposed model of change based on power-will and discontent hypotheses.

One of the important avenues to understanding individual and collective violence is to probe into the behavior of individuals with the purpose of determining why and under what circumstances they resort to violence instead of trying to solve their problems by use of legitimate means. In terms of the power-will hypothesis, one can postulate the following basic theorem: propensity to violence is a function of both preference for violence and opportunity for violence. Each of the two latter, taken separately, are necessary conditions, while taken together they represent a sufficient condition for the occurrence of violence.

Since under similar circumstances some persons resort to violence while others do not, the cause for the difference should be found in their personality structures. According to Fromm, "the most important factor in determining the occurrence and intensity of frustration is the character of a person. . . . The character of the person determines in the first place what frustrates him and in the second place the intensity of his reaction to frustration."[32] Due to space limitation, I will mention only one important characteristic of a personality structure: its threshold of frustration.

Figure 3. Schematic Outline of the Model of Change

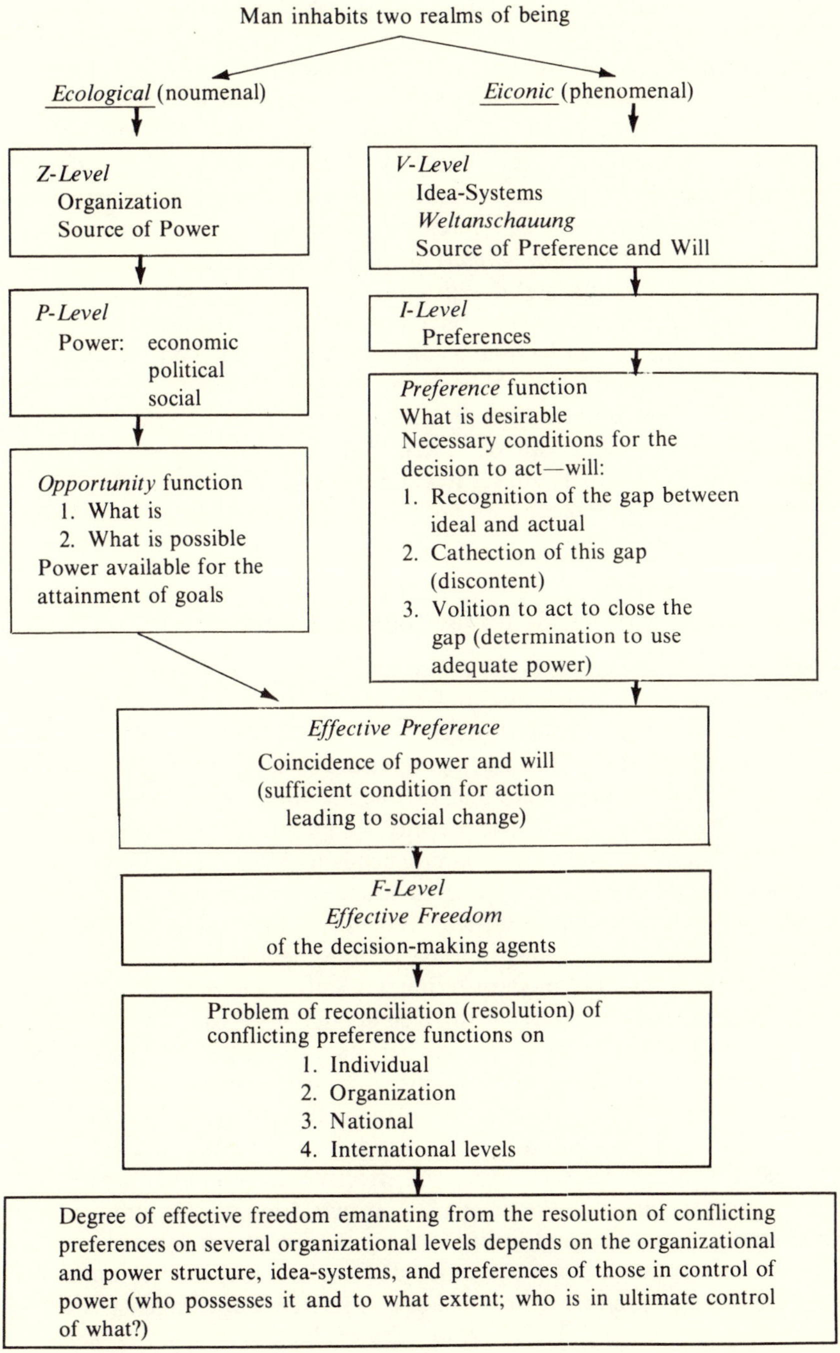

Man inhabits two realms of being

Ecological (noumenal)   *Eiconic* (phenomenal)

Z-Level
Organization
Source of Power

↓

P-Level
Power: economic
         political
         social

↓

Opportunity function
1. What is
2. What is possible
Power available for the
attainment of goals

V-Level
Idea-Systems
Weltanschauung
Source of Preference and Will

↓

I-Level
Preferences

↓

Preference function
What is desirable
Necessary conditions for the
decision to act—will:
1. Recognition of the gap between
ideal and actual
2. Cathection of this gap
(discontent)
3. Volition to act to close the
gap (determination to use
adequate power)

Effective Preference
Coincidence of power and will
(sufficient condition for action
leading to social change)

↓

F-Level
Effective Freedom
of the decision-making agents

↓

Problem of reconciliation (resolution) of
conflicting preference functions on
         1. Individual
         2. Organization
         3. National
         4. International levels

↓

Degree of effective freedom emanating from the resolution of conflicting
preferences on several organizational levels depends on the organizational
and power structure, idea-systems, and preferences of those in control of
power (who possesses it and to what extent; who is in ultimate control
of what?)

Threshold of frustration[33] is here defined as that point at which a person, facing a rising aspiration-attainment gap, becomes frustrated and stops considering legitimate socially acceptable means for closing the gap. He might remain passive and suppress his emotions which might be converted into pent-up discontent, or resort to deviant or socially disapproved behavior, possibly violence, against himself or others. The concept of threshold of frustration is very complex. A person might have different points of threshold of frustration in different areas of interest and activities. But generally one can speak of a relatively low level of frustration tolerance which, in common parlance, is referred to as a "low boiling point." On the macro-societal level, as a useful approximation, one can use the term average threshold of frustration for a given society at a given historical point. This average concept can be used as an indicator of one important component part of the "spirit" of the time in the Weberian sense.

The apparent paradox of high propensity for violence in wealthy, industrially advanced nations can be interpreted in terms of discontent and threshold of frustration. To do so, it will be necessary to analyze the impact of the forces of modernization on both preference for violence and opportunity for violence.

Impact of Modernization on Propensity for Violence

Since modernization is a complex and multidimensional social phenomenon and since numerous and frequently conflicting definitions of modernization are not easily brought to the least common denominator, modernization is here defined as "a process of social change engineered by a set of mutually interdependent and interacting forces which have brought society to its present state of modernity."[34] Forces of modernization are numerous, complex, and closely interdependent. Modernization has many dimensions and facets like "Westernization, rationalization and bureaucratization, systemic and persistent transformation, economic development, social mobilization, institutional politics, democracy, etc."[35] Among the multitude of forces of modernization, six will be selected for the purpose of the present study: three from the eiconic and three from the ecological realms. On the eiconic side, the forces pertinent to the present analysis are: (1) the revolution of rising expectations, (2) anomie or normlessness, and (3) spread of pseudo-humanitarianism. Among the ecological forces are: (1) increasing complexity, interdependence and dynamism of the social order; (2) rapid advance in destructiveness and effectiveness of modern weaponry, and (3) great advances in the means of transportation and communication which improve mobility and facilitate the gathering of intelligence.

The factors operating on the eiconic side have had a substantial impact on society's average preference for violence. Preference for violence has increased in the past because of at least three interdependent changes in the basic components in preference functions and personality structures: (1) increase in the discontent gap, (2) higher elasticity of discontent, and (3) lowering of the average threshold of frustration.

The revolution of rising expectations would not have much of a disruptive effect on society if it were coupled with the revolution of rising efforts to satisfy the demands for higher standards of living. Unfortunately, "the revolution of rising expectations," which has been one of the chief features of Western society in the past twenty-five years, is being transformed into a "revolution of rising entitlements for the next 25."[36] In the United States, the revolution of rising expectations may be considered a part of American ideology, the other part being faith in abundant opportunities for all citizens. The latter "may be regarded functional in terms of their blaming themselves rather than the society for their deprivation," while the former, "from the standpoint of maintaining social order . . . is considered dysfunctional for those people suffering from objective deprivation as Merton's anomie theory suggests."[37]

The rapidly rising level of aspirations not accompanied by increasing efforts to raise the level of attainments tends to widen the aspiration-attainment gap and to increase the coefficient of personal discontent: $D = F (I/A)$. The tendency of the rate of increase in the aspiration level to outstrip the rate of increase in the level of attainment increases elasticity of discontent: $Ed = dI/I - dA/A$. This discontent and its elasticity have a potential for rapid escalation. According to Durkheim, unrestrained aspirations contribute to a higher suicide rate.[38] For him, "a flight of unbridled aspirations has largely its own inherent pitfall of instability and thus a strong potential for frustration."[39] Given the average threshold level of frustration, a higher coefficient of personal discontent and elasticity of discontent lead to a higher preference for violence. If opportunity for violence remains unchanged increased preference for violence leads to increased propensity for violence.

Closely related to the revolution of rising expectations is a phenomenon called *anomie* which follows in its footsteps. Expectations of infinite future improvements in the standard of living and quality of life based on "confidence in the power of science plus education to generate infinite progress"[40] and the belief that the possibilities of organizational and managerial arts are boundless lead to "a general tendency toward overexpectation that began to rise in the U.S. in the fifties and has accelerated rapidly through the sixties."[41] Expectations underlying the modern revolution of rising expectations tend to be "infinitely elastic because they contain a reflection of infinity, a yearning toward absolute justice, absolute happiness."[42]

The impact of the revolution of rising expectations would have been beneficial if the American success ideology, containing the doctrine of "abundant success opportunities for all,"[43] did not conflict with "some pleasant structural realities of opportunity inequality."[44] When the level of aspirations moves rapidly up, while the expected level of attainments falls behind, when "contradiction between legitimized cultural aspirations and socially restricted opportunities"[45] becomes grossly evident, healthy discontent might in many cases be replaced by frustration. If the threshold of frustration is relatively low, the incidence of deviant behavior with its possible violence component is on the rise. Continual and persistent frustration caused by an "acute disjunction between cultural norms and the socially structured capacities of members of the group to act in accord with them" tends to lead to anomie.[46]

Anomie manifests itself in both loss of faith in authority and in societal normative standards. "What we are witnessing," writes Nisbet, "is rising opposition to the central values of the political community as we have known them for the better part of the past two centuries: freedom, rights, due process, privacy and welfare." He believes that "a crisis of the most serious magnitude now exists in the response and assessment of the people to their government."[47] These two related attitudinal changes lower the level of discontent which people are still capable of tolerating without resorting to deviant behavior and possibly violence. Moreover, loss of faith in authority and social value systems blur the lines drawn by legality and legitimacy which separate force from violence. This strengthens the preference and propensity for violence and, therefore, increases the probability of its occurrence.

Since World War II, the revolution of rising expectations and anomie were reinforced in shaping people's attitudes by a so-called philosophy of pseudo-humanitarianism based on acceptance of determinism and faith in the perfectibility of human nature. The traditional American success ideology based on belief in "the equality of success opportunities" contributed to "the internalization of the ethic of self-responsibility for one's own life conditions."[48] But the gradual spread of the notion that human actions are determined by social circumstances undermined the basic belief in personal responsibility. It is only logical then, to put the blame for an individual's deviant behavior on society itself, especially if one accepts the postulate of the inherent goodness of human nature.[49]

One consequence of the diminishing faith in personal responsibility has been a gradual transformation of the revolution of rising expectations into a revolution of rising entitlements and a concomitant lowering of the average societal threshold of frustration, a situation which under normal circumstances enhances preference for deviant and violent behavior and increases societal average propensity for violence. It has been observed that people "many times suffer frustrations without having an aggressive response" if they believe that they themselves are responsible for the situation causing frustration. "What produces the aggression," says Fromm, "is not frustration as such, but the injustice or rejection involved in the situation."[50] Two important corollaries of pseudo-humanitarianism following from its basic premises are: (1) the principle of nonfrustration[51] and (2) misdirected compassion for criminals accompanied by very little compassion for the victims of crime. The former systematically lowers the average threshold of frustration by spreading and enhancing the "spoiled child's temper tantrums" mentality which contributes to the rise in preference for violence. The latter softens the attitude of law-creating, enforcing, and interpreting agencies. The indirect effect of this change in attitude has been to expand the opportunity for committing violence and getting away with it. Thus, technological advance in weaponry, communication, and gathering intelligence, which in itself is neutral, turned out to benefit organized violence and crime instead of helping society to protect its innocent members from the violent acts of lawbreakers.

On the objective (ecological) side, the forces of modernization are manifested, among others, in increasing complexity, interdependence, and dynamism of social organization,[52] in the frightening advance in the development of potential instruments of terror,[53] and in the perfection of means of transportation and communication.[54] All of them tend to make people more vulnerable to acts of violence and terrorism and facilitate their unprecedented dissemination. They contribute to expanding the opportunity for violence and terrorism. This coincidence of increasing preference and opportunity for violence in modern society, caused by some powerful forces of modernization, increases the average propensity for violence and augments the incidence of violence, crime, and terrorism.

Objective forces of modernization can be used by an organized society to prevent and combat violence. Unfortunately, deterministic philosophy downgrading personal responsibility combined with permissiveness on the part of authorities, especially the judiciary and law-enforcing agencies, continues to hamper the effective use of modern legal surveillance, intelligence, and application of effective means of social control to prevent and combat acts of violence and terrorism. See Figure 4 for a tabulated presentation of the impact of modernization forces on the propensity for violence.

Whether the motivation of terrorists is economic, political, ideological, or just purely psychopathic, the rapid spread of organized violence threatens to tear apart the very fiber of modern society and endangers the foundation of our civilization.

Changes in Understanding and Attitudes Needed to Reduce Violence

Since growing violence and its apex—terrorism—present a serious threat to domestic and international peace, they must be subjected to careful study

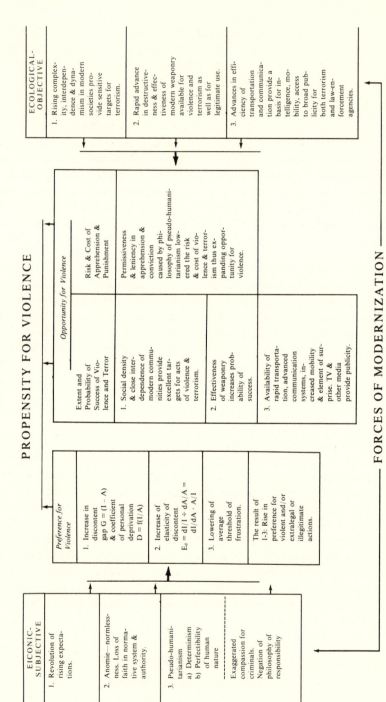

Figure 4.
Impact of Modernization Forces
on Propensity for Violence

PROPENSITY FOR VIOLENCE

FORCES OF MODERNIZATION

by scholars, civic leaders, governmental agencies, business and labor leaders, and all people interested in the protection of basic human rights against the illegitimate use of force.

Antiviolence and terrorism policies are of two categories: (1) short-run measures for combating violence and (2) long-run efforts of a preventive character.

Immediate combating of violence is necessary for survival of the social order and for protection of innocent law-abiding citizens. Short-run measures must be decisive and successful. One should recognize the fact that one of the most potent "determinants of the perceived utility of political violence is people's previous success in attaining their ends by such means: One of the strongest inducements to the spread of violent actions is provided by the demonstration effect of other groups' successful use or threat of violence."[55] Short-run prevention is, of course, the most efficient way of combating violence. This places a great importance on efficient intelligence work which can, if successful, prevent much bloodshed and property loss. The success of violence-combating agencies greatly depends on the cooperation and support of the general public and on the absence of unduly restrictive regulations preventing a swift gathering of information on potential sources of violence.

According to Wilkinson, the following are effective countermeasures to political terrorism—one of the most dangerous kinds of organized violence: "(1) Government must not be seen to give in to terrorist blackmail or intimidation. . . . (2) The authorities must convince the general population that they can protect them against the terrorists. . . . (3) Above all, the government must seek to avoid alienating the support of the mass of the population. . . . (4) While government is dealing effectively with the military and security threat posed by the terrorists, it must also be engaged in a political struggle with the political wing of the terrorist movement to win allegiance of the people."[56] But above all, in its efforts to combat terrorism, "the anti-terrorist policy must be never to surrender to blackmail or extortion. . . . Governments must aim to combat terrorism and win."[57]

Since no governmental security agency is capable of protecting all potential targets, "what is required is to devise a careful balance between reasonable protection and cost in funds and freedom."[58] To be able to attain such a balance, the general public must understand the fundamentals of violence, especially the line dividing it from legitimate use of force. If people, due to a lack of understanding of the problem, fail to circumscribe the area of legitimate actions, "the distinction between violence and nonviolence may be relinquished by the dissenters as well as by their critics."[59]

Unfortunately, even the most outrageous acts of violence and terrorism seem, at times, to fail to arouse strong public reaction. "The nation's besieged lawmen," writes Wiedrich, "have been waiting for a wave of citizen outrage against rising crime, but all they have witnessed is a listless pool of public apathy."[60] Without participation of an informed public, the fight against violence and terrorism is doomed to failure.

Therefore, there exists a need for a two-pronged, long-range intellectual attack on two interrelated problems: (1) presenting to people the fundamental problems involved in drawing the dividing line between legitimate and illegitimate use of force (violence) on the cognitional, cathectic (emotional), and volitional levels and (2) explaining to the public the present general attitudes in educational (in the broadest sense, including all information media) organizations conducive to preference for violence and suggesting the changes in attitudes needed for reducing it. Figures 5 and 6 represent a schematic presentation of factors in determining the legitimate use of force and the changes in attitudes required to reduce preference for violence.

In the process of drawing the line between legitimate and illegitimate acts every society must search for a precarious balance within the three basic dichotomies. On the level of cognition, it must search for an optimum point between absolute order and infinite freedom never forgetting that "total freedom is anarchy; total order is tyranny."[61] Society, to survive, must be able to reconcile freedom and order by limiting individual freedom to insure freedom for both its strong and weak members.

On the emotional level, society is always in search of an optimum point on the scale between the extreme value represented by absolute fear and infinite pity (compassion). Rule by absolute fear—a reign of boundless terror—is self-defeating and usually short-lived, but so is the society which goes to the extreme of showing infinite compassion for both criminals and their innocent victims.

Finally, on the level of volition, people face a dichotomy between absolute pragmatism and infinite morality. The former position sees all means justifiable by a lofty end, whereas the latter contends that no wrong means can ever be justified by an end, no matter how desirable. The line of legitimacy, separating socially approvable use of force from violence, cannot be effectively drawn without an agreement on what constitutes the optimum amount of force necessary to maintain social order and to protect human rights against encroachment. A society subscribing to infinite morality which condemns all use of force as immoral is doomed no less than a society accepting the absolute pragmatism of tyrants.

All organizations and institutions responsible for educating the general public are also caught in a perennial struggle consisting of reconciling the triple dichotomy. On the level of knowledge (cognition), the opposite poles are need for immediate relevance and true relevance in a holistic sense. The predominant trend is toward pseudo-relevance of immediate applicability to jobs presently available in the market. And yet, no true relevance can be

Figure 5. Factors in Determining Legitimate Use of Force

EXTREME POSITION	THE PROBLEM OF DETERMINING AN OPTIMUM POSITION	EXTREME POSITION
1. LEVEL OF COGNITION: DICHOTOMY OF FREEDOM AND ORDER		
Infinite freedom for all No freedom for anyone	Reconciliation of freedom and order by limiting individual freedoms to insure freedom for all: strong & weak members of society.	*Absolute order:* precluding any exercise of freedom except for rulers.
2. LEVEL OF CATHECTION: DICHOTOMY OF PITY (COMPASSION) AND FEAR		
Society based on *infinite pity* (compassion) for all—criminals & victims alike	Compassion for all, but for law-abiding citizens first. Fear of inexorable punishment for those who willfully violate human rights of others.	*Absolute fear:* government of men based on fear.
3. LEVEL OF VOLITION: DICHOTOMY OF ENDS AND MEANS		
Infinite morality Wrong means cannot be justified by a lofty end. Use of force is never justifiable	Optimum amount of use of force to maintain social order and protect human rights against encroachment.	*Absolute pragmatism* All means are justified by lofty ends. All use of force is justifiable to attain the objective.

Figure 6. Need for Long-Range Change in Attitudes to Reduce Preference for Violence.

Factors Reducing Preference for Violence	Direction of Long-Range Change	Factors Conducive to Preference for Violence
	I. LEVEL OF COGNITION (KNOWLEDGE)	
NEED FOR: RELEVANCE Holistic View: Global & Historical Perspective	*Symptoms:* 1. Lack of global perspective of problems: "fallacy of composition" 2. Lack of historical perspective: full satisfaction of all wants *now* 3. Revolution of rapidly rising entitlements 4. Overspecialization	*Harmful Present Attitude: Pseudorelevance* (Immediate relevance for today's job performance)
	II. LEVEL OF CATHECTION (FEELINGS)	
VALUES—CENTRAL THEME IN STUDY OF SOCIAL REALITY	*Symptoms:* 1. Anomie—normlessness 2. Twilight of authority 3. Indifference 4. Boredom	*Irrational Passion for Dispassionate Rationality—* Avoidance of "value judgments"
	III. LEVEL OF VOLITION (DETERMINATION)	
VOLUNTARY COMMITMENT TO Consciously Selected Scale of Values and Decision to Attain & Defend It.	*Symptoms:* 1. Loss of devotion to nobler purposes 2. Devotion to personal & collective self-aggrandizement 3. Disillusionment and alienation of those searching for commitment & sacrifice 4. Commitment to extremists' ideologies that promise utopias	*Commitment to Noncommitment*

attained without a global and historic perspective of the problems torment-ing modern society. The symptoms of this phenomenon are many; among them are the trend toward overspecialization, a lack of understanding of the "fallacy of composition" which greatly contributed to the revolution of rising entitlements, and a lack of historical perspective.

The second dichotomy is found on the emotional level. At one pole, one finds a "valueless" educational ideal, while the other is occupied with a value-oriented educational ideal. The present tendency is toward "irrational passion for dispassionate rationality." Deliberate avoidance of values has greatly contributed to anomie, the "twilight of authority," indifference, boredom, and alienation. And yet, without understanding and deep feelings for values, which must be internalized to make society viable, no social order can persist. Social cohesion depends on adherence to a common normative system, "it does not come about automatically and cannot be taken for granted: it requires continuous attention and concern."[62] "This society has a shortage of things to believe in,"[63] and "new society wide ideals must be forged. People do not conduct themselves ethically unless they believe ethical conduct has some merit—which is only the case where large numbers of people share a devotion to nobler purposes than their own personal or collective self-aggrandizement."[64]

Society is also faced, on the level of volition, with a dichotomy between the "commitment to non-commitment" position and the decisive need for a strong commitment to a set of values needed to preserve society's integrity and survival. "What new or rejuvenated ideals might be capable of evoking a recommitment to shared purposes is hard to foresee from our current vantage point of demoralization," says Etzioni. "Nor can one guarantee that such a recommitment will come about just because it is so badly needed."[65]

If harmful present attitudes of pseudo-relevance, irrational passion for dispassionate rationality, and commitment to noncommitment continue to persist in institutions responsible for conveying knowledge to the people, no one can expect that the dividing line between the legitimate use of force and violence will be adequately drawn. Adherence to true relevance, value-centered education, and insistence on voluntary commitment to a con-sciously selected scale of ethical norms and values will remove this defi-ciency and provide a hopeful avenue which will, in the long run, lead toward a reduction in the preference and propensity for violence.

Summary and Conclusion

The central theme of this study is concerned with the impact of some selected forces of modernization operating on the ecological and eiconic sides of existence—on societal opportunity and preference for violence, the two component parts of the propensity for violence. Concepts of the legitimacy and legality of actions were defined to separate the terms, violence and force. An attempt was made to interpret the rise in violence and terrorism in modern times in terms of such concepts as discontent, elasticity of discontent, and threshold of frustration.

It was found that a general lowering of the threshold of frustration, combined with rapidly growing discontent and its elasticity, contributed to an increase in preference and, therefore, to propensity for violence. The revolution of rising expectations and entitlements, anomie, and the spread of a philosophy of pseudo-humanitarianism with its downgrading of personal responsibility and growing permissiveness on the part of law-creating, interpreting, and enforcing agencies, have contributed to the preference for violence and greatly expanded the opportunity for it.

In this discussion, the long-range suggestions for lowering the propensity for violence were given precedence over short-range policies for the immediate prevention and combating of violence and terrorism. The need for reversing the trend toward pseudo-relevance, irrational passion for dispassionate rationality, and commitment to noncommitment in the educational system and for moving toward true relevance, reintroduction of values, and commitments to voluntarily selected ethical standards and norms was stressed. There is definitely a need for recommitment to values, but no one can "guarantee that such a recommitment will come about just because it is so badly needed."[66] And though presently the outlook seems to be gloomy, one may draw hope from the history of our civilization and join Nisbet in his strong belief that "values and social structures which had survived as many vicissitudes and environmental changes as those had over two and a half millenia of their existence in Western society would go on for at least a few more centuries."[67]

So much for hope in the long run. In the short run, however, our society is facing the immediate problem of "how to nourish the hope without having gigantic expectations pull down the structure of order"[68] and without being drowned in a sea of violence, lawlessness, and terror.

Notes

1. Lewis A. Coser, "Some Social Functions of Violence," *Patterns of Violence, The Annals of the American Academy of Political and Social Science,* vol. 364, March 1966, p. 13.

2. Edwin M. Schur, "Reactions to Deviance: A Critical Assessment," *American Journal of Sociology,* vol. 75, no. 3, November 1969, p. 309.

3. Elton B. McNeil, "Violence and Human Development," *Patterns of Violence, The Annals,* p. 149.

4. Hugh Davis Graham and Ted Robert Gurr, *Violence in America: Historical and Comparative Perspectives,* A Report to the National Commission on the Causes and Prevention of Violence, June 1969, p. XII.

5. Oleg Zinam, "Theory of Discontent: Heart of Theory of Economic Development," *Rivista Internazionale di Scienze Economiche e Commerciali,* anno XVII, November 1971, p. 1111.

6. Max Weber, *The Theory of Social and Economic Organization,* trans. by A. M. Henderson and Talcott Parsons (New York: Oxford University Press, 1947), p. 152.

7. H. L. Nieburg, *Political Violence: The Behavioral Process* (New York: St. Martin's Press, 1969), p. 10; Lewis Mumford, *The Myth of the Machine: Technics and Human Development* (New York: Harcourt, Brace & World, Inc., 1967), pp. 234-262, and E. V. Walter, "Power and Violence," *American Political Science Review,* vol. 29, no. 3, June 1964, p. 350.

8. Robert L. Holmes, "Violence and Nonviolence," *Violence,* Jerome A. Shaffer, ed. (New York: David McKay Co., Inc., 1971), pp. 109-110.

9. Glenn J. Gray, *On Understanding Violence Philosophically* (New York: Harper and Row, 1970), pp. 12, 16.

10. Vilfredo Pareto, *Sociological Writings,* introduction by S. E. Finer, trans. by Denck Mirfin (New York: Frederick A. Praeger, 1966), p. 135.

11. Hugh Davis Graham and Ted Robert Gurr, *Violence in America: Historical and Comparative Perspectives,* p. xiv.

12. Eugene Victor Walters, *Terror and Resistance: A Study of Political Violence* (New York: Oxford University Press, 1969), p. 23.

13. Marvin E. Wolfgang, "A Preface to Violence," *Patterns of Violence, The Annals,* p. 1.

14. H. L. Nieburg, *Political Violence: The Behavioral Process* (New York: St. Martin's Press, 1969).

15. Ernest Van den Haag, *Political Violence and Civil Disobedience* (New York: Harper and Row, 1972), p. 54.

16. Graham and Gurr, *Violence in America,* p. xv.

17. Monica D. Blumenthal et al., *Justifying Violence: Attitudes of American Man,* Institute for Social Research (University of Michigan, Ann Arbor, 1972), p. 13.

18. Walters, *Terror and Resistance,* p. 13.

19. Paul Wilkinson, *Political Terrorism* (New York: Wiley Press, 1975), p. 137.

20. Walters, *Terror and Resistance,* p. 5.

21. M. Cherif Bassiouni, *International Terrorism and Political Crimes* (Springfield, Illinois: Charles C. Thomas, 1975).

22. Lester A. Sobel, ed., *Political Terrorism,* (New York: Facts on File, Inc., 1975), p. 1.

23. Wilkinson, *Political Terrorism,* p. 18.

24. Edwin F. Black, "If Terrorism Goes Nuclear . . ." *Washington Report,* May 1976, p. 3.

25. Oleg Zinam, "Interaction of Preference and Opportunity Functions and Long-Range Economic Development," Dissertation, University of Cincinnati, 1963; "Theory of Discontent: Heart of Theory of Economic Development," *Rivista Internazionale di Scienze Economiche e Commerciali,* anno XVIII, no. 11, November 1971; "A Note on Elasticity of Discontent," *Rivista Internazionale di Scienze Economiche e Commerciali,* anno XVII, vol. 1, January 1970; "Socio-Economic Change and Discontent: A Search for a Broader Paradigm in Economics," *Eastern Economic Journal,* vol. 1, no. 4, October 1974.

26. The term ecology is used here in its broadest sense, including human ecology. Eiconics is a term coined by K. Boulding. It overlaps with the Kantian concept.

27. Alfred North Whitehead, *Adventure of Ideas* (New York, The MacMillan Company, 1933), p. 21.

28. Kenneth E. Boulding, *The Skills of the Economist* (Cleveland, Ohio: Howard Allen, Inc., 1958), p. 14.

29. Zinam, "Theory of Discontent: Heart of Theory of Economic Development," p. 1109.

30. *Ibid.*, pp. 1109, 1110.

31. Oleg Zinam, *A Note on Elasticity of Discontent,* p. 76.

32. Erich Fromm, *The Anatomy of Human Destructiveness* (New York: Holt, Rinehart and Winston, 1973), p. 68.

33. In this study the term frustration is given a special meaning. It is juxtaposed to the concept of discontent which leads to a socially approved action. Here frustration means the breaking point on the discontent continuum—called threshold of frustration—at which the actor gives up accepted channels to attain his objective and either resorts to illegitimate ones, or unable to act, transforms his mobilized mental energy into pent-up discontent. Making discontent synonymous or coextensive with frustration is analogous to equating violence with force, a notion rejected in this study.

34. Oleg Zinam, "Modernization, Convergence Thesis and US-USSR Detente," published in Spanish as "La modernización, la tésis de la convérgencia y la distensión entre Rusia y Estados Unidos," *Revista de Política Internacional,* no. 144, marzo-abril 1976, p. 89.

35. Henry Bienen, *Violence and Social Change* (Chicago: The University of Chicago Press, 1968), p. 3.

36. Daniel Bell, *The Cultural Contradictions of Capitalism* (New York: Basic Books, Inc., 1976), p. 233.

37. Alex Thio, "Toward a Fuller View of American Success Ideology," *Pacific Sociological Review,* July 1972, p. 381.

38. Emile Durkheim, *Suicide* (New York: Free Press, 1951).

39. Thio, *Toward a Fuller View*, p. 382.

40. "The Dynamite of Rising Expectations," *Fortune,* May 1968, p. 135.

41. *Ibid.*, p. 134.

42. *Ibid.*, p. 251.

43. Amitai Etzioni, "Basic Human Needs, Alienation and Inauthenticity," *American Sociological Review,* no. 33, December 1968.

44. Alex Thio, *Toward a Fuller View*, p. 384.

45. Robert K. Merton, *Social Theory and Social Structure* (Illinois: Free Press, 1957), p. 178.

46. *Ibid.*, p. 146.

47. Robert Nisbet, *Twilight of Authority* (New York: Oxford University Press, 1975), pp. 5, 15.

48. Alex Thio, *Toward a Fuller View*, p. 387.

49. For some relevant discussion of determinism and the perfectibility of human nature, see Marian J. Morton, *The Terrors of Ideological Politics* (Cleveland: The

Press of Case Western Reserve University, 1972), pp. 5, 12, 13, and Arthur M. Schlesinger, Jr., *The Vital Center: The Politics of Freedom* (Boston: Houghton Mifflin Co., 1949), p. ix. For refutal of the notion of perfectibility, consult Robert Nisbet, *Twilight of Authority*, especially his statement on p. 76: "The makers of the American Constitutional Democracy thought it best to presume, if anything at all about human nature, a certain ineradicable tendency toward mischief and even evil."

50. Erich Fromm, *The Anatomy of Human Destructiveness* (New York: Holt, Rinehart and Winston, 1973).

51. Oleg Zinam, "Note on the Principle of Non-Frustration," an unpublished paper (University of Cincinnati, 1960), pp. 1-18.

52. "The world has become increasingly interdependent, [and therefore] it has become more vulnerable to assault." J. Bowyer Bell, *Transnational Terror* (Washington, D.C.: American Enterprise Institute for Public Policy Research, 1975), p. 4, and "Western governments, with their relatively open and mobile societies and their complex communications systems, are increasingly vulnerable to . . . terrorist attacks," Paul Wilkinson, *Political Terrorism* (New York: Wiley Press, 1975), p. 145.

53. "A surprising lacuna in strategic studies of revolutionary terrorism is the absence of a full treatment of weapon availability and supply and of the implications of new weapon technology for terrorism." Paul Wilkinson, *Political Terrorism*, p. 135.

54. Advance in transportation and communication "has made possible both the magnification of violence and also created complex and vulnerable targets for that violence." J. Bowyer Bell, *Transnational Terror*, p. 89. "Technological advances afford the terrorist . . . an instant world-wide audience. TV, radio and press coverage are critically valuable to the terrorist, who relies on attracting public attention to his cause." Department of State, *Gist*, March 1976.

55. Ted Robert Gurr, *Why Men Rebel* (New Jersey: Princeton University Press, 1971), pp. 218, 222.

56. Paul Wilkinson, *Political Terrorism*, pp. 137, 138.

57. *Ibid.*, p. 151.

58. J. Bowyer Bell, *Transnational Terror*, p. 88.

59. Monica D. Blumenthal et al., *Justifying Violence*, p. 249.

60. Bob Wiedrich (*Chicago Tribune*), "The Citizen Has a Duty to Combat Crime," *Cincinnati Post*, 30 May 1976.

61. A statement by the commissioner of London's Metropolitan Police, Sir Robert Mark, quoted in Richard Clutterbuck, *Protest and the Urban Guerrilla* (New York: Abelard Schuman, 1973), p. x.

62. H. L. Nieburg, *Political Violence*, p. 3.

63. "The Call to Violence," *Enquirer Magazine*, 9 November 1975, p. 45.

64. Amitai Etzioni, "Our National Shortage of Confidence and Commitment," Public Affairs, *Human Behavior*, January 1976, p. 13.

65. *Ibid.*, p. 13.

66. *Ibid.*, p. 13.

67. Robert Nisbet, *Twilight of Authority*, p. 77.

68. "The Dynamite of Rising Expectations," *Fortune*, May 1968, p. 248.

Selected Bibliography

Alexander, Yonah, ed. *International Terrorism: National, Regional and Global Perspectives.* New York: Praeger, 1975.

Annals of the American Academy of Political and Social Science. "Patterns of Violence," vol. 364, March 1966.

Aron, Raymond. *Histoire et Dialectique de la Violence.* Gallimard, 1973.

Bell, Daniel. *The Cultural Contradictions of Capitalism.* New York: Basic Books, 1976.

Bell, J. Bowyer. *Transnational Terror.* Washington, D.C.: American Enterprise Institute for Public Policy Research, 1975.

Bienen, Henry. *Violence and Social Change.* Chicago: The University of Chicago Press, 1968.

Black, Edwin F. *Washington Report,* "If Terrorism Goes Nuclear, "May 1976.

Burton, A. M. *Urban Terrorism.* New York: Free Press, 1975.

Clutterbuck, R. L. *Protest and the Urban Guerrilla.* New York: Abelard-Schuman, 1974.

Conquest, Robert. *The Great Terror.* New York: Macmillan Co., 1973.

Cressey, Donald R. *Theft of the Nation.* New York: Harper and Row, 1969.

Dallin, Alexander, and Breslauer, George W. *Political Terror in Communist Systems.* California: Stanford University Press, 1970.

Durkheim, Emile. *Le Suicide,* Travaux de L'Annee Sociologique, Libraire Felix Alcan, Paris, 1930.

Endleman, Shalom, ed. *Violence in the Streets.* Chicago: Quadrangle Books, 1968.

Fromm, Erich. *The Anatomy of Human Destructiveness.* New York: Rinehart and Winston, 1973.

Gist, ed. Fahey Black. "Terrorism," Bureau of Public Affairs, Department of State, March 1976.

Gray, Glenn J. *On Understanding Violence Philosophically.* New York: Harper and Row, 1970.

Gurr, Ted Robert. *Why Men Rebel.* New Jersey: Princeton University Press, 1971.

Kelley, Clarence. "Terrorism, The Ultimate Evil," *Washington Report,* Washington, D.C., January 1976.

Lambrick, H. T. *The Terrorist.* London: Ernest Benn Limited, 1972.

Mallin, Jay, ed. *Terror and Urban Guerrillas.* Coral Gables, Florida: University of Miami Press, 1971.

Merleau-Ponty, Maurice. *Humanism and Terror.* Boston: Beacon Press, 1969.

Moore, Barrington. *Terror and Progress, USSR.* Cambridge: Harvard University Press, 1954.

Morton, Marian J. *The Terrors of Ideological Politics.* Cleveland: The Press of Case Western Reserve, 1972.

Moss, Robert. *The War for the Cities.* New York: Collier, 1972.

Nisbet, Robert. *Twilight of Authority.* New York: Oxford University Press, 1975.

Roucek, Joseph S. *Juvenile Delinquency.* New York: Philosophical Library, 1958.

———. *Sociology of Crime.* New York: Greenwood Press, 1969.

———. ed. *Contemporary Sociology.* New York: Philosophical Library, 1958.

Shaffer, Jerome A., ed. *Violence.* New York: David McKay Co., 1971.

Sobel, Lester A., ed. *Political Terrorism*. New York: Facts on File, Inc., 1975.

Trotsky, L. *The Defence of Terrorism*. London: George Allen and Unwin, 1935.

Walters, Eugene. *Terror and Resistance*. New York: Oxford University Press, 1969.

Wilkinson, Paul. *Political Terrorism*. New York: Wiley, 1975.

Zinam, Oleg. "Interaction of Preference and Opportunity Functions, and Long-Range Economic Development," Doctoral dissertation, University of Cincinnati, 1963.

———. "Theory of Discontent: Heart of Theory of Economic Development," *Rivista Internazionale di Scienze Economiche e Commerciali*, anno XVIII, no. 11, November 1971.

———. "A Note on Elasticity of Discontent," *Rivista Internazionale di Scienze Economiche e Commerciali*, anno XVII, no. 1, January 1970.

———. "Impact of Modernization on USSR: Two Revolutions in Conflict," *Economia Internazionale*, Genova, Italy, vol. XXVI, no. 2, May 1973.

———. "Socio-Economic Change and Discontent: A Search for a Broader Paradigm in Economics," *Eastern Economic Journal*, vol. 1, no. 4, October 1974.

PART IV

Some Political Consequences of International Terrorism

EUGENE ALESEVICH

Police Terrorism

Usually condemned in the "civilized" world, the devices and techniques of police terror and violence have always been, and are still today, very frequently used, legally and illegally, as a means of social control. There is no difference between American and Soviet police terror; it is one of the techniques used by all police to achieve domination. Sociologically, it is a person, thing, or practice that causes intense fear and suffering, whose aim is to intimidate and subjugate. Targets of terror and violence in the American police system at the federal, state, and municipal level are criminals (organized and individual), extremists, radicals, and the like, who under pressure curtail or cease criminal activity within the jurisdiction of the agency.

Terror and violence as techniques are limited by the cultural standards which determine the extent and the ways in which these are expressed, inhibited, and sublimated. It is important to note that public knowledge of such activity by the police, through exposure, will result in stopping such operations and practices. However, after the public outcry and probable ensuing investigation, the practice will begin again as the criminal elements cannot be controlled by orthodox enforcement measures. Application of equal or superior force when dealing with criminal elements becomes a must at times in establishing superiority.

Psychological-terror methods, coupled with intimidation, aim to force the terror object to behave in a manner most favorable for the subject. These methods have an indirect, preventive character, with the intention of producing a psychological effect. All these steps aim to strike fear in the potential critics (criminal individuals) and impress on the masses that similar steps, even harsher ones, will follow in case of additional illegal activity.

An application of police terror directed at criminal elements is the Street Crime Unit (SCU) of the New York City Police Department. This unit fills the gap between routine, visible police patrol and after-the-fact criminal investigations. The unit focuses on street crimes—robbery, personal grand larceny, and assault. Its primary strategy employs officers disguised as potential crime victims placed in an area where they are likely to be victimized. A plainclothes back-up team waits nearby, ready to come to the decoy's aid and make an arrest. Only criminals perpetrating criminal acts are the object of this group's attention. Unsure as to which citizen is the policeman terrorizes criminals, throws them into uncertainty, and reduces their activity on most occasions.

But decoy work also raises the serious legal question of entrapment. Are the rights of individuals—whether they be criminals or not—being violated? Authorities claim they do not induce persons to commit crimes. The intent exists in the criminal's mind. Police do not alter that intent, but only substitute the victim. One decoy police officer was mugged thirty-nine times and another retiring in Philadelphia about fifty times.

The Nazis and Communists introduced another type of terror, "chronic terror." A persistent and well-organized series of terrorist acts leaves the criminal uncertain when and where another step will be taken.

The use of terror against those trafficking in narcotics and dangerous drugs has been used often with desired results. Disorientation of pushers and interdiction of supply routes have resulted in some operations. Force (terror) has become a must in many apprehensions. The magnitude of such operations became known on several occasions when the wrong suspects were the targets.

A residence in Winthrop, Massachusetts, was broken into by fifteen burly men, wielding shotguns and terrifying the family. The intruders, it turned out, were not burglars but state and federal narcotic agents who had staged their no-knock raid at the wrong address. This raid was not an isolated episode. It was part of a dark trail of similar incidents in the battle against narcotics dealers.

The battle involves tough and dangerous action (terrorism) against a ruthless enemy. The terror raids have already claimed a number of innocent lives including that of a police officer killed by a woman who fired through the door at the unidentified intruder.

Police intimidation has crippled sex parlors in Los Angeles. Called a police "abatement" program, the object is for the police to be present in the area long enough to close down those establishments. Methods used include finding out who the people are and why they are there. Police stop customers outside and tell them not to go in. Identifications are checked, and if the customers are married, the police imply that their wives will somehow be notified.

Studies of Police Behavior

In May 1971, Dr. Albert Reiss in a report entitled "Our Criminal Police," charged policemen in Boston, Washington, and Chicago with criminal violations. Reiss's thesis was that the greatest failure of American police departments is the failure of any unit to police the police. He said that one in three officers committed a criminal violation in Chicago, one in four in Boston, and one in five in Washington. Misdemeanors were more common than felonies, but in one city roughly one in ten officers committed a felony in the presence of an observer. The policemen were told the observers riding with them were studying citizen reaction to police.

The most common felony, the sociologist said, was assault on a citizen. Such assaults were rarely in response to physical aggression by the citizen and never necessary to sustain an arrest. Actually, no arrest was made in 59 percent of the observed assaults. The next most common felony was theft from a place that had already been burglarized. "This is an interesting form of police crime," Reiss said, "in that the value of stolen property can be charged, so to speak, to the ordinary burglar since just what was taken on the original entry cannot be established."[1] The most common criminal violations, he continued, were extortion or shakedowns of citizens and the acceptance of gratuities as bribes.

Within major metropolitan cities, the rates of violation by police officers are highest in the high-crime areas. The study produced evidence of police misconduct far in excess of that reported by the department's own intelligence units. Reiss said a more effective outside monitoring of police is necessary, perhaps a state, national, or some other system of inspection.

Rubenstein, in his book *City Police,* portrays the average policeman as neither very good, nor very bad. He is a man caught in a crossfire of pressures that few of us could withstand. If he sometimes seems brutal and violent, it is because he must establish his physical authority to survive, and physical authority can only be established physically.

Stark, author of *Police Riots: Collective Violence and Law Enforcement,* believes that both internal and external controls over the police were weakening and that rank-and-file policemen were taking things into their own hands and effectively resisting efforts to control their use of violence.

Specialized units such as the mobile tactical forces have for years applied pressure on criminal elements to force them off the streets, and when desired goals are not achieved, more intense pressure is exerted. These special tactical crime forces vary from a few men in a small department to 200 or more in larger departments. Cities having such units include New York with 690 men and the District of Columbia and Los Angeles with over 200 men each. Other agencies are in Honolulu, Kalamazoo, Syracuse, Amarillo, Savannah, and Chicago, as well as in many other cities. These units are often secretive in their operations, with membership by invitation. More brutality charges are leveled at these units than most other operations in police agencies.

The United States government has recommended the creation of such units in police agencies employing more than seventy-five personnel. These agencies should have immediately available, highly mobile tactical forces for rapid deployment against special crime problems. The general weapon is violence in various forms, which is applied at the proper time, strength, and form. The proper time is when the use of terror will be a surprise to the object. The proper strength is that which will disrupt even the most resistant and strongest group. The proper form is that which has the most damaging psychological effect.

In 1973, the New York Police Department had compiled a list of 150 of the force's 30,000 men who were considered to be violent-prone, unusually excitable, or unstable. This was the first step toward weeding out the undesirable. Numerous other departments have been using preemployment screening methods to eliminate individuals before hiring.

Electronic and Dossier Terrorism

Police have come under fire for snooping into the lives of private citizens. Their spying has stirred criticism since it is not directed at suspected criminals, but at such individuals as bank presidents, civic leaders, politicians, and businessmen. Those attending various protest rallies or involved in civic action may find a dossier on them at police headquarters. Illegal wiretaps may have been used to gather the information. Homosexual arrest records, prostitution charges, and wife-beating reports become useful during political campaigns. This information is made available to other law enforcement agencies on a need-to-know or routine basis.

There is evidence uncovered by Maryland State Senator Edward T. Conroy that the Baltimore police regularly spy on meetings of community organizations, school boards, and utility rate-increase hearings; they take names of everyone in attendance and amass as much information about them as possible. One extreme abuse that was reported recently was the use of computerized criminal histories by city officials to check the names of signers of a recall petition against those same officials. Strict government guidelines prohibit such activity, but abuses are numerous. A 1974 lawsuit in Chicago has charged the police with infiltrating groups, harassment, illegal wiretaps and break-ins, and physical assaults—all against individuals and groups not guilty of criminal activity as far as can be determined.

The Law Enforcement Assistance Administration has been aiding local police for years by funding the purchase of staggering amounts of "electronic surveillance equipment." A total of $160.8 million was designated to support 1,929 intelligence-related projects around the country. Approximately $2.5 million was earmarked directly for the purchase of electronic surveillance equipment. More than $1.3 million worth of bugging equipment went to states which either prohibited wiretaps or had no special laws on bugging. The state of California, which outlaws wiretapping except in unique circumstances, was given $98,565 for sophisticated surveillance. After receiving money from LEAA for such equipment, twenty-five states simply refused to provide LEAA with itemized breakdowns for the bugging equipment.

Federal Terrorism

Recent Federal Bureau of Investigation "political abuses" uncovered by the Justice Department and the Senate Intelligence Committee have shocked government leaders and the American people. This agency's intelligence system had developed to such a degree that no one inside or outside it was willing or able to tell the difference between legitimate national security or law-enforcement information and purely political intelligence gathering. Particularly interesting is that to date no physical violence or terror has been uncovered which would more closely compare this agency with Soviet-style police terror. This absence of physical methods of intimidation, technically removes the agency from a KGB-style organization.

Some examples cited by the report include the following:

1. Hitting at the credit ratings and job status of group members by notifying credit bureaus, creditors, employers, and prospective employers of illegal, immoral, or radical activities.
2. Obtaining tax returns of group members.
3. Interfering in "political or judicial processes" by such actions as revealing arrest records or group affiliations of candidates or defendants. Although there were "only 12 instances" of this type, the report said, they "are among the most troubling in all of the COINTELPRO efforts."
4. Staging an arrest by local police on a narcotics pretext, then using a police radio call to make one of the persons in custody think his companion was a police informer.
5. Forging business and recruiting cards of groups and reproducing the signature stamp of a group leader.
6. Investigating the love life of one civil-rights leader and leaking the information to the press.
7. Making anonymous telephone calls to the families and friends of group members, telling them of immoral or radical conduct.
8. Attempting to use religious and civil leaders to disrupt a group by putting pressure on local governments, landlords, and employers.[2]

A December 1975 Gallup Poll illustrates all too clearly the plunging public esteem for the organization. A decade ago, 84 percent of the Americans surveyed gave the FBI a "highly favorable" rating. Today, only 37 percent do so.

Continual disclosures of FBI abuses and new financial wrongdoings within the bureau are reportedly causing "a fresh and devastating erosion of morale" among the more than 8,500 agents. Still more recently, Attorney General Levi has just ordered a new investigation into charges of corruption in the FBI's ranks—for the first time in the bureau's long and virtually corruption-free history.

Last fall, FBI Director Kelley ordered an inquiry into activities of one of the bureau's top-ranking executives. Reportedly, the probe was quietly suffocated by the impenetrable blanket of secrecy under which the executive operated. Attorney General Levi ordered a second investigation with entirely new investigators. Shock waves are still going through the bureau as of this date. Analysis of accounts of ongoing investigations into the bureau's activities are beginning to point to possibly the number one abuses of position, the top executives of this agency and others at the federal level.

"Look," explained one agent, "the guys who sanctioned the report are the bosses of the FBI. They supervise the investigations, administrations and internal inspections of the bureau—the whole shebang. If they goofed, whitewashed or covered up a case as sensitive as that, what have they done with others? This same cadre of officials, for example, failed last year to find the bureau man who, after the assassination of John F. Kennedy, ordered a Dallas agent to destroy a note written by Lee Harvey Oswald before the killing."[3]

Protection from Government Agencies

The Privacy Act of 1974 aims at reducing the amount of information to be collected and to lessen the flow of information between federal agencies. The Federal government has gone too far in collecting personal data, data that goes beyond what is absolutely necessary. With such information, organization members have been intimidated and politicians threatened and made to vote on issues against the desires of the voters. They are also intimidated to increase appropriations for aging funds to expand the power of the top echelon. These unchecked expansions of power could in time become so powerful as to subvert and destroy democracy.

Conclusion

Previous attempts to put an end to police brutality, harassment and terror, especially at the local level, have not had the desired results. The word terror could easily replace selective enforcement and harassment when pertaining to efforts designed to suppress criminal activity. It is becoming increasingly clear that orthodox, by-the-book policing techniques are not producing reduced crime rates and less criminal activity.

In many cases those responsible for allowing and instigating terror tactics are above the rank-and-file members of a law-enforcement agency. Internal investigations rarely, if ever, are directed at the upper echelon. No agency can effectively investigate itself when those in control direct the investigations. Even the FBI and CIA investigations have shown all too clearly the suppression of such investigations.

Until the law-enforcement bureaucracy is thoroughly investigated by impartial, outside investigative agencies, we will continue to see less results on the streets, more frustrated law-enforcement officers, and a deeper entrenched threat to all directed by many untouchable agency directors.

Notes

1. Albert Reiss, "Our Criminal Police," Russell Sage Foundation, 1971, p. 88.
2. "Using FBI For 'Dirty Tricks'—Behind a Hot Debate," *Time,* 2 December 1974, pp. 37-38.
3. "The FBI: Just How Incorruptible?" *Time,* 5 April 1976, pp. 23-24.

Bibliography

Daley, Robert. *Target Blue: An Insider's View of the N.Y.P.D.* Delacorte, New York, 1973.

Gross, Felix. *The Seizure of Political Power in a Century of Revolution.* Philosophical Library, New York, 1958.

Larson, Richard C. *Urban Police Patrol Analysis.* M.I.T. Press, Cambridge, Massachusetts, 1972.

Merrian, Charles E. *Political Power.* McGraw-Hill, New York, 1934.

Reiss, Albert. "Our Criminal Police," Russell Sage Foundation, 1971.

Rubenstein, Jonathan. *City Police.* Farras, Straus & Girous, New York, 1973.

Stark, Rodney. *Police Riots: Collective Violence and Law Enforcement.* Wadsworth Publishing Company, Belmont, California, 1972.

"The FBI: Just How Incorruptible?" *Time,* 5 April 1976.

"Using the FBI For 'Dirty Tricks'—Behind a Hot Debate," *Time,* 2 December 1974.

Westley, William. *Violence and the Police: A Sociological Study of Law, Custom, and Morality.* M.I.T. Press, Cambridge, Massachusetts, 1970.

Whited, Charles. *The Decoy Man.* Simon & Schuster, New York, 1973.

BROOKS McCLURE

Hostage Survival

Of all the tactics used by political terrorists, kidnapping has probably been the most effective. During the past four years, as much as $80 million in ransoms for hostages have been collected in Latin America alone. Other returns also from kidnapping have been substantial: scores of prisoners have been released; governments have been embarrassed; relations between nations have been strained; and worldwide publicity for terrorist causes has been realized.

All this social disruption has been accomplished at relatively small cost to the perpetrators. About 80 percent of the terrorists involved in political kidnapping have gotten away unscathed, although the odds for success have diminished in several countries during the past year. Countermeasures are improving, but kidnapping remains a low-risk, high-return activity for many terrorist groups.

Further progress in dealing with the kidnap weapon depends in large measure upon improved antisubversion tactics by governments, still more effective protection of prime targets, increased international cooperation, and the elimination of terrorist safe-havens. Until more of these adjustments can be made, political kidnappings are likely to continue.

In the face of this threat, therefore, it has been necessary to take a look at the problem from the other end, that is, what can be done to help prepare a prospective kidnap victim and improve his chance of surviving the experience? To answer this question, a number of researchers have analyzed hostage situations to see whether defense measures can be devised for vulnerable individuals—particularly international businessmen, diplomats, and military officers.

The result is interesting. Anyone with experience abroad might assume that cultural factors alone would create vastly different conditions for terrorist operations in different parts of the world. And to this fact must be added a multitude of other variables, such as the personality and temperament of the victim, the character of his captors, the nature of the terrorist cause, the immediate objective of the kidnapping, and the reaction of the authorities.

Indeed, the key question is whether hostage incidents are subject to so many diverse influences that each case must be considered basically unique. If so, any standard approach to the problem would appear nearly impossible. Any rules for hostage defense would then have to be so vague and qualified as to be practically useless.

Fortunately, the study of more than two dozen cases of political kidnapping in Latin America, Europe, and the Middle East indicates this is not so. While it is certainly no easy matter to develop concrete hostage countermeasures, and there is a danger of trying to set hard-and-fast rules, the task of providing useful guidelines for political kidnap victims is feasible. There are, in fact, several significant similarities in widely disparate incidents from which general lessons can be learned.

The first of these similarities is the psychological reaction of almost any individual to being kidnapped. It does not matter much who the victim is, or where he is taken; he will nearly always react in a predictable fashion. And it helps him to understand in advance what his reaction will be.

Second, again in the psychological realm, the confrontation of prisoner and captor follows a pattern. When the victim knows the basic dynamics of this type of encounter, he can assume his "prisoner role" in such a way as to make the most of what is, at best, an exceedingly difficult situation.

Third, there are basic types of hostage situations with different stresses and challenges to the victim. By understanding the nature of these different circumstances and being able to assess the character and aims of his captors, the hostage can act intelligently in his own interest. Some hostages have helped save their own lives because of this ability to analyze their predicament.

Fourth, ideologically motivated terrorists often follow the same thought process and use similar operating techniques—they, in fact, have all had much the same Marxist-activist schooling. An understanding of this mentality can be a help to any hostage.

Finally, there is a set of prisoner survival techniques which can help a hostage maintain his mental stability and physical condition wherever he may be held.

It is possible, therefore, to give a potential hostage a certain amount of useful training so that he is better able to endure the truly traumatic experience of political kidnapping. The danger, of course, is that the instruction may become oversystematized, resulting in dogmatic "answers" to infinitely varied problems. The most valuable single point that can be made to a possible victim is that he cannot be prepared for precisely what he will encounter; he must above all remain flexible and mentally alert. He has to make his own decisions. But he can draw from the experiences of earlier victims, and he can put his predicament into a framework for effective analysis, again based on the experiences of others.

Specifically, just what advice can be given to the would-be hostage? First are the things he should do before he is taken. Any prospective target should make sure his affairs are in order and his will up-to-date. Logical enough; but hostages often regret not having taken such simple precautions, and the primary concern of most victims in captivity is about the welfare of family members if they do not return.

It is well for a vulnerable person also to be alert to signs that he is marked for seizure. He might sense that he is being watched; he may catch glimpses of the same people in various parts of town; he may become aware that his car is being followed. Such warnings often occur, as some hostages come to realize only in retrospect after they have been taken. Once warned, there are a number of things a targeted person can do to discourage and possibly prevent seizure. He should consult security specialists immediately.

A second precaution is to learn to understand what a kidnapping is like. Just as the well-trained soldier has been taught to anticipate and cope with the dangers of combat, so the potential hostage should be prepared to face his possible travail. In neither case, of course, is it possible to synthesize the true "combat" experience, but psychological preparation can sometimes make a difference between life and death when the real test comes. It is difficult to exaggerate the shock effect of a kidnapping. From a state of total well-being, the victim in seconds finds himself in mortal peril. At first he cannot believe what is happening; he is stunned, disoriented, often paralyzed with fear—but then, he may also reflexively try to defend himself or to escape. If he has been properly briefed, the victim will know something about the time and techniques for attempting escape and when to yield because the odds are hopelessly against him. He should know that he is expendable. His assailants, no matter how experienced, are tense, and their first objective is to get away. They also probably have planning, initiative, manpower, and firepower in their favor. Resistance in this situation is no game for the novice, but certain well-trained and determined victims can raise the price of kidnapping assaults substantially.

Again depending upon his psychological preparation, temperament, and previous life experience, the victim—in anything from minutes to an hour or more after the surprise attack—regains some of his composure. He now recognizes the full reality of his predicament and begins to assess his chances for long-range survival. Most ordinary people make this transition fairly well, although some naturally do better than others. The important lesson here, however, is that the average person's capacity for shock, mental stress, and physical abuse is far greater than he would ever suspect. People of quite different backgrounds and dispositions can find ways of coping with extraordinary hardships. With some psychological preparation for such an experience and an awareness of his innate ability to survive, the potential kidnapping victim can be even better fortified.

Only the beginning of psychological conditioning for possible hostages has been touched on here. There are, as well, several other useful aids for potential victims, which are too involved to discuss in depth. Among these, for example, is recognition of the different general types of terrorists, which the hostage should be able to distinguish; his treatment by various captors may vary predictably, and his response should be adjusted accordingly. Significant differences can exist between terrorists with a nationalist-ethnic motivation and those with an ideological (usually Marxist) motivation. Some general grounding in the characteristic behavior of terrorist types—while avoiding stereotyping, of course—can also be a help to the hostage.

For every rule which might be proposed on this subject, one can always find the classic exception in some actual case. But, while avoiding over-generalization, certain circumstances arise often enough in widely separated incidents to make it an odds-on possibility that the average potential hostage will encounter them. Here are a few examples:

In the kidnap-imprisonment situation—in which the victim is hidden and may be held for months—urban terrorist groups nearly always keep the hostage in isolation, at least for the first weeks, usually in a cellar or other confined place shut off from daylight. They almost invariably take his watch and often make other attempts to cause him to lose track of time as a means of disorienting him.

From these circumstances there are three obvious psychological hazards for which the hostage should be prepared. The first is isolation; he must be able to counter the demoralizing effect of being alone and avoid being overwhelmed by the realization that his only human contact for periods stretching into months may be consistently hostile. This is particularly true when his captors are his declared ideological enemy.

The second hazard is claustrophobia. Darkness and confined quarters for long periods are common conditions of urban terrorist imprisonment, but again this suffocating environment can be endured. Consider one American who was held nearly three months in a cell only a little over five feet high; he was unable to stand erect during his entire imprisonment. Or a British hostage who spent three months in a cell measuring five by seven feet, and then five months in another cell only slightly larger with eighteen inches between his bunk and the wall and three and one-half feet of space at one end. Or still another prisoner who for four months occupied a totally unfurnished, windowless cell with as many as three other prisoners; where the usable floor sleeping space measured a mere seven feet square, including a hole used as a toilet, and the only light bulb was out for days at a time. Hostages have survived such conditions, and others can do as well with some preparation.

A third hazard suggested by the general pattern of urban terrorist hostage-treatment is the victim's loss of a sense of time and complete insulation from the outside world. Here the experiences of former hostages provide valuable hints: how to keep calendars, how to tell night from day in an underground cell, how to establish mental ties with the unseen world and link one's daily routine—no matter how simple—with the reality which exists outside the prison walls.

From this quick review, it might seem that the whole effort of terrorist groups is to brainwash the prisoner. One need not be reminded that there is no Geneva Convention to protect prisoners in the so-called people's war of liberation, and that terrorists feel no constraint of the law which governs the establishment world outside. But as harsh as conditions are in the "people's prisons," only part of the abuse is calculated psychological coercion.

One aim of the terrorists is to make the prisoner as malleable and cooperative as possible. Otherwise, however, much of the abuse is probably due to the terrorists' ineptitude and, in the case of the ideological types, their general urge to punish the hated "class enemy." It does not seem to occur to the middle-class, self-perceived intellectuals who populate Marxist terrorist movements that they have turned civilization back to the Dark Ages in terms of human rights and dignity. And, to compound this singular indifference, they just simply make lousy housekeepers.

Discussed here have been those areas where the hostage might have some influence—however small—on his fate. It stands to reason he should try to find a way to deal with his captors and reduce their hostility toward him. But it must never be forgotten that the hostage is a terrorist pawn in negotiations with the authorities, and his life is the threatened forfeit if they fail to meet acceptable terms. No amount of ingratiation or personal appeal to his captors will save the victim's life if his death clearly furthers the terrorist organization's purposes.

It is this Damoclean sword suspended perilously over the hostage which tests his mettle. He stands in the shadow of death—death which might come today, tomorrow, next month, or perhaps (and hopefully) not at all. The hostage—if he is a gambler or statistician—might take comfort in the fact that, according to a survey of 300 kidnap victims of international terrorists, only 4 percent of these were "executed"—and the odds for survival may be improving. But the cruel uncertainty cannot help but weigh heavily on the hostage as he spends day after interminable day cooped up in his prison. Here he must draw strength from his religion or his fatalism.

But it is still important that the hostage understand the complex set of circumstances under which he is held. The ideological attitudes and emotional makeup of his captors bear careful analysis. The ability of a mature person to divorce his subconscious sense of indignation and his anxiety over his own safety from his assessment of his tormentors can be a factor in his surviving captivity in reasonably good mental condition. At best—and there are notable examples of this—the hostage should try to understand the motivations, perspectives, and internal justifications of the terrorists. He need not make concessions of principle or compromise his own sense of values, but an open and honest approach to his captors is likely to change their view of him for the better.

There are other dangers, however. For entirely plausible psychological reasons, the totally dependent prisoner instinctively tends to identify with his captors. This can occur in a barricade-hostage situation, wherein the terrorist and hostage are besieged by police, and the victim shares the likely fate of the captor if the authorities attack. The victim's sense of deadly contest between "us" and "them" is only natural in the circumstances.

The identification syndrome also arises in the protracted kidnap-imprisonment situation. Again the total dependence of the victim on his jailer—the same sense of utter helplessness which, when it first occurred in infancy, led to his complete submission to mother—impels him now, subconsciously, to support the person who wields life-or-death power over him. In some cases, however, this very impulse to please may be misinterpreted by the ideological terrorist to the victim's serious disadvantage.

It is, therefore, essential that the would-be hostage understand something of these psychological quirks and seek to control them for his own benefit. The maintenance of a natural dignity, where possible and compatible with the personality of the hostage, has been demonstrated to have good effect on the captors. It should not be forgotten that the identification between opposites can operate, for other reasons, in the reverse direction: hostage-takers have, in the crucible of a siege situation, developed an affection for the human beings they have forced to share their fate. In a showdown, they have found themselves no longer able to kill their helpless prisoners.

In the end, the basic defenses of the hostage are relatively simple. To some extent, of course, his stamina and ability to absorb physical punishment are important. But then again, in two notable cases of long-term hostage survival, the victims were past middle age and had health problems. So a philosophical disposition and emotional stability are perhaps, overall, more important survival factors than is excellent physical condition.

Then there is that immeasurable quality of spiritual strength which gives some people a kind of charismatic power and a natural aura of presence and leadership. This obviously is a very useful trait for the would-be kidnap victim. Other more common personality characteristics which are helpful include patience, a sense of humor, sympathy, self-control, and capacity for objectivity.

No one person probably combines all the qualities which would make him the ideally survivable hostage, and one cannot select as actual victims those who might naturally fare best. But political kidnap targets are usually persons of recognized worth, who have accomplished something in their lives, and who therefore are likely to have above-average qualities of intelligence and personality. When such people are properly prepared for the role they may someday be forced to play, as a political hostage, it should be possible to improve their chances of surviving the experience with a minimum of aftereffects.

HILDE L. MOSSE, M. D.

The Media and Terrorism

One cannot understand terrorism without being aware of the role played by the mass media in violence conditioning. Although it is a background role, it is still of far-reaching and sometimes crucial importance. The mass media are television, movies, newspapers, magazines, and comic books directed to children and adolescents.

The basis for terrorism is human violence. An act of terror consists of killing people or threatening to kill them. The threat of killing, however, is very close to actual killing for two reasons: (1) Criminological and historical experience shows that the threat is very often translated into fact; and (2) even more important is that the position in which the terrorized person is put makes killing very easy and very likely. For example, when a robber enters your home, he has you at his mercy. The same is true for customers in a bank during a holdup, and for peaceful demonstrators such as the Kent State students. Terrorist tactics have been used against all these victims. The temptation to use the gun and not just threaten with it is very great indeed.

How thrilling it is to have power over a helpless creature, to sneer at him or her, to humiliate, to torture, to rape, and in the end, to kill, has been shown to more than a generation of children in the United States, first in comic books, and then on television and in the movies. Violence has entered their homes, glorified and in profusion, via the mass media. This has contributed mightily to the implicit acceptance of violence as a means of getting things done. It has distorted the natural attitudes of children, their openness to ideas and experiences, their curiosity, their spontaneous and unbiased interest in other people, and has moved them in the direction of cynicism, greed, hostility, callousness, and insensitivity.[1]

There are endless examples of this when one analyzes television shows, movies, comic books, and the many monster and other sadistic magazines young people raised on this violent intellectual diet buy. In one comic book story alone, I counted thirty-seven murders and fifteen pools of blood. One single television station showed 334 completed or attempted killings in one week. Children spend more time in front of the television screen than in school. They absorb a fantastic dose of pictorial violence. Fortunately, there are also wonderfully constructive shows interspersed among the violent ones. However, shows with a truly antiviolence tendency are by far in the minority.

Millions of children knew about kidnapping and the use of terror tactics at a much earlier age than their parents. They saw it described in great detail in comic books and later on, on television. All the best techniques were shown clearly: how to capture the victim without being recognized; how to transport him; where to hide him or her; how to communicate with the relatives; how to secure the ransom without being observed, and on and on. The victim was usually killed in the end, in spite of promises to let him go, so that he could not possibly become a witness. Policemen and other officials were usually portrayed as stupid and ineffective.

Fredric Wertham was the first and only psychiatrist to point out as long ago as 1947 that the intellectual and emotional development of millions of children was endangered by this attractive portrayal of violence, first in comic books and then on television. I was a member of his Lafargue Clinic group where the original research was done. We used the clinical method which alone makes it possible to study a person as a whole, with all the subtle ramifications involving many psychological levels. It is based on a thorough psychiatric examination. It includes psychological tests, observation within the family (in the case of children, also within the classroom), and in a group (in the case of children, in a playgroup), and longitudinal follow-up studies. A social history with home visits and investigation of the work and economic background forms an indispensable part of this method.

When Wertham's classic book about the influence of mass media on children, *Seduction of the Innocent,* came out in 1954, 100 million comic books were being published each month. This was the greatest publishing success in history. The result of these studies inspired parent organizations all over the country to fight against crime- and violence-portraying comic books. Their fight was successful for a while. The worst comic books disappeared from the market, and the number of comic book publishers declined. Collecting comic books has, however, become a big business, and the worst of them are again on the market.

Television is, of course, a totally different medium. It is one of the greatest inventions of mankind. President Kennedy stressed this when he said that three new inventions dominate our era: rockets, nuclear energy, and television. However, television took over many of the violent comic book heroes, for instance, Superman, Batman, the Hulk, Aquaman, and so forth, and violent themes dominate its cartoons and other shows directed specifically at children.[2]

Wertham's research showed that, as he put it, "the opposite of violence is communiciation," and that "where communication ends, violence starts".[3] Television is for this reason alone potentially the single most important antiviolence device. It makes communication between all people on earth possible as never before. It has already opened the eyes of millions to what goes on in other parts of the world, how other people live, what they think, how they organize their society. It has enabled them to participate in the cultural and intellectual life of all mankind. Why is it then that television fosters violence in such profusion? Is it perhaps due to ignorance of its destructive effects on the part of those who control this crucial mass medium? I don't think so. Violence is very effective in fact and in fiction. It attracts attention and therefore viewers faster and more predictably than any other theme. Fast, gory, brutal action is much easier to write about and to portray than the complicated subtleties of genuine and humane human relationships. To kill someone settles a conflict quickly. It takes time, careful reasoning, and emotional restraint to solve it nonviolently. If you combine violence with sex, as is presently customary, you make the show or the movie even more exciting and attractive.[4]

Children cannot be expected to understand what excessive viewing of this type of show does to them, how it changes their fantasies, attitudes, and behavior. Their very conscience becomes affected; an ethical confusion ensues. They are tempted to solve conflicts in real life also fast and furiously, with fists and weapons rather than with careful thought, consideration of the feelings of others, and by restraining their emotions.

The presently so prevalent terror in the schools cannot be fully understood and most certainly not alleviated without understanding the role played by violent and crime-oriented television shows, movies, and comic books in forming these youngsters' fantasy life from preschool-age on. This has nothing to do with busing and is not primarily caused by racial tensions. What a distraught mother told me recently (in 1976) is unfortunately typical. She was white and living in an affluent suburb. She said: "I have seven children. This is the first time in my life that I am fearful for them in school." Her nine-year-old daughter had been so brutally beaten by another child that she had to be hospitalized with a concussion. One of her sons, age fourteen, was hit so hard that he, too, had to be hospitalized because a ruptured spleen was suspected. I know from my own work in schools that the fear of physical violence permeates many junior and senior high schools. The students are afraid of each other, and the teachers are afraid of the students. The Subcommittee to Investigate Juvenile Delinquency of the Senate of the United States found in 1975 that almost 70,000 teachers are assaulted annually and that hundreds of thousands of students are beaten, robbed, or threatened with violence. As the *New York Times* of March 19, 1976, reported, a federally financed study found "a virtual reign of school-house terror." All violent crimes have increased in the schools, including bomb threats, extortions, and rapes of students as well as teachers.[5]

One of the most pernicious of all violence-fostering attitudes is race hatred. Violent shows in the movies and on television have fostered this hatred and all sorts of discrimination in subtle and not-so-subtle ways.

An example is Superman and most other superheroes. They belong to the strong, admirable, white super-race. The villains usually are people considered inferior in real life, for instance, women, black and Spanish-speaking people, and people of Italian descent as in "The Untouchables."

As a rule, children do not watch the news on television. A spectacular event may, however, arouse their curiosity, and they are apt to watch it. Such an event is often one of violence and tragedy. Many small children get this kind of news mixed up with their favorite show. The shock of the reality which ought to arouse a horror of violence in them is thus blunted. As a number of children told me: "I watch crime shows and I am used to it."

Television and films have an immediate impact on emotions. They reach feelings directly, not via the intellect as reading does. This effect is often subtle and far reaching. It enters our unconscious sphere. This subliminal impact is used very cleverly by advertisers for their own gain. Shouldn't it rather be used for the gain of the great masses of people who watch? Television can, like no other mass medium, manipulate not only the ideas, but also the mood of entire populations. The people who control it, officially or unofficially, have a key position in the power structure of any society. Violence is contagious. Television has the power to spread it or to prevent it from spreading further.

No individual violent act is ever committed for one single reason. Behind it is always a constellation of psychological (conscious as well as unconscious) and social forces interacting with one another.[6] Wertham has so clearly shown in *The Circle of Guilt,* which deals with a juvenile gang killing and terror in the streets, that "there is a continuous dynamic interaction between conscious, unconscious and social forces." The mass media are one of these social forces. They should take their responsibility for the prevention of violence and terror and for arresting their spread much more seriously than they have done to date.

Notes

1. Fredric Wertham, *A Sign for Cain.*
2. Hilde L. Mosse, "The Influence of Mass Media on the Mental Health of Children"; *Seelische Storungen.*
3. Wertham, *A Sign for Cain; The Show of Violence.*
4. Mosse, "Aggression and Violence"; "The Influence of Mass Media on the Sex Problems of Teenagers"; Wertham, *A Sign for Cain.*
5. Mosse, *Masked Depression;* Wertham, *Seduction of the Innocent; A Sign for Cain.*
6. Mosse, *"Individual and Collective Violence."*

Bibliography

Mosse, Hilde L. "Aggression and Violence in Fantasy and Fact," *American Journal of Psychotherapy* 2, no. 3, July 1948.

Mosse, Hilde L. "The Influence of Mass Media on the Mental Health of Children," *Acta Paedopsychiatrica* 30, fascicule 3, 1963.

Mosse, Hilde L. "The Influence of Mass Media on the Sex Problems of Teenagers," *Journal of Sex Research* 2, no. 1, April 1966.

Mosse, Hilde L. "Individual and Collective Violence," *Journal of Psychoanalysis in Groups,* vol. 2, no. 3, 1969.

Mosse, Hilde L. Massenmedien. Chapter in: *Seelische Storungen* (Emotional Disorders), edited by H. H. Meyer. Umschau Verlag, Frankfurt-am-Main, Germany, 1970.

Mosse, Hilde L. The Psychotherapeutic Management of Children with Masked Depressions. Chapter in: *Masked Depression,* edited by Stanley Lesse and Jason Aronson, New York, 1974.

Wertham, Fredric. *Seduction of the Innocent.* New York: Rinehart, 1954. Port Washington, New York; Kennikat Press, 1972.

Wertham, Fredric. *A Sign for Cain.* New York: Macmillan, 1966. New York: Warner Paperback Library, 1969.

Wertham, Fredric. *The Circle of Guilt.* New York: Rinehart, 1956. London: Four Square Books, 1961.

Wertham, Fredric. *The Show of Violence.* New York: Doubleday, 1949. Westport, Conn.: Greenwood Press, 1976.

Wertham, Fredric. "The Scientific Study of Mass Media Effects," *American Journal of Psychiatry* 119, no. 4, October 1962.

Wertham, Fredric. *The World of Fanzines.* Carbondale: Southern Illinois University Press, 1973.

H. H. A. COOPER

Terrorism and the Intelligence Function

Introduction

From a juridical-political point of view, the term terrorism poses considerable definitional problems.[1] Any attempt to produce a universally acceptable normative definition is certain to prove illusory.[2] Yet, as has been well observed, "To the layman terrorism presents no problem of definition."[3] Without some adjectival qualification, the term is really too broad to be useful. It can embrace the "putting in fear" of the victim, which is an essential part of the normative content of the common crime of robbery; the incidental fear induced by a reckless rampage of teen-age street gangs; the deliberately engendered sensations evoked and utilized by a Mafia enforcer; or the "violence for effect" expressly designed to coerce or disrupt the normal workings of some social or political system.

It is with this last phenomenon, increasingly well-known in our days, that we are concerned with. Political terrorism, whether of the domestic or transnational variety, means acts or threats of violence intended to affect the social and political life of the community. The identity and suffering of the instant victims are generally less important than the prime purpose of producing panic, disorder, paralyzing fear, and a certain, official reaction against those who have been responsible for the acts. Terrorism, restricted by way of description to such activities, implies a specific relationship between the forces of action and those of reaction. It has been well said that, "Terrorism is the weapon of the weak."[4] In the sense the term is used here, terrorism implies the use of a particular criminal technique against the community and against those who have legitimate authority to act in the name of the community.

The terrorist is, thus, always the outsider, always operating in contravention of law and, indeed, in contravention, to a large extent, of the generally held standards of decency and fair play of the community. There is an unwritten law even in the realm of criminality and the subculture of violence which is strikingly paralleled by similar developments in the law of warfare. In conventional warfare, there are "understandings" which in some cases have hardened into international agreements and to which there has, even in situations of total warfare, been substantial adherence. The true terrorist has no such respect for any of these conventions of crime or warfare; indeed, it is his very business to flout them. The true terrorist, if he indeed is to be true to his creed, can have no scruples and no kindliness toward his fellow man.[5] He must steel his heart against such emotions in order to be able to perform the awful task before him. to adapt Nechaeyev's famous dicta, "Day and night he may have only one thought, one purpose: merciless destruction."[6]

Thus, by these means and by adherence to this philosophy, the terrorist makes himself the outsider, the outcast, or the self-imposed exile from the society he seeks to destroy or convert. The terrorist may be many things, but, by his very nature and that of his purposes, he cannot openly and pacifically work within the system for the changes he wishes or seeks to bring about. By definition, then, terrorism, as the term has been employed here is a clandestine, unlawful activity of a violent and undiscriminating kind. However much the terrorist may seek to rationalize or justify his actions (and we are not concerned here with judgmental matters) he is always of the minority in terms of legitimate, political power. His efforts are designed expressly to redress that balance in his own favor and in favor of those in whose name he claims to act. It should never be lost sight of that the terrorism which we have described here is fundamentally political.

Terrorists are small in numbers, but possess the powerful advantages of initiative. In the first place, at least, it is the terrorist who is on the offensive, the protagonist who can strike first and then retire into obscurity. His military weakness, as guerrilla strategists have been quick to recognize, is his strength. In our times, the terrorist enjoys the inestimable additional advantages of rapid, transnational mobility; adequate financing for his operations or the means to acquire it; an extraordinary degree of anonymity, if it is desired; a variety of safe havens; the possibilities of exploiting for gain international dissensions; and differences and the supreme advantage of that greatest leveler of all, modern technology.

It is a sobering thought that the modern terrorist can transgress all laws, both domestic and international, and even cause the very subjects of international law, the nation states, to act contrary to another's laws and their own best interests. It is extraordinary yet shockingly true that a terrorist can single-handedly, for a short while at least, hold entire nations for ransom. Modern-day terrorism is the War of the Flea,[7] but modern technology has enlarged the potency of the flea's bite to titanically lethal proportions. We are living in an age when the secrets of mass destruction are no longer confined to a few and the economic resources necessary to bring it about are no longer under the exclusive control of nation states. Political terrorism, particularly transnational terrorism, has, as yet, nowhere near realized its full potential. Terrorist tactics are designed to exploit these advantages and to play upon the weaknesses of the enemy. Terrorism, at its most successful, puts all and everything at risk. In this War of the Flea, society has much to lose not only of a material, but also of a spiritual character. The "war" is meant to be debilitating. It is essentially a species of psychological warfare, a war of nerves with a Scarlet Pimpernel type of opponent. Terror is extreme fear, and we fear most that which we cannot see and do not know.

Wars are won by seeking out the weaknesses of the enemy and devising and employing tactics which might effectively exploit them to advantage. Society's weaknesses have been well studied and documented by terrorist theoreticians. Those entrusted with society's responses to terrorism must take equal pains to study the weaknesses of their opponents, both in theory and practice. The war against the terrorist is not won by overkill, taking a sledgehammer to crack an eggshell. The brilliant terrorist campaign in Cyprus of General Grivas tied up an enormous, well-trained army, enjoying a superiority in firepower it was never able to bring to bear upon a crucial target. The terrorist nucleus at most times did not exceed one hundred persons. Even to survive clandestinely, the terrorist organization must be tight to the point of impenetrability. Terrorists also need a safe haven, whether it be in natural terrain, such as the Sierra Maestra of Cuba, or adapted urban hiding places such as those from which the Tupamaros sallied forth in Uruguay. The old adage that a secret shared is a secret lost is particularly applicable to the terrorist. For the terrorist, there is no safety in numbers, but, rather, the reverse. Yet if the terrorist is to accomplish more than mere destruction for destruction's sake, that is, if he is to be political at all, he needs to have organization and command structure, resources, and the pos-. sibility of expansion. There comes a point when the political terrorist needs to convert his military potency into legitimacy. Therein lies his greatest danger and his inherent weakness. This is well recognized by terrorist movements and their tactics and procedures are designed to give the greatest possible protection.

What Is Intelligence?

This simple question has, over the years, become bedeviled by Hollywood images of Bulldog Drummond and James Bond and the activities of many intelligence agencies throughout the world which have sought, for their own purposes and after their own fashion, to emulate the exploits of these celluloid secret agents. The true intelligence function, although it has its moments of high excitement, is, like so many law-enforcement activities, much more prosaic. Unfortunately, the public impression persists, and it is not difficult to encourage the notion that the intelligence function is really quite different from what, in the main, it is. The impression has received solid, if somewhat unfortunate reinforcement in recent years.

Sir Kenneth Strong has written, "The intelligence process is neither complex nor obscure. It is based on two premises: that sensible policies can be developed and sensible decisions made only when the facts of the case are known; and that warning concerning decisions that must be made in the nearer or distant future is useful. Just as a television receiver searches for and accepts raw signals from outside itself, transforming these signals into an intelligible and useful picture, so the intelligence machine collects, collates and evaluates information, and interprets it to provide both 'facts' and 'forecasts'."[8] This is the true intelligence function and, as such, indispensable to informed decision-making. While the desire for privacy is strong in most individuals and stronger than most in American society, few would argue that the intelligence function so characterized is unnecessary, objectionable, or offensive to the democratic way of life. No one likes intrusion into his private affairs, but the necessity for informed, governmental action to protect society's interests in a number of well-defined areas is manifest. The only question is in relation to the limitations on government and the safeguards necessary to see that it does not stray beyond the bounds. Even the most sensitive and civil libertarian would agree that government should not make decisions blindly; such argument as exists turns upon the degree of intrusiveness acceptable into private affairs.

These are, however, the least objectionable features of the intelligence scene. Those which are disquieting are of a wholly different order. There is a more active aspect of intelligence work which is essentially a counterintelligence, or more properly a countermeasure activity, which is of a very different type. This involves, essentially, the concrete application, in tactical fashion, of the information gathered and the systematic use of it against individuals or organizations so as to affect their purposes and designs. Clearly, a very wide range of matters is comprehended here, some of which, at one end of the scale, would seem reasonable and necessary tactics in the constant struggle against those who threaten the fabric of society. At the other end of the scale, however, are activities, which, while permissible and permitted in some societies, are not such as we would wish to encourage in our own. It is this department of intelligence work, which is not true intelligence as we have defined it here, which has given the intelligence community a bad name over the last few years. In the United States in particular, it is the indiscriminate association of the true intelligence function with such extended activities, some permissible and some clearly not, under the umbrella of a single agency, that has tainted the whole process. The now well-known "dirty tricks" have soiled the entire intelligence apparatus and have engendered doubts, which should never have arisen, about the legitimacy and the desirability of some true intelligence functions. It is time to make the distinction in very clear terms, in order that a sensible discussion of these matters, in relation to terrorism and the intelligence function, can proceed.

Terrorism and True Intelligence

Terroristic activities are planned and organized by small, highly protective groups in the highest degree of secrecy they can attain. The illegality of their activities is unquestionable and their purposes are to inflict damage in human and material terms, to create disorder and panic with a view to affecting the normal workings of society. Before any action at all can be taken against such persons, there is a need to know who they are and what they are doing, and to relate it to what may be known of their earlier activities. Here we come up against what might be called the intelligence mystique.[9] Those engaged in these functions logically have to collect a great deal of information, by a variety of techniques, much of which will be quite valueless for strict law-enforcement purposes. This part of the intelligence operation might be compared with panning for gold or mining diamonds from Kimberly Lode. The problem is what to do with the dross.

It should be borne in mind that terrorists do not, generally, advertise themselves before the event; they hide, they masquerade, they put up a false front. It is part of the War of the Flea to hop and hide and cause the authorities to scratch and to treat as fleas those who are not and thereby cause all to become uncomfortable. There has been a massive attack on all intelligence gathering in the United States during the past few years as part of the post-Watergate syndrome and the general public disquiet over "dirty tricks."[10] There has been a wholesale dismantling of the intelligence-gathering apparatus of many law-enforcement agencies and an indiscriminate purging of much vital information which is now wholly lost to those entrusted with the tactical responses to terrorism. This has seriously impeded law-enforcement efforts in a number of important cases.[11] Law enforcement has, naturally, become very sensitive to these issues and much misguided effort has been directed at embarrassing the intelligence community still further. It is not difficult to see how this has enabled the flea not only to survive but to multiply. The terrorist can only be detected by a proper use of diligent and sophisticated intelligence. Just as the law-abiding have learned to accept for their own better protection the inconvenience of standing in line at airports to be searched, we must all be prepared to allow these intrusions in order that the terrorist be discovered before the Slaughter of the Innocents.

Counter-Terrorist Measures

Here we start to tread upon more controversial ground. We enter the realm of the informer, the police spy, and undercover activities of a wide and ingenious nature designed to attack and break up these movements before they can cause harm. That great tactician of the urban guerrilla movement, Carlos Marighella, has said:

The urban guerrilla lives in constant danger of the possibility of being discovered or denounced. The chief security problem is to make certain that we are well hidden and well guarded, and that there are secure methods to keep the police from locating us or our whereabouts. The worst enemy of the urban guerrilla and the major danger we run is infiltration into our organization by a spy or an informer. The spy trapped within the organization will be punished to death. The same goes for those who desert and inform the police. A good security is the certainty that the enemy has no spies and agents infiltrated in our midst and can receive no information about us even by indirect or distant means. The fundamental way to ensure this is to be cautious and strict in recruiting. Nor is it permissible for everyone to know everyone and everything else. Each person should know only what relates to his work. This rule is a fundamental point in the ABC's of urban guerrilla activity.[12]

The enemy must be presumed to know his own weaknesses, for here he is a witness against his own interest. In practice, all successful actions against organized terrorist groups have involved infiltration, penetration, and often acts of a more violent nature in consequence.[13] We come up against the crucial problem of what our society might be prepared to permit. That we should sit back powerless and wait for some devastating blow simply because legally admissible evidence of a criminal activity cannot be obtained until the blow has been struck seems unconscionable. Yet in many cases, as the law stands at the moment, that may well be the position.[14] No intelligence agency wishes to be accused of harrassment in the present climate of affairs. We clearly would not sanction the preemptive strike against the terrorist that has been so favored in some countries.[15] This is to fight terror with terror, a temptation that the counsels of the wise agree should be resisted.[16]

However efficacious this process of social hygiene may be in removing the individual terrorist from our midst, it is certain that the cost in terms of damage to our society and its fundamentals would be far in excess of what we would wish to pay. Society has to find a means to preserve itself without harm to its principles. We must look carefully at our laws and, while being ever alert against abuse, free the hands of those who have entrusted to them the tactical countermeasures against the terrorist. It has been said that: "Society has never taken pride in its secret agents; informers, like hangmen, are despised in the worthiest of causes. And if an individual spy is unsavory, the threat of an informer state arouses deeper disquiet."[17] Yet for the greater good of society these things must be. The flea must not be allowed to hide safely among us protected by those who are simply too delicate or sensitive either to admit the problem or to scratch in consequence. Countermeasures which are not destructive of fundamental liberties can and should be taken. The safeguards of our system that the terrorist is so anxious to destroy should be employed fully to ensure against excessive zeal and abuse.

Safeguards

All power is capable of being abused. This is not a condemnation of power itself but of those entrusted with its exercise. The intelligence arm is an indispensable one in the fight against terrorism. That the powers entrusted to those charged with the intelligence function are susceptible of abuse is without question; it is wrong that we should deny society the proper use of the intelligence arm on this account. Responsible control and public accountability are the key words. It has been well said that: "Individual freedoms and privacy are fundamental in our society. Constitutional government must be maintained. An effective and efficient intelligence system is necessary; and to be effective, many of its activities must be conducted in secrecy."[18] Secrecy on the part of public servants does not mean either lack of control or accountability. It does not mean autonomy nor an arrogant usurpation of authority. It does not mean law-breaking nor the substitution of subjective criteria for what is laid down as law or policy. The day that any part of the public service, be it the intelligence arm or any other, can regard itself as above the law and not accountable to its political masters, this society of ours is doomed. After the fashion of the eighteenth-century military theorists, the terrorist will have won the war without ever having engaged in a battle.

There is no need for such calamitous consequences if the appropriate safeguards are constructed and sensibly used. First, there must be a clear, overall philosophy with regard to the intelligence function, its uses, and the proper countermeasures to terrorist activity. Second, this philosophy must be translated into clear, practical policy guidelines to inform those who carry out these operations in the name of society.[19] Third, there must be clear and practical laws which combine due respect for the rights of all subjects with the overall interest of society in preserving itself against the terrorist threat. Fourth, the legislature, through its appropriate committees, must exercise vigilant and constant oversight of both law and policy on a strictly nonpartisan basis. Finally, the courts must never be excluded from examining and adjudicating upon what has been done under the color of the law.

A number of specific areas require review and regulation. It is suggested that there is far too much hysteria about electronic surveillance.[20] While it ought not to be used indiscriminately nor in unregulated fashion and excluded as an investigatory tool where less intrusive methods are available, it should be used wherever it is capable of exposing potential terroristic activity in a way that other methods cannot.[21] Let those who claim to be harmed by its use take their cases to the courts. Purging of unnecessary or unhelpful materials should be regularly undertaken and subject to oversight. Strategic intelligence files should certainly not be consigned wholesale to the trashcan as so much useful material currently is. It is essential that those entrusted with the tactical responses to terrorism be allowed to build up comprehensive sources of strategic intelligence.[22] It is equally vital that these sources be available for exchange on an international as well as on a domestic basis. The use of informants should be closely regulated. Prior judicial involvement in this matter is unrealistic and constitutionally questionable, but, again, proper oversight is likely to curb the overzealous and lead to the early detection of the unlawful.

Conclusion

Most authorities are in agreement that terrorism is a growth industry. While it has not grown as quickly and vigorously as some have anticipated, the potential for growth has in no way diminished. That the dire prophecies of mass destruction foreseen by some have not, as yet, been fulfilled, ought not to be taken as evidence of any lack of resolve or ingenuity on the part of individual terrorists or groups. It would be a great mistake to regard terrorism as a phenomenon that has been contained. Whatever steps have to be taken to address the underlying conditions out of which terrorism and, particularly, political terrorism seem to derive, the need for a more direct preventive strategy is still paramount. Intelligence plays a key role in such a strategy. We need to develop an effective intelligence capability which will enable us to protect society from the threat of growing terrorist sophistication. We need to know before the bullet is fired, before the bomb explodes, before the terror, before the disorder and chaos. Such capability is not built upon clairvoyance or the betting man's hunch. It is founded upon tried and tested techniques, the product of patient research and development. Senator Strom Thurmond has said:

I do not say there have not been some excesses and errors by our law enforcement intelligence units. The scale of the operation, nationally, would make a small quota of errors and judgment almost unavoidable. But the answer to such errors is not the abolition of our law enforcement intelligence files and law enforcement intelligence units—this would invite the destruction of our society. The answer lies, rather, in establishing carefully defined standards governing the operations of law enforcement intelligence, so that the officers involved will know what kinds of organizations and individuals require surveillance, and what methods are proper and what methods improper. We have to strike a balance between protecting our constitutional liberties and protecting our society against those who would destroy it.[23]

That excellent summary is respectfully adopted, by way of conclusion, here.

Notes

1. This subject gives rise to endless debate and much sophistry. One of the principal problems lies in trying to make a substantive criminal offense out of something which is essentially a technique. Compare Bruce Palmer. "Codification of Terrorism as an International Crime," *International Terrorism and Political Crimes*, M. Cherif Bassiouni, ed. (Springfield, Ill.: Charles C. Thomas, 1975).

2. This is really part of the wider problem of producing an acceptable, international criminal law. For obvious reasons, this is a remote prospect, in such wide terms, at the present time. On the narrow question of terrorism, the debates of the Fifth United Nations Congress on the Prevention of Crime and the Treatment of Offenders inspire little confidence in the prospects for a speedy consensus.

3. John Dugard, "Towards the Definition of International Terrorism," proceed-

ings of the 67th Annual Meeting of the American Society of International Law 67, *American Journal of International Law,* November 1975, no. 5, p. 94.

4. Brian Crozier, *In Terroristic Activity: International Terrorism,* hearings before the Sub-Committee to Investigate the Administration of the Internal Security Act and Other Internal Security Laws of the Committee of the Judiciary, United States Senate (Washington, D.C.: United States Government Printing Office, 1975), p. 181.

5. The true terrorist operates on the theory, whether by conviction or rationalization, that there are no innocent victims. The callousness of the terrorist is exemplified by the IRA bombings on July 21, 1972, the principal victims being mothers and young children. The victims at Lod Airport of those courageous freedom fighters who callously shot them down with automatic weapons were mainly unarmed Christian pilgrims whose association with the political situation involved was as tenuous as that of the cowardly perpetrators of the massacre.

6. "The Catechism of a Revolutionary," cited with commentary in Edward Hyans, *Terrorists and Terrorism* (New York: St. Martin's Press, 1977), pp. 26-30.

7. Robert Taber, *The War of the Flea* (New York: Lyle Stuart, 1965).

8. *Men of Intelligence* (New York: St. Martin's Press, 1971), p. 152.

9. Frank J. Donner, "Political Intelligence: Cameras, Informers and Files," *Privacy in a Free Society,* final report Annual Chief Justice Earl Warren Conference on Advocacy in the United States, Cambridge, Mass. The Roscoe Pound-American Trial Lawyers Foundation, 1974, pp. 56-71 at page 67.

10. See *The Nationwide Drive against the Law Enforcement Intelligence Operations,* hearings before the Sub-Committee to Investigate the Administration of the Internal Security Act and Other Internal Security Laws of the Committee on the Judiciary, United States Senate (Washington, D.C.: United States Government Printing Office, 1975).

11. "In New York early this year, the Puerto Rican liberation army (FALN) blew up the Fraunces Tavern, killing four people and wounding more than 50. The police were unable to get any kind of a lead on this group, because 2 years earlier they had destroyed the entire file on Puerto Rican suspects." Brooks McClure, *Terroristic Activity: Hostage Defense Measures,* hearings before the Sub-Committee to Investigate the Administration of the Internal Security Act and Other Internal Security Laws of the Committee on the Judiciary, United States Senate (Washington, D.C.: United States Government Printing Office, 1975), p. 293.

12. *Mini-Manual of the Urban Guerilla,* Havana, Tricontinental, N.D.

13. Prime examples of this technique are the British actions in Malaya and Kenya.

14. See, for example, the interview with Clarence Kelley, Director of the FBI, published in the *Washington Star,* 17 February 1976. Mr. Kelley gave a very vivid example in that interview of the type of situation which might well occur.

15. Such measures came to their fullest fruition in Nazi Germany. The Nuremberg Proceedings recall a conversation between Dönitz and Hitler where it is said, "Regarding the general strike in Copenhagen, the Fuhrer says that the only weapon to deal with terror is terror. Court martial proceedings create martyrs. History shows that the names of such men are on everybody's lips, whereas there is silence with regard to the many thousands who have lost their lives in similar circumstances

without court martial proceedings." Proceedings, vol. 5, Nuremberg, 1947, p. 253.

16. Dr. Frederick J. Hacker, an internationally renowned authority on terrorism, has said: "One of the alternatives to terrorism is terror. In other words, sustained governmental terror is a very effective way of wiping out individual and small group terrorism. Historically speaking, terror regimes always offer themselves to be the only remedy against terrorism. Terror, unfortunately, is an option for the combat of terrorism and I say 'unfortunately' deliberately because many people ask why not?" In *Terrorism Part 1*, hearings before the Committee on Internal Security, House of Representatives (Washington, D.C.: United States Government Printing Office, 1975), p. 3033.

17. William D. Iverson, "Judicial Control of Secret Agents," 76 *Yale Law Journal* no. 5, April 1967, pp. 994-1019 at page 994. The true value of the information obtained from the spy or informer has been doubted by many. Sir Kenneth Strong, who is among the doubters, cites the comments of Admiral Wemyss, British First Sea Lord at the end of World War I, that the product of secret intelligence is "uncertain information from unquestionable people." 76 *Yale Law Journal*, note 8, p. 142.

18. *Report to the President by the Commission on CIA Activities within the United States* (Washington, D.C.: United States Government Printing Office, 1975), p. 5.

19. See the *Watergate Special Prosecution Force Report* (Washington, D.C.: United States Government Printing Office, 1975), p. 144. "The intelligence function should be subject to the same policy procedures as any other important government enterprise."

20. See, for example, the debates and resolutions in *Privacy in a Free Society*, final report Annual Chief Justice Earl Warren Conference on Advocacy in the United States, Cambridge, Mass., The Roscoe Pound-American Trial Lawyers Foundation, 1974.

21. There are a number of situations in which electronic surveillance is of particular value. There are some crimes, such as bombings, where it is extremely difficult to get a lead by conventional investigation methods and where the success rate in terms of detection and prosecution is extremely low. It may well be that a more intensified form of surveillance of terrorist groups would produce a higher rate of success in this area and avoid the loss of innocent lives.

22. A distinction needs to be made between tactical and strategic intelligence. It is the latter, involving the long-term collection, storage, and use of information, which is generally under attack by those who fear an encroachment upon civil liberties. Yet if law enforcement is to function effectively and is to have the ability of rapid recall of information in an instant case it must have this information available over a long period.

23. In *The Nationwide Drive against Law Enforcement Intelligence Operations*, hearings before the Sub-Committee to Investigate the Administration of the Internal Security Act and Other Internal Security Laws of the Committee on the Judiciary United States Senate (Washington, D.C.: United States Government Printing Office, 1975), p. 2.

JOHN B. WOLF

Terrorist Manipulation of the Democratic Process

The political process is often conceived of as a bargaining process whereby an assortment of goals and values are maximized relative to the amount of power that can be marshaled on their behalf. However, competition within this process is not often free as it is many times manipulated in the interest of certain groups who, due to particular qualities, are able to maximize their ends at the expense of other, less fortunate groups. Occasionally these disadvantaged groups become dissatisfied with their subordinate position and seek to tilt the political process in such a way so as to create a climate which is more open to their demands. Often they accomplish this objective by introducing new methods of political action which enhance their ability to compete. Frequently, however, these new methods are quite violent in nature.

These groups see violence not as the repudiation of the political process but rather as an indication that their involvement in the bargaining related to it is being intensified and carried on by other means. Consequently, the introduction of violence is regarded by some as an indication that the values at stake are so fundamental that the existing political process is no longer adequate. Actually the central issue of their struggle is viewed by a disadvantaged group as involving no less than the opportunity for them to survive as a recognizable political element.

Occasionally this widened political struggle assumes an especially intense form and the urban environment, in which it is most frequently conducted, becomes the arena for a series of terrorist acts. Cities are the setting for many of these struggles because they embody characteristics which facilitate political organization and cast into sharp contrast positions of disparate power. Consequently, metropolitan areas become the scene of violence whenever a disadvantaged group of people seek to aggrandize themselves by altering the present allocation of power through the use of force or other extralegal means. Almost without exception, however, these attempts have ended in failure when the power of the urban police force was brought to bear.

While it is true that most urban political violence is caused by crowds running amuck, some of it is a highly organized material type of terror which is directed against railway bridges, power lines, or public buildings. Personal terror is also frequently employed by urban insurgents. This brand of terror involves the assassination of their opponents; such people as police chiefs, members of the government, popular figures, and businessmen.

Occasionally, urban insurgents will also indiscriminately employ personal terror against the general public for the purpose of undermining morale. Primarily, however, the intent of terrorism is not to kill or to injure people, but to advertise the fact that a group with a real potential for revolutionary violence exists. Even a token bomb set off somewhere in a capital city each night for a week, a terrorist calculates, will keep the police on the run and let the populace know that his cause is alive.

Yet terrorism by itself will not win a revolution, nor is it likely even to lead to negotiations for the settling of grievances. Most frequently it is strangled by the strict discipline and technical superiority of the police forces which are supplemented by military units in critical situations. Friedrich Engels, an associate of Karl Marx, seemed convinced of this point when speaking about certain of his unpleasant experiences of the mid-nineteenth century. Engles remarked that the era of the barricade and of street-corner revolution had passed. He came to this conclusion because he felt that improved technology and military techniques had rendered street fighting ineffective, while urban redevelopment in the form of broad boulevards and the gridlike patterns of streets facilitated the employment of these new techniques.

Regardless of Engels's observation, many contemporary terrorist groups insist that terror is a weapon which, when intelligently employed, can circumvent the technological capabilities of their opponents and bring final victory. Therefore, contemporary terrorists continue to refine and adopt the techniques of their trade. They regularly attack targets whose destruction or abduction is calculated to gain for them the international publicity which will force the government they view as an anathema to concentrate on the repression of terror for a long period of time. The obvious purpose of their strategy is to cause the government in power to neglect all of its other duties in the interest of public security which, when continued over an extended period, might cause a popular revolution of the masses with the terrorists as the vanguard.

This contemporary notion of terrorism is tied somewhat to the ideas of Serguis Stepniak, a nineteenth-century Russian terrorist, who believed that terrorism was not employed to overthrow a government but to compel it to neglect everything else. It does not, however, embrace the ideas of Ernesto "Che" Guevara who called terrorism a "negative weapon" because it often produces results that are detrimental to the revolutionary cause, including indiscriminate bombings of public places and assassinations of public officials. However, modern terrorists claim that the efficacy of the terrorist should never be evaluated in terms of his tactical targets, as Guevara attempts to do, but rather in some measurable reduction in the political flexibility and morale of his opponent as a consequence of an extended terrorist campaign. A trained terrorist, therefore, never selects a target on the basis of its intrinsic value, but primarily for the political and psychological impact which it will have upon people once it is seized or destroyed.

Strategically, terrorism when employed on an international scope is used simply to convince major world powers that there is a real, immediate, and urgent need for them to correct the conditions responsible for its existence. Terrorist campaigns of this type, therefore, are needful of a supportive publicity campaign which emphasized that moderation over an extended period is not capable of bringing about the required political change, be it the termination of a colonial situation or the achievement of social equality. Furthermore, the press accounts must emphasize that the employment of terror is clearly a response to the denial of basic freedoms of a politically identifiable and deprived people whom the major powers, in the interest of their own national security, should "liberate." Without a credible publicity campaign skewed to this consideration, the terrorist risks not having his activities accepted as logical and tolerable behavior. Therefore, the international terrorist particularly seeks to demonstrate to the world that he is a desperate person who is grimly determined to end the injustice and humiliation of his people.

In pursuance of this objective, the terrorist must also demonstrate to the international community his capability to be militant and withstand prolonged suffering. Consequently, he seeks an environment for his actions which is dominated not by terrain and physical factors but mostly by human beings and political and psychological factors. It is this emphasis on personal terror which lends credence to the terrorist threat, since its employment makes sense only when its advocates understand that terrorism is not so much a military technique as it is the creation of a political condition. The international terrorist, therefore, knows that he must predicate his strategy upon his ability to convince the major world powers that his plight must be resolved in the interest of world peace. He also knows that he must somehow alienate most people everywhere from his enemy.

Thus a public relations assessment would be a prerequisite of any terrorist plan and the controlling factor relative to its intensity, direction, and duration. The release unharmed of Sir Geoffrey Jackson after his capture by the Uruguayan Tupamaros may indicate that his captors realized that there was nothing further to be gained and much to be lost by his continued retention or death. The media already knew them; the British government would give nothing in return for his life; and by the time they kidnapped him, the Robin Hood Tupamaros were already an Uruguayan institution.

However, the Tupamaros and other contemporary Latin American terrorist groups do not conduct their operations on an international scope but rather confine their activities to a particular locale. Furthermore, all of these groups have a cause which is related to a rather isolated domestic political situation which in no immediate way has ramifications which require them to attempt manipulation of the existing international balance of power. The

IRA also, can be included in this group. The Arab terrorists, however, are examples of groups whose structure, strategy, and operations closely conform to the theoretical aspects previously mentioned which pertain to the worldwide utilization of terror as a weapon. These groups realize that all of their actions and inactions have a dramatic impact upon the Middle East where both the United States and the Soviet Union have vital, but divergent, national interests.

Consequently, Arab terrorist strategy is to claim that their people are unable to redeem their lost lands inside Israel through diplomacy, conventional warfare, or a Maoist-type guerrilla struggle. Thus they present themselves as people who are free to employ the tactics of terror against the Israelis and their international supporters everywhere. They use terror to intimidate the world community into believing that the cost of maintaining the status quo in the Middle East will be an eventual nuclear confrontation between the United States and the Soviet Union. Consequently, Arab terrorism supplements those aspects of conventional Arab diplomacy and propaganda which emphasize that a lasting peace in the Middle East is dependent upon a resolution of the "Palestinian Question."

Although aware of the threat posed by terrorist groups, the urban police departments, particularly of the United States, lack the resources and training required to control it. Furthermore, to combat the terrorist it is necessary for municipal American police departments to cooperate with every Federal investigatory agency in a pooled effort against this menace. The Federal agencies, however, have found it most difficult to effect cooperation among themselves, and consequently they are unable to develop any lasting and mutually beneficial liaison with local police departments.

Evidence of this shortcoming in American law enforcement is plainly visible. Eighteen Federal strike forces have been established to combat Mafia-dominated organized crime throughout the United States. The record of these forces has been mixed, and, until recently, the United States Attorney's Office had been urging their dissolution since it is known that the various Federal agencies pooled in the strike forces tend to be competitive and distrustful of each other. Included among the federal agencies normally grouped into the strike forces are the Federal Bureau of Investigation (FBI), Drug Enforcement Administration (DEA), United States Immigration and Naturalization Service (USINS) and Alcohol, Tobacco and Firearms Division of the United States Treasury Department (ATF).

There is some justification, however, for the competition and distrust which exist among these various agencies. One strike-force attorney who had been asked, for example, if he could show a reporter FBI charts on the Mafia, said cynically: "They'll hardly show them to us." "Why is that?" he was asked. "Well, the Bureau has the attitude that one day you're a prosecutor, and the next day you're a defense attorney," he said. That is frequently true of the young attorneys who work in the Federal Strike Forces and the United States Attorney's Office, where a prosecutor's term averages three years.

Fettered both politically and economically, most American police departments also are unable to construct the top-level operational intelligence network which is required to keep records on extremist groups. Yet these same intelligence networks are an effective terrorist countermeasure since they consist of components which will allow rapid acquisition, analysis, and dissemination of current data from a specially constituted and specially skilled group. Once convinced of the need for sophisticated intelligence networks, however, most American police departments would still find it very difficult to conduct any intelligence operation of a prolonged basis which cannot be justified by the performance statistics required to support budgetary appropriations for additional financing. Thus the drive of the American police for statistics tends to divert investigative energy to a succession of low-level arrests most of which have little or no impact on any organized criminal group. Furthermore, most urban American police commanders also realize that intelligence operations normally yield a low number of arrests; consequently, they are often reluctant to undertake them as the size of their budget is often related to the total number of arrests made during the previous twelve-month period.

Yet it is absolutely necessary for a free society to build into its structure the safeguards which it needs to protect basic freedoms. Aware of this situation, the terrorist is often able, sometimes openly, to manipulate the democratic process to create a climate favorable to himself. This is evidenced by the following recent example. More than twenty-five years ago, fearful of the designs of the Soviet Union, Congress authorized the creation of the Central Intelligence Agency (CIA). But Congress was also concerned about the designs of the agency itself, and the National Security Act of 1947 specifically provided that the CIA "shall have no police, subpoena, law enforcement or internal security functions."[1] But in February, 1973, the CIA acknowledged training policemen from about one dozen domestic police departments, including fourteen men from the New York City Police Department, in the storage, processing, filing, and retrieval of intelligence data and security devices and procedures. This acknowledgment came in response to an inquiry from a New York congressman pertaining to press accounts about such training sessions.[2]

Meanwhile a suit was brought in federal court which challenged the constitutionality of many New York City police intelligence activities. Police Commissioner Patrick V. Murphy subsequently announced that the names of more than a million persons and organizations had been purged from the files and new restrictions were established to regulate the collection and dissemination of such material in the future. The commissioner stated further that there was legitimate and absolute need for his department to gather intelligence. "However, there is always the possibility that some police practices may infringe on individual rights. The line between public and private interest is so fine that any system which is required to collect information about individuals and groups is susceptible to such infringement."[3]

As previously indicated, however, most American municipal police departments are not equipped to conduct a meaningful counter-terrorist effort in the area of intelligence-gathering of the kind which could serve as the basis for the implementation of a nationwide program of preventive countermeasures. Therefore, the national government is placed in the position of assessing a situation without the extensive hard intelligence data which could readily be supplied by municipal police forces once they have been trained, financed, and equipped for this mission.[4]

If a nationwide counter-terrorist intelligence system is implemented, however, its managers must be extremely careful that its operations do not include activities which, in the words of Attorney General William B. Saxbe, are "abhorrent in a free society." The American attorney general recently used this expression to condemn some of the COINTELPRO secret counterintelligence operations. COINTELPRO was used by the Federal Bureau of Investigation to spy on and disrupt extremist groups. Its tactics included the spreading of information to create dissension and cause disruptions in militant organizations. For example, FBI informers planted false information identifying prominent members of the extremist organizations as federal agents and distributed false or unsubstantiated damaging information about these leaders to friendly members of the press, employers, business associates, credit agencies, family members, and local law-enforcement agencies. Although COINTELPRO was disbanded in 1971, FBI Director Clarence M. Kelley continues to see some future applications for its use. But he also recognizes that a policy decision is involved which would have to come from the Attorney General.[5]

The CIA, meanwhile, maintains a computerized file in its headquarters in Langley, Virginia, which it calls Octopus. Octopus has the capability of matching television pictures of known terrorists and their associates against profiles contained in its system. These television pictures are taken in various overseas airports, bus terminals, and other transportation centers. Within microseconds, Octopus can analyze a picture along with information already in its file on targets in the area and the equipment and talents required to attack them. Within a few minutes after this computerized analysis takes place, a radio alarm is transmitted to a counter-terrorist team who apprehend the terrorist. When terrorists are picked up and accused in this manner, "they often are flabbergasted at being presented with plans they hadn't yet made."[6] The use of television surveillance in a free society, however, must be carefully controlled and tightly monitored, and all people who are within view of the camera's lens should be aware of its presence.

Yet a democracy, even when confronted with a serious terrorist threat, is still reluctant to suspend basic freedoms as a countermeasure in the belief that this action is a greater danger to the legitimacy of the democratic state and the mass consensus vital to its preservation than a terrorist challenge itself. It is exactly this hesitancy, however, which the terrorist group seizes for the prime input into its strategic plan. This plan is a strategy for eventual conquest which makes sense only when it is understood that terrorism is not so much a military technique as it is a political condition. Always, the strategic aim of the terrorist is not the military defeat of the forces of the incumbent regime, for him an impossible task, but an objective predicated upon the moral alienation of the masses from the existing government until such isolation has become total and irreversible.

The Brazilian guerrilla leader, Carlos Marighella, mapped out part of that strategy when he wrote that "it is necessary to turn political crisis into armed conflict by performing violent actions that will force those in power to transform the political situation of the country into a military situation. That will alienate the masses, who, from then on, will revolt against the army and the police and blame them for this state of things." Consequently, democratic states confronted with an outbreak of insurgency are truly "damned if they do and doomed if they do not."

Also, the citizens of a free society must be prepared to accept restrictions of their basic freedoms once terrorists gain a foothold in regions where they live. For example, on November 22, 1974, the British Government, following a bombing of two pubs in Birmingham, announced that it would quickly introduce legislation to give emergency powers to the police to help combat terrorism by the Irish Republican Army (IRA). One of the major questions was whether to introduce identity cards as was done during World War II. There were strong objections on the ground that identity cards would give the British government too much control over the individual. Yet, regardless of their misgivings and the evidence of recent abuses, citizens of democratic states should insist that selected municipal police officers receive intelligence training for the purpose of containing terrorism in its incipient stage. Otherwise the use of identity cards and a broader interpretation of the existing laws of arrest, search, and seizure might one day become commonplace in every democratic state.

However, there always remains the temptation for the military forces of a democratic state to act outside the law when confronting terrorists. There are two excuses for this action: (1) that the normal safeguards in the law for the individual are not designed for a terrorist and (2) that a terrorist deserves to be treated as an outlaw anyway. Sir Robert Thompson, British expert on counterinsurgency, in his book *Defeating Communist Insur-*

gency, makes the following comment. According to him, action outside the law:

. . . not only is morally wrong, but, over a period, it will create more practical difficulties for a government than it solves. A government which does not act in accordance with the law forfeits the right to be called a government and cannot then expect its people to obey the law. Functioning in accordance with the law is a very small price to pay in return for the advantage of being the government.

But unless the municipal police forces of a free society have a real and reliable intelligence capability which can be used to nip insurgency before it constitutes a real threat to a free society, the use of the army, regardless of the grave consequences of such action, is the only option left.[7]

To avoid the consequences resulting from the use of military force to quell domestic insurrections, the United States has adopted a policy of "gradualism," its sole remaining alternative to autocracy to meet the insurgent challenge. This policy, which seeks to correct the political, social, and economic conditions responsible for the violence, intends to administer a long-range cure when an immediate action response is required. Also, such a policy has the potential to hinder the government's causes as its pronouncements are usually interpreted by the insurgents as mere sops and twisted by their propagandists to indicate the efficacy of their own movement.[8]

It is evident, therefore, that American law-enforcement agencies lack a well-developed and coordinated program to meet the challenge posed by terrorism while simultaneously maintaining the fabric of a free society. We perhaps should adopt the British solution to this threat. Once confronted with insurgency, the British strengthen the social sanctions and thereby act upon the supposition that counterinsurgency is normal police work and not social engineering. This approach seems more sensible than the American methods. After an insurgency explodes into the streets, it is foolish to undertake preventive measures which contain the potential of being manipulated by the insurgents to serve their own cause.[9] A prerequisite to the implementation of the British approach, however, is the establishment of statewide and uniform penal codes which many of the fifty states presently lack.

Another conspicuous feature of the British approach is that military units are not committed against the insurgents until the police operations have been given a reasonable opportunity to quell the insurrection. Police operations, therefore, are intended by the British to buy the time they need to evaluate and contain a situation. Meanwhile they try to devise a strategy which will hopefully prevent alienation of the civilian population and a shattering of the national image.

A demonstration of this sort of British police response took place on the island of Bermuda in March 1973. It was triggered as a consequence of the murder on the island of the governor general and his aide. Although the media reported the possible implication in the affair of a politically motivated insurgent group called the Black Cadre, the British felt that a team of detectives from Scotland Yard should investigate the matter and prepare the normal report. The police reports were then used by the British to assess the parameters of the situation and shape their future response, if indeed any should be required. Meanwhile, the Black Cadre group did not become the beneficiary of publicity which it might be seeking nor were its activities considered by the media as a formidable factor in Bermudian affairs.

But what of the tremendous repressive capability of American police departments? Is it not possible for them to use this capacity to seize the initiative from the terrorists? If terror is such a powerful tactic in the hands of the insurgent can it not be equally efficacious when employed by the police? The answer to these questions is not as obvious as it would appear at first glance. There seems to be little doubt that counterterror by the police can be just as effective as the terror employed by the insurgents. However, whether or not it is an alternative which is open to the government of a free society is an entirely different matter.

Actually, pure repression has become virtually impossible for American police departments, exposed as they are to the shifts of governmental debate and an unfettered press.[10] This, however, may be an oversimplification unless one takes account of the political culture within which these police organizations function. In American life, for example, there are certain preconceptions as to what the government may legitimately do and an exact definition of the fundamental rights of man. Thus its democratic system is both a necessary and a sufficient limitation on the employment of repressive force.

Yet for American police departments to adequately deal with the terrorist challenge they must eventually request that certain constitutional safeguards be suspended. This action, however, places the rights of the entire population in jeopardy and there is great reluctance to give the police the extraordinary powers they require to uncover evidence of terrorist activity. Public opinion aside, it may not be farfetched to say that in certain cases the socialization process by which these values are inculcated into American life may be so intense as to render the government officials and police officers themselves reluctant to contravene cultural norms.

In American societies it is a fact of life that police repression draws more attention to itself than does provocation. As long as this is the case the police are at a decided disadvantage due to the public opposition which any forceful reactions might invoke. Thus, American police agencies are unable to respond early enough and in a sufficiently forceful way so as to catch a terrorist scheme in the incipient stages, the time when it is most vulnerable. After this the suppression of the terrorists requires a much more intense application of force, the use of which becomes ever more open and more costly, thereby increasing the obstacles to the government's freedom of action.

The American police organizations are, therefore, in a difficult position. Whether from political pressure or through personal dislike, they are unable to employ the measures they must use to detect and to crush a terrorist threat. Yet failure to adequately deal with this threat may lead citizens to question the ability of the police to act as a proper authority. Thus, when faced with such a quandary, the police are forced to deploy their forces in accordance with regular operating principles. This sort of strategy is really a compromise by which they seek to stay within what are considered constitutional levels of force while at the same time endeavoring to give the impression that they are actively engaged in combating the terrorist menace. Thus the terrorist infrastructures can easily be established and thrive within American cities since it is unlikely that the police will implement the intelligence system or the courts grant the suspensions of civil liberties necessary to uncover them.

Notes

1. Lyman B. Kirkpatrick Jr., *The U. S. Intelligence Community* (New York: Hill and Wang, 1973), pp. 25-27.

2. "Why Did CIA Train Police?", *New York Times,* 11 February 1973, p. 3.

3. *Ibid.*

4. President's Commission on Law Enforcement and Administration of Justice, *Task Force Report: Organized Crime* (Washington, D.C.: U.S. Government Printing Office, 1967), pp. 16-24.

5. *New York Times,* 24 November 1974, p. 3.

6. Miles Copeland, *Without Cloak or Dagger, the Truth about the New Espionage* (New York: Simon and Schuster, 1970), pp. 96-97.

7. Sir Robert Thompson, *Defeating Communist Insurgency* (New York: Praeger, 1970), pp. 52-55.

8. Lucian W. Pye, *Aspects of Political Development* (Boston: Little, Brown and Company, 1966), pp. 129-131.

9. *Ibid.*, pp. 131-134.

10. Brian Crozier, *The Rebels: A Study of Post War Insurrections* (London, Chatto and Windus, 1960), p. 12.

FELIKS GROSS

Political Assassination [1]

> How does it happen, that certain changes from liberty to
> servitude and from servitude to liberty occur without bloodshed,
> others are full of blood? . . . It depends on this: whether the state
> which is subject to change was born in violence or no; because
> when it was born in violence, accordingly it was also born in
> injury of many. In consequence, it is unavoidable that when
> the state weakens and declines, those who suffered want to
> vindicate; and this desire of vengeance breeds blood and death
> of men. . . .
>
> Machiavelli, *Discorsi Sopra*
> *La Prima Deca di Tito Livio,*
> Book Three

The humanizing effects of democracy and our civilization had an impact on
our perception of past history. It seems almost forgotten that use of violence and assassination to achieve political power, remove an adversary, or
change a dynasty was a general historical phenomenon for centuries in
societies organized into the complex political form of the state. Next to
assassination as a means to gain wealth and property, assassination to
gain political power seems to be tragically frequent in the past.

Western civilization in a slow, historical process humanized political
institutions. Humanization means here above all limitation, reduction, or
abolition of the use of violence, cruelty, and killing in the business of internal government. It seems that reduction of political murder and assassination as a means of transferring power or changing dynasties appears in a
slow development influenced in medieval times by the Western church and
philosophy.

The major concept which reduced political assassination in transmission
and succession of royal power at this period was the concept of legitimacy
rooted in the duality of church and state. It was the ecclesiastic hierarchy
which validated the hereditary legitimacy of the dynasties and maintained
control over the orderly transfer of power. Of course, political murder was
still abundant in medieval times. The church itself indulged in mass terror
toward dissidents. There were ups and downs in this early and long proc-

SOURCE: This article is reprinted by permission of the author. It originally appeared in *Socio-
logia Internationalis,* 1972.

ess. Henry Pirenne, the Belgian historian, writes about the great intensification of "unspeakable violence and treachery" and calls the tenth and fifteenth centuries "epochs of political assassination." Nonetheless, a foundation was laid toward the concept of power based on legal and philosophical (or theological) premises as the only "legitimate" power.

The paramount legitimacy of elective and representative power, established already in antiquity, whether in Greece or Rome, continued in medieval cities and corporations. Advanced and formulated in England, diffused from there to distant corners of the world, representative and democratic legitimacy has greatly contributed to the humanization of politics, especially of those crisis stages of transmission and succession. The complex legal and philosophical concept of legitimacy of power became fundamental in Occidental politics. Few ideas in our civilization could be found which contributed more to the political and cultural continuity of Europe and America. Only late, and in few states, where well-established concepts of democratic legitimacy, based on "general will" or "majority rule," were associated with political freedom and relative equality or absence of excessive exploitation, did a nonviolent power transfer and nonviolent political struggle become fully accepted, that is, "institutionalized." It became a shared value, a political custom or way of life.

In imperial Rome political assassination was frequent. In the time of Emperor Constantin, it became a method later called "sultanism," a continuous murder of all possible pretenders to power, or competitors, until no one but the ruler survived. The Swiss historian, Jacob Burkhardt, coined this term in *The Age of Constantin the Great*. Sultanism reappeared in totalitarian states. Hitler's elimination of competitors Roehm, General Schleicher, and so many others in the infamous blood bath of 1934 and Stalin's purges were assassinations of possible competitors.

In the fourth century, Licinius, a competitor for power with future emperor Constantin, did away with the "families of Galerius Severus, Maximus Daia, including their innocent children." Even the widow and daughter of Emperor Diocletian were assassinated, while Constantin later arranged for the assassination of Licinius. After the death of Constantin, his brothers, first Constantius, then Dalmatius, were murdered, relates the historian Burkhardt. It was the same Constantin the Great whose merits for the establishment of the Christian church as a ruling religion of the Roman Empire are well known. This was, however, a period of transition and disintegration of old value systems and legitimacy. At such times power is based rather on personal loyalty of the bodyguards than on legitimacy.

Byzantium inherited this political pattern. Sultanism continued in a variety of shockingly cruel ways almost until the fall of the empire. Between 477 and 1374 as many as twenty-nine emperors of Byzantium were murdered, poisoned, blinded, or mutilated. This procedure reappears in the Third

Rome—Moscovy and Russia. Ivan the Dread assassinated his own son. Peter the Great plotted the murder of his son Alexis, who died, however, before the "official" execution in consequence of torture. Catherine the Great conspired and was instrumental in the assassination of her own husband, Tsar Peter III, who was murdered in prison. Diplomats reported this political murder without emotion, as a kind of normal procedure, writes historian Albert Sorel. After the death of Catherine, Tsar Paul, more liberal than his predecessors, was assassinated, and his son, the glamorous Tsar Alexander, was directly involved in this conspiracy. Nor is Western history free of royal assassins. But the sequence and consistency in Russian history is perhaps characteristic. The continuity can be traced back to the late Roman Empire.

While principles of legitimacy grew slowly, Western Europe was by no means free from political murder. In highly civilized Muslim Spain in the eighth century political assassination was frequently practiced. "Of a total of twenty [governors, appointed from Damascus or North Africa] only three survived as long as five years: those who did not fall in battle were murdered by their rivals." (Harold Livermore, *A History of Spain.*) In the Ottoman Empire political assassination as a process of consolidation and transfer of power was part of the general use of violence in politics and absolute rule and, as we shall see, may have contributed to a "political style" or political cultural pattern in which assassination and individual terror became one of few avenues of struggle against autocratic rule. When Sultan Murad III (1574-1595) left twenty sons (out of forty-seven children who survived), his successor Mohammed III (1595-1603) ordered the murder of his nineteen brothers to eliminate competitors. (L. S. Stavrianos, *The Balkans Since 1453.*) This pattern of elimination of competing dynasties by assassination, in a far milder form, however, in terms of means and number of victims, continued in the Balkans, especially in Serbia, even after liberation from the Ottoman yoke, from 1817 until 1903. Once a political pattern is well established and "internalized" in the political behavior of individuals, or "institutionalized" in groups, it has a tendency to continue, and it is difficult to terminate such a pattern. Turkey is no exception, but rather a representative of a pattern. In Persia the succession of the two major dynasties was "seldom undisputed and decided without bloodshed." (W. S. Haas, *Iran.*) Sultanism was a major political device in Persia.

Political assassination became an art in the time of the Renaissance. It reappeared when the old, medieval legitimacy based on dynastic heredity with a succession validated and legitimized by the ecclesiastic authority was considerably weakened and the old, elective or aristocratic power in parts of Italy was eroded by violent transfers (capture), conquest, and treason.

This very short historical account could be extended into a voluminous survey and validate a hypothesis that elimination of naked violence and assassination in internal, domestic transmission and succession of political power is a consequence of a long historical development, perhaps of paramount cultural significance, and that nonviolent succession and transmission of political power is not necessarily universally typical in a history stained with blood and violence.

The patterns and incidence of individual political assassination of chief executives and political personalities vary between nations and political cultures. Historical experience, ethnic and religious values, and distribution and patterns of political power, as well as social stratification and socioeconomic conditions, are among the major contributing variables. To blame the economic situation solely for political terror is a gross oversimplification and frequently a fallacy. In times of intense class tensions and class violence in the past, individual terror as a tactic was seldom, if ever, practiced. This was primarily a political tactic. One single variable—legitimacy—seems to be of singular interest. Although by no means a sufficient one, it is perhaps only an indication that such a legitimacy supplies continuity of institutions and facilitates and enhances social change in modern times. When the legitimacy of power, the value structure which supplies the legal and philosophical basis of exercise of power, is weak, unstable, or disintegrating, a tendency toward high-level political assassination seems to increase.

Political assassination persisted and reappeared in the Balkans and in part of the Middle East which was under Ottoman rule. Political assassination and government by violence was widely practiced. Iraqis and Syrians today practice violence and individual assassination in succession of power. This was frequent among the Arabs of the eighth or ninth centuries, but there is not necessarily an historical connection. Professor Karl M. Schmitt of Texas University, in his report submitted to the task force of the U.S. National Commission on Causes and Prevention of Violence,[2] estimates that over thirty rulers or former rulers were murdered in South America in the 162 years since the assassination of Dessalines in Haiti. Bolivia, with about ten victims, tops the list. However, Guatemala and Colombia, two nations of intense political violence, had a very low incidence of assassination of presidents or chief executives. According to the estimates of Schmitt, in Guatemala in the last two or three years the number of victims of political violence runs as high as 3,000, and Colombian political violence was continued for twenty years (1940-60) at a cost of 250,000 people murdered, or killed, to put it more mildly. Argentina, Brazil, Chile, and Cuba (according to Schmitt) did not have even one single occurrence of assassination of any of their chiefs of state, but there were several attempts. None of these nations enjoyed political stability; none was free of violence.

The low level of assassination of chief executives or leading personalities in stable democracies is rather striking. Professor Murray Havens in his report submitted to the commission lists two such attempts in the entire history of Australia: the first in 1868 (by an Irishman) against Alfred Duke of Edinburgh and another in 1966 against the leader of the Labour party, Calwell. Since 1792, there were only two assassination attempts of this kind in Sweden, the second in 1910 directed against a foreign and oppressive ruler, the visiting czar of Russia.

In both nations the legitimacy of power is strong, generally accepted, and recognized by the people. Few question the legal and philosophical basis of power, the underlying values of democracy and of constitutional monarchy. The political institutions are here firm and at the same time elastic; they absorb without significant shocks political and social changes. Sweden is ethnically homogeneous. Both have high standards of living, a relative prosperity of the working classes, and an extensive system of social services.

This strong legitimacy of institutions is not, however, the sole variable of the relative safety of presidents and chief executives. Ethnic values and behavioral patterns, frequently included in our definitions of this vague concept of "national character," do influence political behavior in internal politics. We should not overlook such simple, physical data as frequency of contact and exposure in public meetings of the chief executives. The latter is very high in the United States.

We shall, however, realize the shortcomings of comparative statistics in defining the act, the subject of quantification. The figures are used here for orientation and should be considered as rather tentative.

We may proceed, with this reservation, to the attempts of assassination against officeholders in the United States. According to the research prepared for the commission by Professor Rita James Simon (with the assistance of S. Phillips), the entire history of the United States, since 1789, records eighty-one assassination attempts, both successful and unsuccessful, against all officeholders. Nine of these, of which five were successful, were directed against presidents or candidates (high-level assassinations). In most cases, they were a result of "individual passion and derangement." "Cross national quantitative analyses"—we read in this report of the Task Force I—"show that the incidence of assassination correlates strongly with intense levels of general political violence and political instability." We learn also from the commission's report that the higher the office the higher the probability of an attempt of assassination. However, of the approximately 1,100 men elected to the United States Senate in its entire history, only two were assassinated; of the 8,350 Congressmen, three were assassinated, and there were seven unsuccessful attempts (five, however, in one single attempt in 1954). It is also a higher probability that an attempt will be directed against an elected public officer rather than an appointed one, even if the latter is powerful and prominent, for example, secretary of state or justice of the Supreme Court. The legitimacy of power, the democratic principle, and ideology, despite the present violent experience, seems to be widely shared and has contributed to a basic political continuity already observed more than a hundred years ago by Alexis de Tocqueville. The political assassination in most cases was here an individual act, a result of psychological obsession or derangement, frequently in times of political crisis or rapid political change. Professor Simon concludes that "the level of assassination correlates strongly with the level of political violence."

Not only does the assassination vary in time and space in a quantitative sense, it varies also in its quality and nature, scope and objectives, motivation and tactics.

Roughly we may distinguish:

1. Political assassination as an isolated act, frequently accomplished by a deranged person. The assassins of American presidents, perhaps with the exception of the Puerto Rican nationalists who attacked President Truman, "evidenced serious mental illness," according to a careful study of the Task Force of the National Commission on Violence.

2. Sultanism, assassination of competitors to power. Related to the latter are assassinations to secure power for a new elite, to remove the one which controls political power.

3. Individual terror, systematic and tactical assassination directed against the representatives of the ruling groups or government with an objective toward weakening the government and the political system, destroying the existing legitimacy, and effecting ideological, political, and social change. Individual terror was thus far a tactic for achieving power; mass terror was applied in the past and present to consolidate and maintain power.

"Political" assassination as a systematic activity, a part, even a major one, of political tactics, advanced by an organized political group for achievement of an ideological goal, seems to be a nineteenth-century occurrence, a consequence of struggle against autocracy and foreign rule.

After the French Revolution, what is called "the reaction" in Central and Western Europe closed the avenues of peaceful development of representative and democratic institutions. Monarchies and autocracies representing the interests of the ruling classes lacked will and initiative to resolve the burning social problems of the new industrial society. Here the traditions of the French Revolution suggested the once established and effective type of revolutionary tactics. In Russia, however, which lacked this tradition of a popular revolution "from below," where the people—the peasantry—were either passive, or loyal to the tsar, or rebellious at times, but without broader political goals of basic change, where the government was autocratic in the Oriental sense rather than in terms of contemporary European monarchs, assassination appeared as a political tactic. It spread to the Balkans, again as a tactic in response to foreign oppression and massacres.

During the second half of the nineteenth century, a theory of individual terror developed among revolutionary Russians in their struggle against autocracy. Unlike political assassination as an isolated act, individual terror—in terms of nineteenth-century revolutionaries and later in terms of some resistance groups during World War II—is a systematic, tactical course of action with political objectives. Individual terror attacked directly, above all, key decision makers or administrators, or acted in lieu of punishment against persons responsible for cruelties and oppression. One of its functions was retribution and deterrence. The leaders of the organization expected that assassination of an oppressive administrator would deter his successors from inhuman, oppressive acts.

Such was the goal of assassination of high German Gestapo officers in Poland during World War II. The major function of individual terror in Tsarist Russia was, however, weakening of the government and of the autocratic institutions of the Tsarist Empire.

Still, it was in this terroristic revolutionary group in autocratic Russia where democratic ideas flourished. There were several factions of course, some minor, whose objective was—as was said before—establishment of dictatorship, as the means or a transitory stage toward a true free society, free of any coercion. Here rationalism worked in harmony with perfect ideals and logical contradictions, impressive and convincing for novices. Theories were also advanced (by Morozov and Tkachev) that terror should continue under constitutional rule, since even under such rule a tyranny might appear; they indicated contemporaries—Bismarck or Napoleon III. Individual terror by its power of intimidation and elimination of future tyrants would keep the future, perfect world free from autocracy. Those late regicides were, however, in a minority and formed an insignificant faction or separate party. The main party, the core of the "People's Will," had democratic traditions and clear democratic objectives. In 1878, the "People's Will" stated clearly and sharply in an "Urgent Note" its differences with the group which "indulges in Jacobinistic tendencies and methods of a centralistic organization." The Russian revolutionary movement of those times was not economic; it was primarily political. As Thomas Masaryk put it, "It was an aristocratic struggle for freedom waged against Tsarist absolutism."

We found ourselves, rather suddenly, in an historical period of intellectual confusion and physical violence. The issue of violence and past experiences became of practical significance in a time of appeal to physical violence in domestic politics, as a way of interfering with the business of education and government.

There are times in history when violence is one of the few roads left open for those who fight for the rights of man against the bestiality of others. Man was and is forced sometimes to use violence in his struggle for freedom and emancipation. The experience of a hundred years teaches that a clear distinction must be made between struggle and (1) violence against domestic autocracy, (2) foreign conquerors who exterminate nations or reduce them to servitude changing them into slaves, and (3) individual violence waged against a republic and democratic institutions, as fascists, Nazis, and their satellites did in the past and at present is being practiced by the "extraparliamentary" extremists on the so-called left and right (identification of their goals is not a simple matter).

Violence generated violence; blood called, in the past, for more blood. Individual terror, even in the name of the highest ideals, created at the end political habits which moved into the patterns of political life, and continued even when conditions were changed.

Individual terror was to a large extent a tool of those who were "outs" and stormed the political institutions. After World War I, systematic individual assassination was used by the extreme right against democracy. Political techniques are similar to tools. Some—not all, of course—are "neutral" *per se*; they can be used for a variety of contradictory objectives. The objectives are decisive in a political and above all a moral sense, since ideology and objectives control the choice of means. On the contrary, mass terror is a political tactic of the "ins," of those in the saddle, in an effort to consolidate power, and usually to eliminate groups of innocent people defined as class, race, or a nation. Thus, objectives of mass terror are broader than solely a rule by fear.

Political assassination and violence are not abstract occurrences. This type of individual violence is sociologically meaningless or necessarily misinterpreted by an outside observer unless it is viewed in its three major contexts: personality, group, and situation.

Most of the European and Russian political assassinations were organized and planned by an ideological or political group, or when the terrorist was a lonely actor, he had to count on support, at least moral support, of certain ethnic, ideological groups or politically oriented social classes. The goals, values, ideology, and tactics of the terroristic party suggested the purpose of the act, the function the act should play. The act first must be analyzed within this party context (called here, group context).

The party, again, does not act in isolation; it responds to a situation. The act of individual violence is an act of response to the social and political situation; therefore, the social act should be studied in this context (called here, situation context).

The assassination of a Turkish Pasha by a Dashnak (Armenian) revolutionary as an isolated juridical issue is a crime. The same assassination in a context of a situation of persecution and extermination of Armenians is an act of self-defense and "counterterror": it is a political act. In the context of ideology of the Dashnaks and their perception, this is a revolutionary act of a democratic and socialist Armenian party, an act of killing an enemy in a revolutionary war. In those terms the act has its ideological legitimacy.

The relationship of these three variables is essential. In a very oppressive situation, such as under the Nazi rule during the World War II, an otherwise humane person may resort to violence and organize a terroristic group. On the other hand, in a humane democracy, individuals obsessed by a drive for power, combined with ethnic or racial hostilities, some of them deviant, may embark on terroristic action against democratic institutions. Various situations appeal in this sense to different personality types. But the situation is frequently closely related to the act. We may suggest a simple model to illustrate the three interdependent variables:

G = group or political party
P = personality
S = situation

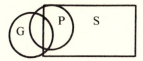

Notes

1. This paper is concerned primarily with the individual, "high-level" assassination, that is, assassination of heads of state, kings, presidents, chief executives, members of government, and leading political personalities.

2. The Report to the National Commission on Causes and Prevention of Violence, *Assassination and Political Violence,* vol. 8, James F. Kirkham, Sheldon G. Levy, and William J. Crotty, eds. (Washington, D.C.: U.S. Government Printing Office, October 1969).

ROBERT A. FRIEDLANDER

Terrorism and Political Violence: Do the Ends Justify the Means?

The wanton and willful taking of human life, the purposeful commission of serious bodily harm, and the intentional infliction of severe mental distress by force or by threat of force are phrases that are legal terms of art (lawyers' words) describing actions and activities designated as common crimes by every civilized society on this earth. The victims of these purposive and, I think, indefensible acts are persons whose selection as victims, whether randomized or calculated, was due solely to their waiting in a hotel lobby, sitting in an outdoor cafe, standing on a street corner, flying on an airplane, riding on a train, or representing corporate interests in a country other than their own.

"No cause," argues French author Albert Camus, "justifies the death of the innocent," and terrorism is the slaughter of the innocent. No matter how we want to look at it, terrorism is a *moral* problem in addition to being a criminal act. As newspaper columnist, Father Andrew Greely has written: "Either terror is moral for everyone or it is moral for no one." To save oneself by killing another is destructive not only of law and legal systems but of civilized society itself. Our Anglo-American common law system is based upon the worth, the sanctity of one human life, and this conforms to the basic human rights principles which have come to be accepted in public international law since the end of World War II. The admonition of legal philosopher Edmund Cahn still rings true: "Whoever kills one kills mankind."

Traditional Anglo-American criminal law permits what are called "excusing conditions"—or, to use once again lawyers' terminology, mistake, necessity, provocation, duress, and insanity—to excuse or to mitigate what otherwise would be criminal acts. However, neither duress nor necessity may operate as an excuse for the taking of human life. The civil law system of Europe and Latin America permits the defense to be raised of a "political crime" and, thereby, it may prevent extradition of a wanted felon. The Third World, in national politics and in the international arena, has given a large measure of support to perpetrators of political crimes. Their attitude is that the end justifies the means. As a result, the continuing public debate over the nature of international terrorism has unleashed a cacophony of national self-interest in the council of nations. Political terrorism has become largely a matter of global perspective. The fundamental issue is whether the primary focus should be upon the *causes* of violence or upon the *acts* of violence.

According to Eric Suy, Deputy Undersecretary General of the United Nations and its general counsel, "(t)he cause of terrorism is not a legal question." And the cure, he suggests, will not be found in international treaties or conventions, but by states acting alone, bilaterally, or multilaterally. In fact, Suy is highly skeptical as to "the efficiency of international treaties." One of my critics likewise suggests that the answer to terrorism cannot be found in the law, but may be discovered in the hearts or the souls (if they have them) of the terrorizers themselves. Again, I must vigorously dissent, for reasons which I shall now discuss.

For more than a decade the specter of international terrorism has been identified with the spread of ideological violence and the fragmentation or dismantling of existing sociopolitical structures. According to Frantz Fanon, the ideological godfather of the Algerian independence movement: "National liberation, national renaissance, the restoration of nationhood to the people . . . is always a violent phenomenon." Thus, terror has become a political weapon to be used wherever and whenever a dissident group is unable to achieve its basic objectives by any legitimized means.

The term itself originated during the French Revolution and the Jacobin Reign of Terror. At first it was identified with state action. Later it was applied to individual or group violence. Contemporary legal scholars and prevailing international legal standards divide terrorism into two major components: (1) individual or group terrorist activities and (2) national or governmental repression. The United States has been primarily concerned with the former category, as reflected in its Draft Convention for the Prevention and Punishment of Acts of International Terrorism submitted to the U.N. General Assembly during September 1972. The Third World nations have emphasized the latter view, particularly in the debates of the assembly's Ad Hoc Committee on International Terrorism which concentrated on the "repressive and terrorist acts by colonial, racist and alien regimes. . . ."

Surprisingly, a legal definition of terrorism has yet to be formulated, and the lack of specificity about the nature of the subject continues to plague the international community. The Algerian analysis submitted to the Committee was actually a description of the United States role in South Viet Nam, while Professor Tran-Tam, formerly of the University of Minh Duc in Saigon, in his contribution to a significant study of international criminal law, defined political terrorism as the activities of the Vietcong.

Terrorism in microcosm is a struggle for power, and its purpose is totally destructive. The quintessence of the terrorist process, according to Professor E. V. Walter, centers on three factors: the source of violence, the victim, and the audience. The necessary concomitant of terrorism is fear and the ultimate objective is coercion. Writing in 1891 on *Siberia and the Exile Sys-*

tem, the American journalist George Kennan commented: "Wrong a man . . . deny him all redress, exile him again if he complains, gag him if he cries out, strike him in the face if he struggles, and at last he will stab and throw bombs."

The terrorist act is one of political desperation rooted in the belief that violence is legitimized when it becomes a form of public protest designed to coerce governmental entities to act in a particular fashion. Camus's protagonist in *The Just Assassins* has convinced himself that he only throws bombs at tyranny, though men die. "Day and night," according to the *Revolutionary Catechism* of Nechayev and Bakunin, the terror-activist "must have one single thought, one single purpose: merciless destruction." Terrorism is thus nothing more nor less than a manifestation of intellectual fanaticism, and there is, on the part of the terrorist, an absolute commitment to engage in or to endure any atrocity for the higher revolutionary goal.

Ironically, the rising level of violence in this country during the past decade as reflected in the news media generally, and especially in television programming, has disoriented community values to such an extent that the victim is often confused with the victimizer. The strange saga of the Symbionese Liberation Army and Patty Hearst, and their implicit media glorification, has turned the public focus away from the plight of the injured parties and, instead, publicizes those responsible for the criminal attacks upon them. The expected condition of society is lawless rather than lawful, and acceptance of crime as the natural order of things engenders still more criminal attacks.

British journalist Robert Moss has divided the terrorist phenomenon into three tactical categories: repressive terror, defensive terror, and offensive terror. The first refers to governmental repression (Reign of Terror, Soviet purges, Nazi occupation). The second stands for the activities of private groups reacting to a foreign invader (guerrillas), or to members of a community attempting to defend what they consider to be their traditional rights (vigilantes). The third category refers to individual political systems (FLN, EOKA, PLO). All three concepts are interrelated, and the appearance of one frequently occasions the response of another. There is, for example, a direct correlation between the oppressive internal and external policies of national governments and the incidence of international terrorist activities. To quote the 1972 study of the United Nations Secretariat: "As violence breeds violence, so terrorism begets counter-terrorism, which in turn leads to more terrorism in an ever-increasing spiral."

Western Europe has had a long tradition of granting asylum to offenders of political crimes dating from the late eighteenth century and the era of the French Revolution. In 1833, the Belgian government formally prohibited extradition for a political offense, and this prohibition was then recognized by international agreement between Belgium and France the following year.

Modern extradition treaties among Western nations (with the exception of the United States) have incorporated this concept into international law but, as with the problem of international terrorism, no one has been able to develop a workable definition of political crimes.

The landmark British case dealing with the subject, *In Re Castioni* (1890), established two basic requirements which had to be met before an exception could be granted to an extradition request: (1) the act must have occurred during a political revolt or disturbance; (2) the act must have been incidental to and have formed part of that same revolt or disturbance. A further qualification was added by the British courts more than two generations later. In *Ex Parte Kolczynski* (1955), it was held that "(t)he words 'offense of a political character' must always be considered according to the circumstances existing at the time when they have to be considered."

Concomitantly, the rapid rise of the revolutionary movement in nineteenth-century Europe necessitated certain limitations to be placed upon the political offense exception to preserve societal order. The *attentat* clause, resulting from an attempt on the life of French Emperor Napoleon III and later broadened as a result of the assassination of President Garfield, placed a reservation on the Belgian law of 1833. The murder of a chief of state or any members of his family was designated as a common crime, and this concept was incorporated into Article 3 of the 1957 European Convention on Extradition.

A recurrence of transnational political violence during the 1930s, dramatized by the twin slaying in Marseilles of King Alexander of Yugoslavia and French Foreign Minister Barthou, along with the assassination of the Austrian Chancellor Englebert Dollfuss that same year (1934), resulted in the calling of a conference by the League of Nations to deal with the resurgent problem of international terrorism. The Geneva Conference of 1937 produced two conventions—one for the prevention and repression of terrorism, and the other for the creation of an international criminal court. Prohibited acts included attempts directed against the life, physical well-being, or freedom of heads of state, their spouses, and other government officials if the attack is upon their public capacity; the impairment of public property; and a general impairment of human lives if made by a citizen of one state against another. But the two conventions failed to obtain a sufficient number of ratifications and, consequently, never entered into force. It appears that the December 14, 1974, U.N. General Assembly Convention on Prevention and Punishment of Crimes Against Internationally Protected Persons, including Diplomatic Agents, will meet a similar fate.

The proposal for an international criminal court has served as a source of much debate and frustration among international legal scholars. It has become a favorite cause of many distinguished authorities but is, in reality, a mere academic placebo. During the past four decades, a vast literature supporting the creation of an international criminal court has reflected the continuing concern of international legal scholarship as to the inadequacy of existing municipal law in controlling international terrorism. The 1971 World Peace Through Law Conference, held at Belgrade, approved a resolution favoring such a court, and the Foundation for the Establishment of an International Criminal Court has drawn up a draft statute. There the matter rests, except for periodic appeals by scholars to an unsympathetic world community.

Murder or kidnapping *per se,* although treated as criminal activities in all national legal systems, are not in themsleves international crimes, unless they include one of the following elements: (1) the act or acts must take place in more than one state; (2) the act or acts must involve citizens of more than one state; (3) the act or acts must be directed against internationally protected persons; (4) the act or acts must occur outside of an exclusively national jurisdiction; and (5) the act or acts must be directed against internationally protected property (that is, aircraft). If one or more of these requirements are satisfied, then the activity in question no longer falls within the category of common crimes, but becomes a new international crime affecting world public order.

The U.N. General Assembly resolutions of the past quarter-century provide a disturbing commentary on the attitude of that august body to the growth of international terrorism and political violence. In the words of one pro-Third World commentator: "[t]he terror-violence of colonization cannot be condoned while the terror-violence of liberation is condemned." Significantly, a prominent Soviet journalist, in an article titled, *Revolutionary Terror: What Does It Lead To?,* vigorously opposes the terrorist solution, arguing that "Terrorists discredit the very idea of revolutionary struggle."

Terrorism is undeniably criminal conduct, and to grant any political exception to offenders who have perpetrated indiscriminate death and destruction upon innocent third parties is a patent denial of the rule of law. The international legal maxim, *aut dedere aut punire* (extradite or prosecute), must be applied to those actors who, by the very nature of their acts, are placed outside customary international law. The recent holding of the Canadian Federal Court of Appeal, as stated by *In Re State of Wisconsin and Armstrong* (1973), leaves no doubt whatsoever that urban terrorists, in Anglo-American law, are to be considered common criminals. It should always be remembered that the function of terror is to terrorize.

Not surprisingly, given the sovereignty explosion and prevailing international alignments, there has been almost a total lack of agreement within the world community on either the cause or the cure of the terrorist phenomenon. The cult of violence has become a ritual substitute for the use of reason in the political arena. Although there is widespread acknowledgment of the necessity for measures to deal with political terrorism, there has been almost no sense of international urgency toward creating viable judicial procedures and implementing effective legal controls. Until such time as a remedial consensus is reached, the politics of power will continue to make a mockery of the law of nations.

To say that randomized terror-violence utilized as a politico-legal strategy for ostensible revolutionary ends can be condoned and even encouraged, simply because there is no peaceful or legitimate remedy for redress, is to replace the rule of law with the ancient credo of might makes right. Terrorism, to use once more the phrase of Albert Camus, is "the murder of the innocent." The observation of Raymond Aron cannot be gainsaid: "Without law and without rules, fear reduces all men to a common impotence."

Professor Lador-Lederer has argued that terrorism is actually humanicide bit-by-bit. Unbridled terrorism in a disordered world is also patent criminality on the internal level. Terrorists operating on their own initiative during an armed conflict, a so-called war of national liberation, or an internal rebellion are outside of the Hague and Geneva conventions, and should be totally outside the protection of any members of the world community. Penalties against nation-states aiding and abetting terrorist crimes should be enacted and enforced by international treaty and convention. To achieve this end, there must be a greater commitment to mutual interdependence and international collaborative enterprise instead of the current ambience of power politics and institutionalized violence. The civilized community must label terrorism, once and for all time, as the criminal activity it truly represents. We must begin to turn the corner on the seemingly endless road toward violence in the world societal structure. It is the only hope for a rational and relatively stable world order.

But then, given the historical events of the last half-century, perhaps the world community itself is on the edge of madness.

PART V

Some Legal Problems and International Terrorism

W. THOMAS MALLISON
SALLY V. MALLISON

The Control of State Terror Through the Application of the International Humanitarian Law of Armed Conflict

Introduction

An empirical perspective must recognize that the practice of extreme coercion and violence to achieve political objectives includes the activities of
governments as well as nongovernmental groups. This requires a corres-
pondingly comprehensive juridical conception of public purpose terror
activities.[1] While there is no desire to minimize the importance of reducing
or eliminating nongovernmental terrorism, the present analysis focuses
exclusively upon the international law prohibitions on the use of terror
which are applicable in international and internal conflict fact situations.

In armed conflict, states are seeking to implement their political objectives by the systematic and institutionalized use of coercion and violence.
Because of the recognition of the urgent necessity to protect noncombatants
in conflict situations, attempts have been made since early history to formulate limits in law upon the use of such coercion and violence which would
prohibit the use of terror. Because state terror has frequently been carried
out through the destruction of human and material values which is not justified by military necessity or which does not advance a lawful military objective, the limitations upon the use of coercion and violence in international
conflicts reflect the common interest of states in avoiding violence as an end
in itself. The humanitarian law of international conflict (traditionally termed
"the law of war") has been used by states to impose restrictions of degree
and kind upon its use.

One of the principal purposes of the humanitarian law is to protect noncombatants, or civilians, from the more destructive consequences of armed
conflict. Civilians are usually defined as individuals who are not members
of the armed forces and who do not participate in military operations. Civilians who need protection from terror in international conflict situations fall
into two categories: enemy civilians who are under the direct control of, or
"in the hands of," a state of which they are not nationals, or are living under
military occupation; and civilians who are living in territory which, while not

under the control of an enemy, is subject to attack by an enemy state. Civilians who need protection from the terror aspects of widespread internal conflict or civil war comprise a third distinct category. The participants in such a conflict are typically a government and a revolutionary movement. Since each category involves a different fact situation, they will be treated separately.

The law of armed conflict applies to intensive and extensive internal conflicts as well as to international ones. Because it is a practical law designed to protect human values, it is applied to *de facto* conflict situations. Both historically and presently, the existence or not of a declaration of war or of a so-called technical state of war is irrelevant. Since the international humanitarian law of armed conflict has been created and agreed to by states, it seems reasonable to expect states to comply with it. Such compliance by states, however, is not the invariable rule. There are substantial enforcement and sanctions problems in this branch of international law just as there are in domestic criminal law.

The Protection of Civilians in Territories under Belligerent Occupation

The Hague Convention IV of 1907 Respecting the Laws and Customs of War on Land, and its Annexed Regulations,[2] comprises a multilateral treaty that is still binding on the United States and most other states which were independent in 1907. The third section of the Annexed Regulations deals with belligerent occupation and provides protections for civilians living in occupied territories. Article 46, for example, provides:

Family honour and rights, the lives of persons, and private property, as well as religious convictions and practice, must be respected.
Private property cannot be confiscated.

It is important to note that both human and property rights are involved since civilians may be terrorized by attacks upon either human or property values. Other articles of the Hague regulations of 1907 prohibit the belligerent state from coercing civilians to supply military information or to swear allegiance to the enemy state. The regulations are a substantial improvement over the prior treaty law on the subject, but even if all of the relevant articles should be considered, these regulations provide, at best, an incomplete protection for civilians. The famous DeMartens clause in the preamble indicates that the treaty law provisions may not be considered alone but that they must be applied along with the customary humanitarian law.

Even the modest provisions of the convention and its regulations, along with the customary law, were violated by the practices of both the Nazis and the Japanese militarists during World War II. The Geneva Diplomatic Conference of 1949 met in the shadow of those grim events and aimed at prevent-

ing the repetition of the state terror which characterized that war. The first
two conventions produced by the conference provided for the protection of
sick, wounded, and shipwrecked military personnel, and the third provided
protections for prisoners of war. The fourth, the Geneva Convention for the
Protection of Civilian Persons, is an entirely new convention.[3] This convention deals primarily with the situation of belligerent occupation, and accordingly, Article 4 defines protected civilian persons as those who are "in the
hands of a Party to the conflict or Occupying Power of which they are not
nationals."

In provisions which are applicable in the territories of the parties to the
conflict as well as in occupied territories, a number of substantial and specific protections are provided for civilians. Article 27 is entirely inconsistent
with terror directed at protected persons and provides:

> Protected Persons are entitled, in all circumstances, to respect for their persons,
> their honour, their family rights, their religious conventions and practices, and their
> manners and customs. . . .

Article 27 (3) prohibits adverse distinctions of any kind in the treatment of
protected persons and in particular discriminations based on race, religion,
or political opinion. Article 31 prohibits physical or moral coercion for any
purpose including the obtaining of information.

It is undoubtedly a sad commentary on the condition of the human race
that the prohibitions of Article 32 are deemed necessary. This article provides in part:

> The High Contracting Parties specifically agree that each of them is prohibited
> from taking any measure of such a character as to cause the physical suffering or
> extermination of protected persons in their hands. This prohibition applies not only
> to murder, torture, corporal punishment, mutilation. . . .

Unfortunately, the experience of World War II as well as more recent events
indicate the urgent need for such prohibitions against these reprehensible
methods of state terror directed against individuals.

Article 33, which also reflects the wartime experience, provides in full:

> No protected person may be punished for an offence he or she has not personally
> committed. Collective penalties and likewise all measures of intimidation or of ter-
> rorism are prohibited.
> Pillage is prohibited.
> Reprisals against protected persons and their property are prohibited.

This article sets forth the only prohibition upon "terrorism" in exact word-
ing which appears in the four Geneva Conventions of 1949. The permissible
extent of and the limitations upon the use of reprisals against civilians was

a major issue in the post-World War II War Crimes Trials. In view of the flat prohibition in Article 33, this issue has now been eliminated. In the same way, Article 34 of the Civilians Convention has prohibited the taking of hostages without qualification or exception.

It is important that the Civilians Convention not be frustrated by domestic law decisions of the belligerent occupant. Article 47 provides that protected civilian persons shall not be deprived of the benefits of the convention by any change introduced into the institutions or government of the occupied territory by the belligerent occupant nor by an annexation "of the whole or part of the occupied territory."

The negotiating history of Article 49 reflects the purpose of preventing repetition of practices which were particularly associated with the Nazis in World War II. The first paragraph prohibits forced transfers and deportations of protected persons from the occupied territory; the sixth paragraph prohibits the transfer of the occupant's civilians into the occupied territory. These provisions constitute a prohibition on "creating facts" in occupied territory which would amount to the implementation of a policy of creeping conquest and aggression.

The Protection of Civilians in Unoccupied Territories

The Civilians Convention, as has been shown, is directed primarily at the protection of civilians in territory under the occupation of an enemy state. Civilians in unoccupied territories have, nevertheless, been exposed to great danger and destruction by the military operations of enemy states. In both Southeast Asia and Southwest Asia (also known as the Middle East) the principal method of state terror against such civilians has been massive aerial bombardment. It should also be mentioned that the so-called free fire zones involve the probability of the infliction of terror, in the form of death and destruction, upon any civilians who have the misfortune to live in the zone or indeed are merely passing through it.

The Third Session of the Diplomatic Conference on the Reaffirmation and Development of International Humanitarian Law Applicable in Armed Conflicts met in Geneva from April 21 to June 11, 1976. The purpose of this conference was not to supercede, but to supplement the four existing Geneva Conventions for the Protection of War Victims. With this objective in view, the conference is working on two draft additional protocols which it is hoped will produce agreed upon texts at the end of this year's session. Protocol I deals with international conflicts and Protocol II deals with internal conflicts.[4]

Some of the most significant articles of Protocol I concern the protection of civilians in international conflict situations. Draft Article 46, already agreed upon in committee, codifies the customary law doctrine that the civilian population as such, as well as individual civilians, may not be made the object of direct military attack. In a significant provision it specifies that: "Acts or threats of violence which have the primary object of spreading terror among the civilian population are prohibited." The article also prohibits indiscriminate attacks which are "of a nature to strike military objectives and civilians or civilian objects without distinction." The article further specifies that a bombardment which treats as a single military objective a number of clearly separated and distinct military objectives located in a city, town, village, or other area containing a concentration of civilians is indiscriminate and consequently prohibited.

If this article is adopted by the diplomatic conference and thereafter ratified by the states represented at Geneva (which are substantially the same as the membership of the United Nations) the result will be a specific prohibition upon area bombardment which, if it is enforced, will provide significant protection for civilians which they do not now have. The development of precision guided missiles, including so-called smart bombs, makes it possible for the states possessing sophisticated weaponry to support this draft article without reducing military efficiency. The Third World states require no persuasion in order to support the article.

Draft Article 50, which has also been adopted in committee, concerns precautions which must be taken in conducting an attack. This article codifies the customary international law rule of proportionality by providing that those who plan or decide upon an attack shall:

refrain from deciding to launch any attack which may be expected to cause incidental loss of civilian life . . . which would be excessive in relation to the concrete and direct military advantage anticipated.

Other provisions of the article require that all feasible precautions to avoid injury to civilians be taken if an attack is launched.

The Protection of Civilians in Internal Conflicts

It may seem surprising that international humanitarian law contains doctrines which are applicable to internal or civil conflicts. However, the objective characteristics, including the terrorization of civilians, in internal or civil wars are not mitigated by their classification as internal rather than as international.

The modern international law of war, including the protection of civilians, traces its origin to the United States Civil War. In 1863 President Lincoln promulgated General Order #100 prescribing "Instructions for the Government of Armies of the United States in the Field."[5] This code, prepared mainly by Professor Francis Lieber of Columbia College, New York, was widely recognized as applying the most advanced rules of international humanitarian law. It was later taken as the starting point by international conferences charged with the development and improvement of the international law of land warfare.

The common Article 3 of each of the four Geneva Conventions of 1949 for the Protection of War Victims provides certain rules which must be applied, as a minimum standard, in internal conflicts. This article has been aptly described as a "mini-convention" on the subject and, like the Civilians Convention, it deals with the protection of civilians in the hands of the enemy. It specifies that persons who take no part in the hostilities (including members of armed forces who have surrendered or are wounded or sick) must "in all circumstances" be treated humanely, without any adverse distinction based on considerations of race, color, religion or faith, sex, birth, or wealth, or any similar criteria.

The article also provides that the application of its provisions shall not affect the legal status of the parties to the internal conflict. This is necessary since without it a government would be concerned that a revolutionary movement might obtain a more recognized position under international law by being accorded the elementary humanitarian standards prescribed.

Draft Protocol II which is under consideration by the Geneva Diplomatic Conference provides much more detailed protections for civilians in the hands of an enemy in an internal or civil war than does the common Article 3. In addition, it includes protections for civilians who are present during the conduct of military operations in internal conflicts similar to those provided for civilians in unoccupied territories in Protocol I. It is important to mention that Protocol II does not apply to internal disturbances such as riots and isolated and sporadic acts of violence. These matters are to be dealt with under the applicable domestic law. The protocol concerning internal conflicts applies in situations where the internal conflict takes place between the armed forces of the government in power and dissident armed groups which are under responsible military command and which exercise such control over a part of the state's territory as to enable them to carry out sustained military operations and to fulfill the obligation of implementing the provisions of Protocol II.

Conclusions and Recommendations

International humanitarian law, like domestic law, is not self-enforcing. If the protections which it specifies are to be implemented in reality, they must be enforced. The common Article 1 of the four Geneva Conventions of 1949 provides in full:

The High Contracting Parties undertake to respect and to ensure respect for the present Convention in all circumstances.

This is a new provision in international law in that the state parties to the agreement not only assent to its provisions themselves, but also undertake to ensure the compliance of other parties as well. This means that if any state party violates a provision of the four existing Geneva Conventions and any other state party does not take urgent measures "to ensure respect" for the convention which is violated, the other state parties are also in violation of the convention.[6] This provision was particularly intended to impose enforcement obligations on the great powers.

The realities of international interdependencies are becoming increasingly apparent. In southern Africa the white elites have long acted on the underlying assumption that their own values may be protected without regard to the protection of the values of the black majority. It must be doubted whether or not it is any longer possible to protect elites without also protecting the masses. International humanitarian law, including that which is applicable in internal as well as in international conflicts, is designed to protect the interests of all states and all individuals on a nondiscriminatory basis. Those who attempt to deny its protections to others today may succeed only in denying themselves the same protections tomorrow.

In an era of increasingly sophisticated weapons technology, it is apparent that law and legal institutions must at least keep pace. Perhaps our thinking is still too much dominated by the sixteenth-century conception of sovereignty which was formulated by Jean Bodin to provide a theoretical justification for the French absolutist monarchy. Such a conception today could cause us to deny the existence of common values which we in fact share with those who express conflicting ideologies. The protection of civilians from the terror aspects of armed conflict should be accorded a preeminent place in the listing of such values. This presents a significant opportunity to the Third Session of the Geneva Conference on the Humanitarian Law of Armed Conflict to improve both the substantive law and its enforcement. Harold Lasswell has put the central point succinctly:

From your perspective or mine the creative opportunity is to achieve a self-system larger than the primary ego; larger than the ego components of family, friends, profession, or nation; and inclusive of mankind.[7]

Notes

1. See W. Thomas Mallison and Sally V. Mallison, "The Concept of Public Purpose Terror in International Law: Doctrines and Sanctions to Reduce the Destruction of Human and Material Values," 18 *Howard Law Journal* 12 (1973).

2. 36 *U.S. Statutes at Large* 2310.

3. The four conventions appear in 6 *U.S. Treaties and Other International Agreements* at pp. 3114, 3217, 3316, and 3516 (Washington D.C.: U.S. Government Printing Office, 1956).

4. International Committee of the Red Cross, Draft Additional Protocols to the Geneva Conventions of August 12, 1949 (Geneva, June 1973).

5. Reprinted in Schindler and Toman, eds., *The Laws of Armed Conflict: A Collection of Conventions, Resolutions and Other Documents* 3 (Leiden: Sijthoff, 1973).

6. Pictet, ed., 4 "Commentary on the Geneva Convention" 15-17 (ICRC, 1958).

7. In the Introduction to Myres S. McDougal and Florentino P. Feliciano, *Law and Minimum World Public Order* (New Haven: Yale University Press, 1961).

L. KOS-RABCEWICZ-ZUBKOWSKI

Essential Features of an International Criminal Court

Efforts to Establish an International Criminal Court

There is abundant literature on the need and the possibility for the creation of an international criminal court (see the author's previous studies).[1] It may be recalled that in 1953 a Committee on International Criminal Jurisdiction appointed by the General Assembly of the United Nations prepared a draft statute of an international criminal court.[2] The General Assembly of the United Nations decided to postpone its decision in this matter until the elaboration of the definition of aggression.[3]

On December 14, 1974, the twenty-ninth U.N. General Assembly adopted Resolution 3314 which defines aggression as "the use of armed force by a State against the sovereign territorial integrity, or political independence of another state, or in any other manner inconsistent with the Charter of the United Nations, as set out in this definition."[4] Thus, the formal obstacle within the United Nations has been eliminated and therefore further international cooperation in the establishment of an international criminal court appears to be timely.

Important nongovernmental bodies continue to deal with this problem. The International Association of Penal Law organized on September 5, 1975, at Geneva during the Fifth United Nations Congress on the Prevention of Crime and Treatment of Offenders, a session devoted to the "International Criminal Tribunal." During this session, presided over by Dean Pierre Bouzat (University of Rennes, France), president of the association, Professor M. Cherif Bassiouni (De Paul University, Chicago), its secretary general, and Gerhard Grebing (Max Planck Institute for Foreign and International Penal Law, Freiburg in Breisgau, Federal Republic of Germany), its associate secretary general, submitted their reports which were followed by expositions by Professor Bart De Schutter (Free University of Brussels, Belgium) and by Professor Louis Kos-Rabcewicz-Zubkowski (University of Ottawa, Canada).[5]

The statute of an international criminal court was the subject of the work of experts from many countries during international criminal law conferences organized by the Foundation for the Establishment of an International Criminal Court and presided over by its president, Professor Robert K. Woetzel (Boston College—Jesuit University of Boston).[6]

Defendants Before an International Criminal Court

There is a general consensus that natural persons who committed serious crimes of international concern may be accused before an international criminal court. According to the present international law, states may be defendants before the International Court of Justice,[7] and therefore there is no need to provide for them an additional international jurisdiction. Furthermore, it is improbable that any government would submit to an international criminal jurisdiction.

Should a possibility of a trial of a state before an international criminal court exist, the final outcome of such a case would not differ much, insofar as possible sanctions are concerned, from a condemnation to pay damages according to a judgment of the International Court of Justice of The Hague. Obviously also in a criminal jurisdiction, a state could be subject only to economic-type sanctions.

In addition, from a moral point of view it is questionable whether a state, that is, the whole of its population, should be held criminally responsible for acts of its governing bodies. It seems more appropriate to hold criminally responsible the individuals including the highest state officials even when they acted in performance of their official state functions.

There remains, however, the problem of legal persons known under various names in various countries which may be called here corporations. National laws of some states provide for criminal responsibility of corporations while in others only natural persons are subject to jurisdiction of criminal courts. Should it be accepted that certain economic crimes qualify for an international jurisdiction, then corporations—authors of such crimes—could be held internationally criminally responsible. In the states which recognize domestic criminal responsibility of corporations there is no apparent reason why such a responsibility should not be extended to an international forum.

Insofar as conspiracy is concerned, a corporation could be responsible for all types of international crimes. As to the states that do not hold corporations criminally responsible their acceptance of such an international concept could lead to corresponding modifications of their national laws.

A shareholder of a criminally condemned corporation may suffer a loss, but this is also true in cases of other errors of judgment or negligence, and the like, of the officers of a corporation within the field of civil and commercial law. A shareholder may try to change the policy of the corporation, vote to remove an officer, or refrain from reelecting a person whom he considers unsuitable for a directorship and, in a last resort, sell his shares in the corporation and in this way dissociate himself from the same.

This last possibility is not available to a citizen who would like to dissociate himself from the acts of his government. He may choose an exile from his state but such a step is obviously more serious than a sale of shares in a corporation.

Jurisdiction as to International Crimes—"Nullum Crimen sine Lege"

MULTILATERAL CONVENTIONS

There is no international criminal code. This is a serious problem in view of the principle of legality *nullum crimen sine lege.* Nevertheless numerous multilateral conventions recognize certain acts as criminal. Examples of these are: piracy as defined in Article 15 of the Convention on the High Seas of 1958;[8] hijacking and related offenses as defined in the Convention for the Suppression of Unlawful Seizure of Aircraft of 1970 and in the Convention for the Suppression of Unlawful Acts against the Safety of Civil Aviation of 1971; international traffic in drugs and other related acts as defined in the Single Convention on Narcotic Drugs of 1961[9] and the Amending Protocol of 1972, as well as in the Convention on Psychotropic Substances of 1971; slavery, slave trade, and related practices as defined in the Slavery Convention of 1926,[10] the Protocol of 1953,[11] and the Supplementary Convention of 1956;[12] genocide as defined in the Convention on the Prevention and Punishment of the Crime of Genocide of 1948;[13] acts subject to criminal sanctions under the Convention on the Prevention and Punishment of Crimes against Internationally Protected Persons, including Diplomatic Agents of 1973; and war crimes under four Geneva conventions of 1949.[14] All these crimes could be submitted to the jurisdiction of an international criminal court.

INTERNATIONAL CRIMINAL CODE—GENERAL PART

Conventions on international crimes do not contain provisions which are usually in general parts of penal codes, for example, on defenses, complicity, minimum age of criminal responsibility, and so forth. When a crime defined in an international convention is tried by a national court, the latter applies the general part of its national penal or criminal code. The question arises as to which provisions are to be applied when such a case is before an international criminal court. It seems that at least a general part of an international criminal code is needed for this purpose.

Jurisdiction as to International Crimes—"Nulla Poena sine Lege"

The multilateral conventions presently in force do not specify penalties for the international crimes mentioned therein. Such penalties are provided in national laws into which states incorporated the international crimes, with perhaps the most striking difference being capital punishment, which has been entirely abolished in certain states but is still applied in several other jurisdictions. To satisfy the generally accepted principle that only such punishment may be imposed by a court which is stated in law (*nulla poena sine lege*), it would appear necessary to include in the international criminal code provisions on maximum and also minimum sanctions which may be imposed by the international criminal court. Should it be the same minimum-maximum range for all crimes submitted to the court? Such a solution could be justified by the argument that all such crimes are very serious and dangerous. Furthermore, the court could exercise the judicial individualization within the possible maximum-minimum range in a given case according to various mitigating or aggravating circumstances, the latter not being codified but left to the judgment of the court.

Another solution would be to provide in the international criminal code separate provisions on punishment for each of the international crimes. This method would require references to conventions defining such crimes or a definition of the same in the international code.

Both solutions may create a problem of acceptance of capital punishment. The states which abolished capital punishment in their respective national laws would most likely refuse to accept this punishment in an international court.

The method used in some extradition treaties may be of assistance here, namely that the state which detained a suspect may refer him to the international criminal court under condition that capital punishment will not be imposed in his case. This solution may result, however, in a situation whereby one of the two coauthors of the same crime tried in the court is exposed to a capital punishment while the other, extradited to the court by a state which abolished the punishment by death, faces only a sentence of imprisonment. This difficulty may be overcome by elimination of capital punishment from the court. It is doubtful, however, that it would be widely accepted.

Non-exclusive Character of International Jurisdiction

It may happen that in certain cases a state would prefer to try in its national court an author of an international crime while in other cases, even the same type of crime, this state would be willing to surrender the suspect to an international court. This may result, for example, from the national principle of non-extradition of a state's own nationals. It is suggested that, at least during a certain initial period of the existence of an international criminal court, its non-exclusive jurisdiction would be preferable as it would be easier to accept by the states, which in each specific case would be at liberty to decide whether to try a suspect in the state's national court or to surrender him to an international criminal court.

An Open International Criminal Court

While the recognition of the jurisdiction of an international criminal court may be assured by an international multilateral convention, other methods could also be employed subsidiarily.

Thus, submissions to the court may result from:
1. New bilateral treaties.
2. Amendments to existing treaties.
3. Special agreements.
4. Unilateral declarations.
5. National legislation.
6. Ad hoc submission of a case.
7. Tacit recognition of the jurisdiction of the international criminal court in a given case.

Such submissions may apply to a certain crime or to certain types of crimes and not necessarily to all international crimes. In addition, states may recognize only the jurisdiction of the fact-finding international commission of inquiry but not that of the International Criminal Court.

Structure of International Administration of Criminal Justice

TWO-TIER SYSTEM

The positive experience of the two-tier system of the European Commission of Human Rights and of the European Court of Human Rights shows the advantages of an extensive preliminary fact-finding process. It is proposed therefore to envisage: (1) an international commission of inquiry and (2) an international criminal court.

INTERNATIONAL COMMISSION OF INQUIRY

It is suggested that general rules of procedure before the international commission of inquiry could be as follows: Any state, legal person, or natural person is entitled to file information with the commission. The complainant may appoint his attorney for the purposes of the procedure. Furthermore, the public prosecutor acts ex officio before the ICI. The commission examines the information in order to decide whether it is within its jurisdiction and either rejects it or accepts it for an inquiry. This decision is final.

The inquiry is made in a nonpublic session except when the defendant requests that it be public. The purpose of this provision is to avoid unnecessary publicity, especially when the commission finds ultimately that the allegations against the defendant are unfounded. In all cases the public prosecutor must be present at the sessions of the commission. The attorney for the defendant has the right to be present at sessions, to cross-examine witnesses, to examine evidence, and to submit testimonial and documentary evidence. Victims of the crime may intervene in the inquiry and be represented by attorneys, the latter having the right to submit and examine evidence, and cross-examine all witnesses.

The inquiry is terminated by a fact-finding decision and either a decision dismissing the complaint or a referral to the international criminal court for trial (only when the state which surrendered the defendant recognized the jurisdiction of the court), or a termination by a settlement involving the defendant and the victim, the commission having a discretionary power to approve such settlement.

International Criminal Court

Cases referred by the international commission of inquiry to the international criminal court are tried in public. All parties, that is, the public prosecutor, the attorneys for victims-complainants, and the attorneys for defendants, have the right to submit evidence and to question witnesses. Also the court, upon its own initiative, may summon witnesses and order other evidence.

Detention Prior To and During Trial

The simplest solution would be to provide for detention of the suspect prior to and during the trial in a prison of the state where the international commission of inquiry and the international criminal court have their main offices. A special agreement with this state would assure the extranational control of such a suspect. It seems that the initial arrest of the suspect would require the cooperation of a national court and police. National authorities would act on behalf of the international commission of inquiry and/or of the international criminal court.[15] Should the defendant be released prior to the trial, the necessary surveillance, if any, would have to be provided by the organs of the same state.

Enforcement of Decisions of the Court

Sentences of the international criminal court could be enforced by the state of its main office. There may be a problem with the execution of the capital punishment as this would require that the state in question recognize such type of punishment.

The decisions on parole and temporary leaves should be made by the international criminal court. The parolee could be transferred to the state of his citizenship or perhaps even of his permanent residence, provided the latter state accepts it.[16]

International Prison

While detention in a national prison is an economically easy solution, in certain cases, for example, international terrorists, pressure may be made on the state in which the prison is situated in order to obtain the release of such terrorists against hostages, and so forth. An international prison could perhaps be a better solution as it would be known that there is no chance that the international criminal court controlling such a prison would yield to blackmail.

Appeals to The International Criminal Court

While the main purpose of an international criminal court would be to act as a court of the first instance (trial court), it could also hear appeals in certain matters such as: (1) appeals from final decisions of national courts in cases of international crimes; (2) appeals from the decisions of national courts on the qualification as political of a given international crime; (3) appeals from final decisions of national courts of asylum and deportation; and (4) appeals from final decisions of national courts in extradition matters.

The international criminal court could also deal with international conflicts of jurisdiction between national courts of two or more states.

International Participation in National Administration of Justice in Matters of International Crimes

International participation in cases of international crimes tried before national courts might constitute an intermediate solution between an exclusively national trial on one side and an exclusively international trial on the other.

It is suggested that an international attorney for prosecution and/or international attorney for defense could act in a subsidiary but independent manner before national courts. Such an international participation could be envisaged in addition to a national prosecutor and attorney for defense. The international attorneys would *inter alia* strive to submit all pertinent evidence.

National Assistance to the International Criminal Court

National police, prosecutors, investigating magistrates, and judges may help the international criminal court significantly in fulfilling requests of this court for implementation of its various orders in their respective states.

Notes

1. L. Kos-Rabcewicz-Zubkowski, "The Creation of an International Criminal Court," *International Terrorism and Political Crimes,* M. Charles Bassiouni, ed.

(Springfield, Ill.: Charles C. Thomas, 1975), p. 519; "Towards a Feasible International Criminal Court," 5 *World Law Review* 1972, p. 392.

2. United Nations, Report of the 1953 Committee on International Criminal Jurisdiction, 27 July-20 August 1953. General Assembly: Ninth Session, Supplement no. 12, (A/2645).

3. G.A. Res. 898, 9 U.N. GAOR Supp. 21, at 50 U.N. Doc. A/2890 (1954); G.A. Res. 1187, 12 U.N. GAOR Supp. 18, at 52, U.N. Doc. A/3805 (1957).

4. G.A. Res. 3314 (XXIX).

5. 46 *Revue Internationale de Droit Penal* 1975, nos. 1, 2.

6. For example, *Establishment of an International Criminal Court, A Report on the First and Second International Criminal Law Conferences and Commentary* by Robert K. Woetzel, Newton, Mass., 1973.

7. Article 34 of the Statute of the International Court of Justice.

8. *UNTS,* vol. 450, p. 11.

9. *UNTS,* vol. 521, p. 151.

10. *UNTS,* vol. 60, p. 253.

11. *UNTS,* vol. 182, p. 51.

12. *UNTS,* vol. 266, p. 3.

13. *UNTS,* vol. 78, p. 277.

14. I—for the Amelioration of the Condition of the Wounded and Sick in Armed Forces in the Field; II—for the Amelioration of the Condition of the Wounded, Sick and Shipwrecked Members of Armed Forces at Sea; III—Relative to the Treatment of Prisoners of War; IV— Relative to the Protection of Civilian Persons in Time of War. *UNTS,* vol. 75.

15. This would be a sort of *dedoublement fonctionnel,* a double function of state organs, both for national and international purposes (compare this theory of the eminent French jurist Georges Scelle in his *International Public Law*).

16. Compare the European Convention on the Supervision of Conditionally Sentenced or Conditionally Released Offenders of 1964, *European Treaty Series,* no. 51.

ROBERT K. WOETZEL

Détente in Action:
A Convention on International Crimes

French President Valery Giscard d'Estaing described detente in his address to Congress on May 18, 1976, as an attitude of remaining open to others' ideas without giving up one's own sense of values. Secretary of State Henry Kissinger most often equates detente with relaxation of tensions, and Soviet Party Chairman Leonid Brezhnev sees detente as cooperation when this is in the mutual interest. Former President Ford decided not to use the word for fear of misunderstanding.

Whatever connotation one ascribes to detente, it is clear that relaxation of tensions between any two parties in the world arena may not be considered relaxing by others. This explains the current Chinese nightmares about a United States-Soviet detente. Domestically, one leader may not consider relaxing what another one does; Ronald Reagan's campaign against detente is a case in point. In a global context, detente to be truly relaxing to all must take into consideration mankind's interests as a whole. The following Convention on International Crimes, presented here for the first time, may speak more eloquently for global detente than any definition can. It was drafted by experts from different ideological and legal systems under the auspices of the Foundation for the Establishment of an International Criminal Court and edited by this writer who is also president of the foundation which is in consultative status with the United Nations. It represents an international code of conduct which proscribes certain actions which are in nobody's interest and which outrage the conscience of mankind. It is open-ended, and other categories may be added on later. It depoliticizes certain actions which constitute obstacles to peace and relaxation of tensions and establishes responsibility and accountability without denigrating states or state sovereignty.

Perhaps it seems ironic that this approach to global detente rests on defining obstacles to peace and categories of international criminal behavior. But it must be remembered that since Cain slew Abel it has been outrages against civilized conduct that have caused war and bloodshed. It is hoped that by isolating the worst of these and by bringing to justice their perpetrators, the causes of international tensions as well as their consequences may be diminished. One may legitimately speculate whether earlier reactions to major violations of human rights in the concentration camps of the

1930s might have prevented some of the excesses that followed during World War II.

Convention on International Crimes

ARTICLE I

The Parties to this Convention agree that, in addition to acts which are crimes under existing international law,

a. the offenses in respect of which they make a declaration under Article II hereof shall be international crimes for the commission of which individuals are liable, and

b. the offenses in respect of which they make a declaration under Article II, paragraph 4, subparagraphs j to l inclusive, hereof shall be international crimes for the commission of which not only individuals but also corporations, associations and other commercial, industrial or financial organizations are liable, whether or not they constitute crimes under national law.

ARTICLE II

1. In ratifying or acceding to this Convention, each Party shall make a declaration with respect to which of the acts under paragraphs 2, 3, 4, and 5 of this Article it accepts the obligations under this Convention.

2. Acts specified by the following international agreements:

a. crimes against peace as they are defined in the Charter of the International Military Tribunal for the Trial of the Major War Criminals of 1945;

b. war crimes as they are defined in the Charter of the International Military Tribunal for the Trial of the Major War Criminals of 1945;

c. crimes against humanity as they are defined in the Charter of the International Military Tribunal for the Trial of the Major War Criminals of 1945;

d. genocide as defined in the Convention on the Prevention and Punishment of the Crime of Genocide of 1948;

e. acts subject to criminal sanctions under the Geneva Conventions of 1949;

f. slavery, slave trade, and related practices as provided for in the Slavery Convention of 1926, the Protocol of 1953, and the Supplementary Convention of 1956;

g. piracy as defined in the Convention on the High Seas of 1958;

h. hijacking and related offenses as defined in the Convention for the Suppression of Unlawful Seizure of Aircraft of 1970 and the Convention for the Suppression of Unlawful Acts against the Safety of Civil Aviation of 1971;

i. acts subject to criminal sanctions under the International Convention on the Suppression and Punishment of the Crime of Apartheid of 1973;

j. acts subject to criminal sanctions under the Convention on the Prevention and Punishment of Crimes against Internationally Protected Persons, including Diplomatic Agents of 1973.

3. Acts subject to criminal sanctions specified in the following Resolutions of the United Nations General Assembly:

a. Resolution on the Formulation of the Nuremberg Principles of 1950 (GA/Res/488 (V));

b. Resolution on Human Rights in Armed Conflict of 1970 (GA/Res/2673-2677 (XXV));

c. Resolution on Basic Principles of the Legal Status of the Combatants Struggling against Colonial and Alien Domination and Racist Regimes of 1973 (GA/Res/3103 (XXVIII));

d. Resolution on the Definition of Aggression of 1974 (GA/Res/3314 (XXIX)).

4. Acts belonging to any of the following general categories:

a. the planning, preparation, initiation, or waging of a war of aggression; or a war in violation of international treaties, agreements, or assurances;

b. war crimes including violations of the laws and customs of war committed in armed conflicts of an international or non-international character;

c. violations of humanitarian rules under international law applicable in armed conflicts of an international or non-international character;

d. crimes against humanity being:

(i)   genocide;

(ii) mass murder, extermination, enslavement, deportation, torture, rape, or other inhuman acts committed against any civilian population;

(iii) persecutions on political, racial, religious or cultural grounds;

(iv) apartheid;

e. slavery, slave trade and related practices;

f. piracy;

g. unlawful seizure of aircraft or unlawful acts against the safety of civil aviation;

h. unlawfully taking across a national frontier a person kidnapped for political, racial, or religious reasons who was engaged in governmental or public activities;

i. acts of violence directed against persons who enjoy protection under international law in respect of their functions or office;

j. external interference in the affairs of a state by the commission of acts, of whatever nature, for the purpose of subverting, controlling, or destroying the economy of that state;

k. violations of mandatory sanctions of the United Nations Security Council irrespective of applicable domestic law;

l. acts which impede the exercise of the right of self-determination by peoples under colonial, racist or apartheid regimes in accordance with the United Nations Declaration on the Granting of Independence to Colonial Countries and Peoples of 1960.

5. Acts which constitute—

a. complicity in, or willful failure to prevent, the commission of any of the above offenses; or

b. attempts to commit any of the offenses defined under paragraphs 2, subparagraphs b to j inclusive; paragraph 3, subparagraphs a to d inclusive; and paragraph 4, subparagraphs b to l inclusive;

c. participation in a common plan or conspiracy for the accomplishment of any of the acts mentioned under paragraph 4, subparagraph a.

6. After ratifying or acceding to this Convention, a Party may at any time give notice of modification of the declaration referred to in paragraph 1 of this Article so as to specify with respect to which acts it will or will not accept such obligations.

7. In the case where such notice of modification specified additional acts in respect of which a Party will accept such obligations, it shall take effect immediately upon deposit with the competent authority.

8. In the case where such notice specifies acts in respect of which the Party will no longer accept such obligations, it shall take effect one year following the date on which notification is received by the competent authority.

ARTICLE III

The fact that an individual charged with an international crime under this Convention acted in his official capacity shall not relieve him of responsibility, irrespective of rank or status.

ARTICLE IV

Obedience to national law or superior orders shall not free an individual charged with an international crime under this Convention from responsibility but may be considered in the award of punishment if justice so requires.

ARTICLE V

1. Each Party to this Convention undertakes to take the necessary steps, in accordance with its constitutional processes and the provisions of this Convention, to adopt such legislative or other measures as may be necessary to give effect to the obligations recognized in the Convention.

2. Each Party to this Convention shall be under the obligation to search for and detain persons alleged to have committed any offenses to which this Convention applies.

3. Each Party to this Convention shall have jurisdiction to try and punish any persons for having committed any offenses to which this Convention applies.

4. Each Party to this Convention undertakes to prosecute an alleged offender of this Convention in its custody, or to extradite him, or to surrender him to an international criminal court.

5. Persons accused of crimes under this Convention are entitled to generally recognized judicial safeguards.

6. Nothing in this Convention shall derogate from the application of other treaties which define or deal with the prevention or punishment of international crimes, provided that application of such treaties is not inconsistent with any provisions of this Convention.

ARTICLE VI

Reservations to this Convention shall be governed by the applicable provisions of the Vienna Convention on the Law of Treaties of 1969.

ARTICLE VII

1. Any Party to this Convention may denounce it by written notification to the competent depository authority.

2. Denunciation shall take effect one year following the date on which notification is received by the competent authority.

ARTICLE VIII

Any dispute between two or more Parties with respect to the interpretation or application of this Convention which is not resolved by other means of peaceful settlement shall, at the request of any of the parties to the dispute, be referred to the International Court of Justice for decision.

ARTICLE IX

Nothing in this Convention shall preclude a Party from accepting obligations hereof with respect to crimes defined in any international agreement or resolution of the United Nations General Assembly in addition to those enumerated in Article II.

ARTICLE X

This Convention shall enter into force thirty days after the deposit of the tenth instrument of ratification.

The Foundation for the Establishment of an International Criminal Court is in the process of setting up a commission of inquiry which will be empowered to receive and investigate complaints. The results will be made available to international agencies and the governments concerned. The procedures envisage close observance of defendants' rights. Cases not settled by any other means may then be brought before a projected international tribunal of criminal justice for trial and judgment. The statute for such a tribunal is now being drafted by the foundation. There is no statute of limitations in international law, and individuals may be held responsible for criminal violations at any time during their lives. This should serve as a deterrent to potential wrongdoers.

IMRE BEKES

The Legal Problems of
Hijacking and Taking of Hostages

In the decade following World War II, new forms of behavior appeared and spread to the field of criminality. Airplanes were diverted, and both passengers and crew were subjected to terrorism. Diplomats were kidnapped and held as hostages compelling governments to make decisions whether or not to pay for their lives and release. Bombs were exploded on busy streets, in department stores, at railway stations, in amusement places, and entire buildings were destroyed. During the last decade, these actions became an epiphenomenon of regional wars and other international conflicts. But they also showed themselves in civil wars and in some other social, political, and religious conflicts within states as methods and means of belligerent activity.

The circle of potential victims has constantly widened because terrorists have captured and taken as hostages not only diplomats but ordinary citizens without influence. Kidnappings and assassinations became a way of expressing political power. As we know from experience, victims of these terrorist attacks were innocent civilians, diplomats, members of international boards, members of international civil air crews, members of international mass media services, members of nonbelligerent armed forces, or members of nonbelligerent governments. Simultaneously, kidnapping has appeared in countries free of civil war or other armed crisis, such as Italy, and has become a lucrative form of criminality. Similarly, since 1951, not only political motives but ransom have played a part in some hijackings.

This diversity of motives has made it more difficult to understand these actions. The political question has been raised whether or not hijacking, kidnapping, or assassination aimed at helping rational and justifiable national goals should be considered as legitimate national wars or struggles for freedom. If the answer is affirmative, the terrorist should be regarded as a hero instead of a criminal. If terrorism can be conceived by the law as a political crime, there should be no extradition. The terrorist who escapes to another country should be granted political asylum. Acceptance of this conception would lead us to perceive hijacking, kidnapping, and assassination as common crimes or as political crimes according to the motives of the offender.

In an earlier century and in another situation, this problem had appeared already. Sea law made a distinction between piracy and privateer. The pirate was seeking private and lucrative goals in his use of illegal force, holding up and looting on the open seas ships of any nationality. Privateers, however, being authorized or commanded by a belligerent partner, applied force on the open seas against ships of an enemy nation only. But in spite of the historical analogy, essential differences exist. The privateer got his authority from a belligerent partner and was subject to international law, but the modern terrorist acts according to the instructions of a secret organization.

To this day no common definition or interpretation of terrorism has been agreed upon. A satisfactory legal definition covers only one part of terrorism, namely, hijacking.

The fight against terrorism has been carried on now for over two decades. Apart from technical means, this fight has another important aspect—and this is in the area of criminal law. The first offenders in these crimes appeared as adventurers seeking their own personal goals. Typical personal goals frequently drove them to reach a land or a country which could not be reached by any other means. The unexpected success of this activity called the attention of criminals to the advantages of ransoming both the passengers and crew of a plane. The insufficient defense against kidnapping and the willingness of flight companies to give in to criminal demands then drove illegal political organizations to add this method to their political arsenal. They could, for example, use hostages to have their own confined members released. Their first actions meant the criminalization of domestic politics. After the Arab-Israeli war in 1967, hijacking was applied by Arab guerrillas to help freedom fighters and to acquaint foreign politicians about the Palestinian movement. Attacks were thus made on planes and passengers of countries that were completely uninvolved in the Middle East conflict. International air transportation was menaced by a serious crisis.

Countries which had international airlines sought effective legal defense against the attacks through conventions held in The Hague and Montreal. Special equipment was set up in national and international airports, and preventive control over passengers became universally accepted. These are effective means of security to which legal enforcement has supplementary importance. Nevertheless, one can trust in the effectiveness of criminal law especially in cases when the offender is motivated by a private aim, and the crime was committed alone or by a small group. According to experience, the criminal punishment could not have preventive force since attackers are persons who volunteered for death and who even in the case of capture often have a chance to get out of prison in exchange for hostages from other hijackings.

As a phenomenon, hijacking can be divided into two categories: (a) attacks committed by organizations of guerrillas, (b) all other attacks. Liquidation of the former depends on political decisions, with unknown components, but elimination of the latter may demand the measures and instruments of criminal law.

The Hague Convention of 1970, however, makes one differentiation between the two types of attacks or their legal evaluation. According to this convention, hijacking is to be considered a common crime, and its motive allows differentiated evaluation. Hence this convention—on the basis of international law—refuses to accept hijacking as a form of political and military offensive, aiming at victory through national efforts. Experience shows, however, that the motives of hijacking have wider range: (a) a demand of ransom for captured passengers and crew; (b) an exchange of hostages for political prisoners convicted of civil crimes; (c) an exchange of hostages for prisoners convicted of political crimes or prisoners imprisoned with no sentence; (d) an illegal emigration by forcing a plane from one state to fly to another; and (e) an expression of the power of an illegal political or military group. Ultimately, hijacking may correspond to any kind of target. The Hague Convention underlined the fact that effective international control of that crime can be achieved if states do not give recognition to one or another motive or target. Conversely, the criminal codes of some states would excuse offenders when they request a receiving state for asylum.

Practically speaking, the different forms of hijacking show great variety. Earlier hijackings were committed by single offenders; one of the passengers forced the pilot to divert the plane. Lately this method has completely changed. To reduce the risk involved in the crime, offenders organized themselves into groups and began holding passengers and crew as hostages.

Since the very beginning several governments—including that of the Hungarian People's Republic—were anxious about the growing threat to the security of flight. On the occasion of a diplomatic conference held on this subject, socialist countries clearly expressed their stand: hijacking is to be considered a common crime.

The struggle to reestablish the security of flight has had two different stages. The first lasted until 1970 and was determined by the Convention of Tokyo (1963). It did not, however, establish solid ground for coordinated defense. Lacking cooperation in security measures governments could give but insufficient protection against hijacking and other crimes endangering the security of flight.

The year 1970 was a turning point both in the course of terrorism and the struggle against it. At the beginning of that year, the number of attempted hijackings and assassinations rose to unprecedented heights and the need for new defensive devices became obvious as did the recognition that without them the most dynamic branch of transportation would fall into crisis.

The reestablishment of the security of flight was equivalent to complying with two requirements: (a) to introduce preventive measures of a technical nature and (b) to accede to international conventions serving this prevention.

Today, international regulations compel nations to introduce complex equipment, methods, and procedures of control at international airports. Systematic application of these security measures has greatly contributed to the detection of potential offenders. No doubt these measures are rather expensive and, in addition, they make the waiting period at the airport longer. Compared with the radically shortened flying time, this seems a very anachronistic development. However, these methods contributed quite effectively to the improvement of the security of flight. The present view is that security should be based on the ground. Even in the case of an attack during flight, we cannot endanger the lives of passengers and crew or the great value of a plane with resistance of dubious value once the plane is in the air.

Besides the existing horizontal-technical defense, another solution is the standardization of criminal investigation and the unification of the actions of various nations. The Hague Convention in 1970 made an effort to unify— through the aspect of criminal law—the qualification of hijacking. This convention set up a concrete criminal codification on hijacking and the acceptance of that codification by national criminal codes which would render the possibility of a homogeneous judgment under unified criteria. If this could be joined with a unified criminal investigation, we would be able to say that the principle of universality prevails in criminal law. This indicates that hijacking has made nations aware to a great degree of the fact that to overcome such terrorism, cooperation is unavoidable. This is the benefit which international law and criminal law (perhaps we might call it international criminal law) has gained from hijacking.

Considering methods of a legal solution, we can see that both the form and the content of the regulations have to be decided. The Hague and Montreal Conventions were multilateral, and this form seems to be the most effective for international cooperation. But there are some bilateral agreements, too, supporting an energetic defense against hijackings. An example of a successful one of this kind is the Caribbean agreement, where Cuba has cooperated with the United States, Canada, and Venezuela to overcome the hijacking of planes and vessels. It appears that Cuba is preparing similar arrangements between itself and other countries of South America. Recently obtained information shows that with the signing of the Caribbean agreement, the incidence of hijackings has radically decreased in this area. Mention must also be made of the International Civil Airway Organization which prefers bilateral agreements in the event of attacks against the security of flight. The fight against hijacking is thus based on three international legal documents: the conventions of Tokyo (1963), the Hague (1970), and of Montreal (1971). The conference of ICAO held in Rome (1973) is considered an amendment of the latter.

The results of the past five years can be characterized as follows:

1. The convention of the Hague (1970) defined it to be a crime if a person

on board a plane (a) illegally, by force, or by threat of force or terrorization of any kind, captures or plans or attempts to capture a plane; (b) becomes an accessory to a person who either commits or attempts to commit these actions (Article 1).

The Montreal Convention (September 23, 1971) dealt with the technical questions of criminal investigation. The Hague Convention was quickly ratified by the various states and came into force on October 14, 1971. Article 2 of the convention obliged signatory states to impose serious punishment upon offenders who committed a crime defined by Article 1. A new paragraph has been enacted into the Hungarian Penal Code (paragraph 192) in accordance with this obligation. This law enables judges to impose prison sentences of from five to twelve years. Offenders can be sentenced either to life imprisonment or to capital punishment when this crime simultaneously causes the death of anyone involved. The punishment for an attempt under this law is equal to that of the accomplished crime. Advance preparation for a hijacking not actually attempted can be punished with imprisonment of from one to five years.

Speakers for the convention have agreed on the interpretation of serious punishment, which means imprisonment. But they did not want to confine the signatory states by determining the upper and lower levels of imprisonment. Despite this, the suggestion of Austria's delegate that the offender in such crimes must be punished equally with the offender charged with battery and manslaughter was well-received. The Hungarian Penal Code has seemingly adopted this proposition. Under the provision of this code, an offender, who by intentional bodily injury causes an unanticipated death of someone, should be imprisoned from two to eight years. The punishment for manslaughter extends from five to fifteen years but in aggravated cases can be from ten to fifteen, or life imprisonment or, alternatively, capital punishment. This shows that among crimes of hijacking, manslaughter, and battery, some kind of proportionality exists. The convention of the Hague has not prescribed the minimal level of punishment either, but a comparison with manslaughter and battery seems to be reasonable at this range, too, mostly because the minimal punishments for these crimes adopted by the European Criminal Code generally exceed one year of imprisonment. This is in keeping with many other extradition treaties, which order the extradition of offenders committing common crimes and those who have been imprisoned over one year. According to the sense of the Hague Convention "serious punishment" cannot be less than imprisonment for one year.

2. The Hague Convention decided to recognize the nonpolitical character of these crimes, and hijacking has thus been declared an ordinary crime. Offenders in such crimes are excluded from the favored treatment of the political criminal, namely, from otherwise prohibited extradition.

3. The problem of extradition was a very essential topic at the conference

and it brought the convention very close to failure. Fortunately, the delegates succeeded in achieving a compromise on this question which saved the article of extradition (Article 8) and, at the same time, the success of the convention. By this compromise, signatory states—at their discretion—may consider this agreement as a basis of extradition in connection with states with which they had not previously had such an agreement.

4. The convention mentioned above has not obliged the signatories to grant extradition but offers it as a possible option. States capturing an offender may have a choice of punishing him in accordance with the convention, or they might apply the rule of extradition. There was no debate on the extradition of a state's own citizens. In this way the convention has provided states with the alternative of *aut dedere aut punire*. At the diplomatic conference of ICAO, held in Rome on September 21, 1973, the implementation of extradition was restricted to the demand that states conducting criminal procedures on hijacking should be requested to take into consideration the primary necessity of extradition.

The Hague Convention did not deal with problems of asylum. But we have to differentiate between political asylum and asylum springing from criminal law. Asylum based on criminal law can be enjoyed by an offender whose action cannot be considered a crime according to the law of the receiving state. Lack of double incrimination hinders extradition of such a person because his action is not qualified as a crime by the state of his residence. Asylum of a political character, however, is quite another matter. It contains no more than the prohibition of extradition. In this case a state—by *ius deprehensionis*—may take the offender into custody and may sentence and convict him, but after his release he can obtain a grant of asylum.

Since the convention came into force, experience has shown that states prefer to rely upon their own criminal procedures rather than extradition. But in this way a nation having suffered the greatest harm, for example, the state which registered the plane, is deprived of the possibility of prosecuting the offender. There is no doubt that among the anticipated solutions (*aut dedere aut punire*) the progress of extradition should bring about the most success because this has unquestionably the greatest deterring effect upon potential offenders. Since December 1970 most of the states have expressed their official stand on this question without, however, having accomplished anything essential.

There is no question that the legal solutions of the international agreements mentioned above could theoretically be developed further. The hope of such development stimulated both the Symposium of Criminal Law at Syracuse, Italy, in 1973, and the Congress of AIDP at Budapest, to put forward proposals setting up an international criminal court. It may happen that a state, which is the custodian of a hijacker, does not care, for reasons of its own, to pursue either criminal prosecution or extradition. In this situation the international criminal court—as an independent legal entity—could protect such a state by calling the offender into court. The establishment of such a court could further increase the possibility of international cooperation by operating on the territory of some other state.

Arguments against an international criminal court have rather a more practical than a theoretical character. For example: (a) What kind of law should be applied by this court? (b) What should be the location of the prison which receives those convicted? (c) Which organ should supply the maintenance of this prison? (d) Who should have the right to release a prisoner on parole? (e) Who should have the power of mercy?

There is also a conception which would reduce the authority of an international criminal court to sentencing, while the administration of imprisonment would be the responsibility of any other country which chose to undertake this task. It is difficult to believe that this idea would work. Presumably, very few nations would want the administration of a conviction of this kind, which would possibly endanger the lives of their own citizens through a potential act of terrorism aimed at securing the release of the imprisoned.

We must conclude, then, that further expansion of these agreements cannot presently be achieved. The main trend today is to make the acceptance of the conventions of the Hague and of Montreal universal. Experience has shown that some countries have failed to observe these resolutions and, according to their interests, have received the hijacker and have granted him political and legal asylum. Obviously, insofar as nations cannot be in agreement on the control of this crime, they cannot achieve any definite success at such control.

Hijacking in the classical sense, however, is a very rare occurrence nowadays. Technical equipment and devices set up at airports are usually capable of detecting potential offenders. Experience shows that at a well-controlled airport it is impossible for such a person to board a plane with the intention of hijacking it during the flight. Subsequently, this sort of crime will be converted to crimes committed on the ground, that is, on the field, at the airport (such as occurred in Rome), or in some other part of the country. Kidnappings are going to supersede hijacking; offenders will capture hostages on the ground, then demand an airplane for their transportation. This type of crime, however, will need considerably better organization than before.

Practically speaking, success of such kidnappings depends on the following conditions:

1. Prior exploration of possibilities and opportunities, clearing of customs, behavior and purposes of potential hostages, and previous detection on the spot.

2. The smuggling of necessary instructions to fellow conspirators.

3. The smuggling of arms to a certain location close to the spot of the proposed kidnapping.

4. Since kidnapping is to be committed on the ground and usually in a criminal partnership, it is necessary to organize the implementation of periodic catering, rest, and guarding of hostages, and to provide the conspirators with security measures.

5. To avoid traps, offenders are obliged to know the roads leading to the airport and to search the interior of the plane for hiding places of different types.

6. To determine the country of landing without the risk of being punished or extradited by the country of *locus deprehensionis*. Today, to commit a hijacking, offenders need both the sympathy and the cooperation—at least subsequently—of another government, including permission to land. Practically, the meeting of these conditions is impossible for private persons, so that this crime can only be committed by an organization well-equipped with special apparatus and having excellent organizers. The risk such organizers undertake can be reduced in two ways: (a) They must have a guarantee against unexpected failure based on the taking of a new hostage, who can be freed in exchange for the party they want released; (b) They must acquire prior permission from a foreign government to land freely on its territory after the hijacking.

Since this new form of preflight action, hijacking can be placed in the category of kidnappings committed on the ground. Acquisition of a plane is merely designed to serve as an escape and for the transportation of the hostages. Presently, the conventions of Montreal and of The Hague are not able to give sufficient legal protection against such kidnappings. Similarly, the technical devices at airports cannot provide as much security as is expected.

After World War II, the Geneva Convention of August 12, 1949, aimed at the protection of the civilian population, proscribed the taking of hostages (Article 3). This convention forbids attacks against human life and body (that is, manslaughter, inquisition, or torture), the taking of hostages, the imposing of punishment, or the execution of it without the sentence of a court having been brought into session by due process. The best we can hope to do is to turn to the Geneva Convention for an international agreement similar to the conventions of Montreal and of The Hague which would enable nations to have access to a unified system of investigation of kidnapping. Some basic principles of the conventions of Montreal and of The Hague (depolitization, severe punishment, *aut dedere aut punire*) should also be applied to kidnapping.

NICHOLAS N. KITTRIE

A New Look at Political Offenses and Terrorism

In recent years the international community has witnessed a growing number of unorthodox political activists and movements whose tactical arsenal has ranged from civil disobedience to coups d'etat, from tyrannicide to guerrilla war and terrorism. Their proclaimed goals have included self-determination and human rights, but unorthodox activism need not be confused with exclusively liberal and human pursuits. Both recent and earlier history has demonstrated that reactionary and oppressive goals may also be served by resort to extralegal or violent means.

Political activists have attracted an inordinate degree of public attention. More inches of newsprint have been devoted the past year in America and in many other countries to the adventures and trials of Patricia Hearst, Lynette "Squeeky" Fromme, and Sarah Moore than to any other topic in the field of criminal justice. What was uniquely common to all three was not merely their gender but the political character of their crimes. As one adds to these domestic headliners the coverage of such transnational violence as the South Moluccan train hijackers in Holland, the kidnapping of the OPEC oil ministers in Vienna, and the increasing worldwide speculations regarding the mysterious Carlos, it is apparent that political crime and terrorism are this decade's favorite cops-and-robbers stories.

It is not the sheer number of those killed, injured, or otherwise affected by political crime and terrorism which accounts for the widespread public attention given this phenomenon. In the four worst years of domestic turmoil in America (1965-1968), a grand total of 214 were killed and 9,000 were injured as a result of terrorism, protests, and ghetto riots. But this compares with a national total of 12,000 murders and 250,000 aggravated assaults annually. During the height of the aircraft hijacking epidemic (1968-1972), the number of persons who lost their lives or were injured in all domestic and international flights did not exceed 200. In the same period, the number of internationally protected persons subjected to attack, kidnapping, or threat of violence did not exceed forty-six, with sixteen meeting eventual death. The most recent statement issued by FBI Director Clarence Kelley, pointing to the growing threat posed by terrorist activities, lists eleven victims killed and seventy-two injured through bombings and other violence in America during 1975.[1] Worldwide, it is estimated that in 1975 at least fifty people lost their lives and more than 150 were taken hostage in seventeen major acts of international terrorism.[2] Thus, it is apparent that political crime and terrorism account for a mere fraction of all domestic and international crime. There are more people murdered annually in intrafamily strife or killed in automobile accidents in America alone than are killed as a result of political and terrorist activities worldwide.[3]

What then underlies the significance of the public's as well as the media's preoccupation with terrorism and other forms of political crime? Others have commented on the political offender's denial of the very legality of the challenged system of justice and the terrorist's resort to "violence for effect," viewing a grip of panic as his ultimate goal.

Some additional observations need to be made regarding the functions of political violence in modern Western societies. In the first place, political offenses—frequently reflected in highly colorful deeds and offenders—are antidotes to public apathy and boredom. They appeal to the news consumer's prurient interest in the unexpected, the unpredictable, and the adventurous. There were times when motiveless psychopathic mass-killers had the major claim to public attention. At other times, the media spotlighted organized crime and its "godfatherly" management system. There are growing indications that white-collar crime and business criminality—ranging from corporate disregard for safety and ethics to the practices of multinational corporations—might gain more attention in the future. But the current stage belongs to two major classes of political crime, posed like the obverse faces of the Roman god Janus.

On one side are the crimes perpetrated by those holding the reins of political power. These official or quasi-official offenses range from such relatively "mild" abuses of justice as Watergate and election law frauds[4] (what Kirchheimer terms "political justice") to such atrocities as the "reigns of terror" employed in postrevolutionary France, the Soviet Union and Nazi Germany. On the other side are the crimes undertaken by those who view themselves as being out of power: those politically, economically, racially, ethnically, or otherwise subjected to discrimination. This second group of offenses likewise ranges from mild displays of protest and civil disobedience (at times described as "political offenses") to a full arsenal of violent tactics against authority and established institutions, sometimes labeled as a "siege of terror."

As often as not, political offenses are directed against persons who have achieved high position (heads of state, politicians, diplomatic personnel, and captains of industry) and it is the victim's status that endows the offender with identity. The loss of such leaders is likely to dramatically affect political, social, or economic conditions, nationally and worldwide, and the offender at least temporarily senses the pulse of power. In a society suffering from a high degree of alienation and individual feelings of impotence in the face of government and big business, the political offense symbolizes the little man or woman's remaining power to be noticed. He or she can at least disrupt if not direct the flow of distant and unaccountable government powers. Most political offenders thus carry the message of many others who feel aggrieved and without adequate opportunities to be heard. Moreover, when government or other established institutions are increasingly perceived to be in the wrong—when they become the dispensers of injustice —the political offender becomes a crystallization of popular discontent and opposition, much like Robin Hood, antislavery leader John Brown, or the patriots of the American Revolution.

In the councils of international affairs and law, political crime and terrorism have equally received growing attention because of their adverse impact on fundamental international institutions and doctrines of international law. First, by seeking out weak links in the international air-traffic system, political terrorists have been able to render not only air carriers, but also governments, virtually helpless in the face of blackmail demands. Not since the heyday of classical piracy has international traffic been so seriously affected. To a lesser degree, letter-bombs, for a period, had similarly jeopardized the flow of international mail, traditionally immune to such interferences. Second, the historical inviolability and special protection of diplomats, both in peace and in war, has been totally rejected, if not in theory then at least in practice, by terrorist organizations. Frequently, these agents of international communications are specifically singled out as targets for terrorist activities. Third, previous international efforts to protect the innocent and noncombatants from the ravages of uncontrolled violence through codifications of the law of war have again been contradicted both by the practices and doctrines of modern terrorism. The Hague and Geneva conventions sought through firm standards to confine and restrain the theaters of war. Yet, modern terrorism denies the very concept of innocence and noncombatancy and seeks to make the whole globe accountable to violence.

It is not surprising, therefore, that despite evidence of relatively limited victimizations, transnational political crime and terrorism have become of grave concern to the international community. For regardless of doctrinal shadings, the security of international commerce and travel, diplomatic protection, and the safeguarding of noncombatant civilian populations are long-standing and indeed classical pillars of the international community.

To these concerns one should add the terrifying hazards posed by present-day technological progress. A shrinking world, due to the revolution in transportation, has so redefined the theaters of violence that no place is safe from terrorism. Progress in mass-destruction weaponry, and its ready availability, further affords terrorists an almost boundless expansion of destructive capabilities.

Despite terrorism's challenges to the basic institutions of society, newly coupled with fears of potential exposure to nuclear or other high-risk blackmail, the community of nations has not produced a joint plan of antiterrorist action. Lack of consensus affects not only the ability of governments to agree on how to respond to these manifestations of violence but also on how to classify and differentiate among various types of politically motivated offenders.

In the face of these disagreements, the two major international attempts of the past forty years to define and control terrorism have not proven successful. The League of Nations, in 1937, prepared an international convention against terrorism, to have it ratified by one country only.[5] In 1972, the United States presented a draft convention to the United Nations which languishes in committee. However, the prevalence of transnational violence places the topic once again on the international agenda and revives attempts to seek new and acceptable solutions.

Political Crime in National and International Law

A productive analysis of the new efforts cannot be undertaken without due attention to past political and legal traditions. It is this heritage which in part accounts for the present impasse. Yet these very traditions might help dictate fruitful future directions. Because most nations have not recognized the existence of political crime in their domestic law, the phenomenon has not been subjected to close scrutiny by courts or commentators. The significance of the political nature of an offense has been recognized primarily in the law of extradition. In this limited sphere, the framework for a conceptual analysis of political crime has been developed. Moreover, several attempts to define terrorism have been made in the context of international agreements to control transnational crimes.

The terms *political crime* and *terrorism* cannot be readily defined through a review of the standard literature of the social and behavioral sciences. Similarly, legal materials provide little assistance.[6] In the Anglo-American tradition, crimes are usually classified according to the objects of the offenses—crimes against the person (such as murder and rape), against the habitation (such as burglary and arson), against property (such as larceny), and against public order (such as disturbing the peace). Another system relied primarily upon the severity of the offenses and their requisite penalties, thus drawing a line between felonies, which always called for capital punishment, and misdemeanors, which merited lighter dispositions. Both English and American jurisprudence also distinguish ordinary offenses from treason, the most despised of all crimes and one which required, in the common law, the corruption of blood in addition to drawing and quartering.

The United States Constitution delegated the law-making power to Congress. Only one crime is listed and defined in the Constitution: treason, the levying of war against the United States or the aiding and comforting of its enemies. But despite this constitutional identification of the political crime par excellence, American law retains the unique distinction (which it shares with its English predecessor) of failing to list, identify, or recognize political crimes as a distinguishable class.[7] An offender's political motive is never to be afforded a forum or hearing.

Some legal systems specifically define political crimes in their domestic codes. In so addressing themselves openly and directly to the problems of political crimes, the laws might also decree a differential treatment for political offenders. Alexsandr Solzhenitsyn points out that to draw a distinction between political offenders and common prisoners "is the equivalent of showing their respect as equal opponents, of recognizing that people may have views of their own."[8] Reflecting this respect, the German penal system in the Weimar Republic offered imprisonment in a fortress (Festungshaft) as a symbolic confinement when the offender's motives were considered "honorable." It was the benefit of this differentiation which permitted Adolph Hitler, after the failure of his 1923 Munich Putsch, the leisure for writing *Mein Kampf.*

Describing Tsarist practices, Solzhenitsyn reported:

Criminals were teamed up and driven along the streets to the station so as to expose them to public disgrace. And politicals could go there in carriages. Politicals were not fed from the common pot but were given a food allowance instead and had their meals brought from public eating places.[9]

But while a great number of countries have treated their political offenders leniently, others have responded more harshly. After the tsar came the revolution, and the pursued of the past became the new pursuers. The lenient tsarist practice gave way to a totally different and much harsher Soviet response to political crime in the name of socialist justice. Equally, the Nazi and Fascist regimes, as well as other totalitarian governments in the post-World War II era, have singled out their domestic political offenders for particularly oppressive controls and punishment.

The major recognition and differential treatment of political offenders occurred not in domestic law but in international practice. In antiquity and throughout the Middle Ages, the offender who committed a crime against the sovereign was the most despised of all criminals. He had challenged the most sacred of all institutions—divinely ordained government.[10] In the Middle Ages, political offenders, persons guilty of crimes of lese majeste, thus became the most important targets of extradition to facilitate the meting out of punishments. The first known European treaty dealing with the surrender of political offenders was entered in 1174 between England and Scotland, followed by a 1303 treaty between France and Savoy. But the Age of Enlightenment and the subsequent Ages of Revolution revealed government to be less than godly. How, therefore, could all rebels against authority be labeled evil?

One commentator has noted that "the French Revolution of 1789 and its aftermath started the transformation of what was the extraditable offense par excellence to what has since become the nonextraditable offense par excellence."[11] Recognizing the nobler motives of political offenders and the growing diversity of political regimes, Belgium, in 1833, became the first country to enact a law withholding the extradition of political offenders. By the middle of the century, the doctrine was widely established throughout the continent. Virtually every European treaty gave a refugee political offender protection against extradition back to the country in which an offense was committed. While a domestic political offender was often accorded no differential treatment, the offender who committed his crime abroad and sought refuge elsewhere was afforded a safe haven.

Who was this privileged offender? The term political offense is seldom defined in either treaties or domestic legislation. The determination of what constitutes a political offense is reached according to the laws of the haven country, and the decision is usually made by the courts of the state. Seeking to establish the proper boundaries for political crime, most courts have drawn a distinction between "pure" political offense and "complex" or "connected" offenses. Treason, sedition, espionage, other acts endangering the external security of the state, rebellion, and incitement to civil war are all viewed as offenses exclusively against sovereign authority and are considered pure political offenses. Other offenses that endanger the life or property of individuals but are carried out in connection with and in furtherance of a crime against the state, might be classified as either complex or connected political offenses. Viewed alone the latter offenses are common crimes. But if a criminal act (such as the assassination of a head of state) was primarily the "means, method or cloak"[12] for carrying out a political offense, the act will be viewed as a complex political crime. When an act primarily affects individual life or property yet is closely connected with other acts against the security of the state, it would be described as a connected political offense (for example, a bank robbery by revolutionaries).

The political offense exception was not designed to accommodate the individual conscience of each malcontent or rebel. In the common law approach, represented by the classic case of In re Castioni,[13] the requirement was established that recognized political offenses must be "incidental to and formed part of a political disturbance." In the absence of a general political revolt or disturbance, the individual offender, regardless of his political or ideological motivation, was to be viewed as a common criminal. Moreover, the European, and primarily Swiss practice, had further sought to curtail excessive violence by conditioning the political offense exception upon objective standards of proportionality. Accordingly, the ideological beliefs and goals of the offender must be correlated to the effect of his acts and offenses. In the Ktir case, a member of the Algerian Liberation movement (FLN) was charged in France with the murder of another FLN member suspected of treason. Ktir fled to Switzerland and contested the French request for extradition. In granting the request, the Swiss court held that "the damage had to be proportionate to the aim sought; in the case of murder, this had to be shown to be the sole means of attaining the political aim."[14]

While domestic laws have found it difficult if not impossible to allow the political offender's challenge to the legal order, the international legal system has found a way to accommodate the conflicting interests. The political offender exception to extradition was certainly an innovative answer. In his own country, the political offender often remained a common criminal, but the civilized world community was willing to listen to the defense of conscience. This accommodation was reached in the last century. However, in recent years, the old conflict between individual conscience and public order has once more returned to haunt the international arena. Once again the right to resist injustice is being heatedly debated in world councils.

Since the creation of the political offense exception, new international standards of justice have gained world acceptance. World War I ended with a commitment to international self-determination. And the movement which started with President Wilson's Fourteen Points reached its peak in the post-World War II era. Little of this commitment has been reflected in positive international law,[15] but the climate of the world community has certainly supported the most expeditious roads to self-determination. The conclusion of World War II has also witnessed a renewed international commitment to the protection and promotion of individual human rights worldwide. In 1948, the General Assembly of the United Nations adopted the Universal Declaration of Human Rights. In the following quarter century, a host of other declarations, conventions, covenants, and proclamations were advanced by the United Nations on such topics as economic, social, and cultural rights, civil and political rights, racial discrimination, slavery, collective bargaining, rights of children, and the right to asylum.[16] While these documents have not been uniformly accepted, nor do they share the same legal status, they have, nevertheless, made an indelible mark upon world opinion. Even stronger undertakings for the advancement of human rights have come into being on a regional basis. The European Convention on Human Rights and its enforcement process is a notable example.[17]

The terrible experiences with Nazi and Fascist policies and practices produced, after World War II, a special sensitivity to the rights of minorities. The Genocide Convention of 1948[18] sought to protect national, ethnic, racial, and religious groups. It defined as an international crime the killing of members of a group, causing them serious bodily or mental harm, or deliberately inflicting conditions of life calculated to bring physical destruction. In the recent past, the General Assembly of the United Nations, after a discussion of the South African practice of apartheid, labeled it "a crime against humanity."[19]

The Shrinking Political Offense and the Growth of
International Crime

Despite the unwillingness of many countries to condemn acts committed under claims of self-determination and human rights as terrorist, there has been an evident trend in international law to narrow the traditional exception granted to political offenders. As early as 1856, Belgium, the first country to embody the political offense protection in its law, amended its requirements by excluding assassinations of chiefs of state from this safeguard. This limitation, called a *clause d'attentat,* was widely copied in both bilateral and regional treaties among European, South American, and African states. In several recent treaties, all assassinations are excluded from the political offense protection.[20]

Another narrowing of the scope of political offenses came at the end of the last century in the face of the growing threat of anarchism. The earlier tolerance toward those seeking to violently overthrow a regime turned into a suspicion of those viewed as a danger to all governments. The case of *In re Meunier*[21] held, in 1894, that confessed anarchists are not political offenders exempt from extradition. To constitute a political offense, the English court held, there must be two or more parties, each seeking to impose the government of its own choice, but "the party with which the accused is identified . . . is the enemy of all governments. Their efforts are directed primarily against the general body of citizens."[22]

In subsequent years, domestic laws, international conventions, and judicial decisions further confined the political offense exception. The French Extradition Law of 1927 provided that the exception was not to apply to "acts of odious barbarism and vandalism prohibited by the laws of war."[23] The extradition agreement approved by the League of Arab States in 1952 also exempted from the exception premeditated murder or acts of terrorism.[24] Similarly, the Supreme Court of Argentina declared in 1968: "Extradition will not be denied where we are dealing with cruel or immoral acts which clearly shock the conscience of civilized peoples."[25]

In the post-World War II era, an even more drastic restriction was placed on the benefits of the political offense claim. World revulsion against the Nazi and Fascist excesses resulted in the designation of crimes against humanity and war crimes as international crimes not entitled to the benefit of any political offense exception. Both the Nuremberg Trial and the subsequent formulation of its principles by the United Nations General Assembly established crimes against humanity to be universally condemned.[26] War crimes, as defined by the 1912 Hague Convention and 1949 Geneva Conventions, also constitute international crimes to which the political offense exception does not apply.

The origins of international criminal law date to the crime of piracy, long considered an offense against all civilized nations.[27] Other early international efforts concentrated on white slavery and traffic in narcotics. However, in more recent years, there has been a growing international commitment to limit, through international criminalization, conduct which could be viewed as political yet which threatens basic institutions of the world community. The definition of counterfeiting as an international crime after World War I was such a step.[28] Even more demonstrative of the world community's willingness to condemn universally disruptive political violence have been the recent treaties making aircraft hijacking[29] and the kidnapping of diplomats (internationally protected persons) international crimes.[30] So condemned by international law, these crimes can no longer be viewed as political offenses affording their perpetrators protection from extradition. Instead, it has become the duty of all civilized nations to apprehend the offenders and subject them to either prosecution or extradition.

While the terminology of political crime has had nearly a century and a half to reach a degree of maturity, terrorism is a relatively unstable newcomer. Most commentators find the origins of modern terrorism in the Reign of Terror after the French Revolution and in the anarchist movement of the last century. But neither domestic legislation nor international treaties specify its elements. Like the political offender, the terrorist may be motivated by political considerations. He might also claim to act out of an altruistic rather than an egoistic motive, and unlike the common offender, proclaim the goal of serving humanity rather than his own baser interests.

What distinguishes the terrorist from political offenders generally is the nature of his deeds, his strategy, and his goals. The political offender is not necessarily committed to violence. Breaking censorship laws or publishing official secrets is as much a political offense as the assassination of a head of state. The political offender usually seeks to assert rights that he believes the state has improperly denied him, for example, freedom of speech and assembly or the right to travel. At times a reactionary political offender might seek a restriction of civil rights. The offender need not be militant; he may prefer to depart for more compatible societies. The political offender's deed is usually directed against those he views as specifically responsible for the conceived ills. The terrorist, however, has a commitment to the violent process as an end, "as a catharsis not therapy." The political offense might be "a passing deed, an event. Terrorism is a process, a way to life, a dedication."[31]

While the political offender seeks to remove the specific causes of his discontent, the terrorist believes the social order to be so corrupt as to require its total destruction. For the deprived, says Franz Fanon in *The Wretched of the Earth,* violence is a purifying force. The true terrorist consciously employs terror. The goal is to spread panic by maximizing uncertainty. The final erosion of popular support of the system is to be attained through indiscriminate terrorism which produces equally brutal countermeasures. A leading nineteenth-century Russian revolutionary once proclaimed that "the object is perpetually the same: the quickest and surest way of destroying this whole filthy order."[32] To the terrorist, this objective can be best attained through bold actions which demonstrate the terrorist's complete unconditional and irrevocable opposition to the existing order. Frequently the strategy is to attack the masses, "the very people he wants to liberate, but to attack them in such a way that it is government which appears to be their enemy."[33]

Codes of Conduct for Political Offenders and Terrorists

Political offenses, as previously seen, may range from "pure" offenses, such as sedition, to a "siege of terror," involving random and indiscriminate violence. Political offenders may be within the confines of international legality even though in violation of domestic laws. The so-called pure political offense—which challenges the state but affects no innocent private rights—continues to benefit from a privileged status in international law and practice. Those who violate state laws limiting freedom of speech or assembly, those who disregard censorship and other secrecy laws, those who break laws restricting religion or other exercises of human rights may benefit from international asylum at the very least. Hopefully they may gain additional protective shelters, both internationally and domestically, through expanding international standards of human rights.

On the other extreme of the political offense spectrum, there is a growing list of activities which have been prohibited as outright international crimes. This group includes crimes against humanity, aircraft hijacking, and the kidnapping of diplomats. Some of this conduct might be classed as complex political crime, while other acts could be described as connected political offenses. Aircraft hijacking and other offenses against innocent victims would fall within the category of connected offenses. But both assassinations and diplomatic abductions might be categorized as complex offenses. All the political offenses which have been designated as international crimes are not "pure" political offenses, but beyond that they do not readily respond to any further classification. They do reflect, by and large, a universal reaffirmation of classical international law commitments to the preservation of transportation and communication routes.

There is an area in the center of the political offense spectrum which remains unaffected by the growing recognition of human rights on the one hand and the increasing expansion of international crimes on the other. Typical of this middle conduct are what might generally be regarded as both complex political offenses and connected political offenses. The assassination of a governmental official in the course of a political uprising, the bombing of military headquarters, and violent resistance to an oppressive arrest all come within this class. But also included are such practices as bank robberies for the replenishing of a political treasury, the kidnapping of a business executive for extortion, and the taking of hostages for exchange with political offenders.

It is the legal status of this wide range of conduct in the middle spectrum that has become increasingly uncertain in light of recent international developments. To these examples could be added some of the contemporary manifestations of international terrorism, for instance, when violence is used indiscriminately against innocent victims only marginally associated with an opposing political regime or party. The assault against such victims, furthermore, might increasingly take place in neutral countries remote from the battlefield. A machine gun assault against a bus carrying school children in Northern Ireland, the Munich Olympics kidnappings, and the massacre of Christian Puerto Rican pilgrims upon their arrival at Israel's Lod Airport come within this category. How should this conduct be treated by the international community? And to what extent would the conventions previously offered in response to terrorism have affected such conduct?

The most comprehensive convention for the prevention and punishment of terrorism was proposed by the League of Nations in 1937. Following the assassination of King Alexander I of Yugoslavia at Marseilles on October 9, 1934, the French government urged the Council of the League of Nations to prepare an international agreement for the suppression of terrorism. A committee of experts prepared a draft convention which was later opened for signature at a conference held at Geneva in November of 1937. An international criminal court was also proposed, to help in the enforcement of terrorist violations. On January 1, 1941, India became the only country ever to ratify the convention.

Viewing the League of Nations Convention today, from the vantage point of some thirty-five years of historical developments, the shortcomings of that effort are readily apparent. The document required all signatories to make acts of terrorism committed on their territories criminal offenses. Similarly, signatories were required to either extradite or punish persons who committed these offenses abroad. Acts of terrorism were defined by Article 2 to include: (1) causing death, grievous bodily harm, or loss of liberty to heads of state, their spouses, and others holding public office; (2) willful destruction of public property; and (3) acts endangering the lives of members of the public. Article 3 specified further that conspiracy to commit the above acts, and incitement and assistance in performing such acts were, likewise, criminal offenses.

The attempted assassination of Hitler and the successful execution of Mussolini could have readily qualified as internationally condemned terrorist acts under the proposed League of Nations Convention. Many of the post-World War II liberation movements would have been defined as terroristic under it. Broadcasting to an oppressed people to encourage them to rise against an exploiting regime would have been condemned as an incitement to commit international crime. No wonder that there were few takers for the 1937 document.

The League Convention clearly attempted to perpetuate the pre-World War II status quo and manifested a willingness to label any future revolutionary or national liberation movement as terrorist. But what about the terrorist excesses of recent years? Why could international consensus not be reached with regard to the suppression of these?

A more reasonable effort to suppress international terrorism was contained in the draft convention introduced at the United Nations on September 25, 1972, by the United States. The major, and limited, intent of the proposed draft was to require countries to either prosecute or extradite those engaging in the exportation of terrorism. To come within the scope of the convention, an offender must intend to damage the interests of, or to obtain concessions from, a state or international organization. The prohibited acts include killing, causing serious bodily harm, and kidnapping. Acts are defined as international offenses if they are committed outside the offender's own country, and (1) also outside the country against which they are intended, or, (2) within the country against which they are intended but against persons who are not nationals of that state.

The narrower scope of the United States draft convention makes it much less subject to criticism for being oppressive to unorthodox political change. Indeed, the convention has been criticized for having defined its goals so narrowly as to be farfetched and irrelevant. A German terrorist acting against his own regime would not come under the draft convention. An Irish offender bombing a London cafe inhabited only by Englishmen would also be exempt. It is only, for example, when a Greek terrorist commits an act of violence against a Turkish national living in Switzerland, or against a non-Turkish national in Turkey, that he would come within the confines of the treaty. The basic principle of the United States convention is simple: "Fight your enemies in your country or theirs. Do not export your grievances to distant places where innocent persons are likely to be affected." But even these limited goals, which steer clear of ideological conflicts, have not assured the draft convention widespread support. In part, the American authorship had doomed it from the start. And today any revival of this effort remains unlikely.

Despite the existence of some historical and legal insights into the nature of modern terrorism, there has been little success in reaching an internationally acceptable definition. To most Western writers, the term connotes an undiscriminating commitment to violence. In the view of Third World countries, the terrorist label has too frequently and improperly been attached to "legitimate" national liberation and revolutionary movements. The misapplication of labels, however, is evident in many camps. Even nonviolent conduct has been tagged "terroristic" in socialist and other use. For example, an East Berlin court recently sentenced a West Berliner to fifteen years in prison for having helped ninety-six East Germans to flee to the West. The East Berlin City Court found him guilty of "organized human trafficking, sabotage, espionage and terrorism."[34] Similarly, South African law provides that a person who has written letters to Africans likely "to encourage feelings of hostility between the white and other inhabitants" will be presumed to have done so with "intent to endanger the maintenance of law and order." Defined by law as a terrorist, such letter writer is subject to the death penalty.[35]

What makes the international definition of terrorism difficult is the conflict between diverse camps and ideologies in the world community. What is terrorism to some is heroism to others. The international disagreement on whether political violence should be universally condemned is not unlike the domestic debate on whether political offenders should be accorded differential treatment.

One who disobeys the law does so at his peril. It is a fundamental premise of most legal systems that obedience to the law is an absolute obligation of all citizens, irrespective of the morality of the legal command.[36] But while "render unto Caesar" remains the imperative, what about the individuals or groups who are bound by the conviction that the law is cruel, unjust, immoral, or plainly outdated? What about those whose conviction, ideology, conscience, or political motivation propels them to disobey or to break the law? In 1849, Henry David Thoreau cried out: "Must the citizen even for a moment, or in the least degree, resign his conscience to the legislator? Why has every man a conscience, then?"[37] But despite the compelling resurgence of this question, few legal systems have found satisfactory solutions to the conflict between individual conscience and the dictates of public order. Once the law has been made, it is said, individual conscience may not override it. Indeed, no society can survive if the subjective values and judgments of individual citizens are allowed to contradict community rules.

Comparing the expanding boundaries of international crime with the narrowing perspective on political offenses, one soon confronts two central questions:

1. Within the confines of international legality, what may persons deprived of recognized human rights do in the defense of their claims?
2. In view of the recent expansion of international crimes, notwithstanding past failures to define terrorism, what are the future prospects for the regulation of terrorist excesses?

In the light of the international commitment to self-determination, human rights, and ethnic and racial survival, one must examine the acceptable tools for the enforcement of these rights. How is the international community to judge those who claim merely to assert these recognized rights? May people press for these rights through force of arms? May they protect themselves against abuse? To the "haves," to many others committed to the gradual peaceful processes for remedying the claims of the aggrieved—to all those fearing international chaos and anarchy—the tools of violent opposition and rebellion remain unacceptable.

In the eyes of the "have nots"—and many others who believe that the international machinery for bringing about political, social, and economic justice is at best defective—the self-help approach is totally justifiable. Viewed from these diverse perspectives, those who are terrorists to some are evident freedom fighters and legitimate revolutionaries to others.

So long as these ideological and definitional schisms exist, no honest cooperation, with regard to the control of terrorism, can be expected in the international community. Each country might develop its own domestic machinery for the prevention and suppression of terrorist violence. It might further seek assistance and cooperation from those nations with a common mind. But as long as a significant number of safe-haven countries remain for terrorists—to supply the weapons for destruction, the training grounds, and, finally, the escape routes—effective prevention, control, and punishment will be difficult. Recent efforts to bridge these schisms have not been successful. Typically, most efforts in the United Nations and elsewhere designed to condemn and to impose sanctions upon terrorist "sieges of terror" have resulted in Third World and other countries calling for a parallel curbing of official "reigns of terror."[38]

Given the present freeze in the movement toward an international agreement for the control of terrorism, how should civilized nations respond to the problems posed by transnational and domestic political violence?

One approach would be to encourage self-policing and greater conformity by guerrillas and others with the traditional rules of war, in exchange for granting them recognition as belligerents rather than criminals. There has been considerable writing recently concerning the status of guerrillas and other irregular belligerents in international law.[39] Especially with the decline of all-out formal wars, the movement for the regulation of military conflicts short of war has gained momentum. Attention has centered particularly on the question of whether guerrillas and other irregulars in transnational conflicts should benefit from the privileges traditionally afforded belligerents under international law, in particular the prisoner-of-war status. By and large, the Geneva Convention III of 1949 on Prisoners of War would condition the grant of those protections upon guerrilla willingness to comply with specified standards of lawful belligerency, including the wearing of insignias, the open bearing of arms, and conformity with the laws and customs of war.

Adherence by guerrillas and other irregulars to these standards might help reduce the outrages of civil war and especially the abuse of innocent parties. But apart from the reluctance of governments to treat domestic terrorists as belligerents, there is little hope of guerrilla conformity since the effectiveness of guerrilla activities depends in great part upon departure from the traditional rules of war. An extension of the belligerency status to terrorists will, therefore, offer little help to governments in their combatting of excessive violence.

Another effort to infuse civilized standards into civil wars might call for greater enforcement of the requirements contained in Article 3 of all four Geneva Conventions of 1949. This article, which deals with domestic armed conflicts, seeks to protect persons taking no active part in the hostilities and applies to all parties to the conflict, governments and rebels alike. The article specifically prohibits: (1) violence to life and person, in particular murder, mutilation, cruel treatment, and torture; (2) taking of hostages; and (3) outrages upon personal dignity, in particular humiliating and degrading treatment. But the fact that these prohibitions do not require reciprocal observance by all parties, and other shortcomings, have resulted in widespread disregard of these rules in recent civil wars.[40] Moreover, it remains uncertain whether these rules for domestic armed conflicts are applicable or enforceable with regard to individual political offenders and terrorists in situations short of an armed conflict.

A different approach with a considerable following calls for an international convention that would define and outlaw all forms of terrorism and related types of political violence. The enforcement of such proposed prohibitions would be handled either through the universal jurisdiction of cooperating states or through the creation of an international criminal tribunal.[41] Not disputing the value of such goals, the likelihood of their adoption in the forseeable future must be seriously questioned. A fourth approach attempts to deal with the problem of terrorism by means of a further narrowing of the extradition exception. This approach was adopted by the Council of Europe in a 1974 resolution[42] in which a Committee of Ministers pointed out correctly its conviction that extradition is a particularly effective means for the control of terrorism. The council urged member states in their response to extradition requests to consider the particular seriousness of terrorist acts which: (1) create a collective danger to life, liberty, or safety; (2) affect innocent persons foreign to the motives behind them, or (3) employ cruel and vicious means. If extradition is refused in such serious instances, submission of the cases for prosecution by competent domestic authorities is required.

Obviously, there is no single or simple solution for the control of the excessive violence posed by political crime and terrorism. The recent efforts to control these increasingly transnational threats, however, suggest several possible approaches. In the concluding section of this discussion, several principles will be advanced as a starting point for further discussion and development.

Reconciling Protection of Human Rights with World Order

Essentially, the crux of the problem of transnational political violence revolves around the fact that, while the permissible spectrum of political crime and terrorism is being narrowed, at the same time the growing international commitment to human rights tends to further legitimize political offenses. Recent international agreements have already proscribed some of the more extreme measures of political violence. At this point, if there is a need for further codification and regulation, it exists primarily with regard to the less extreme middle spectrum of political conduct, consisting mainly of complex and connected political offenses. Since these offenses are, at present, subject to the ad hoc sovereign dispositions of the various countries in extradition cases, and their substance is frequently complex and controversial, they remain resistant to international agreement. Last but not least, while a desire to protect innocent and remote victims exists; there is a fear also that international legislation will unduly assert the rights of existing regimes and overlook the needs of exploited people. This concern is crystallized in the continuing opposition, especially in the Third World, to proposed antiterrorist conventions which might deny self-help measures to those who assert to be struggling to attain political goals. Some of these political goals, moreover, are claimed to have gained general international acceptance. Possibly, what might be required first, before more formal international developments can take place, is a clearer and more open balancing of the conflicting interests.

This article, therefore, does not call for a new antiterrorism convention nor for the creation of an international criminal tribunal. It seeks, instead, to suggest, at present, a more tentative, deliberate, yet more pragmatic step-by-step approach: further national and international studies, deliberations, discussions, and recommendations, and the development of draft resolutions for action by governments and international organizations. Especially, it urges exploring potentials for greater consensus regarding the extradition of political offenders, including terrorists. This avenue seems most capable of support among various governments, and it promises a direct effect upon the imposition of criminal sanctions.[43]

Following the regional model of the Council of Europe, it is likely that what could be attained first, on a more global scale, is not an international convention but a less formal product, similar to the council's Resolution on International Terrorism. Such a universal resolution could be developed and advanced at the United Nations. But a less politicized forum might be more appropriate. One of the nongovernmental organizations in the field of international justice, or a combination of such organizations as the International Association of Penal Law, Amnesty International, and the International Committee of the Red Cross, could support such a development.

However, this will deal only with one side of the problem. Seeking to maintain world order, governments should not overlook the growing international commitment to self-determination and human rights which, of course, tends to further legitimize political activism and consequently seeks better international protection for political offenders. While recognizing that extradition might serve as an effective measure for the control of transnational violence, one should not be unmindful of the *political offense* exception in the extradition law which reflects nineteenth-century and ongoing international recognition that extralegal means are justified in political conflicts. To maintain a balance between human rights and world order, a proposed resolution could not give exclusive support to the proposition that any act is justified if supported by considerations of conscience. Neither could it take the other extreme stand that no opposition to an established regime is permissible by international standards. What could be introduced more vigorously into this arena is the principle of self-defense and a scale of proportionality.

In domestic law, the only justified resort to violence is grounded upon the concept of self-defense. Similarly, in post-World War II international law, the only legal resort to arms is justified in the case of self-defense. A modification of this principle seems to be useful also in the international response to the problems of terrorism and political crime. In essence, assertive conduct by individuals in response to denial of recognized human rights might be viewed as a class of self-defense.[44]

Drawing upon the previous observations, a number of general principles might be advanced. Any person who deliberately commits acts against innocent persons, who uses cruel or vicious means or engages in collective violence, or who otherwise violates the requirements of any international criminal law, should be subject to punishment for what might be designated crimes against humanity. All states should have universal jurisdiction to try offenders who commit crimes against humanity. If extradition is refused in such instances, the case should be submitted to competent local authorities for prosecution, in accordance with the principle *aut dedere aut judicare*.

Those seeking the status of political offenders should be required to circumscribe their conduct. Acts of self-defense should be addressed, as directly as possible, against those exercising the overall or the most applicable state power and must avoid all deliberate, or careless, harm to innocent parties. The force used in such acts of self-defense should be appropriate and proportionate to the right deprived by the authorities, as well as the amount of force utilized by the authorities. States should undertake to grant asylum to all persons who commit such proper acts of self-defense, whatever the country in which such acts occurred, which means that no person should be extradited for acts that come properly within the above principles.

A resolution constructed substantially on these principles, with an emphasis upon the reformation of the extradition principles and practices, will not require new international legislation. There will be continued reliance on a long tradition of exempting political offenders from extradition, with the exception of those who use excessive or indiscriminate violence. This approach recognizes the growing field of international crimes. Yet it will also support the enforcement of international consensus in this area and will also permit states the ultimate decision in extradition cases, based on the facts in each individual case.

As international deliberations and experience progress and consensus grows, it may be possible, as a further step, to provide for an international commission on human rights to be set up by all countries that adhere to these principles. Member states could voluntarily refer to such a commission for advisory opinions in all cases of doubt. Through the work of the commission, a finer line of demarcation would be drawn between political non-extraditable political offenses and crimes against humanity.

Needless to say, this development would constitute a major contribution toward more effective rules and a machinery for international criminal and political justice. These intermediate steps, at some future stage, might culminate in an international criminal tribunal.

One need not be a visionary to foresee that public interest and opinion will also continue to press more and more for effective controls not only over the "siege of terror" but also over "reigns of terror." Thus, in developing proposed principles and resolutions on political crime and terrorism, all concerned should seek to overcome the current ideological breach by dealing both with nongovernmental and governmental violence and illegality. To bridge the current gap, one will have to dispel the serious concern that while "sieges of terror" are being condemned and regulated, "reigns of terror" are left free of international intervention. The outcome must reflect the growing realization that people are entitled to expect all rights enunciated in the Universal Declaration on Human Rights and in similar documents, and that the exercise of such rights should not, in itself, be internationally considered a criminal act.

Some may go further to suggest that on the basis of international law, people, in given circumstances and within certain restrictions, are entitled to engage in acts of resistance and self-defense against governmental denials of basic and universally recognized human rights—including the right to life, liberty, religious, political, and ethnic equality, and self-determination. Such "acts of resistance," even though utilizing extralegal means, may be indispensable as long as the international community lacks the tools for the effective enforcement of such fundamental human rights around the world.

It is to be expected that, within the not-too-distant future, growing support will develop around a call to combat governmental violence and illegality in the government's very core of sovereignty—its relation to its own citizens. Here one should be prepared to face growing public emphasis on the need for further extension of the international recognition that any governmental official who deliberately deprives an individual of fundamental human rights is to be subject to punishment for crimes against humanity.

One cannot avoid the remaining knotty problem of jurisdiction. Who is to apply criminal sanctions against individuals and officials alike who deprive others of recognized rights or who use excessive violence? Two approaches deserve further attention. One will grant all states universal jurisdiction to try offenders in such cases. States within whose boundaries such offenders are found might be required, furthermore, to either extradite them or to submit their cases to competent domestic authorities for prosecution, in accordance with the principle of *aut dedere aut judicare*. Another approach would be to explore more vigorously the creation of an international criminal tribunal. Possibly, the international commission on human rights, which might be set up voluntarily by the countries that adhere to these principles, should be also vested with the mandate to explore the needs and to recommend whether an international criminal court should be constituted to exercise concurrent jurisdiction with the several states in the prosecution of persons turned over to it for crimes against humanity.

Political crime and terrorism are destined to remain with us in years to come. Excesses by both those in power and out will continue. The agenda for research, deliberations, and resolution-making—designed to seek a reduction in the climate of violence—is long and difficult. A number of general principles have been proposed. Once these principles have undergone more precise development by scholars or by appropriate international bodies, public or private, they could be offered to the community of nations for guidance in the operation of existing or future extradition treaties. Beyond extradition, these principles could provide guidelines for a more comprehensive response to the conflict between human rights and world order. In endorsing and adhering to these principles, states will have an opportunity to condemn those forms of conduct which are destructive of a civilized world community. At the same time, they will be able to more effectively commit themselves to support those universal human rights which they proclaimed nearly three decades ago.

Notes

1. *Washington Post,* 14 January 1976, p. 3, col. 3.

2. *U.S. News and World Report,* 19 January 1976, p. 27.

3. In some parts of the world, however, political violence has developed into large-scale civil or guerrilla war and presents a major public-safety problem. For example, former British Prime Minister Harold Wilson claimed that 1,400 political killings were committed in Ireland since 1969 (*Washington Post,* 31 January 1976, A. p. 17, col. 1).

4. Otto Kirchheimer, *Political Justice* (Princeton, N.J.: Princeton University Press, 1961).

5. See Appendix Q. *International Terrorism and Political Crimes 546,* M. Cherif Bassiouni, ed. (1975); M. Hudson, *International Legislation 862* (1941).

6. For a review of the status of political crime in the United States, see "Comment, Criminal Responsibility and the Political Offender," 24 *Am. U.L. Rev.* 797 (1975).

7. American law parallels that of the United Kingdom. Thus Brendan Behan commented upon "the usual hypocrisy of the English not giving anyone political treatment and then being able to say that alone among the Empires she had no political prisoners." Brendan Behan, *Borstal Boy* (New York: Knopf, 1958), p. 271.

8. Alexsandr Solzhenitsyn, *The Gulag Archipelago* (New York: Harper and Row, 1973), p. 500.

9. *Ibid.*

10. See the biblical account of King David's execution of the messenger reporting to him that he slew David's archenemy, King Saul. "Thy blood be upon thy head; for thy mouth hath testified against thee, saying I have slain the Lord's anointed." 2 Sam. 1:16.

11. M. Cherif Bassiouni, *International Extradition and World Public Order* (Oceana, 1974), p. 371.

12. *In re* Fabijan (Supreme Court of Germany, 1933) 6 *Digest of International Law* 802, Whiteman, ed. (1968).

13. *I.Q.B.* 149 (1891) p. 152.

14. 34 *I.L.R.* 143 (1961), pp. 143-144.

15. For one of the few examples of an attempt to implement the international commitment to self-determination, see the Declaration on the Granting of Independence to Colonial Countries and Peoples, General Assembly Resolution 1514 (xv) of 14 December (1960).

16. U.N., Human Rights, A Compilation of International Instruments of the United Nations (1973), no. E. 73. XIV. 2.

17. See generally, Robertson, "United Nations Covenant on Civil and Political Rights and the European Convention on Human Rights," XLIII *British Yearbook of International Law* 21 (1968-69); O'Hanlon, Brussels Colloquy on the European Convention on Human Rights, 5 *Irish Jurist* 252 (1970); Comte, "Application of the European Convention on Human Rights in Municipal Law," 4 *Journal International Commission of Jurists* 94 (1962-63).

18. UN, Human Rights, p. 41.

19. GA. Res 2923, 27 UN GAOR Supp. 30, p. 25, UN Doc. A/8730 (1972).

20. Bassiouni, *International Extradition,* p. 410.

21. 2 Q.B. 415 (1894).

22. *Ibid.,* p. 419.

23. French Extradition Law of 1927, Act of March 10, 1927, Art. 5 (2) quoted in I. Shearer, *Extradition in International Law* 185 (Manchester University Press, 1971).

24. Extradition Agreement Approved by the Council of the League of Arab States, September 14, 1952, 159 British and Foreign State Papers (HMSO) quoted in Shearer, *Extradition,* p. 52.

25. *In re* Bohme, 62 *American Journal of International Law* 784-85 (1968), Supreme Court of Argentina, quoted in Shearer, *Extradition,* p. 186.

26. G.A. Res. 177 (II) (1947).

27. For the most recent statement on piracy, see the 1958 Geneva Convention on the High Seas, 4 Whitman, *Digest* 657 (1963).

28. Convention for the Suppression of Counterfeiting Currency, 20 April 1920; 4 Hudson, International Legislation, pp. 692-705 (1931).

29. *See,* 1971 Montreal Convention, U.S.T.I.A.S. 7570 (sabotage of aircraft), 1970 Hague Convention, USTIAS 7192 (hijacking), 1963 Tokyo Convention, USTIAS 6768 (offenses committed on board aircraft).

30. Convention to Prevent and Punish Acts of Terrorism Taking the Form of Crimes Against Persons and Related Extortions That Are of International Significance, OAS/Off. Rec./Ser. p./Doc. 68, 13 January 1971; Convention on the Prevention and Punishment of Crimes Against Internationally Protected Persons Including Diplomatic Agents, G.A. Res. A/3166 (XXVIIII) 5 February 1974.

31. David C. Rapoport, *Assassination and Terrorism* (CBS, 1971), p. 37.

32. Nachaeyeff, "Revolutionary Catechism, in Rapoport," *Assassination* (CBS, 1971), p. 40.

33. Rapoport, *Assassination,* p. 47.

34. *New York Times,* 27 January 1976, p. 2, col. 4.

35. Terrorism Act, no. 83 of 1967, sec. 2, quoted in Leslie Rubin, "Apartheid in Practice," UN Publication OPI/553 (1976), p. 40.

36. A. Fortas, *Concerning Dissent and Civil Disobedience* (1968), pp. 59-64.

37. Henry David Thoreau, *On the Duty of Civil Disobedience* (Lancer Books, 1968), pp. 413-14.

38. See, e.g., Bennett, "U.S. Initiatives in the United Nations to Combat International Terrorism," 7 *International Lawyer* (1973), pp. 753, 759.

39. See, e.g., J. Bond, *The Rules of Riot; Internal Conflict and the Law of War* (Princeton, 1974); George Schwarzenberger, "Terrorists, Guerrilleros, and Mercenaries," 1971 *Toledo Law Review* 71; "Comment, Civilian Protection in Modern Warfare: A Critical Analysis of the Geneva Civilian Convention of 1941," 14 *Virginia Journal of International Law* 123 (1973).

40. Higgins, "International Law and Civil Conflict," *International Regulation of Civil Wars,* Evan Luard, ed. (New York University Press, 1972), p. 183.

41. See, e.g., Dautricourt, "The International Criminal Court: The Concept of International Criminal Jurisdiction," in M. Bassiouni and V. Nanda, *A Treatise on International Criminal Law* 636 (1973).

42. See Resolution (74) 3, 24 January 1974.

43. Since 1970, a total of 267 transnational terrorists were apprehended. Of these, 50 were released after serving prison terms, and 104 were still confined in mid-September 1975. But another 39 were freed without punishment, 58 avoided punishment by getting safe conduct to other countries, and 16 were released from confinement on the demand of fellow terrorists. *US News and World Report,* 29 September 1975, p. 79.

44. For discussion of such an approach see Bassiouni, "Ideologically Motivated Offense and the Political Offense Exception in Extradition—A Proposed Juridical Standard for an Unruly Problem," 19 *DePaul Law Review* 217 (1969), pp. 254-57.

ERNEST H. EVANS

American Policy Response to International Terrorism: Problems of Deterrence

There have been several American efforts to deter acts of international terrorism. Among them are the Latin American Diplomats Convention, the United Nations Convention on the Protection of Diplomats and Diplomatic Agents, and the policy of "no negotiations, no ransoms" with terrorist groups. Of particular interest, however, was one specific effort, namely, the 1972 Draft Convention on International Terrorism, which was introduced by the United States in the fall of 1972 in the General Assembly of the United Nations, debated in the Sixth (Legal) Committee, and finally quite effectively killed by that committee.

The 1972 American Draft Convention and the accompanying debates are interesting because they provide an answer as to why it has been so difficult to negotiate a general multilateral accord to deal with the problem of transnational terrorism. There are, to be sure, numerous extradition treaties between states that provide for the extradition or punishment not only of common criminals, but also of certain categories of political offenders, such as individuals who have assassinated or attempted to assassinate a head of state or a member of a head of state's family. (This is the so-called Belgium clause in extradition treaties.) In addition, there are several multilateral conventions in effect that deal with certain specialized forms of international terrorism: the Latin American Diplomats Convention (negotiated in 1971), the United Nations Convention on the Protection of Diplomats and Diplomatic Agents (adopted by the General Assembly in 1973), and the three conventions on aircraft hijacking: the 1963 Tokyo Convention, the 1970 Hague Convention, and the 1971 Montreal Convention. However, the two major efforts to negotiate multilateral conventions against the general problem of international terrorism have both failed. The first was the 1937 League of Nations Conference on the Suppression of Terrorism, which produced a convention for that purpose. The convention never received sufficient ratification to be enacted and so has remained a dead issue. The second was the previously mentioned 1972 American Draft Convention on International Terrorism.

I will concentrate on explaining the 1972 convention's failure to be accepted. The 1937 convention is not without interest, but it was considered in a very different era and by a far more limited number of nations than the 1972 convention; an analysis of why it failed would shed light only indirectly on the problem of the response to terrorism in the contemporary world.

The American Draft Convention on International Terrorism was formulated with the intention of securing maximum possible support. Thus those who drew it up took care to exclude from its scope acts of domestic terrorism. The convention applied only to terrorist acts of "international significance." For a terrorist act to be of international significance four conditions had to be fulfilled: First, the act had to take place or have effects outside of the territory of the state of which the offender was a national; second, the victims of the attack had to be citizens of a state other than the one on whose soil the attack took place; third, the attack had to be committed neither by nor against a member of the armed forces in the course of military hostilities; fourth, the attack had to be intended to damage the interests of or to obtain concessions from a state or international organization.[1] Even with these fairly precise guidelines, exactly what acts the convention would have covered is open to dispute, but the drafters went to great pains to note that wars being waged by indigenous rebels in such places as South Africa were not within the jurisdiction of the convention.[2]

The key provision of the convention pledges its signatories to either extradite or punish any individuals within their territory who were deemed to have committed an act of international terrorism as defined by the convention. The convention's articles dealing with what constituted an extraditable offense were to be considered as being included in the existing extradition treaties of the signatory states.

Accompanying the draft convention, the United States introduced a resolution which urged states to ratify the three antihijacking conventions and which called for prompt measures against international terrorism. It soon became apparent in the debates in the legal committee that the American resolution commanded little support, so the United States switched its support to a second resolution that had been introduced by some West European and Latin American states. This resolution, unlike the American resolution, had a paragraph reaffirming the right of national self-determination, and therefore it was hoped it would meet the objections concerning wars of liberation raised by the Arab, African, Asian, and Communist states to the original American resolution. However, this coalition of Third World and Communist states refused to accept the second resolution either, and instead introduced and passed a resolution of their own which condemned racist and repressive regimes as terroristic and called for an *ad hoc* committee to meet in 1973 to consider the problem of international terrorism. This committee did meet for several weeks in 1973, but nothing came out of its deliberations, as was probably the intention of the coalition of states that voted through the resolution referring the issue to the *ad hoc* committee. (Table 1 lists the vote on the resolution.) In short, the American

**Table 1. The Vote on the Resolution Referring Action
on Terrorism to an Ad Hoc Committee**

IN FAVOR: Afghanistan, Albania, Algeria, Bahrain, Botswana, Bulgaria, Burma,
Burundi, Beylorussian SSR, Cameroon, Central African Republic, Chad, Chile,
Congo, Cyprus, Czechoslovakia, Dahomey, Democratic Yemen, Ecuador, Egypt,
Equatorial Guinea, Ethiopia, Gabon, Gambia, Ghana, Guinea, Guyana, Hungary,
India, Indonesia, Iraq, Jamaica, Jordan, Kenya, Kuwait, Lebanon, Liberia, Libya,
Madagascar, Malaysia, Mali, Mauritania, Mexico, Mongolia, Morocco, Niger,
Nigeria, Oman, Pakistan, Panama, Peru, Poland, Qatar, Romania, Rwanda, Saudi
Arabia, Senegal, Sierra Leone, Somalia, Sri Lanka, Sudan, Syria, Togo, Trinidad
and Tobago, Tunisia, Uganda, Ukrainian SSR, USSR, United Arab Emirates,
United Republic of Tanzania, Upper Volta, Venezuela, Yemen, Yugoslavia, Zambia
(76)

IN OPPOSITION: Australia, Austria, Belgium, Bolivia, Brazil, Canada, Colombia, Costa Rica, Cuba*, Denmark, Dominican Republic, Fiji, Guatemala, Haiti,
Honduras, Iceland, Iran, Israel, Italy, Japan, Laos, Lesotho, Luxemburg, Netherlands, New Zealand, Nicaragua, Paraguay, Philippines, Portugal, South Africa,
Turkey, United Kingdom, United States, Uruguay (34)

ABSTAINING: Argentina, Barbados, El Salvador, Finland, France, Greece,
Ireland, Ivory Coast, Malawi, Nepal, Norway, Singapore, Spain, Sweden, Thai-
land, Zaire (16)

*Cuba voted against the resolution not because it wanted immediate steps against ter-
rorism but because it opposed the whole idea of discussing terrorism; the Cuban representative said that such discussions were an attempt to stifle wars of national liberation.

efforts to pass a multilateral convention had been wholly unsuccessful.

The question remains, why did the convention never gain momentum? To
answer this, it is necessary to examine in detail the arguments of both the
states who opposed and the states who supported the convention.

Since the convention was a U.S.-sponsored effort, we might consider first
the arguments made by American representatives on the legal committee.
The fundamental American position stressed the need to protect innocent
people. It was argued that terrorist attacks were a matter of grave concern to
the international community both because such attacks sacrificed innocent
lives (in itself a serious matter) and because the sacrifice of such lives endangered international order. The following quotations from speeches by
W. Tapley Bennett, the chief U.S. delegate during the debate, illustrate how
the United States presented its arguments:

[Mr. Bennett] recalled that the United States Secretary of State, addressing the General Assembly, had said that the issue was not an issue of war, whether between

States, civil war or revolutionary war and was not the striving of people to achieve self-determination and independence. Rather, it was whether millions of air travellers could continue to fly in safety each year, whether a person could open his mail without fear of being blown up, whether diplomats could carry out their duties safely and whether international meetings could carry out their duties safely without the ever-present threat of violence. It was not an issue which should divide the international community. It was a human problem.[3]

. . . he wished to observe, in reply to the comments made by the representative of Saudi Arabia, that while it was true that George Washington had been a rebel—and a brilliantly successful one—he had not hijacked the boat in which he had crossed the Delaware and had not endangered innocent lives. This was a not unimportant point as far as the item under consideration was concerned.[4]

The basic thrust of the American position can thus be summarized as an attempt to portray terrorism as a humanitarian issue and an attempt to prevent the destruction of innocent human life.

The delegations that supported the American efforts made similar arguments. Of the thirty-six nations that voted against the final resolution (which, as noted earlier, referred all action on international terrorism to an *ad hoc* committee, thereby effectively preventing any action) some thirty made speeches in the Sixth Committee. Of these thirty, some twenty-one made references to the problem of the killing of innocent people. (Table 2 lists the states that stressed this theme of the need to protect innocent lives as well as three other themes that were an elaboration on it.) First, there was the argument that attacks on innocent people, in addition to being wrong in and of themselves, were also a grave threat to international order. Second, it was argued that even morally legitimate policies (such as fighting for one's national independence) did not justify the immoral means of attacks on innocent people. Third, it was held that the issue of the loss of life was serious and did not brook delay.

One can say that the reason why no steps were taken against international terrorism by the United Nations in the fall of 1972 was that the opponents of any such steps saw the problem of terrorism quite differently from the United States and its supporters. To the coalition of Arab, African, Asian, and Communist-bloc countries that voted down the American-backed initiative, terrorism was not a human problem at all, but rather a political problem. Specifically, it was a political problem concerning the struggles of the Palestinians to regain their national rights and of the blacks in southern Africa to end rule by white minorities. An analysis of the speeches made by the opponents of the American convention reveals that the most common objection was the fear that such a convention would hinder wars of national liberation against racism, colonialism, and Zionism. The following quotations express this fear:

Libya:

Mr. Abdulaziz said that both in the General Committee and in plenary his delegation had opposed including the item on terrorism in the agenda of the current session
on the grounds that delegations were being asked to take measures against a phenomenon that had never been defined. In the absence of a definition, racist and
colonialist regimes could be expected to take advantage of the debate in order to
justify their acts in territories under their control.[5]

Table 2. The Arguments of the States in Favor of Action Against Terrorism

	Protection of Innocent Lives	Defense of International Order	Immoral Methods	Delay Not Justified
Australia			X	X
Austria	X	X	X	X
Belgium	X	X		X
Bolivia	X			
Brazil	X			
Canada	X			
Colombia			X	
Costa Rica	X	X		
Denmark	X		X	X
Dominican Republic				
Fiji	X			
Guatemala				
Haiti		X		
Iceland	X	X	X	X
Iran	X	X	X	X
Israel	X			
Italy	X	X		X
Japan	X			
Lesotho	X			
Netherlands	X			X
New Zealand			X	X
Nicaragua	X	X	X	
Paraguay	X			X
Philippines				
Portugal				
South Africa	X			
Turkey		X		X
United Kingdom	X	X	X	X
USA	X	X	X	X
Uruguay	X	X	X	X
30 countries	21	12	11	14

Senegal:
An attempt was being made to raise the spectre of international terrorism as a pretext for calling for severe measures and sanctions against all who were seeking to make radical changes in the order established by a minority of racist and colonialist opportunists.[6]

India:
. . . great care must be taken to ensure that the offense was so defined as not to affect the exercise of the right of self-determination and the legitimacy of the struggle against colonial and racist regimes and all forms of foreign domination.[7]

USSR:
. . . a moral and political distinction must be drawn between the concept of international terrorism and the use of force in the struggle of peoples for their freedom. There was a tendency to confuse the two. His delegation was on principle opposed to any attempt to use the discussion on international terrorism perpetrated by individuals in order to prejudice the struggle of peoples for their liberation or to discredit on the international political scene a struggle which had been recognized as legitimate by the United Nations.[8]

A total of seventy-six states voted in favor of the Third World-sponsored resolution referring action on international terrorism to an *ad hoc* committee. Of these states, some fifty-seven made speeches during the course of the debates. Of these fifty-seven, a total of fifty-two made statements to the effect that there was a danger that measures against international terrorism would hinder wars of national liberation. This was clearly the most frequently expressed rationale for opposing the American-sponsored initiatives against international terrorism. (Table 3 lists the states that made speeches against the American-supported convention and resolution.) The other reasons given for opposing the American proposals, namely, that the term "international terrorism" had not been defined, that the causes of terrorism must be studied as well as the phenomenon itself, and that the United Nations was being asked to act in haste, were all related directly or indirectly to the objection concerning wars of national liberation. It was claimed that unless the term terrorism was defined there would be a tendency to confuse wars of national liberation and terrorism. The causes of terrorism were usually held to be racism and colonialism. In addition, the states opposing any steps against international terrorism demanded that nothing be done in haste because there was a need to study these root causes of terrorism.

There was thus a very wide divergence of perceptions between the United States and its supporters and the coalition of Arab, African, Asian, and Communist states concerning the problem of international terrorism. Since the latter group had a very large majority, no steps were taken on the subject.

In conclusion, I would argue that the major lesson to be drawn from the 1972 United Nations debates on international terrorism is that while terrorism may be perceived in the West in general and in the United States in particular as a humanitarian problem, this is *not* the way it is perceived by most of the rest of the world. Most countries regard international terrorism as basically a political manifestation of the struggles against regimes such as South Africa, Rhodesia, and Israel which, it must be admitted, are very unpopular among the community of nations.

So the question remains, is multilateral action against international terrorism possible at all? Based on the 1972 United Nations debates, the outlook must be conceded to be rather gloomy; however, it is possible that certain actions can be taken, especially if the number of terrorist events increases significantly. If anything at all is ever to be done at the multilateral level to cope with international terrorism, the nations concerned about the problem (above all, the United States) must adjust their perceptions of the issue. They must come to see that terrorism is regarded by most nations as a political problem and must be approached as such. Whether in the final analysis terrorism is *really* a humanitarian or *really* a political problem is irrelevant; the important point is that the problem is perceived by most nations as a political problem.

Specifically, the nations that want action on the issue of international terrorism must be prepared to make concessions to the political demands of the countries that opposed the 1972 convention. It is difficult to speculate regarding the form such concessions might take, but several possible areas of negotiation can be highlighted: (1) The United States can perhaps partially satisfy the objections of the Arab states by pressing Israel to accept some sort of Palestinian state on the land now occupied by Israel as a result of the 1967 war; (2) The United States can also, perhaps, in part meet the demands of certain of the African states by agreeing to take a firmer stand in the United Nations and elsewhere against Rhodesia and South Africa.

It is beyond the scope of this discussion to say whether in the grand scheme of American foreign policy such measures should be undertaken. All that is intended here is to indicate that given the intensity of the feelings on the part of the Arab, African, Asian, and Communist countries regarding the question of wars of national liberation, little can be accomplished in the United Nations concerning international terrorism unless some concession is made to these feelings. It remains another question whether terrorism is considered a problem of sufficient magnitude to justify such concessions on the part of the United States and other Western nations.

Table 3. The Arguments of the States Opposed to Action Against Terrorism

	Liberation Struggles	Definitions Unclear	Causes Must Be Studied	Acting in Haste
Albania	X			
Algeria	X			
Bulgaria	X			
Burundi	X		X	
Beylorussian SSR	X	X		
Cameroon	X	X	X	
Chad	X			
China	X			
Cuba	X			
Cyprus	X		X	
Czechoslovakia	X			
Dem. Yemen	X		X	
Ecuador	X			
Egypt	X	X	X	
Ghana	X			X
Guinea	X		X	
Guyana	X			
Hungary	X			
India	X			X
Indonesia	X		X	
Iraq	X	X		X
Jamaica	X		X	X
Jordan	X	X		X
Kuwait	X			X
Lebanon	X		X	
Liberia			X	
Libya	X	X		X
Madagascar	X	X		X
Malaysia			X	
Mali	X		X	
Mauritania	X		X	
Mexico			X	
Mongolia	X		X	
Niger	X	X		
Nigeria			X	
Oman	X			
Pakistan	X		X	
Peru	X			X
Poland	X		X	
Romania	X			
Saudi Arabia	X		X	X
Senegal	X	X	X	X

Table 3. The Arguments of the States Opposed to Action Against Terrorism (Continued)

	Liberation Struggles	Definitions Unclear	Causes Must Be Studied	Acting in Haste
Sierra Leone	X			
Somalia	X	X	X	X
Sri Lanka	X	X		
Sudan	X		X	X
Syria	X		X	
Tanzania	X	X	X	X
Tunisia	X		X	X
Uganda	X	X		
Ukrainian SSR	X			
USSR	X			
UAE	X		X	
Venezuela	X	X	X	
Yemen	X	X	X	
Yugoslavia	X			
Zambia	X			
57 countries	53	16	29	15

Notes

1. "American Draft Convention on Terrorism," *Survival,* vol. XV, no. 1, January-February 1973, p. 32.

2. John R. Stevenson, "International Law and the Export of Terrorism," *Department of State Bulletin,* 4 December 1972, p. 651.

3. Official Records of the General Assembly, 27th Session, 6th Committee, 1386 meeting, pp. 452-453.

4. Official Records of the General Assembly, 27th Session, 6th Committee, 1357 meeting, pp. 254-255.

5. Official Records of the General Assembly, 27th Session, 6th Committee, 1369 meeting, p. 345.

6. Official Records of the General Assembly, 27th Session, 6th Committee, 1359 meeting, p. 271.

7. Official Records of the General Assembly, 27th Session, 6th Committee, 1365 meeting, p. 308.

8. Official Records of the General Assembly, 27th Session, 6th Committee, 1363 meeting, p. 294.

PART VI

International Terrorism and the Military

JAY MALLIN

Terrorism As a Military Weapon

> "It is a dress which is justly supposed to carry no small terror to the enemy, who think every such person a complete marksman."
>
> General George Washington[1]

Terrorism is a disease of modern society, a virus growing in an ill body. The effects of this virus can sometimes be ameliorated, but there is no certain cure.

The causes of terrorism are diverse and often one overlaps another or several. It may be social, as was the case of the Uruguayan young people denied their rightful place in a stagnating society. Or it may be racial, as is the case of black and Indian militant groups in the United States. And, of course, there is the political cause: Israelis seeking independence from Great Britain; Cuban rebels seeking freedom from dictators Batista and Castro; Algerians seeking independence from France; northern Irish Catholics trying to destroy British rule and, conversely, Irish Protestants attempting to neutralize the Catholics.

Each case cited was or is one of armed conflict; in a word, of war. Whether the cause be social discontent or national aspirations, a larger or smaller segment of a population wars on another or on a foreign adversary. The feasible weapon is terrorism. A military observer noted, "Terror, it is obvious, is a legitimate instrument of national policy."[2]

The complexity of terrorism's causes, the diverse ideologies that have employed it, the variety of arms and tactics available to terrorists—all these factors have made terrorism one of the most complicated problems of our times. Certainly the scope of the problem defies understanding by any single discipline. Terrorism is a tangled skein of varied human motivations, actions, hopes, emotions, and goals. A 1973 conference on terrorism and political crimes concluded in part:

The problem of the prevention and suppression of "terrorism" arises in part because there is no clear understanding of the causes leading to conduct constituting "terrorism." The International Community has been unable to arrive at a universally accepted definition of "terrorism" and has so far failed to control such activity.[3]

Note: This article has been printed in *Air University Review*, January-February 1977.

Terrorism cannot be explained by psychologists who construct facile theories. It cannot be countered by police who view it as simply one more type of criminal activity: Identify the culprits, arrest them, throw them in prison, or perhaps shoot them, and the problem is solved. Nor can terrorism be handled by conventional military men who scoff at it as being beneath their notice. Even the academician who wishes to study terrorism dispassionately finds theories, explanations, and chronological statistics, but little else. Penetrating interviews with genuine terrorists, for example, are minimal in availability.

Terrorism is indeed a tangled skein, and any observer attempting to unravel and separate even one thread leaves himself open to criticism, justified criticism. For example, one might say terrorism is a military weapon. But what about the kidnappings solely for financial gain in Italy and the brigandage in Argentina motivated by monetary profit?

Thus, the skein is a mess of threads; it may not be possible to separate cleanly any one. Nevertheless, the effort is worth the attempt if it contributes even a pinpoint of light in what is certainly a long and dark tunnel. This discussion will attempt to focus on one thread: terrorism as a military weapon.

In September of 1972, the world was stunned to hear that the Twentieth Olympic Games, a symbol of international harmony, had been attacked by political terrorists. A group of urban guerrillas belonging to the Palestinian Black September movement had forced their way into the Israeli quarters at the Olympic site and seized nine hostages.

The guerrillas issued a number of demands, including one for the release of 200 Palestinian prisoners in Israel. Day-long negotiations took place between the guerrillas and the West German government, and eventually the government appeared to accede to the Palestinian demands. An accord was reached whereby the terrorists, together with their hostages, were to be taken to an airport and there provided with air transportation to Egypt. At Fuerstenfeldbruck Airport, however, German snipers opened fire on the terrorists, and in the resulting battle all Israeli hostages died, as well as four guerrillas, a police officer, and a helicopter pilot.

Thanks to the miracle of modern communications, people in many lands were kept abreast of developments minute by minute. Americans watched television in fascination as events unfolded before their eyes. When the final holocaust occurred at the German airport, shock, horror, and revulsion swept the civilized world.

The question was repeatedly asked, what did the Palestinians hope to gain by their action? Did not the kidnappings—and the resultant killings— do their cause far more harm than good? The actions of terrorists, however, cannot be measured in the way other acts of war or revolution are appraised. Urban guerrillas do not march to the same drummer as regular soldiers, or even rural guerrillas. Colonel William D. Neale (USA, ret.), the previously quoted observer, stated:

Terroristic violence must be totally ruthless, for moral scruples and terror do not mix and one or the other must be rejected. There can be no such thing as a weak dose of terror. The hand that controls the whip must be firm and implacable.[4]

Although not generally viewed as such, the Olympic action was nevertheless fundamentally a military move. Having failed in four conventional wars to defeat the Israelis, the Arabs and Palestinians resorted to unconventional tactics—specifically, terrorism in the border zones and against Israeli installations in foreign lands. If the Arab leaders had not themselves been conventional, they might have utilized unconventional tactics much earlier—perhaps more successfully than their efforts to defeat the Israelis in "regular" warfare.

Basically, terrorism is a form of psychological warfare (frighten your enemy, publicize your cause). Seen within this context, the Olympic attack achieved its purpose. Kidnapping the Israeli athletes did no military harm to Israel. As a psychological blow, however, it probably boosted Palestinian morale and it certainly spotlighted worldwide the Palestinian cause. It encouraged future moves by Palestinian terrorists—the historical record attests to this. As a psychological blow, the Olympic attack demonstrated that wherever Israeli figures of prominence went abroad, whether they be diplomats or athletes or whatever, they were susceptible to terrorist attack.

War is armed conflict, and armed conflict is the province of the military. Terrorism is a form of armed conflict; it is, therefore, within the military sphere. When diplomats fail, soldiers take over. When soldiers fail, terrorists take over. The political terrorist, however, is a soldier, too. He wears no uniform, he may have received little or no training, he may accept minimal discipline, his organization may be ephemeral—but he is a soldier. He engages in armed conflict in pursuit of a cause. His weapons are the gun and the explosive. His battlefield is the city street, and his targets are the vulnerable points of modern society.

Certainly not all terrorists are soldiers, nor is all terrorism military. For our purposes, however, it is postulated that terrorism is military when:

1. It is utilized as a substitute for "regular" warfare, as in the case of the Palestinians against the Israelis.

2. It is used in conjunction with other military activities, as in the cases of Cuba (against Batista) and Vietnam (against the Saigon administrations).

3. It is used as the chosen weapon of conflict by a population segment against another segment and/or a foreign power, as in the case of Northern Ireland.

Terrorism is sometimes believed to be synonymous with urban guerrilla warfare. Urban guerrilla warfare, however, is a broader term: it encompasses urban terrorism but other actions as well, for example, street skirmishes, assaults on official installations, and other types of hit-and-run urban combat. Also, it may be noted that terrorism is not confined to urban zones; it can be conducted in rural areas as well, as was notably the case in South Vietnam.

Thus terrorism in certain circumstances is conducted as a military tactic. The purpose of military action is often to achieve political goals. "For political aims are the end and war is the means . . .," states Clausewitz.[5] In some cases terrorism is a part of the means, or is *the* means.

Terrorism as a tactic can be traced to ancient times. Today's terrorists take human hostages; the Incas seized the idols of people they had conquered and held these as hostages to insure that the defeated would not rebel. Terrorism as a tactic of urban guerrilla warfare dates to the struggles in the past century and in this century of Russian revolutionaries against the tsars. The concept of terrorism as a military instrument, however, is comparatively new. One of the papers developed at the first National Security Affairs Conference held at the National War College in 1974 noted:

Despite Mao's emphasis on the relationship between guerrilla warfare and the rural peasant, despite the doctrinaire vision of armed, revolutionary conflict culminating on the open battlefield, and despite the role of rural warfare in the most important revolutions of the past half-century, the rapid urbanization of much of the world now suggests new opportunities and hence new strategies for a revolutionary warfare, and, in particular, a new attitude toward the role of the city as the ultimate revolutionary battlefield.[6]

For the political militant, urban guerrilla warfare offers clear advantages over rural guerrilla warfare. If he is a city youth, he can remain in the cities and need not meet the rugged demands of rural and hill fighting. In the cities there are an abundance of potential targets. The countryside offers few. In the cities there are opportunities for militant action (such the as placing of bombs) which does not necessarily entail direct personal conflict with the police. In the countryside guerrillas must eventually prove themselves by combat with units of the regular army. Rural guerrilla warfare requires a great deal of physical exertion with few gratifying results over a long period. In urban areas guerrillas can commit spectacular acts which garner great publicity and then, if they have not been identified by the authorities, can return to "normal" lives until the time comes for their next violent action.

The growing technological complexity of our times increases the vulnerability of modern life. Not only does technology engender vulnerability, it also develops more sophisticated weapons that can kill or endanger more people and do more damage. Professor Zbigniew Brzezinski aptly referred to "the global nervous system";[7] Swedish Premier Olof Palme discussed at the United Nations "technology's multiplication of the power to destroy."[8]

One has but to look about a modern city to see a plethora of targets. Aqueduct pumping stations and conduits, power stations and lines, telephone exchanges, post offices, airport control towers, radio and television stations—all these form part of a city's nervous system. Terrorists can shoot at policemen, rob banks, sabotage industrial machinery, kill government officials, incapacitate vehicles, and set bombs in theaters and other public localities. Destruction of an enemy's cities is an accepted strategy of modern warfare; whether it be accomplished by aerial bombers or by land-bound terrorists is merely a matter of means. The National War College paper previously noted also pointed out:

The destruction of a hydroelectric system, the crippling of a central computer bank, the acceleration of a social disorder by racist and counterracist assassination, the undermining of an economy by the pollution of an entire wheat crop . . . all these are but mere samples of the kind of violence which would lend itself to a strategic manipulation. Although disguised in the name of revolution or rebellion, such violence could be decisive in terms of distracting a nation, or isolating it, or even paralyzing it. It would be, in effect, a new form of war. . . .[9]

As previously postulated, terrorism could be used in conjunction with "regular" military activities. Or it could be used as a substitute. Colonel Seale R. Doss sets forth in the aforementioned paper that, "with the rapidly shifting alliances and animosities of the modern world, no nation could be quite sure in any case just which foreign power had (or even *if* some foreign power had) sponsored its disasters, for such violence would lend itself, like underworld money, to political launderings."[10]

Because terrorism as an instrument of war is a relatively new concept, there has been little specific doctrinal categorization or interpretation of, or doctrinal direction for, this type of warfare. The three foremost warrior-theoreticians of guerrilla warfare, Mao Tse-tung, Vo Nguyen Giap, and Ernesto "Che" Guevara, virtually ignored this method of combat. Giap has said only that *"to the counter-revolutionary violence of the enemy, our people must definitely oppose [place in opposition] revolutionary violence,"* and that *"the most correct path to be followed by the peoples to liberate themselves is revolutionary violence and revolutionary war."*[11] (Emphasis is Giap's.) By "revolutionary violence," Giap probably meant all available means of warfare, including terrorism.

Guevara alone approached the subject of urban guerrilla warfare as a specific type of combat, and then he did so only in brief. In his book *La guerra de guerrillas* he provided limited recognition to what he called "sub-urban warfare." The sub-urban guerrilla group, he stated, should not carry out "independent actions" but rather should "second the action of the larger groups in another area."[12] This Guevara book has been considered the basic instructional volume for Latin American guerrillas. It has, however, no instructions for urban guerrilla warfare. This is especially interesting in view of the fact that the urban guerrilla movement played as important a role, perhaps a more decisive role, than did the rural guerrillas in the 1956-1958

Cuban civil war. Fidel Castro and Guevara preferred, however, to promote the mystique of the rural guerrilla. They had been rural guerrilla captains, and it did not suit the historic position they envisioned for themselves to grant recognition to the urban clandestine movement that participated so significantly in the conflict.[13]

There was a practical consideration as well in the Castro-Guevara effort to develop the mystique of the rural guerrilla. Almost as soon as Castro came to power in Cuba, that small country launched an extensive program of subversion, with most of the effort concentrated on creating *fidelista* guerrilla movements in rural areas of Latin America. Castro and Guevara sought to duplicate their own guerrilla operation; launched from abroad, it had functioned in isolated rural areas. Guerrilla warfare, declared Guevara, is "the central axis of the struggle" in Latin America.[14] So deeply did Guevara believe in the guerrilla mystique that eventually it led him to his death in Bolivia. It was only after repeated failures, including Guevara's death, that Castro turned his attention to urban movements.

A perusal of other military instructional literature reveals a similar dearth of attention to urban guerrilla warfare. North Vietnamese Lieutenant General Hoang Van Thai's *Some Aspects of Guerrilla Warfare in Vietnam*[15] deals entirely with rural combat. The *Handbook for Volunteers of the Irish Republican Army*[16] is a fine basic book on rural guerrilla warfare, and much that it says is applicable to urban guerrilla combat, but it does not touch on this specifically despite the long utilization of urban terrorist tactics by the IRA. Bert "Yank" Levy's *Guerrilla Warfare*[17] has a brief chapter on "the city guerrilla" but the book is primarily about rural guerrilla warfare. Spanish General Alberto Bayo's *150 Questions to a Guerrilla*[18] and Swiss Major H. von Dach Bern's *Total Resistance*[19] also have material useful to an urban guerrilla, particularly in regard to sabotage activities, but again the books are concerned mainly with rural guerrillas.

The only document specifically dealing with urban guerrilla warfare that has received international recognition was written by a Brazilian politician-turned-terrorist, Carlos Marighella. Marighella wrote the *Minimanual of the Urban Guerrilla* for use by Brazilian terrorists, but its instructional contents are valid for guerrillas in any city in the world. He stated:

The urban guerrilla is an implacable enemy of the government and systematically inflicts damage on the authorities and on the men who dominate the country and exercise power. The principal task of the urban guerrilla is to distract, to wear out, to demoralize the militarists, the military dictatorship and its repressive forces, and also to attack and destroy the wealth and property of the North Americans, the foreign managers, and the Brazilian upper class.[20]

He also declared: "The urban guerrilla is a man who fights the military dictatorship with arms, using unconventional methods. . . . The urban guerrilla follows a political goal. . . ."[21]

It is interesting to note that just as Mao, prophet of rural guerrilla warfare, believed that type of combat was secondary to "regular" warfare,[22] Marighella, prophet of urban guerrilla warfare, envisioned urban combat as supplementary to rural guerrilla combat. He stated that the function of urban guerrilla warfare was "to wear out, demoralize, and distract the enemy forces, permitting the emergence and survival of rural guerrilla warfare which is destined to play the decisive role in the revolutionary war."[23]

As for terrorism specifically, Marighella said, "Terrorism is an arm the revolutionary can never relinquish."[24] It is also a weapon the military cannot ignore.

Anyone writing about terrorism labors under the difficulty that it has not been possible to develop an entirely satisfactory definition of terrorism. Mainly this is due to the fact that there is no precise understanding of what the term terrorism encompasses. There are too many gray areas of violence and of intimidation that may or may not be labeled as terroristic. Whether any particular area of activity or specific act is indeed terroristic largely depends on the circumstances. Example: Is sabotage a form of terrorism? Seeking an answer, we go full circle, for whether sabotage is terroristic depends on the definition of terrorism. Therefore, the following working definition is offered:

Political terrorism is the threat of violence or an act or series of acts of violence effected through surreptitious means by an individual, an organization, or a people to further his or their political goals.

Under this definition, sabotage committed for political purposes is indeed a form of terrorism.

Perhaps there is no such thing as "military terrorism," or perhaps this is merely a semantic lack. At any rate, terrorism is one form of military activity that can be utilized by an organization or a people in pursuit of their political goals. Terrorism is a military weapon.

Most often, terrorism consists of a series of acts of violence. All terrorism is criminal in the eyes of the government that is assailed. But there may be "criminal terrorism" in which the violence is committed purely for monetary, not political gain. Frequently this type of terrorism will disguise itself as political terrorism, especially in situations wherein genuine political terrorism is rampant, for example, the Argentine situation.

As previously noted, terrorism as a military arm is a weapon of psychological warfare. The purpose, as the very word indicates, is to engender terror in the foe. The terror thrust encompasses the following ingredients:

1. Terrorism publicizes the terrorists' political cause.

2. Terrorism demonstrates the capability of the terrorists to strike blows.

3. Terrorism heartens sympathizers of the terrorists' cause.

4. Terrorism disconcerts the enemy.

5. Terrorism eventually—the ultimate goal—demoralizes the enemy and paralyzes him.

6. Conceivably, in certain circumstances, terrorism could deter potential allies of the terrorists' target country from assisting that country. ("If you provide aid to our enemy, we will unleash our terror tactics against you, too.")

7. Sabotage causes material damage to an enemy's vital installations; the damage, in turn, has a psychological effect on the foe and on the populace. It frightens the foe and emboldens the ally.

Terrorists function within an area controlled by the enemy, whether it be a metropolis or an airliner in flight. The terrorists either:

1. Represent a significant portion of the population (as in the case of a struggle against an unpopular dictator) and their actions are applauded, even when they cause discomfort to the population (as when rebels knocked out a substantial portion of Havana's electric and water systems during the Cuban civil war[25]).

2. Do not receive any significant amount of popular support and are generally condemned as outlaws (the miniscule ethnic militant groups in the United States are an example).

3. Or are foreign or foreign-supported and are seeking to destroy the enemy's control structure or to achieve some other political result (as in the case of the IRA bombs in restaurants and other public places in London).

Whereas with the first alternative the terrorist may try to minimize civilian casualties in order not to turn the population against him, in the third instance the more casualties there are the better the terrorist feels his goals are served; he is applying ruthless pressure against his enemy, and the number of casualties is a measure of his success. With the second possibility, whether the terrorist concerns himself over civilian casualties is largely determined by whether his fanaticism is tempered by mercy.

At what point does terrorism become the concern of the "regular" military? For a military establishment that is *attacking,* terrorism can be used, as previously postulated, as a substitute for conventional warfare or in conjunction with conventional warfare and/or rural guerrilla warfare. For a military establishment that is responsible for *defending* an area or a country, the military role in the handling of a terrorist problem is determined by local circumstances: Is the government of the country under attack run by civilians or by the military? What constitutional and other legal responsibilities and restrictions are placed on the military? What useful capabilities do the military have that the police do not have?

The level of intensity of terrorist activity appears to be a determinant of military response more than any other factor. In most national cases, military activity has been largely limited to guard and military intelligence duties in support of the police authorities. In other cases, however—notably in pre-Israel Palestine, Cyprus, Algeria, Uruguay, Argentina, and Northern Ireland—the military took over primary responsibility for combatting terrorists because the police were overwhelmed.[26] It is significant that in those instances cited where the military sought to maintain foreign control over populations, the independence struggles were nevertheless successful (except in Ireland, where the conflict continues). In the two countries where indigenous military have sought to suppress major terrorist movements, the military were successful in one instance (Uruguay) and the outcome is as yet inconclusive in the other (Argentina). One may reasonably gather from this that terrorism is an effective weapon when used by a substantial portion of a population against foreign occupation troops. As a weapon against indigenous authorities supported by a military establishment, its efficacy is open to question. It appears to have succeeded only in such cases wherein it was used in conjunction with other military tactics (Cuba, South Vietnam).

There appear to be three fundamental functions of terrorism as a military weapon:

1. Psychological warfare—to demoralize the enemy (his government, armed forces, police, even the civilian population) through assassinations, bomb explosions, agitation, and so on. The Vietcong utilized the entire arsenal of violence in their campaign in South Vietnam.

2. Material destruction—to destroy or damage the enemy's utilities, communications, and industries. Destruction by sabotage, particularly against specific targets limited in size, can be as effective as destruction by air raid.

3. Economic damage—to engender a state of psychological unease and uncertainty in a city or a country. Commerce dries up; investment funds vanish. The deterioration of the Cuban economy during the 1956-58 revolution was a major factor in the downfall of the Batista regime.

Terrorism utilized as a military weapon, whether by a foreign power or by domestic insurgents, is somewhat akin to air raids; it is warfare conducted in the enemy's rear. In both cases, the tactic aims at destroying the foe's installations, killing his officials, and battering his morale. Lamentably, in both cases the deaths of civilians are an additional result, unacknowledged as a goal but, nevertheless, often deliberately sought.

If, then, terrorism is a military weapon, a weapon to be used for a military goal—the defeat of an enemy—how much recognition of this weapon has been extended by "regular" military establishments? Traditionally, the regular military have looked askance at any type of unconventional warfare. This remains true today even though the line of differentiation between "conventional" and "unconventional" warfare grows increasingly blurred. In the cases of the British, Israeli, Argentine, and Uruguayan armies, the military have been forced by circumstances to recognize their responsibility in dealing with terrorism. Reality has legitimized the bastard—military terrorism —in fact if not in name.

In South Vietnam, terrorism was a major problem facing the American and South Vietnamese forces. Nevertheless, the main responsibility for combating it was turned over to civilian intelligence organizations, such as the Central Intelligence Agency. In general, of the military branches, only the U.S. Marines recognized the military importance of Vietcong terrorism and sought not only to conquer territory but to hold it and to provide security for its inhabitants.[27] It is interesting to note that the U.S. Joint Chiefs of Staff's *Dictionary of Military and Associated Terms* finds no place for the words "terror" or "terrorism."[28]

United States military interest in terrorism appears to be minimal. The fact that one of the panels at the National War College's National Security Affairs Conference dealt with " 'New' Forms of Violence in the International Milieu" was encouraging. There have been lectures and panels at the Institute for Military Assistance at Fort Bragg, and a protection-against-terrorism manual for U.S. military personnel going overseas has been written there. The *Air University Review* has published a number of relevant articles. This attention, however, must be considered inadequate in view of the enormity of the problem. Major General Edward G. Lansdale (ret.) has warned:

We live in a revolutionary era. My hunch is that history is waiting to play a deadly joke on us. It did so on recent graduates of the Imperial Defence College in London, who now find themselves facing the savagery of revolutionary warfare in Northern Ireland. It did so on Pakistani officers under General Niazi, who undoubtedly wish now that they had learned better ways of coping with the Mukti Bahini guerrillas. It is starting to do so on Argentine graduates of the Escuela Nacional de Guerra in Buenos Aires, who are waking up to the fact that Marxist ERP guerrillas intend to win themselves a country with the methods of the Tupamaros next door.[29]

There are existing situations and possible situations which counsel greater understanding of terrorism by the U.S. military. American military personnel have already been subjected to terrorist attacks in countries as diverse and far apart as Iran and Guatemala. It is not inconceivable that an international terrorist organization might decide, for tactical and ideological reasons, to strike at U.S. military personnel and even installations in a number of countries. (NATO, concerned over the spread of terrorism, conducted a study through the intelligence agencies of its member states of an international terrorist organization which is believed to operate globally.)[30]

The United States provides military equipment and guidance to a substantial number of friendly countries. Of what use is tank warfare doctrine to an army confronted with a major terrorist problem? Are U.S. MAGs prepared to provide the assistance needed? Here is another scenario: U.S. forces are stationed in a foreign country, perhaps as part of an international peacekeeping force, and the local rebels resort to terror tactics. Is the U.S. military prepared to cope with such a situation?

There are additional terror situations that might require military involvement within the United States itself, much as troops were required at critical moments during the civil rights struggle of the sixties. Recognizing the constitutional and historical limitations on the military and recognizing that a terror level akin to that in Argentina and Northern Ireland is not likely to develop in the United States within the foreseeable future, it is still possible to postulate situations in which the military would have to exercise counterterror capabilities. Two possibilities are:

1. Terrorists seize the Capitol in Washington while Congress is in session. Or they take another major edifice in an American city. Handling the crisis is beyond the means of the police.

2. Terrorists have a nuclear device, or a major bacterial weapon. They hold the weapon in a heavily guarded building in the center of a city, and they threaten to devastate the city if their demands are not met. Again the situation is beyond the capability of the police.

Hypothetical situations? Yes. But terrorists have seized buildings in other countries, and the United States government is concerned over the possibility of terrorists obtaining a nuclear bomb. These situations could occur within the United States. The military would do well to prepare to assist if they are called upon.

Beyond that is the necessity of recognizing that in today's world terrorism is often a military weapon. General Robert E. Lee said of the Confederacy's own guerrillas, "I regard the whole system as an unmixed evil."[31] Evil or not, guerrilla warfare has been employed by innumerable combatants down through the ages, always bedeviling the regulars. Disdaining it will not make it go away. Disdaining terrorism will not make it go away, either. Unhappy though it may make the graduate of the Imperial Defence College, or of the Escuela Nacional de Guerra, or of the U.S. Military Academy, it is a tactic that must be dealt with. Far better that the U.S. military be prepared than that they, too, be caught by surprise. Tactics must be studied, doctrines developed, defenses constructed. For, as one writer stated, "Step by step, almost imperceptibly, without anyone being aware that a fatal watershed has been crossed, mankind has descended into the age of terror."[32]

Notes

1. Richard M. Ketchum, *The Winter Soldiers* (New York: Doubleday, 1973). Washington prescribed the "rifle dress" for his troops because it was associated in the minds of the British with the apparel worn by skilled riflemen.

2. Col. William D. Neale, USA (ret.), "Terror—Oldest Weapon in the Arsenal," *Army,* August 1973.

3. M. Cherif Bassiouni, ed., *International Terrorism and Political Crimes* (Springfield, Ill.: Charles C Thomas, 1975).

4. Neale, "Terror."

5. H. Rothfels in *Makers of Modern Strategy,* Edward Mead Earle, ed. (Princeton, N.J.: Princeton University Press, 1970).

6. Col. Seale R. Doss in *Defense Planning for the 1980's and the Changing International Environment* (Washington, D.C., 1975).

7. "The U.S. and the Skyjackers: Where Power Is Vulnerable," *Time,* 21 September 1971.

8. "The City as Battlefield: A Global Concern," *Time,* 2 November 1970.

9. Doss, *Defense Planning.*

10. *Ibid.*

11. Vo Nguyen Giap, *The South Vietnam People Will Win* (Foreign Languages Publishing House, 1965).

12. Ernesto Guevara, *La guerra de guerrillas* (Havana: Departamento del Minfar, 1960).

13. See Jaime Suchlicki's *University Students and Revolution in Cuba 1920-1968* (Coral Gables, Fla.: University of Miami Press, 1969); Ruby Hart Phillip's *Cuba, Island of Paradox* (New York: McDowell, Obolensky, 1959); Jay Mallin's *Fortress Cuba* (Chicago: H. Regnery Co., 1965).

14. Guevara, "Guerrilla Warfare: A Method," *Cuba Socialista,* September 1962.

15. Foreign Languages Publishing House (Hanoi, 1965).

16. Issued by General Headquarters, 1965.

17. Panther Publications (Boulder, Colorado, 1964).

18. Twenty-eighth edition (Havana, 1961).

19. Panther Publications (Boulder, Colorado, 1965).

20. Carlos Marighella, "Minimanual of the Urban Guerrilla," *Tricontinental,* November 1970.

21. *Ibid.*

22. "When we say that in the entire war [against Japan] mobile warfare is primary and guerrilla warfare supplementary, we mean that the outcome of the war depends mainly on regular warfare, especially in its mobile form, and that guerrilla warfare cannot shoulder the main responsibility in deciding the outcome." From "On Protracted War," *Selected Military Writings of Mao Tse-tung* (Peking: Foreign Languages Press, 1963).

23. Marighella, "Minimanual."

24. *Ibid.*

25. Mallin, *Fortress Cuba.*

26. Robert Taber, *The War of the Flea* (New York: L. Stuart, 1965); *Challenge and Response in Internal Conflict* (three volumes, Washington, D.C., 1967, 1968).

27. William R. Corson, *The Betrayal* (New York: W. W. Norton, 1968).

28. Washington, D.C., 1972.

29. Major General Edward G. Lansdale, USAF (ret.), "The Opposite Number," *Air University Review,* July-August 1972.

30. "Radical Nations Aid, Finance Global Terror, NATO Thinks," *Miami Herald,* 6 February 1976.

31. Bruce Catton, *A Stillness at Appomattox* (New York: Doubleday, 1953).

32. Paul Johnson, quoted in David Fromkin's "The Strategy of Terrorism," *Foreign Affairs,* July 1975.

R. WILLIAM MENGEL

The Impact of Nuclear Terrorism on the Military's Role in Society

Introduction

Terrorism is not a new phenomenon, having receiving its name as far back as the late 1700s during the French Revolution. One might argue that terroristic acts have been part of the entire history of our civilization. In each era, whether it was that of anti-tsarist terrorists of the late nineteenth century, the Irish Republican Army in the first quarter of the twentieth century, or any of the numerous others, terrorists have had the capacity for acquiring and employing the technology of the day. Guy Fawkes' attempt to blow up the English Parliament in 1604 with thirty-six barrels of gunpowder is illustrative of employment of state-of-the-art technology for terroristic motives.

Since the early twentieth century, technological advancement within industrialized nations, and to a lesser degree developing states, has occurred at a rate greater than in all previous history combined. Most significantly for this discussion, technologies with mass destruction and mass casualty potential have been widely developed and deployed by the major militaries of the world. Beyond a purely military application, a few of these potent technologies have been adapted to civilian use, including nuclear energy.

One result of this proliferation of technology is that for the first time in history terrorists now have available a broad spectrum of means that carry catastrophic consequences. To date, however, terrorists have foregone the use of those technological leaps which would significantly increase their potential to publicize goals and achieve concessions from government and society in general. Instead, they have elected to apply incremental improvements in existing conventional technologies. The reasons for this choice, if it in fact has been a matter of choice, are too complex to discuss in detail here. Rather, central to this discussion are the propositions that, despite the lack of interest up to now, nuclear technology is reasonably available to terrorists and the employment of this technology represents such a danger to society that the ultimate force of the state—the military—must be used to counter the threat.

The purpose of the following is to present an overview of nuclear terrorism and the potential role of the military in democratic society as an instrument for coping with it. Since the military is not functionally integrated into the day-to-day domestic life of the nation and does not interact with the private citizen on a recurring basis, military intervention into the domestic realm carries ominous connotations. In most democratic societies, a strong tradition of military noninvolvement in domestic matters has been established. For these reasons, both the consequences of nuclear terrorism and military intervention must be examined and weighed before reaching any conclusions.

Recognition of the differences between countries with respect to the military's role in society led to the decision to use the United States as a model for discussion. This selection was made for three reasons.

1. Within the United States are large numbers of nuclear facilities and materials, including fifty-six operational power plants, several weapons and material fabrication facilities, numerous weapon storage sites, a large number of research reactors, and wide application of radioactive isotopes at research and health facilities. These provide a target-rich environment for terrorists in comparison to most other countries.

2. The tradition of civilian control of the armed forces and military nonintervention in domestic matters is equal to that found anywhere in the world today.

3. The sociopolitical environment in the United States today is reflective of peacetime conditions where the military is not involved in the daily lives of most citizens. Guerrilla war, insurgency, or intensified urban warfare environments have been excluded because of the likelihood that the military is already involved in domestic society.

Three principal sections follow. Initially, a typology of nuclear terrorism is developed to provide perspective to its potential magnitude and consequences. In the second part, the role of government, in particular, the military, in responding to nuclear terrorism is explored. Finally, several conclusions are drawn with respect to the use of the military in controlling and responding to nuclear terrorism and the overall impact this involvement might have on society.

Typology of Nuclear Incidents

Rather than attempt to succinctly and clearly define terrorism to the satisfaction of each reader, a feat which has eluded more authors than can be recounted, the issue will be sidestepped by stressing the nuclear aspect of terrorism. Nuclear terrorism encompasses those acts which would normally be considered terroristic, but which include a nuclear element as the principal means of violence. In attempting to provide substantive body to this imprecise definition, a typology of nuclear malevolent actions has been developed. The intent is to offer a broad spectrum of potential nuclear acts which might be appropriate for employment by terrorists. There has been no effort made to enumerate all the possible actions in any one category since the inclusion of this material ad infinitum would provide no special benefit.

But the seven categories do represent, in a generic sense, a continuum of potential malevolent actions.

1. *Threat incident* is one in which no physical violence is involved, but authorities are led to believe that unless certain conditions are met, an act will occur.

2. *Harassment* represents the lowest level of actual violence in the typology, involving acts against facilities which are purely of nuisance value and do not present any nuclear danger. Harassment is usually external to a facility.

3. *Disruption/damage* is accomplished when an overt or covert action stops work or otherwise disrupts operations and may entail damage to components of the installation. This category of action may originate with external or internal perpetrators.

4. *Hostage/barricade* occurs when terrorist elements physically hold a facility for bargaining purposes. In many cases, such as a missile site or a reactor, it is highly unlikely any nuclear danger could be created.

5. *Theft* involves the overt or covert diversion of nuclear material or weapons for an illicit purpose.

6. *Dispersal* is the release of radioactive material into the atmosphere, either at a nuclear site or into the general public domain.

7. *Fabrication of a nuclear weapon* includes implicitly the ability to detonate the weapon.

A second dimension of this typology is the nature of the nuclear material or installation involved in the malevolent action. The potential danger found in each category is dependent upon the characteristics of the nuclear component of the specific incident. In making a determination of the potential danger, two criteria are applied: the objective consequences of the act in terms of casualties and damage to the general public; and the subjective consequences of the act in terms of the extent of probable impact on the current societal structures, norms, and values. For example, the theft of a nuclear weapon from the military creates a totally different situation from the theft of radium needles from a hospital. Similarly, the seizure of a research reactor is markedly less significant than the occupation of a power reactor or a fuel fabrication plant.

Consequences and Societal Impact

Since the focus here is on nuclear terrorism and the role of the military, it is reasonable to proceed and exclude those classes of incidents that clearly have not been, and would not be in the future, of sufficient import to warrant direct military intervention. To accomplish this, the various categories of malevolent actions have been arrayed against the types of nuclear elements that might be part of a nuclear terrorism act. Each of the combinations in the matrix has been evaluated to determine the relative objective and subjective consequences. The result of this judgmental assessment is presented as a score on a scale of one to ten, ten representing the greatest danger to society. (Figure 1 offers a graphic portrayal of the rating of societal consequences.)

Malevolent Action / Nuclear Element	NUCLEAR WEAPONS	WEAPONS GRADE MATERIAL	OTHER RADIOACTIVE MATERIAL	FUEL FABRICATION	REPROCESSING	RESEARCH REACTOR	POWER REACTOR	NUCLEAR WASTE	WEAPONS SITE
Fabrication of a Nuclear Weapon	10								
Dispersal		10	6						
Theft	9	9	3						
Hostage/Barricade				7	7	3	6	5	7
Disruption/Damage				5	5	3	4	4	5
Harassment				3	3	2	2	2	3
Threat Incident	1-10	1-10	1	2	2	1	1	1	2

Figure 1. Societal Consequences for Nuclear Terrorism

CASUALTIES/DAMAGE (OBJECTIVE) CONSEQUENCES

One can conclude that the objective consequences of the majority of malevolent nuclear actions are such that society would not suffer any greater damage than is inflicted on a recurring basis by terrorists today. Even the dispersal of most radioactive material would not create larger numbers of casualties than suffered in today's terrorist attacks. For example, in April 1975 a lone terrorist sprayed railway passenger compartments with Iodine-131 on two occasions. The outcome was that six people suffered temporary upset stomachs, but no permanent damage or even hospitalization resulted. Several accidental incidents and intentional attacks at nuclear facilities themsleves have caused no objective consequences:

1. Two bombs caused heavy damage to the electronic equipment in the control room at the Stanford Linear Accelerator in December 1971, causing about $100,000 in damage. No danger of radioactive leaks resulted (nor could one have because of the nature of the equipment).

2. An accidental fire at the Rocky Flats nuclear weapons fabrication facility in Colorado in May 1969 caused $45 million in damage. Although several Colorado scientists claimed off-site contamination, AEC investigators de-

termined no radiation danger existed beyond the immediate vicinity of the plant. In any case, no casualties or damage to the general public resulted.

3. In May 1975, an accidental fire caused approximately $50 million damage to Brown's Ferry Nuclear Power Plant, Athens, Alabama. Although the fire posed no danger to the public, it was the most serious nuclear incident to date, holding the potential for a reactor core-meltdown at one time.

The point these examples illustrate, and a body of reasonably extensive literature on nuclear dangers supports, is that most nuclear-related incidents have not been and are not now potentially dangerous to the general public. Harassment, disruption, and even damage do not constitute malevolent actions that would have a major impact on society. Hostage situations are to a great degree facility-dependent, but in any case, the objective consequences must be evaluated in terms of the potential results. Threats are an anomaly in the typology in that most do not pose a problem of objective consequences. But a threat involving the theft of a weapon or weapons-grade material must be considered equally as serious as the threatened malevolent action until determined otherwise. At a minimum, threats result in an increased cost to society in terms of security.

Most significant among nuclear malevolent actions are theft, dispersal, and fabrication. Each offers the potential for creating considerable numbers of casualties. Theft is a prerequisite to either a bomb or a dispersal device, so it is rated high on the relative consequence scale. The simplest application of nuclear material is dispersal. This discussion focuses on plutonium since it is considered the most lethal material of those available. Whether the device is employed in a highly sophisticated dispersal mechanism, such as a command-controlled element to ensure systematic distribution of material, or a crude explosive that disperses plutonium dust into the air, the probable results will be more in terms of casualties caused by cancer over a fifteen- to thirty-year period rather than immediate deaths.

Once plutonium or high-enriched uranium has been acquired, an alternative use is the fabrication of a nuclear bomb. Fabrication of a nuclear device is a time-consuming and risky task requiring highly skilled technicians. Given reasonable resources and talent, the expected yield would be 0.1 to 10 kilotons (KT). Damage produced by a fabricated weapon varies with design, yield, and location, but a 1 KT surface burst (detonated in a parked van, for example) in a major city's downtown area would probably kill 100,000 people and cause in excess of a billion dollars damage.

Since the yield and dependability of weapons is a function of expertise in design and component workmanship, the theft of a nuclear weapon from the military eliminates the risks inherent in the manufacture of a weapon while significantly increasing the actual damage potential that might be achieved. The theft of a weapon presents a situation where direct military involvement is realized in the first instance. Whether or not the military will be compelled to transverse that line between civil and military authority in this type situation is open to question and will be addressed later.

SOCIETAL (SUBJECTIVE) CONSEQUENCES

At a more abstract level, the subjective consequences of the employment of nuclear terrorism can be evaluated in terms of impact on the structure, norms, and values of the community. Equally as cogent as the fact that most nuclear actions pose little objective consequences is the demonstrated non-effect that these incidents have had on society from a subjective perspective. Until some catastrophic act of nuclear terrorism is executed, it is unlikely that any changes will occur in public attitudes. Nuclear safeguards have been debated by the anti- and pronuclear forces and highlighted by the media in news stories, magazine articles, books, and even television specials. Still, overall public reaction has not been significant, even in those communities in the vicinity of operational nuclear facilities. For example, no general exodus of the population or shrinking property values are in evidence near these sites.

Until that time when an actual attack involving theft, dispersal, or fabrication causes major objective consequences, it is unlikely that the lower-level malevolent actions will change the public's perception of what is required to protect the community. The public shows little inclination to significantly change its way of life or sacrifice its freedoms for a threat that has not yet touched the community or society. Contributing to this general attitude with respect to nuclear incidents is the fact that to date no serious consequences have resulted.

Evidence from disaster and terrorism research points to three principal conclusions concerning the potential subjective consequences of a major incident. First, as described above, it is unlikely that threats or other low-level nuclear malevolent actions will alter the public's view of the danger. This, in turn, contributes to the limitation of actions by authorities in preparing to respond to nuclear terrorism. Second, the local impact of acts of nuclear terrorism with major objective consequences is far greater than nonlocal. Particularly with respect to overall fear and level of concern, locales directly affected by events will react the strongest. This position is supported by media and violence research which indicates a direct correlation between distance and reaction. Third, those segments of society subjected to major acts of nuclear terrorism will more readily accept increased safeguards and the concomitant decrease in civil liberties. The paramount concern of society is to protect itself from known consequences. Seldom acting until after at least some consequences have been demonstrated, society will be inclined to permit changes in its norms, values, and social structures once an event has occurred.

Probable Forms of Nuclear Terrorism

From the foregoing discussion and evaluation of the consequences of nuclear terrorism for society, it is clear that the full range of nuclear malevolent actions has not in the past, nor would in the future, require military intervention. Although the specter of nuclear terrorism has been broadly represented as the most catastrophic event that could befall society, in reality nuclear terrorism offers neither the greatest threat in terms of consequences nor the most probable with respect to the ability of the group to obtain necessary resources, personnel, and expertise. Much easier to initiate are acts using chemical and biological agents and their related technologies. In fact, several biological agents, such as anthrax, are potentially many times more potent than any use of nuclear material in terms of casualty-producing effects.

However, nuclear terrorism does offer the perpetrator the advantage of creating massive damage without inflicting large numbers of casualties. Other means of mass-destruction terrorism only provide a mechanism for creating tremendously large numbers of casualties. For this reason, as well as the fact that the nuclear industry and its potential dangers have been widely publicized, nuclear terrorism may be the first type of mass-destruction terrorism initiated on a scale that would have significant societal impact with respect to subjective and objective consequences.

Based on the previous analysis and extensive research on the threat to the commercial nuclear industry, lower-level malevolent actions of nuclear terrorism are more likely to occur than those of a higher order. Despite the probability of terrorists using nuclear material to perpetrate attacks, the constraints placed on the groups by resource and personnel requirements will limit activity to the lower end of the malevolent action range. The societal consequences of these attacks will be negligible in terms of both objective and subjective criteria. Thus, threat (outside the context of theft and dispersal), harassment, and damage/disruption are not significant as the likelihood of military involvement appears minimal. Hostage situations, theft, dispersal, and fabrication of a bomb may create incidents where the consequences are such that the military is encouraged to intervene. The most probable application of nuclear terrorism is the occupation of a nuclear facility, establishing a hostage situation. Theft of a weapon or weapons-grade material is the next most probable occurrence, while dispersal and, finally, fabrication of a bomb are the least. The basis for this determination is founded in the evaluation of a mixture of resources, motivations, and target vulnerabilities for each case.

Role of Government in Countering Nuclear Terrorism

In the initial section, the consequences of nuclear terrorism have been discussed and the most significant types of nuclear malevolent actions determined. From this presentation, it is possible to ascertain those situations which might warrant intervention of the military—hostage, theft, dispersal, fabrication and, possibly, threats. Other malevolent actions were found to have less consequential results for the public and do not require the level of resources usually available only within the military. This section briefly outlines the role of government in combating terrorism, the potential and actual roles of the military, and how the military might gain new roles.

Nonmilitary Agencies and Their Roles

The special roles and functions of governmental agencies, including the military, in countering and controlling nuclear terrorism vary from country to country. The role of each agency is dependent on the laws of the particular nation, in most cases a direct result of the initial laws that established and controlled the nuclear program in that country. In some nations, the military has sole responsibility for all nuclear activities, as in Brazil; in others, the military is secondary to the civilian sector, as in India. As a generalization, the nuclear program in all democratic countries is under the direct control of the national government, with the commercial nuclear industry under the auspices of the civilian sector of the government and the nuclear weapons program under the military. Thus, in discussing the role of nonmilitary agencies, the United States resembles to a greater or lesser degree other nations with nuclear programs. One chief difference should be noted; in the United States the civilian nuclear industry makes the weapons for the military, and military responsibility for them begins only with delivery. The Energy Research and Development Administration (ERDA) is charged with this responsibility and has several facilities that support military programs. Minor differences between the civilian-military division of authority and responsibility are to be noted among the nations with both military and commercial programs, with civilian agencies playing a greater role within the United States than elsewhere. By far, the United States has the largest number of civilian agencies with some nuclear-related function and responsibility.

Under the Atomic Energy Act of 1954, as amended, and the Energy Reorganization Act of 1974, the Federal government has been given authority and responsibility to respond to nuclear incidents, either accidental or intentional. The law stresses that the response should be in coordination with state and local governments, but clearly delineates the Federal government as having full authority. Four departments and agencies have primary responsibility for planning and responding to nuclear terrorism: Nuclear Regulatory Commission (NRC), Federal Bureau of Investigation (FBI), ERDA, and Department of Defense (DOD).

Since terrorism is viewed as essentially a criminal activity, under existing laws the principal responsibility for responding to nuclear terrorism resides with the FBI. This agency is charged with:

1. Operational planning in response to extortion, threats, thefts, or sabotage involving nuclear material;

2. Investigating all violations of the Atomic Energy Act of 1954 and successive legislation;

3. Investigating all incidents of sabotage involving nuclear facilities, materials, or weapons, any theft of nuclear weapons or materials, or any extortion using nuclear components, devices, or materials.

In executing these investigative responsibilities, the FBI is charged with coordinating all their activities, as appropriate, with state and local law-enforcement officials. Further, the FBI maintains liaison and coordinates with ERDA, NRC, and DOD. The principal point is that any instance of nuclear terrorism, regardless of its location within the United States, and including military installations, is the primary responsibility of the FBI. Roles of the other major civilian departments and agencies are as follows:

1. The Energy Research and Development Administration (ERDA) supports the FBI with technical assistance as required. Since ERDA is the manufacturer of all United States nuclear weapons and has a number of facilities under its direct control, the FBI will rely on ERDA for threat verification and technical assistance relevant to acts of nuclear terrorism.

2. The Nuclear Regulatory Commission (NRC) supports the FBI with technical information for licensed nuclear facilities and has responsibility for contingency plans for dealing with threats, thefts, hostage situations, and sabotage relating to weapons-grade materials, nuclear waste, and licensed facilities.

3. Other agencies and departments such as the Environmental Protection Agency, Department of Transportation, Department of Housing and Urban Development, and the Federal Preparedness Agency have assorted responsibilities in responding to nuclear terrorism.

4. The President has broad powers under Article II of the Constitution to deal with sudden emergencies that might endanger national security or the safety of the nation's people. Specific authorities are provided for in a wide range of statutes which address a spectrum of emergency situations.

In summary, there appears to be no lack of authority which would bar an effective Federal response to a nuclear terrorist incident. Furthermore, responsibilities have been delegated in such a way that the role of the military is subordinated to other civilian agencies, particularly the FBI, for nuclear terrorism responses and controls.

The Military's Role and Function

The military's role in responding to nuclear terrorism is determined by the nature of the law of each particular country, economies, and the traditional functions of the military. In countries where the military is the principal agency for handling nuclear materials and has been delegated responsibility for responding to criminal activity associated with those materials, the military will intervene directly and control the government's response to the incident. Specific roles of the military have in many cases been dictated, at least in part, by the economies of the country. Economic constraints on expenditures in many countries result in the military, by the nature of the traditional requirements placed upon that organization, controlling the only expertise, manpower, and physical resources available which are capable of coping with nuclear terrorism. These instances create a situation in which the military, by default, is the principal agency in planning for and responding to nuclear terrorism.

Even in cases where the military is not the only organization in a nation capable of responding, the inherent characteristics of the military provide the basis for the argument that the military should have responsibility and authority in cases of nuclear terrorism. The military is the best trained, equipped, organized, and disciplined force in the nation. The very nature of military planning provides a sound basis upon which contingencies might be developed and implemented as necessary. Military training activities offer a means of maintaining ready-response forces. This combination of resources, planning expertise, and understanding of nuclear weapons and technologies creates a situation in which the military is a viable, and even perhaps desirable alternative to civilian organizations. However, the conscious decision to retain civilian preeminence in planning a response to nuclear terrorism reflects two important factors present in most democratic societies. First, the military is not fully qualified to perform law-enforcement functions, a role which will be thrust upon the armed forces if they assume authority. Second, and most importantly, the maintenance of civil-military traditional relationships is fundamental to and at the foundation of democratic society. For these reasons, the United States military has only a supportive role in responding to nuclear terrorism. Specifically, the United States military has a series of tasks which generally support other agencies:

1. Planning for the prevention of, and response to, theft or sabotage of nuclear weapons under its control, coordinating with ERDA, FBI, and other agencies in responding to an incident, and facilitating the FBI investigative activities with respect to the theft or sabotage of weapons under its control.

2. Development of operational responses to the detonation or widespread contamination from a nuclear weapon or materials under DOD control which does not involve major property damage and poses little threat to the general public.

3. Support of other government agencies as authorized by law and as requested by those agencies.

4. Response to Presidential direction under the Constitution and statutory authority in domestic disasters.

It may be concluded from these roles that the military has been quite limited in its authority with respect to nuclear terrorism, reflecting the general premise that military involvement in domestic situations should be constrained. The military has no direct role beyond those actions associated with its own installations and weapons. Even in cases where military weapons are involved, if stolen or sabotaged, the FBI has the investigative responsibility. Should a military weapon or material cause widespread damage or contamination that endangers the public, it is ERDA that has the lead in directing action.

The military does provide assistance in the form of equipment and to a lesser degree personnel on an as-required basis to other agencies in response to nuclear terrorism. The economics of the situation dictate that the unique resources of the military in terms of personnel and equipment be available to the civilian sector. But even in these situations, control of personnel and equipment often passes to the civilian agency that is directing the operation.

Specific note should be made of existing laws which sanction military intervention into domestic society. The Disaster Relief Act of 1974 and other longer-standing legislation authorize the use of the military in times of civil disorders and disasters, including a Presidential declaration of a state of national emergency. In such cases, the military, although still under the civilian control of the commander-in-chief, may have full authority to control the public. Used with discretion in the past, in terms of the situations where this power has been exercised and the extent of the powers granted, a reign of nuclear terrorism might result in the broader application of these laws.

Even more likely and dangerous to the maintenance of traditional civil-military relationships than the imposition of full martial law is the incremental involvement of the military. A series of related or unrelated incidents of nuclear terrorism over a period of time may well result in increased military participation in the civilian sector. During crises that seem to overwhelm civilian authorities, the tendency is to rely on the military. However, each instance in which the military assumes responsibility for a function previously controlled by civilian authorities is a step toward the permanent alteration of civil-military roles in society. If the present civil-military balance in democratic society is to be guarded, the role differentiation between civil and military must be maintained in all respects. From the above, it is clear that adequate mechanisms do exist in the civilian sector for response to, and control of, nuclear terrorism. These should be reviewed and upgraded, as appropriate, to maintain the traditional civil-military relationship that has existed for 200 years in the United States.

Conclusions

The myths that have arisen with respect to the potential for nuclear terrorism are to a great extent just that—myths. More realistic is the assessment that nuclear terrorism, resulting in significant societal consequences in either the objective or subjective sense, is unlikely. The fact that lower-level malevolent actions are not only possible, but have actually happened, should not weigh too heavily in determining what responses are appropriate for nuclear terrorism. Rather, one must examine the entire range of actions and evaluate each in terms of societal consequences. For the most part, these actions do not require the type of response the military is capable of and prone to provide. Even in democratic societies where the military has a preeminent role in the nuclear industry, consideration should be given to altering existing relationships to permit civil authorities to respond to at least the lower-level threats. In United States society there are adequate mechanisms for controlling and responding to nuclear terrorism without reliance on the military, regardless of the level of malevolent action. The military should be, as it has been in the past, retained in support of the civilian sector.

There is a danger that the military will be seen as the best equipped and manned organization to deal with some aspects of nuclear terrorism. There have been some informal suggestions that the Army form special military SWAT teams to be used in nuclear terrorist situations, such as hostage of a weapon site or a nuclear power plant. It is at that point where the military begins to intervene directly that a certain loss of traditional and democratic norms and values has taken place. Beyond the provision of this type unit, once the military actively engages in controlling and responding to nuclear terrorism, the possibility of later encroachments into the civilian sector becomes more likely. Examples of additional duties with respect to terrorism might be domestic collection of intelligence, massive use of military personnel in searches, military units protecting facilities, and other security measures. These might be necessary at some time in the future, but the situation must be entirely different from the environment that now exists in the United States. Within the current context, increased military participation will only erode the balanced civil-military relationship of today.

Bibliography

Atomic Energy Act of 1954, as amended.

Cohen, Bernard L. *The Hazards in Plutonium Dispersal.* Oak Ridge, Tenn.: Institute for Energy Analysis, March 1975 as cited in U.S. Congress. Committee on Government Operations. *Peaceful Nuclear Exports and Weapons Prolifera-*

tion: A Compendium. Washington, D.C.: Government Printing Office, April 1975.

Department of Defense. *Department of Defense Directive 3025.12, as changed, titled "Employment of Military Resources in the Event of Civil Disturbances."* Washington, D.C.: Department of Defense, 1973.

Department of Justice. *Attorney General's Annual Report.* Washington, D.C.: Government Printing Office, 1975.

Federal Preparedness Agency. *Federal Response Plan for Peacetime Nuclear Emergencies (FRPPNE).* Washington, D.C.: Government Printing Office, 1976.

Mengel, R. William; Greisman, Harvey; Karber, Philip A.; Newman, George S.; Novotny, Eric J.; Whitley, A. Grant. *Analysis of the Terrorist Threat to the Commercial Nuclear Industry.* Vienna, Va.: The BDM Corporation, 1975.

Mengel, R. William. *Terrorism and New Technologies of Destruction: An Overview of the Potential Risk.* Prepared for the National Advisory Committee Task Force on Disorder and Terrorism. Vienna, Va: The BDM Corporation, 1976.

U.S. Atomic Energy Commission. *Proposed Final Environmental Statement, LMFBR (WASH 1535).* Washington, D.C.: Government Printing Office, December 1974.

U.S. Congress. Senate. Committee on Government Operations. *Peaceful Nuclear Exports and Weapons Proliferation: A Compendium.* Committee Print. Washington, D.C.: Government Printing Office, 1975.

Willrich, Mason, and Taylor, Theodore B. *Nuclear Theft: Risks and Safeguards.* Cambridge, Mass.: Ballinger Publishing Company, 1974.

EDGAR O'BALLANCE

Terrorism: The New Growth Form of Warfare

Imperceptibly the world balance of power is being changed by a new, and as yet, hardly recognizable, form of warfare that may replace the more familiar ones. It is that of terrorism, which is developing and spreading under the umbrella of the nuclear stalemate, as neither of the two realistic super-powers want to be simultaneously annihilated by the other. During the present nuclear blackmail period, both superpowers have supported, indi-rectly or otherwise, "alternative" forms of warfare, ranging from the conven-tional, as in the Arab-Israeli War of October 1973, to the guerrilla type, as in Vietnam, in an effort to spread their individual power and influence and to balk those of their opponent; such wars, however, tend to escalate, and with escalation comes the danger of nuclear war brought on by accident, loss of nerve, or chagrin.

Terrorism, politically motivated, carefully planned, and shrewdly di-rected, may provide a substitute means of dominating situations that nor-mally could only be influenced by the use of regular armed forces. The new concept is that nations, governments, and peoples might be terrorized into compliance or complacency. While the full potential of organized terrorism has yet to be realized, spasmodic evidence of its potency stares us in the face almost daily. Skyjacking aircraft, seizing hostages and sometimes kill-ing them, causing explosions with loss of life, and political murders have become commonplace. Incidents such as the massacre of the Israeli ath-letes at the World Olympic Games in 1972 seem to belong to the realm of far-fetched fiction, rather than reality. But modern technology enables tiny groups to wield gigantic powers of destruction, and while Guy Fawkes had to laboriously move thirty-six barrels of gunpowder, today the terrorist travels light, using submachine guns, grenades, and easily transportable plastic explosives. If he does not want to travel at all, he can use the postal service to send letter-bombs to unsuspecting victims.

Internationalization

Until a few years ago, the pattern of terrorism seemed to be a random one with terrorists grouping together for a common political aim (terrorism for criminal purposes is not considered here), usually being of the same nation-ality, race, or persuasion. These included national resistance groups, ex-tremist Zionists in Palestine, the Arab fedayeen in the Middle East, the

Note: This article was printed in *East-West Digest,* June 1976.

Japanese Red Army, those in South America, and other diverse organizations with diverse aims. For some years, money, arms, equipment, and training facilities have been given to terrorist groups by both the Soviet Union and China, but selectively, while the several national Communist parties poured out propaganda in selective support, but declaimed the use of force. The Trotskyists, who in 1938 had formed their Fourth International, at a 1974 congress in Sweden attended by Trotskyist groups from forty nations, decided to embark upon guerrilla warfare and terrorism in South America, especially in Argentina and Bolivia. Already coming out in open support of the PLO in 1967, only days after the end of the Six-Day War, the Fourth International consisted of some 11,000 members, distributed worldwide in small groups who had a form of liaison with each other, and the organization gave assistance at times to other terrorists, such as the Baader-Meinhof group in West Germany.

One of the first distinct evidences of international terrorism became apparent when in May 1974 three members of the Japanese Red Army, landing at Lod Airport in Israel, suddenly killed twenty-four people including Puerto Rican pilgrims and injured another seventy-nine. This caused the fedayeen to claim it had international support, but it was really the beginning of a process of penetration of that movement and others by international terrorists. The process began to coagulate, and in the past two years or so, a number of small terrorist networks of an international character have been unearthed. A culmination was the attack in December 1974, ostensibly an Arab one, on the OPEC HQ in Vienna, when people were killed and hostages taken, including eleven oil ministers. This was led by Carlos Martinez, a South American, known as "The Jackal," who had no direct interest in the Palestine problem, declaring at the time that he was simply "working for world revolution."

Poor Man's Warfare

No longer could there be any doubt that international terrorists were penetrating existing terrorist organizations in an attempt to gain control of them. With minuscule costs, as compared with those of even the smallest military campaign or modern sophisticated weapons, terrorism can be thought of both as "poor man's warfare" and as the weapon of the conventionally weak, capable of being used against strong adversaries by repressed or colonial peoples and others suffering restraints or injustices. The terrorist can strike almost anywhere at any time against any installation or unsuspecting victim, and in his violence, men, women, and children are expendable. Terrorism, against which there seems as yet to be no sure or positive defense, may eventually reach such a scale as to force governments to change their policies and adopt others alien to them.

Certain conditions must prevail, and terrorists need determination, dedication, political motive, money, weapons, support, and, above all, a safe sanctuary. Few countries are prepared willingly to provide such a safe refuge for any and every terrorist, the exceptions being some Arab ones, but many do so selectively. Terrorism seems to thrive best in open democratic states, in the developed countries, where it is aided by the media. The terrorists especially need the media to gain publicity so as to transmit fear and apprehension. Under repressive regimes, where there is a controlled press, deprived of this advantage, they are far less successful. All terrorists are not "kamikaze"-conditioned, and the majority, estimated to be some 80 percent, of terrorist acts are explosions, designed to make a political impact and create fear, while at the same time ensuring maximum security for the perpetrators.

The Individual or the Principle?

There are many instances of terrorists taking hostages, usually to try to obtain the release of imprisoned comrades. This is especially true when a demand for a plane to fly them out to a "sanctuary" country has all too often been hastily met, owing to the government's high regard for human life. In kidnapping and hostage situations, the terrorists want something, apart from public impact, and if they have to kill their victims their effort is self-defeating; therefore, if hostages are not killed in the first moments of the incident they have a good chance of survival, and a study of some 300 cases showed that only 4 percent were killed.

When it comes to bargaining for the life of a hostage, a conflict arises between the safety of the individual and the basic principles of justice and resisting blackmail. Attitudes tend to vary; some governments capitulate immediately, as has happened in Germany and Austria, although their policy recently has hardened, while that of the United States is one of no negotiation with terrorists, but with modifying variations that allow discussions and individuals in certain circumstances to intercede privately. Britain seems to be leading the way in evolving a policy of playing for time, of making a siege a long drawn-out test of nerves which has had several successes. A much harder policy is adopted by Israel, where response is swift and deadly, and where the principle of upholding the law seems to override the importance of the individual.

Definition of Terrorism

The most effective deterrent policy would be to make terrorism unprofitable, and if the terrorists could find no sanctuary, and if all countries universally agreed to punish or extradite those seeking refuge, the problem would subside. In 1972, with this in mind, the United States tried to instigate such a measure in the United Nations, but very few countries were interested, most being anxious to avoid condemning anything that smacked of a "national liberation movement": indeed, many of the UN member states had themselves been born of rebellion or revolution. The first essential point, that of legally defining terrorism, has yet to be overcome, as one man's terrorist is another man's freedom fighter, and many regard certain terrorist acts as being justified. The problem is really a doctrinal, and not a legal one. Unresolved issues include whether refugee terrorists should be handed back to "repressive" regimes that demand their extradition.

At this symposium at Glassboro State College, which met to examine the nature, origins, causes, impact, and consequences of terrorist acts, the participants agreed that it was impossible to arrive at a definition of terrorism, the element of terror being the only discernible thread; and that even if one were produced, it would never be sufficiently acceptable to form a basis for a UN treaty for the apprehension, trial, or extradition of terrorists wherever they may be found, because of diverse political doctrinal views. The main conclusions of the symposium seemed to hover around the opinion that the "cause" was more important than the "effect," and that first of all steps should be taken to remove the "grievances" that gave rise to terrorism.

Little that was positive emerged on how terrorism could be curbed or eliminated, although a U.S. Foreign Service officer outlined the measures taken by the U.S. government in establishing a cabinet-level committee and appointing a special assistant to the Secretary of State for combating terrorism, contingency planning, and coordinating action whenever a terrorist incident occurred. One suggestion was that a "handbook" be issued by the government to certain vulnerable potential hostages, who could be briefed on "hostage survival" techniques. The symposium opinion was that not only was international terrorism here to stay, but that it was expected to be on the increase.

Deterrence and Prevention

The best deterrent is a determination, national and governmental, not to give in to international terrorist blackmail; this would involve preventative measures that mean loss of certain civil liberties. Often it is a question of how much terrorism a country can stand before it will accept restrictions willingly, and one constantly wonders at the almost placid way in which the huge numbers of road deaths are accepted annually. Paradoxically, fear helps the public condition itself to restrictions, and while today it is accepted routine to be searched before boarding an aircraft, a decade ago such an indignity would have caused a mass outcry at such an infringement of liberty.

A realistic attitude toward police and security forces is necessary, and the use of identity cards, finger prints, computer dossiers capable of instant identification of individuals at ports and police stations, and other forms of surveillance and detection have to be seriously considered. A fine balance between restrictive safety and civil liberty would have to be struck. Also, a responsible attitude on the part of the media is required, and while news should be fairly and fully reported, there is no need to glorify terrorist deeds, make folk heroes of terrorists or to show them open sympathy or support. The media have a moral responsibility, too. In the absence of a U.N. treaty to deal with international terrorists, and an international court to try them, nations should consider applying drastic sanctions against states harboring or supporting terrorists; that would include severing all communications, including those by air and sea, ceasing all commercial contact, and withholding any aid, goods, or food.

Nations should build on bilateral agreements, such as that between the United States and Cuba, which has drastically reduced the incidence of skyjacking to Cuba.

The other important weapon is that of intelligence, and governments should establish centers to collect and collate information about terrorists to enable attacks to be forestalled. A successful example occurred in 1973, near Rome airport, when terrorists were detected before they were able to fire two SAM-7 missiles at an El Al airliner. Intelligence is also required to identify potential hostages, victims, or targets, so that security measures can be taken. Although they are being studied in several countries, anti-terrorist measures and techniques are as yet in their infancy, and so far international liaison in this sphere has only been spasmodic because of political conflicts, causing the free flow of antiterrorist intelligence to be only partial.

Nuclear Tailpiece

The rapid progress in technology prompts the thought that one day soon terrorists may steal, manufacture, or take over a nuclear installation, or even explode a nuclear device. Experts soothingly say that such an eventuality at the moment is more of a possibility than a probability because of such factors as the radiation hazard, good security of nuclear elements, and the simple fact that a nuclear bomb cannot just be picked up and taken away under one arm. They say the film *The Plutonium Connection* is science fiction and bears no resemblance to reality. However, one is not comforted by the fact that in 1972, a U.S. congressional inquiry indicated that United States security of nuclear installations and the transport of nuclear fuel needed tightening up. Damage had been done amounting to over $45 million to the "Rocky Flats" reactor, where plutonium and nuclear devices were manufactured; there have been losses in the United States of plutonium, which induces cancer if the fumes are inhaled; and in Austria in 1975 some Iodine 131, a noxious substance, was sprayed in some railway carriages. While only limited information about these incidents is available, one wonders how many more have occurred and never been openly reported.

It is of interest to note that experts admit that two people of average education and intelligence, should they be able to obtain the elements, gaining information from readily available scientific journals and papers, would be able to manufacture a nuclear device within fourteen months. There was the case of the student at the Massachusetts Institute of Technology, obtaining his data from unclassified scientific papers, who designed a viable nuclear device in five weeks. As nuclear materials which could ultimately be used to manufacture nuclear devices now exist in some thirty countries, each of which must have varying standards of security; as plutonium and highly enriched uranium are worth over $12,000 a kilogram; and as black markets exist for scarce high-value products, perhaps the probability has overtaken the possibility. Organized terrorism has a great, even nuclear, potential as a new form of warfare, but the weapons needed to successfully combat it have yet to be forged.

PART VII

Some Historical Aspects of International Terrorism

WILLIAM GLICKSMAN

Violence and Terror: The Nazi-German Conception of Killing and Murder

According to the *Universal Oxford Dictionary*, terror is defined as "the state of being terrified or greatly frightened; intense fear, fright or dread. The action or quality of causing dread . . . ," while violence is "the exercise of physical force so as to inflict injury on or damage to persons or property. . . ." How are these definitions applicable to Nazi Germany in its treatment of conquered countries and populations, and particularly of the Jews? In one sense, the Jews were a part of the overall German plan of world conquest and destruction. Nevertheless, the specific manner and method which the Germans devised for the annihilation of the Jews, physically and spiritually, merit special attention, as do the factors which motivated the Nazi government.

It is not necessary to engage in a historical review of the German nation from the date of its appearance on the world scene. Neither should we compare, in historical terms, the terror and violence of Spartacus in Rome, the Sicarii in ancient Judea, the Jacobins in France, or the Social Revolutionaries in tsarist Russia, no matter how one views these phenomena, with the terror and violence of Nazi Germany.

Mention should be made, however, of the myth of Germanic racial superiority which evolved in the nineteenth century. The Germans believed that they were the bearers of true culture, and that what the other peoples ("races" in German terminology) had to offer was either inferior or injurious. For example, since Slavic culture was viewed as inferior, the Slavs were to be slaves. The Jews, however, were not only inferior, they were harmful to the pure race. Therefore, they had to be eliminated.

This was the German concept of racial anti-Semitism, a case of all-out warfare against logic and against all spiritual values. In addition, there was the attitude of the Church toward the Jews. Attention should be called particularly to the following two essays: "The Silence of Pope Pius XII and the Beginning of the 'Jewish Document,'" by Aryeh L. Kubovy, and "Vatican Policy and the 'Jewish Problem' in 'Independent Slovakia'" (1939-1945), by Livia Rothkirchen. Both were published in *Yad Vashem Studies,* volume VI, Jerusalem 1967 [pp. 7-26 and pp. 27-53]. A document on the Church's attitude toward the Holocaust is found in *The Deputy* by Rolf Hochhuth.

Racial Anti-Semitism

In Germany, the most fanatical Jew-haters have in the main been from among the urban rather than the rural population; that is, they have been members of the so-called educated class. According to Paul Massing, "The most virulent kind of anti-Semitism was spread throughout Germany by teachers, students, industrial and commercial employees, petty officials, professional people, and followers of cults of every variety."[1]

It was this *Mittelstand,* with all its social and economic problems, that was the dominant factor in racial anti-Semitism. (It is a fact that Hitler's votes came from the urban element of the population.) Baptism and even total assimilation did not help Jews. To cite Massing again: "The exigencies of competition were such that many participants felt that no individual merit should enable Jews to gain access to spheres from which it was desirable to eliminate them altogether."[2] It was the agricultural population who accepted Jews, whether willingly or unwillingly. The best-known advocates of the anti-Semitic policy to rescind emancipation and foster discrimination were Treitschke and Stoecker. Wilhelm Marr, the creator of the term *anti-Semitism,* maintained that racial anti-Semitism was needed in order to destroy Jews and "Jewishness" and to prevent the *Verjüdung* of humanity.

One need only look at the catalogue of Jewish misdeeds, which the racial anti-Semite Theodor Fritsch compiled in his *Antisemiten-Katechismus* to recognize the founder and progenitor of Hitler's deeds.[3] He merely followed the teachings of Treitschke and Stoecker, which became a *Weltanschauung.* Marr reinforced this in his *"Sieg des Judentums über das Germanentum."* Toward the end of the nineteenth century, racial anti-Semitism in Germany was becoming an "organized myth."[4]

"Aryan blood, embodying the secret of the highest creation, was glorified as the only guarantee of national survival in a hostile world, and consequently, as a providential promise of world domination."[5] "Hitler's . . . prediction that the nation of purest blood would eventually rule the universe was formulated in the anti-Semitic literature of the 1890's."[6]

"The people which first and most thoroughly rids itself of its Jews and thus opens the door to its innate cultural development is predestined to become the bearer of culture and consequently the ruler of the world." Thus wrote Ahlwardt in 1890.[7]

Hitler merely paraphrased this statement in *Mein Kampf.* "A state which in the days of race poisoning endeavors to cultivate its best racial elements is bound to become some day the master of the world."[8]

Hitler expounded Ahlwardt's theory in this way: "This is the great significance of our long, dogged struggle for power, that in it will be born a new master class, chosen to guide the fortunes not only of the German people but of the world."[9] It is no wonder, then, that the "basic principle formulated by Hitler [was] that man does not equal man, but is divided into gods and beasts."[10]

This was his attitude toward the domination of the world. His theory about Jews is stated so often that one would need volumes to document it. I will therefore limit myself to one of Hitler's statements, made during what Fest calls "The Incubation Period."

The press, art, prostitution, land speculation, syphilis, capitalism as well as Marxism, but also pacifism, the idea of world citizenship and liberalism, these were all camouflages adopted at different times to conceal a world conspiracy; and behind all of them stood the figure of the Eternal Jew. The last obstacle to the Jew's plans was the German nation with its high proportion of Aryan blood.[11]

What about Hitler's henchmen?

"Goebbels found in the increasingly unrestrained practice of anti-Semitism by the state new possibilities into which he threw himself with all the zeal of an ambitious man worried by a constant diminution of his power."[12]

"Heydrich set about seizing and herding together the Jews of Europe and sending them to their death, partly by 'national reduction,' that is to say, by hunger, exhaustion or disease, and partly by physical destruction, either with the aid of murder squads or by the so-called 'special treatment' of mass gassing."[13]

Franck is described as "the man who, in the vulgar phraseology characteristic of the officials responsible for the Final Solution, described his task as being to clean Poland of lice and Jews."[14] "We must not be squeamish when we hear the figure of 17,000 shot."[15]

Heinrich Himmler: "The Jewish people is to be exterminated, says every Party member. That's clear, it's part of our program; elimination of the Jews, extermination, right, we'll do it. . . . This is a glorious page in our history that has never been written and never shall be written."[16]

We know by now that the Final Solution to the Jewish Problem was not adopted at the Wannsee Conference on January 20, 1942, but long before that. On January 24, 1939, Goering empowered Himmler and Heydrich "to solve the Jewish Problem." And on July 31, 1939, he requested them to prepare plans that would once and for all liquidate the Jewish Question. On September 21, 1939, Heydrich issued an order to the S.D. (Sicherheitsdienst—Security Service), a document known at the Nuremberg Trial as PS-3363, in which he differentiated between the final act, that is, the gas chambers, which still had to be kept secret, and measures like the concentration of Jews in ghettos, the establishment of Councils of Elders, and "the ejection of Jews from their economic positions and property."[17] Also, document NG-2586-F, dated December 12, 1941, issued by the Ministry of Foreign Affairs, gave detailed steps to be taken for the extermination of the Jews.[18]

In the summer of 1941, Rudolf Hoess, builder and first commandant of Auschwitz, was summoned to Berlin where Himmler told him:

The Fuehrer has ordered the final solution of the Jewish Problem. We in the S.S. have to carry out this order. . . . Keep this order top secret even from your subordinates. The Jews are the eternal enemies of the German nation and must be exterminated. Every Jew that falls into our hands during this war will be exterminated without exception. If we don't succeed in the destruction of Jewry's biological forces, then some day the Jews will destroy the German nation.[19]

I have quoted two prominent representatives of the Nazi-German ideology in order to underscore the following two aspects: (1) the very nature and essence of the regime, and (2) the nature and essence of the men who carried out its program. Not only the government, but the men who worked for it were bestial. Further citations will support my thesis.

For the Germans, violence and terror were not only acts of racial purification; they were also acts of masculinity. For them it was part of human nature to be aggressive, in the sense that the end justifies the means. Peaceful ways were seen almost as emasculating, something that was natural only for people of inferior quality. Hence the destructive forces were not only culturally condoned, but honored, as a natural German trait.

The aforementioned Hoess wrote the following about Eichmann:

Many times and in detail I spoke with Eichmann about everything in connection with the "Final Solution of the Jewish Problem," not revealing my inner torments. I tried very hard to find out how, deep in his soul, he really viewed the "Final Solution." However, Eichmann was simply obsessed with the idea of the complete extermination of all those Jews who would fall into our hands; nor did he change his mind even when he was drunk and when we were alone. Eichmann told me: "We must, as quickly as possible, without compassion and with cold indifference, carry out this extermination. To show any consideration would be to our disadvantage." In view of these kinds of ideas, I had to bury deep any human restraint.[20]

And lest there be any mistake about this, Hoess himself repeats his "confession." "Yes, I must openly admit that human emotion—after my talks with Adolph Eichmann—seemed almost a betrayal of the Fuehrer."[21]

All these ideas, aims, indoctrinations, conquests, and acts of destruction could be achieved only by terror and violence. No nation would let itself be conquered by any other means. *Violence, terror, and murder became a virtue, an honor.* Anti-Semitism became a law. Physical force operated against spiritual values, not merely to change the social order, first in Germany itself and then in the conquered world, but also to change Homo sapiens, the human species, first the German and then the conquered individual, and to make out of him an instrument in accordance with the order of the national-socialist hierarchy. The next step was to educate and prepare the

German to achieve his goal for his fatherland by these means, to suppress, destroy, wipe out other nations, for only the Nordic Germanic race was worthy of ruling the world. Hitler painted this "new man" as possessing demonic features like those of a beast of prey; "fearless and cruel," as he said, so that he himself "shrank from him."[22]

Terrorism began in Germany proper. Hitler applied this method of violence toward his opponents among his own people. Fest writes: "Even the first signs of terrorism could not mute the jubilation, but rather added to it. The brutal behavior with which the regime celebrated its entry into office . . . placed a value on acts of brutality."[23]

If this method was applied to his own people, how much more intensively would it be used on non-German nations, for example, the Poles, and most particularly, the Jews? For the Jews, violence and terrorism was never a positive goal to strive for, except in the case of defending one's right to live. For that reason there were Jewish self-defense groups against the pogroms in the Ukraine and in Poland in the early 1900s. There were Jews in the partisan units in the forests and in the resistance movements in the ghettos. All these units were formed for defense against those trying to destroy Jews. Even when such a group took the offensive, it was always in response to an attack made upon the Jews by their enemies.

In Jewish tradition peace was primary, along with all the positive values that peace makes possible. The Jew saw an end to his suffering not in the elimination of his enemies, as the Germans saw it, but in a messianic age when everyone would dwell together in peace. This was the age-old belief of both religious and nonreligious Jews. The ultimate goal was a messianism on earth—a world of justice and peace—the vision of Isaiah.

In the Nazi-German scheme of things, the Jews had no place, and any available means were right to use against them, including the unspeakable methods of annihilation which are now so well known. *The sufferings— rather, the death—of the Jews began the very moment the Germans occupied a town with a Jewish community in it.* Looting, destroying Jewish property and Jewish homes, mass executions for the sake of terror, inciting Christian mobs against Jews, burning down synagogues, sacking Jewish institutions—these were the first steps to the Final Solution. Next came the ghettos, with the death penalty for leaving. Unknown numbers of Jewish youngsters paid with their lives for trying to leave the ghetto to bring back a loaf of bread or a potato for their starving families.

After that came the deportations, which brought more indescribable terror and violence, and at the end—the gas chamber. The death penalty applied to everything that was illegal according to the German regulations for the Jews. The draconic laws of ancient Greece pale into insignificance when compared with those of Nazi Germany, completely void of any moral or ethical values.

Mankind's vocabulary, I am afraid, has not yet found the proper term for the Nazi-German crimes against humanity. I am beginning to doubt whether "terrorism" and "violence" can render and explain these crimes. Perhaps "barbarism" would come closer to reality. What can we term the act of a German sergeant in my home town who, on April 20, 1943, shot to death a ten-year-old Jewish child—to honor the birthday of the Fuehrer? What else can we call the act of a German who, during a deportation, shot to death a mother because she had turned back to pick up a coat for her three-year-old? Or the acts of the *Einsatz-Gruppen* in Russia or the SS in the concentration camps?

About the latter, a most expressive statement was made by Rudolf Hoess. Asked whether he was convinced of the guilt of the murdered Jews, he said the question was "unrealistic"—he had really "never wasted much thought on it."[24] On another occasion he said, "I am completely normal. Even while I was carrying out the task of extermination, I led a normal family life, and so on."[25]

Did the Jew, hidden somewhere in the cellar of a ruin in Warsaw, commit any crime by leaving his hiding-place to pick up part of a sacred Torah scroll lying in the street? He was shot to death by a German guard. Did the Jew, somewhere in Volynia, commit any crime by trying to rescue from desecration a Torah scroll from the hands of a German? He, too, was shot to death. What violence was committed by eighty-two-year-old Rabbi Kanal, who resisted deportation to the gas chambers and wrestled with a German guard —so that he could be buried according to ritual law?

One could go on and on with more and more facts. They all add up to an overwhelming truth. Jewish resistance, both the physical and the spiritual, was motivated chiefly by moral and ethical values. The goal of a nation, its culture or religion, can be seen in its actions toward outsiders. It may be said that the way of the Germans was death, not only for the Jews but for civilization itself; the way of the Jews was life, even in the jaws of death.

Let me conclude with Hoess's confession made on April 12, 1947, four days before his execution.

In my loneliness in prison, I came to the bitter realization of what monstrous crimes I had committed against mankind. As the first Commandant of the annihilation camp at Oswiecim [Auschwitz], I implemented part of the terrible genocide plans of the Third Reich. In so doing, I inflicted the most grievous harm upon humanity. For this responsibility I pay with my life. . . . May the fact of revealing and confirming these horrible crimes against mankind and humanity prevent, in the future, even concealed thoughts which could lead to such dreadful events.[26]

Notes

1. Paul Massing, *Rehearsal for Destruction,* a study of political anti-Semitism in Imperial Germany (New York: Harper and Brothers, 1949), p. 75.

2. *Ibid.,* p. 76.

3. *Ibid.,* pp. 77-87.

4. *Ibid.,* p. 80.

5. *Ibid.,* p. 83.

6. *Ibid.*

7. Hermann Ahlwardt, "Der Verzweiflungskampf der Arischen Völker mit dem Judentum, Berlin, 1890." Quoted in Massing, *Rehearsal,* p. 234; see Ahlwardt's speech in *Reichstag* 6 March 1895, pp. 300-305.

8. Massing, *Rehearsal,* p. 84.

9. Joachim C. Fest, *The Face of the Third Reich* (New York: Pantheon Books, 1970), p. 292.

10. *Ibid.*

11. *Ibid.,* p. 11.

12. *Ibid.,* p. 93.

13. *Ibid.,* p. 106.

14. *Ibid.,* p. 210.

15. *Ibid.,* p. 209.

16. *Ibid.,* p. 115.

17. Hapisron Hasofi, *The Final Solution* (Israel: Ghetto Fighters House, 1961), p. 10.

18. Robert M. W. Kempner, *Trzecia Rzesza w Krzyzowym Ogniu Pytan (The Third Reich in Cross-Examination),* (Krakow: Wydawnictwe Literackie, 1976), pp. 210-216.

19. R. Hoess, *Wspomnienia* (Warsaw, 1956), p. 181.

20. *Ibid.,* pp. 141-42.

21. *Ibid.*

22. Fest, *Face of Third Reich,* p. 293.

23. *Ibid.,* p. 39.

24. *Ibid.,* p. 284.

25. *Ibid.,* p. 276.

26. Hoess, *Wspomnienia,* p. 351.

ABRAHAM I. KATSH

Terror, Holocaust, and the Will to Live

In the nineteenth century, Victor Hugo wrote, "War will be dead, the scaffold will be dead, hatred will be dead, frontiers will be dead, royalty will be dead, dogmas will be dead, man will begin to live." But here we are in the twentieth century. War is not dead, nor is the scaffold. Dogmas are not dead, and man does not know how to live. Truly this is a killing century, a century of terror, destruction, and devastation, marred by moral cynicism. The mind of man, trained by generations in science and education, is shockingly applying the results to the perfection of weapons of death. As man's capacity for destruction has become almost unlimited, the need becomes even greater to rekindle his awareness of a higher purpose in human destiny.

Our own generation has witnessed the unthinkable horror of the Holocaust and the systematic extermination of six million Jews—men, women, and children. Indeed Israel Zangwill was right when he said, "The people of Christ have become the Christ of the people."

The whole nation is sinking in a sea of horror and cruelty. . . . I do not know whether anyone else is recording the daily events. The conditions of life which surround us are not conducive to such literary labors. . . . Anyone who keeps such a record endangers his life, but this doesn't alarm me. I sense within me the magnitude of this hour and my responsibility to it. I have an inner awareness that I am fulfilling a national obligation. . . . My words are not rewritten, momentary reflexes shape them. Perhaps their value lies in this. . . . My record will serve as source material for the future historian.

KAPLAN DIARY, January 17, 1942

The Holocaust visited on the Jews was different from all earlier massacres in Jewish history because of its conscious and explicit planning, its systematic execution, and the absence of any emotional element in the remorselessly applied decision to exterminate everyone—*everyone*—to ensure that no one might escape or survive. There was no chance for survival!

The terror inflicted on all Hitler's victims, and his total disregard of the commandment, "Thou shalt not kill"—nor take life without proper trial, nor kill the defenseless, nor harm the innocent—was in this case so violent and unprecedented that it is difficult to grasp how even an insane or half-sane fanatic would find it in himself not only to conceive such a plan, but to decree that "Thou shalt kill" millions and an entire nation without evoking the immediate horrified reaction from the world: "Why, you must be out of your mind!"

How, we wonder, did Hitler obtain the consent and cooperation of his closest associates, the compliance of the mass of executioners, and the resigned acceptance of the very many who did not care or who were unwilling to get into trouble? They all knew fully, partially or dimly, what was going on and chose not to rebel or to ask questions.

A vast literature has been written on the Holocaust, but unfortunately, most of the world even in our own time shies away from reading it. Death is always tragic, but when death by murder is multiplied by six million in five years (counting only the Jewish victims) the deed becomes so enormous, so inconceivable that a new term had to be coined for it: *genocide.*

In a symposium on the Holocaust conducted in 1975 by the Joseph and Sally Handleman Communications Center of Dropsie University in Philadelphia, John Cardinal Krol of Philadelphia and Professor Roy A. Eckardt of Lehigh University took opposing views. Cardinal Krol saw the Holocaust as a logical consequence of modern rationalism, which undermined the Judeo-Christian philosophy of life. Beginning with Descartes, who set up the human mind as the only source of truth, going on to Spinoza, Kant, Hegel, Wagner, and Nietzsche, the cardinal saw a continuous process of degeneration which culminated in Hitler's conviction that morality is "a Jewish invention." The Nazi movement offered a "substitute religion" akin to that of the Bolsheviks and equally as destructive. He pointed to three theses as the essence of Judaism—the One God, human dignity, and freedom. Hitlerism resulted from an attack on these basic principles in our society.

Professor Eckardt, on the other hand, asserted that the ultimate root of anti-Semitism can be understood only as the remnants of the medieval heritage. He cited the long and sad litany of Christian mythology, which created the image of the Jew as a mystical enemy, an image that lent plausibility to Nazi propaganda. Luther continued and aggravated the demonic image of the Jew, transferring the medieval myth to modern Protestants.

It seems that both Cardinal Krol and Professor Eckardt were right. Here, precisely, lies the uniqueness of the Holocaust, for the Jew stood at the boundary, assailed by traditional and racial anti-Semitism at the same time. He was still under the old historic attack for refusing to accept Christianity and at the same time was assaulted from the other side for bringing Christianity to the European World. The two kinds of attack were mutually contradictory in logic, but mutually reinforcing in popular feeling. Without the legacy of hatred from the Christian myths, the Nazi terror and triumph was impossible. Yet, Nazism was undoubtedly a massive assault on Christianity as well.

The Holocaust was indeed made possible by the resurgence of primitive paganism in modern guise when Judeo-Christian tradition was undermined. As for the victims, one is not certain who was the real hero—the soldier who marched in battle complete with war song and all modern arms, or the isolated Jew living under tragic conditions in the ghetto, imbued only with a zeal for life and an indomitable faith at a time when there was no hope. This zeal and struggle to resist when resistance was impossible evinced the noblest expression of the will to live.

To live is one thing, to will to live is another. To live is an assignment to which we are conscripted. The will to live is instinct and choice. But then, to will to live with a firmness of purpose, with courage, and with a taste for life, even in the face of pain, frustration, and adversity is something of a resounding vote of open-eyed confidence in the act of being, because it is an enlightened exercise of preference for life over death. This struggle to resist tyranny and to retain dignity and integrity as human beings, at a time when the conscience of the world seemed mute, evidenced the noblest expression of the will to live, with faith in the Almighty that justice would ultimately prevail.

It is true that the Jews were not the only ones to be exterminated in the course of history. Many nations suffered fates like theirs, but the difference came in the *nature* of the struggle for survival. With the Jewish people in the Nazi concentration camps were some five million inmates, representing every European nation from Norway to Greece, from France to Russia. Regardless of how much better their conditions were as compared to the Jews, life for them, too, was horrible and inhuman, yet there was no active rebellion or even self-defense on the part of these non-Jews. The non-Jewish population in Warsaw, in Lidice, in the Ukraine, in white Russia, and in France did not revolt as civilians. It would seem that the only people, *as civilians,* who actually revolted were the Jews. One would be embarking on a hopeless task were he to search in history books for examples of successful revolts by a civilian minority against a majority.

The Jewish people were a small, weak, impoverished minority between two powerful majorities (the local population and the invading enemy), both equally terrifying and both aiming to destroy them. One common point united the enemies, the conquerors and the conquered—the determination to wipe out the Jew completely. History cannot recall such a predicament— as a minority in Europe, helpless, despised, and ostracized, vulnerable to attack on all sides, and lacking in any potentiality for self-defense.

No foreign enemy ever heard from German lips what Jews heard constantly, "The last bullet will be for a Jew!" With all doors closed to him and without weapons of defense, there was no escape from German hands. In contrast to this hopeless situation of the Jews, the world saw how a western army equipped with the best and most modern weapons in the world was facing Hitler, and yet it took six years of war, with the concentration of all forces and strategic intelligence, to finally overcome the Nazis.

The will to live in such a horrible, tragic situation unparalleled in history is clearly described in a published book—a detailed diary of the Warsaw Ghetto written in Hebrew by Chaim A. Kaplan, which I translated and edited. Kaplan lived in Warsaw with dignity even under the indignities of the Nazis, and while in the ghetto he wrote a daily chronicle that could be called a pragmatic poem, which, although it deplored the evils about him, also cheered the existence of life and toasted the life of existence.

Kaplan writes: "In the eyes of the conquerors, we are outside of the category of human beings. This is the Nazi ideology, and its followers, both common soldiers and officers, are turning it into a living reality. Their wickedness reaches the heights of human cruelty." But the will to live gave Kaplan stamina to record the days of misery for history. Kaplan was sure that there would be a tomorrow.

Some of my friends and acquaintances who know the secret of my diary urge me, in their despair, to stop writing. "Why? For what purpose? Will you live to see it published? Will these words of yours reach the ears of future generations? How?" . . . And yet in spite of it all I refuse to listen to them. I feel that continuing this diary to the very end of my physical and spiritual strength is a historical mission which must not be abandoned. My mind is still clear, my need to record unstilled, though it is now five days since any real food has passed my lips. Therefore I will not silence my diary!

And here now *our* today is *his* tomorrow. Kaplan no longer breathes, but the pulse of his passion for life still beats in the diary bequeathed to us. Written in flawless Hebrew, Kaplan's diary is an imposing document of 1,500 pages, from the years 1939 to the end of 1942, each paragraph having been composed with a sense of danger, lest it be discovered by the German invader. Kaplan is believed to have died in 1942 or 1943, but through his writings, we have the story of ghetto living and an overpowering urge of the will to live.

Kaplan writes:

If anyone in the democratic lands is attempting to write a book on the nature of Nazism, I know without seeing it that the author will fail. Descriptive literary accounts cannot suffice to clarify and emphasize its real quality. And, moreover, no writer among the Gentiles is qualified for this task. Even a Jewish writer who lives the life of his people, who feels their disgrace and suffers their agony, cannot find a true path here. Only one who has examined the various nuances of its administrative and legal tactics in relation to the Jews, unequaled in hard-heartedness, sadistic cruelty, warped sensibility, petrification of human feeling, and stupidity—only such a writer, if he is a man of sensitivity, and if his pen flows, might be able to give a true description of this pathological phenomenon called Nazism.

On April 26, 1942, Kaplan made this entry:

The Nazi terror does not stop. The ghetto dwellers fear for their lives. When they go to bed they are doubtful of seeing the light of day; when they go to work or to attend to their "affairs" they are doubtful of returning home; on their way home, they wonder whether they will arrive safely.

The second type of terror is beatings. They attack Jews who are walking along minding their own business, and in the sight of thousands of passers-by beat them up brutally. If a Nazi crooks his finger at a Jew from a distance, that gesture is a command to approach him immediately and "willingly." The intention is of course to give the Jew a merciless beating.

The third type of terror is humiliation, which is as a matter of course followed by physical violence, too. The moans of the tortured one become merged with the Homeric laughter of the torturer and of his colleagues who witness the incident.

Terror stalks up and down the entire ghetto in all its ferocity. Humiliations, beatings, shootings occur by the dozen every day. No private person can possibly check or count them. I shall, therefore, limit myself to what I personally saw only today.

The will to live was there and is beautifully expressed in Kaplan's words:

Logically we should be dead. According to the laws of nature, we ought to have been completely annihilated. How can an entire community feed itself when it has no place in life? There is no occupation, no activity which is not limited, circumscribed for us. But here again we do not conform to the laws of nature. A certain invisible power is embedded in us in spite of all the laws of nature; if it is impossible to live by what is permitted, we live from what is forbidden. The Jewish community is on a battlefield, but the battle is not conducted with weapons. It is conducted by means of various schemes, schemes of smuggling, and so on. *We don't want simply to disappear from the earth.*

The Jewish people have always lived in material and spiritual straits. Our enemies have always engulfed us to destroy us. Yet Jewish creativity never ceased throughout all the days of our exile. Moreover we created more in the lands of the Disapora than we did in our homeland. This is the strength of eternal Judaism, that it continues to spin the fibre of our lives even in hiding.

This fact, that we have hardly any suicides, is worthy of special emphasis. Say what you wish, this will of ours to live in the midst of terrible calamity is the outward manifestation of a certain hidden power whose quality has not yet been examined. It is a wondrous, superlative power with which only the most established communities among our people have been blessed.

We are left naked, but as long as this secret power is still within us we do not give up hope. And the strength of this power lies in the indigenous nature of Polish Jewry, which is rooted in our eternal tradition that commands us to live. Polish Jewry says, together with our poet laureate Bialik:

> One spark is hidden in the stronghold of my heart,
> One little spark, but it is all mine;
> I borrowed it from no one, nor did I steal it
> For it is of me, and within me.

Pastor Niemüller once remarked, when alas it was all too late:

> First it was the Jew, but I wasn't a Jew
> so I didn't react—
> Then it was the worker, but I wasn't a
> worker so I didn't react—
> Then it was the Catholic, but I wasn't a
> Catholic so I didn't react—
> Then it was me, But I was too late. . . .

The martyrs of the ghettos restored the image of God in man, for they did not go to be slaughtered as sheep; rather, humanity as a whole and in its silence and indifference behaved like lambs.

Instead of being attuned to the inability to remain comfortable and at ease in the presence of those who are in trouble and in pain, man has become attuned to complacency. To fight terror means to think of the past and say to yourself: Remember, it could have been the reverse, *they* here and *we* there.

GEORGE M. KREN

The SS: A Social and Psychohistorical Analysis

The black uniform of the SS with its death's-head insignia has come to symbolize cruelty, while the organization's actions—most particularly its administration of the death camps—have come to identify it with a unique kind of evil.

The first stage in the analysis of the SS held that it was a collection of criminal and sadistic individuals. During World War II, Hollywood productions consistently portrayed SS men as lacking all feeling and being sadistic—though the movie producer never seemed to be aware that this portrayal involved a contradiction. Ellie Cohen, in one of the first serious studies of the psychodynamics of the German concentration camp, defined the men as individuals with a criminal superego. This interpretation reached its logical conclusion during the Nuremberg trials which condemned the SS as a criminal organization and made membership in it *ipso facto* proof of criminal guilt. This almost demonic view of the SS was reinforced by the various memoirs of concentration camp inmates, who—with the exception of Kautzky and Kogon—painted a radically undifferentiated picture of evil.

Nor was this view without a foundation, for the prisoner situation had produced a radical cognitive distortion which led inmates to see only the uniform. Thus Reimund Schnable, who had before becoming a prisoner been a Hitler Youth leader and had some acquaintance with the system from another perspective than that of victim, wrote: "The brutal faces of the men in uniform with the symbol of death on their caps and collars, with a lack of expression, a whip in the hand and a pistol around the belt . . . made an unforgettable impression on the new prisoners." Or an academically educated Jewish prisoner comments: "For me they were all the same. If you asked me how they looked I can only reply: they all wore boots. These dull, evil and uncritical automatons, educated for murder in the school of Himmler will whenever they receive an order carry out their shameful craft." Or:

All SS officers have something dominating, almost like supermen. All SS noncoms are brutal individuals, sadists and robbers who attempt wherever possible to organize for themselves. They are convinced that prisoners are not human beings but rather embody all the evil in the world. The prisoner is some kind of animal for them which must be punished and which must be made to suffer with all means available before one finally exterminates it.

On the basis of the available evidence—memoirs of Wiesenthal, Kogon and, above all, Langebein, as well as the evidence from the Auschwitz trial, it becomes quite apparent that SS individuals were not uniform in their behavior, in personality, and even in values. They included pathological sadists—though these were in a minority—a number who would fit Adorno's model of an authoritarian personality, and even some who were able to relate empathetically to others and even within the structure of the camps attempted to help the victims.

Though false, the view that sees almost all SS individuals as alike is a consequence of a distorted cognition and symbolically contains a larger truth. The more basic truth is that, with rare exceptions, from the point of view of the victim, the personality of the SS really did not matter, for it was the organization and not the psychology of its members that defined its actions. Thus Dicks, who in *Licensed Mass Murder* showed some of the personality structures of individual convicted SS murderers, is on a false track as soon as that personality structure is made a causal agent for the destructive actions of the SS. What explains the SS is not the personality of its members, but a unique constellation of ideology, organization, and situation.

As an organization the SS started out in 1922 serving as Hitler's private bodyguard. The men were selected for their personal loyalty and provided Hitler with more efficient protection than the more casually selected Brown Shirts. The SS received little attention until 1926 when a small formation of some 200 SS men paraded during a Nazi rally. They remained subordinate to the SA, and at that time Himmler played a distinctly secondary role within the top Nazi councils. The organization came into its own only following the Night of the Long Knives in 1934, when Hitler disposed of the new "left" element of the Nazi party in a major purge. Here, for the first time, the Hitler regime publicly acted totally outside the law—executing jailed individuals without trials. After Hitler had been convinced to act by Goring, Himmler, and Heydrich, previously planned operations were set in motion. Lists of names, including top SA leaders, conservative opponents, and a mixed bag of personal enemies were given to special SS and Gestapo squads formed specifically for this "counterrevolutionary" mission. The squads operated freely for three days, killing some of their victims wherever they were found, taking others for one-way rides in the country, and holding many under arrest in police and SS barracks until their execution was approved by higher authority.

Roehm was killed after having been arrested and after refusing to commit suicide. Other victims included Generals von Schleicher and von Bredow, Gregor Strasser, and a leader of the Catholic party, and a close friend of von Papen.

The total number of lesser persons killed or literally kidnapped into concentration camps has never been established, and estimates vary widely. As a consequence of the Roehm purge, the SS was now held together by a new view of loyalty to Hitler even to the point of murder, a fact which overshadowed everything else. Hitler recognized the debt he owed and rewarded Himmler and the SS by giving them increasing power, including complete control over the Gestapo and police. At the same time even formally the SS was now, like the medieval clergy, beyond the control of conventional law, having its own internal courts of honor.

While the personality of its members is not sufficient to explain its behavior, the SS did attract certain kinds of persons. Himmler molded the organization to emphasize its elitism based on race. The men had to trace their lineage back to 1740 and could not marry without permission and then only after investigation of the racial purity of the bride-to-be. Using all sorts of revived pagan rituals, Himmler attempted to create a kind of Jesuit order of the Nazi movement. The organization attracted relatively well-educated, somewhat romantic, and enthusiastic young men. Surprisingly, the SS officer corps included a large number of Ph.D.'s, as well as aristocrats. The young SS recruit was typically someone who recognized that the Weimar state had failed and who rejected Weimar's identification with a humiliating defeat. He usually was a person seeking new values, because the old ones had lost meaning for him, and who could meet the fairly tough physical requirements of the SS.

Peter Loewenberg has argued that the trauma of the generation which experienced World War I as children predisposed them toward supporting the Nazi movement and created a psychological conditioning which helps explain the destructiveness of so much of that generation. Loewenberg's thesis is that:

... the war and postwar experiences of the small children and youths of World War I explicitly conditioned the nature and success of national socialism. The new adults who became politically active after 1929 and who filled the ranks of the SA and other paramilitary party organizations such as the Hitler Jugend and the Bund Deutscher Mädchen were the children socialized in the first world war.

The main events in the history of that generation which Loewenberg cites are the prolonged absence of the parents, "the return of the father in defeat, extreme hunger and privation and a national defeat in war, which meant the loss of the prevailing political authority figure and left no viable replacement with which to identify."

Some detailed evidence about the nature of some SS officers who participated in mass killing is provided by Dicks' previously cited work, which emphasizes the generational experience discussed by Loewenberg and further finds a very consistent presence of a strong, authoritarian, harsh family situation. The character structure of SS officers is further illuminated by Rudolf Hoess's autobiography and Sereny's brilliant study of Franz Stangl,

the commandant of Treblinka. What emerges are individuals who have
difficulty relating emotionally to others and possess rigid character structures, a strong sense of duty, and a belief in ideals and authority; in many
ways they fit the type labeled by Freud as anal.

Above all, we have available two important complementary studies of
Heinrich Himmler by Peter Loewenberg and Bradley Smith. Though different in significant points, both emphasize the essential respectability and
undemonic nature of Heinrich Himmler. Loewenberg, in "The Unsuccessful
Adolescence of Heinrich Himmler," points to Himmler's inability to have
any emotional engagement: "He did not act out of rage or intense hatred. He
never personally committed an atrocity; . . . he had no life of his own."
Having studied Himmler's adolescence, Loewenberg concludes that in this
case, the child was very much the father to the man and that "by concentrat-
ing on the precise details of Himmler's youth and on inferences from the
whole range of his life, . . . adolescent patterns can be identified that would
lead the adult to be a police bureaucrat who treats human beings as feces."
Bradley Smith arrives at a similar conclusion.

His conduct and manner of life make it difficult to accept him at face value as a
master of genocide. He was a fussy little man, pedantic to the point of caricature,
who loved dogs, children and family life. He railed against the timid middle class, but
embodied most of the middle class virtues, especially thrift, sobriety and a belief in
hard work. . . . His taste in art, music, furniture and clothing remained within cozy
bourgeois limits, while his men in their awesome black uniforms personified the new
era of sleek political terror.

An important element of the position the SS acquired after 1934 was that
the SA lost and the SS gained control of the concentration camps, which
had been established in 1933. Under "Papa" Eicke, a cadre of SS men was
trained for concentration camp service in a way that systematized brutality
and destroyed feelings of human sympathy. Moral scruples were identified
with weakness or cowardice and threatened with dire consequences. They
were fighting a ubiquitous enemy—a task which did not permit the selfishness of private emotions. (See Dicks, p. 55.) Theodore Eicke, a commander
of Dachau, created it as an ideal example of a concentration camp. The
trained cadres could be found operating in almost all of the camps which
were established later.

What was striking about SS behavior toward prisoners in the camps—
and this applies both to the original concentration camps and to mixed
camps such as Auschwitz—was the seeming contradiction of brutality
without sadism. Eugen Kogon, in one of the earliest systematic books
about the concentration camp system, argued that one of its main aims was
the brutalization of the SS, an aim eminently and successfully carried out.

After war broke out the SS vastly extended its sphere of influence, most particularly, dispensing terror in the various occupied countries of Europe and administrating the genocide program. It is its latter activity that marks a fundamentally unique event in history and has made the SS the epitome of human destructiveness and cruelty. Its role in the final solution started in the east. Special groups of *Einsatzgruppen*, patterned after those which had already successfully operated against the Polish intelligentsia, were organized to follow on the heels of army combat units and destroy what Nazi leaders called the *Jewish origins of bolshevism*. Trained under the careful direction of Heydrich, these groups were composed of men drawn from all components of the SS. The leadership was varied. Arthur Nebe, a lawyer and head of the criminal police, volunteered as a commander in order to earn a military decoration and gain Heydrich's approval. Otto Ohlendorf, another lawyer, was the idealistic head of an SD department which had investigated corrupt practices. He had earlier refused an assignment but now accepted to avoid the accusation of cowardice. Dr. Otto Rasch, an SD functionary, thought it would advance his career. Walter Stahldecker was an old fighter who had run into difficulties and hoped that field duty would pave the way for his return to a position in internal security.

Using various subterfuges, *Einsatzgruppen* concentrated as many Jews together as possible and set them to work digging trenches which would serve as their graves. Groups were counted off and shot down with automatic weapons. The sheer horror of these actions took its toll on the killers. Notwithstanding all of the indoctrination and literal intoxication with death which sometimes overtook them, the sensory impact of these scenes simply overwhelmed many of those who witnessed them. Grisly dreams involving the sights and sounds of slaughter were the most commonly reported symptom of the nervous strain resulting from these activities.

Many turned to heavy drinking, a few arranged transfer to different units, while at least one, Nebe's chauffeur, committed suicide, and still others, such as SS General von dem Bach Zelewski, suffered nervous breakdowns. Himmler himself, witnessing a scene of Jews being killed at Minsk, became ill. Some claim that as a result of this experience he set into motion plans to find new methods of killing which would be less disturbing to the killers.

Simultaneous with the genocide program in Russia, which continued to be carried out by essentially primitive—that is, manual—methods, a new, more carefully organized effort using methods of mass production of modern industry began to be developed in Poland with the aim of killing all Jews inhabiting areas under Nazi control or influence. It was there that the gas chamber technique was first put into operation on a large scale and eventually perfected to such an extent that body disposal was a greater technical problem than killing.

It was Rudolf Hoess, the commander of Auschwitz, who was responsible for the technical breakthrough—the shift from inefficient carbon monoxide using exhaust from diesel engines to Cyklon B—cyanide gas. He tried it out first on some 600 Russian POWs, and the experiment worked well enough to justify start of construction of new gas chambers which could hold up to 2,000 persons each.

Auschwitz quickly became such an impressive model of efficient production of death that after rebellions occurred at Sobibor and Treblinka, these camps were closed. Killings continued throughout the war using the basic techniques required for mass murder which were established in Russia and Poland during 1941 and 1942. All of the SS accomplishments in this relatively brief period were attained with what modern strategic planners call an excellent economy of force. If all and sundry killing operations are taken together it would seem that at most only approximately 25,000 men could have had direct experience with the extermination program.

Considering that their victims could be numbered in the millions, the estimated number of SS men is quite small. On the other hand, the character of the organization could not fail to be influenced when at least one out of every ten men in it must have been aware of his association in acts of murder extending beyond the pale of the traditions of warfare or even social revolution. This awful and awesome secret of genocide, hardly even discussed among themselves except in a special language of euphemisms—so-called language rules—was shared by all the higher-ranking leaders and a good many of the rank and file.

A perennial question that appears whenever SS actions are discussed is "how are such things possible?" Certainly the view that the SS was made up of psychopaths and sadists is no longer tenable. True, sadism played a role in Auschwitz—but it was secondary to bureaucratically administered violence. The camps provided a situation where such individuals could indulge in their proclivities without fear of punishment, but it was not typical behavior. The judgment of Dr. Ella Lingens that "not more than 5 or 10 percent [of the SS] were pathological criminals in the clinical sense" is borne out by all of the increasing evidence.

How were ordinary men able to perform these actions? On the individual level, everything we know about persons engaged in these monstrous activities testifies to their normality and mediocrity. It is in fact the dreadful normality of the individual that is so frightening, something of the order of "war is hell, but we must cope." The most important explanatory element is that the actions were ordered by an authority considered both legal and legitimate. As Kaltenbrunner said in his defense of them: "Just as I, they believed that they were acting under law." Second, few of the individuals involved, such as Hoess, Stangl (except for a few days before his death), or Eichmann, suffered from any serious form of guilt. The proposition may be formulated that if orders derive from an apparently legal and legitimate authority, individuals will carry them out no matter how violent the action may be with a minimum of psychic damage because they are able to shift responsibility from themselves to those who gave the order.

Many of these discussions suffer from an implied view of human nature that derives from the Enlightenment. This almost Rousseauistic view suggests that man is essentially good—that is, not destructive—and that evil is caused only by social and political forces which distort man's inherent goodness. If we assume that there is a substantial and significant component in what is called human nature which enjoys the suffering and destruction of others, and if we assume that there is no natural instinct of kindness toward others, then SS behavior—and other kinds of behavior in situations where civilizing restraints have been removed—becomes much more explicable.

On the organizational level, an important element supporting SS activities was their ideology of "heroic nihilism," a term designating the desire for action for its own sake without the luxurious encumbrance of values. Ernst Junger has summarized this succinctly when describing the contemporary situation. He concludes that:

> . . . we find ourselves in a final and peculiar phase of nihilism, characterized by the fact that the new order has already advanced, but that the values which correspond to this order have not yet become visible. If one grasps the uniqueness of this situation, then the seemingly contradictory appearance . . . becomes illuminated. One perceives the coexistence of highly developed organizational ability and the total colorblindness towards values, faith without content, discipline without legitimacy. . . . One recognizes why . . . technics and ethics have in such a remarkable manner become synonymous.

This new ideology served the SS well—as it did other paramilitary forces. It led to its members looking inward toward their esprit de corps, toward a sense that they represented the wave of the future and that their actions were the embodiment of a new kind of morality devoid of weak humanitarianism, without the bourgeois overvaluation of life. Heroic nihilism involved a contempt for life—both for their own as well as for that of their victims.

Perhaps the ultimate historical and psychological truth about the meaning of the SS is this: It was an authentic expression of a major element of Western civilization. The fact that it represented a logic of personal morality and individual and collective actions which were so atrocious as to dwarf the imagination should not be allowed to obscure this. In the language of existentialism, one must accept the SS as an "authentic" institution just as R. D. Laing and other psychiatric writers have come to accept schizophrenia as an authentic experience of individuals.

It is no contradiction to recognize that evil can be as existentially authentic as goodness. Indeed, if the SS has taught us anything it should be the reality of evil, a reality which since the Enlightenment seems to have been swept under the rug. Cancer may be evil, but it is a genuine determinant of the human condition, and so it was with the SS. The organization grew, prospered, and attained an institutional status because it provided a historically viable form and logical structure for destructive social-emotional impulses. These impulses have become increasingly familiar to psychiatry, for it has been learned that healthy individuality is difficult to maintain when persons are caught in a flux of historical events which make a mockery of individuality. Not for nothing has this century been called the century of mass man. We may yet end up referring to it also as the century of senseless individual and bureaucratic violence. Thus, it is reasonable to suggest that in the face of profoundly disorienting historical upheavals an elitist, romantic, nihilistic, ferociously aggressive psychology could take form in an authoritarian institutional structure capable of extracting almost total commitment from its adherents. Opaque as many aspects of the SS are when viewed from the standpoint of contemporary social science, its organizational vitality is not obscure. Beneath the viciously nihilistic and doctrinaire ideological skin of the SS there was great scope for technically brilliant intelligence.

To grasp the exceptional persona of the SS, it is useful to conceptualize much of its internal dynamic using contemporary antiestablishment terms; "the revolution within the revolution" and "do your own thing" were also significant realities for the youthful antibourgeois and antiestablishment, mystery-ridden SS. The SS, then, was an organization owing its strength to its authenticity as a form for the expression of an evil potential in Western civilization.

In Germany, it was possible for men to believe in values stressing their own innate superiority, the rightness of exploitation, oppression, violence, and the ultimate extermination of others. In America, about 1971, a majority of a national sample responded to a survey by saying that if ordered to do so they would shoot Vietnamese women and children suspected of aiding the enemy—we know many did so even without orders. If there is never to be another SS in human history, it is not because the predisposing social-emotional factors have disappeared. Rather, the SS will become an antiquarian institution only if the kinds of social-historical, political constellations which made it possible can be avoided and if the energy that went into destruction and death can be deflected toward other goals.

ROBERT H. HEWSEN

"Who Speaks Today of the Armenians?"

The Nazi Holocaust is considered by many to be a purely Jewish experience but this was not entirely the case. While some six million Jews were, indeed, murdered in Hitler's death camps, it has been estimated that at least another six million non-Jews perished in the same camps under identical circumstances. Not all of these were merely miscellaneous victims; non-Jews were to a certain extent the victims of genocide as well. It was the usual Nazi policy to exterminate gypsies for example, while a conscious and deliberate attempt was made to "thin out" the Slavic populations of both Poland and Russia during the German occupation. Nazism, as the world knows, was a racist philosophy, and while this racism, applied to the Jews, resulted in genocide, genocide—actually, in part, and potentially, in toto—could be practiced by the Nazis upon all so-called inferior peoples.

It is natural, of course, for many Jews to think of the Holocaust largely in terms of its Jewish victims, a situation akin to a newscaster identifying only the casualties from his local community when describing a plane crash occurring in another city. But to limit the Holocaust to an anti-Jewish phenomenon, as is sometimes done, is not only historically inaccurate but also unwise. Not only does this ignore the sufferings of other people who were victims of the same atrocity, but it also ignores the fact that the Holocaust was in actuality an atrocity committed against all mankind.

To neglect this does the Jews themselves a disservice, too, for limiting the Holocaust to a solely Jewish experience tends to cut non-Jews off from the real lesson of this monstrous episode in recent history and creates at times in some non-Jews one of the following three responses:

1. The Holocaust was a uniquely anti-Semitic phenomenon, another example of the age-old streak of anti-Jewish sentiment which has run throughout Western history and which would not and could not happen to another people.

2. The Nazis were dynamic, efficient, exciting, and even glamorous figures, except for their unfortunate aberration of being anti-Semitic. This is an attitude—in part fostered by Hollywood films—which I have often encountered among my students.

3. Or, finally, the attitude I have heard, occasionally in Germany and once in Russia, that the massacre of the Jews was not such a bad idea after all and that "it is too bad they didn't get the rest of them."

It is my position that no one could take any of the three attitudes just cited if the true extent and nature of the Nazi atrocities were fully realized.

I once doubted if a plan aimed at genocide, however terrifying it might appear, could be classed as an act of terrorism in and of itself. However, I have changed my view. Apart from the fact that the Holocaust can be seen as an attempt to terrorize the opposition both in Germany and in the occupied terrorities, and apart from the step-by-step terror inflicted upon the victims in particular, there is also, I believe, an implicit long-term terror imposed upon humanity at large by the realization that such a monstrosity could take place in modern times and in one of the supposedly most civilized states of Western Europe—perhaps of Christendom, itself. If the land of Goethe, Schiller, and Beethoven could raise to supreme power a man like Adolf Hitler, whose views had been openly presented in his notorious testament *Mein Kampf,* might we not all be potential victims of the would-be Hitlers and their followers who must surely exist in every civilized state not excluding our own?

A large ad appeared in the *Philadelphia Inquirer* on April 13, 1976. It was paid for by the Federation Allied Jewish Appeal—Israeli Emergency Fund and had as its sole caption, "Until we are all free, none of us is free." I would extend this statement to read "until the world is safe from a racist holocaust, none of us is safe from one." And I submit that we cannot appreciate the truth of this dictum unless we realize that the Holocaust was not a crime perpetrated against the Jewish people alone but one against humanity.

Some years ago, the Israeli Parliament passed a law condemning what it called "crimes against the Jewish people," and it was under this law that the infamous Adolf Eichmann was brought to justice and convicted by an Israeli court. While I both understood and sympathized with the motives behind the drafting of this law, I also saw in its passage a great opportunity unfortunately lost. Experience with the liberal Jewish community in the United States has shown us that it has a clear understanding of the fact that the Jews can be safe and flourish only in a situation where all minorities are safe and are free to flourish. This has led this community to defend the rights of blacks, Spanish-speaking Americans, and other minority groups with a zeal one might only expect in the defense of its own. What struck me about the Israeli law was the marvelous opportunity lost for Israel to have become the first nation in history to enact a law condemning crimes against humanity. The surest guarantee against a recurrence of such a horror is the full recognition by the world that, unless such crimes against all mankind are punished, and punished swiftly and certainly, then we are all potential victims of a holocaust.

In 1915, the ruling circles of the Ottoman Empire engineered the slaughter of nearly one and one-half million Armenians in a massacre which, until World War II, was widely regarded as the greatest single crime in history. No punishment or retribution was ever meted out to the Ottoman authorities responsible for this slaughter and no reparations to the survivors were ever made. Twenty-five years later, Adolf Hitler, discussing his proposed

Final Solution to the Jewish Question, when questioned by a coconspirator as to its impact upon world opinion, is said to have answered, "Who speaks today of the Armenians?"

The Armenians are indeed long forgotten. History has shown that we would be wise not so easily or so quickly to forget the victims of the Nazi Holocaust—Jew and Gentile alike.

BERNARD GROS

Terrorism and Literature

It is not at first apparent that any relationship exists between literature and political assassination, which cloaks itself with such labels as armed conflict, a people's struggle for liberation, and so forth. On the one hand, we are confronted with an action that in three out of four cases spills the blood of innocent people; on the other, we are dealing with the writings of intellectuals well out of the range of violence, intellectuals who have been termed the *whiskierda* in Latin America—a word formed by the contraction of *whiskey* and *izquierda,* which means the left. In other words, *whiskierda* signifies intellectuals "from capitalist countries for whom revolution consists of letting one's hair grow a little longer than others' and discussing world equilibrium over a bottle of whiskey."[1]

This discussion will deal exclusively with revolutionary terrorism, excluding entirely any mention of terrorism on the part of the state. This is terrorism of those not in power, with crimes committed to create a state of permanent threat by striking anyone at any time. This kind of terrorism includes an extremely complex etiology, combining the politics, economy, racial struggles, propaganda, and anger—"the ultima ratio" of the scorned and the desperate—as well as fanaticism and utopian visions.

What is particularly interesting in the relationship between this kind of terrorism and literature is the fact that one finds it frequently accepted by many intellectuals, especially in France, where the intelligentsia is most often of the left, indeed, since 1968, of the extreme left. This acceptance may be explained by the need for prestige and for an audience—both of which have become very restricted since the advent of mass media. Our society is a "society of spectacle," as situationalist Guy Debord has called it, and, in order to be regarded, the French intellectual must provoke and challenge. The greatest challenge in the contemporary world is the act of terrorism. The intellectual who turns to it is thus easily able to garner not necessarily sympathy but at least the attention of the masses. The prestige which the writer formerly enjoyed due to his talent and his knowledge, he now finds through his easy acceptance of crimes which stir the entire world.

To be sure, the literary history of terrorism is a very long one, dating to ancient Greece, if one includes the false myth of Electra. It was Rousseau who furnished, in the eighteenth century, the essence of the formulas favorable to terrorism that are used by literature today: "unhappy peoples, groan-

Note: This article was translated from the French by Muriel Onni, associate professor of foreign languages, Glassboro State College, Glassboro, N.J.

ing under an iron yoke . . . human beings crushed by a handful of oppressors
. . . famished masses . . . the rich who, in peace, feed upon blood and tears . . .
and everywhere the strong armed with the awful power of the law against the
weak." I have just quoted briefly from one of the political writings of Jean-
Jacques Rousseau titled *The State of War*.[2] One might almost think one
were listening to a declaration by a member of the Baader Gang or a Tupamaro or a fedayeen, not to a Sartre or a Domenach.

In everything that Dostoevski wrote in and about *The Possessed*, it
seems obvious that the writer was at one time tempted by revolution and the
nihilistic terrorism of Russia. In 1870 he was delivered from this temptation
and he depicted, unfavorably,. men impregnated with Oriental ideologies,
men "possessed," who seemed prisoners of a mysterious power which led
them on to the most atrocious crimes and to the most delirious utterances.
These characters greatly resemble our contemporary terrorists, especially
Verkhovensky. Even if he admits he is a trickster ("I am a rotter and not a
socialist"[3]) he is nevertheless the romanticized version of an authentic terrorist, Netchaiev.

Netchaiev is the author of the greatest text of terrorist literature. Indeed,
he edited *Rules for a Revolutionary,* which is most often called the *Catechism* in view of its dogmatic character. The whole of contemporary terrorism appears in this book which is veritably a treatise on antimorality and at
the same time a program of action. It is short—containing only twenty-six
items—but nevertheless too long to be used here. It can be found in the
excellent booklet by Jean Barrue, *Bakounin and Netchaiev*, published by
Spartacus in 1971 as well as in my own work, *Terrorism*. Speaking of Netchaiev, Brice Parain noted that he was "a precursor in the area of austerity
and self-denial. For he was not only the murderer of the student Ivanov . . .
but equally, during the long years of his imprisonment which followed, the
unflagging life and soul of resistance."[4]

The so-called *Catechism* resembles a kind of charter of contemporary
terrorism: belief in the effects of terror, Machiavellian preparations for
assassination attempts, the isolation of the terrorist, hatred, suicidal
tendencies, and the like. It is much more straightforward and infinitely
more violent than the 1880 resolutions of the International Association of
Workers, which recommended the use of bombs to propagate revolutionary
ideas. It is much more serious than the proposals of a Laurent Tailhade, in
France, at the time of the attempted assassinations by anarchic terrorists:
"What does the death of a few vague humans matter if the gesture is beautiful?"[5] At the end of the nineteenth century in France, one can find a literature
which prefigures today's terrorist violence in the works of Joseph Dejacque
(who lived for a short time in New York) and of Ernest Coeurderoy—works
which have recently been republished by Champ Libre (40 rue de la Mon-
tagne, Ste. Geneviève, Paris).

I cannot fail to mention, even in this very rapid listing, the Marquis de

Sade, Lautreamont, the futurists, the dadaists, the surrealists—although their works, which elicit visions of modern terrorism, are far too literary in this context. I prefer to concentrate on a few contemporary writers for whom terrorism is a serious consideration worthy of interest.

Here and there, throughout his novels and plays, Jean-Paul Sartre "celebrated" violence, the necessity for destruction, for the purifying or creative crime. In *The Flies*, Orestes kills Ebistha and Clytemnestra, and Orestes "achieves" his liberty. In *The Devil and God*, Goetz affirms himself the equal of God as he organizes his massacres and his conflagrations. Sartre loves to present intellectuals who, as Hoederer says in *Dirty Hands*, "dream of action" (Act 3, scene 4). But, there is more than literature in these Sartrean stances. *The Critique of Dialectic Reason*, in 1960, which is a political/philosophic treatise, clearly states that terror is the cement of fraternity and both the justification and the mover of history: terrorism should therefore be eternal—like revolution—according to some.

It is for this reason that, in an article in the periodical *L'Arc*, a professor of philosophy could write that the philosophy of tomorrow (that is, today, ten years afterward) must be terrorist. Here is the central theme of this astonishing declaration:

The philosophy of tomorrow will be terrorist. Not philosophy of terrorism, but terrorist philosophy, allied with terrorist political practices. . . . Philosophy, abandoning its flirtation with novelists and poets, will rediscover its pure theoretical intent and, on the other hand, political "engagement" will no longer arise from the art of the word, because the society in which we live is condemned to refuse, with more and more savagery to listen to reason. Thus we are being led slowly but surely to the necessity of pure violence, since nothing but terror can now make the bourgeoisie retreat.[6]

Again, one might think one were listening to a spokesman for the Baader Gang or the Japanese Red Army. One can understand why Sartre intends, publicly, to visit Andreas Baader in his prison cell. One understands how, in his preface to extracts from the revolutionary works of Ernest Coeurderoy, Rayoul Vaneigem could write:

As long as it has not been everywhere accepted without reservation that the mercantile system must be destroyed and that a basis for general self-government must be established, no repression, no promise, no reason will succeed in turning revolutionaries away from the idea of the continuing validity of social self-destruction and of the current logic according to which it is better to strike down a policeman than to commit suicide, it is better to kill a judge than to strike down a policeman, it is better to lynch a boss than to kill a judge, it is better to pillage department stores, burn down Wall Street, blow up banks, dynmite nhurches than to lynch bosses; because the rules of the terrorist game are to kill the fuzz, judges, bosses, and most of all the defenders of commerce and the system of death which they impose and which is self-multiplying.[7]

In another work, *Treatise on Savoir-Vivre for Young People*, published in Paris in 1967, the same Raoul Vaneigem points out that good tactics, as far as terrorism is concerned, consist in not respecting the rules of the game of traditional armed conflict[8] but in proving oneself creative, as we, who have become accustomed to real terrorism, have learned to our sorrow.

We are aware that not one of the literary men who have dealt with terrorism has committed any crime—neither Sartre, nor Vaneigem, nor the surrealists. Referring to his own lack of participation in terrorist acts, Vaneigem has written that: "He has spoken in order not to be"[9]—thus allying himself with Rene Daumal, according to whom literature is constituted of "words which one places one after the other in order not to have to act or in order to console oneself for being incapable of acting."[10]

Except for Sartre, it is largely in periodicals or newspapers that one finds declarations, clearly or ambiguously, in favor of violence and terrorism. I shall give three examples only.

In *Modern Times* (Sartre's periodical), in November of 1972, a certain Christian Zimmer reviewed an American film by Gordon Davidson, *The Most Beautiful Day of Our Lives*. Zimmer praised the theme of the film, that is, the reenactment of the trial of nine citizens who had napalmed the files of the Catonsville recruitment office as a protest against the war in Vietnam. He also praised the production and then came to what he called the weakness of the film. They show us—this is essentially what he said—defendants who are after all reincorporated into the capitalist system; they fall into the trap which consists of accepting trial and the legal system. What, according to our brilliant journalist, should have happened? The film should have shown us violence—and I quote: "Everything would have doubtlessly been different, if they had not been content with an *illegal* action, one which did not imperil the authorities, and if they had had recourse to violence (illegality simulates violence). In short, *The Most Beautiful Day of Our Lives* illuminates the insufficiency of protests which do not include the necessity of personal, individual violence, that is, they are divested of ideologies, acquired beliefs, accepted principles. . . ."[11]

The second example is a newspaper commentary concerning the criminal arson of a school in Paris in February of 1973. Briefly, here are the facts: Some youngsters had set fire to their school, which burned rapidly and caused the death of some twenty children. This is the commentary which appeared in the newspaper *Combat* under the byline of Rene Scherer:

These children affirmed themselves by taking vengeance for the meanness and the humiliating constraints they suffer each day. Their gesture has obviously nothing to do with ordinary murder. It is rigorously confined: a symbol of exasperated protest against an institution where, as a matter of principle, the child can never take the initiative, be enterprising, or speak up, where the child dies from lack of social responsibility.

As far as I am concerned, those who died are the children caught in the fire, innocent victims of what I call in my book *terrorism by imitation*.

The final example concerns the murder of some diplomats, including an American charge d'affaires, George Moore, in Khartoum by Palestinian commandos. The journalist and "catholic" writer, Jean-Marie Domenach, wrote in *Le Monde* on March 4 and 5, 1973:

Perhaps the spread of terrorism will result in leading us to an examination of our individual political responsibilities. Also . . . we should consider that terrorism denounces the generalized immobility of societies and institutions, both national and international. . . . Technical proliferation is paid for by immobilization and the reduction of other factors in human development. . . . If, tomorrow, anyone can become a target for believers in a cause which he despises or is ignorant of, this is a sign that no one can henceforth escape his responsibility in deciding which world order is to die and which one it is urgent to create. . . .

We should, as we say in France, make a scrupulous *explication* of these three texts, that is, a commentary in which each word would be studied and illuminated by the total context. I cannot do that here and therefore must take recourse in the more expeditious: I wonder how literature has reached the point of praising crimes which the entire world detests?

It was Albert Camus who supplied the first answer to this question when he wrote in *The Fall* (1956): "The Truth is that every intelligent man . . . dreams of being a gangster and of reigning over society through violence alone. As that is not quite as easy as reading novels might lead one to believe, one generally has recourse to politics and joins the cruelest party."[12] Oh well, I guess that's how it is. Literary terrorism is a sort of aggressive dream; it is the manifestation of mental imperialism. It is also, doubtlessly, an attempt to come to terms with a neurosis. Every intellectual is an unquiet soul, tormented by the absolute, who bears, only with difficulty, the given order of the world. To write about terrorism, to write in favor of terrorism, is in some way to enter into a fantastic world which, at least in appearance, offers escape from the everyday. It is—in dream or in thought, it's all the same—to go from nothing to everything, to live the event in a sort of verbal orgasm, to allow oneself to play out sadistic or masochistic fantasies. It is to "make a habit of the unusual," as Paul Virilio, one of the intellectuals most excited by May 1968, said (in *Common Cause*, no. 2, 1972). The petty hoodlum chooses, as the locale for this terrorism by imitation, Saturday night dances, subway corridors or nightclubs; the writer chooses a sheet of paper.

In a most interesting book written in 1973, which has just been translated into French, Friedrich Kacker unconsciously explains why terrorism is a subject for literature: "The fact of being completely centered on the impression produced or the effect obtained makes terrorism—which is normally based in moral polarization, that is, auto-idealization and condemnation of others—an outstanding dramatic, not to say theatrical, form of aggression, capable of evoking pity and fear, indignation or admiration."[13]

As every writer is a little bit theatrical, as an Arab is theatrical, for example, one can understand that the Arab is a man capable of terrorism and that the intellectual loves to dream of his criminal acts.

It must finally be said that there is an intellectual mode of violence. We are witnessing a veritable cerebral intoxication with the myth of justice, the myth of Electra. All our intellectuals see, in the sister of Orestes, a sort of incarnation of pure virtue. Nothing is more false, since Electra cheerfully violates the rules of pity and of moderation. The intellectuals take from this woman/executioner only the concept of the will to purification through death. Most often this is done unconsciously, but it seems clear to me that those who praise the Baader Gang (Emile Marensin, for example) or the criminal acts of the Palestinians (I have already quoted Jean-Marie Domenach) believe, like Electra, that justice must be obtained at any price, even if it costs the lives of innocent people. As Bernanos wrote shortly before his death, there is an "instinct for justice which is perhaps the most destructive of all." And he added: "Passing from reason to instinct, the idea of justice acquires a prodigious capacity for destruction. As a matter of fact, at that point it is no longer any more justice than the sexual instinct is love. . . . The instinct for justice, with every technical resource at its disposal, is preparing to ravage the earth."[14]

In France, we enjoy the unhappy privilege of possessing moralists of murder. They give themselves over to literary terrorism, to journalistic terrorism, to terrorism "of the stomach" (as Julien Gracq said about a certain writer). Their "activism" proceeds from what could be termed a Faustian mentality in the sense that "in the beginning was action." It is true that this is only vicarious and that their violence is only theoretical—I mean contemplative (it is rare, such as in the case of Regis Debray, that they act in reality)—but it is no less true that this literature nourishes many readers and justifies the most unjust of human actions.

Notes

1. Jean-Paul Richard, *Whiskierda* (Albin Michel, 1973).

2. Jean-Jacques Rousseau, *The State of War* (Pleiade, Ecrits Politiques, vol. III), p. 609.

3. Dostoevski, *Les Possedes* (Pleiade), p. 444.

4. Brice Parain, Introduction to *You Can Kill This Man*, edited by Gall, 1950, p. 6.

5. Laurent Tailhade, *The Myth of the Dandy*, A. Colin, ed., U2, 1972, p. 160.

6. *L'Arc*, no. 30, 1966, pp. 30-32.

7. Rayoul Vaneigem, *For Revolution* (Champ Libre, 1972), p. 29.

8. Rayoul Vaneigem, *Treatise on Savoir-Vivre for Young People* (Paris, 1967), p. 273.

9. Rayoul Vaneigem, *The Real Schism in the Internationale* (Champ Libre, 1972), p. 143.

10. Rene Daumal, *The Analagous Mountain* (Gallimard, 1952).

11. *Modern Times*, November 1972, p. 900.

12. Albert Camus, *The Fall, Complete Works*, vol. I (Pleiade, 1962), p. 1052.

13. Friedrich Kacker, *Terror and Terrorism* (Flammarion, 1976), p. 25.

14. Bernanos, "European Spirit," lecture delivered at the International Meetings in Geneva, 12 September 1946, published in *Why Liberty* (Gallimard, 1972), p. 151.

WILLIAM P. YARBOROUGH

Terrorism–The Past As an Indicator of the Future

For reasons known only to the Creator, terrorism has been with mankind since the beginning. Our own American Declaration of Independence refers to the use of terror by King George III of Great Britain in these terms:

He has plundered our seas, ravaged our coasts, burnt our towns, and destroyed the lives of our people. He is at this time transporting large armies of foreign mercenaries to complete the works of death, desolation, and tyranny already begun with circumstances of cruelty and perfidy scarcely paralleled in the most barbarous ages, and totally unworthy of the head of a civilized nation.

He has constrained our fellow citizens, taken captive on the high seas, to bear arms against their country, to become the executioners of their friends and brethren, or to fall themselves by their hands.

He has excited domestic insurrections amongst us, and has endeavored to bring on the inhabitants of our frontiers the merciless Indian savages, whose known rule of warfare is an undistinguished destruction of all ages, sexes and conditions.

The deplorable conditions imposed by Great Britain on our American forebears seem almost wholesome when compared with the bloody chronicle spelled out carefully and painfully by Alexandr Solzhenitsyn in *The Gulag Archipelago*. The odor of the truly evil base upon which the Soviet Union has been built rises from every page of Solzhenitsyn's epic work. Use of terror as a political instrument was a key element of Lenin's strategy for building the first Communist state. At Lenin's direction, the VECHEKA under Comrade Dzerzhinsky systematically brutalized the Russian public into accepting control by one Bolshevik out of every six hundred in the population of that time. As inhuman as the methods of the VECHEKA might have been, they were mild when compared with the scientific and sophisticated terror mechanisms which were brought into play by its successors: the OGPU (1922-34); the NKVD (1934-43); the NKGB (1943-46); the MGB (1946-53); the MVD (1953); and today's KGB. The tactics, techniques, philosophy, and inspiration for a major part of today's deliberate use of terror as a political weapon radiates from the carefully developed Soviet model. There is no indication on the horizon that Soviet political, military, and psychological power is on the wane. Thus the prospects for the continued flow of moral, physical, and conceptual assistance to terrorist activities inside the non-Communist states of the world are good.

Recent events on the continent of Africa illustrate the skillful orchestration of the Soviet psychological warfare strategy in that important area. Having focused upon and progressively inflamed the "contradictions" which still remain from former colonialism, the Soviet propagandists are again selling the doctrine that a new order can only "grow out of the barrel of a gun." Of even greater help to the proponents of violent resolution of sociological problems is the black-white dichotomy which seems to be made expressly for the architects of civil disorder.

It is ironic that much of the non-Communist world, which largely abhors imposition of the death penalty for even the most heinous crimes, looks with little concern at the mutilation and murder of black and white farmers in Rhodesia by Soviet-trained terror squads. With the help of massive Soviet propaganda, much of the Western world has been led to believe that the ends (black majority rule) do in fact justify the means (terror against innocent men, women, and children). This attitude seems to represent support for Lenin's repeatedly stated conviction that it is always the enemy who is to blame if terror has to be employed against him! The use by revolutionary groups in Africa of Communist-supported terror mechanisms for political purposes should strike a familiar note particularly to students of war and conflict.

It was during the very early 1960s that American Army officers had their first chance to study the strategic and tactical uses of terror. Professor Bernard Fall, the eminent French author and historian, was a frequent visitor at the United States Army's Special Warfare School at Fort Bragg, North Carolina. As a guest lecturer he shocked, outraged, intrigued, and stimulated military students who had assembled to try to unravel some of the mysteries surrounding the catastrophic French military failure in Indo-China. There were times when Fall concealed with difficulty his contempt for the purely conventional soldiers' views as to how irregular forces could be destroyed through classical fire and movement. He argued that the "People's Wars" of Mao Tse-tung, Ho Chi Minh, and Vo Nguyen Giap were multidimensional and thus only partially responsive to bombs and bayonets. There were other facets which the United States military would have to understand if they were to avoid the same pitfalls upon which the French had foundered.

Professor Fall invariably went to considerable lengths to trace the pattern of Vietcong terror and to show that it was aimed at very definite objectives. Both the geographic spread as well as the nature of the terrorists' targets were clues to the strategy which was developing. Vietcong and North Vietnamese terror activities were a clearly identifiable projection of psychological operations. Terrorist acts against certain village officials or government functionaries had the calculated effect of placing varying degrees of psychological stress on others in the same categories as those who had been maimed or killed.

In addition to creating chaotic conditions which worked against popular support for the legitimate government, terrorists' acts both forced and enticed new members into the underground. It was the underground and its auxiliary organizations which became the source for guerrillas, saboteurs, and assassins. From the underground flowed intelligence, logistics, and propaganda support for the growing subversive cancer which would eventually be a major factor in the destruction of the Republic of Vietnam.

Most students of the uses of terror as a weapon of war are familiar with Roger Trinquier's book, *Modern Warfare*. In it, Trinquier holds that terrorism has been the basic weapon with which those whose resources and numbers are small have been able to fight effectively and even to defeat conventional forces. In *Modern Warfare*, Trinquier describes the terrorists' battlefield as being among the civilian population—the targets for attack, generally unarmed and defenseless. The goal of terrorism as a form of warfare is, in Trinquier's view, the control of people.

In a world jammed with Communist propaganda, it becomes a nice task to define the differences between a terrorist "criminal" and a courageous, self-sacrificing "freedom fighter." Implicit in the very statement of this problem is the forecast of more rather than less terrorist activity among the states which are on the Communists' target lists.

The shadow of a rising threat from organized terror now looms over our free and open American society. The ritual that we must now perform prior to traveling by air immediately comes to mind. Thanks to the international brotherhood of terrorists, our luggage and even our persons are searched even though we may be flying but a short distance wholly within the United States on a domestic airline. As a result of the terrorists' bomb which exploded at LaGuardia Airport on December 29, 1975, we no longer have the convenience of lockers in which to cache our baggage.

There is little comfort in the knowledge that the police bomb squad in New York City received 4,183 calls during 1975—an average of one bomb alert every half hour, day and night, throughout the entire year! In twenty-two instances the bomb squad was able to find and disarm the explosive charges in time, but in forty-eight others there was death, maiming, and property damage.

Many Americans are surely asking themselves the question "What is so hideous and bad about our society that it deserves attacks of this kind?" Those of us who are familiar with the political goals of the Marxist-Leninists have little doubt concerning the basic incompatibility between our systems, but not all terrorists are Marxist-Leninist. Why are so many members of the American subversive underground, college-educated intellectuals? Dr. Frederick Schwarz answered these questions brilliantly in his testimony before a Subcommittee of the United States Senate Judiciary Committee on July 5, 1974. Dr. Schwarz holds that the alienation and subversion of certain American intellectuals stems from their persuasion that the American system is in its totality, imperialistic. To quote from his testimony, "The doctrine of imperialism is the ideological serum which transforms the gentle, courteous, humane student, Dr. Jekyll, into the malevolent and homicidal revolutionary, Mr. Hyde." Dr. Schwarz goes on to point out that a major focus of the giant Soviet propaganda machine is upon teaching and spreading the doctrine of imperialism and our American classrooms are lamentably lacking in answers to this corrosive propaganda.

How vulnerable is our society to the strategy and tactics of sabotage, terror, and unconventional attack? In addressing this question, there was a most interesting think piece published by the United States Army War College on this theme in the fall of 1973. Two American colonels, one a Marine, one Army, analyzed the problem under the title "Military Implications of Societal Vulnerabilities." They trace the rise of our interdependent societal structure over the past few decades, to find, not suprisingly, that there are innumerable functions supporting the life of any major United States city and that these functions depend upon others. The modern American system is made up of thousands of interwoven individual activities and enterprises which together serve the entire economy. Interruption or destruction of even minor elements of this vast interdependent complex can cause varying degrees of trauma in the overall system. They record, without further comment being necessary, the case of a single circuit breaker activated by a machine error, plunging 50 million Americans into darkness. They quote from an American newspaper headline the sobering intelligence that two revolutionaries in Chicago had threatened to poison the city's water supply by emptying cultures of deadly bacteria into the main filtration plant. The two colonels then point to the rise in the use of nuclear sources of energy and wonder how the environment these nuclear plants will help to create will stand up in an atmosphere of armed internal violence and sabotage. Their conclusion: Our society is definitely vulnerable to a new kind of threat which has little in common with classical military attack.

The mechanisms for carrying out political kidnappings are present here in the United States and *they are linked to the international subversive underground.* Congressman Ichord has stated that no one can predict with certainty whether political kidnappings will become part of the American scene and if they do, what the results will be. He notes that chaos could follow a wave of such actions and that the very principles upon which the nation is founded could be severely shaken.

The American terrorist organization known as the Weathermen illustrates both the nature of the threat to our society and the problems we shall have to solve if we are going to neutralize the danger it poses. Spokesmen for the Weather Underground have stated repeatedly that terrorism, political assassination, in fact, any kind of violence that is considered antisocial is a legitimate form of armed struggle against the "imperialistic American System."

Although the following statement by Bernardine Dohrn speaking from the Weather Underground has been widely published, it still has a decided impact which is both macabre and ominous:

> All over the world, people fighting Amerikan imperialism look to Amerika's youth to use our strategic position behind enemy lines to join forces in the destruction of the Empire. Now we are adopting the classic guerrilla strategy of the Viet Cong and the urban guerrilla strategy of the Tumpamaros to our own situation here in the most technically advanced country in the world.
>
> . . . We fight in many ways. Dope is one of our weapons. The laws against marijuana mean that millions of us are outlaws long before we actually split. Guns and grass are united in the youth underground.
>
> Freaks are revolutionaries and revolutionaries are freaks. If you want to find us, this is where we are. In every tribe, commune, dormitory, farmhouse, barracks and town-house where kids are making love, smoking dope and loading guns—fugitives from American justice are free to go. . . .

It is not a waste of time to remind ourselves that the Weathermen's threat to use revolutionary violence materialized first on June 9, 1970, when one of their bombs exploded in the New York City Police Headquarters on Center Street. This act was followed by a Weathermen bombing on the Marin County Courthouse in San Rafael, California, a National Guard Armory in Santa Barbara, an ROTC facility at the University of Washington, and a bombing attack on the courthouse in Queens, New York.

On March 1, 1971, the Weathermen bombed the United States Capitol itself. On August 28, Weather Underground bombs exploded in the California Department of Corrections in Sacramento. On May 19, 1972, a Weather Underground bomb was detonated in the Pentagon. In May of 1973, two New York City police patrol cars were destroyed by Weathermen explosive charges. In September 1973, the Weathermen bombed the New York City offices of IT&T. In March of 1974, the offices of the Health, Education and Welfare Department in San Francisco were blasted by Weather Underground bombs. The list goes on and on. Brian Crozier, who directs the Institute for the Study of Conflict in London, has recorded over four thousand bombings and incendiary attacks on banks, schools, and offices which he attributes to this American subversive group of terrorists.

As shocking as the terror tactics themselves is the knowledge that after over five years of intensive search, the countersubversive forces of the United States have been unable to lay hands on the leaders of the Weathermen. The National Lawyers Guild attributes this lack of success in catching the Weathermen's "top brass" to the limitations placed upon electronic surveillance as a result of a United States Supreme Court decision in 1972. The same Supreme Court decision also caused Federal charges to be dropped in several cases involving the Weathermen even though a Federal Grand Jury had handed down indictments. Evidence from wiretaps was just not acceptable under the existing law. It is significant to note that this situation is disturbing to many of our judges, among them Chief Justice Walter H. McLaughlin of the Massachusetts Supreme Court who stated in a Law Day address recently, "I would suggest that we start trying the defendent on his guilt and innocence and stop trying the police on how they got the evidence."

The Weathermen, apparently secure in their assessment that current American legal processes hold little danger for them, have entered into the production of a documentary film in which their revolutionary doctrine and activities are featured. The documentary stars the same Bernardine Dohrn who transmitted the appeal to American youth to fight "American imperialism" from their strategic position "behind enemy lines." The Weather Underground film will be the organization's contribution to the celebration of our Bicentennial. Proceeds from the movie will be applied toward furthering subversive activity against the United States.

One can look with divided feelings at Attorney General Levi's refusal to ask for a subpoena against the producers of the Weather Underground film. On the one hand, it can be maintained that the legal formulas available for the control of subversion are less than adequate. On the other hand, the absolute adherence to the letter of the existing law by the attorney general should be a source of deep satisfaction to Americans who are dedicated to a free and open society.

In international forums where the United States has pushed for and agreed to "deter terrorists by eliminating safe havens for them," our spokesmen could experience some problems in explaining why we have ourselves failed to eliminate safe havens for such movements as the Weather Underground.

The much publicized Congressional investigations of the FBI and of our other security organizations have served both to reduce their prestige in the eyes of the American public and to break some of the fragile threads with which any security system in a democratic state must be painstakingly stitched together over a period of many years.

While the strength of the subversive is being improved through growing international links, the American posture for protecting its institutions and society is suffering more and more from self-inflicted wounds. There is little light at the end of this tunnel. The cure for the situation does not seem to lie within our current concepts of personal freedom.

Bernard Fall, during one of his appearances before a military audience at a senior service college in the early 1960s, postulated a situation which could provide ammunition for a lively discussion between hard-core proponents of civil liberties and other citizens who place equally high value on personal security. Professor Fall put the dilemma like this:

Where is your moral standing as a police officer? You know that this fellow has just placed two bombs in a department store. If these bombs go off, about 50 people will be killed and another hundred will be maimed. Now you have 50 minutes to get information out of that guy as to where he placed those bombs. You have a couple of choices. You can stand on your honor and say "I am not a torturer; I'd rather see 50 people dead and another 100 maimed, perhaps your wife among them, rather than to clout this guy in the face."

As difficult as the physical prevention of terrorist acts may be, gathering evidence necessary to convict a suspect can be even more so. The release of Patricia Swinton by the Federal Court in Manhattan in September of 1975 followed the court's refusal to accept evidence from FBI and police who had infiltrated the antiwar sabotage group for which Swinton had been the chief propagandist. The government's witnesses, labeled *agents provocateurs* by the defense, had gathered evidence to show that the underground organization of which she was a member had bombed federal buildings and corporate offices in Manhattan in 1969. Swinton had been a fugitive for the next five years, but the court declined even to prosecute her for unlawful flight. The *Washington Post*'s report on the Swinton acquittal illustrated another aspect of the American scene which tends to nurture rather than dampen terrorist initiatives. The September 26, 1975, issue of the *Washington Post* carried photographs of a smiling, triumphant Patricia Swinton not only on page 1 but elsewhere, together with the assurance that she was now more firmly than ever committed to radical leftist principles.

There is as yet no discernible national trend toward tightening anything but our mechanical protection against the effects of terrorism. Purely protective measures in a physical sense cannot be successful except in a limited way. As long as the terrorist himself holds the initiative, he can strike wherever and whenever he chooses. It is not possible for protective systems to cover every eventuality. As in antiguerrilla warfare, the underground and auxiliary organizations which produce, nurture, and support the kidnappers, assassins, and saboteurs must be neutralized before action against the visible perpetrators of terrorist crimes can be dealt with decisively. There are various forms of subversive action organizations designed for a variety of tasks. They all have at least one characteristic in common—they are *contrived to avoid detection by law-enforcement and counterintelligence agencies*. While existing and functioning outside the framework of the law, they nonetheless rely upon certain aspects of the law for their continued existence.

Certain American lawyers specialize in defending subversives and revolutionaries. One of these, William Kunstler, is the chief counsel for the Symbionese Liberaton Army members William and Emily Harris. The Associated Press on January 28, 1976, quoted him as saying: "I'm not entirely upset by the assassinations of John F. Kennedy and Robert Kennedy —they were two of the most dangerous men America has produced. I don't disagree with murder sometimes, especially political assassinations."

Kunstler and others of his type know all of the tricks of the legal trade. Their strategy was discussed at an annual convention of the Connecticut Bar Association by one participant who was quoted as saying: "Because of the recent (early 1960s) decisions by the United States Supreme Court, in every criminal case that I defend, I file 30 or 40 motions prior to trial with the result that the prosecutor and the court become so exhausted that I can get any deal I want."

Subversive underground organizations are invariably rigidly compartmentalized. Cellular structure denies wide knowledge among its own members as to the size and shape of the overall organization. "Underground" members of a subversive structure are fully committed to the subversive work of their organization. They are often assisted partially, peripherally, or intermittently by so called "auxiliaries." These may be citizens who knowingly or even unwittingly perform services which in some way support the clandestine subversive organization in its mission.

The amorphous relationship among the criminal cadre of an underground organization and others who may be associated with the subversives across a wide spectrum of nonculpable activities explains the reason why dossiers may be gathered on "innocent" American citizens. To trace the connecting lines which explain the functions and mechanism of a terror organization may take months or years of work, checking every lead, no matter how trivial.

The understandable and traditional emphasis that Americans have placed upon civil liberties has also served to reduce the capability of our security forces to cope with a subversive underground. Terrorist "cellular" organizations often exercise command, control, and coordination through live- and dead-letter drops. Under a system where "one gentleman does not read another gentleman's mail," it is possible for a great deal of conspiracy to be conducted on the very steps of the Supreme Court without the FBI or any security force being the wiser.

It seems that we have not yet achieved that fine balance between measures we must take to prevent destruction of our dynamic society by subversion and those essential to its continuation in its free and open form. This problem may loom in the months and years to come as one of the greatest challenges to the leadership of our nation.

Perhaps what is needed at this juncture is a Congressional investigation of the nature of foreign support to American subversive activities. If this were done with the same fanfare, vigor, and public visibility as was displayed by the Pike and Church committees in their analyses of our security and intelligence services, the American public might be able to make up its own mind as to whether temporary surrender of some civil rights would be justified during the emergency which almost certainly lies ahead.

GORDON RATTRAY TAYLOR

Terrorism: How to Avoid the Future

The first step when trying to determine the future of terrorism is to decide what that future is that must be avoided. In other words, what situation will develop in the absence of any conscious attempt to alter present trends.

We must not, of course, make the mistake of simply extrapolating present trends blindly, since trends often level off or even reverse themselves. However, such leveling off may take a very long time, as in the case of a population growth which has continued unabated for thousands of years. I shall consider only the next thirty years or so, since forecasting for longer periods is so chancy as to be a waste of time and, moreover, people find it hard to take serious threats which will not materialize in their own probable lifetime.

I shall also exclude from consideration unpredictable catastrophes, or lucky breaks, including major nuclear war, a worldwide pandemic, a drastic change in climate, such as might follow an ice-wave in the Antarctic, or the arrival of little green men with advanced ideas and a supply of antiaggression pills.

The current trend in terrorism is one of increase both in geographic scope, numerical frequency, and intensity—perhaps also in ingenuity and subtlety. If this trend continues we may expect to see increasingly varied threats to society, accompanied by more powerful weapons and tools. Bombs will get smaller and more powerful, poisons and mind-blowing drugs more insidious, psychological techniques for converting or brainwashing the victims more effective, and psychological tortures more agonizing. New targets will be attacked: bridges destroyed, perhaps. Air-traffic control centers are an obvious target.

The most probable reaction to such an escalation of violence and terror will be, I suspect, to try to control it rather than to remove the cause. The police will be given new weapons and new freedom. Control of personal movement (already far more elaborate than even fifty years ago) will become quite rigid; many countries already require identity cards and registration with the police. This could become universal. And since identity cards can be forged, tattooing will be the next step—perhaps with a tattoo which only shows under ultraviolet light or other special conditions. At the same time, defensive measures will be developed further. Already there are enclaves within which people can shop and take recreation, rather secure in the knowledge that guards check all those who come in and out. This is not uncommon in buildings and will be extended to whole areas. In Belfast, already, there is a shopping precinct operated on these lines. People venturing outside will notify the security control of their intended route and time of return, and check in by phone. Many will carry radio transmitters or bleepers which will indicate their location at all times. Movement will be safer in groups, recalling the days of the eighteenth century, when armed groups set out from the suburbs to visit the theaters in the heart of town.

All this, and more, is predicated on the assumption that terroristic methods will become more general, more intensive. Is this assumption valid? What forces give rise to terrorism, and what countermeasures might be developed to defuse them? And will they be so developed?

Forces Facilitating Terrorism

I cannot attempt here to make an exhaustive list, so I will just identify a few of the factors which may favor terroristic activity, assuming the motive to perform such acts is there.

EDUCATION

Obviously education makes it easier to conceive and plan acts of terror, easier to set up the necessary organization and contact others, and perhaps it makes awareness of injustice more likely; it may also provide rationalizations and political theories and slogans. Education, in the narrow sense, opens people to demagoguery. Now in the world at large enormous efforts are being made to bring education—basics of reading and writing, plus national history, technical skills, and the like—to more and more people—and often without the education in the arts and humanities which might have a modifying influence. The primitive peasant goes his way, accepting the world as he finds it. Education breeds dissatisfaction. (Don't assume from this that I am opposed to education or even assessing it in an overall way: it's just a pragmatic fact that it favors and will continue to favor the growth of terrorism.)

FREEDOM OF MOVEMENT

Transportation and communications favor terrorism in many ways. First, they make it easier to move in, and to get away. Second, they confine potential victims where they cannot readily be helped. Third, in a much larger sense, freer movement helps to break up communities, and brings people into areas with which they feel little sense of affiliation. Fourth, a world which depends on complex transport and communication systems for the means of life is more vulnerable to destructive acts than a world composed of self-sufficient, self-governing communities. Once again, I don't make a judgment: I just note a fact which is conducive to the growth of terrorism. All signs are that transport will become ever more widely available to more people. That is a plus for terrorism.

TECHNIQUES

The techniques of destruction are constantly improving. More powerful, more compact explosives are the most obvious example. I note that kidnappers now often inject their victims with a soporific drug—much more effective and reliable than old-fashioned chloroform. But no one is going to stop the march of technical progress, and I can readily imagine quite subtle wrecking techniques, such as feeding the wrong instructions to computers, while the CIA and KGB have shown what can be done in the way of concealed weapons, fancy gadgets which could be used for blackmail, and so on. And the case of Patricia Hearst shows what the technique of brainwashing can do.

DECAY OF SOCIAL CONTROLS

The member of a closely knit community is somewhat inhibited from attaining his ends by force, not simply from fear of counterforce—meaning the law and punishment—but also by his need to live with the community afterwards, his dependence upon approval and acceptance, perhaps upon help if he is struck by illness and misfortune. In past times, to be an *outcast* was very serious for it deprived you of this vital support. In the modern world, the perpetrator of an antisocial act can get away to other communities where he can be anonymous, or even be approved. He may even call upon the state which he is attacking to care for him in the hospital, or to support him. It recently turned out that some of the Irish terrorists exploding bombs in Britain had been living on British unemployment insurance. Biting the hand that feeds you no doubt gives an extra kick. I'm sure you'll agree that social controls of this informal kind are becoming and will continue to become less and less effective against alienated individuals.

DECAY OF CONSCIENCE

Perhaps the most important force restraining a person from the wanton wounding and killing of innocent third parties is the built-in restraint we call conscience. I can see that the "freedom fighter" who kidnaps a foreign diplomat in the hope of forcing his government to release his friends from prison (to take an example) can reconcile this with his conscience. I find it harder to understand the Irish Provisional who tosses a bomb into a supermarket where innocent persons, children, and maybe even his own political supporters are shopping. The question needs more detailed discussion, but I think it is beyond doubt that *some* terrorists are pathological personalities, incapable of feeling, actually getting a kick from destruction, even attracted by the idea of a holocaust in which they may themselves perish.

I suspect that the number of such personalities produced by Western (and maybe some Eastern) societies is increasing. The growth of schizophrenia, which is marked by emotional blunting, is a clue. Why this should occur is something I have written about at length in my book *Rethink* and elsewhere. Here I need only say that if the output of pathological individuals is increasing, violence—including terrorism—will certainly increase, too.

To recap: All these five factors, to name no others, are likely to become more marked and thus promote an increase of terrorism and violence over the next twenty or thirty years—education, freedom of movement, techniques of destruction and disruption, decay of social controls, decay of conscience. Don't overlook the obvious point that the terrorists of the year 2000 have already been born. They are *now* undergoing experiences which will turn them toward terrorism.

Motives for Terrorism

The above remarks were prefaced by the statement that these factors would favor terrorism if the motive were there. Are the motives for terrorism likely to weaken or fade away? A good deal has already been said by others on this matter, so I shall only point briefly to trends which seem particularly relevant.

All governments tend to think their policies are wise and right and that those of opponents are wrong; they therefore feel that the use of force and trickery against such opponents is justified. Where critics see no hope of achieving their aims by peaceful means, they are liable to resort to violence, and at this point the pathological types are likely to move in. I don't foresee governments becoming any humbler in the next twenty years or so.

At the same time, we must concede that dissident groups may make demands which are impossible to meet or which would inflict great hardship on another group. It is inevitable that such demands will be resisted—and if they are not, we simply exchange one angry lot of dissidents for another. The Arab-Jewish conflict is a case in point; but even if this is negotiated to a settlement, there are plenty of others coming up.

There are governments which favor a particular group in the community, notably religious groups, racial groups, the rich, landowners, and the like. There are even governments which favor the poor at the expense of the rich, or which favor trade union members at the expense of the self-employed and the retired. As the number of governments multiplies, the number of such conflicts increases. Preoccupied as Americans are with the black-white issue, they may not have noticed what is happening to, say, the Tamils in Sri Lanka.

However, there are two trends to which I want to draw attention. First, the case of governments who are blind to the interests of people in other countries whose lives they can affect. In the modern world, it is increasingly easy for the actions of one country to affect the citizens of another. One can think of cartels to push up the price of raw materials; or of holding big grain reserves when other countries are short of food. One can think of techniques for changing the climate or the dumping of atomic wastes. One can think of over-fishing the sea or punching holes in the van Allen belts. One can even think of bribing foreign government officials, or provoking changes of regime, or of assassinations. I think the world is going to see more and more resentment between countries—and particularly between countries of the poor and rich worlds. And this is the situation I have just referred to, where people feel they cannot influence those who have the power by any means but force.

Finally, I believe that more and more people are fighting for the preservation of cultural identity. This is what powers the Basques, the Welsh, the French in Canada, and many others. The creation of a single world culture—a single clothing pattern, diet pattern, music pattern, and so on—is felt as a loss of personal identity. Hence the demand for devolution. On the whole, governments distrust this demand as a weakening of their power. (In America, of course, the states have always had some devolved power, and states' rights is still a touchy subject.) When Americans ask why European states don't coordinate, they need only look at the American experience. Here again, we have a minority demand which won't go away, but which governments find it hard to take with due seriousness.

The real focus of violence lies in pathological individuals for whom these perfectly valid issues are no more than excuses for violence. They are simply rationalizations. Thus even if governments were suddenly seized with a fit of sweet reason and all demands were met, the pathological terrorists would speedily find some other cause to justify their taste for destruction. In short, discussion of the political motives for terrorism won't get very far. One must also look for the psychological factors and the social patterns for channeling violence.

Feedbacks

Trends produce countertrends. Feedback loops arise. What likely reactions are there to a steady escalation of violence and how effective might they be?

1. The usual reaction is an attempt to control violence by force, by counterviolence. Larger, better-equipped police forces; heavier legal penalties; closer control of the activities of the citizen. A glance at history suggests that this does not work too well.

2. When life becomes unbearably disorganized, people turn to a dictator who looks as if he will be able to restore a measure of normality, however tough his methods. So one possible feedback is a trend to authoritarianism.

3. Another reaction is a trend toward a severer upbringing for children. I believe there are some faint signs of this in Europe. As one child indignantly

said to his parents: "You gave me everything I wanted." He won't repeat the mistake.

4. A religious revival? In the university nearest my home, Bristol, I was told that Christian movements are very strong, and in Cambridge, where I spoke recently, I heard much the same thing. Is this a flash in the pan or a straw in the wind?

5. The feedback for which I should hope would be for a worldwide recognition of terrorism as a symptom of loss of social cohesion and a comprehensive attempt to restore cohesion on a basis of consent rather than indoctrination or force.

Policies for Social Cohesion

Obviously, there is no easy one-shot solution—which is what people always hope for. You have to do a lot of different things in many different fields; I have indicated below the main areas of attack.

At present, the growth of terrorism has not yet been accorded the status of an admitted problem; it is just something which happens. Twenty years ago, pollution was just something that happened; nowadays, in the West, we recognize it as a legitimate focus of concern demanding adequate response. Perhaps this conference is a significant step toward identifying terrorism as a problem. Then, I think we have to distinguish between what we might call *avoidable* terrorism from *unavoidable* terrorism. For instance, I find it easy to understand that an Arab, born perhaps in some kind of transit camp, with little hope of making a satisfying life for himself and fed on stories of injustice, could feel that violence was the only feasible method, and that the alternative was apathy. I find it much harder to understand the Symbionese Army or the Weathermen. Of course, I know there is poverty and injustice, that there are problems of segregation, and I know that one can be psychologically wounded even if brought up in bourgeois luxury—but all the same, in a country with extensive social care, education, opportunity, it really is a different problem. If the rich world can't control violence with all its resources, what hope is there for the poor world? I can't help feeling that Western violence is, in principle, *avoidable* violence.

I'm surprised that we don't devote far more scientific effort to analyzing and learning from the violence which occurs in our society. I would like to see a highly motivated organization, comparable with the NASA, assembling data on every violent episode. When the rocket develops trouble on the way to the moon, a team is formed with the duty to identify the cause and determine measures to avoid a recurrence. An event like the Manson killings calls for equally determined investigative response. In this way, a pool of information about social pathology could be built up. Of course, to apply the knowledge gained would be far harder than in the case of the space race because people outside the organization are affected and emotions are involved. But the fact remains, it is only by objective, organized study that the roots of social cohesion can be traced and legislators convinced. Then small-scale experiments in modifying the social pattern could be attempted. If they worked at all, if any reduction in violence, crime, schizophrenia rates, or social pathology was effected, the idea would begin to spread, and finally would influence other countries.

I suspect that such an investigation—and, of course, we have a great deal of data already in the files about such matters as delinquency, attitudes to authority, racial relations, and so on—would reveal three things: the importance of father figures in the formation of conscience; the importance of giving children an ordered, comprehensible environment; and the importance of local group structure. Social policy would have to be modified to minimize the dissolution of the family group, as well as the regional group. Just as we provide skilled attention to individuals who are in a pathological condition, we may have to assist pathological family groups and local communities.

At the teen-age level, I believe we have to do much more to simplify the transition to adult status, and to provide more opportunities for risk-taking and discovering one's self-respect. Social policy lags far behind sociological know-how here.

And with all this, of course, we must tackle genuine political injustice and resolve supposed injustices. Everyone who has run an office, a factory, or a military or naval unit, or any other organization, knows how often people seize on an apparent injustice simply because they don't know the reason behind it. Above all, we must recognize and respond to the demand for the preservation of cultural identity.

In France, for example, the *departements* were decreed 150 years ago without reference to regional culture areas, and control was highly centralized. The European Cultural Commission is slowly unraveling some of these mistakes, but governments lag behind. Outside Europe, there is still more to do.

Finally, we must learn to work on an international scale. While governments actually finance terrorist groups, or give them training, or allow this to be done, or even promote terroristic acts themselves, and if they give sanctuary to terrorists, the problem cannot be solved. But that raises the insoluble problem of how to get good government!

LEE BRUCE KRESS

Selected Bibliography

This bibliography is not intended to be an authoritative or exhaustive listing. Rather, it is designed to serve as an introduction to the voluminous works on terrorism existent.

Aaron, Harold R. "The Anatomy of Guerrilla Terror," *Infantry,* LVIII, March-April 1967, 14-18.

Abramovsky, Abraham. "Multilateral Conventions for the Suppression of Unlawful Seizure and Interference with Aircraft; Part I: The Hague Convention," *Columbia Journal of Transnational Law,* XIII (1974), 381.

Abu-Lughad, Ibrahim. "Unconventional Violence and International Politics," *American Journal of International Law,* LXVII, November 1973, 100-103.

Achinard, Andre. "La Suisse et les Infractions Non Aeriennes Commises a Bord des Aeronets Civile," *ASDA Bulletin,* no. 3 (1968), 3; no. 1 (1969), 2.

Adelson, Alan. *SDS: A Profile.* New York: Scribner's, 1972.

Aggarwala, Narinder. "Political Aspects of Hijacking," *International Conciliation,* DLXXXVI, November 1971, 1.

Ahmad, Eqbal. "The Theory and Fallacy of Counter-Insurgency," *Nation,* CCXIII (1970), 70.

Aines, Ronald C. *The Jewish Underground against the British Mandate in Palestine,* thesis (1973), Union College, Schenectady, New York.

Akehurst, Michael. "Arab-Israeli Conflict and International Law," *New Zealand Universities Law Review,* V (1973), 231.

Alexander, Yonah, and Kittrie, Nicholas N., eds. *Crescent and Star: Arab-Israeli Perspectives on the Middle East Conflict.* New York: AMS Press, 1972.

Alexander, Yonah, ed. *International Terrorism: National, Regional, and Global Perspectives.* New York: Praeger, 1976.

Alexander, Yonah. *The Role of Communications in the Middle East Conflict: Ideological and Religious Aspects.* New York: Praeger, 1973.

Alexander, Yonah. "Some Perspectives on International Terrorism," *International Problems,* XIV: 3-4, Fall 1975, 24-29.

Ali, T., ed. *The New Revolutionaries: A Handbook of the International New Left.* New York: McClelland, 1969.

Allen, Rodney F., and Adair, Charles H., eds. *Violence and Riots in Urban America.* Worthington, Ohio: Jones Publishing, 1969.

Allon, Yigal. *Shield of David.* New York: Random House, 1970.

Alves, Marcio Moreira. *A Grain of Mustard Seed.* Garden City, N.Y.: Doubleday Anchor Press, 1973.

Alves, Marcio Moreira. "Kidnapped Diplomats: Greek Tragedy in a Latin State," *Commonweal,* XCII, 26 June 1970, 311-314.

Alsina, Gerónimo. "The War and the Tupamaros," *Bulletin Tricontinental,* August 1972.

Amadou, Fode. "Le Tigre, La Guele Ouverte," *Afrique-Asie* 10 March 1975, 51.

Anable, David. "Tackling the International Problem," *Current History,* CLXXX, February 1976, 51-60.

Anable, David. "Terrorism: Violence as Theater," *The Inter-Dependent,* III: 1, January 1976, 1, 6.

Andics, Hellmut. *Rule of Terror.* New York: Holt, Rinehart and Winston, 1969.

Antonius, George. *The Arab Awakening.* Beirut: Khayat, 1955.

Arendt, Hannah. "Ideologie und Terror," in *Offener Horizont: Festschrift für Karl Jaspers.* Munich: R. Piper, 1953.

Arendt, Hannah. *On Revolutions.* New York: Viking Press, 1965.

Arendt, Hannah. *On Violence.* London: Penguin, 1970.

Arendt, Hannah. "Reflections on Violence," *Journal of International Affairs,* XXIII (1969), 1.

Arey, James A. *The Sky Pirates.* New York: Charles Scribner's and Sons, 1972.

Ariel, Dan. *Explosion!.* Tel Aviv: Olive Books, 1972.

Arnold, Theodor. *Der Revolutionare Krieg.* Pfaffenhofen: Ilmgau Verlag, 1961.

Ashab, Naim. "To Overcome the Crisis of the Palestinian Resistance," *World Marxist Review,* 15:5 (1972), 71.

Astorg, Bertrand d'. *Introduction au Monde de la Terreur.* Paris: Editions du Sevil, 1945.

Atala, Charles, and Jacquemin, G. *Le Hijacking Aerien ou La Maitrise Illicite d'Aérnef, Hier, Aujourd'hui, Demain.* Montreal: Lemeac, 1973.

Atala, Charles, and Groffier, Ethel. *Terrorisme et Guerrilla; La Revolte Armee Devant les Nations.* Montreal: Leméac, 1973.

Atwater, James. "Time to Get Tough with Terrorists: An Interview with Brian Crozier," *Reader's Digest,* April 1973, 89-93.

Avineri, Shlomo, ed. *Israel and the Palestinians; Reflections on the Clash of Two National Movements.* New York: St. Martin's Press, 1971.

Azak, Abul Kalam. *India Wins Freedom.* Calcutta: Orient Longmans, 1959.

BDM Corporation, *Analysis of the Terrorist Threat to the Commercial Nuclear Industry,* Washington, Report submitted to the Special Safeguards Study, Nuclear Regulatory Commission, 1975.

Baccelli, Guido Rinaldi. "Pirateria Aerea: Realta Effettiva e Disciplina Giuridica," *Diritto Aereo,* IX:35 (1970), 150.

Bacheller, Don. "Guerrillaism, the Peasantry, and the N.L.F.," *Independent Socialist,* April 1968, n.p.

Bain, Chester A. *Vietnam—The Roots of Conflict.* Englewood Cliffs, N.J.: Prentice-Hall, 1967.

Baker, Robert K., and Ball, Sandra J. *Mass Media and Violence, A Staff Report to the National Commission on the Causes and Prevention of Violence.* Washington: Government Printing Office, 1969.

Baldwin, D. A. "Thinking About Threats," *Journal of Conflict Resolution,* IX (1971), n.p.

Bambirra, Vania, et al. *Diez años de insurrección en América Latina,* Santiago, Chile, 1971.

Band, R. E., "Havana Knows; Castro's Assassins Strike Again," *American Opinion*, XVII, June 1974, 23-25.

Barrie, G. N. "Crimes Committed Aboard Aircraft," *South African Law Journal*, LXXXIII (1968), 203.

Barron, John. *KGB: The Secret Work of Soviet Secret Agents*. New York: Reader's Digest Press, 1974.

Bartos, M. "International Terrorism," *Review of International Affairs*, XXIII, 20 April 1972, 25-26.

Bassiouni, M. Cherif. *Criminal Law and Its Processes*. Springfield, Ill.: Charles C. Thomas, 1970.

Bassiouni, M. Cherif. "Ideologically Motivated Offenses and the Political Offense Exceptions in Extradition—A Proposed Judicial Standard for an Unruly Problem," *De Paul Law Review*, XIX (1969), 217.

Bassiouni, M. Cherif. "International Extradition in the American Practice and World Public Order," *Tennessee Law Review*, XXXVI (1969), 1.

Bassiouni, M. Cherif, ed. *International Terrorism and Political Crimes*. Springfield, Ill.: Charles C. Thomas, 1975.

Baudouin, Jean Louis, Fortin, Jacques, and Szabo, Denis. *Terrorisme et Justice: Entre la Liberte et L'ordre: Le Crime Politique*. Montreal: Editions du Jour, 1970.

Baumann, Carol Edler. *The Diplomatic Kidnappings. A Revolutionary Tactic of Urban Terrorism*. The Hague: Martinus Nijhoff, 1973.

Bayo, Alberto. *150 Questions to a Guerrilla*. Montgomery, Ala.: Air University, n.d.

Beals, Carl. *The Nature of Revolution*. New York: Cromwell, 1970.

Beaton, Leonard. "Crisis in Quebec," *Round Table*, CCXLI, January 1971, 147-152.

Beaton, Leonard. *Must the Bomb Spread?* London: Penguin Books, 1968.

Beckett, J. C. "Northern Ireland," *Journal of Contemporary History*, VI:1 (1971), 121.

Bell, J. Bowyer. "Assassination in International Politics, Lord Moyne, Count Bernadotte, and the Lehi," *International Studies Quarterly*, XVI:1, March 1972, 59-82.

Bell, J. Bowyer. "Dealing with Terrorist Acts," *Intellect*, CIV, May 1976, 551.

Bell, J. Bowyer. "The Escalation of Insurgency: The Provisional Irish Republican Army's Experience, 1969-1971," *Review of Politics*, XXXV:3, July 1973, 398-411.

Bell, J. Bowyer. "The Gun in Europe," *New Republic*, 22 Nov. 1975, 1.

Bell, J. Bowyer. *The Long War: Israel and the Arabs since 1946*, n.p., 1969.

Bell, J. Bowyer. *The Myth of the Guerrilla; Revolutionary Theory and Malpractice*. New York: Knopf, 1971.

Bell, J. Bowyer. *On Revolt: Strategies of National Liberation*. Cambridge, Mass.: Harvard University Press, 1976.

Bell, J. Bowyer. *The Profile of a Terrorist*. New York: Columbia Institute of War and Peace Studies, n.d.

Bell, J. Bowyer. *The Secret Army, The I.R.A. 1916-1974*. Cambridge, Mass.: MIT Press, 1974.

Bell, J. Bowyer. *Terror Out of Zion*, n.p., 1977.

Bell, J. Bowyer. *Transnational Terror*. Washington: American Enterprise Institute for Public Policy Research, 1975.

Bell, J. Bowyer. "Transnational Terror and World Order," *South Atlantic Quarterly,* Autumn 1975, 404-417.

Bennett, R. K. "Terrorists Among Us: An Intelligence Report," *Reader's Digest,* October 1971, 115.

Bennett, R. K. "Brotherhood of the Bomb," *Reader's Digest,* December 1970, 102.

Bennett, Richard L. *The Black and Tans.* Boston: Houghton Mifflin, 1959.

Bennett, W. T., Jr. "U.S. Initiatives in the United Nations to Combat International Terrorism," *International Lawyer,* VII (1973), 753-759.

Beres, Louis Rene. "Guerrillas, Terrorists, and Polarity: New Structural Models of World Politics," *Western Political Quarterly,* December 1974, 624-636.

Bergier, Jacques. *La Troisieme Guerre Mondial Est Comencee.* Paris: Albin Michel, 1976.

Beristain, A. "Terrorism and Aircraft Hijackings," *International Journal of Criminology and Penology,* II (1974), 327.

Berkowitz, B. J., et al. *Superviolence; The Civil Threat of Mass Destructive Weapons.* Santa Barbara, Cal.: ADCON Corp., 1972.

Bern, Major H. von Dach. *Total Resistance.* Boulder, Col.: Panther Publications, 1965.

Bienen, Henry. *Violence and Social Change; A Review of Current Literature.* Chicago: University of Chicago Press, 1968.

Bingham, Jonathan B., and Bingham, Alfred M. *Violence and Democracy.* New York: World Publishing Co., 1971.

Bite, Vita. "International Terrorism," Library of Congress, Congressional Research Service, 31 October 1975.

Black, Cyril E., and Thornton, Thomas P., eds. *Communism and Revolution: The Strategic Uses of Political Violence.* Princeton University Press, 1964.

Black, Edwin F. "If Terrorism Goes Nuclear . . . ," *Washington Report,* May 1976, n.p.

Black, Harold, and Labes, Marvin J. "Guerrilla Warfare: An Analogy to Police-Criminal Interaction," *American Journal of Orthopsychiatry,* XXXVII, July 1967, 666-670.

Black, Robert J. "A Change in Tactics? The Urban Insurgent," *Air University Review,* XXIII:2 (1972), 50-58.

Blackstock, Paul W. *The Strategy of Subversion.* Chicago: Quadrangle Books, 1964.

Blanco Munoz, Agustin. *Modelos de violencia en Venezuela.* Caracus: Ediciones Desorden, 1974.

Blanco Munoz, Agustin. *Revolucion e investigacion social.* Caracus: Ediciones Desorden, 1972.

Bloomfield, Louis M., and Fitzgerald, Gerald F. *Crimes against Internationally Protected Persons, Prevention and Punishment: An Analysis of the U.N. Convention.* New York: Praeger, 1975.

Blumenthal, M. D., and Kahn, R. L. *Justifying Violence—Attitudes of American Men.* Ann Arbor: University of Michigan Press, 1972.

Bocca, Geoffrey. *The Secret Army.* Englewood Cliffs, N.J.: Prentice-Hall, 1968.

Bond, James. "Application of the Law of War to Internal Conflicts," *Georgia Journal of International and Comparative Law,* III (1973), 345.

Borisov, J. *Palestine Underground; The Story of Jewish Resistance.* New York: Judea Publishing Co., 1947.

Boston, Guy D., Marcus, Marvin, and Weaton, Robert J. *Terrorism—A Selected Bibliography*. Washington: National Institute of Law Enforcement and Criminal Justice; U.S. Dept. of Justice, 1976.

Boulton, David. *The Making of Tania Hearst*. London: New English Library, 1975.

Bouthoul, Gaston. "Le Terrorisme," *Etudes Polemolgiques*, No. 8 April 1973, 37.

Boyle, Robert P. "International Action to Combat Aircraft Hijacking," *Lawyer of the Americas*, IV, October 1964, 460.

Boyle, Robert P., and Pulsifer, Roy. "The Tokyo Convention on Offenses and Certain Other Acts Committed On Board Aircraft," *Journal of Air Law and Commerce*, XXX (1964), 305.

Bozakis, Christos L. "Terrorism and the Internationally Protected Persons in the Light of the I.L.C.'s Draft Articles," *International and Comparative Law Quarterly*, XXII (1974), 32.

Brach, R. S. "The Inter-American Convention on the Kidnapping of Diplomats," *Columbia Journal of Transnational Law*, X, Fall 1971, 393-412.

Bradford, A. L. "Legal Ramifications of Hijacking Airplanes," *American Bar Association Journal*, XLVIII (1962), 1034.

Bravo, Navarro M. "Apoderamiento ilícito de aeronaves en vuelo," *Revista Española de Derecho Internacional*, XXII (1969), 788.

Breton, J. M. "Piraterie Aerienne et Droit International Publique," *Revue Generale de Droit International Publique*, LXXV (1971), 392.

Brigham, Daniel T. *Blueprint for Conflict*. New York: American-African Affairs Assoc., 1969.

Brimmel, J. H. *Communism in Southeast Asia*. London: Oxford University Press, 1959.

Brinton, Crane. *The Anatomy of a Revolution*. Englewood Cliffs, N.J.: Prentice-Hall, 1965.

Brodie, T. G. *Bombs and Bombings*. Springfield, Ill.: Charles C. Thomas, 1972.

Brown, Robert K., ed. *150 Questions for a Guerrilla*, Denver, 1963.

Brown, Thomas N. *Irish-American Nationalism*. Philadelphia: Lippincott, 1966.

Browne, Jeffrey T. *International Terrorism: The American Response*, Washington, School of International Service, The American University, 1973.

Browne, Malcom W. *The New Face of War*, Indianapolis: Bobbs-Merrill Co., 1965.

Buchanan, J. R., ed. "Safeguards Against the Theft or Diversion of Nuclear Materials," *Nuclear Safety*, XV, September-October 1974, 513-619.

Buckman, Peter. *The Limits of Protest*. Indianapolis: Bobbs-Merrill, 1970.

Budenz, Louis F. *The Techniques of Communism*. Chicago: Henry Regnery Co., 1954.

Bugliosi, Vincent, and Gentry, Curt. *Helter Skelter; The True Story of the Manson Murders*. New York: W. W. Norton, 1974.

Burki, S. J. "Social and Economic Detriments of Political Violence: A Case Study of the Punjab," *Middle East Journal*, XXV, August 1971, 465-480.

Burnham, James. "Notes on Terrorism," *National Review*, XXIV, 13 October 1972, 1116.

Burnham, James. "The Protracted Conflict," *National Review*, XXV, 5 January 1973, 22.

Burnham, James. "Roots of Terrorism," *National Review*, XXVI, 16 March 1974, 311.

Burton, Anthony M. *Urban Terrorism*. New York: Macmillan, 1975.
Burton, Anthony M. *Urban Terrorism: Theory, Practice, and Response*. New York: The Free Press, 1975.
Byford-Jones, W. *Grivas and the Story of EOKA*. London: Robert Hale, 1959.

Callanan, Edward F. "Terror in Venezuela, 1960-64," *Military Review*, XLIX:2, February 1969, 49-56.
Calvert, Michael. "The Characteristics of Guerrilla Leaders and Their Rank and File," *The Practitioner*. London: December 1973, n.p.
Calvert, P. "The Diminishing Returns of Political Violence," *New Middle East*, LVI, May 1973, 25-27.
Calvert, P. *A Study of Revolution*. Oxford: Clarendon Press, 1970.
Carlton, David, and Schaef, Carlo, eds. *International Terrorism and World Security*. New York: Wiley, 1975.
Carr, Gordon. *The Angry Brigade. A History of Britain's First Urban Guerrilla Group*. London: Gollancz, 1975.
Chaliand, G. *La Resistance Palestinenne*. Paris: Le Seuil, 1970.
Central de Droit International et Association Belge Des Juristes Democrates. *Reflexions sur la Definition et al Repression du Terrorisme: Actes du Colloque: Universite Libre de Bruxelles, 19 et 20 Mars, 1973*, Bruxelles, Editions de l'Universite de Bruxelles, 1974.
Chappell, Duncan, and Monahan, John. *Violence and Criminal Justice*. Lexington, Mass.: Lexington Books, 1975.
Chaturvedi, S. C. "Hijacking and the Law," *Indian Journal of International Law*, XI (1971), 89.
Chauncey, Robert. "Deterrence: Certainty, Severity, and Skyjacking," *Criminology*, XII, February 1975, 447.
Cheng, Bin. "Crimes On Board Aircraft," *Current Legal Problems*, XII (1959), 177.
Chilcote, Ronald H. *Revolution and Structural Change in Latin America: A Bibliography on Ideology, Development, and the Radical Left (1930-1965)*, 2 vols., Stanford: Stanford University Press, 1970.
Chisholm, Henry J. *The Function of Terror and Violence in Revolution, Georgetown University*. Unpublished Master's thesis, 1948.
Clark, Dennis. "Which Way the IRA?," *Commonweal*, XIII (1973), 294.
Clark, Lorne S. "The Struggle to Cure Hijacking," *International Perspectives*, XLVII, January-February 1973.
Clutterbuck, Richard L. *Living with Terrorism*. London: Faber and Faber, 1975.
Clutterbuck, Richard L. *Protest and the Urban Guerrilla*. New York: Abelard-Schuman, 1974.
Clyne, Peter. *An Anatomy of Skyjacking*. London: Abelard-Schuman, 1973.
Coblentz, S. A. *The Militant Dissenters*. South Brunswick, N.J.: Barnes, 1970.
Cobo, J. "The Roots of 'Violencia'," *New Times*, 5 August 1970, 25-27.
Cohen, Bernard L. *The Hazards in Plutonium Dispersal*, Oak Ridge, Tenn.: Institute for Energy Analysis, 1975.
Cohen, G. *Woman of Violence: Memoirs of a Young Terrorist, (1943-1948)*. Stanford: Stanford University Press, 1966.
Colebrook, Joan. "Israel with Terrorists," *Commonweal*, LVIII:1, July 1974, 30.

Conant, R. *The Prospects for Revolution: A Study of Riots, Civil Disobedience, and Insurrection in Contemporary America.* New York: Harper's Magazine Press, 1971.

Condit, D. M., et al. *Counterinsurgency Bibliography,* Washington, Special Operations Research Office, The American University, 1963.

Conley, Michael C. "The Strategy of Communist-Directed Insurgency and the Conduct of Counter-insurgency," *Naval War College Review,* XXI:9 (1969), 73-79.

Conquest, Robert. *The Great Terror.* New York: Macmillan, 1968.

Conrad, Thomas R. "Coercion, Assassination, Conspiracy: Pejorative Political Language," *Polity,* VI (1974), 418-423.

Conte, Aguero, Luis. *!Paredon!.* Miami: Ta-Cuba Printing, 1962.

Coogan, Tim Patrick. *The I. R. A.* New York: Praeger, 1970.

Cooley, John K. "China and the Palestinians," *Journal of Palestinian Studies,* I:2 (1972), 19.

Cooley, John K. "Moscow Faces a Palestinian Dilemma," *Mid East,* XI:3 (1970), 32.

Cooper, H. H. A. "Terrorism and the Media," *Chitty's Law Journal.* XXXIV:7, September 1976, 226-232.

Cooper, H. H. A. "Terrorism and the Intelligence Function," *Chitty's Law Journal,* XXIV:3, March 1976, 73.

Cooper, H. H. A. "The Terrorist and His Victim," *Victimology,* I:2, June 1976.

Copeland, M. "Unmentionable Uses of a C.I.A.; Counterterrorist Activity," *National Review,* XXV, 14 September 1973, 990-997.

Copeland, Miles. *Without Cloak or Dagger; The Truth About the New Espionage.* New York: Simon and Schuster, 1970.

Corning, Peter A., and Corning, C. H. "Toward a General Theory of Violent Aggression," *Social Science Information,* XI:3, 4 (1972), 7.

Cornog, Douglas. *Unconventional Warfare: A Bibliography of Bibliographies.* Washington: Government Printing Office, 1964.

Cosyns-Verhaegen, Roger. *Actualite du Terrorisme; Selection Bibliographique.* Bruxelles: Wavre, 1973.

Coussirat-Coustere, V., and Eismann, P. M. "Enlevement de Personnes Privees et le Droit International," *Revue de Droit International Publique,* LXXVI, April-June 1972, 346.

Craig, Alexander. "Urban Guerrillas in Latin America," *Survey,* XVII:3 (1971), 112-128.

Cross, James Eliot. *Conflict in the Shadows: The Nature and Politics of Guerrilla Warfare.* London: Constable and Co., 1964.

Crowley, Fred R. "Insurgency in the Urban Areas," *Marine Corps Gazette,* LVI:2 (1972), 55-56.

Crozier, Brian. "Anatomy of Terrorism," *Nation,* CLXXXVIII (1959), 250-252.

Crozier, Brian, ed. *Annual of Power and Conflict 1972-73; A Survey of Political Violence and International Influence,* London, Institute for the Study of Conflict, 1973. Similar annuals have been issued for 1973-74, 1974-75, 1975-76.

Crozier, Brian, ed. *New Dimensions of Security in Europe,* London, Institute for the Study of Conflict, 1973.

Crozier, Brian. *The Rebels: A Study in Postwar Insurrection.* Boston: Beacon Press, 1960.

Crozier, Brian. "The Study of Conflict," *Conflict Studies,* no. 7, October 1970.

Crozier, Brian. *A Theory of Conflict.* New York: Charles Scribner's Sons, 1974.

Culley, John A. "Hostage Negotiation," *FBI Law Enforcement Bulletin,* XLIII, October 1974, 10.

Curtis, Lynn A. *Violence, Race and Culture.* Lexington, Mass.: Lexington Books, 1975.

Curtis, Michael, et al., eds. *The Palestinians; People, History, Politics.* Edison, N.J.: Transaction Books, 1975.

Curtis, Richard, and Hogan, Elizabeth. *Perils of the Peaceful Atom.* London: Gollancz, 1970.

Cyr, Anne V. *Cuban Revolutionary Strategy: Lessons Drawn from Insurgency Movements in Bolivia and Venezuela,* McLean, Va., 1970.

Dallin, Alexander, and Breslauer, George W. *Political Terror in Communist Systems.* Stanford: Stanford University Press, 1970.

Davidson, W. Philips. *International Political Communication.* New York: Praeger, 1965.

Davies, Donald M. "Terrorism: Motives and Means," *Foreign Service Journal,* September 1962, 19-21.

Davies, James C., ed. *When Men Revolt and Why,* New York: Free Press, 1971.

Davies, James Chowning. "Toward a Theory of Revolution," *American Sociological Review,* XXVII (1962). 19-21.

Davis, Jack. *Political Violence in Latin America.* London: International Institute for Strategic Studies, 1972.

Davis, M. *Jews Fight Too!.* New York: Jordan, 1945.

Deakin, T. J. *Legacy of Carlos Marighella.* Washington: NCJRS Microogram, 1974.

Deas, Malcolm. "Guerrillas in Latin America," *World Today,* XXIV:2 (1968), 72-78.

Debray, Régis. *Algunos problemas de estrategia revolucionaria.* Buenos Aires: Ensayos Latino-Americanos, 1968.

Debray, Régis. *El Castrismo; La march de América Latina.* Buenos Aires: Ensayos Latino-Americanos, 1968.

Debray, Régis. *Che's Guerrilla War.* Baltimore: Penguin Books, 1975.

Debray, Régis. *La Critique des Armes.* Paris: Editions du Seuil, n.d.

Debray, Régis. *Revolution in the Revolution? Armed Struggle in Latin America.* New York: MR Press, 1967.

De Dios Marin, Juan. "Inside A Castro 'Terror School'" *The Reader's Digest,* December 1964, 119-123.

DeGramont, A. "How One Pleasant, Scholarly Young Man from Brazil Became a Kidnapping, Gun-Toting, Bombing Revolutionary," *New York Times Magazine,* 15 November 1970.

de Onis, Juan. "Isabelita's Terrible Legacy," *New York Times Magazine,* 12 March 1976, 15.

Delmas, Claude. *La Guerre Revolutionnaire.* Paris: Editorial P.U.F., 1959.

Dekel, Ephraim (Krasner). *Shai; Historical Exploits of Haganah Intelligence.* New York: Yoseloff, 1959.

Denaro, Jacob M. "Inflight Crimes; The Tokyo Convention and Federal Judicial Jurisdiction," *Journal of Air Law and Commerce,* XXXV (1969), 171.

Derber, M. "Terrorism and the Movement," *Monthly Review*, XXII, February 1971, 36.

De Rocquigny, Colonel. "Urban Terrorism," *Military Review*, XXXVIII (1969), 93-99.

Dershowitz, Alan M. "Terrorism and Preventive Detention: The Case of Israel," *Commentary*, L, December 1976, 67.

Dillon, Martin, and Lehane, Dennis. *Political Murder in Northern Ireland*. London: Penguin Books, 1973.

Dimitrijevie, Vojin. "Aktuelna Prava Pitanja Medunarodnog Terorizma," *Jugoslovenska Revija za Medunarodno Pravo*, XXI:1-3 (1974), 55.

Dinstein, Yoram. "Criminal Jurisdiction over Aircraft Hijacking," *Israel Law Review*, VII (1972), 195.

Dinstein, Yoram. "Terrorism and Wars of Liberation Applied to the Arab-Israeli Conflict: An Israeli Perspective," *Israel Yearbook on Human Rights*, III (1973), 78.

Dixon, C. Aubrey, and Heilbrunn, Otto. *Communist Guerrilla Warfare*. New York: Praeger, 1954.

Dobson, Christopher. *Black September; Its Short, Violent History*. New York: Macmillan, 1974.

Dody, Lawrence. "Anti-Hijacking Drive Gains Impetus," *Aviation Week and Space Technology*, 19 October 1970, 27.

D'Oliveria, Sergio L. "Uruguay and the Tupamaro Myth," *Military Review*, LIII:4 (1973), 25-36.

Dror, Yehezkel. *Crazy States; A Counterconventional Strategic Problem*. Lexington, Mass.: D.C. Heath, 1971.

Drummond, William J., and Zycher, Augustine, "Arafat's Press Agents." *Harper's*, March 1976, 24.

Duff, Ernest A., and McCamant, John F., *Violence and Repression in Latin America: A Quantitative and Historical Analysis*. New York: Macmillan Co., 1976.

Dugard, John. "International Terrorism: Problems of Definition," *International Affairs*, L:1, January 1974, 67-81.

Dugard, John. "Towards the Definition of International Terrorism," *American Journal of International Law*, LXVII, November 1973, 94-99.

Eave, L. "Political Terrorism: Hysteria on the Left," *New York Times Magazine*, 12 April 1970, 25.

Eayrs, James. *Diplomacy and Its Discontents*. Toronto: University of Toronto Press, 1971.

Eckstein, Harry, ed. *Internal War: Problems and Approaches*. New York: The Free Press, 1964.

Eckstein, Harry. "On the Etiology of Internal Wars," *History and Theory*, IV (1965), 133.

Eggers, William. *Terrorism; The Slaughter of Innocents*. Chatsworth, Cal.: Major Books, 1975.

Ellenberg, Edward. *International Terrorism vs. Democracy*, n.p., 1972.

Ellenberg, Edward. *The PLO and Its Place in Violence and Terror*, n.p., 1976.

Ellenberg, Edward. *Western Democracies vs. Terrorism, A Study of Ineffectiveness,* n.p., 1974.

Elliott, Major John D. "Primers on Terrorism," *Military Review,* October 1976.

El-Rayyes, Riad N., and Nahas, Dunia, eds. *Guerrillas for Palestine; A Study of the Palestinian Commando Organization.* Beirut: An-Nahar Press Services, 1974.

Endleman, Shalom. *Violence in the Streets.* New York: Quadrangle Books, 1968.

Esson, D. M. R. "The Secret Weapon—Terrorism," *Army Quarterly,* LXXVIII (1959), 167-180.

Evans. Alona E. "Aircraft Hijacking: Its Cause and Cure," *American Journal of International Law,* LXIII (1969), 695.

Evans, Alona E. "Aircraft Hijacking: What Is Being Done," *American Journal of International Law,* LXVII (1973), 641-671.

Evans, Alona E. "A Proposed Method of Control," *Journal of Air Law and Commerce,* XXXVII (1971), 171-182.

Evans, Alona E. "Reflections upon the Political Offenses in International Practice," *American Journal of International Law,* LVII (1963), 1.

Faleroni, Alberto D. "What Is an Urban Guerrilla?," *Military Review,* XLVII:1 (1969), 94-96.

Falk, Richard A. "Terror, Liberation Movements, and the Processes of Social Change," *American Journal of International Law,* LXIII (1969), 423-427.

Fallaci, Oriana. "A Leader of the Fedayeen: 'We Want a War like the Vietnam War': Interview with George Habash," *Life,* 12 June 1970, 32.

Fanon, Franz. *The Wretched of the Earth.* New York: Grove Press, 1968.

Farrell, Barry. "A Let-Burn Situation," *Harper's Magazine,* September 1974, 31-36.

Fawcett, J. E. S. "Kidnapping Versus Government Protection," *World Today,* XXVI, September 1970, 359-362.

Felgas, Helio A. Esteves. *Os movimentos terroristas de Angola, Guine, Mocambique (influencia externa),* Lisboa, 1966.

Feierabend, Ivo K., and Feierabend, Rosalind L., eds. *Anger, Violence and Politics; Theories and Research.* Englewood Cliffs, N.J.: Prentice-Hall, 1972.

Feller, S. Z. "Comment on Criminal Jurisdiction over Aircraft Hijacking," *Israel Law Review,* VII (1972), 207.

Fenston, John, and de Saussure, Hamilton. "Conflict in the Competence and Jurisdiction of Courts of Different States to Deal with Crimes Committed on Board Aircraft and Persons Involved Therein," *McGill Law Journal,* LVI (1952), 66.

Fenwick, C. G. "'Piracy' in the Caribbean," *American Journal of International Law,* LV (1961), 426.

Ferreira, J. C. *Carlos Marighella.* Havana: Tricontinental, 1970.

Fick, Ronald L., Gordon, Jon I., and Patterson, John C. "Aircraft Hijacking: Criminal and Civil Aspects," *University of Florida Law Review,* XX (1969), 72.

Fisk, Robert. *The Point of No Return; The Strike which Broke the British in Ulster.* London: Andre Deutsch, Ltd., 1975.

FitzGerald, G. F. "Development of International Rules Concerning Offenses and Certain Other Acts Committed on Board Aircraft," *Canadian Yearbook of International Law,* I (1963), 230.

FitzGerald, G. F. "Offenses and Certain Other Acts Committed on Board Aircraft: The Tokyo Convention of 1963," *Canadian Yearbook of International Law*, II (1964), 191.

FitzGerald, G. F. "Recent Proposals for Concerted Action against States in Respect of Unlawful Interference with International Civil Aviation," *Journal of Air Law and Commerce*, XL (1974), 161.

FitzGerald, G. F. "Towards Legal Separation of Acts against Civil Aviation," *International Conciliation*, DLXXXV, November 1971, 42.

Flores Castro Altamirano, Enrique. *El delito de terrorismo*, Mexico, n.p., 1963.

Fly, Claude L. *No Hope But God*. New York: Hawthorne Books, Inc., 1973.

Forman, J. *Journal, 1955-1962*. Paris: Seuil, 1962.

Franck, Thomas M., and Lockwood, Bert B. Jr., "Preliminary Thoughts Towards an International Convention on Terrorism," *American Journal of International Law*, LXVIII, January 1974, 69-94.

Frank, Gerold. *The Deed*. New York: Simon and Schuster, 1963.

Frank, Gerold. "The Moyne Case: A Tragic History," *Commentary*, December 1945, 64.

Franklin, W. M. *Protection of Foreign Interests*. New York: Greenwood, 1969.

Friedlander, Robert A. "Terrorism," *Barrister*, II, Summer 1975, 10.

Friedlander, Robert A. "Terrorism and Political Violence: Some Preliminary Observations," *International Studies Notes*, II, Summer 1976, 4.

Friedmann, W. "Terrorist and Subversive Activities," *American Journal of International Law*, L (1956), 475.

Friedrich, C. J. "Uses of Terror," *Problems of Communism*, XIX, November 1970, 46.

Fromkin, David. "Strategy of Terrorism," *Foreign Affairs*, LIII:4, July 1975, 683-698.

Galeano, Edvardo. "With the Guerrillas in Guatemala," *Ramparts*, VI:2 (1967), 56-59.

Galula, David. *Counterinsurgency Warfare: Theory and Practice*. New York: Praeger, 1964.

Galyean, T. E. "Acts of Terrorism and Combat by Irregular Forces—An Insurance 'War Risk'," *California Western International Law Journal*, IV (1974), 314.

Garcia-Mora, Manuel R. "Crimes against Humanity and the Principle of Nonextradition of Political Offenders," *Michigan Law Review*, LXII (1964), 927.

Garcia-Mora, Manuel R. *International Law and Asylum as a Human Right*. Washington: Public Affairs Press, 1956.

Garcia-Mora, Manuel R. *International Responsibility for Hostile Acts of Private Persons against Foreign States*. The Hague: Martinus Nijhoff, 1962.

Gaucher, Roland. *The Terrorists, from Tsarist Russia to the O.A.S.* London: Secker & Worburg, 1968.

Gellner, John. *Bayonets in the Streets; Urban Guerrilla At Home and Abroad*. Don Mills, Ontario, Canada: Collier-Macmillan, 1974.

George, A. L., et al. *The Limits of Coercive Diplomacy*. Boston: Little, Brown & Co., 1971.

Gerassi, Marysa N. "Uruguay's Urban Guerrilla," *Nation*, CCIX:10 (1969), 306-310.

Gerbasi, Frank. "Terror in Palestine," *Colliers,* August 1945, 64.

German Federal Republic, Bundestag, Wissenschaftliche Dienste. *Terrorismus und Gewalt: Auswahlbibliographie mit Annotationen,* Bon, Deutscher Bundestag, 1975.

Gertler, Z. J. "Amendments to the Chicago Convention, Lessons from Proposals That Failed," *Journal of Air Law and Commerce,* XL (1974), 225.

Geyer, Georgie Anne. "The Blood of Guatemala," *Nation,* CCVII:1 (1968), 8-11.

Geyer, Georgie Anne. "Guatemala and the Guerrillas," *New Republic,* CLXIII:1 (1970), 17-19.

Gilio, Maria Esther. *The Tupamaro Guerrillas; The Structure of the Urban Guerrilla Movement.* New York: Saturday Review Press, 1972.

Glaser, S. "Terrorisme International et Sus Divers Aspects," *Revue Internationale de Droit Compare,* XXV (1973), 825.

Goldberg, Yona. *Haganah or Terror.* New York: Hechalvtz, 1947.

Goldenberg, Boris. "The Strategy of Castroism," *Studies on the Soviet Union* (Munich), VIII:2 (1968), 127-145.

Gomez, Alberto. "The Revolutionary Forces of Colombia and Their Perspectives," *World Marxist Review* (Toronto), X:4 (1967), 59-67.

Gonzàlez Lapayre, Edison. *Aspectos jurídicos del terrorismo.* Montevideo: A. M. Fernandez, 1972.

Gonzàlez Lapayre, Edison. "El secuestro de diplomáticos y consules," *Revista Uruguaya de Derecho International,* I (1972), 161.

Goodhart, Philip. *The Climate of Collapse: The Terrorist Threat to Britain and Her Allies.* Richmond, Eng.: Foreign Affairs Publishing Co., 1975.

Goodsell, James Nelson. "Guatemala: Edge of an Abyss?," *Current History,* LXII:366 (1972), 104-108.

Goodsell, James N. "Terrorism in Latin America," *Commentator,* March 1966, 9.

Gott, Richard. *Guerrilla Movements in Latin America.* London: Thomas Nelson and Sons, 1970.

Gott, Richard. "Latin America Guerrillas," *Listener,* LXXXIV:2166 (1970), 437-440.

Great Britain, Commission on Legal Procedures to Deal with Terrorist Activities in North Ireland, *Report,* London, H.M.S.O., 1972.

Great Britain, Committee of Privy Counsellors Appointed to Consider Authorized Procedures for the Interrogation of Persons Suspected of Terrorism, *Report,* London, H.M.S.O., 1972.

Green, G. *Terrorism—Is It Revolutionary?* New York: Outlook Publications, 1970.

Green, L. C. *The Nature and Control of International Terrorism,* Atlanta, University of Atlanta, Department of Political Science, Occasional Paper, no. 1, 1974.

Green, Nan. "Revolutionary Upsurge in Latin America," *Marxism Today* (Toronto), XII:2 (1968), 38-45.

Greene, Thomas H. *Comparative Revolutionary Movements.* Englewood Cliffs, N.J.: Prentice-Hall, 1974.

Greene, T. N., ed. *The Guerrilla—And How to Fight Him.* New York: Praeger, 1962.

Greene, W., and Cockburn, A., "Case of the Paranoid Hijacker," *Esquire,* July 1975, 10.

Greene, Wase. "The Militants Who Play with Dynamite," *New York Times Magazine,* 25 October 1970, 38.

Grivas-Dighenis, Gen. George. *Guerrilla Warfare and EOKA's Struggle*. London: Longmans, Green, 1964.

Gros, Bernard. *Le Terrorisme,* Paris: Ed. Hatier, 1976,

Gross, Feliks. *The Revolutionary Party; Essays in the Sociology of Politics*. Westport, Conn.: Greenwood Press, 1974.

Gross, Feliks. *The Seizure of Political Power in a Century of Revolutions*. New York: Philosophical Library, 1958.

Gross, Feliks. *Violence in Politics, Terror, and Political Assassination in Eastern Europe and Russia*. The Hague: Mouton, 1972.

Gross, Feliks. *World Politics and Tension Areas*. New York: New York University Press, 1966.

Gross, Leo, "International Terrorism and International Criminal Jurisdiction," *American Journal of International Law*, LXVII, 11 July 1973, 506-511.

Grundy, Kenneth W. *Guerrilla Struggle in Africa; An Analysis and Preview*. New York: Grossman, 1971.

Grundy, Kenneth W., and Weinstein, M. A. *Ideologies of Violence*. Columbus, Ohio: Ohio State University Press, 1975.

Gude, E. W. "Dealing with Worldwide Terror," *Society*, X, January 1973, 9.

Guevara, Ernesto. *Obras completes*, 5 vols., Buenos Aires: Editiones Argentinas, 1973.

Guillen, Abraham. *Desafio al pentagono*. Montevideo: Ed. Andes, 1969.

Guillen, Abraham. *Estrategía de la guerrilla urban*. Montevideo: Editorial Manuales del Pueblo, 1966.

Guillen, Abraham, ed. *Philosophy of the Urban Guerrilla*. New York: Wm. Morrow and Co., 1973.

Guillen, Abraham. *La rebelion del tercer mundo*. Montevideo: Ed. Andes, 1969.

Guillen, Abraham. *Teoría de la violencia*. Buenos Aires: Editorial Jamcana, 1965.

Gurr, Ted R. *The Conditions of Civil Violence; First Tests of a Causal Model*. Princeton, N.J.: Center of International Studies, 1970.

Gurr, Ted R. "Psychological Factors in Civil Violence," *World Politics*, II, 2 November 1968, 245.

Gurr, Ted R. *Why Men Rebel*. Princeton: Princeton University Press, 1970.

Guzmán, Campos, Borda, Orlando Fals, and Luna, Eduardo Umaña. *La Violencia en Colombia*, 2 vols., Bogota: Ediciones Tercer Mundo, 1963.

Hachey, Thomas. *Voices of Revolution; Rebels and Rhetoric*. Hinsdale, Ill.: Dryden Press, 1973.

Hacker, Frederick J. *Crusaders, Criminals, Crazies; Terror and Terrorism in our Time*. New York: W. W. Norton and Co., 1976.

Hacker, Frederick. *Terror: Myths, Realitat, Analyse*. Wien: Verlog Fritz Molden, 1973.

Haggman, Bertil. *Sweden's Maoist "Subversives"—A Case Study*. London: Institute for the Study of Conflict, 1975.

Halperin, Ernst. *Terrorism in Latin America*. Beverly Hills, Cal.: Sage Publications, 1976.

Hamer, John. "Protection of Diplomats," *Editorial Research Reports*, II (1973), 759.

Hannay, William A. "International Terrorism; The Need for a Fresh Perspective," *The International Lawyer*, VIII:2 (1974), 268-284.

Harkabi, Y. "Fedayeen Action and Arab Strategy." London: Adelphi Papers, no. 53, December 1968.

Havens, Murray C., Leiden, Carl, and Schmitt, Karl M. *The Politics of Assassination*. Englewood Cliffs, N.J.: Prentice-Hall, 1970.

Hawkins, Jack. "Guerrilla Wars: Threat in Latin America," *World Affairs*, CXXVI:3 (1963), 169-175.

Healy, R. J. *Design for Security*. New York: Wiley, 1968.

Heath, G. Louis. *Vandals in the Bomb Factory; The History and Literature of the Students for a Democratic Society*. Metuchen, N.J.: Scarecrow Press, 1976.

Heer, Friedrich. *Siebenkapitel aus der Geschichte des Schreckens*. Zurich: M. Niehans, 1957.

Heilbrunn, Otto. *Partisan Warfare*. New York: Praeger, 1962.

Heilbrunn, Otto. "When the Counterinsurgents Cannot Win," *Journal of the Royal United Service Institution* (London), CXIV:653 (1969), 55-58.

Hempstone, S. *Rebels, Mercenaries, and Dividends; The Katanga Story*. New York: Praeger, 1962.

Hendel, Samuel, ed. *The Politics of Confrontation*. New York: Appleton-Century-Crofts, 1971.

Heron, Paddy. "Television's Role in Reporting Ulster Violence," *Harrangue, A Political and Social Review* (Belfast), I, Summer 1974, 2.

Hibbs, Douglas A., Jr. *Mass Political Violence; A Cross-National Causal Analysis*, New York: Wiley, 1973.

Hilsman, Roger. "Internal War: The New Communist Tactic," *Military Review*, XLII, April 1962, 11-22.

Hirano, R. "Convention on Offenses and Certain Other Acts Committed on Board Aircraft of 1963," *Japanese Annual of International Law*, VIII (1964), 44.

Hirsch, Arthur I., and Fuller, David. "Aircraft Piracy and Extradition," *New York Law Forum*, XVI (1970), 392.

Hoagland, John H. "Changing Patterns of Insurgency and American Response," *Journal of International Affairs*, XXV:1 (1971), 120-141.

Hobsbawn, Eric J. *Les Bandits*. Paris: Maspero, 1972.

Hobsbawn, Eric J. *Primitive Rebels: Studies in Archaic Forms of Social Movements in the 19th and 20th Centuries*. New York: Praeger, 1959.

Hosbawn, Eric J. *Revolutionies*. New York: Pantheon Books, 1973.

Hodges, Donald C., Elias, Robert, and Shanab, Abu. *National Liberation Fronts: 1960-1970*. New York: Morrow, 1972.

Hoffacker, Lewis. "The United States Government Response to Terrorism: A Global Approach," *Department of State Bulletin*, LXX, 18 March 1974, 274-278.

Holt, Simma. *Terrorism in the Name of God*. New York: Crown Publishers, 1965.

Hook, Sidney. *Revolution, Reform, and Social Justice*. New York: New York University Press, 1973.

Horlick, Gary. "The Developing Law of Air Hijacking," *Harvard International Law Journal*, XXI (1971), 33.

Horlick, Gary. "The Public and Private International Response to Aircraft Hijacking," *Vanderbilt Journal of Transnational Law*, VI (1972), 144.

Horne, Alistair. "The Guerrillas of Teoponte," *Encounter*, December 1971.

Horowitz, J., et al. *Latin American Radicalism*. New York: Vintage, 1969.

Horowitz, Irving L. "Political Terrorism and State Power," *Journal of Political and Military Sociology*, I, Spring 1973, 147-157.

Horowitz, Irving L. *The Struggle is the Message*. Berkeley: The Glendessary Press, 1970.

Horrell, Muriel. *Terrorism in Southern Africa*. Johannesburg: South African Institute of Race Relations, 1968.

Hosmer, Stephen T. *Viet Cong Repression and Its Implications for the Future*. Lexington, Mass.; Heath Lexington Books, 1970.

Hotz, R. "Hijacking Turns Murderous," *Aviation Week*, C, 21 January 1975, 7.

Hotz, R. "More on Hijacking," *Aviation Week and Space Technology*, XCIV, 10 November 1969, 11.

Hotz, R. "Rising Tide of Terror," *Aviation Week*, XCVII, 7 October 1972, 7.

Howard, Alan. "With the Guerrillas in Guatemala," *New York Times Magazine*, 26 June 1966, 8.

Howe, Irving. "Political Terrorism: Hysteria on the Left," *New York Times Magazine*, 12 April 1970, 25.

Hubbard, David G. *The Skyjacker: His Flights of Fancy*. New York: Macmillan, 1971.

Hubbard, David G. *The Skyjackers*. New York: Collier Books, 1973.

Huberman, Leo, and Sweezy, Paul M., eds. *Regis Debray and the Latin American Revolution*. New York: Month Review, 1968

Huntington, Samuel P. *Civil Violence and the Process of Development*. London, Adelphia Papers, no. 89 (1973).

Hussain, Mehmodd. *The Palestine Liberation Organization: A Study in Ideology and Tactics*. New York: International Publications Service, 1975.

Hutchinson, Martha Crenshaw. "The Concept of Revolutionary Terrorism," *The Journal of Conflict Resolution*, XVI:3, September 1972, 383-396.

Hutchinson, Martha Crenshaw. Transnational Terrorism and World Politics," *Jerusalem Journal of International Relations* I:2, Winter 1975, 109-129.

Hyams, Edward S. *Terrorists and Terrorism*. New York: St. Martin's Press, 1975.

Hyde, Douglas A. *The Roots of Guerrilla Warfare*. Chester Springs, Pa.: Dufour Editions, 1968.

Ikor, Roger. *Lettre Ouverte a de Gentils Terroristes*. Paris: A. Michel, 1976.

Institute for Strategic Studies. *Civil Violence and the International System*, 2 vols. London, 1971.

Institute for the Study of Conflict. *New Dimensions of Security in Europe*. London, 1975.

Inter-American Defense College. *Bibliografía: guerra revolucionaria y subversión en el continente*. Washington, 1973.

International Centre for Comparative Criminology. *Hostage Taking: Problems of Prevention and Control*. Montreal, 1976.

Irish, Joss. *Terrorismo internacional*. Barcelona: Producciones Editoriales, 1975.

Israel, Embassy to the United States. *Efforts Continue to Check Arab Terrorism*. Washington, 1973.

Israel, Ministry of Foreign Affairs. *The ICAO and Arab Terrorists Operations; A Record of Resolutions.* Jerusalem, 1973.

Israel, Ministry of Foreign Affairs. *Nasser Terror Gangs; The Story of the Fedayun.* Jerusalem, 1956.

Jack, H. A. "Terrorism; Another U.N. Failure," *America,* 20 October 1973, 282.

Jackson, Geoffrey. *Surviving the Long Night.* New York: Vanguard, 1974.

Jacobs, Harold, ed. *Weatherman.* Berkeley: Ramparts Press, 1970.

Jacobs, Walter Darnell, Peterson, Carl A., and Yarborough, William P. *Terrorism in Southern Africa: Portents and Prospects.* New York: American-African Affairs Association, 1973.

Jacobson, Peter M. "From Piracy on the High Seas to Piracy in the High Skies: A Study of Aircraft Hijacking," *Cornell,International Law Journal,* V (1972), 161.

James, Daniel. *Che Guevara; A Biography.* New York: Stein and Day, 1969.

James, Daniel, comp., *The Complete Bolivian Diaries of Che Guevara and Other Captured Documents.* New York: Stein and Day, 1968.

Janke, Geoffrey. "Terrorism in Argentina," *RUSI Journal* (London), September 1974.

Jay, Martin, "Politics of Terror," *Partisan Review,* XXXVIII:1 (1972), 95-103.

Jenkins, Brian M. *The Five Stages of Urban Guerrilla Warfare.* Santa Monica, Cal.: RAND Corporation, 1971.

Jenkins, Brian M. *High Technology Terrorism and Surrogate War: The Impact of New Technology on Low-Level Violence.* Santa Monica, Cal.: RAND Corporation, 1975.

Jenkins, Brian M. "Hostage Survival: Some Preliminary Observations." Santa Monica, Cal.: The RAND Corporation, 1976.

Jenkins, Brian M. "International Terrorism: A Balance Sheet," *Survival,* July-August 1975, 158-164.

Jenkins, Brian M. *International Terrorism: A New Kind of Warfare.* Santa Monica, Cal.: RAND Corporation, 1974.

Jenkins, Brian M. *International Terrorism: A New Mode of Conflict.* Los Angeles: Crescent Publications, 1975.

Jenkins, Brian M. *Terrorism and Kidnapping.* Santa Monica, Cal.: RAND Corporation, 1974.

Jenkins, Brian M. *Terrorism Works—Sometimes.* Santa Monica, Cal.: RAND Corporation, 1974.

Jenkins, Brian M. *An Urban Strategy for Guerrillas and Governments.* Santa Monica, Cal.: The RAND Corporation, 1972.

Jenkins, Brian M., and Johnson, Janera, eds. *International Terrorism: A Chronology, 1968-1974.* Santa Monica, Cal.: RAND Corporation, 1975.

Joesten, Joachim. *The Red Hand; The Sinister Account of the Terrorist Arm of the French Right-Wing "Ultras" in Algeria and on the Continent.* New York: Abelard-Schuman, 1962.

Johnson, Chalmers. *Revolution and the Social System.* Stanford: Hoover Institution, Stanford University Press, 1964.

Johnson, Chalmers. *Revolutionary Change.* Boston: Little, Brown, 1966.

Johnson, D. H. N. "Piracy in Modern International Law," *Transactions of the Grotius Society,* XLIII (1957), 63.

Johnson, Kenneth F. *Guatemala: From Terrorism to Terror*. London: Institute for the Study of Conflict, 1972.

Johnson, K. F. "On the Guatamalan Political Violence," *Politics and Society*, IV, Fall 1973, 55.

Johnson, Paul. "Age of Terror," *New Statesman*, LXXXVIII (1974), 763,

Johnson, Paul. "The Resources of Civilization," *New Statesman*, LXXXIX, 31 October 1975, 531.

Johnson, Paul. "Wrath of the Righteous," *New Statesman*, LXXXVII, June 1974, 871.

Johnston, L. D. "Aviation Crimes Act of 1972," *New Zealand University Law Review*, V (1973), 305.

Joll, James. *The Anarchists*. Boston: Little, Brown, 1964.

Jova, J. J. "OAS Asked to Consider Problem of Kidnapping," *Department of State Bulletin*, LXII, 25 May 1970, 662.

Juillard, P. "Les Enlevements de Diplomates," *Annuaire Francais de Droit International* (1971), 205-231.

Kaplan, John. "The Assassins," *Stanford Law Review*, IX:5, May 1967, 1110-1151.

Karber, Phillip A. "Newspaper Coverage of Domestic Bombings: Reporting Patterns of American Violence," *Bomb Incident Bulletin*, March 1973.

Karber, Phillip A. "Psychological Dimensions of Bombing Motivations," *Bomb Incident Bulletin* (1973).

Karber, Philip A. "Urban Terrorism: Baseline Data and a Conceptual Framework," *Social Science Quartly,* December 1971, 521-533.

Karber, Phillip A., Nengel, R. William, and Novotny, Eric J. *A Behavioral Analysis of the Terrorist Threat to Nuclear Installations*. Unpublished manuscript prepared for U.S. Atomic Energy Commission, 1974.

Karber, Phillip A., and Novotny, Eric J. "Radical Bombings in the United States: What Happened to the Revolution?," *Bomb Incident Bulletin*, January 1973.

Katsh, Abraham I., ed. and trans. *The Warsaw Diary of Chaim A. Kaplan*. New York: Collier Books, 1973.

Katz, S. *Days of Fire—The Secret History of the Irgun Zvai Leumi*. Garden City, N.Y.: Doubleday, 1968.

Kaufman, Edy. "La estrategia de las guerrillas," *Problemas Internacionales*, XX:1 (1973), 12-27.

Kelly, George A. "Revolutionary Warfare and Psychological Action," *Military Review,* IX, October 1960, 4.

Kelly, George A., and Miller, Linda B. *Internal War and International Systems: Perspectives on Methods*. Cambridge, Mass.: Center for International Affairs, Harvard University, 1969.

Kelly, R. J. *New Political Crimes and the Emergence of Revolutionary Nationalist Ideology*. Chicago: Rand-McNally 1973.

Kelman, Herbert C. "Violence without Moral Restraint: Reflections on the Dehumanization of Victims and Victimizers," *Journal of Social Issues*, XXIX (1974), 25-62.

Keohane, Robert O., and Nye, Joseph S., Jr., eds. *Transnational Relations and World Politics*. Cambridge: Harvard University Press, 1973.

Khan, M. A. *Guerrilla Warfare; Its Past, Present and Future*. Karachi: Rangrut, 1960.

Kahn, Rahmatullah. "Hijacking and International Law," *Africa Quarterly*, X (1971), 398.

Khashaf, Al. *Arab Terrorism, American Style*. Gaithersburg, Md.: International Association of Chiefs of Police, 1974.

Kim, B. S. "Student Activism in Korea and Japan: A Comparative Analysis," *Asian Journal of Columbia University*, I:1 (1973), 3-13.

Kirkham, James F., Levy, Sheldon G., and Crotty, William J., eds. *Assassination and Violence, A Report to the National Commission on Causes and Prevention of Violence*. New York: Bantam Books, 1970.

Kissinger, Henry, A. "Hijacking, Terrorism and War," *Department of State Bulletin*, LXXIII, 8 September 1975, 360-361.

Kitson, Frank. *Low Intensity Operations: Subversion, Insurgency, Peace-Keeping*. London: Faber and Faber, 1972.

Kittrie, N. N. "Comments on Terrorism," *American Journal of International Law*, 62, November 1973.

Klare, Mike. "Urban Counterinsurgency: An Introduction," *Viet-Report*, Summer 1968.

Klein, Milton M. "The Fact of Violence in America: A Historical Perspective," *Social Education*, XXXVII (1973), 540.

Klovis, J. J. *Guerrilla Warfare: Analysis and Projections*. New York: Speller, 1972.

Kohl, James, and Litt, John. *Urban Guerrilla War in Latin America*. Cambridge: MIT Press, 1976.

Kren, George. "Another Aspect of War: The Holocaust, A Generation After," *Military Affairs*, December 1976.

Kren, George M., and Rappoport, L. "S.S. Atrocities: A Psychohistorical Perspective," *History of Childhood Quarterly*, III:1, Summer 1975.

Kren, George, and Rappoport, L. "The Waffen SS," *Armed Forces and Society*, November 1976.

Krieger, D. M. "Terrorists and Nuclear Technology," *Bulletin of the Atomic Scientists*, XXXI, June, 1975, 28-34.

Kumar, Mahendra. *Violence and Nonviolence in International Relations*. New Delhi: Thompson Press, 1975.

Kurado, Yasumasa. "Young Palestinian Commandos in Political Socialization Perspective," *Middle East Journal*, XXVI (1972), 253.

Kuriyama, Y. "Terrorism at Tel Aviv Airport and a 'New Left' Group in Japan," *Asian Survey*, XIII, March, 1973, 336.

Kutner, Luis. "Constructive Notice, A Proposal to End International Terrorism," *New York Law Forum*, XIX (1973), 325.

Kyo, Jo. *Revolt is Spreading*. Tokyo: Jo Kyo Sa, 1968.

Labrousse, Alain. *Les Tuparmaros; Guerrilla Urbaine en Uruguay*. Paris, 1971.

Lador-Lederer, J. J. "Legal Approach to International Terrorism," *Israel Law Review*, IX, April 1974, 194.

Laffin, John. *Fedayeen*. New York: Macmillan, 1973.

Lamberg, Robert F. "La guerrilla-urbana; conditiones y perspectivas de la 'segunda ola' guerrillera," *Foro Internacional* XI:3 (1971), 431-443.

Lamberg, Robert F. "Latin America's Urban Guerrillas," *Swiss Review of World Affairs,* XX:3 (1970), 18-19.

Lamberg, Vera B. de. "La guerrilla castrista en América Latina; bibliografía selecta, 1960-1970," *Foro Internacional,* XXI:1 (1970), 95-111.

Lambrick, H. T. *The Terrorist.* Totowa, N.J.: Rowan & Littlefield, 1972.

Lamont, Norman. "The Urban Guerrilla," *Crossbow,* April 1971, 32-33.

Landazabel R., Fernando. *Política y táctica de la guerra revolucionaria.* Bogota, 1966.

Lapp, Ralph E. "The Ultimate Blackmail," *New York Times Magazine,* 4 February 1973, 13.

Laqueur, Walter. "The Futility of Terrorism," *Harper's Magazine,* CCLII, March 1976, 99-105

Laqueur, Walter. "Guerrillas and Terrorists," *Commentary,* LVIII, October 1974, 40-48.

Larsson, Janerik. *Politisk terror i Sverige.* Goteborg: Solna, Seelig, 1968.

Lartéguy, Jean. *The Guerrillas; New Patterns in Revolution in Latin America.* New York: Signet, 1972.

Larus, J. *Nuclear Weapons Safety and the Common Defense.* Columbus: Ohio State University Press, 1967.

Lasch, Christopher. *The Agony of the American Left.* New York: Vintage, 1969.

Lasky, Melvin J. "Ulrike Meinhof and the Baader-Meinhof Gang," *Encounter,* XLIV, June 1975, 9-23.

Lasswell, Harold D. *World Revolutionary Propaganda.* Westport, Conn.: Greenwood Press, 1973.

Lasswell, H. D., and Cleveland, H., eds. *The Ethics of Power.* New York: Harper and Brothers, 1962.

Lasswell, Harold D., and Lerner, D., eds. *World Revolutionary Elites: Studies in Coercive Ideological Movements.* Cambridge: MIT Press, 1965.

Leachman, Robert B., and Althoff, Philip, eds. *Preventing Nuclear Theft: Guidelines for Industry and Government.* New York: Praeger, 1972.

Legun, C. "How to Curb International Terrorism," *Current History,* CXLVII, January 1973, 3-9.

Leiden, Carl, and Schmitt, Karl M., eds. *The Politics of Violence: Revolution in the Modern World.* Englewood Cliffs, N.J.: Prentice-Hall, 1968.

Leites, Nathan, and Wolf, C. *Rebellion and Authority: An Analytic Essay on Insurgent Conflicts.* Chicago: Markham Publishing Co., 1970.

Lewis, Flora. "The Anatomy of Terror," *New York Times Magazine,* 18 November 1956, 67-69.

Lieberman, J. *The Scorpion and the Tarantula—The Struggle to Control Atomic Weapons.* Boston: Houghton Mifflin, 1970.

Liebert, R. *Radical and Militant Youth: A Psychiatrist's Report.* New York: Praeger, 1971.

Lipset, Seymour Martin. "On the Politics of Conscience and Extreme Commitment," *Encounter,* August 1971, 66.

Lissitzyn, Oliver J. "International Control of Aerial Hijacking: The Role of Values and Interests," *American Journal of International Law,* LXV (1971), 80.

Lora, Guillermo. *Revolución y foquísmo; balance de la discusión sobre la desviación "guerrillerista."* Buenos Aires: El Yunque Editorial, 1975.

Loy, Frank E. "Department of Transportation Reviews Problem of Aircraft Hijacking and Proposals for International Action," *Department of State Bulletin*, LX (1969), 212.

Loy, Frank E. "Some International Approaches to Dealing with Hijacking of Aircraft," *The International Lawyer*, IV, April 1970, 444.

Luard, Evan, ed. *International Regulation of Civil Wars*. New York: New York University Press, 1972.

La Lutte Internationale contra Le Terrorisme. Paris: La Documentation Francaise, 1975.

Lynn, Robert H. "Air Hijacking as a Political Crime—Who Should Judge?," *California Western International Law Journal*, II (1971), 2.

McClintock, Michael C. "Skyjacking: Its Domestic Civil and Criminal Ramifications," *Journal of Air Law and Commerce*, XXXIX (1971), 29.

McCuen, John J. *Art of Counter Revolutionary War: The Strategy of Counter-Insurgency*. London: Faber and Faber, 1966.

McGuire, Maria. *To Take Arms; My Year in the Provisional IRA*. New York: Viking Press, 1973.

McKnight, Gerald. *The Terrorist Mind*. Indianapolis: Bobbs-Merrill, 1974.

McLellan, Vin, and Avery, Paul. *The Voices of Guns; The Definitive and Dramatic Story of the 22-Month Career of the Symbionese Liberation Army*. New York: Putnam, 1976.

McMahan, John P. "Air Hijacking: Extradition as a Deterrent," *The Georgetown Law Journal*, LVIII (1970), 1135.

McNeil, Mark S. "Aerial Hijacking and the Protection of Diplomats," *Harvard International Law Journal*, XIV (1973), 595.

MacStiofain, Sean. *Memoirs of a Revolutionary*. Dublin: Cremonesi, 1975.

McWhinney, Edward. "New Developments in the Law of International Aviation: The Control of Aerial Hijacking," *American Journal of International Law*, LV (1971), 71.

Mahoney, H. T. "After a Terrorist Attack—Business as Usual," *Security Management*, XIX, March 1975, 16.

Malawer, Stuart S. "United States Foreign Policy and International Law; The Jordanian Civil War and Air Piracy," *International Problems*, X (1971), 31.

Malik, Sushman. "Legal Aspects of the Problem of Unlawful Seizure of Aircraft," *Indian Journal of International Law*, IX (1969), 61.

Mallin, Jay, ed. *Che Guevara on Revolution: A Documentary Overview*. Coral Gables: University of Miami Press, 1969.

Mallin, Jay, ed. *Strategy for Conquest; Communist Documents on Guerrilla Warfare*. Coral Gables, Fla.: University of Miami Press, 1970.

Mallin, Jay, ed. *Terror and Urban Guerrillas; A Study of Tactics and Documents*. Coral Gables, Fla.: University of Miami Press, 1971.

Mallin, Jay. *Terror in Viet Nam*. Princeton N.J.: Van Nostrand, 1966.

Mallin, Jay. "Terrorism as a Political Weapon," *Air University Review*, XXII, July-August 1971, 45-52.

Mallin, Jay. "Terrorism Is Revolutionary Warfare," *Strategic Review*, II, Fall 1974, 48-55.

Mallison, W. T., Jr., and Mallison, S. V. "Concept of Public Purpose Terror in International Law, Doctrines and Sanctions to Reduce the Destruction of Human and Material Values," *Howard Law Journal*, XVIII (1973), 12.

Malmborg, K. E. "New Developments in the Law of International Aviation; The Control of Aerial Hijacking," *Proceedings of the American Society of International Law* (1971), 75.

Mankiewicz, R. H. "The 1970 Hague Convention," *Journal of Air Law and Commerce*, XXXVII (1971), 195-210.

Mao Tse-tung. *Basic Tactics*. New York: Praeger, 1966.

Mao Tse-tung. *On Guerrilla Warfare*. New York: Praeger, 1961.

Ma'oz, Moshe. "Soviet and Chinese Relations with the Palestinian Guerrilla Organizations," *Jerusalem Papers on Peace Problems*, no. 4, March 1974.

Mardor, Muhyd. *Haganah*. New York: New American Library, 1966.

Marighella, Carlos. *For the Liberation of Brazil*. Harmondsworth, Eng.: Penguin Books, 1971.

Marighella, Carlos. *Mini-Manual of Guerrilla Warfare*. Havana: Tricontinental, 1970.

Martin, Bill. "The Politics of Violence—The Urban Guerrilla in Brazil," *Ramparts*, October 1970, 35.

Martin, Peter. "The Unlawful Seizure of Aircraft," *The Law Society's Gazette*, LXVI (1969), 714.

Martìnes, Lauro, ed. *Violence and Civil Disorder in Italian Cities*. Berkeley: University of California Press, 1972.

Martìnez Codo, Enrique. "Communist Guerrillas in Argentina," *Marine Corps Gazette*, XLIX:9 (1965), 43-50

Martìnez Codo, Enrique. "Continental Defense and Counterinsurgency," *Military Review*, L:4 (1970) 71-74

Martìnez Codo, Enrique. *Guerrillas y subversión en América Latina*. Buenos Aires: Manuales de Información, n.d.

Martìnez Codo, Enrique. "Guerrilla Warfare after Guevara," *Military Review*, XLIX:7 (1969), 24-30.

Martìnez Codo, Enrique. "Insurgency: Latin Américan Style," *Military Review*, XLVII:11 (1967), 3-12.

Martìnez Codo, Enrique. "The Urban Guerrilla," *Military Review*, LI:8 (1971), 3-10.

Masotti, L. H., and Bowen, D. R. *Riots and Rebellions—Civil Violence in the Urban Community*. Beverly Hills, Cal.: Sage Publications, 1968.

Matekalo, Ivan. *Les Dessous du Terrorisme International*. Paris: Julliard, 1973.

Mathews, A. S. "Terrors of Terrorism," *South African Law Journal*, XLI, August 1974, 381.

Maulnier, Thierry. *La Face de Méduse de Communisme*. Paris: Gallimard, 1951.

Max, Alphonse. *Tupamaros—A Pattern for Urban Guerrilla Warfare in Latin America*. The Hague: International Documentation and Information Centre, 1970.

May, W. F. "Terrorism as Strategy and Ecstasy," *Social Research*, XLI, Summer 1974, 277-298.

Mayans, Ernesto, ed. *Tupamaros, antología documental*. Cuernavaca, Mex.: Centro Intercultural de Documentación, 1971.

Mazrui, Ali A. "Thoughts on Assassination in Africa," *Political Science Quarterly*, LXXXIII:1, March 1968, 40-52.

Means, J. "Political Kidnappings and Terrorism," *North American Review*, Winter 1970, 5.

Melander, Göran. *Terroristlagen: ett onodigt ont*. Stockholm: PAN/Norstedt, 1975.

Melo, Artemio Luis. "La inviolabilidad diplomática y el caso del Embajador Von Spreti," *Revista de Derecho International y Ciencias Diplomáticas*, XIX:37-38 (1970), 147.

Mendelsohn, A. I. "In-Flight Crime: The International and Domestic Picture under the Tokyo Convention," *Virginia Law Review*, LIII (1967), 509.

Mengel, R. William. *Terrorism and New Technologies of Destruction*. Vienna, Va.: The BDM Corporation, 1976.

Mengel, R. William, Greisman, Harvey, et al. *Analysis of the Terrorist Threat to the Commercial Nuclear Industry*. Vienna, Va.: The BDM Corporation, 1975.

Mercadier, Antonio, and de Vera, Jorge. *Tupamaros: estrategía y acción*. Montevideo, 1969.

Mercier Vega, Luis, ed. *Guerrillas in Latin America: The Technique of the Counter-state*. New York: Praeger, 1969.

Merleau-Ponty, Maurice. *Humanism and Terror; An Essay on the Communist Problem*. Boston: Beacon Press, 1969.

Meron, T. "Some Legal Aspects of Arab Terrorists' Claim to Privileged Combatancy," *Mordisk Tidasakrift for International Ret*, XL (1970), 47-85.

Meron, Theodor. *Some Legal Aspects of Arab Terrorists' Claims to Privileged Combatancy*. New York: Sabra Books, 1970.

Methvin, Eugene H. *The Riot Makers; The Technology of Social Demolition*. New Rochelle, N.Y.: Arlington House, 1970.

Methvin, Eugene H. *The Rise of Radicalism; The Social Psychology of Messianic Extremism*. New Rochelle, N.Y.: Arlington House, 1973.

Metrowich, F. R. *Terrorism in Southern Africa*. Pretoria; Africa Institute of South Africa, 1973.

Meyrowitz, H. "Statut des Guerilleros dans le Droit International," *Journal du Droit International*, October-December 1973, 875.

Mieres, Francisco. "Lessons of October and Contemporary Revolutionary Movements in Latin America," *World Marxist Review* (Toronto), X:11 (1967), 77-81.

Mickolus, Edward F. *Annotated Bibliography on International and Transnational Terrorism*. Washington: Central Intelligence Agency, Office of Political Research, 1976.

Mickolus, Edward F. *Assessing the Degrees of Error in Public Reporting of Transnational Terrorism*. Washington: Central Intelligence Agency, Office of Political Research, 1976.

Mickolus, Edward. *Codebook: ITERATE (International Terrorism: Attributes of Terrorist Events)*. Ann Arbor: Inter-University Consortium for Political and Social Research, University of Michigan, 1976.

Mickolus, Edward F. "Negotiating for Hostages: A Policy Dilemma," *Orbis*, XIX:4, Winter 1976, 1309-1325.

Milbank, David L., and Mickolus, Edward. *International and Transnational Terrorism: Diagnosis and Prognosis*. Washington: Central Intelligence Agency, Office of Political Research, 1976.

Milte, Kerry. Terrorism and International Order," *The Australian and New Zealand Journal of Criminology*, VIII, June 1975, 101.

Molnar, Andrew R. *Human Factors—Considerations of Undergrounds in Insurgencies*. Washington: Special Operations Research Office, American University, 1966.

Molnar, Andrew R., et al. *Undergrounds in Insurgent, Revolutionary, and Resistance Warfare*. Washington: The American University Special Operations Research Office, 1963.

Montellano, Julian V. *Terror y angustía en el corazón de América*. Santiago (Chile): Impr. Gutenberg, 1954.

Moore, Barrington. *Terror and Progress, U.S.S.R.* Cambridge: Harvard University Press, 1954.

Moore, John N., et al. "Terrorism and Political Crimes in International Law," *American Journal of International Law*, LXVII, November 1973, 88-93.

Morales, Emilio. *Uturunco y las guerrillas en la Argentina*. Montevideo: Editorial SEPE, 1964.

Morf, Gustave. *Terror in Quebec; Case Studies of the FLQ*. Toronto: Clarke, Irwin, 1970.

Moreno, Francisco José, and Mitrani, Barbara, eds. *Conflict and Violence in Latin American Politics*. New York: Thomas Y. Cromwell and Co., 1971.

Moreno, José Antonio. "Che Guevara on Guerrilla Warfare: Doctrine, Practice and Evaluation," *Comparative Studies in Society and History*, XII:2 (1970), 114-133.

Morris, Michael. *Armed Conflict in Southern Africa: A Survey of Regional Terrorisms from Their Beginnings to the Present, with a Comprehensive Examination of the Portuguese Position*. Cape Town: Jeremy Spence, 1974.

Morris, Michael. *Terrorism, The First Full Account in Detail of Terrorism and Insurgency in Southern Africa*. Cape Town: H. Timmins, 1971.

Morris, Robert. "Patty Hearst and the New Terror," *New Republic*, CLXXIII:21, 27 November 1975, 8-10.

Morton, Marian J. *The Terrors of Ideological Politics*. Cleveland: Press of Case-Western Reserve University, 1972.

Moss, Robert. "International Terrorism and Western Societies," *International Journal*, XXVIII:3, Summer 1973, 418-430.

Moss, Robert. "Urban Guerrillas in Uruguay," *Problems of Communism*, XX:5 (1971), 14-23.

Moss, Robert. "Urban Guerrillas in Latin America," *Conflict Studies*, no. 8 (1970).

Moss, Robert. *Urban Guerrillas: The New Face of Political Violence*. London: Maurice Temple Smith, Ltd., 1972.

Moss, Robert. "Urban Guerrilla Warfare," *Adelphi Papers*, no. 79 (1971).

Moss, Robert. "Uruguay: Terrorism versus Democracy," *Conflict Studies*, no. 14 (1971).

Moss, Robert. *The War for the Cities*. New York: Coward, McCann, and Geoghegan, 1972.

Movimiento de Liberación Nacional, *Actas tupamaras*. Buenos Aires: Schapire, 1971.

Mullen, Robert K. *The International Clandestine Nuclear Threat*. Santa Barbara, Cal.: Mission Research Corporation, 1975.

Murphy, John F. "International Legal Controls of International Terrorism, Performance and Prospects," *Illinois Bar Journal,* LXIII, April 1975, 444.

Mydans, Carl, and Mydans, Shelley. *The Violent Peace.* New York: Atheneum, 1968.

Namruddin, D. "Kidnappings of Diplomatic Personnel," *Police Chief,* XL, February 1973, 18.

Nasution, Abdul Harris. *Fundamentals of Guerrilla Warfare.* New York: Praeger, 1965.

Nawful al-Sayyid, Muhammad Ali. *Israel's Crime Record.* Cairo Information Dept. 1965.

Neale, William D. "Oldest Weapon in the Arsenal: Terror," *Army,* August 1973, 10-13.

Nekhlek, E. A. "Anatomy of Violence: Theoretical Reflections on Palestinian Resistance," *Middle East Journal,* XXV, Spring 1971, 180-200.

Nieburg, H. L. *Political Violence; The Behavioral Process.* New York: St. Martin's Press, 1969.

Niezing, John, ed. *Urban Guerrilla: Studies on the Theory, Strategy, and Practice of Political Violence in Modern Societies.* Rotterdam: Rotterdam University Press, 1976.

Nolin, Thierry. *La Hagannah; L'Armee Secrete d'Israel.* Paris: Ballard, 1971.

Nomad, M. *Aspects of Revolt.* New York: Bookman Associated, 1959.

Novick, S. "Basement H-Bombs," *Scientist and Citizen,* December 1968.

Novotny, Eric J., and Karber, Phillip A. "Organized Terror and Politics," in American Political Science Association, *Short Essays in Political Science,* Washington, 1973.

Nuñez, Carlos. *Los Tupamaros; vanguardia armada en el Uruguay.* Montevideo: Ediciones Provincias Unidas, 1969.

O'Ballance, Edgar. *The Algerian Insurrection, 1954-62.* London: Faber and Faber, 1967.

O'Ballance, Edgar. *Arab Guerrilla Power, 1967-1972.* Hamden, Conn.: Archon Books, 1973.

O'Ballance, Edgar. *The Indo-China War, 1945-1954; A Study in Guerrilla Warfare.* London: Faber and Faber, 1964.

O'Ballance, Edgar. *The Wars in Vietnam, 1954-1973.* New York: Hippocene Books, 1975.

O'Mara, Richard. "New Terror in Latin America; Snatching the Diplomats," *Nation,* CCX:17 (1970), 518-519.

Oppenheimer, Martin. *The Urban Guerrilla.* Chicago: Quadrangle Books, 1969.

Organization of American States, Pan American Union, "Convention to Prevent and Punish the Acts of Terrorism Taking the Form of Crimes against Persons and Related Extortions that Are of International Significance," in *Serie sobre Tratados,* 37, 2 February 1971.

Orlou, A. *Handbook of Intelligence and Guerrilla Warfare.* Ann Arbor: University of Michigan Press, 1963.

Paine, Lauran. *The Terrorists.* London: Hale, 1975.

Panhuys, Haro F. van. "Aircraft Hijacking and International Law," *Columbia Journal of Transnational Law,* IX (1970), 1.

Paret, Peter, and Shy, John W. *Guerrillas in the 1960's.* New York: Praeger, 1962.

Parry, Albert. *Terrorism: From Robespierre to Arafat.* New York: Vanguard, 1976.

Paust, Jordan J. "Some Thoughts on 'Preliminary Thoughts' on Terrorism," *American Journal of International Law,* LXVIII (1974), 502.

Paust, Jordan J. "A Survey of Possible Legal Responses to International Terrorism; Prevention, Punishment, and Cooperative Action," *Georgia Journal of International and Comparative Law,* V (1975), 431.

Paust, Jordan J. "Terrorism and the International Law of War," *Military Law Review,* LXIV (1974), 1.

Payne, Pierre Stephen Robert. *Zero, The Story of Terrorism.* New York: Wingate, 1951.

Perrera, Victor. "Guatemala: Always La Violencia," *New York Times Magazine,* 13 June 1971, 13.

Peters, R. "Terrorists at Work: Report from Argentina," *National Review,* 28 July 1964, 63.

Peterson, Edward A. "Jurisdiction-Construction of Statute-Aircraft Piracy," *Journal of Air Law and Commerce,* XXX (1964), 292.

Peterson, William H. "Urban Guerrilla Warfare," *Military Review,* March 1972, 82.

Petras, James. "Guerrilla Movements in Latin America," *New Politics,* VI:1 (1967), 80-94; VI:2 (1967), 58-72.

Petras, James. "New Forms of Struggle in Latin America," *New Politics,* VIII:1 (1969), 58-61.

Pike, Douglas. *The Viet-Cong Strategy of Terror.* Saigon: U.S. Mission to Vietnam, 1970.

Pike, Douglas. *Viet Cong: The Organization and Techniques of the National Liberation Front of South Vietnam.* Cambridge: M.I.T. Press, 1966.

Plastrik, S. "On Terrorism," *Dissent,* XXI, Spring 1974, 143.

Pomeroy, William J. *Guerrilla and Counter-Guerrilla Warfare; Liberation and Suppression in the Present Period.* New York: International Publishers, 1969.

Pomeroy, William J., ed. *Guerrilla Warfare and Marxism; A Collection of Writings from Karl Marx to the Present on Armed Struggles for Liberation and for Socialism.* New York: International Publishers, 1968.

Ponte, Lowell. "Better Do As We Say: This Is an Atom Bomb and We're Not Fooling," *Penthouse,* February 1972.

Popper, F. J. "Internal War as a Stimulant of Political Development," *Comparative Political Studies,* III, January 1971, 413.

Possony, Stefan T. "Terrorism: A Global Concern," *Defense/Foreign Affairs Digest,* January 1973, 4-5.

Potter, D. "Violence Out of a Box," *New Statesman,* LXXXVIII, 29 November 1974, 796.

Powell, W. *The Anarchist Cookbook.* New York: Lyle Stuart, 1971.

Powers, Thomas. *Diana: The Making of a Terrorist.* Boston: Houghton Mifflin, 1970.

Poulantzas, Nicholas M. "The Hague Convention for the Suppression of Unlawful Seizure of Aircraft," *Nederlands Tijdschrift voor International Recht,* XVIII:1 (1971), 25.

Poulantzas, Nicholas M. "Hijacking or Air Piracy?," *Nederlands Juristenblad,* XX (1970), 566.

Poulantzas, Nicholas M. "Hijacking v. Piracy; A Substantial Misunderstanding, Not a Quarrel over Semantics," *Revue Hellenique de Droit International,* XXIII:1-4 (1970), 80.

Poulantzas, Nicholas M. "Some Problems of International Law Connected with Urban Guerrilla Warfare: The Kidnapping of Members of Diplomatic Missions, Consular Offices and Other Foreign Personnel," *Annales d'Etudes Internationales,* III (1972), 137.

Proceedings of the Second International Conference on the History of the Resistance Movements, Milan, Italy, 26-29 March 1961. New York: Macmillan, 1964.

Przetacznik, Franciszek. "Convention on the Special Protection of Officials of Foreign States and International Organizations," *Revue Belge de Droit International,* IX:2 (1973), 455.

Przetacznik, Franciszek. "Prevention and Punishment of Crimes against Internationally Protected Persons," *Indian Journal of International Law,* XXIII, January-March 1973, 65.

Przetacznik, Franciszek. "Special Protection of Diplomatic Agents," *Revue de Droit International de Sciences Diplomatiques et Politiques,* L, October-December 1972, 270-289.

Pulsifer, Roy, and Boyle, Robert. "The Tokyo Convention of Offenses and Certain Other Acts Committed on Board Aircraft," *Journal of Air Law and Commerce,* XX, Fall 1964, 305.

Pye, A. Kenneth, and Lowell, Cym H. "The Criminal Process during Civil Disorder," *Duke Law Journal,* III, August 1975, 581-690.

Pye, Lucian. *Guerrilla Communism in Malaya.* Princeton: Princeton University Press, 1956.

Quartim, João. "Dictatorship and Armed Struggle in Brazil," *New Left Review,* 1971.

Quartim, João. "Régis Debray and the Brazilian Revolution," *New Left Review,* January-February 1970, 61-82.

Quintero Morente, Frederico. "Terrorism," *Military Review,* XLV, December 1965, 55-57.

Radovanovic, Ljubomir. "The Problem of International Terrorism," *Review of International Affairs,* XXIII, October 1972, 5-20.

Rafat, Amir, "Control of Aircraft Hijacking: The Law of International Civil Aviation," *World Affairs,* CXXXIV, Fall 1971, 143.

Ransom, David. "The Berkeley Mafia and the Indonesian Massacre," *Ramparts,* October 1970, 24.

Rapoport, David C. *Assassination and Terrorism.* Toronto: Canadian Broadcasting Corp., 1971.

Rauch, Elmar. "The Compatibility of the Detention of Terrorists Order (Northern Ireland) with the European Convention for the Protection of Human Rights," *New York University Journal of International Law and Politics,* VI (1973), 1.

Rayne, F. "Executive Protection and Terrorism," *Top Security* (England), 1:6, October 1975, 220-225.

Rein, Bert. "A Government Perspective," *Journal of Air Law and Commerce,* XXXVII (1971), 183-194.

Rejai, Mostafa. *The Strategy of Political Revolution.* Garden City, N.Y.: Doubleday, 1973.

Reisman, W. M. "Private Armies in a Global War System, Prologue to Decision," *Virginia Journal of International Law,* XIV (1973), 1.

Rivers, Charles R., and Switzer, Kenneth A. *Violence.* Rochelle Park, N.J.: Hayden, 1976.

Roberts, Adam, ed. *Civilian Resistance as a National Defense.* Harrisburg, Pa.: Stackpole Press, 1968.

Rojo, Ricardo. *My Friend Che.* New York: Dial Press, 1968.

Romaniecki, Leon. *The Arab Terrorists in the Middle East and the Soviet Union.* Jerusalem: Soviet and East European Research Center of the Hebrew University of Jerusalem, 1973.

Romaniecki, Leon. "The Soviet Union and International Terrorism," *Soviet Studies,* XXVI:3, July 1974, 417-440.

Roquet, Claude, and Rowe, Allen. "Task Force on Kidnapping," *External Affairs,* XXIII (1971), 6-11.

Rose, Richard. *Governing Without Consensus.* London: Faber and Faber, 1971.

Rosenau, James N., ed. *International Aspects of Civil Strife.* Princeton: Princeton University Press, 1964.

Rosenfield, Stanley B. "Air Piracy, Is It Time to Relax Our Security?," *New England Law Review,* IX (1973), 81.

Rothstein, Andrew. "Terrorism—Some Plain Words," *Labour Monthly,* September 1973, 413-417.

Roucek, Joseph S. "Sociological Elements of a Theory of Terror and Violence," *American Journal of Economics and Sociology,* XXI:2, April 1962, 165-172.

Roy, Suprakesh. *Bharatera Baiplabika Samgramera Itihasa.* Karachi, 1955.

Rozakis, C. L. "Terrorism and the Internationally Protected Persons in the Light of ICL's Draft Articles," *International and Comparative Law Quarterly,* XXIII (1974), 32.

Ruppenthal, Karl M. "World Law and the Hijackers," *Nation,* 3 February 1969, 144.

Russell, Charles A., Schenkel, James F., and Miller, James A. "Urban Guerrillas in Argentina: A Select Bibliography," *Latin American Research Review,* IX:3, Fall 1974, 53-89.

Russell, Charles A., Miller, James A., and Hildner, Robert E. "The Urban Guerrilla in Latin America: A Selected Bibliography," *Latin American Research Review,* IX:1, Spring 1974, 37-80.

Russell, Charles A., and Hildner, Robert E. "Urban Insurgency in Latin America; Its Implications for the Future," *Air University Review,* XXII:6, September-October 1971, 55-64.

Ryter, Lt. Stephen L. "Terror: A Psychological Weapon," *The Review,* May-June 1966, 21, 145-150.

Said, A. A., and Collier, D. M. *Revolutionism.* Boston: Allyn, 1971.

St. George, Andrew. "How the U.S. Got Che," *True,* April 1969, 29.

Sale, Kirkpatrick. *SDS.* New York: Random House, 1973.

Samuels, Alec. "Crimes Committed on Board Aircraft; Tokyo Convention Act, 1967," *British Yearbook of International Law,* XLII (1967), 271.

Samuels, Alec. "The Legal Problems; An Introduction," *Journal of Air Law and Commerce,* XXXVII (1971), 163-170.

Santos, M. Barbero. "Delitos de bandolerismo, rebelión militar y terrorismo regulados por el Decreto de 21 de septiembre de 1960," *La Justicia* (Mexico), XXXIII, January 1974, 43.

Sarkesian, Sam C., ed. *Revolutionary Guerrilla Warfare.* Chicago: Precedent Publishing, Inc., 1975.

Schelling, Thomas C. *Arms and Influence.* New Haven, Conn.: Yale University Press, 1964.

Schiff, Zeev, and Rothstein, Raphael. *Fedayeen; Guerrillas Against Israel.* New York: David McKay, 1972.

Schloesing, E. "La Repression International du Terrorism," *Rue Politique et Parlementaire,* DCCCXLI, April 1973, 50-61.

Schwarzenberger, Georg. "Terrorists, Guerrilleros, and Mercenaries," *Toledo Law Review,* Fall-Winter 1971, 71-81.

Schwarzenberger, Georg. "Terrorists, Hijackers, Guerrilleros, and Mercenaries," *Current Legal Problems,* XXIV (1971), 257-282.

Schwarzenberger, Georg. "Title to Territory: Response to a Challenge," *American Journal of International Law,* LI.

Scott, Andrew M., et al. *Insurgency.* Chapel Hill, N.C.: University of North Carolina Press, 1971.

Segre, D. V., and Adler, J. H. "The Ecology of Terrorism," *Encounter,* XL, February 1973, 17-24.

Segal, Ronald. *Whose Jerusalem?* London: Jonathan Cape, 1973.

Selznick, Philip. *The Organizational Weapon: A Study of Bolshevik Strategy and Tactics.* New York: Free Press of Glencoe, 1960.

Shaffer, Helen B. "Political Terrorism," *Editorial Research Reports,* I, 13 May 1970, 340-360.

Sharabi, Hisham. *Palestine Guerrillas: Their Credibility and Effectiveness.* Washington: Center for Strategic and International Studies, Georgetown University, 1970.

Sharp, J. M. "Canada and the Hijacking of Aircraft," *Manitoba Law Journal,* V (1973), 451.

Shay, Reg, and Vermaak, Chris. *The Silent War.* Salisbury, Rhodesia: Galaxie Press, 1971.

Sheehan, William M. "Hijacking and World Law," *World Federalist; U.S. Edition,* XVI (1970), 14.

Shepard, Ira M. "Air Piracy: The Role of the International Federation of Airline Pilots Associations," *Cornell International Law Journal,* III (1970), 79.

Shepard, N. "Israel and the Air Gangsters," *New Statesman* 27 February 1970, 280.

Shubber, Sami. "Aircraft Hijacking under the Hague Convention 1970—A New Regime?," *International and Comparative Law Quarterly,* XXII, October 1973, 687-726.

Shubber, Sami. "Aircraft Hijacking under the Hague Convention upon Asylum," *Harvard International Law Journal,* XVI (1975), 93.

Siekman, Philip. "When Executives Turned Revolutionaries," *Fortune,* September 1964, 147.

Silverman, Jerry M., and Jackson, Peter M. "Terror in Insurgency Warfare," *Military Review,* L:10 (1970), 61-67.

Simandjuntak, L., and Oman, T. I. *Fitnah Sebagai Suatu Sistim Perebutan Kekuasaan.* Djakarta: Penerbit Matoa, 1966.

Simpson, Howard R. "Counter-Guerrilla Operations," *U.S. Naval Institute Proceedings,* XLVI:6 (1970), 56-63.

Simpson, Howard R. "Terror," *U.S. Naval Institute Proceedings,* XCVI, April 1970, 64-80.

Smith, Chester Lee. "The Probable Necessity of an International Prison in Solving Aircraft Hijacking," *The International Lawyer,* V (1971), 269.

Smith, Colin. *Carlos; Portrait of a Terrorist.* New York: Holt, Rinehart, and Winston, 1976.

Smith, D. "Scenario Reality; A New Brand of Terrorism," *Nation,* 30 March 1974, 392-394.

Sobel, Lester A., and Kosut, Hal. *Political Terrorism.* New York: Facts on File, Inc., 1975.

Sorenson, John L. *Urban Insurgency Cases.* Santa Barbara, Cal.: Defense Research Corporation, 1965.

Sponsler, T. H. "International Kidnapping," *International Lawyer,* V (1970), 27-52.

Stechel, Ira. "Terrorist Kidnapping of Diplomatic Personnel," *Cornell Journal of International Law,* V (1972), 189-217.

Stephen, John E. "Going South—Air Piracy and Unlawful Interference with Air Commerce," *International Lawyer,* IV (1970), 433.

Stevenson, John R. "International Law and the Export of Terrorism," *Record of the Association of the Bar of the City of New York,* XXVII (1972), 716-730.

Stevenson, John R. "International Law and the Export of Terrorism," *Department of State Bulletin,* LXVII, 4 December 1972, 645-652.

Stewart, Anthony T. Q. *The Ulster Crisis.* London: Faber, 1967.

Stockholm International Peace Research Institute, *The Nuclear Age.* Cambridge: MIT Press, 1974.

Stoffel, J. *Explosives and Homemade Bombs.* Springfield, Ill.: Charles C. Thomas, 1972.

Stohl, Michael, ed. *The Politics of Terror: A Reader in Theory and Practice,* 2 vols. New York: Marcel Dekker, 1977.

Strafford, David. "Anarchists in Britain Today," *Government and Opposition,* VI:3 (1971), 345.

Strauss, Harlan. "Revolutionary Types," *Journal of Conflict Resolution,* XIV (1973), 307.

Strother, Robert S., and Methvin, Eugene H. "Terrorism on the Rampage," *Reader's Digest,* CVII, November 1975, 73-77.

Stumper, A. "Considerations a propos de L'affaire Baader-Meinhof," *Revue de Droit Penal et de Criminologie,* LIV, October 1973, 33.

Stupack, Ronald J., and Booher, D. C. "Guerrilla Warfare; A Strategic Analysis in the Superpower Context," *Journal of Southeast Asia and the Far East,* 2 November 1970, 181.

Suárez, Carlos, and Sarmiento, Rubén Anaya. *Los Tupamaros,* Mexico, D.F., Editorial Extemporaneos, 1971.

Sundberg, Jacob W. F. "The Case for an International Criminal Court," *Journal of Air Law and Commerce,* XXXVII (1971), 211.

Symposium on Skyjacking. "Problems and Potential Solutions," *Villanova Law Review,* no. 18 (1973).

Symser, Willis M., et al. *Annotated Bibliography on Internal Defense.* Washington: Center for Research in Social Systems, 1968.

Syrkin, Marie. "Political Terrorism," *Midstream,* XVIII:9 (1972), 3-11.

Szabo, M. O., "Political Crimes: A Historical Perspective," *Denver Journal of International Law and Politics,* II (1972), 7.

Taulbee, J. L. "Retaliation and Irregular Warfare in Contemporary International Law," *International Lawyer,* VII, January 1973, 195-204.

Taylor, Edmund. "Terrorists," *Horizon,* XV, Summer 1973, 58-65.

Taylor, Telford, and Willrich, M. *Nuclear Theft: Risks and Safeguards.* New York: Ballinger, 1974.

Teixeira, Bernardo. *The Fabric of Terror—Three Days in Angola.* New York: Devin-Adair, 1965.

Terekhov, Vladimir. "International Terrorism and the Fight Against It," *New Times* (Moscow), XI (1974), 20-22.

Thomas, C. S., and Kirby, M. J. "Convention for the Suppression of Unlawful Acts against the Safety of Civil Aviation," *International and Comparative Law Quarterly,* XX, June 1973.

Thompson, Sir Robert. *Defeating Communist Insurgency.* New York: Praeger, 1970.

Thompson, W. Scott. "Political Violence and the 'Correlation of Forces'," *Orbis,* XIX:4, Winter 1976, 1270-1288.

Tiewul, S. A. "Terrorism: A Step Towards International Control," *Harvard International Law Journal,* XIV, Summer 1973, 585-595.

Toch, Hans. *Violent Men.* Chicago: Aldine Publishing Co., 1969.

Tophoven, Rolf, Hrsg. *Politik Durch Gewalt: Guerilla u Terrorismus Heute.* Koblenz: Wehr-und Wissen-Verlags-gesellschaft, 1976.

Tran, Tam. "Terrorisme et le Droit Penal International Contemporain," *Revue de Droit International de Sciences Diplomatiques et Politiques,* XLV, January-March 1976, 11-25.

Truskier, Andy. "The Politics of Violence: The Urban Guerrillas in Brazil," *Ramparts,* IX (1970), 30-34, 39.

Tuckerman, A. "U.N.; New Look for 1972—Debate on Terrorism," *Nation,* 2 October 1972, 258.

Turner, James S. G. "Piracy in the Air," *Naval War College Review,* XXII (1969), 86.

Uboldi, Raffaello. "La parabola della guerriglia urbana," *Est. Rome,* IV (1971), 81-86.

U.N., *Causes and Preventions of International Terrorism, A Study,* A/C. 6/418 Corr 1/ Add 1/ 2 November 1972.

U.N., *Convention for the Suppression of Unlawful Acts against the Safety of Civil Aviation, Montreal, 23 September 1971,* A/C. 6/418 Annex 4—2 November 1972.

U.N., *Convention for the Suppression of the Unlawful Seizure of Aircraft, The Hague, 16 December 1970,* A/C. 6/418 Annex 3—2 November 1972.

U.N., *Convention on Offenses and Certain Other Acts Committed on Board Aircraft, Tokyo, 14 September 1963,* A/C. 6/418 Annex 2² November 1972.

U.N., *The General Assembly Resolution on Terrorism: The Final Text and Member Votes,* A/Res/3034 (XXVII), 18 December 1972.

U.N., *Legal Committee Report on the Terrorism Issue,* A/8069, 16 December 1972.

U.N., *League of Nations Convention for the Prevention and Punishment of Terrorism, Geneva. 16 November 1937,* A/C. 6/418 Annex 1—2 November 1972.

U.N., *A Select Bibliography on Aerial Piracy,* List no. 6, 20 November 1972.

U.N., *A Select Bibliography on International Terrorism,* List no. 5/Rev. 1, 25 October 1972.

U.N., *State Responsibility to Deter, Prevent or Suppress Skyjacking Activities in Their Territory, 1970,* A/Res/2645 (XXV), 25 November 1970.

U.N., *Report of the Ad Hoc Committee on International Terrorism,* A/9028, 1970.

U.S., Central Intelligence Agency, *International and Transnational Terrorism: Diagnosis and Prognosis,* Washington, D.C., 1976.

U.S., Congress, House of Representatives, Committee on Foreign Affairs, Subcommittee on the Near East and South Asia, *International Terrorism, Hearings before the Subcommittee.* Washington: Government Printing Office, 1974.

U.S., Congress, House of Representatives, Committee on Internal Security, *Political Kidnappings, 1968-1973.* Washington: Government Printing Office, 1973.

U.S., Congress, House of Representatives, Committee on Internal Security, *Terrorism—A Staff Study.* Washington: Government Printing Office, 1974.

U.S., Congress, Senate, Committee on Banking, Housing, and Urban Affairs, Subcommittee on International Finance, *Exports of Nuclear Materials and Technology.* Washington: Government Printing Office, 1974.

U.S., Congress, Senate, Committee on Government Operations, *Peaceful Nuclear Exports and Weapons Proliferation: A Compendium.* Washington: Government Printing Office, 1975.

U.S., Congress, Senate, Committee on the Judiciary, Subcommittee to Investigate the Administration of the Internal Security Act and Other Internal Security Laws, *Terrorist Activity.* Washington: Government Printing Office, 1974.

U.S., Congress, Senate, Committee on the Judiciary, Subcommittee to Investigate the Administration of the Internal Security Act and Other Internal Security Laws, *Terrorist Activity; Hostage Defense Measures.* Washington: Government Printing Office, 1975.

U.S., Congress, Senate, Committee on the Judiciary, Subcommittee to Investigate the Administration of the Internal Security Act and Other Internal Security Laws, *Terrorist Activity—International Terrorism.* Washington: Government Printing Office, 1975.

U.S., Congress, Senate, Committee on the Judiciary, Subcommittee to Investigate the Administration of the Internal Security Act and Other Internal Security Laws, *Trotskyite Terrorist International.* Washington: Government Printing Office, 1975.

U.S., Congress, Senate, Committee on the Judiciary, Subcommittee to Investigate the Administration of the Internal Security Act and Other Internal Security Laws, *Terrorist Activity: Inside the Weather Movement.* Washington: Government Printing Office, 1974.

U.S., Department of Justice, *Terrorism: Statistics and Techniques—An F.B.I. Special Study.* Washington: 1973.

U.S., Department of State, *The Role of International Law in Combatting Terrorism.* Washington: Government Printing Office, 1973.

U.S., Department of State, Bureau of Public Affairs, Office of Media Services, *U.S. Action to Combat Terrorism.* Washington: 1973.

U.S., Department of State, *Viet Cong Terror Tactics in South Viet Nam.* Washington: Government Printing Office, 1967.

U.S., Department of Transportation, Federal Aviation Administration, Civil Aviation Security Service, *Bomb Threats Against U.S. Airports.* Washington: 1974.

U.S., Department of Transportation, *Hijackings: Selected Readings.* Washington: 1971.

U.S., National Advisory Committee on Criminal Justice Standards and Goals, *Report of the Task Force on Disorders and Terrorism.* Washington: 1976.

U.S., National Commission on the Causes and Prevention of Violence, *Staff Reports.* Washington: Government Printing Office, 1969.

Valeriano, Napoleon, and Bohannan, Charles T. *Counter-Guerrilla Operations: The Philippine Experience.* New York: Praeger, 1962.

Van Der Haag, Ernest. *Political Violence and Civil Disobedience.* New York: Harper and Row, 1972.

Van Panhuys, Haro F. "Aircraft Hijacking and International Law," *Columbia Journal of Transnational Law,* IX, Spring 1970, 1.

Vasilijevic, V. A. "Essai de Determination du Terrorisme en tant que Crime International," *Jugoslavenska Revija za Medunarodno Pravo* (Yug.), XX (1973), 169.

Vayrynen, Raimo. "Some Aspects of Theory and Strategy of Kidnapping," *Instant Research on Peace and Violence,* I (1971), 3.

Venter, Al J. *Africa at War.* Old Greenwich, Conn.: Devin-Adair, 1974.

Venter, Al J. *The Terror Fighters; A Profile of Guerrilla Warfare in Southern Africa.* Cape Town: Purnell, 1969.

Volpe, J. A., and Stewart, J. T. "Aircraft Hijacking: Some Domestic and International Responses," *Kentucky Law Journal,* LIX (1970-71).

Von Baeyer-Katte, W. "Terrorism," in Kernig, C. D., ed. *Marxism, Communism and Western Society,* vol. 8. New York: Herder & Herder, 1973.

Vucinic, Milan. "The Responsibility of States for Acts of International Terrorism," *Review of International Affairs,* XXIII:536-537 (1972), 11.

Wahl, Jonathan. "Responses to Terrorism; Self-Defense or Reprisal?," *International Problems,* V:1-2 (1973), 28.

Walter, Eugene Victor. *Terror and Resistance; A Study of Political Violence with Case Studies of Some Primitive African Communities.* London: Oxford University Press, 1972.

Walter, Eugene V. "Violence and the Process of Terror," *American Sociological Review,* XXIX:2, April 1964, 248-257.

Walzer, Michael. "The New Terrorists," *New Republic, CLXXIII:9,* 30 August 1975, 12-14.

Walzer, Michael, Bell, J. Bowyer, and Morris, Roger. "Terrorism: A Debate," *New Republic,* CLXXIII:26, 27 December 1975, 12-15.

Watson, Francis M. *Political Terrorism: The Threat and the Response.* Washington: R. B. Luce Co., 1976.

Weigert, Gideon. *Whoso Killeth a Believer.* Jerusalem: Israeli Communications, 1971 or 72.

Whelton, Charles. *Skyjack.* New York: Tower Publications, 1970.

White, Gillian M. E. "The Hague Convention for the Suppression of Unlawful Seizure of Aircraft," *Review of the International Commission of Jurists,* VI, April-June 1971, 39.

Wijne, J. S. *Terreur in de politiek; Politieke Geheime Genootschappen in Deze Tijd.* The Hague: Kruseman, 1967.

Wilkinson, Paul. *Political Terrorism.* New York: Macmillan, 1974.

Wilkinson, Paul. "Three Questions on Terrorism," *Government and Opposition,* VII:3 (1973), 290-312.

Willrich, Mason, ed. *Civil Nuclear Power and International Security.* New York: Praeger, 1971.

Willrich, Mason. *Global Politics of Nuclear Energy.* New York: Praeger, 1971.

Willrich, Mason, ed. *International Safeguards and Nuclear Industry.* Baltimore: Johns Hopkins University Press, 1973.

Willrich, Mason. "Terrorist Keep Out! Problem of Safe-Guarding Nuclear Material," *Bulletin of the Atomic Scientists,* XXXI, May 1975, 12-16.

Willrich, Mason, and Taylor, Theodore B. *Nuclear Theft: Risks and Safeguards.* Cambridge, Mass.: Ballinger Publishing Co., 1974.

Winchester, Simon. *In Holy Terror: Reporting the Ulster Troubles.* London: Faber, 1975.

Winegarten, R. "Literary Terrorism," *Commentary,* LVII, March 1974, 58-65.

Wohl, J. "Responses to Terrorism: Self Defense or Reprisal?," *International Problems,* XII, June 1973, 28-34.

Wolfenstein, E. V. *The Revolutionary Personality.* Princeton: Princeton University Press, 1967.

Wolin, Simon, and Slusser, Robert M., eds. *The Soviet Secret Police.* New York: Praeger, 1957.

Wood, M. C. "Convention on the Prevention and Punishment of Crimes against Internationally Protected Persons, Including Diplomatic Agents," *International and Comparative Law Quarterly,* XXIII (1974), 791.

Woddis, Jack. *New Theories of Revolution.* New York: 1972.

Wurfel, Seymour W. "Aircraft Piracy—Crime or Fun?," *William and Mary Law Review,* LXX (1969), 820.

Yaari, Ehud. "The Decline of Al-Fatah," *Midstream,* May 1971, 3.

Yaari, Ehud. *Strike Terror.* New York: Sabra Books, 1970.

Yahalom, Dan. *Fire on Arab Terrorism.* Jerusalem: Carta, 1973.

Yahalom, Yivtah. *Arab Terror*. Tel Aviv: World Labour Zionist Movement, 1969.

Yamamoto, Soji. "The Japanese Enactment for the Suppression of Unlawful Seizure of Aircraft and International Law," *Japanese Annual of International Law*, XV (1971), 70.

Yearbook of the United Nations. "Questions Relating to International Terrorism." New York: United Nations, 1972.

Zahn, G. C. "Terrorism for Peace and Justice," *Commonweal*, XCIII, 23 October 1970, 84-85.

Zawodny, J. K. "Guerrilla and Sabotage: Organization, Operations, Motivation, Escalation," *Annals of the American Academy of Political and Social Science*, CCCXLI, May 1962.

Zivic, J. "The Nonaligned and the Problem of International Terrorism," *Review of International Affairs* (Belgrade), XXIV, 20 January 1973, 6-8.

Zotiades, George B. "The International Criminal Prosecution of Persons Charged with an Unlawful Seizure of Aircraft," *Revue Hellenique de Droit International*, XXIII:1-4 (1970), 12.

APPENDIX

Symposium Participants

Aronfreed, Eva, Department of Political Science/Economics, Glassboro State College, New Jersey.

Alesevich, Eugene, Criminal Justice Program, University of Nevada at Las Vegas, Nevada.

Alexander, Yonah, Department of History, State University of New York at Oneonta, New York.

Anable, David, Staff Correspondent, *Christian Science Monitor,* Boston, Massachusetts.

Anderson, Thomas P., Department of History, Eastern Connecticut State College, Willimantic, Connecticut.

Ballester, A. N. F., Vice President and Executive Director, Foundation for the Establishment of an International Criminal Court and International Criminal Law Commission, Newton, Massachusetts.

Barrett, Raymond J., Department of Administrative Studies, Glassboro State College, New Jersey.

Bassiouni, M. Cherif, College of Law, DePaul University, Chicago, Illinois.

Bekes, Imre, Criminal Law, University of Budapest, Hungary.

Bell, J. Bowyer, Institute of War and Peace Studies, Columbia University, New York, New York.

Bender, Aaron, Department of History, Glassboro State College, New Jersey.

Bennett, Lt. Gershom, Police Department, Willingboro, New Jersey.

Blanco-Muñoz, Agustín, Universidad Central de Venezuela, Caracas, Venezuela.

Blanken, Maurice, Department of Political Science/Economics, Glassboro State College, New Jersey.

Byrne, The Honorable Brendan T., Governor of New Jersey, Trenton, New Jersey.

Clark, Dennis J., Philadelphia, Pennsylvania.

Clarke, John Henrik, Department of Black and Puerto Rican Studies, Hunter College, New York, New York.

Cook, Blanche, Department of History, John Jay College of Criminal Justice, The City University of New York, New York, New York.

Cooper, H. H. A., Staff Director, National Advisory Committee Task Force on Disorders and Terrorism, Washington, D.C.

Croker, Stanley W., Callison College, University of the Pacific, Stockton, California.

Dautricourt, J. Y., Faculteit der Rechtsgeleerdheid, School voor Criminologie, Katholieke Universiteit, Leuven, Belgium.

Dinstein, Yoram, Department of International Law, Tel Aviv University, Israel.

Dowling, Joseph A., Department of History, Lehigh University, Bethlehem, Pennsylvania.

Edelman, Murray, Department of Political Science, University of Wisconsin at Madison, Wisconsin.

Eisenstein, Ira, President, Reconstructionist Rabbinical College, New York City, New York.

Ellenberg, Edward S., President, Institute of International Sociological Research, Cologne, West Germany.

Evans, Ernest H., Cambridge, Massachusetts.

Fearey, Robert A., Special Assistant to the Secretary for Combating Terrorism, Department of State, Washington, D.C.

Fisk, Robert, Foreign Staff, *The Times* of London, London, England.

Frank, Robert S., Research Scientist, University City Science Center, Philadelphia, Pennsylvania.

Friedlander, Robert A., Department of International Law, Lewis University, Lockport, Illinois.

Gilmore, William J., Department of History, Lehigh University, Bethlehem, Pennsylvania.

Glicksman, William, Author, Philadelphia, Pennsylvania.

Goldie, L. F. E., College of Law, Syracuse University, Syracuse, New York.

Golin, Steve, History Department, Bloomfield College, Bloomfield, New Jersey.

Gros, Bernard, Critique Litteraire, Lille, France.

Gross, Feliks, Department of Sociology, Graduate School of C.U.N.Y., New York, New York.

Guannu, Joseph, Political Science/Economics Department, Glassboro State College, New Jersey.

Harper, Robert W., Department of History, Glassboro State College, New Jersey.

Hazen, William, Abbott Associates, Incorporated, Alexandria, Virginia.

Hendel, Samuel, Department of Political Science, Trinity College, Hartford, Connecticut.

Hewsen, Robert H., Department of History, Glassboro State College, New Jersey.

Hitchner, Benjamin, Political Science/Economics Department, Glassboro State College, New Jersey.

Hutchinson, Martha Crenshaw, Department of Government, Wesleyan University, Middletown, Connecticut.

Johnson, Richard, Department of Political Science/Economics, Glassboro State College, New Jersey.

Johnson, Roger, School of Theoretical and Applied Science, Ramapo College, Mahwah, New Jersey.

Kato, Shuichi, Department of History, Yale University, New Haven, Connecticut.

Katsh, Abraham I., President, The Dropsie University, Philadelphia, Pennsylvania.

Kerr, Louise, Department of History, The Newberry Library, Chicago, Illinois.

Kessler, Sidney H., Department of History, Glassboro State College, New Jersey.

Khan, Mohammad I., Department of History, Clarion State College, Clarion, Pennsylvania.

Kittrie, Nicholas N., Director, Institute for Advanced Studies in Justice, Washington, D.C.

Kos-Rabcewicz-Zubkowski, L., Department of Criminology, University of Ottawa, Ottawa, Canada.

Kren, George M., Department of History, Kansas State University, Manhattan, Kansas.

Kress, Lee Bruce, Department of History, Glassboro State College, New Jersey.

Livingston, Marius H., Chairman, Symposium, Department of History, Glassboro State College, New Jersey.

McCloskey, The Honorable Paul N. Jr., Member of Congress, Washington, D.C.

McClure, Brooks, Special Assistant, Department of Defense, Washington, D.C.

Mallin, Jay, Author, Coral Gables, Florida.

Mallison, Sally V., The National Law Center, International Law Program, The George Washington University, Washington, D.C.

Mallison, W. T., Director, International Law Program, The National Law Center, The George Washington University, Washington, D.C.

Maurer, Marvin, Department of Government, Monmouth College, West Long Branch, New Jersey.

Melander, Goran, Department of Law, University of Lund, Lund, Sweden.

Mengel, R. W., Project Manager, Nuclear Assessments Department, The B.D.M. Corporation, Vienna, Virginia.

Methvin, Eugene, Senior Editor, *The Reader's Digest*, Washington, D.C.

Mickolus, Edward, Department of Political Science, Yale University, New Haven, Connecticut.

Miller, James A., The American University, Washington, D.C.

Miszczak, Edward, Department of History, Glassboro State College, New Jersey.

Mojekwu, Christopher C., Department of Politics, Lake Forest College, Illinois.

Moodie, Michael L., Research Associate, Foreign Policy Research Institute, Philadelphia, Pennsylvania.

Mosse, Hilde L., Clinical Professor of Psychiatry, New York Medical College, New York, New York.

Moyer, Kenneth E., Department of Psychology, Carnegie-Mellon University, Pittsburgh, Pennsylvania.

Murphy, John F., Associate Dean, School of Law, The University of Kansas, Lawrence, Kansas.

Myers, Robert P., Assistant Coordinator for Combating Terrorism, Department of State, Washington, D.C.

Naftzinger, Lt. Col. Joseph E., Office of the Secretary of Defense (I.S.A.), Pentagon, Washington, D.C.

O'Ballance, Edgar, Author, Nottingham, England.

Pate, Clarence W., History Department, Montclair State College, Upper Montclair, New Jersey.

Pine, Alan S., Department of History, Monmouth College, West Long Branch, New Jersey.

Pizzillo, Carole M., Administrative Assistant, History Department, Glassboro State College, New Jersey.

Porterfield, Richard, Department of History, Glassboro State College, New Jersey.

Price, Joedd, Department of History, East Texas State University, Commerce, Texas.

Rappoport, Leon H., Department of Psychology, Kansas State University, Manhattan, Kansas.

Standstrom, Harold M., Department of Political Science, University of Hartford, West Hartford, Connecticut.

Smith, Donald E., Department of Political Science, University of Pennsylvania, Philadelphia, Pennsylvania.

Spragens, William C., Department of Political Science, Bowling Green University, Ohio.

Storr, Anthony, Consultant Psychotherapist, The Warneford Hospital, Oxford, England.

Sullivan, Eileen, Department of Behavioral Studies, University of Florida, Gainesville, Florida.

Sundberg, Jacob, Institutet for Offentlig Och Internationell Ratt, Stockholm, Sweden.

Sundiata, Ibrahim K., Department of History, Northwestern University, Evanston, Illinois.

Taylor, Gordon Rattray, Author, Bath, England.

Vacca, Roberto, Rome, Italy.

Wagenlehner, Gunther, President, Association des Journalistes Europeens, Bonn-Bad Godesberg, West Germany.

Wanek, Marie G., Department of History, Glassboro State College, New Jersey.

West, Gerald T., Foreign Policy Research Institute, Philadelphia, Pennsylvania.

Wilkinson, Paul, Department of Politics, University College, Cardiff, Wales.

Woetzel, Robert K., President, Foundation for the Establishment of an International Criminal Court and International Criminal Law Commission, Newton, Massachusetts.

Wolf, John B., Department of Criminal Justice, Union College, Cranford, New Jersey.

Yarborough, Lt. General William P., United States Army, Retired, Southern Pines, North Carolina.

Zinam, Oleg, Department of Economics, University of Cincinnati, Ohio.

CONTRIBUTORS

Eugene Alesevich is Assistant Professor of Criminal Justice at the University of Nevada, Las Vegas. A Ph.D. candidate at New York University, N.Y., he was made a Life Fellow of the Institute for Sociological Research and is Executive Secretary of Delta Tau Kappa, International Social Science Honor Society. Among his publications are: "The Sociology of Law and Jurisprudence," *International Journal of Legal Research;* and "American Heritage of Violence," *International Behavioral Scientist.*

Thomas P. Anderson, a Latin Americanist, received his Ph.D. from Loyola University, Chicago. He is the author of *Matanza: El Salvador's Communist Revolt of 1932* and other studies of Latin American society. He is Professor of History at Eastern Connecticut State College.

J. Bowyer Bell, authority on twentieth-century revolutionary movements, is with the Institute of War and Peace, Columbia University, N.Y. He received his Ph.D. from Duke University in 1958, has taught international studies, and was a Fulbright Fellow (Italy) in 1956-57 and a Guggenheim Fellow (Ireland, Middle East, Africa) in 1972-73. His numerous publications include: *The Secret Army: The IRA 1916-74* (1974); *On Revolt: Strategies of National Liberation* (1976); and *Terror out of Zion* (1977).

Brendan T. Byrne is Governor of the State of New Jersey and Chairman of the National Advisory Committee on Criminal Justice Standards and Goals.

Dennis J. Clark is an historian and expert on Irish immigration and U.S. minority groups. He has been Executive Director of the Samuel S. Fels Fund in Philadelphia since 1974. He was born in Philadelphia and received his Ph.D. in urban history from Temple University. His publications include: *The Irish in Philadelphia: Ten Generations of Urban Experience* (1974); and *Irish Blood: Northern Ireland and the American Conscience* (1977).

H. H. A. Cooper, of the Institute for Advanced Studies in Justice of The American University, is adjunct professor of the Center for Administration of Justice of that university, on the faculty of the National College of State Judiciary, Staff Director of the National Advisory Committee, Task Force on Disorders and Terrorism, and is deputy director of the Center of Forensic Psychiatry at New York University. He holds the bachelor of law degree from the University of London, a master of arts in legal history from the University of Liverpool, and a master of laws in criminal justice from New York University. He was chairman of the United Nations N.G.O. Alliance from 1973 to 1975. As a member of the Executive Board of the International Society of Social Defense, he has represented that society before the United Nations since 1972. He has written numerous books and articles on crime prevention and control in both English and Spanish.

Joseph A. Dowling received his A.B. at Lincoln Memorial University and his M.A. and Ph.D. at New York University. He has taught at Shorter College, Bates College, and is presently Distinguished Professor of History at Lehigh University. A student of American intellectual history and psychohistory, he has published articles in those fields and edited *American Issues: The Social Record* in collaboration with Merle Curti, Willard Thorp, and Carlos Baker. He is a member of the American Historical Association, American Studies Association and the Organization of American Historians. He received the Lindback Foundation Award for Outstanding Teaching in 1966 and is listed in *Who's Who in America* (1977).

Edward S. Ellenberg is the founder, Chairman of the Executive Committee, and President of the Institute for International Sociological Research in Cologne. Born in Vienna, he is also President of the International Academy of Social and Moral Sciences, Arts and Letters (Cologne) and of the Academy of Diplomacy and International Affairs (Cologne), and was former Consul-General (hon.) of the Ivory Coast and Lesotho. He holds the degrees of LL.B. and Doctor in Political Sciences. Publications include: *International Terrorism vs. Democracy* (1972); *Western Democracies vs. Terrorism, A Study of Ineffectiveness* (1974); and *The PLO and Its Place in Violence and Terror* (1976).

Ernest H. Evans is at present a research assistant with the Senate Armed Services Committee. He holds a Ph.D. degree in political science from M.I.T. and has done field research on terrorism in Ireland and in the Middle East through a grant by the Ford Foundation.

Robert A. Fearey was born in New York and attended Harvard University. He is presently an Advisor for the Agency for International Development (AID). He has served in numerous official and diplomatic posts, including: Special Assistant to the Secretary of State and Coordinator for Combatting Terrorism (1975-76); Chairman, Department of International Relations and Area Studies, National War College faculty, 1972-75; Civil Administrator of the Ryukyu Islands (Okinawa), with personal rank of Minister, 1969-72; Political Advisor to the Commander in Chief, Pacific, with personal rank of Minister, 1966-69; Deputy Director, and then Director, for East Asian Affairs, responsible for Japan, Republic of Korea, Republic of China, Department of State, 1963-66; Chief, Political-Military Affairs Branch, American Embassy, Tokyo, concerned with negotiation of U.S.-Japan Security Treaty, 1959-61; member of U.S. delegation to NATO, Paris, 1952-56; Japanese Desk Officer in Department of State, 1946-50; Special Assistant to Ambassador George Atcheson, U.S. political advisor to General MacArthur, in Tokyo, 1945-46.

Mr. Fearey was awarded the Department of the Army's Decoration for Distinguished Civilian Service, Okinawa, 1972, and is the author of *The Occupation of Japan* (1950) and *The US Versus the USSR—Ideologies in Conflict* (1959). He made the preceding address at Los Angeles, California, on February 19, 1976, before the Los Angeles World Affairs Council and the World Affairs Council of Orange County.

Robert Fisk is on the foreign staff of the *Times* of London. He received his Ed.D. from Columbia University, was a visiting scholar at the Institute of Education, University of London, a Fulbright lecturer and Chairman of the National Conference of Professional Educational Administrators. He is the author of *The Point of No Return* and numerous articles and is co-editor of *Faculty Unions and Collective Bargaining*. His many articles appear in various professional journals.

Robert A. Friedlander is Professor of Law at Lewis University in Illinois. He earned his B.A., M.A., and Ph.D. at Northwestern University and a J.D. at DePaul University. He is listed in *Who's Who in the Midwest* and has published *International Law Is What the Lawyers Say It Is* (1975) and *The Origins of International Terrorism* (1976).

William Glicksman was born and educated in Poland and survived the ghettos and concentration camps. After coming to the United States in 1946, he received his Ph.D. in Jewish history from Dropsie College. He is a retired teacher and lecturer and is affiliated with, among others, the Diaspora Research Institute at Tel-Aviv University and the Association for Jewish Studies, Harvard University. His publications include: "In the Mirror of Literature"; "A Kehillah in Poland During the Inter-War Years"; and "Jewish Social Welfare Institutions in Poland."

Bernard Gros was born in France and educated in literary studies at the University of Lille. He teaches literature and culture agrégé there and was awarded the Chevalier de la Légion d'Honneur, 1970. His publications include: *Victor Hugo Le Vissionaire de Guernesey* (1975); *Le terrorisme* (1976); and *Profil de "l'Homme revolte" d'A. Camus* (1977).

Feliks Gross was born in Poland, where he earned the LL.M. and LL.D. degrees. Following postgraduate work in Paris, he came to the United States in 1941 and has been Professor of Sociology and Anthropology at the City University of New York. He was a Fulbright lecturer at the University of Rome and has lectured at several other European and American universities. In 1968 he was a consultant to the National Commission on Causes and Prevention of Violence. Among his publications are: *World Politics and Tension Areas* (1967); *Violence in Politics* (1973); *The Revolutionary Party* (1974); and *Ethnics in the Borderland: Slavs and Latins in a Border Region* (in progress).

Samuel Hendel is Professor of Political Science at Trinity College, Connecticut. He taught for many years at the City College of the City University of New York and directed its Russian Area Studies Graduate Program. He has been a visiting professor in the Ph.D. programs at Columbia University, CUNY, and Claremont Graduate School. Dr. Hendel is the editor of *The Soviet Crucible,* a widely used textbook, now in its fourth edition, and a contributing author of *The U.S.S.R. After 50 Years; The Communist World;* and *European Politics I.* He is listed in *Who's Who in America* and *Who's Who in the World.*

Robert H. Hewsen is Professor of Russian and Middle East History at Glassboro State College, N.J. Born in New York City, Dr. Hewsen is a specialist in Caucasian studies who has published extensively in this field. He was drawn to the question of terrorism through his acquaintance with the Armenian massacres.

Abraham I. Katsh is President Emeritus and distinguished research professor at Dropsie University. Dr. Katsh earned his Doctorate of Jurisprudence from New York University in 1936 and since then has been extensively teaching in a number of universities. At New York University he founded the Jewish Cultural Foundation in 1937 and established the New York University Library of Judaica and Hebraica. From 1947 to 1967 he directed the American Israel Student and Professional Workshop in Israel. In 1965, New York University established a fellowship in the field of Hebrew studies in his honor. He has written twenty books, among them the *Scroll of Agony, The Chaim A. Kaplan Diary of the Warsaw Ghetto,* and the *Hebraica Heritage of American Democracy.* In addition, Dr. Katsh has written three hundred articles for learned and professional publications, such as the *Encyclopedia of Religion.*

Byong-Suh Kim is Associate Professor of Sociology and Chairman of the Sociology Department at Montclair State College, N.J. He earned his Ph.D. at Emory University and studied further at the University of Chicago.

He has published articles on youth activism and student revolt in Japan and Korea in *The Asia Journal,* and is currently working on a study of religious deprogramming of American youths in the Eastern religions.

Nicholas N. Kittrie is Professor of Law and Director, Institute for Advanced Studies in Justice, at The American University, Washington, D.C. Secretary-General of the American Section of the International Association of Penal Law and former Counsel to the Judiciary Committee of the United States Senate, Professor Kittrie is also Past President of the American Society of Criminology.

Louis Kos-Rabcewicz-Zubkowski is Doctor of Laws of the University of Paris, member of the Bar of Montreal, Professor at the University of Ottawa, Chairman of the International Criminal Law Committee, International Law Association, President of the Canadian Section, Inter-American Commercial Arbitration Commission, Chairman of the Private International Law Committee, Inter-American Bar Association, Vice-President, Canadian International Academy of Humanities and Social Sciences, and Honorary Secretary, Canadian Branch, International Law Association. He is a member of numerous international, inter-American and national learned societies and professional associations and has lectured and done research work at various universities in Canada, the United States, Mexico, Peru, England, France, Germany, Poland, and the Netherlands. During his professional and academic career, he has published books and papers in English, French, Spanish, German, and Polish in thirteen European and American countries.

George M. Kren is Professor of History at Kansas State University. He earned his M.A. and Ph.D. at the University of Wisconsin and has taught at several colleges and universities. Among his publications are: "SS Atrocities: A Psychohistorical Perspective" (with L. Rappoport), *History of Childhood Quarterly* (Summer 1975); "The Waffen SS" (with L. Rappoport), *Armed Forces and Society* (November 1976); and "Another Aspect of War: The Holocaust, A Generation After," *Military Affairs* (December 1976).

Lee Bruce Kress is Assistant Professor of History at Glassboro State College, N.J., where he has acted as Coordinator of World Studies, an interdisciplinary program, and Director of Latin American Studies. He earned his B.A. at The Johns Hopkins University and his M.A. and Ph.D. at Columbia University with majors in Latin American and United States history. Research grants have taken him to Mexico and Argentina. Among his publications are: "Centralism and Federalism in Latin America: The Argentine Case," *Journal of International and Comparative Studies* (Winter

1973); "Argentine Liberalism and the Church," *The Americas* (January 1974); and "The Development of the Spanish-Speaking Community in New Jersey," to appear in *New Jersey History,* 1978.

Marius H. Livingston was Associate Professor and Chairman of the Glassboro State College History Department. He died in December 1977. He was the Director of the 1976 International Symposium on Terrorism held at Glassboro State College and has taught courses on the subject of terrorism.

Brooks McClure follows developments in transnational terrorism as International Security Advisor to the U.S. Information Agency (USIA) and as a member of the Working Group of the Cabinet Committee to Combat Terrorism. His paper is based upon an analysis of actual hostage cases drawn from after-action reports and debriefings of kidnap victims.

McClure holds a B.A., *magna cum laude,* in political science from the University of Maryland, and is a distinguished graduate of the Naval War College. He worked as a New York and Washington newspaperman for ten years before joining the State Department Foreign Service in 1951. Two years later he transferred to USIA and served more than eighteen years in Europe, the Middle East, and Asia. His Washington assignments include three years as USIA Policy Officer for Europe and four years as Special Assistant in the Directorate of Policy Plans and National Security Council Affairs, International Security Affairs, Department of Defense.

An Army veteran of World War II, McClure has written extensively for such military publications as the *Infantry Journal, Air Force Magazine, Combat Forces Journal,* and *Army,* and he is the author of a study of Soviet partisan operations in World War II in an anthology, *Modern Guerrilla Warfare.* He has also contributed articles on hostage behavior and terrorist tactics and organization to professional journals and in 1975 testified on hostage defense measures before the Senate Internal Security Subcommittee.

Jay Mallin, a journalist, has witnessed terrorism firsthand in Cuba, Vietnam, Uruguay, Argentina, and elsewhere. He holds an A.B. from Florida Southern College and is the author of six books, two of which deal entirely with terrorism. He has lectured on this subject at the Pentagon, Fort Bragg, North Carolina, and the Air Force Special Operations School, as well as at civilian seminars and college conferences. He is a regular contributor to the *Air University Review;* his "Terrorism as a Political Weapon" appeared in the July-August 1971 issue.

Sally V. Mallison is a research associate in the International and Comparative Law Program at the George Washington University Law Center,

Washington, D.C. She studied the behavioral sciences and international affairs at the University of Washington. She and Dr. Mallison work together on legal research and writing projects. They share a major professional interest in the control and reduction of international coercion, and they have vigorously opposed acts of terrorism whether committed by groups or by governments.

Their most recent writing is a study of the juridical status of irregular forces under the humanitarian law of armed conflict which will appear in the symposium on this subject to be published this spring by Case-Western Reserve International Law Journal.

W. T. Mallison, Professor of Law and Director of the International Law Program at George Washington University Law Center, Washington, D.C., holds the J.S.D. degree from Yale University. In 1957 and 1958, he worked with the U.S. Atomic Energy Commission where he was the principal United States negotiator of the "Atoms for Peace" agreements with Asian and Middle Eastern countries. He has served twice in the Stockton Chair of International Law at the Naval War College, and was Visiting Professor of Law at the Law Faculty and the Center of Advanced International Studies at the University of Tehran in Iran in 1968.

Marvin Maurer is Professor of Political Science at Monmouth College, West Long Branch, N.J. He received his Ph.D. from Columbia University and was President of the Northeastern Political Science Association, 1975-76. He is the coauthor of *Political Behavior in the United States.*

R. William Mengel is Director, Washington Operations, of the BDM Corporation. Over the past several years he has specialized in the study of terrorism including the behavioral attributes associated with that phenomenon. He has contributed to numerous studies and authored "Terrorism and New Technologies of Destruction" in the *National Advisory Committee Task Force Report on Disorder and Terrorism.*

Edward Francis Mickolus is with the Central Intelligence Agency, engaged in a number of projects for the Office of Training, Office of Data Processing, and Office of Regional and Political Analysis. In 1976 he was involved in contract research on transnational terrorism for the Office of Political Research, Central Intelligence Agency. Educated in political science at Georgetown University and Yale University through various fellowships and awards, he is currently working on a Ph.D. dissertation for Yale and is a member of several professional and honorary societies. Among his many papers and articles are: *Annotated Bibliography on International and Transnational Terrorism* (1976, available from Library of Congress DOCEX Project); "Transnational Terrorism" in *Political Terrorism: A*

Reader in Theory and Practice, Volume II (1977); and *Transnational Terrorism: Analysis of Terrorists, Events and Environments* (Ph.D. dissertation in progress).

Christopher Chukwuemeka Mojekwu, Associate Professor of Politics, Lake Forest College, Illinois, earned an LL.B. at London School of Economics and an LL.M. and S.J.D. at Northwestern University. A Barrister-at-Law and member of the Honourable Society of Gray's Inn, London, he was a former Civil Service Commissioner for the Federal Government of Nigeria; Attorney-General of the then Eastern Region of Nigeria; and commissioner for Home Affairs and Local Government in the erstwhile Biafran regime. His publications include: *Faith in Ourselves* (1964); *Law and Development in Eastern Nigeria* (1964); and *African Society, Culture and Politics* (co-editor, 1977).

Michael L. Moodie is Research Associate at the Institute for Foreign Policy Analysis, Inc., in Cambridge, Mass., and a doctoral candidate at the Fletcher School of Law and Diplomacy, Tufts University. He has recently coauthored a monograph titled *Defense Technology and the Atlantic Alliance: Competition or Collaboration?* as well as an article on India's nuclear politics for the May/June 1977 issue of *Survival.* He has also published articles on British policy options in Northern Ireland and the problem of international terrorism in general.

Hilde L. Mosse, M.D., is Clinical Associate Professor in Psychiatry at New York Medical College where she teaches child and adolescent psychiatry. She was a Fulbright lecturer on child psychiatry at the University of Marburg, Germany, and is a Diplomate in Psychiatry, certified by the American Board of Psychiatry. She has published numerous studies on the influence of mass media on children, on violence and other forms of criminal behavior and, most recently, had a chapter in *Masked Depression* titled "The Psychotherapeutic Management of Children with Masked Depression."

Edgar O'Ballance is a journalist, commentator, and lecturer, specializing in foreign affairs, defense, and strategical matters. Born in Dublin, he is a member of the International Institute of Strategical Studies and the Foreign Affairs Research Institute, both in London. Among his writings are *Arab Guerrilla Power and International Terrorism* (in progress).

Charles Anthony Storr holds the degrees of M.A., F.R.C.P., and F.R.C. Psych. and is Clinical Lecturer in Psychiatry at the University of Oxford and Consultant in Psychotherapy in the Oxfordshire area. He is qualified as a physician and trained as a psychiatrist at Runwell Mental Hospital and the Maudsley Hospital. He has held various psychiatric posts at hospitals in Britain. Among his numerous books, papers, chapters, and articles are: *Human Aggression* (1968); *The Dynamics of Aggression* (1972); and *Human Destructiveness* (1972).

Jacob W. F. Sundberg is Professor of Jurisprudence at the Faculty of Law, University of Stockholm. He was born and educated in Stockholm and, after studies at New York University Law School, was made Master of Comparative Jurisprudence at that university in 1961. He has had extensive Swedish juridical experience and his authorship includes articles in foreign and Swedish legal periodicals on such topics as air law, criminal law, private law, international law, and jurisprudence. In 1975, he received a Presidential Citation of the American Society of Criminology for his contributions to the understanding of international crime. He also served as expert to the 5th UN Congress on the Prevention of Crime and the Treatment of Offenders.

Ibrahim K. Sundiata is Assistant Professor of History at Northwestern University. He earned his B.A. at Ohio Wesleyan and his Ph.D. at Northwestern University in 1972. He was a State Department Foreign Affairs Scholar in 1965.

Gordon Rattray Taylor is an author whose main interest is how society changes and why. Born in Eastbourne, Sussex, he was educated at St. Peter's College, Radley, and Trinity College, Cambridge. He has served as the BBC's chief science advisor and contributed a regular feature to the monthly, *Science Journal.* Founder of the International Science Writers Association, he is the author of several books, among which are: *The Biological Time Bomb* and *The Doomsday Book,* both world bestsellers; *Rethink;* and *How to Avoid the Future.*

Robert W. Taylor is Assistant Professor of Urban Studies and Coordinator of the Urban Studies Program at Montclair State College, N.J. He earned his Ph.D. at Saint Louis University and studied at Columbia University on a postdoctoral grant from the National Endowment for the Humanities. He has published a mongraph on the suburbanization of the elderly, and is currently working on a study of the revitalization of American central cities through planned alternatives.

Gunther Wagenlehner is President of the Association of European Journalists and lives in Bad-Godesberg. He teaches Military Problems and European Politics at the University of Munich. Since 1971 he has given annual lectures at various American universities on East and West problems. He is considered an outstanding specialist in that field and has written extensively, as well as having appeared on radio and television. Among his publications are: *The Soviet Economic System and Karl Marx* (1960); *Communism Without a Future* (1962); and *Escalation in the Near East* (1968). In 1945 Dr. Wagenlehner became a prisoner of war of the Russians and was not released until 1955. He studied at the University of Hamburg and got his doctorate with a ·dissertation on Lenin. Since 1962 he has been working as an expert on Eastern affairs in the West German Defense Ministry.

Marie G. Wanek, Professor of History at Glassboro State College, received her Ph.D. degree from Georgetown University. She holds membership in various professional organizations and has several times held office in the Mid-Atlantic Regional Conference of the Association for Asian Studies. She has received grants or fellowships from Columbia, Yale and Seton Hall universities and under the Fulbright, National Defense, and National Endowment for the Humanities programs. Her review of *The City of the Gods* and *The Myth of Christian Beginnings* appeared in *The Catholic Historical Review.*

Robert K. Woetzel is President of the United Nations Assocation of Greater Boston and the Massachusetts Division, President of the Foundation for the Establishment of an International Criminal Court and International Criminal Law Commission, and Chairman of the International Human Rights Conference and of the International Inter-University Seminar. He is the Senior Professor of International Law and Politics at Boston College and has served as Consultant to the Attorney General of the Commonwealth of Massachusetts and the National Commission on the Causes and Prevention of Violence. He was awarded the Distinguished International Criminal Law Award, the Einstein Prize for American Diplomacy, and the Stokes Prize in Political Theory. He is the author of ten books including *The Nuremberg Trials in International Law, The Philosophy of Freedom,* and *Toward a Feasible International Criminal Court.*

John B. Wolf is a management consultant specializing in the design and implementation of intelligence systems for criminal justice agencies and private corporations. He has served as a consultant to the New York City Police Department, New Jersey State Police, Illinois State Police, and other law-enforcement agencies. His published articles and research concern aspects of urban insurgency, international terrorism, and police intelligence. He has rendered expert testimony on terrorism before the Congress of the United States, Committee on Foreign Affairs, serves as a member of the

New Jersey Criminal Justice Standards and Goals Advisory Committee, and as Chairman of the Department of Criminal Justice at Union College, Cranford, N.J.

William Pelham Yarborough, a 1936 graduate of the United States Military Academy at West Point, retired from the U.S. Army in 1971 to become a writer, lecturer, and research consultant. His military service led to the Far East, Europe, and Africa and to the British Staff College at Camberley. He was appointed in 1965 to the post of Senior Member of the United Nations Military Armistice Commission at Panmunjom and studied at close range the North Korean and Chinese propaganda mechanisms revealed at the conference table. In 1968 he moved from "Special Operations" in the Pentagon to the top position in U.S. Army Intelligence. During the past four years he has made a number of fact-finding visits to various parts of Africa, studying sociological, political, economic, and security aspects of the changing African scene. General Yarborough is presently a member of the Board of Directors of the American African Affairs Association, a nonprofit organization. His publications include: *At the Sharp Edge in Africa: Alternatives for America* (coauthored with Dr. Walter Darnell Jacobs, 1975); *Terrorism in South Africa* (coauthored with Dr. Walter Darnell Jacobs and Carl Peterson, 1973); and *Trial in Africa—The Failure of US Policy* (1976).

Oleg Zinam, Professor of Economics, University of Cincinnati, received his B.S. in Military Science from the Belgrade Military Academy, Yugoslavia, in 1939, a B.S. in Economics and an M.B.A. from Xavier University in Cincinnati, Ohio, in 1956 and 1958 respectively, and a Doctorate in Economics from the University of Cincinnati in 1963. He has published numerous articles on economics and sociology in professional journals in the U.S., Canada, Germany, Italy, Spain, and India. His areas of special interest and specialization are: comparative economic systems; economic history; history of economic thought; economic growth and development; economic and political systems of Eastern Europe; theory of socioeconomic change; theory of population; and theory of discontent. Before embarking on his academic career in the U.S., Professor Zinam spent many years in administrative, banking, and business work. At the present time he is teaching economics at the University of Cincinnati and Russian language at Xavier University.

INDEX